Marriage Records of Accomack County Virginia

1854-1895

Recorded in Licenses & Ministers' Returns

Barry W. Miles and Moody K. Miles, III

HERITAGE BOOKS
2006

HERITAGE BOOKS
AN IMPRINT OF HERITAGE BOOKS, INC.

Books, CDs, and more—Worldwide

For our listing of thousands of titles see our website at
www.HeritageBooks.com

Published 2006 by
HERITAGE BOOKS, INC.
Publishing Division
65 East Main Street
Westminster, Maryland 21157-5026

Copyright © 1997 Barry W. Miles and Moody K. Miles, III

All rights reserved. No part of this book may be reproduced or transmitted in any form or by any means, electronic or mechanical, including photocopying, recording or by any information storage and retrieval system without written permission from the author, except for the inclusion of brief quotations in a review.

International Standard Book Number: 978-0-7884-0680-9

Table of Contents

Acknowledgments v

Introduction 1

Production Process 3

Female Nicknames 5

Surname Spelling 7

Ministers 9

Clerks of Court 13

Abbreviations 13

Explanation of Entries 15

Illustrative Documents 17

Marriages 27

Bride Index 371

Acknowledgements

The compilers would like to express their appreciation to those who helped make this book possible. First, to Dr. Brooks Miles Barnes, Eastern Shore Public Library, for making arrangements to have the microfilmed records duplicated by the Virginia State Library and Archives and making them available to the compilers, without which this project would not have been possible. Also for his suggestions and review of the introductory material. To Gail M. Walczyk, Coram, NY, for handling the printing of the microfilm in hardcopy for use by the compilers. To Caretta S. Harris, Deputy Clerk of Court, Accomack County, for providing copies of a number of the licenses, including those used in the illustrations. To Rev. Kirk Mariner, Arlington, VA, for reviewing, correcting and providing the denominations for the Ministers. A special appreciation goes to Mary Frances Carey, New Church, VA, for providing hand written copies of 2,218 marriage licenses for the 21 year period, 1854 through 1874. Since these records were never microfilmed, she made numerous visits to the Accomack County Clerk's Office between September 1995 and October 1996 to accomplish this task. She also verified many names in the orginal Marriage Register No. 3 that could not be read with confidence on the hardcopy or microfilm. Her knowledge of local family names, based on almost 20 years of genealogical research, was key to this effort. She also contributed significantly to the introductory material and provided the list of female nicknames. We would also like to express our sincere appreciation to our wives, Leslyn and Linda, for continuing to tolerate our genealogy hobby as it consumes more and more of our lives.

Barry W. Miles
120 Cherwell Ct.
Williamsburg, VA 23188

Moody K. Miles, III
13568 Adrian Ct.
Woodbridge, VA 22191

December 1996

Introduction

The Virginia General Assembly passed an act on 11 Apr 1853 that required any person solemnizing a marriage to return this information to the Clerk of the County Court beginning on 1 Jan 1854 or risk losing their licenses to perform marriages. These returns were to be signed by the minister and were to include the full name and ages of both parties, names of parents, whether single or widowed, place of birth and residence, the husband's occupation, date and place of the marriage. The Clerk of Court was to put a summary of these marriages in the marriage registers. All this information was not required on the license, nor was there a place provided for it on the license form, until another act was passed on 15 Mar 1861. The marriage license forms changed in Accomack County on 1 Apr 1861 to reflect this law. The bottom of the form stated that it was to be annexed to the license. Copies of several typical licenses from this period are included herein for reference.

This book contains the 6,225 marriages listed in the Accomack County, Virginia, Marriage Register No. 3, labeled 1853-1896. Marriage dates range from 8 Jul 1852 to 29 Dec 1895 with certificate return dates from 30 Jan 1854 to 31 Dec 1895. The 8 Jul 1852 marriage certificate was returned on 26 Apr 1854, almost 2 years after the marriage. There are 7 marriages from 1852, most of which were returned in Apr and Mar 1854 by Reverends P. Bowdin and J. Allen. There are 14 marriages from 1853, most of which were returned in Mar, Apr and May 1854.

The first listed return was dated 30 Jan 1854 for a 5 Jan 1854 marriage, which was the only return in Jan 1854. There were only 2 returns in Feb 1854. However, on 7 Mar 1854 Rev. J. Allen returned 11 marriages, 3 from 1852, 3 from 1853, and 5 from 1854. This illustrates the practice of some of the ministers of that time to accumulate several marriage certificates before returning them to the County Clerk, spanning many months or years. One of the most exaggerated cases was by Rev. W. Fisher, who returned a certificate on 17 Apr 1858 for a 17 Nov 1853 marriage, almost 5 years later. Several such marriage dates have been marked with a (?) after the date to bring this to the reader's attention. In these cases the return date has also been included to show the discrepancy. In at least one case the marriage date was after the return date, which would seem to be an impossible situation, implying that the Clerk may have made a mistake in entering either the marriage date or the return date in the register. This could also have been the case with Rev. W. Fisher's return in 1858. The Clerk may have also accumulated the returned certificates and only entered them into the register a few times per year.

This book also contains 322 marriage licenses in the Accomack County Clerk's Office dated from 1 Jan 1854 to 21 Jan 1875 that were not included in Marriage Register No. 3. The reason for this is that all marriages were not consistently reported to the County Clerk by local ministers until after the Civil War. There may have even been a few that were not reported after that time. The existence of a marriage license, however, does not assure that the marriage actually took place.

Marriage Records of Accomack County, Virginia, 1854-1895

Due to the extensive time required to be spent in the Clerk's Office at Accomac to compare the licenses to the marriage register and the relatively small number of unrecorded licenses in the marriage register, which could in fact be those persons deciding not to get married after a license was issued, it was decided to not continue the cross check after 1874. Some of the largest number of unrecorded marriages (licenses issued but no minister's returns) occurred in 1864 and 1865, the last two years of the Civil War. George H. Ewell was the only minister making returns from Nov 1864 through Feb 1865. The following listing illustrates the inconsistency of the ministers' returns of this period and how it improved after the Civil War.

Year	Lic Issued	Not in Register	(%)	Year	Lic Issued	Not in Register	(%)
1854	103	44	43	1865	89	27	30
1855	110	34	31	1866	107	2	2
1856	120	42	35	1867	127	3	2
1857	88	22	25	1868	107	5	5
1858	87	27	31	1869	149	1	1
1859	84	26	31	1870	131	2	2
1860	81	22	27	1871	127	9	7
1861	78	9	12	1872	136	5	4
1862	49	3	6	1873	142	3	2
1863	55	0	0	1874	177	4	2
1864	71	32	45	Totals	2218	322	15

There were free African Americans in Accomack County from the time of the earliest records (1632) and they came to be called "free-negro" in marriage records. Slavery was prohibited in Federally-occupied Virginia by the new constitution of Apr 1864, at which time all Accomack County African Americans became free. The last license marked "free-negro" was on 20 Aug 1866, except for one on 4 Apr 1868. The first license marked "colored" was on 18 Oct 1869, except for one on 30 Jan 1865, which showed a colored man and a colored woman. It appears that a number of African Americans were married between Aug 1866 and Oct 1869 who were not labeled as either "F.N." or "Col^d," and some were marked "Col^d" on the license, but not on the minister's returns after Oct 1869.

It was common practice about 1856 to include the mother's maiden name as well as the father's surname. If only the mother's name was given, it could mean the father had been deceased for some time. The widow/widower status was not always used consistently as some considered themselves single again after a spouse had died. Licenses were sometimes procured by others who did not have all the information required on the license. For example, a note was found with some licenses which stated: "Dear Sir, You will please at your most convenient and opportune time fix up the following marriage licenses:
- Wm. J. Bayly son of Thos. & Margaret A. Copes daughter of Solomon
- Wm H. Prewit son of Henry & Henrietta M. Fedderman of Jno. W.
- A. Frank Byrd son of Colmore S. & Charlotte E. Matthews daughter of Wm. S. Please not say any thing about this as they do not want the matter known.
Monday Apr 25 1858   Yours   W.S. Byrd
J.W. Gillet, Esq"

Introduction

It was also common practice during this period for Accomack County residents to go to Somerset and Worcester Counties, MD, to marry, where no consent was needed if the persons were under age and parents' names were not required. The marrying tree at the MD/VA line was a popular choice of location for Worcester County marriages by Accomack County people. After the railroad was built in 1884 local couples could go to Princess Anne in Somerset County, MD, easily. Tangier and Smith Island residents and other baysiders had access by boat to the courthouse there before the railroad was built.

The time of year of the marriages of this period is shown below:

Month	% of Yr	Month	% of Yr	Month	% of Yr
Jan	14	May	7	Sept	7
Feb	8	Jun	5	Oct	7
Mar	6	Jul	6	Nov	9
Apr	6	Aug	6	Dec	19

Late fall and early winter were the most popular times of the year to be married. The most popular day of the year was Christmas, followed closely by the days between Christmas and New Years' Day. The currently popular marriage month, June, was the least popular of all. As Accomack County was a rural area with farming and seafood as its primary industries, there was little time for weddings during the peak planting and harvesting times.

Production Process

The compilers worked on this book from December 1995 to December 1996. Mary Frances Carey also worked from September 1995 to October 1996 on the licenses. In all, over 700 hours, of which one-fourth was spent on checking. We began by entering the data into a computer database which was set up to match the marriage register's rows and columns, see figures on pages 24 and 25. This facilitated data entry and checking. Checks included sorting the database on each of the 23 fields, e.g., dates, places, names, etc. This allowed the comparison of the various spelling of the surnames, given names, place names, etc. and correcting most of the data entry errors, such as misspelling common names and places. The most time-consuming parts were the checking of the index in the marriage register to the database and the 2,218 marriage licenses from 1854 to 1874 to the database. Any mismatches were corrected by looking again at individual entries on the microfilm and, in some cases, the original marriage register in the Clerk's Office. Licenses or items on licenses that were not in the register were added to the database. Once the database was believed to be as accurate as possible, it was sorted by the husbands' names and exported to a word processor for generation of the bride's index and printing. It is hoped that the errors that remain are a very small percentage of the 130,000 pieces of information contained in this book.

Female Nicknames

The following female nicknames were used in Accomack County Records:

Name	Nickname
Adaline	Addie
Amelia/Permelia	Milly
Caroline	Lina, Lena, Carrie
Charlotte	Lottie
Clarissa	Lottie
Cornelia	Neely
Demaris	Daisy, Damy
Eleanor/Ellen	Nelly
Elizabeth	Eliza, Betsy, Betty, Lizzie
Esther/Hester	Hessy, Essie
Frances	Fanny
Gertrude	Gatty, Gattie, Trudy
Harriet	Hetty
Henrietta	Henny, Ritter
Isabelle/Isabella	Bell
Leticia	Letty
Lucretia	Critty, Luky
Mariah	Rida, Ridie
Margaret	Peggy
Martha	Patty
Mary	Polly, Molly, Manie, Mamie
Mildred	Milly
Nancy/Ann	Nanny
Rebecca	Becky, Beky
Sarah	Sally, Sary, Sadie
Susan/Susanna	Suky
Tabitha	Tabby, Tibbie
Trephenia	Tippy
Uphamia/Euphamia	Famey
Zipporah	Zippy

Surname Spelling

The first spelling in each of the following surname groupings was the most widely used in the marriage register and licenses. For alphabetizing purposes, the first spelling was used. The actual spelling that appeared in the records, if different than the first spelling, is shown after the given name in brackets [ ] if from the register and in parenthesis ( ) if from the license. Some of the variations are due to the compilers' inability to distinguish between certain letters in the records. Especially difficult were the letters 'e' and 'i,' and 'r' and 's,' especially if at the end of a name. Also difficult were "L" and "S" when at the beginning of a name, such as Lemuel and Samuel. In some of the handwritings they are practically identical, as evidenced by entries in the occupation column, such as in Laborer and Sailor, were the first letters of each appear to be the same.

Abbott, Abbitt
Allen, Allens
Anderton, Andertson
Andrews, Andress
Aydelotte, Aydelott
Babbitt, Bobbitt
Bayly, Bayley, Bailey, Baily
Beasley, Beasly
Beauchamp, Beacham
Beavans, Beavins, Bevans, Bivans, Bivens, Bivins
Bibbins, Bibins
Becket, Beckett
Beloate, Beloat, Belote
Bennett, Bennet
Birch, Burch
Bloxom, Bloxome, Bloxsom
Bonnewell, Bonawell, Bonewell, Boniwell, Bonnowell, Bonowell
Bowden, Bowdin
Brasure, Brasine
Brimer, Brimore, Brymer
Broadwater, Brodwater
Brown, Browne
Burton, Burten
Byrd, Bird
Carmine, Carmines
Cathell, Cathel
Charnock, Charnick
Cherricks, Cherick, Cherich, Chericks, Cherix, Cherrix

Clark, Clarke
Claville, Clavel, Clavelle, Clayville
Coleburn, Colbourn, Colburn, Colburne
Colonna, Colona, Colna
Conner, Connor
Conworton, Corworton
Coryell, Caryell
Crippin, Crippen
Crockett, Crocket
Cullen, Culling
Daisey, Daizy, Dasey, Daysey, Dazsey, Dazy
Daugherty, Dougherety, Dougherty
Dies, Dise, Dize, Dye, Dyes, Dyer
Douglass, Douglas, Doughlas
Duffy, Duffie, Duffee
Dunton, Dunston
Edmonds, Edmunds
Eichelberger, Eichelbeger, Eichilberger
Eskridge, Eschridge
Evans, Evins
Feddeman, Fedderman
Ferguson, Forguson, Furguson
Fleming, Flemings, Flemming
Garrison, Garison
Gaskins, Gaskin
Giddings, Giddins
Gillett, Gillet, Guillette
Gray, Grey

Grinnalds, Grinnald, Grinalds, Grinals
Groton, Groten
Harmon, Harman
Harmonson, Harmanson
Hart, Heart
Hateney, Hatney, Hateny
Hathway, Harthway, Hathaway
Holden, Holdings, Houlding
Hyslop, Hyslup
Jacobs, Jacob
Jeffries, Jeffers, Jeffreys
Johnson, Johnston
Jubilee, Jublie, Jubliee
Justice, Justis, Jestis
Kelly, Kelley
Kerr, Ker
Killman, Killmon, Kilmon, Kilman
Lankford, Langford
Laws, Law
Lescallette, Lescalitte
Logan, Logen, Login
Manuel, Manuell
Mariner, Marriner
Marshall, Marshal
Martin, Marten, Marting
Mason, Mayson
Matthews, Mathews
McMath, Mackmath
Merritt, Marriett
Milbourn, Milbourne, Milburne, Melburn
Milliner, Millines
Moffitt, Moffett
Nedab, Needab
Onions, Onion
Onley, Only
Outten, Outen
Parkes, Parks
Payne, Pane
Pettitt, Pettit
Phillips, Philips, Philip
Pollitt, Polliet, Politte
Poole, Pool
Poulson, Polson
Powell, Powel
Pruitt, Prewitt, Pruoitt
Pryor, Prior

Purnell, Parinell, Paunell
Read, Reed, Reid
Revell, Revel
Reynolds, Raynolds
Robins, Robbins
Rogers, Rodgers
Ross, Rossa
Rowley, Rawley, Roley, Rolly
Ruediger, Rusdiger
Russell, Russel
Satchell, Satchel
Scarborough, Scarborogh, Scarburgh
Shaw, Shaws
Shepherd, Shepard, Shepperd
Shield, Shields
Shrieves, Shreaves, Shreeves, Shreives, Shreves, Shrevis, Shrives
Spence, Spense
Staton, Staten
Sterling, Starling, Starlin
Stevens, Stephens
Stewart, Steward
Stokes, Stakes, Staks
Stran, Strann, Stram, Strame
Strigle, Streggle, Striggle
Summers, Sommers, Somers
Tatem, Tatum
Teagle, Teackle
Teague, Tigue
Thorns, Thornes, Thorms
Tindall, Tindal, Tindle, Tyndall
Trehearn, Trehurn
Trower, Trowers
Twiford, Twyford, Tryford
Tyler, Tiler
Wallace, Wallis
Waples, Wapler
Warrington, Warrenton
Watkinson, Wadkinson, Witkinson
Wescott, Wescot, Wescoat
Wessells, Wessels, Vessels
Wilkerson, Wilkinson
Willett, Willet
Williams, William
Wimbrough, Wambough, Wimbro, Wimber
Winder, Window

Ministers

A list of the ministers who submitted marriage returns to the Accomack County Clerk from 1854 to 1895 follows. The denomination of most of them is also given. Their full names are given here as either listed in the Marriage Register or from other sources including, *Revival's Children, A Religious History of Virginia's Eastern Shore*, Peninsula Press, Salisbury, Maryland, 1979, by Kirk Mariner and from Rev. Mariner's and Mary Frances Carey's private research. For more on these ministers and the history of their churches see *Revival's Children*.

Adams, George F - Baptist
Adams, James K
Adams, Peter J
Addison, James H
Addison, James C
Adkins, Isaac Tunnel - Methodist
Allen, John
Ames, Benjamin T - Methodist
Amiss, Joseph H - Methodist
Amos, A S
Anderson, Henry M
Anderson, J M - Methodist
Anderson, John F - Methodist
Anderson, John G - Presbyterian
Anderson, Richard W - Episcopalian
Arnett, Charles S - Methodist
Atkins, E C
Atkinson, John
Ayler, Junius C
Ayres, T O
Baker, Charles S - Methodist
Banning, E T
Bargamin, Vincent Walter - Methodist
Barker, John A - Baptist
Barrett, Louis E - Methodist
Battersby, G S
Beadles, Robert Blackwell - Methodist
Bean, Addison S - Methodist
Bean, E H
Bean, H S
Berkeley, Alex L
Berryman, Albert C - Methodist

Betty, Lewis Bond - Methodist
Birch, Francis M
Bledsoe, Adam Clarke - Methodist
Bonen, Wm S P
Booker, George E - Methodist
Boon, J A
Bosman, John Thomas - Methodist
Boston, Frank R - Baptist
Boston, Solomon Charles - Baptist
Bowdin, Parker Sr - CSH Ch, Chinco:
Bowdin, Parker Jr - CSH Ch, Chinco:
Boyd, Reuben T - Methodist
Bradford, George - Baptist
Broaddus, Andrew Jr - Baptist
Brown, S A
Bryan, E M
Bundick, John E
Burke, George W - Methodist
Burris, G W
Burris, G C
Burriss, Caleb - Baptist (black)
Burton, Joshua - Methodist
Burton, Thomas - Methodist
Butler, J B -
Butts, Daniel Gregory Claibourne - Methodist
Byrd, George H T - Baptist (black)
Carroll, James - Methodist
Carroll, John William - Methodist
Carroll, W H
Chandler, E Gunter
Chaplain, John Francis - Methodist

Charlton, John W - Methodist
Cheveis(?), John Mark
Chinn, William
Clark, Byron - Presbyterian
Clayton, William A
Clement, Charles - Baptist
Cluff, James C - Baptist (black)
Coe, William Gwynn - Methodist
Cole, Thomas M - AME (black)
Coleburn, R H
Coleman, R H
Collin, C
Colton, C
Compton, Robert Asbury - Methodist
Connor, James - Methodist
Converse, James B
Cook, Jacob W
Copeland, S M G
Corbin, William H - Baptist (black)
Corrd, Felix
Coulling, David - Baptist
Councill, J G - Baptist
Cowan, Horace G
Cox, William
Craighill, James B - Episcopalian
Crawley, Charles D - Methodist
Crosdale, John - Episcopalian
Crouse, William A - Methodist
Cummins, George - Methodist
Davis, Andrew D - Methodist
Davis, Fielding A - Methodist
Davis, Robert - AME
Dennis, John M
Derby, Henry L - Episcopalian
Derrickson, Edmund Handy - Methodist
Diggs, John W
Dixon, William - Baptist (black)
Dolly, Adam B
Dougherty, Beverly Waugh
Drunning, H
Duckett, Joseph
Duhadaway, William J - Methodist
Dulany, Henry S
Dunaway, James Manning - Baptist
Duncan, Levi - Baptist (black)
Easley, James W - Methodist
Eason, Samuel Washington - Methodist
Easter, George W - Episcopalian

Edmonston, George D - Methodist
Edmundson, John T
Edward, Joseph John - Methodist
Elderdice, Hugh L - Methodist
Ellegood, J H - Methodist
Elliott, John Wesley Andros - Methodist
Evans, William
Ewell, George H
Ewell, John W
Ewell, John E T
Farring, George F
Felton, Daniel
Ferguson, Samuel T - Methodist
Fisher, William - Baptist
Fletcher, O Frank
Flippo, Oscar Farish - Methodist
Fosnocht, Isaac G - Methodist
Fristoe, A J - Baptist
Garner, Emmett Francis - Methodist
Govans, Richard H
Grant, Edward S
Grice, C A - Methodist
Griffith, Joseph Richard - Methodist
Grimsley, Simeon U - Baptist
Gwinn, William R - Methodist
Hains, C R
Hall, Alexander McCaine - Methodist
Hammer, James G
Handy, Aaron
Hardesty, G L
Harmonsley, James H
Harrell, Emmett E - Methodist
Harris, Alexander
Hayes, William Franklin - Methodist
Haynes, James A
Hazzard, Robert B - Methodist
Hebard, Edward
Hill, Charles - Methodist
Hill, George J - Methodist
Hilldrup, John Wesley - Methodist
Hitt, Luther - Methodist
Hoblitzell, Solomon A - Methodist
Holmes, William L
Hopkins, William
Horsey, Charles A
Houghton, Thomas G - Episcopalian
Hubbard, J H B - Meth (black female)
Hughes, Josiah H

Ministers

Humphreys, Joshua E - Methodist
Hundley, John W - Baptist
Hundley, William T - Baptist
Irvin, Edward G - Methodist
James, Abel
Jester, Benjamin F - Methodist
Johns, Stephen
Johnson, James H A - AME
Jones, George P - Methodist
Jones, Richard C - Methodist
Joynes, Abel
King, J L - Baptist
Laws, William - Baptist
Lawson, R E C
Leatherbury, Perry A - Methodist
LeCato, Littleton K - Methodist
Lee, Lemuel W
Lee, Paul W
Lee, Robert E
Lennon, Joseph G - Methodist
Lenox, D M
Lewis, J B
Lewis, Joseph
Lewis, P M
Lindsay, William C
Littleton, Oscar - Methodist
Lodge, James L - Baptist
Long, Handy - Methodist (black)
Lynch, Joseph B - CSH Ch
Maloy, J Earle - Methodist
Marshall, Samuel
Martin, James G
Martin, James Cameron - Methodist
Massey, James Augustus - Methodist
Matthews, Charles W
Matthews, George W
May, George S
McCluer, E B
McKenry, M L
McLean, L A
McNabb, John - Episcopalian
McSparran, James E - Methodist
Mears, Julius C
Melvin, Adolphus D - Methodist
Merrill, William - Methodist
Merritt, Joseph B - Methodist
Mickle, Edward - Roman Catholic
Miller, E Hamline - Methodist

Moore, J E W
Moore, John T - Methodist
Moore, Lloyd - Methodist
Morely, A S
Morris, Noah
Morris, Samuel James - Methodist
Moss, James Obadiah - Methodist
Mullineaux, Franklin H - Methodist
Nettles, T W - Baptist (black)
Nichols, M
Nichols, R W
Nicholson, John Wesley - Methodist
Norris, J Wright - Methodist
Nutter, John Henry
Offer, John Henry - AME (black)
Oldham, Montcalm Sr. - Methodist
Only, P M
Outen, Elisha T - Methodist (black)
Overton, Frank Warren - AME (black)
O'Brien, T A H - Methodist
Peeden, Thaddeus
Pernell, P H - Baptist
Petty, Henry - Baptist
Phillips, John H - Baptist
Phillips, William - Methodist
Pinder, A
Plato, J K
Polk, J L
Potts, Joseph Ezekial - Methodist
Poulson, Thomas L - Methodist
Poulson, Thomas M - Baptist
Powers, Samuel - Methodist
Pritchell, Edgar Herndon - Methodist
Pruitt, John Benjamin - Baptist
Pullen, Thomas Granville - Methodist
Quinn, William - Methodist
Ray, George Henry - Methodist
Read, Miles S - Baptist
Reamy, Adoniram Judson - Baptist
Reed, James C - Methodist
Reese, James D - Methodist
Rich, Harrison G
Riddick, J E R
Riddick, Joseph Henry - Methodist
Robins, John H
Roper, Lee
Rosser, Leonidas - Methodist
Royall, William Woolridge - Methodist

Ruff, John W - AME (black)
Rutledge, G P
Sample, W B
Sanford, Millard F - Baptist
Sanford, R B - Baptist
Satchell, Abel J - Baptist (black)
Satchell, C W
Savage, Dennis B - Baptist (black?)
Savage, Jasper - Baptist (black)
Scott, R B - Methodist
Sheppard, Peter - AME (black)
Simmerman, H S
Sledd, Robert Newton - Methodist
Snow, Charles P
Spencer, L E
Stern, H C
Stickney, Ezekeil W - Methodist
Stiff, James Willard - Methodist
Stimson, R D - Presbyterian
Stone, Walter H - Methodist
Street, W A - Baptist
Sturgis, Joseph Rodgers - Methodist
Swain, Charles P - Methodist
Taft, John Leroy - Methodist
Talbott, William F - Methodist
Tennent, John E
Thomas, J H - AME (black)
Thomas, James Dunlap - Presbyterian
Thornton, William P - Baptist
Tidball, Thomas Allen
Tillery, John R
Titlow, Daniel - Methodist
Tomkinson, T Lessey - Methodist
Toulson, Lewis E
Traynham, David James - Methodist
Truitt, Benjamin P - Methodist
Tuelley, W C
Tull, Willam T
Turlington, Thomas - Baptist (black)
Turner, Joseph W - Baptist
Twiford, Obed P
Twilley, William James - Methodist
Tyler, Geroge Thomas - Methodist
Vaden, Wesley Childs - Methodist
Wallace, Adam - Methodist
Wallace, Andrew J
Wallace, David M - Methodist
Wallace, John Silas - Methodist

Walsh, Richard
Walter, A J
Walton, Olin Scott - Methodist
Ward, John Wyatt - Baptist
Warren, Patrick - Baptist (father)
Warren, Patrick Thomas - Baptist (son)
Waterfield, Robert Tankard - Methodist
Waters, Joshua N
Waters, Robert J
Waters, Thomas - Baptist
Watkins, R Irving - Methodist
Watkins, S W
Watson, J Carson - Methodist
Watts, Charles Edward - Methodist
Waugh, C V - Baptist
Webster, Zachariah H - Methodist
Wellman, E H - Episcopalian
Wertenbaker, Charles C - Methodist
West, John R - AME (black)
Wharton, J S - Baptist
Wharton, M B
White, D B
Whittington, Stephen P
Wiggins, Alexander M - Methodist
Wiles, A
Wilkerson, William T - Baptist
Williams, A J
Williams, Charles Henley - Methodist
Williams, J C
Williams, Milton Lee -Methodist (Saxis)
Williams, Robert - Baptist
Williams, William F - AME (black)
Williamson, Riley S - Methodist
Williamson, Robert - Baptist
Wilson, J Harry - Methodist
Wise, Henry A Jr
Wood, Felix or Phoenix
Wood, George E
Wood, W W - Baptist
Wooden, J Fred
Woodson, Drury A - Baptist
Woodyard, Almarine - Baptist
Workman, James B - CSH Ch
Wright, William P - Methodist
Young, George W - Methodist (black)
Young, J C
Zeaue, A S

Clerks of Court

The following is a list of the Clerks of Court of Accomack County between 1854 and 1895 as taken from *The Eastern Shore of Virginia, 1603-1964*, by Nora Miller Turman, Heritage Books, Inc., Bowie, MD 1988.

        John W. Gillett 1850-1862
        John B. Ailworth 1862-1865
        John W. Gillett 1865-1869
        William H.B. Custis 1869-1887
        Montcalm Oldham, Jr. 1887-1900

Abbreviations

( )	from License	ME	Methodist Episcopal
[ ]	from Register	Meth	Methodist
Acc	Accomack County, VA	Mkr	maker
Acc CH	Accomack Court House	Mt	Mount
AME	African Methodist Episcopal	Nk	Neck
Ave	Avenue	N'hamp:	Northampton County, VA
b:	birth place	orp/o	orphan of
Bapt	Baptist	Par	Parsonage
Br	Branch	r:	residence
Capt	Captain	r/o	residence of
Ch	Church	Rd	Road(s)
Chinco:	Chincoteague	Rev	Reverend
Chp	Chapel	RR	Rail Road
Ck	Creek	s/o	son of
Co	County	S	single
Col	colored	So	south
CSH	Christ's Sanctified Holy	Som	Somerset
d/o	daughter of	Sr	Senior
D	divorced	Sta	Station
dec'd	deceased	Temp'ville	Temperanceville
div	divorced	W	Widow, Widower
Dr	Doctor	ward/o	ward of
Drum'tn	Drummondtown	Wic	Wicomico
FN	Free Negro	wid/o	widow of
Isld	Island	widr	widower
Jr	Junior	Wor	Worcester
lic:	license date		
marr:	marriage date		

Current standard 2 letter state abbreviations codes were used.

Explanation of Entries

Sample Entry from Register:
ADAMS William L 22 S Fireman Burlington Co NJ Acc s/o Thomas & Fannie to Effie L Evans 18 S Acc Acc d/o William & Sally on 4 Dec 1889 at bride's mother's by JM Anderson

Explanation: William L. Adams, age 22, single, occupation: fireman, born in Burlington Co, NJ, residing in Accomack Co, VA, the son of Thomas and Fannie Adams was married to Effie L Evans, age 18, single, born in Accomack Co, VA, residing in Accomack Co, VA, the daughter of William & Sally Evans on 4 Dec 1889 at the bride's mother's house by Rev. J.M. Anderson

Sample Entry from License:
BLOXOM William ward/o Jesse Dickerson who gave consent to Mary Wessells d/o John dec'd & ward/o Thorogood Mason who gave consent lic: 31 Dec 1855

Explanation: William Bloxom, the ward of Jesse Dickerson who gave consent (implying William's father was deceased and he was under age 21) and Mary Wessells, the daughter of John Wessells who is deceased and the ward of Thorogood Mason who gave consent (implying Mary was under age 21) were issued a marriage license on 31 Dec 1855. The use of the "lic:" date indicates that the marriage was not recorded in the marriage register and that all of the information in the entry came from the license.

Sample Entry from Register supplemented by information from License:
BROADWATER William (Brodwater) (Col) 60 W Laborer Acc Acc s/o Brutchey to Eliza Mills (Col) 40 S Acc Acc on 22 Jan 1871 near Modest Town by WF Williams

Explanation: William Broadwater (spelled Brodwater on the license and shown as colored on the license, but not in the Register), age 60, a widower, who was a laborer, born in Accomack Co, VA, residing in Accomack Co, VA, the son of Brutchey Broadwater was married to Eliza Mills (shown as colored on the license, but not in the Register), age 40, single, born in Accomack Co, VA, residing in Accomack Co, VA, were married on 22 Jan 1871 near Modest Town by W.F. Williams (the Ministers' Full Names list shows him as William F. Williams).

Marriage Records of Accomack County, Virginia, 1854-1895

Sample Entry from Register supplemented by information from License:
CLOWS Peter J (Claws) 50 W Steward b: Sussex Co DE s/o Isaac & Sarah to Sarah Jane Mears 42 W b: Acc d/o Benj & Ann Annis & (wid/o John B Mears) on 7 Nov 1855 at Pungo: by M Oldham

Explanation: Peter J Clows (spelled Claws on the license), age 50, a widower, born in Sussex Co, DE, the son of Isaac and Sarah Clows was married to Sarah Jane Mears, age 42, a widow, born in Accomack Co, VA, the daughter of Benjamin and Ann Ames and (from the license, the widow of John B. Mears) on 7 Nov 1855 at Pungoteague by Rev. Montcalm Oldham.

Notes:
1. If the age was given, the martial status is shown as either S-single, D-divorced, W-widow or widower. If the age was not given, the martial status is shown as either single, div-divorced, wid-widow, widr-widower to avoid confusing the martial status with the middle initial.
2. If both a birth place and residence is given they are listed in that order . If only one of these is listed it will be preceded by b: for born or r: for residence.
3. If the parents' surname is the same as the husband's or wife's, it will not be shown. If it is different it will be shown.
4. Only the ministers' initials are shown. Refer to the list of Ministers for their full names and denominations, if they were available.
5. Supplemental information from the licenses is shown in ( ).
6. Surname spelling from the register is shown in [ ] if different from the most common spelling of that surname, which was used to alphabetize the entries.
7. (?) after a marriage date indicates it is either considerably after the license date or before the certificate return date. The license date or certificate return date will then be shown at the end of the entry.
8. (?) after a name indicates the inability of the compilers to read it with certainty.

Illustrative Documents

The following copies of documents are representative of the various forms of marriage licenses, certificates and notes of consent found in the Accomack County Clerk's Office for the period 1854-1874. Also shown are representative pages from the Accomack County Marriage Register No. 3. All of these documents were photographically reduced in size to fit on these pages. Some of these copies are less than half of their original size.

Marriage License issued on 1 Apr 1854 by J.W. Gillet
to marry Edward W. Kellam (son of Argyle)
and Rose Ann Hyslop (daughter of James)

Marriage License issued on 3 Jan 1863 by J.B. Ailworth
to marry Thomas Trader (son of Parker & Nancy)
and Sarah J. Marshall (daughter of Ann Marshall)

Illustrative Documents

> To the Clerk of Accomack County Court
> you are authorised to issue License
> to celebrate the rites of matrimony between
> Authaer. C. Landen and my Daughter
> Margaret. J. Thomas Witness my
> hand this 1st day of May 1865.
> Witness
> Lybrand Thomas   Joshua Thomas

A Note of Consent (for underage child) attached to the back of a License.
Joshua Thomas gave consent for his daughter Margaret to marry Author Landen.
Dated 1 May 1865, witnessed by Lybrand Thomas.

> To the Clerk of Accomac County Court: I hereby
> authorize you to grant license to marry my
> daughter Georgiana to Samuel Wessels of John.
> Given under my hand this the 29th May 1865
> Witness   her
> Thomas. S. Lewis   Margret X Thorns
>   mark

A Note of Consent (for underage child) attached to the back of a License.
Margaret (her X mark) Thorns gave consent for her daughter Georgiana
to marry Samuel Wessels (son of John).
Dated 29 May 1865, witnessed by Thomas S. Lewis.

MARRIAGE LICENSE.

Virginia—County of Accomack, to wit:

To any Person Licensed to Celebrate Marriages:

You are hereby authorized to join together in the Holy State of Matrimony according to the rites and ceremonies of your Church, or religious denomination, and the laws of the Commonwealth of Virginia, _Gilbert Webb Jr,_ and _Ailey Morris Jr,_

Given under my hand, as Clerk of the County Court of said County, this _8th_ day of _May_ 186_6_.

L.R. Warren Dy. for J.W. Gillet, Clerk.

CERTIFICATE TO OBTAIN A MARRIAGE LICENSE,

TO BE ANNEXED TO THE LICENSE, REQUIRED BY THE ACT PASSED 15TH MARCH, 1861.

Time of Marriage, _May 9th 1866._
Place of Marriage, _Accomack County Va._
Full Names of Parties Married, _Gilbert Webb & Ailey Morris_
Age of Husband, _24 years_
Age of Wife, _28 "_
Condition of Husband, widowed or single, _Single_
Condition of Wife, widowed or single, _do_
Place of Husband's Birth, _Accomack County Va._
Place of Wife's Birth, _Do._
Place of Husband's Residence, _Do._
Place of Wife's Residence, _Do._
Names of Husband's Parents, _John Webb & Harriet, his wife._
Names of Wife's Parents, _Levin Morris & Tabitha, his wife._
Occupation of Husband, _Sawyer_

Given under my hand, this _8th_ day of _May_ 186_6_.

L.R. Warren Dy. for J.W. Gillet, Clerk.

Marriage License issued 8 May 1866 by L.R. Warren, Deputy Clerk to marry Gilbert Webb, FN, (son of John & Harriet) and Ailey Morris, FN, (daughter of Levin & Tabitha)

I acknowledge that I this day made oath before L. R. Warren, Depy by Jno John W. Gillet _____ Clerk of Accomack County Court, in his Office, that the within named Gilbert Webb and Ailey Morris are each upwards of twenty-one years of age, this 5th day of May A. D. 1866.

                                                                                his
                                                           George X Bagwell
                                                                 mark

Sworn to and Subscribed }
  in presence of

L. R. Warren Dy.
Jno J. W. Gillet. C.A.C.

Oath, on the back of the License (see previous page),
by George (his X mark) Bagwell that Gilbert Webb and
Ailey Morris are each upwards of 21 years of age

Hand written Marriage License (when Clerk was out of printed pages)
issued on 23 Dec 1867 by L.R. Warren, Deputy Clerk,
to Charles Ames (son of Easter) and Lucy Chase (daughter of Nanny)
for a marriage to occur on 25 Dec 1867

Illustrative Documents

Marriage License issued on 28 Dec 1870 by M. Oldham, Deputy Clerk
to John W Rogers (son of Wm and Eliz'th) of York Co, VA
and Sarah M Cobb (daughter of James and Leah) of Acco Co, VA
with oath as to age by Nathaniel T. Rayfield

Marriage Register No. 3 (left hand part of page)

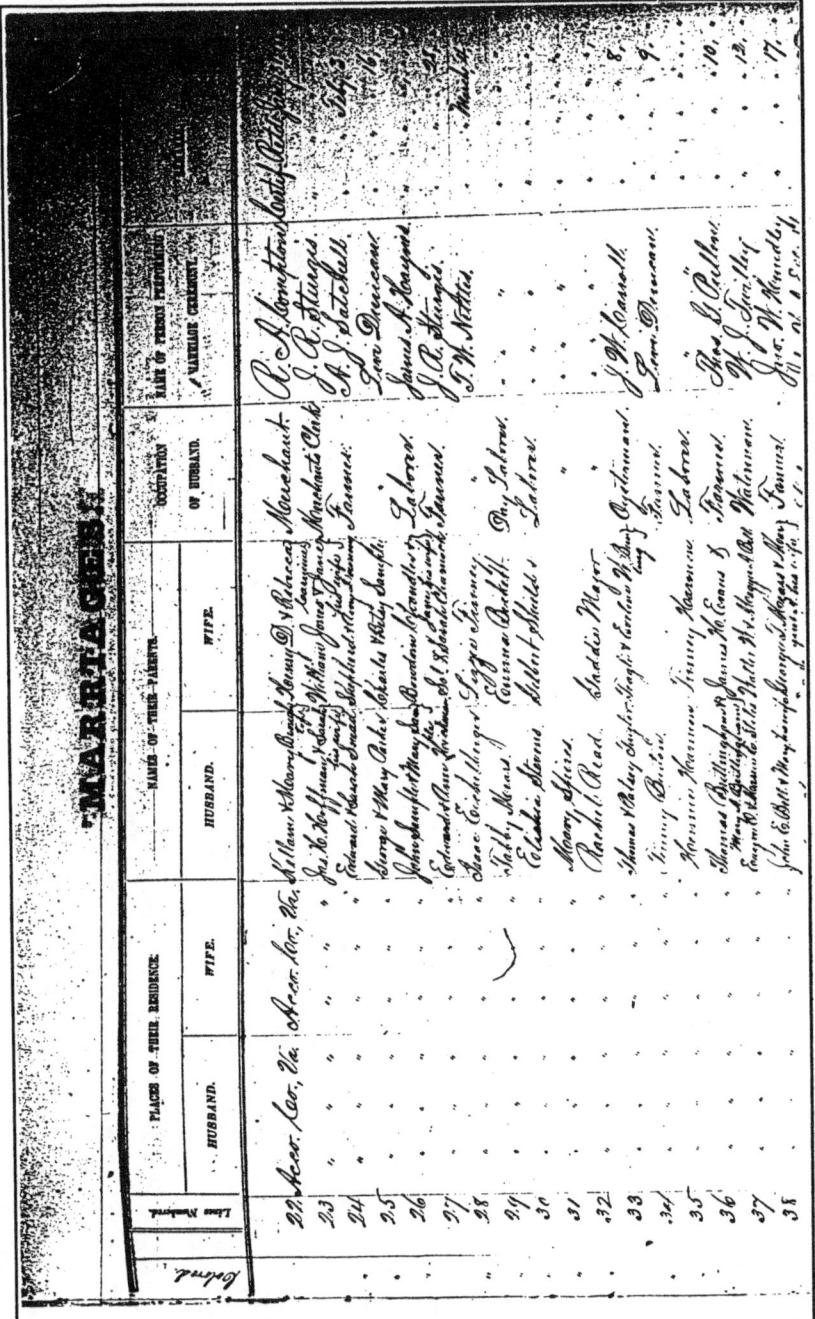

Marriage Register No. 3 (right hand part of page)

Marriages

(-----) (-----) to Mary E Savage lic: 17 Feb 1864

ABBOTT David D 22 S Farmer Acc Acc s/o Saml C & Anna to Mary Warner 22 S Acc Acc d/o Critty on 28 Jan 1863 at Acc by ES Grant

ABBOTT Samuel C 22 S Farmer Acc Acc s/o David & Mary A to Elizabeth Y Ewell 19 S Acc Acc d/o Charels & Susan on 20 Apr 1887 at Acc by WA Street

ABBOTT Wm Col 22 S Laborer Acc Acc s/o George Abbott & Esther Outten to Sarah Mapp Col 16 S Acc Acc d/o Peter & Mary on 2 Jan 1870 at Acc by A Joynes

ABRAMS John T 18 S Farmer Acc Acc s/o John & Eliz'th to Margaret S Elliott 19 S Acc Acc d/o John & Margaret on 6 Jun 1888 at Keller by JWA Elliott

ACKLEY J Wallace 38 S Paper Hanger Philadelphia PA Acc s/o John T & Marietta to Arinthia J Scott 42 W Acc Acc d/o Selby & Margaret Lankford on 14 Jun 1893 at Parksley by JET Ewell

ACKLEY Orlando A 23 S Manger [Mgr] Saw Mill Philadelphia PA Acc s/o Jno T & Maryetta to Grace W [Bowdin] Bowden 21 S Acc Acc d/o Jno R & Amanda on 1 Oct 1878 near Guilford by JW Hundley

ADAIR Geo H 29 W Merchant b: Acc s/o Theadore & Mary to Harriet Susan Nottingham 20 S b: N'hamp: d/o Severn & Rosa & (ward/o Jacob Nottingham) on 29 Mar 1854 at Belle Haven by W Fisher

ADAMS Daniel J 32 S Steamboating NJ Acc s/o T J & Maria L to Maggie W Dies 16 S Acc Acc d/o Peter H & Mary W on 3 Dec 1890 at Acc by JM Anderson

ADAMS Ellis 26 W Sailor NJ NJ s/o Jas & Elma to Sarah A Berry 21 S Acc NY City d/o Saml & Susan on 30 Jan 1865 at r/o Jas Lewis by ES Grant

ADAMS Ezra T 21 S Seaman NJ Chinco: Isld s/o Jeremia & Alsey to Matilda Claville 21 S Chinco: Isld Chinco: Isld d/o Jas & Amy on 7 Jun 1877 at Chinco: Isld by R Williamson

ADAMS Henry D 30 S Farmer Som Co MD Acc s/o Henry D & Elizth to Mary A Baker 17 S Acc Acc d/o Jno S & Emma on 14 Aug 1878 at Modest Town by DA Woodson

ADAMS John E 23 S Blacksmith Som Co MD Acc s/o Henry & Elizth to Nancy E West 18 S Acc Acc d/o Solemon & Margt on 27 Aug 1868 at Acc by JE Bundick

ADAMS Leonard H to Virginia S Joynes d/o Edward D who gave consent lic: 8 Apr 1857 H C Walker says he over 21

ADAMS Oswald J 26 S Farmer Acc Acc s/o James C & Mary to Sarah [Millines] Milliner 24 S Acc Acc d/o Southey & Susan on 7 Dec 1881 at Acc C H by JG Anderson

ADAMS Thomas H 57 S Merchant Som Co MD Som Co MD s/o Elijah to Maggie I Willis 42 S Acc Acc d/o Adah on 21 Mar 1894 at Onancock by GE Booker

ADAMS William L 22 S Fireman Burlington Co NJ Acc s/o Thomas & Fannie to Effie L Evans 18 S Acc Acc d/o William & Sally on 4 Dec 1889 at bride's mother's by JM Anderson

ADAMS Wm T 22 S Waterman b: Acc s/o Thomas Adams & Mary Wilson to Mary Hopkins 37 S b: Acc d/o Nathaniel Hopkins & Elizth Thornton on 14 Jun 1885 at New Church by T Waters (George Fletcher says both over 21)

ADKINS Emory A 22 S Wage-earner Salisbury MD Acc s/o James & Olivia to Mary F Wright 21 S Acc Acc d/o Charles & Margaret on 2 Jul 1890 at Masonville by HS Dulany

AGATHORN Dion S 36 W Engineer Niagara Ont CA Acc s/o John & Eliz'th Nisbet to Ella B Wise 21 S Acc Acc d/o Benj B & Louisa S on 25 May 1892 at Pungo: by JM Anderson

AILWORTH Frank 28 S Oysterman Acc Acc s/o Lenor & Ann to Brunetta J Hickman 28 S Acc Acc d/o Asa & Jane on 9 Apr 1884 at Modest Town by JW Hundley

AILWORTH James E 19 S Farmer Acc Acc s/o Lenox & Ann to Emily Thornton 28 W Acc Acc d/o Delight & Mary Christopher on 12 Jan 1869 at Acc by M Oldham

AILWORTH William 23 S Farming Acc Acc s/o Lenox & Ann to Elizabeth Northam 24 S Acc Acc d/o Gillet & Elizabeth on 22 Jan 1873 at New Church by TM Poulson

ALEXANDER Wm 23 S Engineer DE Acc s/o George & Elizabeth to Alice Marshall 16 S Acc Acc d/o Samuel S on 5 Jul 1891 near Mappsville by JL King

ALLEE Winfield K 25 S Farmer Kent Co DE Caroline Co MD s/o Jacob R & Sallie R to Annie L Dennis 22 S Som Co MD Acc d/o David H & Mary E on 1 Jun 1887 at Temp'ville by JW Carroll

ALLEN Charles 30 S Mariner b: Nautes France s/o Ephiane Allen & Rebecca Jurrd to Elizabeth Scott 20 S b: Acc d/o Major Scott & Mahala Justic on 28 Jan 1857 at Acc by P Warren (E B Waples says he over 21)

ALLEN Edmond Col 44 W Farmer Acc Acc s/o Margaret to Jane Davis Col 26 S Acc Acc d/o Center on 16 Jul 1891 at Fair Oaks by RH Coleman

ALLEN Edmund Col 27 S Laborer Acc Acc s/o Margaret Perkins to Annie Custis Col 22 S Acc Acc d/o Betsy on 29 Dec 1872 at Acc by N Morris

ALLEN Edward Col 23 S Farmer Acc Acc s/o Thomas & Rachel to Mary E Boggs Col 16 S Acc Acc d/o Ibby on 13 Feb 1889 at Drum'tn by P Sheppard

ALLEN George A Col 25 S Laborer Acc Acc s/o Mary to Ella Allen Col 17 S Acc Acc d/o Thos & Rachel on 14 Jan 1880 at Drum'tn by RH Govans

ALLEN Jacob Col 68 W Farmer Acc Acc s/o Lurie Custis to Candice Parker Col 50 S Acc Acc on 23 Jun 1888 at Drum'tn by P Sheppard

ALLEN James Col 60 S Sawyer Acc Acc to Margaret Bayly Col 45 S Acc Acc d/o Anna on 1 Mar 1874 near Drum'tn by JH Offer

ALLEN James Col 24 S Laborer Acc Acc s/o Joise Ashby to Easter Snead Col 22 S Acc Acc d/o Peter Snead & Any on 4 Jun 1874 at St Luke Ch by LK LeCato

ALLEN James H Col 21 S Wage-earner Acc Acc s/o Esther Taylor to Susan [Scarburgh] Scarborough 22 S Acc Acc d/o Tillie on 15 Dec 1895 at Acc by JH Robins

ALLEN John Col 21 S Laborer Acc Acc s/o Jim & Ada to Patsy Simpkins

Col 21 S Acc Acc d/o Jim & Patsy on 14 Jan 1872 near Locust Mount by JWA Elliott

ALLEN John Col 43 S Wage-earner Acc Acc to Arinthia J Dennis Col 37 S Acc Acc d/o Fairy on 13 Jan 1895 at Acc by JC Cluff

ALLEN John H Col 22 S Farm Laborer Acc Acc s/o James & Margt to Margie Coleburn Col 21 S Acc Acc d/o Rebecca on 19 Jun 1884 at Acc by LW Lee

ALLEN Levin T Col 50 S Farmer Acc Acc s/o Tabby to Clarissa Gunter Col 35 S Acc Acc d/o Tinsey Fisher on 28 Mar 1883 at Drum'tn by LW Lee

ALLEN Obediance Col 35 S Laborer Acc Acc to Maria Coard Col 36 S Acc Acc on 28 Jan 1880 at Drum'tn by RH Govans

ALLEN Robert E Col 23 S Farmer Acc Acc s/o Esther to Maggie E White Col 22 S Acc Acc d/o Henry & Susan on 22 Nov 1894 at Drum'tn by R Davis

ALLEN Severn Thos Col 21 S Wage-earner Acc Acc s/o Elizabeth to Daisey Allen Col 18 S Acc Acc d/o James & Hester on 1 Dec 1895 at Acc by JH Robins

ALLEN Thomas Col 24 S Laborer Acc Acc s/o Esther to Sarah Ann Taylor Col 24 S Acc Acc on 6 Dec 1874 at Acc by JK Plato

ALLEN Thomas Col 60 S Farmer Acc Acc s/o Daniel to Rachel Allen Col 50 S Acc Acc on 1 Dec 1895 at Acc by JR West

ALLEN William Col 24 S Farmer Acc Acc s/o Mary to Missouri Burton Col 21 S Acc Acc d/o Mary on 28 May 1876 at Little Rest by HT Rich

ALLEN William 22 S Farmer Acc Acc s/o Hester to Sarah C Bull 20 S Acc Acc d/o Geo W & Elizth on 3 Jan 1886 near Parksley by HG Cowan

ALLEN William R 26 S Farmer Acc Acc s/o Edwd R & Mary to Mary Crowson 25 S Acc Acc d/o Jas & Sarah on 14 Jan 1886 at Mappsville by WA Street

ALLEN Wm H 25 S Oysterman Acc Acc s/o Wm H to Elizabeth Marshall 21 S Acc Acc d/o Dennard & Elizth on 19 Dec 1884 at Temp'ville by JW Carroll

ALLENDER John E 21 S Farmer Baltimore Co MD Baltimore Co MD s/o J E & Hannah to Jane S Coard 20 S Acc Acc d/o Wm R & E W on 20 Jan 1870 at r/o Wm R Coard by JET Ewell

AMES Alexander Col 33 S Farmer Acc Acc s/o Lauretta to Louisa Finney Col 18 S Acc Acc d/o Mary on 20 Dec 1885 at Drum'tn by LW Lee

AMES Benjamin Col 24 S Wage-earner Acc Acc s/o Nancy to Mary Byrd Col 19 S Acc Acc d/o Sally Garrison on 6 Feb 1889 at Acc by JK Adams

AMES Charles 30 S Farmer Acc Acc s/o Esther to Lucy Chase 21 S Acc Acc d/o Nanny on 25 Dec 1867 at Acc by JH Offer

AMES Douglas Col 19 S Wage-earner Acc Acc s/o Louis to Martha [Hateny] Hateney Col 17 S Acc Acc d/o Mary on 10 Oct 1890 at Acc by JWA Elliott

AMES Edward Alma 35 S Farmer Acc Acc s/o John & Margaret S to Lena E Trower 23 S Acc Acc d/o Thomas L & Ann A on 15 May 1895 at Acc by EF Garner

AMES Elijah M 27 S Merchant Acc Acc s/o Levin L & Margt to Vandalia E Mears 25 S Acc Acc d/o Jno W A & Hester on 5 Feb 1873 at Pungo: by JE Humphreys

AMES Geo T 22 S Merchant Acc Acc s/o Richd W & Susan E to Sallie G Smith 20 S Acc Acc d/o Jno E & Margt E on 24 Oct 1877 at Belle Haven by E Hebard

AMES Geo W Col 21 S Farm LaborerAcc Acc s/o Mary to Mary Custis Col 15 S Acc Acc d/o Lydis Topping on 10 Jan 1884 at Morris Chp by JH Nutter

AMES George Col 21 S Laborer Acc Acc s/o Mary to Ellen Drummond Col 19 S Acc Acc d/o Eliza on 31 Oct 1880 at Cashville by JW Diggs

AMES George Col 46 S Farmer Acc Acc s/o Letty to Mary Jubilee Col 31 S Acc Acc d/o Diana on 6 Nov 1881 at St Luke Ch by PM Lewis

AMES George L 26 S Physician Acc Acc s/o George I & Bettie B to Gabriella Susan Mapp 22 S Acc Acc d/o George S & Sarah on 6 Dec 1893 at Pungo: by HL Derby

AMES George T 28 S Merchant Acc Baltimore MD s/o Levin S & Margt to Bettie B Doughty 22 S Acc Acc d/o John R & Mary on 19 Nov 1866 at Acc by JWA Elliott

AMES Henry T Col 20 S Farming Acc Acc s/o Kessey Hatton to Jane Trower Col 22 S Acc Acc on 1 Apr 1874 at Pungo: by R Davis

AMES Isaiah T Col 21 S Farmer Acc Acc s/o Alexander & Annie to Mary E Short Col 20 S Acc Acc d/o Leah Joynes on 25 Nov 1891 at Acc by J Duckett

AMES J S 46 W Farmer Acc Acc s/o Stinger & Rachel to Julia Winder 36 W Acc Acc d/o Thorogood Mears on 3 Dec 1874 near Pungo: by JE Humphreys

AMES James widr to Catherine Savage d/o Littleton who gave consent lic: 16 Aug 1858

AMES James 31 D Laborer Acc Acc to Mary A B Richardson 15 S Acc Acc d/o Mary J on 11 Dec 1867 at Acc by D Felton

AMES James P 20 S Farmer Acc Acc s/o James S & Margt to Mary Scott 20 S Acc Acc d/o John & Maria on 4 Jan 1874 near Job Town by LK LeCato

AMES Jesse Col 34 S Farmer Acc Acc s/o Ann to Sarah Harmon Col 28 S Acc Acc d/o Tabbie on 30 Jun 1873 at Acc by N Morris

AMES Jno Col 57 S Laborer Acc Acc s/o Ann Jubilee to Sarah Joynes Col 45 S Acc Acc on 12 Nov 1884 at Acc by CA Horsey

AMES Jno Alfred 26 S Merchant b: Ames Ridge s/o Tho H (Decd) & Sally to Margt V Bull 23 S b: Scarborough Nk d/o Thos S & Polly on 11 Dec 1854 near Pungo: by A Wallace (Alfred J Mason says both over 21)

AMES John (FN) 38 W Laborer N'hamp: N'hamp: s/o Sambo & Jennie to Maria Upshur (FN) 23 S Acc Acc d/o Custis Revel & Rose Major on 28 Dec 1865 at Acc by GS May

AMES John H 21 S Farmer Acc Acc s/o John E & Margt S to Mary T Ashby 18 S Acc Acc d/o Saml & Sarah on 28 Nov 1866 at Acc by BT Ames

AMES John S 24 S Farmer Acc Acc s/o Edwd & Sally to Charlotte M Downing 18 S Acc Acc d/o Edwd T & Anna on 12 Dec 1877 at Ames Ridge by CC Wertenbaker

AMES Joseph B to Isabella Sarah Ames (ward/o George P Cutler who gave consent) on 18 Apr 1860 at N'hamp: by M Oldham (John McLand says he over 21)

AMES Julius A 22 S Farmer Acc Acc s/o Edward H & Ann K to Susan Beach 25 S Acc Acc d/o George & Susan on 7 Jan 1857 at Pungo: by M Oldham (Abel J Beach says both over 21)

AMES Leonard H 25 S Carriage Mkr Acc Acc s/o Levin S & Ann to Virginia S Joynes 17 S Acc Acc d/o

Edward D & Ann on 9 Apr 1857 at Warehouse by M Oldham

AMES Leonard O 20 S Farmer Acc Acc s/o Leonard H & Virginia S to Lillian S Doughty 23 S Acc Acc d/o John B on 7 Jan 1890 at Acc by JM Anderson

AMES Levin (T) 25 S Blacksmith b: Acc s/o Lewis Ames & Margt Brittingham to Charlott (E) Bull 20 S b: Acc d/o Thomas Bull & Polly Mapp on 25 Nov 1860 at Burtons Ch by LK LeCato (George A Holt says both over 21)

AMES Levin G 23 S Farmer Acc Acc s/o Denard H & Virginia J to Ella E Kellam 23 S Acc Acc d/o Shepherd S & Mary on 14 Nov 1894 at Acc by GE Booker

AMES Louis Col 42 S Farmer Acc Acc s/o Annie to Emma Doughty Col 31 S Acc Acc d/o Lizzie on 27 May 1895 at Locust Mount by JWA Elliott

AMES Orris Sidney 25 S Clerking Acc Acc s/o John H & Mary T to Virginia M Dean 25 S Sussex Co DE Acc d/o Charles H & Annie S on 26 Mar 1894 at Acc C H by JM Dunaway

AMES Robert L 24 S Merchant Acc Acc s/o Edward T & Sallie to Mary J Turner 20 S Acc Acc d/o John T & Virginia on 23 Oct 1889 at Jno T Turner's by JH Riddick

AMES Samuel H Col 23 S Waterman Acc Acc s/o Saml & Margaret to Mary A [Giddins] Giddings Col 18 S Acc Acc d/o Matthew & Lettie on 23 Sep 1880 at Belle Haven by SMG Copeland

AMES Samuel W 22 S Merchant s/o Leonard H & Jennie to Sarah A Mears 19 S d/o Benjamin W & Emma S lic: 27 Oct 1884 marr: 28 Oct 1884

AMES Smith Col (mulatto) 23 S Laborer Acc Acc s/o Lnay to Henrietta Finney Col (dark) 17 S Acc Acc d/o Maria on 28 Jan 1872 at Belle Haven by TM Cole

AMES Smith H Col 21 S Farmer Acc Acc s/o Smith K & Hannie to Lizzie Hutchinson Col 21 S Acc Acc d/o Daniel & Mary on 23 Jun 1895 at Acc by J Duckett

AMES Thomas 22 S Farmer Acc Acc s/o Juliet to Mary Hack 21 S Acc Acc d/o Sarah on 15 May 1867 at Acc by WT Tull

AMES William E 35 S Farmer Acc Acc s/o Edward & Sally to Virginia E Beloate 21 S Acc Acc d/o Levin B & Sarah on 18 Sep 1887 at Acc by CD Crawley

AMES William H 22 S Merchant Acc Acc s/o Levin to Susan W Doughty 20 S Acc Acc d/o Jno A & Emily on 20 Jan 1875 at Craddockville by HM Anderson

ANDERSON James M 42 W Minister Richmond City Danville s/o Louis M & Susan A to Maggie O Robins 36 S Acc Acc d/o Jno S & Drucilla B on 7 Jul 1879 at Jenkins Bridge by JW Hilldrup

ANDERTON John L 26 S Light House Keeper Acc Assateague Isld s/o E H to Clara E W Holland 20 S Acc Horntown d/o John & Sally on 22 Dec 1875 at John Davis' by IT Adkins

ANDERTON John T 22 S Oysterman Acc Acc s/o James E & Joanna to Elizabeth J Stant 19 S Acc Acc d/o Edward T & Angannette on 6 Jun 1888 at Temp'ville by WF Hayes

ANDREWS Alfred widr to Cath Lucas wid/o Elijah lic: 27 Dec 1856

ANDREWS Benjamin to Ellen Wessells ward/o James Mason who gave consent lic: 19 Jan 1858 James Mason says he over 21

ANDREWS Isaac [Andress] 22 S Fisherman Chinco: Isld Chinco: Isld s/o Mordicas & Nancy to Sarah Daisey 16 S Chinco: Isld Chinco: Isld d/o Jas & Elenor on 19 Feb 1859 at Chinco: Isld by P Bowdin

ANDREWS John 22 S Farmer to Catherine Colonna 21 W d/o James & Nancy lic: 12 Jan 1865 marr: 12 Jan 1865

ANDREWS John 24 S Farmer Acc Acc s/o Wm & Eveline to Rachel Ann [Bonewell] Bonnewell 21 S Acc Acc d/o Geo & Ellen on 25 Sep 1867 at Acc by JO Moss

ANDREWS John T 21 S Waterman Acc Acc s/o John & Kate to Daisy B Sterling 15 S Crisfield MD Acc d/o Wm Thos & Rachel on 22 Oct 1894 at Acc by J Connor

ANDREWS John W 22 S Farmer Acc Acc s/o John & Rachel to Ella D Holly 19 S Acc Acc d/o Benj T & Charolette on 20 Mar 1892 at Winterville by JW Nicholson

ANDREWS Joseph (Andrews) 22 S Mariner Chinco: Isld Chinco: Isld s/o Mardicai & Nancy to Nancy (R) [Cherics] Cherricks 21 S Chinco: Isld Chinco: Isld d/o Wm & Mary Cherricks (Mary Watson gave consent for her dauther) on 27 Apr 1854 at r/o Andress by P Bowdin (Tegel Sharpley said both over 21)

ANDREWS Joshua 20 S Oysterman Chinco: Isld Chinco: Isld s/o Isaac & Sarah to Elizabeth A Daisey 16 S Chinco: Isld Chinco: Isld d/o Wm h & Mary on 7 Oct 1883 at Chinco: Isld by WP Thornton

ANDREWS Selby J 22 S Sailor Chinco: Isld Chinco: Isld s/o Isaac & Sarah to Annie L Taylor 16 S Chinco: Isld Chinco: Isld d/o Samuel R & Jane Taylor (now Daisey) on 5 Nov 1890 at Chinco: Isld by JW Turner

ANDREWS William 21 S Sailor Acc Acc s/o John & Catherine to Lottie E Galloway 19 S Page Co VA Acc d/o Wm H & Lydia on 21 Sep 1887 at Onancock by JW Easley

ANDREWS William D 24 S Sailor N'hamp: Acc to Ida Collins 17 S Acc Acc d/o Littleton & S on 5 Aug 1874 at Pocomoke by M Oldham

ANNIS Franklin 27 S Sailor Acc Acc s/o James & Margt to Margaret Twiford 23 S Acc Acc d/o Julius & Margt on 8 Mar 1877 near Wiseville by FH Mullineaux

ANNIS Franklin 26 S Waterman Acc Acc s/o Wm & Elizabeth to Mary James single Acc Acc d/o Margaret Thorns on 30 Nov 1880 near Guilford by M Oldham

ANNIS Franklin P 21 S Oysterman Acc Acc s/o Sylvester & Rebecca to Cornelia J Thorns 22 S Acc Acc d/o Wm & Margt on 1 Sep 1875 near Guilford by DA Woodson

ANNIS George Col 20 S Laborer Acc Acc to Caroline Matthews Col 21 S Acc Acc on 5 Sep 1872 at Log Chp by A Joynes

ANNIS Jas T 34 S Oysterman Acc Acc s/o Sylvester & Rebecca to Melissa Taylor 35 W Acc Acc d/o William & Jane Killman on 26 Nov 1891 at Lee Mont by AJ Fristoe

ANNIS John Col 24 S Farmer Acc Acc s/o Mary to Sarah Hope Col 21 S Acc Acc d/o Rosa on 15 May 1887 at Modest Town by AJ Satchell

ANNIS John D 24 S Oysterman Acc Acc s/o Delila to Amanda Jane Taylor 21 S Acc Acc d/o Thorogood M & Mary on 5 Oct 1875 at Guilford by JM Anderson

ANNIS Levy (Levi Annis) 60 W Farmer b: Ames Ridge s/o Levy & Nancy to Sarah Collins 35 W b: Acc on 6 Jul 1856 at r/o Levy Annis by GH Ewell (Southy Grinnalds says she over 21)

ANNIS William 46 W Oysterman Acc Acc s/o Levi & Tabitha to Margaret Fisher 22 S New York City Acc d/o

Marriages

Thos & Margaret on 22 Oct 1870 at Acc by JET Ewell

ANTHONY James F Col 24 S Farmer Acc Acc s/o Eliza Major to Frances Nettles Col 22 S Iele of Wrigh Co Acc d/o Cary & Mary on 9 Feb 1879 at New Boston by TW Nettles

ANTHONY Severn Jr Col 25 S Wage-earner Acc Acc s/o Severn Sr & Isabella to Susan Sample Col 21 S Acc Acc d/o Peggie on 26 Jan 1890 at Acc by TW Nettles

ARDIS David T 30 S Farmer Acc Acc s/o William to Sallie A Taylor 18 S Acc Acc d/o Rixon on 6 Dec 1888 at Acc by JS Wallace

ARDIS Edward T to Margaret J Taylor lic: 9 Oct 1860 Wm H Dennis says both over 21

ARDIS George 22 S Farmer Acc Acc s/o Rosa to Clara S Mitchell 16 S Acc Acc d/o George W & Mary on 27 Dec 1885 at Zion Ch by WA Street

ARMSTRONG Jesse L Col 24 S Oysterman Acc Acc s/o Parker Brittingham & Margt Armstrong to Hannah [Douglas] Douglass Col 23 S Acc Acc d/o Wm Douglas & Mary Ewell on 20 Oct 1886 at Horntown by RJ Waters

ARMSTRONG Thomas 25 S Laborer Acc Acc s/o Saha to Nellie Marshall 22 S Acc Acc d/o Jane on 28 Jan 1869 at Acc by S Marshall

ARMSTRONG Williams (Col) 30 S Laborer Acc Acc to Mary Edwards (Col) 25 S Acc Acc on 4 Apr 1870 at Horntown by S Marshall

ARNOLD Alfred J 25 S Printer NY Carmal NY to Minnie S Reeder 22 S Perry Co PA Acc d/o Daniel K & Eliza J on 28 Oct 1891 at Lee Mont by AJ Fristoe

ASHBY Bayly 24 S Farmer Acc Acc s/o Wm Thos & Sarah to Elizth F Chandler 21 S Acc Acc d/o Sylvester R & Mary on 30 Nov 1881 at Acc by JC Watson

ASHBY Benjamin Col 28 S Sailor Acc Acc s/o Charles & Mary to Sarah Dunton Col 23 S N'hamp: Acc d/o Peter on 9 May 1875 at Savageville by JK Plato

ASHBY Benjamin Col 37 S Farmer Acc Acc s/o Charles & Mary to Mary Mapp Col 30 S Acc Acc d/o Leah on 15 Oct 1882 at Savageville by F Corrd

ASHBY Charles FN 25 S Laborer Acc Acc to Mary Floyd FN 40 S Acc Acc d/o Exor & Betsy on 26 Dec 1852 at r/o theirs by J Burton

ASHBY Daniel Col 23 S Farmer Acc Acc s/o George & Leah to Maria Byrd Col 25 S Acc Acc on 2 Jan 1887 at his parents' by JK Adams

ASHBY Edmond Col 26 S Laborer Acc Acc s/o George & Margaret to Harriet Johnson Col 30 W Acc Acc d/o James on 21 Aug 1887 at Locust Mount by JWA Elliott

ASHBY Edward Col 21 S Farmer Acc Acc s/o Leah to Belle Watson Col 21 S Acc Acc d/o Arie on 2 Oct 1873 at Locust Mount by N Morris

ASHBY Francis Col 34 S Sailor Acc Acc s/o Easter to Mary Joynes Col 38 S Acc Acc d/o Sary on 27 Dec 1874 near Locust Mount by JWA Elliott

ASHBY George Col 62 S Fisherman Acc Acc s/o Alice Coleburn to Caroline Custis Col 30 S Acc Acc d/o Margaret on 15 Aug 1890 at Acc by BJ Hargarves

ASHBY Henry Col 39 S Farmer Acc Acc s/o Eliza to Sarah LeCato Col 35 S Acc Acc d/o Annie on 27 Aug 1890 at Acc by JWA Elliott

ASHBY John A Col 22 S Acc Acc s/o Char & Mary to Ellen Nock Col 17 S Acc Acc d/o Thomas & Eliza on 13 Jul 1881 at St Luke Ch by PM Lewis

ASHBY John T 24 S Farmer Acc Acc s/o Saml & Sarah A C to Ella F Goffigon 22 S Acc Acc d/o Wm P & Margt S on 28 May 1879 near Locust Mount by JWA Elliott

ASHBY John Wm Col 37 S Wage-earner Acc Acc s/o Mary to Rose Ayres Col 24 S Acc Acc d/o Jay & Sarah on 16 Jun 1888 at Locust Mount by JWA Elliott

ASHBY Louis Col 50 S Farmer Acc Acc s/o Tamar to Mary Floyd Col 50 S Acc Acc d/o Henny Byrd on 6 Jan 1890 at Acc by JH Thomas

ASHBY Robert C 48 W Farmer Acc N'hamp: s/o Samuel & Sarah E to Mary E Shield 34 S Acc Acc d/o Samuel A & Mary on 19 Dec 1894 at Acc by JR Griffith

ASHBY Robert T 22 S Farmer Acc Acc s/o Saml & Sarah A to Nervilla E Ames 22 S Acc Acc d/o Jno E & Marget S on 16 Dec 1868 at Acc by LK LeCato

ASHBY Smith T Col 25 S Wage-earner Acc Acc s/o George & Belle to Rachel Byrd Col 22 S Acc Acc d/o Maria on 29 Oct 1890 at Savageville by JB Lewis

ASHBY William T 20 S Farmer b: Acc s/o Benjamin & Margaret to Sarah E Beloate 18 S b: Acc d/o William & Keziah on 30 Sep 1855 at r/o Wm Beloat by LK LeCato

ASHBY William T 50 W Farmer Acc N'hamp: s/o Benj & Margaret A to Margaret A White 48 S Acc Acc d/o Nepolian O & Eliza on 11 Nov 1886 at Belle Haven by CD Crawley

ASHBY Wilson (Col) 31 S Laborer Acc Acc s/o James & Harriet to Caroline Becket Col 25 S Acc Acc d/o Luky on 5 May 1871 at Locust Mount by JWA Elliott

ASHBY Wm Col 27 S Farmer Acc Acc s/o Charles & Mary to Margt Va Parker Col 20 S Acc Acc d/o Elizabeth on 29 Jan 1879 near Locust Mount by JWA Elliott

ASHMEAD John W 20 S Mechanic Acc Acc s/o Francis A & Elizth to Charlotte A Mason 26 S Acc Acc d/o Stephen & Ann on 6 Aug 1873 at Craddockville by JE Humphreys

ATCHKINS Charles H 38 S Carpenter DE Acc to Catharine Budd 22 S Acc Acc d/o McKell on 25 Jan 1877 at Chesconessex by JH Amiss

ATKINS Robert 23 S Milling DE Acc to Bettie Trader 23 S Acc Acc d/o John & Eliza on 2 Jan 1890 at Temp'ville by WF Hayes

AULD John H G 21 S Sawyer Boston MA Acc s/o John T & Eliz'th to Alice D Webster 19 S Clark Co WI Acc d/o Asa & Emily M on 5 Apr 1892 at Belle Haven by T Burton

AYARS Heritage 25 S Minister b: Salem Co NJ s/o Mark & C M to Arinthia P Taylor 24 S b: Guilford d/o David C & Margt on 16 May 1854 at Popular Grove by JJ Edward (Thomas H Kellam said Ayres over 21)

AYDELOTT Peter 23 S Laborer s/o Scarborough Johnson to Mary Ewell 33 S d/o Esther Welbourn lic: 7 Dec 1866

AYRES Alfred Col 22 S Wage-earner Acc Acc s/o Littleton & Sally to Mary H Rew Col 21 S Acc Acc d/o Georgianna on 29 Jun 1890 at Onancock by GHT Byrd

AYRES Arthur Col 23 S Farmer Acc Acc s/o Rose Ayres to Margaret Parramore Col 25 S N'hamp: Acc d/o Ann Ames on 2 Jul 1879 at Belle Haven by JE Humphreys

AYRES Edward 20 S Watermna Acc Acc s/o Thos & Mary to Manie Evans 14 S Acc Acc d/o Jno & Mary on 24 Dec 1879 at Chesconessex by PA Leatherbury

AYRES Edward T 32 W Sailor Acc Acc

Marriages

s/o Thos & Nancy to Triphemia A Evans 40 W Som Co MD Acc d/o John H & Marg't Marsh on 7 Sep 1892 at Acc by EC Atkins

AYRES George Col 22 S Laborer Acc Acc s/o Littleton & Sally to Rose Ashby Col 19 S Acc Acc d/o Nicy on 25 Jun 1882 at Acc by JE Humphreys

AYRES George W 24 S Farmer Acc Acc s/o Thos R & Sally A to Bertha L [Belote] Beloate 17 S Acc Acc d/o Julius D & Edna B on 4 Feb 1891 at Savageville by AC Berryman

AYRES Henry 28 S Farmer Acc Acc s/o Kennie to Margaret Evans 22 S Acc Acc d/o Geo & Easter on 7 Aug 1867 at Acc by JL Taft

AYRES Henry C 30 S Carpenter Acc Acc s/o Edmund & Betsy to Annie W Coleburn 26 S Acc Acc d/o James & Sallie on 28 Feb 1867 at Acc by BT Ames

AYRES Isaac Col 21 S Laborer Acc Acc s/o Littleton & Sallie to Mary Snead Col 18 S Acc Acc d/o Abel & Nancy on 14 Mar 1883 at Savageville by F Wood

AYRES James 18 S Farmer Acc Acc s/o Jas & Polly to Margaret A Hickman 18 S Acc Acc d/o Edwd & Polly on 13 Nov 1867 at Acc by M Oldham

AYRES James E F 38 S Farmer Acc Acc s/o Levin R & Susan M to Bettie U Chandler 28 S Acc Acc d/o Thos B & Sarah A on 6 Mar 1892 at Acc by GW Burke

AYRES James Kellam 24 S Farmer Acc Acc s/o Richard J & Leah to Sally Upshur Hack 33 S Acc Acc d/o (Dr) Thomas U (Decd) & Sally on 26 Nov 1856 at r/o Peter J Hack by JM Cheveis(?) (Abel T Johnson says both over 21)

AYRES Jay Col 22 S Wage-earner Acc Acc s/o Jay & Sarah to Maggie Jacobs Col 16 S Acc Acc d/o Benj & Rosey on 25 May 1890 at Pungo: by JB Lewis

AYRES Jay Col 55 W Wage-earner Acc Acc s/o Leah to Ann Cutler Col 55 W Acc Acc d/o Nancy Ames on 12 Apr 1893 at Locust Mount by JWA Elliott

AYRES John Col 21 S Laborer Acc Acc s/o Molly to Sarah Bradford Col 21 S Acc Acc d/o barney & Maria on 21 Jan 1880 at Hank's Nest by JE Humphreys

AYRES John 24 S Oysterman Acc Acc s/o Littleton L & Eliza to Lizzie Mister 18 S Crisfield MD Acc d/o James & Mary on 28 Dec 1881 near Onancock by LE Barrett

AYRES John H 30 S Physician Acc Acc s/o Richard S & Elizabeth A to Mary C Derby 21 S Lancaster Co VA Acc d/o Henry L & Charlotte on 6 Nov 1895 at Drum'tn by HS Simmerman

AYRES John R 25 S Carpenter Acc Acc s/o Edwd & Sally A to Manie A Bull 23 S Acc Acc d/o Jas H & Elizth on 12 Dec 1883 at Pungo: by JWA Elliott

AYRES Levin Col 23 S Farm Hand Acc Acc s/o Molly to Hennie Smith Col 22 S Acc Acc d/o Ann on 7 Mar 1877 near Hawk's Nest by RH Govans

AYRES Levin R 34 S Farmer b: Acc s/o Francis R & Susan to Susan M Gunter 20 S b: Acc d/o Edwd & Agness on 27 Oct 1853 at Ayres Chp by ES Grant

AYRES Levin R 32 S Farmer Acc Acc s/o Levin R & Susan M to Mary F [Shreaves] Shrieves 19 S Acc Acc d/o Thos W & Frances on 6 Dec 1893 at Onancock by EC Atkins

AYRES Littl 21 S Waterman b: Acc s/o Thos & Nancy to Elizth Mister 17 S b: Acc d/o Jno M & Lovey on 7 Sep 1854 at r/o Jno M Mister by ES

Grant
AYRES Littleton Col 46 S Laborer Acc Acc to Sallie Becket Col 35 S Acc Acc d/o Lukey on 21 Jul 1872 at Acc by N Morris
AYRES Peter T H 21 S Farmer Acc Acc s/o Jas K & Sallie U to Ella J E Warren 18 S Acc Acc d/o Laws & Francie S on 5 Jun 1879 at Pungo: by RD Stimson
AYRES Richard Stephen 23 S Carriage Trm b: Acc s/o John J & Margt B to Betsy Ann Hack 25 S b: Acc d/o John Wm & Saha C on 13 Mar 1856 at Acc by M Oldham (Arthur Jacob says both over 21)
AYRES Robert 32 S Farmer Acc Acc s/o Elijah & Sally to Evelin J White 32 W Acc Acc d/o Wm & Cathr Powell on 4 Sep 1862 at Acc by ES Grant
AYRES Stephen Col 22 S Farmer Acc Acc s/o Isaac & Betsy to Elizabeth Ames 18 S Acc Acc d/o Alexander & Anne E on 25 Dec 1895 at Acc by FW Overton
AYRES Thomas Col 21 S Farm Labor Acc Acc s/o Litt & Sally to Belle Sarah Mears Col 24 S Acc Acc d/o Rachel on 30 Dec 1882 at Savageville by F Wood
AYRES Thomas 50 W Oysterman Acc Acc s/o Thos & Nancy to Henrietta Scott 35 W Acc Acc d/o Joshua Johnson on 21 Feb 1884 at Acc by PA Leatherbury
AYRES Thomas 18 S Sailor Acc Acc s/o James E & Marg't to Julia E [Tyndall] Tindall 16 S Acc Acc d/o Washington on 31 Aug 1893 at Mappsville by JL King
AYRES Thos 36 W Farmer Drum'tn Acc s/o Littl & Racheal to Sally Crockett 26 S Saxes Isld Acc d/o Armanica & Polly on 2 Feb 1854 at Onancock by C Hill
AYRES Thos 26 S Waterman b: Acc s/o Thos & Nancy to Nancy (wid/o Thomas) Gray 35 W b: Acc d/o Scarborough Melson on 11 Mar 1858 at r/o Thos Ayres by ES Grant
AYRES William FN to Elizabeth Taylor FN lic: 25 Dec 1854 John E Smith says both over 21
BADGER Levin T 26 S Farmer Acc Acc s/o Susan to Lizzie Ann Showard 28 S Acc Acc d/o Henry C & Mary on 25 Dec 1861 at Acc by BT Ames
BADGER Levin T 39 W Laborer Acc Acc s/o Susan to Margaret Charnock 37 S Acc Acc d/o James & Sally on 30 Aug 1874 at Bull Br by O Littleton
BAGWELL Anthony Col 22 S Wage-earner Acc Acc s/o Daniel & Harriet to Clara Parramore Col 18 S Acc Acc d/o Ellen on 17 Feb 1892 at Acc by JA Boon
BAGWELL Charles Col 26 S Laborer Acc Acc s/o Alsie to Margaret Fosque Col 24 W Acc Acc d/o Solomon & Ada on 3 Aug 1876 at Savageville by JK Plato
BAGWELL Edward Col 21 S Wage-earner Acc Acc s/o Ephraim & Ann to Martha Parker Col 15 S Acc Acc d/o Joseph & Amy on 15 Sep 1895 at Onley by JR West
BAGWELL Ephraim Jr Col 25 S Wage-earner Acc Acc s/o Ephraim Sr & Ann to Cordie Boggs Col 22 S Acc Acc d/o Bowdoin & Jane on 24 May 1891 at Savageville by JH Offer
BAGWELL Geo Col 30 S Laborer Acc Acc s/o Moses & Emeline to Docia Walker Col 18 S Acc Acc d/o Harriet Pettit on 2 Apr 1879 near News Town by A Joynes
BAGWELL George Col 35 S Farmer Acc Acc s/o Comfort to Mary Fletcher Col 21 S Acc Acc d/o Esther Poulson on 12 Jan 1876 at Acc by RH Govans

Marriages

BAGWELL George E 25 S Farmer Acc Acc s/o Arena to Caroline Lewis 22 S Acc Acc d/o Thos & Margt on 4 Mar 1877 at Guilford Ch by JB Merritt

BAGWELL George H (W) 35 S Druggist Acc Acc s/o Thos P & Sally H to Rose D Twiford 19 S Acc Acc d/o Robert on 7 May 1868 at Acc by HA Wise Jr

BAGWELL George S Col 21 S Wage-earner Acc Acc s/o Ephraim & Sarah to Laura A Jacobs Col 21 S Acc Acc d/o Benjamin & Rosie on 10 Sep 1890 at Savageville by JB Lewis

BAGWELL Henry Col 20 S Farm Laborer Acc Acc s/o Enna Dix to Jane Blake Col 17 S Acc Acc d/o Mary Bayley on 28 Nov 1883 at Acc by AJ Satchell

BAGWELL Henry R Col 26 W Laborer Acc Acc s/o Edmund Warner & Emma Bagwell to Martha J Custis Col 24 S Acc Acc d/o Kitty on 20 Nov 1887 at Acc by AJ Satchell

BAGWELL Isaiah Col 26 S Laborer Acc Acc s/o Moses & Emaline to Sarah [Duffie] Duffy Col 22 S Acc Acc d/o Eliza on 5 Jun 1881 near News Town by AJ Satchell

BAGWELL Isaiah N 41 W Farmer Drum'tn Acc s/o Wm (Jr) (Decd) & Margt to Leah Finney 39 S Onancock Acc d/o Wm & Rose on 11 Jan 1854 at Drum'tn by C Hill (John D Tyler says she over 21)

BAGWELL John FN to Violet Guy FN lic: 17 Jan 1857 Thos B Gray says both over 21

BAGWELL John A [Begwell] 25 S Steam Fitter Baltimore City MD Baltimore City MD s/o John & Emma to Kate C Hurst 24 S Acc Acc d/o John & Mary on 17 Oct 1894 at Acc by JET Ewell

BAGWELL Levi J Col 58 W Wage-earner Acc Acc s/o Comfort to Lottie Major Col 39 W Acc Acc d/o Mary Hatton on 27 Dec 1894 at Acc by JC Young

BAGWELL Moses FN widr to Sabra White FN lic: 26 Jul 1858 W O White says she over 21

BAGWELL Moses Col 25 S Laborer Acc Acc s/o Moses & Emaline to Mary A Rew Col 19 S Acc Acc d/o Upshur & Maris on 15 Jan 1880 near News Town by A Joynes

BAGWELL Nathaniel Col 21 S Farmer Acc Acc s/o Kitty to Sarah Alice Bayly Col 21 S Acc Acc d/o Sewell & Eliz'th on 3 Sep 1893 at Drum'tn by R Davis

BAGWELL Spencer Col 21 S Wage-earner Acc Acc s/o Daniel to Margie Savage Col 21 S Acc Acc d/o Easter on 2 Mar 1890 at Acc by JH Thomas

BAGWELL Thomas 25 S Farmer Acc Acc s/o Moses to Rosa Pitts 26 S Acc Acc d/o Jannie on 1 Jun 1868 at Acc by A Joynes

BAGWELL Thomas Col 30 S Farmer Acc Acc s/o Moses to Ayrie Gibbons Col 35 S Acc Acc on 8 Jan 1885 at Acc by AJ Satchell

BAKER Benj L 18 S Farmer Acc Acc s/o Ezekiel & Nancy to Maggie S Walker 18 S Acc Acc d/o Robert W & Mary on 16 Nov 1892 at Acc by WW Wood

BAKER Charles S 29 W Minister Sussex Co DE Acc s/o Joseph D & Larinia E to C Annie Ross 23 S Som Co MD Acc d/o Edwd W & Sarah M on 24 Apr 1884 at Onancock by GT Tyler

BAKER Chas C 27 S Farmer Acc Acc s/o Ezekiel & Nancy to Mary E Crowson 17 S Acc Acc d/o Joseph W & Mollie on 11 Oct 1893 at Lee Mont by JET Ewell

BAKER Ezekiel 22 S Farmer Acc Baker Town s/o Asa & Tabitha to Nancy

[Parks] Parkes 23 S Acc Guilford d/o Benj & Polly on 29 Dec 1864 at r/o Benj Parker by GH Ewell

BAKER George Col 45 W Wage-earner Acc Acc s/o Adah to Emeline Bayly 30 S Acc Acc d/o Clarissa on 14 Dec 1895 at Acc by AJ Satchell

BAKER Jas H (John H) 44 W Miller Acc Acc s/o Edwd & Sally to Hetty (Ketty) Mears 35 W Acc Acc d/o Meshai & Margt on 23 Jan 1864 at Acc by ES Grant

BAKER John 35 W Farmer Acc Acc s/o Edmund & Sallie to Tabitha Coxton 33 S Acc Acc on 24 Nov 1869 at Acc by G Bradford

BAKER John S to Emma Baker lic: 15 Mar 1860 Edward Baker says both are over 21

BAKER Joseph A 28 S Teacher Delmar DE Acc s/o David & Lavinia A to Marthella [Corworton] Conworton 19 S Acc Acc d/o Patrick H & Matilda on 6 May 1886 at Tangier Isld by CS Baker

BAKER Joseph J 27 S Merchant Salesman Wic Co MD Acc s/o Absalom W & Margaret to Ellie Jester 18 S Acc Acc d/o William J & Libbie on 19 Feb 1890 at Chinco: Isld by EH Miller

BAKER Josiah P 27 S House Carpenter Wor Co MD Acc s/o James & Julia A to Elizabeth J Jones 19 S Acc Acc d/o Burton & Mary on 27 Aug 1866 at Acc by WP Thornton

BAKER Josiah P 38 W Carpenter Wor Co MD Acc s/o Jas & Julia A to Mary Hester Hudson 30 W Acc Acc d/o Selby & Elizth Lewis on 12 Dec 1877 at Chinco: Isld by P Bowdin Sr

BAKER Josiah P 49 W Carpenter Wor Co MD Acc s/o James & Julia to Cora A Pruitt 38 W Acc Acc d/o John & Elizabeth Sturgis on 4 Jul 1888 at Chinco: Isld by SU Grimsley

BAKER Josiah P 55 W Carpenter Wor Co MD Acc s/o James & Julia A to Elizabeth C Coard 46 W Acc Acc d/o John & Betsy Russell on 1 Feb 1894 at Acc by GP Jones

BAKER Oliver 20 S Farmer Acc Acc s/o Asa & Elizth to Nancy Tatham 20 S Acc Acc d/o Steven & Nancy on 28 Dec 1858 at Acc by D Coulling

BAKER Oliver 35 W Farmer Acc Acc s/o Asa & Tabitha to Polly Northam 18 S Acc Acc d/o Jno T & Adaline on 5 Nov 1879 at Modest Town by DA Woodson

BAKER Samuel s/o Edmond to Hester Wright orp/o Edith lic: 14 Jan 1858 Thomas Baker says he over 21 & Hester is ward/o said Baker

BAKER Wash 24 S Farming Acc Acc s/o George & Sinia to Licia A Ayres 18 S Acc Acc d/o James on 12 Jun 1861 at Acc by W Laws (John Bell says he over 21)

BAKER Washington 35 W Farmer Acc Acc s/o George & Sina Baker to Ambret [Wambough] Wimbrough 26 W Acc Acc d/o James & Polly Ayres on 30 Nov 1871 near Modest Town by DA Woodson

BAKER Wiley L 37 S Farmer Acc Acc s/o James H & Susan to Mary S Adams 18 S Acc Acc d/o John & Nancy on 18 Dec 1887 at Mappsville by WA Street

BAKER William 50 S Farming Acc Acc s/o Ezekeil & Nancy to Caty Mears 46 S Acc Acc d/o Meshack & Margt on 6 Jul 1865 at Acc by ES Grant

BAKER William T 23 S Farmer Acc Acc s/o Oliver & Nancy to Sallie S Bloxom 19 S Acc Acc d/o Perry & Nettie on 26 Jan 1887 at Mappsville by WA Street

BAKER Wm A 41 S Farmer Acc Acc s/o Edwd & Sally to Annie Lee Taylor 19 S Acc Acc d/o Thos & Emily S on 21 Mar 1886 at Zion Ch by WA Street

BALL Benjamin T 23 S Oysterman Baltimore MD Acc s/o Danl M & Sally to Cynthiana Parker 23 S Acc Acc d/o Henry on 3 Mar 1875 at Acc by WJ Twilley

BALL Edward F 21 S Farmer Acc Acc s/o Dan'l M & Elisha to Vernetta E Davis 17 S Acc Acc d/o Wm R & Mary on 4 Jan 1883 at Acc by JW Hundley

BALL John S 20 S Oysterman Acc Acc s/o David to Sarah P Kelly 18 S Acc Acc d/o Edwd & Sarah on 1 Dec 1886 at Acc by WA Street

BALL Noah D Col 24 S Oysterman Acc Acc s/o Danl M & Lititia to Mary Christopher Col 24 S Acc Acc d/o Levin & Nancy on 9 Mar 1882 at Levin Christopher's by JW Hundley

BALL Richard F 21 S Oysterman Acc Acc s/o Daniel & Elishea to Martha J Chesser 17 S Acc Acc d/o Trorogood & Elizth on 29 Apr 1885 at Messongo by WA Street

BALL Wm D 23 S Sailor Acc Acc s/o Danl & Lydia to Mary Jane Kelly 18 S Acc Acc d/o Edwd F & Sarah on 3 Sep 1879 at Muddy Ck by JE Bundick

BALLARD Charles Col 22 S Wage-earner Wor Co MD MD s/o William & Rosa to Bertie Wise Col 21 S Acc Acc d/o Thomas & Hester on 29 Dec 1891 at Acc by L Duncan

BALLARD Emory Col 23 S Teamster MD Acc s/o Mary Ann to Sarah Collins Col 22 S Acc Acc d/o James & Elizth on 13 Jun 1877 at Bapt Ch by TW Nettles

BALLARD William Col 30 S Farmer Acc Acc s/o Tabitha Ballard to Rose Ann Gumby Col 30 S Acc Acc d/o Sarah on 12 Oct 1881 at New Church by JC Cluff

BALLTRAP Wm A Col 40 W Farmer NC Acc s/o Lucretia to Sarah A Staton Col 40 W Acc Acc d/o Alsey White on 1 Dec 1886 at Acc by AJ Satchell

BALTRIP Wm A Col 45 S Farmer near Raleigh NC Acc s/o Lucretia to Mary A Hinman Col 40 S Acc Acc d/o Lottie on 30 Nov 1881 at Acc by AJ Satchell

BANCROFT Louis J 21 S Farmer Acc Acc s/o Amanda to Rosey A Hickman 21 S Acc Acc d/o Edwd & Ann on 22 Jun 1881 at Acc by LE Barrett

BARKER Victor FN 35 S Laborer s/o Preson & Lucretia to Ailsey Bowen FN 23 d/o James & Elzy lic: 31 Oct 1864

BARKER Victor Col 49 S Farmer Acc Acc s/o Craca Hermons to Lillie Washington Col 28 S Acc Acc d/o Mary on 25 Apr 1886 at Jenkins Bridge by RJ Waters

BARNES Alfred 20 S Waterman b: Acc s/o Parker & Elizth to Mary Johnson 14 S b: Acc d/o Jno S S & Elizth on 27 Mar 1856 at bride's mother's by ES Grant

BARNES Alfred F 22 S Mechanic Acc Acc s/o Parker & Jane to Polly Susan Young 19 S Acc Acc d/o Saml T & Rachel on 28 Dec 1881 near White's Store by M Oldham

BARNES Arthur J 21 S Milling Acc Acc s/o Thomas to Maggie E Matthews 18 S Acc Acc d/o Samuel H & Margaret on 5 Sep 1888 at Woodbury by WF Hayes

BARNES Arthur R 23 S Waterman Acc Acc s/o Jno of Authur & Sally to Arinthia J Parkes 22 S Acc Acc d/o Mark & Eliz W on 14 Jan 1871 at Guilford by JET Ewell

BARNES Charles 20 S Oysterman Acc Acc s/o John & Margaret to Manie E Justice 18 S Acc Acc d/o Sallie Bundick on 14 May 1890 at Acc by HS Dulany

BARNES Edmond P 25 S Waterman

Acc Acc s/o John & Sally to Susan A Barnes 19 S Acc Acc d/o James & Emaline on 20 Dec 1876 at Hunting Ck by FH Mullineaux

BARNES Franklin J 20 S Merchant Acc Wor Co MD s/o Geo W & Evaline to Sadie D Lewis 17 S Acc Acc d/o Levin D & Anna on 16 Jul 1884 at Acc by AJ Walter

BARNES Geo 19 S Mariner b: Acc s/o Jno (of A) & Sally to Emaline Justice 21 S b: Acc d/o Wm (of B) & Sally on 1 Mar 1855 at Wm Justice's by ES Grant

BARNES Geo W 21 S Farmer Acc Acc s/o Arthur & A to Mary A (Ann) Groton 18 S Acc Acc d/o Wm & Lovy on 18 Nov 1863 at Acc by D Titlow

BARNES Geo W 24 S Sailor PA Acc s/o Louis S & Fanny to Margt Taylor 18 S Acc Acc d/o Susan on 12 Sep 1866 at Acc by ES Grant

BARNES George 30 W Sailor Acc Acc s/o Arthur & Anna to Isabella Killman 20 S Acc Acc d/o Thomas & Ann on 7 Jan 1874 at Acc by O Littleton

BARNES George W 40 W Farmer Acc Acc s/o Arthur & Julia to Elizabeth Gardner 27 S Acc Acc on 24 Jan 1883 at Onancock by WC Vaden

BARNES Hanson P 24 S Farmer Acc Acc s/o William G & Mary to Olive P Baker 18 S Acc Acc d/o Samuel & Hester on 30 Nov 1887 at Zion Ch by WA Street

BARNES Isaiah Tully 28 S Merchant Acc Acc s/o John (of P) & Sallie to Maud S Coard 18 S Acc Acc d/o Charles R & Mary on 6 Aug 1890 at Acc by GF Farring

BARNES Jacob D 19 S Waterman Acc Acc s/o Arthur & Arinthia to Mahie A East 27 S Acc Acc d/o William & Elizabeth on 29 Dec 1895 at Acc by HS Dulany

BARNES James A 25 S Farmer Acc Acc s/o Samuel & Lidia to Olivia S Parkes 22 S Acc Acc d/o Edward & Ann on 14 Nov 1880 at Maronville by FH Mullineaux

BARNES James W 21 S Oysterman Acc Acc s/o James & Emeline to Mary Jane Lewis 16 S Acc Acc d/o Major & Elizth on 25 Sep 1866 at Acc by JH Ellegood

BARNES John Columbus 42 S Oysterman Acc Acc s/o John of I & Sallie to Sarah J Lewis 43 S Acc Acc d/o Major & Elizabeth on 29 Jan 1893 at Acc by JET Ewell

BARNES John F 21 S Oysterman Acc Acc s/o John Jr & Margaret to Sallie E Barnes 16 S Acc Acc d/o Arthur J & Arintha on 7 Jul 1895 at Acc by JW Charlton

BARNES John P to Sally W Gibbons wid lic: 13 Jan 1858 Wm T Wright says he over 21

BARNES John W 21 S Oysterman Acc Acc s/o Jas (of A) & Emeline to Margaret Bundick 19 S Acc Acc d/o Geo H & Annie on 6 May 1866 at Acc by ES Grant

BARNES John W 25 S Waterman Acc Acc s/o Alfred & Mary to Mary E Rayfield 22 S Acc Acc d/o Major & Elizth on 6 Feb 1884 at Mappsville by M Oldham

BARNES Levin J 25 S Waterman Acc Acc s/o Jno & Sally to Margaret Ewell 21 S Acc Acc d/o Harry & Patsy on 9 Jun 1864 at Acc by ES Grant

BARNES Louis A 27 S Sailor Acc Acc s/o Lewis S & Margt M to Clara D Twiford 17 S Acc Acc d/o Julius & Annie on 8 Oct 1876 near Deep Ck by RC Jones

BARNES Oliver J 20 S Sailor Acc Acc s/o George W & Margaret S to Lizzie S Twiford 20 S Acc Acc d/o George D & Elizabeth on 5 May

Marriages

BARNES Oliver T 20 S Farmer Acc Acc s/o Thomas H & Nancy to Isorah Matthews 20 S Acc Acc d/o Samuel H & Margaret on 1 Sep 1880 at Guilford Ch by WW Royall

BARNES Oscar T 22 S Farmer Acc Acc s/o Geo W & Eveline T to Mary J Mason 18 S Acc Acc d/o Haury P & Jane E on 13 Jan 1892 at Acc by AJ Fristoe

BARNES Parker Jr 32 S Mariner b: Acc s/o Parker & Elizth to Jane Matthews 23 S b: Acc d/o Jacob & Seymour on 4 Dec 1856 at Reese Chp by ES Grant (Samuel Mason says both over 21)

BARNES Samuel C 20 S Farmer Acc Acc s/o Parker & Jane to Pamelia A C Justice 22 S Acc Acc d/o Wm & Sally on 24 Dec 1876 at Hunting Ck by FH Mullineaux

BARNES Thomas 20 S Farmer & Oysterman b: Ames Ridge s/o Parker & Betsey to Nancy Wessells 21 S b: Back Ck d/o Arthur & Ann on 25 Jun 1856 at r/o Thos Wessels by GH Ewell

BARNES Thomas 23 S Farmer Guilford Guilford s/o Robt & Aneritta to Ann E [Killmon] Killman 21 S Guilford Guilford d/o Jno & Nancy on 20 Dec 1857 at r/o George H Ewell by GH Ewell (Burwell B Ewell says both over 21)

BARNES Thomas Col 21 S Farmer Acc Acc s/o Ibby Parkes to Ann Bunting Col 21 S Acc Acc d/o Millie on 8 Jun 1879 at Belle Haven by JE Humphreys

BARNES Webster 22 S Farmer Acc Acc s/o William G & Mary to Mollie Mears 17 S Acc Acc d/o Meshack & Betsey on 23 Nov 1892 at Oak Hall by WW Wood

BARNES William 21 S Sailor Acc Acc s/o Lewis & Margaret to Mary Gray 1889 at Crowsontown by HS Dulany

17 S Acc Acc d/o Shephard & Mary on 17 Mar 1880 at Deep Ck by PA Leatherbury

BARNES William J 22 S Sailor Acc Acc s/o Jno (of P) & Sally to Brunetta Justice 17 S Acc Acc d/o William & Sallie on 17 Aug 1870 at Acc by J Carroll

BARNES William T 25 S Farmer Acc Acc s/o Joshna & Betsy to Julia F Bunting 22 S Acc Acc d/o George & Rose on 24 Jan 1869 at Acc by JE Bundick

BARNES William T 24 S Merchant Acc Acc s/o James & Evaline to Georgianna Lewis 23 S Acc Acc d/o James & Mary on 22 Dec 1875 near Onancock by RC Jones

BARNES Wm 24 S Waterman b: Acc s/o Parker & Eliz to Mary Mason 21 S b: Acc d/o Wm & Mary J on 26 Nov 1857 at r/o Wm Mason by ES Grant (Revell Justice says both over 21)

BARNES Wm F 22 S Sailor Dorchester Co MD Acc s/o Geo W & Elizth C to Lydia S East 16 S Acc Acc d/o Geo W & Bettie on 2 Aug 1882 at Onancock by SC Boston

BARRETT Elva 22 S Oysterman Acc Acc s/o Alfred P & Nancy to Rebecca Hill 16 S Acc Acc d/o Littleton & Mary on 23 Dec 1891 at Chinco: Isld by JW Turner

BARRETT George W 26 S Merchant N'hamp: N'hamp: s/o John & Izetta to Mary V Beloate 19 S Acc Acc d/o John W & Joice on 19 Dec 1888 at Acc by JW Hundley

BARRETT Mark S 20 S Oysterman Acc Acc s/o Alfred P & Nana to Lizzie Andrews 19 S Acc Acc d/o Joseph & Nancy on 26 Oct 1894 at Chinco: Isld by SU Grimsley

BARRETT Peter M 29 S Brick Maker DE Acc s/o Morris to Millie Godwin 26 S Acc Acc d/o Obadiah W &

Eliz'th on 13 Jan 1892 at Acc by JW Nicholson

BARULSON Henry O 24 S Sailor Norway Acc s/o John & Maria to Nellie T Evans 20 S Acc Acc d/o Wm T & Sally on 23 Dec 1885 at Acc by L Roper

BASSETT Charles E 28 S Merchant Norfolk VA Norfolk VA s/o John W & Josephine V to Janie T Matthews 26 S Norfolk VA Acc d/o Maria on 3 Jun 1889 at Belle Haven by J McNabb

BATTAILE Henry 31 S Teacher Carol Co Acc s/o F W & Ellen to Addie M Rogers 23 S Acc Acc d/o Geo S & Margt on 19 Dec 1861 at Acc by JH Phillips

BAXTER William V single House Joiner b: Qn Ann Co s/o John & Elizth to Eliza Ann Thompson single b: Acc d/o Robert & Eliza on 15 Nov 1855 at Acc by M Oldham (Benj Kellam says both over 21)

BAYLY Andrew Col 21 S Farmer Acc Acc s/o Louis & Noria to Anna Allen Col 21 S Acc Acc d/o Clarissa on 24 Jan 1895 at Acc by PW Lee

BAYLY Arthur 50 S Blacksmith Acc Acc s/o Jas & Nicey to Mary Jane Burton Col 49 S Acc Acc d/o Leah on 22 Sep 1881 at Locust Mount by JWA Elliott

BAYLY Asher J 21 S Farmer Acc Acc s/o Richard & Sally A to Emma [Tyndall] Tindall 21 S Acc Acc d/o Samuel on 13 Sep 1891 at Mappsville by JL King

BAYLY Custis [Bayley] Col 23 S Wage-earner Acc Acc s/o Leah to Martha Wise Col 22 S Acc Acc on 17 Apr 1889 at Acc by JA Haynes

BAYLY Edmond 18 S Wage-earner Acc Acc s/o Louis & Marie to Lottie Garrison 18 S Acc Acc d/o Leah Gardner on 23 Jan 1889 at St Luke Ch by P Sheppard

BAYLY Edmund Col 65 S Farmer N'hamp: Acc s/o Edie Elliott to Sally Parramore Col 36 S Acc Acc d/o Tabby on 27 Dec 1877 at Parsonage by A Handy

BAYLY Egbert G 68 W Farmer Acc Acc to Margt A Bennett 15 S Acc Acc d/o Teackle & Margt on 29 Dec 1879 at Hacks Nk by CC Wertenbaker

BAYLY Frank Col 21 S Laborer Acc Acc to Comeliac Sample Col 18 S Acc Acc d/o Geo F & Eliza on 25 Jun 1882 at Pungo: by F Wood

BAYLY Frank Col 35 S Wage-earner Acc Acc s/o Custis & Eliza to Martha Laws Col 30 S Acc Acc on 23 Oct 1890 at Pungo: by TW Nettles

BAYLY Frederick Col 21 S Farmer Acc Acc s/o Louis & Maria to Juliet Ann Ashby 19 S Acc Acc d/o Benj & Belle Sarah on 22 Dec 1895 at Acc by JN Waters

BAYLY George 24 W Farmer North Co VA Acc s/o Adah to Ann Case 25 S Acc Acc d/o Chas & Nancy on 15 Apr 1868 at Acc by E Hebard

BAYLY George Col 22 S Farmer Acc Acc s/o Peter & Mary to Annie Floyd Col 21 S Acc Acc d/o Isaac & Rachel on 3 Jun 1883 at Snead's Chp by GW Young

BAYLY George Col 23 S Farm Laborer Acc Acc s/o Clarissa to Mary J Parker Col 23 S Acc Acc d/o Margaret on 13 Jun 1886 at Belle Haven by JE Humphreys

BAYLY George [Bailey] Col 21 S Wage-earner Acc Acc s/o Frank & Jane to Cordelia Snead Col 15 S Acc Acc d/o Jane on 21 Jan 1892 at Acc by L Duncan

BAYLY George E Col 24 W Farmer Acc Acc s/o Alfred & Jenima to Alsie Harmon Col 18 S Acc Acc d/o John & Sabra on 2 Jan 1890 at Acc by L Duncan

BAYLY Gilbert [Bailey] Col 23 S Laborer Acc Acc s/o Easther Hickman to Hester Northam Col 21 S Acc Acc d/o Mary on 28 Mar 1877 near Modest Town by JE Bundick

BAYLY Harry Col 22 S Farmer Acc Acc s/o Emily Bull to Esther Brickhouse Col 22 S Acc Acc d/o Johnson & Juliet on 2 Dec 1882 at Locust Mount by JWA Elliott

BAYLY Henry 17 S Laborer Acc Acc s/o Kitty Ailworth to Louisa Ashby 26 S Acc Acc d/o Joise on 16 May 1875 at Savageville by JK Plato

BAYLY Henry Col 23 S Laborer Acc Acc s/o Lydia to Harriet Wise Col 25 S Acc Acc d/o Leah on 2 Jun 1877 at Onancock by PA Leatherbury

BAYLY Henry C Col 29 S Farmer Acc Acc s/o Wallace & Margaret to Sarah Parker Col 32 S Acc Acc d/o George & Mary on 31 Jan 1894 at Acc by TW Nettles

BAYLY Henry P [Baily] Col 19 S Wage-earner Acc Acc s/o Margie to Sadie Poulson Col 17 S Acc Acc d/o Henry J & Harriet on 11 Jul 1895 at Acc by AJ Satchell

BAYLY Isaac Col 21 S Laborer Acc Acc s/o Isaac & Sarah to Mary Kellam Col 21 S Acc Acc d/o Saml & Mary on 12 Mar 1884 at Acc by P Sheppard

BAYLY Jacob Col 26 S Day Laborer Acc Acc s/o Polly Bobbins to Mary West Col 17 S Acc Acc d/o Jno R & Elsie on 31 Jan 1886(?) at St Luke Ch by LW Lee Certificate returned 8 Jan 1886

BAYLY James Col 30 S Farmer Acc Acc s/o Sarah to Georgianna Stewart Col 29 S Acc Acc d/o Smith & Jane on 10 Nov 1886 at Acc by L Rosser

BAYLY James A Col 24 S Laborer Acc Acc s/o Esther to Maria Nock Col 26 S Acc Acc d/o Airida on 26 Mar 1880 at Locust Mount by JWA Elliott

BAYLY James A Col 30 S Farmer Acc Acc s/o Jacob Heath & Leah Bayly to Elizabeth Sample Col 29 S Acc Acc d/o Emma on 17 Nov 1886 at Acc by JA Haynes

BAYLY James E Col 22 S Farmer Acc Acc s/o Mark & Virginia to Sarah V Fosque Col 16 S Acc Acc d/o Henry K & Louisa on 5 May 1889 at Onancock by GHT Byrd

BAYLY James H 23 S Farmer Acc Acc s/o John & Sally to Mary Elizth Chandler 21 S Acc Acc d/o John W & Elizth on 11 Jan 1860 at Acc by JH Addison (Wm P Bayly says he over 21)

BAYLY John 30 S Sailor Acc Acc s/o Bridget to Mary Ann Upshur 29 S Acc Acc d/o Delia on 23 Dec 1868 at Acc by DB White

BAYLY John Col 23 S Farm Laborer Acc Acc s/o Cliarissa Justis to Mary H Justice Col 15 S Acc Acc d/o Moses & Mary on 19 Jun 1884 at Acc by AJ Satchell

BAYLY John Col 35 S Farmer Acc Acc s/o John & Betsy to Lydia Gunter Col 40 S Acc Acc on 2 Oct 1887 at Locustville by P Sheppard

BAYLY John J [Bailey] 28 S Clerking Acc Acc s/o James H & Mary E to Ellen T Lilliston 21 S Acc Acc d/o Alexander W & Betty S on 25 Jul 1894 at Onancock by EF Garner

BAYLY John R Col 29 S Farmer Acc Acc s/o Wallace & Margaret to Addie Savage Col 21 S Acc Acc d/o Custis & Alice on 20 Mar 1895 at Acc by L Duncan

BAYLY John T Col 26 S Farmer Acc Acc s/o Arthur & Mary to Vandalia A Jubilee Col 21 S Acc Acc d/o Mary on 6 Jan 1884 at r/o Thos Nock by GW Young

BAYLY Josiah L [Bailey] 29 S Farmer Acc Acc s/o James H & Mary E to Fannie L Harris 29 S Acc Acc d/o

John W & Mary J on 22 Jun 1893 at Acc by JR Sturgis

BAYLY Julius L 24 S Carpenter Acc Acc s/o Thomas & Elizabeth to Drucilla Trader 18 S Acc Acc d/o Raymond Elizabeth on 26 Oct 1887 at Mappsville by WA Street

BAYLY Lewis 26 S Sailor b: Messongo s/o Arfaxey & Polly to Leticha Smith 16 S b: Messongo d/o Valentine on 31 Jul 1855 at r/o Geo H Ewell by GH Ewell

BAYLY Lewis Col 34 S Laborer Acc Acc s/o Leah to Mary [Stram] Stran Col 25 S Acc Acc d/o Lura on 4 Jun 1874 at Doe Ck by HT Rich

BAYLY Lewis Col 35 S Farmer Acc Acc s/o Adah to Maria Bowdoin Col 34 S Acc Acc d/o Candace Mapp on 17 Mar 1886 at Locustville by LW Lee

BAYLY Lewis R 25 S Oysterman Acc Acc s/o Lewis & Letiha to Mary A Pecor 16 S Acc Acc d/o Edwd & Emeline on 3 Dec 1884 at Acc by A Woodyard

BAYLY Littleton [Bailey] Col 45 S Sailor Acc Acc s/o Kissy Wyatt to Margaret [Beavains] (Beavans) Beavans 22 S Acc Acc d/o Lney on 11 Sep 1873 at Belle Haven by JE Humphreys

BAYLY Lorenzo [Bailey] Col 23 S Farmer Acc Acc s/o Polly to Martha A Upshur Col 22 S Acc Acc d/o Wm Upshur & Ann Wescott on 30 Dec 1885 at Wardtown N'hamp by J Savage

BAYLY Louis J Col 21 S Wage-earner Acc Acc s/o Mark & Virginia to Matilda Finney Col 16 S Acc Acc d/o Edward & Mary on 25 Feb 1892 at Acc by J Duckett

BAYLY Perry L [Bailey] Col 24 S Seaman Acc Acc s/o Martha to Harriet Hateney Col 18 S Acc Acc d/o Lizzie on 11 Nov 1884 at Acc by GW Young

BAYLY Peter FN to Sarah Wise FN lic: 6 Nov 1854 Thos Budd says both over 21

BAYLY Peter FN 23 S Farmer Acc Acc s/o Custis & Susan to Mary Downing FN 26 S Acc Acc d/o George & Sarah on 4 Jan 1860 at Locust Mount by JWA Elliott (Thomas H Selby says both over 21)

BAYLY Peter Col 40 W Laborer Acc Acc s/o Comfort to Mary Dix Col 38 S Acc Acc d/o Lewis & Margt on 24 May 1877 at Acc by A Joynes

BAYLY Peter Henry Col 23 S Farmer Acc Acc s/o Peter & Mary to Harriet Ann White Col 25 S Acc Acc d/o Peter & Elizabeth on 22 Sep 1889 at Savageville by JB Lewis

BAYLY Phelix FN to Angeline Mears FN lic: 25 Apr 1859 John D Winder says both over 21

BAYLY Phillip Col 47 W Farmer Acc Acc s/o Nannie to Nancy Downing Col 27 S Acc Acc d/o Edwd & Emma on 30 Dec 1886 at Acc by L Duncan

BAYLY Richard 53 W Merchant Acc Acc s/o Robt & Polly to Sally Johnson 25 S Acc Acc d/o Gillet & Elizabeth Northam on 12 May 1868 at Acc by M Oldham

BAYLY Richard Col 45 S Laborer Acc Acc s/o James & Nicy to Mary Garrison Col 31 S N'hamp: Acc on 20 Dec 1871 near Drum'tn by A Joynes

BAYLY Robert Col 45 S Laborer Acc Acc s/o Maria Browne to Mary Wise Col 46 S Acc Acc d/o Sarah on 12 May 1881 at Onancock by JC Ayler

BAYLY Sewel (Sewell) Col 26 S Sailor Acc Acc s/o Richd & Anna to Elizabeth Custis Col 26 S Acc Acc d/o Robt & Eliza on 2 Jan 1874 at Drum'tn by A Joynes

BAYLY Sewell H 24 S Mechanic Acc

Marriages

Acc s/o Thos & Elizth to Clara F Northam 23 S Acc Acc d/o Wm & Drucilla on 24 Jan 1883 at Mappsville by JW Hundley

BAYLY Solomon [Baily] 22 S Farmer Acc Acc s/o Martha to Martha Bowdoin Col 22 S Acc Acc d/o Candace on 23 Feb 1881 at Locust Mount by JWA Elliott

BAYLY Southey Col 27 S Laborer Acc Acc s/o Leah to Patience Parker Col 21 S Acc Acc d/o Eliza on 10 Nov 1880 at Acc by SMG Copeland

BAYLY Theo A Col 24 S Wage-earner Acc Acc s/o Daniel & Mary to Sarah A Snead Col 18 S Acc Acc d/o Ellen Custis on 31 May 1891 at Savageville by JH Offer

BAYLY Thomas Col 23 S Farmer Acc Acc s/o Harriet to Susan Sturgis Col 18 S Acc Acc d/o John H & Ann on 4 Jan 1893 at Acc by L Duncan

BAYLY Thomas [Bailey] 27 S Farmer Acc Acc s/o Edward & Lovey to Amie C Leatherburry 18 S Acc Acc d/o Nicetty on 29 Jul 1888 at Mason's Corner by HS Dulany

BAYLY Thos S 24 S Farmer b: Acc s/o Jno J & Sally to Elizth M Boggs 27 S b: Acc d/o Jas S & Elizth on 6 Dec 1854 at Acc by JH Addison (Wm H White says both over 21)

BAYLY Upshur Col 21 S Saloon Keeper Acc Acc s/o Harriet to Neville Parker Col 21 S Acc Acc d/o Emma Susan on 24 Aug 1886 at Pungo: by GHT Byrd

BAYLY William Col 30 S Farmer Acc Acc s/o Adah to Sally Allen Col 28 S Acc Acc d/o Robert & Jennie on 6 Nov 1881 at St Luke Ch by PM Lewis

BAYLY William Col 25 S Laborer Acc Acc s/o Emma to Alice Drummond Col 23 S Acc Acc d/o Tabbie on 19 Aug 1881 at Acc by RJ Waters

BAYLY William 25 S Oysterman Acc Acc s/o Lewis & Letetia to Catharine Stant 21 S Acc Acc d/o John & Susan on 11 Apr 1883 at Acc by WP Wright

BAYLY William Col 35 S Farmer Acc Acc s/o Eliza to Cordelia West Col 30 S Acc Acc d/o Nellie on 21 Sep 1892 at Acc by L Duncan

BAYLY William H 21 S Farmer Acc Acc s/o Thos & Hennie to Margaret Rachel West 16 S Acc Acc d/o Jesse & Susan on 9 Dec 1868 at Acc by D Titlow

BAYLY William S 28 S Farmer Acc Acc s/o Thomas W & Sarah E to Esther F Kellam 28 S Acc Acc d/o Augustus F & Mary E on 22 Nov 1871 at Pungo: by JE Humphreys

BAYLY Wm H Col 30 S Laborer Acc Acc to Frances Weeks Col 28 S N'hamp: Acc d/o Elizabeth Bibbins on 24 Aug 1876 at Belle Haven by JE Humphreys

BAYLY Wm H Col 20 S Farmer Acc Acc s/o Peter & Sarah to Hester Johnson Col 24 W Acc Acc d/o Lewis & Margaret Dix on 18 Oct 1882 near Poor House by AJ Satchell

BAYLY Wm James 24 S Shoemaker Acc Acc s/o Thos & Mary to Margt Arinthia Copes 21 S Acc Acc d/o Solomon & Henrietta on 27 Apr 1858 near Temp'ville by JF Chaplain (Wm S Byrd says both over 21)

BAYLY Wm T 22 S Merchant b: Acc s/o Jno J & Sally to Cath C (wid/o Hugh S) Powell 22 W b: Acc d/o Jno R & Eliza W Wise on 24 May 1855 at Pungo: by M Oldham (H C Walker says both over 21)

BAYNE James B Col 20 S Farmer Acc Acc s/o James H & Emma to Maggie S [Beckett] Becket Col 21 S Acc Acc d/o Peter & Margaret on 14 Jan 1891 near Savageville by JB Lewis

BEACH Charles Col 40 S Farmer Acc Acc s/o Selby to Selby Burton Col 40

S Acc Acc d/o Ann on 1 Oct 1873 at Burtons Chp by N Morris

BEACH Charles Col 21 S Wage-earner Acc Acc s/o Daniel & Sarah to Lauretta Taylor 21 S Acc Acc d/o Arthur & Catharine on 31 Dec 1895 at Wachapreague by JN Waters

BEACH Charles H Col 25 S Blacksmith Acc Acc s/o Charlse & Sylva to Martha Becket Col 26 S Acc Acc d/o Lukey Taylor on 25 Apr 1875 at Acc by HT Rich

BEACH Custis Col 22 S Farmer Acc Acc s/o Eliza Carpenter to Virginia [Reed] Read Col 20 S Acc Acc d/o Lucy on 10 Jan 1879 at Acc by JW Diggs

BEACH George Col 22 S Laborer Acc Acc s/o Charles & Sylvia to Arinthia Savage Col 23 S Acc Acc d/o Comfort on 15 Oct 1882 at Locust Mount by JWA Elliott

BEACH George W 29 S Farmer Acc Acc s/o Wm P & Virginia to Lizzie W Nock 19 S Acc Acc d/o John E & Sarah A on 4 Mar 1889 at Acc by JWA Elliott

BEACH John R Col 39 S Oysterman Acc Acc s/o Charles & Sylvia to Eliza Ashby Col 32 S Acc Acc d/o Geo & Isabell on 29 Jun 1892 at Acc by RH Coleman

BEACH Lewis M Col 21 S Farm Laborer Acc Acc s/o Charles & Sylvania to Laura Harmon Col 17 S Acc Acc d/o Bomlia on 9 Jan 1881 at Acc by JWA Elliott

BEACH Louis M Col 23 W Laborer Acc Acc s/o Charles & Sylva to Sarah A Hateney Col 19 S Acc Acc d/o George & Margaret on 19 Nov 1882 at Locust Mount by GW Young

BEACH Walter Col 22 S Farmer N'hamp: Acc s/o Eliza Nelson to Lottie [Reed] Read Col 22 S Acc Acc d/o Martha on 11 Jun 1885 near Pungo: by GHT Byrd

BEACH William P 25 S Carpenter b: Acc s/o Geo & Rosey to Virga E (Virginia) Roberts 21 S b: Acc d/o Edwm S & Elizth on 29 Mar 1855 at r/o Geo Roberts by JWA Elliott

BEACH Wilson 60 S Laborer Acc Acc s/o Sarah to Luky Becket 33 S Acc Acc d/o Rachel on 1 Jan 1867 at Acc by JWA Elliott

BEASLEY Alfred 21 S Farmer Acc Acc s/o Elizabeth to Mary C Rossey 16 S Acc Acc d/o Jacob & Elizth on 28 Nov 1883 at Acc C H by JG Anderson

BEASLEY Elijah 22 S Farmer Acc Acc s/o Thomas & Tabitha to Alice Hopkins 18 S Acc Acc d/o William H & Cornelia on 3 Dec 1890 at Acc by JA Barker

BEASLEY Fred S 22 S Farmer Acc Acc s/o Thos & Tabitha to Bettie Gretrude Owens 17 S Acc Acc d/o George C & Catharine on 25 Dec 1892 at Locust Mount by JWA Elliott

BEASLEY George 17 S Farm Laborer Acc Acc s/o Mary J to Laura Mears 15 S Acc Acc d/o George & Betsy on 7 Jan 1885 at Acc by AJ Walter

BEASLEY George Coleburn 23 S Farmer Acc Acc s/o Thomas & Tabithia to Adalaide Turner 20 S Acc Acc d/o James S & Margaret on 27 Dec 1894 at Acc C H by JM Dunaway

BEASLEY Henry [Beasly] 23 S Farmer Acc Acc s/o William & Betsy to Rosa Turner 23 S Acc Acc d/o Jno & Mary on 29 Dec 1875 near Onancock by FR Boston

BEASLEY James 25 S Farmer Acc Acc s/o Elizabeth to Margaret A Lilliston 22 S Acc Acc d/o Edwd & Rose on 3 Jan 1880 near The Folly by JG Anderson

BEASLEY John 21 S Farmer Acc Acc s/o Jno & Mary to Margaret Hargis 18 S Acc Acc d/o Belle Purnell on 18

Dec 1878 near Locustville by LK LeCato

BEASLEY Lewis 29 S Farmer Acc Acc s/o John & Susan to Arminda Hart 28 S Acc Acc on 1 Sep 1880 at Acc by JG Anderson

BEASLEY Thomas H 36 W Farmer Acc Acc s/o William & Betsy to Melissa Harris 33 D Acc Acc d/o Sally Cropper on 11 Sep 1887 at Acc C H by J McNabb

BEASLEY William 30 S Farmer Acc Acc s/o John & Leavina to Mary R Hutchinson 17 S Acc Acc d/o James H & Donnda W on 20 Jan 1871 at Acc by AC Bledsoe

BEASLEY William T 22 S Farmer Acc Acc s/o William & Elizth to Tabitha A East 30 S Acc Acc d/o Daugherty on 5 Aug 1867 at Acc by JWA Elliott

BEASLEY Wm 41 W Laborer b: Acc s/o Jno & Elizabeth to Elizth Watson 25 S b: Acc d/o Jas Phillips & Cath Watson on 9 Nov 1854 at r/o Wn Beasley by LK LeCato (Wm S Kellam says she over 21)

BEASLEY Wm 20 S Farmer Acc Acc s/o Perry to Alitia Parkes 20 S Acc Acc d/o Jno P & Margaret on 4 Jan 1877 near Guilford by JE Bundick

BEAUCHAMP Burton J H [Beacham] 23 S Farmer Som Co MD Acc s/o Elisha & Jane to Elizabeth J Waterfield 22 S Acc Acc d/o Wm & Margt on 24 Feb 1870 at Acc by TM Poulson

BEAUCHAMP Samuel Col 30 S Wage-earner Som Co MD Acc s/o Harriet to Sarah J Ashby Col 28 S Acc Acc d/o Eliza on 13 Jun 1894 at Acc by PW Lee

BEAUCHAMP Wm K 29 S Livery Keeper Wor Co MD Acc s/o Jas M & Emiline C to Marg't B Guy 37 W Acc Acc d/o John S & Sarah A Hopkins on 20 Jan 1892 at Onancock by JB Pruitt

BEAVANS Charles [Bivens] Col 22 S Wage-earner Acc Acc s/o Moses & Hester to Fannie Stran Col 16 S Acc Acc d/o Mary on 11 Mar 1891 at Acc by L Duncan

BEAVANS Charles C [Bivins] 24 S Farmer Acc Acc s/o Severn & Elizabeth to Henrietta Byrd 21 S Acc Acc d/o Edward & Fanny on 17 Dec 1885 at Acc by P Sheppard

BEAVANS David Col 22 S Laborer Acc Acc s/o Lucy to Nancy Satchell Col 24 W Acc Acc on 8 May 1881 at Shilo Bapt Ch by TW Nettles

BEAVANS Dennis FN 21 S Farming Acc Acc s/o Henry & Atha to Susan Ann Nedab FN 17 S Acc Acc d/o Levi & Margt (who gave consent) on 1 May 1861 at Acc by D Titlow (John D Window says he over 21)

BEAVANS Dennis [Beavins] Col 35 W Farmer Acc Acc s/o Henry & Alsie to Elizabeth Harmon Col 20 S Acc Acc d/o Jas & Laura on 25 Jan 1880 at Onancock by JW Diggs

BEAVANS Edward H [Bivins] Col 21 S Farmer Acc Acc s/o Charlotte Wimbrough to Annie F J A Laws Col 19 S Acc Acc on 10 Jan 1886 at Acc by AJ Satchell

BEAVANS Henry [Bevans] Col 21 S Sailor Acc Acc s/o Severn & Nancy to Mary S Phillips Col 22 S Acc Acc d/o Robert & Mary on 23 Dec 1885 near Craddockville by GHT Byrd

BEAVANS James [Beavins] Col 54 S Farmer Acc Acc s/o Rosey to Mary Ann Bayly Col 56 S Acc Acc on 25 Oct 1874 at Savageville by JK Plato

BEAVANS James [Bevins] Col 22 S Farmer Acc Acc s/o Leah Maddux to Mary Savage Col 17 S Acc Acc d/o Rachel on 29 Jan 1890 near Temp'ville by JC Cluff

BEAVANS James [Bevins] Col 38 W Farmer Acc Acc s/o Eldred to Jimma Johnson Col 38 S Acc Acc d/o Stran

& Mollie on 30 Nov 1892 at Pungo: by JH Offer
BEAVANS Jno W Col 40 S Acc Acc to Margaret Bayly Col 30 S Acc Acc on 4 Dec 1879 at Acc by TW Nettles
BEAVANS John [Bivins] FN s/o Henry to Mary Susan Martin FN d/o James who gave consent lic: 28 Feb 1859
BEAVANS John Wm s/o Joshua to Henrietta Taylor d/o Bundick Taylor dec'd lic: 8 Mar 1856 Edward Smith says both over 21
BEAVANS Moses [Bevans] Col 75 W Farmer N'hamp: Acc s/o Thomas & Esther to Jane Sample Col 45 S Acc Acc d/o Rose on 14 Jul 1892 at Acc by L Duncan
BEAVANS Moses [Bevans] Col 24 S Farmer Acc Acc s/o Moses Sr & Kesiah to Charlotte Ames Col 32 S Acc Acc d/o Smith W & Mary J on 17 Jun 1894 at Belle Haven by ET Outen
BEAVANS Obed S [Bevans] Col 22 S Laborer Acc Acc s/o Margaret to Betty Wise Col 20 S Acc Acc d/o Lotty on 12 Oct 1881 at Acc by RJ Waters
BEAVANS Riley [Bevans] Col 23 S Farmer Acc Acc s/o Eli to Emma [Doughlas] Douglass Col 18 S Acc Acc d/o Jacob & Jane on 24 Feb 1884 at Mappsville by AJ Satchell
BEAVANS Riley W [Bevans] Col 34 W Farmer Acc Acc s/o Edmund to Sallie Williams Col 28 W Acc Acc d/o Isaac & Lydia on 17 Jul 1892 at Acc by AJ Satchell
BEAVANS Saml [Bivans] Col 21 S Farmer Acc Acc s/o Mary to Mary Johnson Col 17 S Acc Acc d/o Sarah on 5 Dec 1877 near Savageville by JK Plato
BEAVANS Severn FN to Nancy West FN d/o Mary who gave consent lic: 13 Mar 1861 Wm S Sturgis says he over 21

BECKET Arthur Col 22 S Laborer Acc Acc s/o Sam'l & Sally to Rose Poulson Col 21 S Acc Acc d/o Eser & Julia A on 14 Dec 1887 at Acc by JA Haynes
BECKET Charles S Col 22 S Farmer Acc Acc s/o Peter & Margaret to Mary Boggs Col 19 S Acc Acc d/o Samuel & Margaret on 30 Dec 1894 at Acc by J Duckett
BECKET Daniel FN 23 S Farmer Acc Acc s/o Jas & Sally to Lesh Downing FN 18 S Acc Acc d/o S Downing on 7 Jan 1863 at Acc by JWA Elliott
BECKET George Col 21 S Farmer Acc Acc s/o Peter & Margaret to Mary Stran Col 18 S Acc Acc d/o Perry & Rosey on 17 Dec 1887 at Acc by JA Haynes
BECKET Henry E Col 32 W Farmer Acc Acc s/o Weston & Susan to Kessie Sample Col 33 S Acc Acc d/o William & Mary on 19 May 1895 at Acc by JH Offer
BECKET Henry M Col 21 S Farm Labor Acc Acc s/o Emma to Easter Badger Col 18 S Acc Acc d/o Arcena on 5 Oct 1882 at Savageville by F Corrd
BECKET James Col 30 S Farmer Acc Acc s/o Leah to Margaret Colonna Col 25 S Acc Acc d/o Esther on 6 Mar 1878 at Pungo: by JK Plato
BECKET James Col 44 W Wage-earner Acc Acc s/o Leah to Mary Thomas Col 45 W Acc Acc d/o Virginia Nock on 24 Sep 1893 at Savageville by JH Offer
BECKET John FN to Susan Evans FN lic: 28 Mar 1854
BECKET John [Beckett] 45 S Sawyer Acc Acc to Susan Gaskins 40 S Acc Acc d/o Geo & Elizth on 18 Nov 1866 at Acc by JH Addison
BECKET John A Col 22 S Farmer Acc Acc s/o Jno & Sarah to Mary J Smith Col 25 S Acc Acc d/o Geo & Esther

BECKET John T [Beckett] Col 23 S Wage-earner Acc Acc s/o Margaret to Mary S [Parks] Parkes Col 22 S Acc Acc d/o Jesse & Ann on 20 Mar 1889 at Acc by JA Haynes
BECKET Lewis FN to Harriet Roane FN lic: 27 Aug 1855 Wm J Beloate says both over 21
BECKET Michael 22 S Farmer Acc Acc s/o Eliza Poulson to Sarah Dix 19 S Acc Acc d/o Lewis & Margt on 11 Aug 1867 at Acc by ES Grant
BECKET Peter FN s/o Rachel to Polly Becket FN lic: 27 Sep 1858 John T Hutchinson & Wm Harmon both say both over 21
BECKET Peter 25 S Farmer Acc Acc s/o Peter & Rosa to Margaret [Bird] Byrd 18 S Acc Acc d/o Ann on 23 Dec 1866 at Acc by BT Ames
BECKET Peter Col 38 W Farmer Acc Acc s/o Peter & Rosey to Maggie [Ker] Kerr Col 24 S Acc Acc d/o Jno & Susan on 2 Jan 1884 at Drum'tn by LW Lee
BECKET Smith [Beckett] Col 23 S Wage-earner Acc Acc s/o Leah to Ella [Bevans] Beavans Col 22 S Acc Acc d/o Margaret on 30 Oct 1890 at Savageville by JB Lewis
BECKET Wm Thos [Beckett] Col 22 S Farmer Acc Acc s/o Littleton to Hester Moore Col 19 S Acc Acc d/o Edmund & Nellie on 31 Dec 1890 at Pungo: by JB Lewis
BECKNER Wm M 32 S Merchant Philadelphia PA Acc to Willianna Ackley 26 S Philadelphia PA Acc d/o Jno T & Mary on 3 Jan 1877 at Guilford by JB Merritt
BEEBY Andrew J 21 S Oysterman Acc Acc s/o Burton & Arinthia to Maggie Taylor 17 S Acc Acc d/o Samuel R & Jane on 27 Oct 1892 at Chinco: Isld by RB Sanford
BEEBY Daniel J 21 S Oysterman Acc Acc s/o John & Nancy to Elizabeth Daisey 16 S Acc Acc d/o W J & Peggy on 26 Mar 1892 at Chinco: Isld by JF Wooden
BEEBY John B 17 S Oysterman Acc Acc s/o Silas B & Arinthia to Henrietta Williams 16 S Acc Acc d/o William & Henrietta on 25 Jun 1892 at Chinco: Isld by JW Turner
BEEBY Silas B 18 S Oysterman Acc Acc s/o John & Mary to Arinthia Andrews 17 S Acc Acc d/o Wm & Mary on 6 Dec 1868 at Acc by WP Thornton
BEEBY Thomas 20 S Waterman St Martins MD Acc s/o Jno & Mary to Mary Ann Bowden 17 S Acc Acc d/o Crippen Sr & Nancy on 4 Oct 1865 at Acc by WP Thornton
BELL Abel A 24 S Farmer Acc Acc s/o James & Elizth to Emory E Davis 22 S Acc Acc d/o Littleton on 3 Oct 1869 at Acc by JE Humphreys
BELL Abel J 21 S Farmer Acc Acc s/o Abel to Sadie E Byrd 18 S N'hamp: Acc d/o Thos T & Bettie A on 24 Feb 1892 at Acc by JWA Elliott
BELL Burwell O 20 S Farmer Acc Acc s/o Gilbert & Cathe to Sarah E Bell 20 S Acc Acc d/o Robin & Sarah on 5 Aug 1866 at Acc by JWA Elliott
BELL Custis 28 S Laborer Acc Acc to Mary Turlington 24 S Acc Acc on 27 Aug 1867 at Acc by JWA Elliott
BELL Edward (J) 28 W Harness Mkr Acc Acc s/o Jacob & Margaret to Margaret (A) Harmon 30 S Acc Acc d/o Abel Harmon & Nancy Chance on 2 Sep 1860 at r/o L K LeCato by LK LeCato (Abel Mears of A says she over 21)
BELL Edward T 20 S Farmer Acc Acc s/o John E & Lucretia to Mary Scott 16 S Acc Acc d/o James E & Elizabeth on 29 Dec 1889 at Drum'tn by WJ Twilley
BELL Francis 26 W Sailor to Mary

Gardner 21 S d/o James & Eliza lic: 7 Dec 1871 marr: 10 Dec 1871 at Onancock

BELL George E 25 S Farmer Acc Acc s/o John E & Mary to Catherine E Mears 21 S Acc Acc d/o George T & Margaret A on 13 Mar 1887 at Onley Sta by JW Hundley

BELL George W 33 S Sailor Acc Acc s/o James S & Eliz'th to Ida J Davis 24 S Acc Acc d/o Littleton B & Hester Ann on 2 Aug 1891 at Acc by JR Strugis

BELL George W T 21 S Life Saving Station Acc Acc s/o Walter W & Margaret A to Rachel J Sterling 19 S Acc Acc d/o Annie J. on 25 May 1887 at Pungo: by JW Hundley

BELL Isaiah Col 21 S Wage-earner Acc Acc s/o Keziah Wise to Sophia Rew Col 19 S Acc Acc d/o Handy & Ellen on 4 Dec 1890 at Acc by AJ Satchell

BELL Jacob Col 40 W Farmer Acc Acc to Caroline Ashby Col 38 S Acc Acc d/o Lucretia Johnson on 13 Jan 1886 at Acc by CA Horsey

BELL James 22 S Farmer Acc Acc s/o Gilbert & Catharine to Theodocea Ward 18 S Acc Acc d/o Golden & Margaret on 10 Nov 1874 near Locust Mount by JWA Elliott

BELL James B 20 S Farmer Acc Acc s/o Bayly & Mary to Lottie E Ames 20 S Acc Acc d/o John A & Margt V on 24 Nov 1875 at Oak Grove Ch by E Hebard

BELL James F 29 S Farmer Acc Acc s/o James S & Virginia to Maggie E Mears 17 S Acc Acc d/o James E & Virginia on 8 May 1889 at Locust Mount by JWA Elliott

BELL James H 43 S Farmer Acc Acc s/o Elias to Ann Eliza Mason 43 S Acc Acc d/o Major & Polly on 2 Apr 1872 near Wood Stock by JET Ewell

BELL John 26 S Laborer Acc Acc to Ellen Smith 21 S N'hamp: Acc d/o Dinah on 20 May 1868 at Acc by LK LeCato

BELL John E 22 S Farmer Acc Acc s/o Lorenzo D & Eliz Ann to (Mary) Esther LeCato 17 S Acc Acc d/o Wm R & Jain & (ward/o Nathaniel B LeCato who gave consent) on 23 Nov 1856 at Bradford Nk by JWA Elliott

BELL John E 22 S Farmer Acc Acc s/o Thorogood & Cath to Lucretia Satchell 35 W Acc Acc d/o George & Nancy Bundick on 7 Feb 1867 at Acc by ES Grant

BELL John Herbert 20 S Farmer Acc Acc s/o John E & Lucretia to Lucy A Savage 30 W Acc Acc d/o Wm S & Mary Evans on 18 Dec 1895 at Acc C H by JM Dunaway

BELL Lorenzo D 22 S Oysterman Acc Acc s/o Jodiah & Elizabeth to Drucilla Mears 23 S Acc Acc d/o Robert & Nancy on 1 May 1860 at Pocomoke Ch by EW Stickney (Raymond Stant says both over 21)

BELL Nebraska P 29 S Merchant N'hamp: N'hamp: s/o Bayly & Mary to Elizabeth A Warren 29 S Acc Acc d/o Patrick & Elizabeth on 12 Sep 1888 at Acc by PT Warren

BELL Robert J 25 S Farmer Acc Acc s/o Elias to Margaret S Savage 24 S Acc Acc d/o Susan A on 3 Dec 1868 at Acc by EG Irvin

BELL Seth E 24 S Laborer Acc Acc s/o Victor & Emaline to Mittie C Franklin 22 S Acc Acc d/o Philip C & Harriet on 31 Jan 1873 at Acc by TM Poulson

BELL Walter P 24 S Farmer Acc Acc s/o Wm H & Peggy to Margt Mears 22 S Acc Acc d/o James on 19 Nov 1854 at r/o Wm H Bell by J Burton

BELL William G 25 S Farmer N'hamp: N'hamp: s/o Bayly & Mary to Rose S Doughty 30 S N'hamp: Acc d/o James & Susan on 24 Feb 1874 at

Marriages

Acc by LK LeCato
BELL William of R 43 S Variable b: Acc s/o Wm to Atta Ann (Cropper) Harris 15 S b: Acc d/o Sally on 25 Jan 1855 at Acc by JWA Elliott
BELL William P 27 S Druggist Acc Acc s/o Lorenzo J & Bettie C to Margaret D Blackstone 25 S Acc Acc d/o John J & Bettie on 26 Oct 1887 at Drum'tn by J McNabb
BELL William T 34 S Brick Mason Acc Acc s/o Wm & Ann E to Bettie C Hinman 34 S Acc Acc d/o Thos & Mary on 11 Feb 1883 at Acc by WP Wright
BELOATE Alfred Col 21 S Farmer Acc Acc s/o Clarissa to Mary [Mathews] Matthews Col 21 S Acc Acc d/o Susan on 25 Dec 1874 at Burton by JW Ruff
BELOATE Arthur T 28 S Sailor Acc Acc s/o Lewis & Mollie to Catharine Hurst 17 S Acc Acc d/o James & Susan on 17 Sep 1867 at Acc by ES Grant
BELOATE Benjamin (T) 22 S Farmer b: Acc s/o William & Kesiah Dunton to Susan Ward 26 S b: Acc d/o William & Margaret Lewis on 4 Feb 1857 at my house by LK LeCato (James H Beloate says both over 21)
BELOATE Benjamin W 23 S Laborer Acc Acc s/o Benjamin & Susan to Mary Bunting 18 S Acc Acc d/o Jacob & Mary on 23 Nov 1881 at Warrington Br by SC Boston
BELOATE Charlie T 22 S Farmer Acc Acc s/o James L & Mary T to Virginia T Gray 19 S Acc Acc d/o Thomas R (Decd) & Sally on 4 Jan 1882 at Onancock by JC Watson
BELOATE Edward 22 S Farmer Acc Acc s/o Edward A & Annie B to Mary C Drummond 16 S Acc Acc d/o George E & Ada J on 6 Feb 1895 at Acc by JR Sturgis
BELOATE Edward A 28 S Farmer Acc Acc s/o Jos G & Elizth to Ann B Harris 23 S Acc Acc d/o Geo B & Rachel on 27 Dec 1866 at Acc by BT Ames
BELOATE Everett J 22 S Farmer Acc Acc s/o Jas L & Mary T to Emma S Haley 20 S Acc Acc d/o James P & Rosetta on 24 Dec 1879 near Savageville by JC Watson
BELOATE Frederick H 24 S Farmer Acc Acc s/o Benj T & Susan to Annie M Custis 26 S Acc Acc d/o Benj F & Mary E on 25 Dec 1883 at Hollybrook by JW Hundley
BELOATE George B 34 S Laborer Acc Acc s/o Mary to Edie White Col 21 S Acc Acc d/o Harriet on 1 Jun 1881 at Acc by PM Lewis
BELOATE George W (Belote) 30 S Sailor s/o Lewis & Molly to Sarah Jane Hurst 22 d/o James & Susan lic: 23 Nov 1864 marr: 24 Nov 1864
BELOATE Gwynell L 21 S Farmer Acc Acc s/o James L & Mary T to Mary Gray 18 S Acc Acc d/o Thos R & Sally on 24 Dec 1884 at Acc by WC Vaden
BELOATE Herbert [Beloatt] 24 S Farmer Acc Acc s/o Levin B & Sally to Missouri Turlington 17 S Acc Acc d/o Wm T on 12 Mar 1879 at Oak Grove by CC Wertenbaker
BELOATE James L (S) 27 S Farmer b: Acc s/o Lewis & Molly to Mary T Williams 21 S b: N'hamp: d/o John & Esther on 15 Jan 1857 at Reese Chp by ES Grant (Thomas Mears says he over 21 & Eliz T Williams says she over 21)
BELOATE Jas 23 S Farmer Acc Acc s/o Levin & Nancy to Emily Warrington 20 S Acc Acc d/o Jas & Margt on 29 Mar 1864 at Acc by JWA Elliott
BELOATE Jno W 21 S Drummer Acc Acc s/o John W to Alice Lee Coard 23 S Acc Acc d/o John & Nancy on

9 Jun 1886 at Zion Ch by JW Carroll

BELOATE John R 21 S Farmer Acc Acc s/o James F & Emma S to Maggie C Savage 23 S Acc Acc d/o John & Susan on 6 Feb 1895 at Acc by SW Eason

BELOATE John W 23 S Farming Acc Acc s/o Wm J & Sally to Susan S Harris 19 S Acc Acc d/o George B & (ward/o John A M Whealton who gave consent) on 9 May 1860 at Acc by P Warren

BELOATE John W 22 S Farmer Acc Acc s/o Levin & Sally to Joice M Mears 21 S Acc Acc d/o Fanny on 10 Jan 1869 at Acc by JE Humphreys

BELOATE Julius D 23 S Farming Acc Acc s/o Lewis & Molly to Edna B Martin 16 S Acc Acc d/o John S & Anna on 6 Nov 1861 at Acc by BT Ames

BELOATE Louis S 23 S Farmer Acc Acc s/o Wm H & Keziah to Mary S Martin 17 S Acc Acc d/o Jno S & Ann on 7 Jan 1866 at Acc by P Warren

BELOATE Nath'l 42 S Merchant Acc Acc s/o Jas G & Betsy to Susan Beloate 42 W Acc Acc d/o Geo & Rachel Harris on 31 Dec 1882 at Acc by SC Boston

BELOATE Robert T 22 S Farming b: Acc s/o Wm J & Sally to Euphemia Finney 33 S b: Acc d/o Walter & Sally on 17 Feb 1857 at r/o Benj Ames by BT Ames (Wm J Mason says both over 21)

BELOATE Wellington 21 S Farming Acc Acc s/o Levin & Sally to Sarah Ann Charnock 21 S Acc Acc d/o Edward & Sally on 10 Mar 1870 at Acc by OP Twiford

BELOATE William L 27 S Farmer Acc Acc s/o Louis S & Mary S to Manie A Guy 26 S Acc Acc d/o John W & Mary A on 14 Jan 1894 at Locust Mount by JWA Elliott

BELOATE William T [Beloat] 25 S Merchant Acc Acc s/o James L & Mary T to Alice L Beloate 26 W Acc Acc d/o John W & Nancy B Coard on 29 Apr 1891 at Acc C H by GF Farring & JT Moore

BENNETT George W 20 S Farming Acc Acc s/o Covington & Peggie to Laura H Shrieves 18 S Acc Acc d/o Abraham & Louisa on 25 Feb 1869 at Acc by E Hebard

BENNETT James H 52 W Farmer Acc Acc s/o Covington & Peggy to Bettie Killman 45 W Acc Acc on 31 Mar 1887 at Edw'd Joynes' Gate by JR Strugis

BENNETT James H [Bennet] 28 W Sailor Acc Acc s/o Covington & Margt to Rachel S Shrieves 19 S Acc Acc d/o Abraham & V Louisa on 26 Nov 1868 at Acc by OP Twiford

BENNETT John 52 W Farmer Acc Acc s/o Covington & Margaret to Hester Parker 20 S Acc Acc d/o Wm & Susan on 11 Jun 1879 at Acc by CC Wertenbaker

BENNETT John T to Mary [Killmon] Killman on 8 Sep 1858 by M Oldham (James Killman says both over 21)

BENNETT Leonard James 22 S Sailor Acc Acc s/o John & Mary to Betsy Davis Charnock 22 S Acc Acc d/o Solomon & Sarah A on 18 Jan 1888 at Acc by JH Riddick

BENNETT Teakle [Bennet] 26 W Sailor Acc Acc s/o Covington & M to Mary E [Shreaves] Shrieves 19 S Acc Acc d/o Chas & Lavine on 17 Aug 1863 at Acc by JWA Elliott

BENNETT Walter 21 S Waterman Acc Acc s/o John & Mary to Lillie C Bennett 21 S Acc Acc d/o George & Laura on 19 May 1891 at Acc by JM Anderson

BENSON George T 23 S Blacksmith Acc Acc s/o Kealy & Anna to Ida L

Mears 19 S Acc Acc d/o Alfred J & Leah Ann on 23 Nov 1882 at Acc by JWA Elliott

BENSON Henry 25 S Sailor Pocomoke City MD Acc to Delia Evans 31 S Acc Acc d/o Lewis & Patsey on 23 Mar 1883 at Tangier Isld by CS Baker

BENSTON William 35 W Oysterman DE Acc s/o Wm & Hulda to Elizabeth Jester 41 W Acc Acc d/o Parker & Mary Ann Bowden on 13 Jul 1872 at Chinco: Isld by P Bowdin Sr

BENSWANGER Emannel 34 S Merchant b: Germany s/o David & Sarah to Ann R Kellam 27 S b: Locustville d/o Nathl & Nancy on 13 Feb 1856 at Locustville by J Allen (John W Mears says both over 21)

BERRY Edward 22 S Oysterman Acc Acc s/o Agness to Sabra Griffin 31 S Acc Acc d/o Jane Cropper on 2 Mar 1870 near Horntown by S Marshall

BERRY George W of C 23 S Farmer Acc Acc s/o Charles & Margt to Ann Eliza [Shreaves] Shrieves 25 S Acc Acc d/o George & Hetty on 14 Feb 1875 near News Town by JE Bundick

BERRY John N 29 S Farmer Acc Acc s/o Chas C & Margt to Elizabeth Hickman 28 S Acc Acc d/o Elijah & Rachel on 30 Nov 1879 at Modest Town by DA Woodson

BERRY Jonathan 40 S Blacksmith Princess Ann Co VA Acc s/o Jonathan & Mary to Mary [Pettit] Pettitt 28 S Acc Acc d/o James & Mary on Jun 1877 at r/o Jas Pettitt by CC Wertenbaker

BERRY Robert H 20 S Merchant Som Co MD Acc s/o George N & Margaret to Fannie E Watson 17 S Acc Acc d/o Ellison T & Cascia on 11 Apr 1888 at Craddockville by JH Riddick

BERRY William 21 S Farmer Acc Acc s/o John & Jane to Scarborough Melson 18 S Acc Acc d/o John H & Susan on 10 Nov 1880 at Reese Chp by JC Watson

BIBBINS George [Bibins] Col 22 S Laborer Acc Acc s/o Elizabeth to Martha Downing Col 18 S Acc Acc d/o Sally on 29 May 1882 at Drum'tn by AJ Satchell

BIBBINS James Col 26 S Farmer Acc Acc s/o Elizth Martin to Elizth Sarah West Col 20 S Acc Acc d/o Sophia on 23 Sep 1874 at Belle Haven by JE Humphreys

BIBBINS John S Col 24 S Sailor Acc Acc s/o Severn & Nancy to Betsy Ann Major Col 22 S Acc Acc d/o Thomas & Louisa on 14 Apr 1887 at Middlesex by L Duncan

BIBBINS Moses Col 45 S Farmer Acc Acc to Ibby Nock Col 38 S Acc Acc on 22 Dec 1875 at Savageville by JK Plato

BIBBINS Peter Col 35 S Farmer Acc Acc to Jane Hyslop Col 30 S Acc Acc on 7 Jan 1876 at Belle Haven by JE Humphreys

BIBBINS Robert [Bibins] Col 22 S Laborer Acc Acc s/o Kessy to Ellen Bull Col 24 S Acc Acc on 6 Oct 1878 near Pungo: by TW Nettles

BIRCH Andrew 22 S Oysterman Acc Acc s/o William F & Phoebe to Harriet Clark 20 S Acc Acc d/o Samuel & Comfort on 9 Feb 1892 at Chinco: Isld by JW Turner

BIRCH Charles 22 S Sailor Acc Acc s/o Henry & Rosetta to Minor Williams 17 S Acc Acc d/o Selby & Susan on 7 Mar 1888 at Chinco: Isld by SU Grimsley

BIRCH Charles H 24 S Oysterman Wor Co MD Acc s/o John E & Elizabeth to Jannie E Bloxom 16 S Acc Acc d/o John W & Martha A on 22 Apr 1891 at Chinco: Isld by JW Turner

BIRCH David 22 S Oysterman Acc Acc s/o Jas to Caroline C Loan 18 S Acc Acc d/o James & Elizabeth on 11 Mar 1869 at Acc by WP Thornton

BIRCH David 23 W Oysterman Acc Acc s/o Joseph & Ruth to Mary F Hopkins 18 S Acc Acc d/o Henry & Mary on 9 Jun 1870 at Chinco: Isld by WP Thornton

BIRCH Eba 22 S Oysterman Acc Acc s/o Henry & Rosa to Susan Jones 15 S Acc Acc d/o Jas S Sr & Rebecca on 24 Oct 1895 at Chinco: Isld by SU Grimsley

BIRCH George to Trany M Lewis lic: 3 Oct 1860 John A M Whealton says both over 21

BIRCH George C 57 W US Life Saving Service Acc Acc s/o Thomas & Mary C to Mary E Mumford 47 W Wor Co MD Acc d/o Benjamin & Charlott A Timmons on 11 Oct 1892 at Chinco: Isld by JF Wooden

BIRCH George H 20 S Oysterman Acc Acc s/o David H & Mary F to Henrietta Watson 20 S Acc Acc d/o Littleton & Eliza A on 14 Feb 1894 at Chinco: Isld by JT Edmondson

BIRCH Henry 61 W Oysterman Acc Acc s/o Joseph & Betsey to Frany Wharton 27 S Wor Co MD Acc d/o Henry & Ellen on 13 Jan 1891 at Chinco: Isld by GE Wood

BIRCH James L 23 S to Martha A M Jones 19 S d/o Susan Williams lic: 5 Apr 1865

BIRCH James M 32 S Oyster Dealer Chinco: Isld Chinco: Isld s/o Thos & Mary to Louisa A Burton 25 S Acc Acc d/o Wm & Margt on 12 Feb 1876 at Horntown by JM Anderson

BIRCH James T 21 S Oysterman Acc Acc s/o Wm & Nancy to Jane Savage 21 S MD Acc d/o Elisha & Ellen on 10 Jul 1896 at Acc by P Bowdin Jr

BIRCH James T [Burch] 26 W Sailor Acc Acc s/o Wm F & Mary to Sally J Clayton 22 S Acc Acc d/o Anna on 2 May 1866 at Acc by ES Grant

BIRCH John 50 W Oysterman Acc Acc s/o Jos & Elizabeth to Mary Hopkins 40 S Acc Acc d/o Eli & Elizabeth Matthews on 12 Sep 1872 at Chinco: Isld by WP Thornton

BIRCH John 20 S Oysterman Acc Acc s/o W F & Phoebe to Mary A Sharpley 16 S Acc Acc d/o John W & Elizabeth on 12 May 1888 at Chinco: Isld by RI Watkins

BIRCH Joseph 23 S Sailor Acc Acc s/o John & Margt to Mary Ann [Monger] Munger 17 S Acc Acc d/o Parker & Mary on 4 Apr 1874 at Chinco: Isld by WP Thornton

BIRCH Peter Col 69 S Wage-earner Acc Acc to Jane Taylor Col 52 S Acc Acc d/o Sarah Brown on 13 Jan 1892 at Acc by JC Cluff

BIRCH Peter R 21 S Oysterman Acc Acc s/o Wm F & Phebear to Maria Daisey 24 S Acc Acc d/o Wm & Peggy on 12 Dec 1881 at Chinco: Isld by WP Thornton

BIRCH Thomas B 23 S Waterman Acc Acc s/o Thomas & Mary to Sarah E Burton 27 S Acc Acc d/o Wm & Margt on 15 Sep 1875(?) at Brutons Shores by JH Amiss Certificate returned 5 Apr 1877

BIRCH Thomas J 21 S Oysterman MD Acc s/o George & Eliza Anna to Comfort A Beeby 17 S Acc Acc d/o John & Nancy on 14 Jan 1877 at Chinco: Isld by P Bowdin Sr

BIRCH Thomas L 66 W Oysterman Acc Acc s/o Joseph & Elizabeth to Mary Hudson 46 W Acc Acc d/o James & Eliza Wheeler on 31 May 1889 at Chinco: Isld by SU Grimsley

BIRCH William D (Decatur) [Burch] 24 S Sailor Acc Acc s/o John & Mrgaret to Rebecca Claville 17 S Acc Acc d/o Geo W & Lydia on 8 Jun 1872 at Chinco: Isld by P Bowdin Sr

Marriages

BIRCH William Junr (Burch) s/o Nancy to Sarah Walker d/o Mary lic: 30 Jan 1864 John A M Whealton says she is illegitimate

BIRCH Wm [Burch] 38 W Ship Carpenter Chinco: Isld Chinco: Isld s/o Joseph & Betsey to Phoba Thornton single Chinco: Isld Chinco: Isld d/o Jno & Betsey on 18 Mar 1854 at my house by P Bowdin

BIRCH Wm F 20 S Sailor Chinco: Isld Chinco: Isld s/o James T & Mary to Matilda Andrews 17 S Chinco: Isld Chinco: Isld d/o Isaac & Sarah on 10 Nov 1883 at Chinco: Isld by WP Thornton

BISHOP Charles 22 S Oysterman Sussex Co DE Acc s/o Reuben W to Angeline M Conner 18 S Acc Acc d/o Martin G & Charlotte on 13 Apr 1884(?) at Chinco: Isld by JD Reese Certificate returned 12 Jan 1889

BISHOP Daniel 21 S Oystering Sussex Co DE Acc s/o Reuben W & Mary to Mary E Bloxom 16 S Acc Acc d/o Richard F & Mary S on 5 Apr 1893 at Chinco: Isld by JB Workman

BISHOP Geo 26 S Farmer Acc Acc s/o Henry & Betsy to Susan Annis 26 S Acc Acc d/o Major & Polly on 5 May 1864 at Acc by ES Grant

BISHOP James A 22 S Oysterman Sussex Co Acc s/o Henry & Jane to Lucinda [Brasine] Brasure 17 S Sussex Co Acc d/o Joshua H & Elizth on 21 Dec 1876 at Chinco: Isld by P Bowdin Sr

BISHOP Reuben E 22 S Oysterman Acc Acc s/o Reuben to Henrietta Thornton 16 S Acc Acc d/o William S & Elizabeth on 15 May 1887 at Chinco: Isld by SU Grimsley

BISHOP Reuben W 36 S Oysterman Sussex Co DE Chinco: Isld s/o Joshua & Comfort to Margt E Whealton 18 S Chinco: Isld Chinco: Isld d/o Joshua & Nancy on 13 May 1877 at Chinco: Isld by P Bowdin Sr

BLACKSTONE John J 39 W Sheriff Acc Acc s/o Wm B & Elizabeth to Elizabeth D Gillett 32 S Acc Acc d/o Wm & Henrietta on 4 Dec 1857 at St James Ch Drum'tn by JE Tennent (George D Wise says she over 21)

BLACKSTONE Thomas W 26 S Merchant Acc Acc s/o Thos W & Ann to Sarah A Kellam 19 S Acc Acc d/o Fred C A & Eliza on 20 Dec 1860 at Acc by P Warren

BLACKSTONE Thomas W 33 S Druggist Acc Acc s/o John J & Bettie D to Sarah P Walston 24 S Acc Acc d/o Samuel I & Bettie T on 1 Jun 1893 at Acc C H by WC Lindsay

BLACKWELL Asher J 25 W Oysterman Mercer Co NJ Acc s/o J M & Emma to Mary O Busby 21 S Norfolk VA Acc d/o A J & Olena on 15 Jan 1886 at Temp'ville by JW Carroll

BLAKE Archie Col 25 S Farmer Acc Acc s/o Sarah Duncan to Mania D J White Col 25 S Acc Acc d/o Harriet Ann Poolman on 10 Jul 1884 at Acc by LW Lee

BLAKE David 68 W Carpenter s/o Major to Harriet A Smith 40 W lic: 12 Dec 1866 marr: 16 Dec 1866

BLAKE Frank Col 30 S Oysterman Acc Acc s/o Rachel Williams to Elizabeth Crippen Col 30 S Acc Acc d/o Wilson & Sarah on 18 May 1880 at Chinco: Isld by R Williamson

BLAKE Glenn Col 60 W Farmer Acc Acc s/o Oakey to Esther Marshall Col 50 W Acc Acc on 12 Dec 1889 at Winders Neck by N Morris

BLAKE Henry Col (mulatto) 33 S Oysterman Acc Acc s/o Leah to Arinthia Holden Col (mulatto) 22 S Acc Acc d/o Lydia on 27 Nov 1872 at Acc by M Oldham

BLAKE Llewellyn A 46 S Salesman Middlesex Co VA Baltimore MD s/o

James & Ann K to Leonora G Bullman 22 S King & Queen VA Acc d/o Leroy C & Elizabeth on 2 Jul 1884 at Locust Mount by JWA Elliott

BLAKE Oakey Col 28 S Laborer Acc Acc s/o Oakey & Mary to Leah Ewell Col 26 S Acc Acc d/o Peter & Amelia on 25 May 1887 at Chinco: Isld by SU Grimsley

BLAKE Samuel J Col (mulatto) 30 S Oysterman Acc Acc s/o Leah to Elizabeth Susan Harmon Col (mulatto) 30 S Acc Acc d/o Margt on 24 Nov 1872 at Temp'ville by M Oldham

BLOXOM Alfred Col 49 S Farmer Acc Acc s/o Alsie to Sabra Mason Col 49 S Acc Acc d/o Rachel on 6 Apr 1882 near News Town by AJ Satchell

BLOXOM Alonzo F 26 S Farmer Acc Acc s/o Alfred & Catharine to Mary C Young 22 S Acc Acc d/o Benj F & Elizabeth on 13 Dec 1885 at Bethel by JW Carroll

BLOXOM Asher C H 24 S Farmer Acc Acc s/o Thos H & Phoebe to Ruth T Barnes 22 S Acc Acc d/o Jno P & Sally on 27 Dec 1882 at Modest Town by MS Read

BLOXOM Custis W 23 S Farmer Acc Acc s/o Wm C & Eliza to Maggie S East 21 S Acc Acc d/o Peter & Susan on 29 Aug 1866 at Acc by LK LeCato

BLOXOM David F 22 S Farmer Acc Acc s/o Percy & Birnetta P to Sarah L Rayfield 23 S Acc Acc d/o Major & Elizth on 11 Feb 1880 at Bethel Bapt Ch by DA Woodson

BLOXOM Elias H 23 S Merchant Acc Acc s/o Wm T & Nancy to Maggie F Gaskill 17 S Acc Acc d/o John T & Elizabeth on 1 Feb 1888 at Mappsville by WA Street

BLOXOM Ezikeil A 22 S Farmer Acc Acc s/o Ezikiel & Sally to Georgia T James 18 S Acc Acc d/o Jno T & Susan on 23 Dec 1883 near Locustville by JG Anderson

BLOXOM George FN to Easter Taylor FN wid lic: 20 Oct 1860 T J Rayfield says both over 21

BLOXOM George Col 21 S Farmer Acc Acc s/o Edward to Grace Riley Col 24 W Acc Acc d/o Dinah Corbin on 27 Feb 1890 at Acc by AJ Satchell

BLOXOM George T Col 23 S Farmer Acc Acc s/o Labra to Henrietta Rayfield Col 19 S Acc Acc d/o Sarah Wise on 29 Dec 1881 at Acc by AJ Satchell

BLOXOM George Y 36 S Merchant Acc Acc s/o George & Elizabeth to Laura S Clayton 22 S Acc Acc d/o Henry & Sally on 27 Dec 1885 at Guilford by JW Carroll

BLOXOM James 40 S Oysterman Acc Acc s/o Richd & Rosa to Catharine W Lilliston 27 S Acc Acc d/o Edmd & Rosa on 31 Dec 1871 at Locustville by H Petty

BLOXOM James W 28 S Merchant Acc Acc s/o Geo & Elizth to Arinthia G [Hinmon] Hinman 18 S Acc Acc d/o John R & Elizth on 29 Nov 1866 at Acc by ES Grant

BLOXOM James W 38 W Farmer Acc Acc s/o Geo & Betsy to Sally M Clayton 38 W Acc Acc d/o Wm Rew on 23 Jan 1880 at Guilford by M Oldham

BLOXOM John M 22 S Sailor Acc Acc s/o Wm H & Mary to Ocianna Bundick 21 S Acc Acc d/o Wm J & Seymons on 18 Dec 1878 at Modest Town by DA Woodson

BLOXOM John M 25 S Merchant Acc Acc s/o Ezekiel & Sallie to Louisa Elliott 23 S Acc Acc d/o Geo Wm & Elizabeth on 4 Jun 1893 at Locust Mount by JWA Elliott

BLOXOM John W 23 S Sailor b: Acc s/o Stephen & Nancy to Catharine Jones 22 S b: Acc d/o Smith & Mary on 12 Aug 1857 at Acc by T Waters (Wm W Selby says both over 21)

BLOXOM John W 20 S Sailor Acc Acc s/o Wm & Tabitha to Martha Collins 20 S Sussex Co DE Acc d/o Chls & Hester on 20 Jan 1872 at Chinco: Isld by P Bowdin Sr

BLOXOM Levin W 21 S Laborer Acc Acc s/o Alex to Mary Finney 19 S Acc Acc d/o Tabbie on 2 Jun 1868 at Acc by A Joynes

BLOXOM Major to Clarissa Byrd d/o Selby who gave consent lic: 5 Dec 1859 Perry Bloxom says he over 21

BLOXOM Martin 22 S Farmer Acc Acc s/o George & Narcissa to Susan [Killmon] Killman 18 S Acc Acc d/o Saml on 28 Mar 1867 at Acc by GW Matthews

BLOXOM Nehemiah [Bloxome] 24 S Farmer Acc Acc s/o John & Mary to Sallie A Nock 21 S Acc Acc d/o James & Rachel on 22 Feb 1874 at Bethel Ch by JE Bundick

BLOXOM Perry L 22 S Farmer Acc Acc s/o Perry & Brunetta P to Danice R Parkes 20 S Acc Acc d/o Jas & Polly on 25 Feb 1886 at Mappsville by WA Street

BLOXOM Richard 45 W Sailor Acc Acc s/o Elijah & Mary to Elizabeth Whealton 40 W Acc Acc d/o Daniel & Comfort Jones on 4 Apr 1867 at Acc by P Bowdin Sr

BLOXOM Richard F 24 S Oysterman Acc Chinco: Isld s/o Wm & Tabitha to Ellen Beeby 16 S Wor Co MD Chinco: Isld d/o John & Nancy on 25 May 1873 at Chinco: Isld by P Bowdin Sr

BLOXOM Samuel Col 63 S Miller Acc Acc to Surena Crippen Col 48 S Acc Acc d/o Sarah on 28 Aug 1888 at Temp'ville by JC Cluff

BLOXOM Sealamore 54 W Keeper of US Light Ship Station Acc Acc s/o Stephen & Nancy to Martha E [Cherrick] Cherricks 28 W Wor Co MD Acc d/o George & Nancy Dennis on 8 Aug 1893 at Chinco: Isld by RB Sanford

BLOXOM Sewell 19 S Farmer Acc Acc s/o Major & Clarissa to Sadie Ewell 16 S Acc Acc d/o Charles & Susan on 5 Apr 1882 at Wm Ewell's by JW Hundley

BLOXOM Thomas Col 35 S Laborer Acc Acc s/o Alsie to Emily Catharine Davis Col 23 S Acc Acc d/o Labra Bagwell on 8 Apr 1875 near Metompkin by A Joynes

BLOXOM Thomas H widr to Phebe Eliz'th Bull d/o Thomas lic: 3 Jan 1855

BLOXOM Thos 25 S Farming Acc Acc s/o George & Eliz to Elizabeth Parkes 22 S Acc Acc d/o Benja & Polly on 27 Dec 1870 at Acc by JET Ewell

BLOXOM Wesley A 21 S Farmer Acc Acc s/o Wm T & Nancy to Martha J Schley 22 S Acc Acc d/o Wm T & Nancy on 27 Dec 1883 at Temp'ville by M Oldham

BLOXOM William ward/o Jesse Dickerson who gave consent to Mary Wessells d/o John dec'd & ward/o Thorogood Mason who gave consent lic: 31 Dec 1855

BLOXOM William B 21 S Oysterman Acc Acc s/o Comfort Bowdoin to Ida V Fisher 18 S Wor Co MD Acc d/o Obadiah & Iallie M on 17 Apr 1893 at Acc by GP Jones

BLOXOM William H 23 S Farmer Acc Acc s/o Martin L & Amanda S to Miranda T [Killmon] Killman 21 S Acc Acc d/o Henry T & Georgianna on 27 Dec 1893 at Acc by JL King

BLOXOM William P 26 S Farming Acc Acc s/o David & Lucretia to Anna Dix 23 S Acc Acc d/o Thorogood & Nancy on 17 Oct 1861 at Acc by T Waters

BLOXOM William P 19 S Oysterman Acc Acc s/o Richard & Patience to Manie S Thornton 18 S Acc Acc d/o Parker & Eliza on 12 Jun 1880 at Chinco: Isld by WP Thornton

BLOXOM William T 22 S Farmer Acc Acc s/o Custis W & Maggie S to Maggie [Shreaves] Shrieves 19 S Acc Acc d/o William J & Pollie on 22 Mar 1891 at Lee Mont by AJ Fristoe

BLOXOM William T Jr 22 S Farmer Acc Acc s/o Wm T Sr & Annie M to Mary E Hall 21 S Acc Acc d/o Eliza J on 10 Jul 1889 at Oak Hall by JS Wallace

BLOXOM Wm 41 S Waterman Acc Acc s/o Richd & Rosa to Margt Tignal 41 S Acc Acc d/o Geo & Lotiha on 27 Jan 1864 at Acc by D Titlow

BLOXOM Wm L 24 S Merchant Acc Acc s/o Wm H & Mary A to Eliz'th S Abbott 20 S Acc Acc d/o David D & Mary on 2 Sep 1891 at Acc by JL King

BOCHEM Saml R 34 W Cabinet Maker Shenandoah Co VA Baltimore City MD to Sarah Elizth Stevenson 24 S Acc Acc d/o Isaac K & Elizth on 3 Dec 1879 at Drum'tn by JC Watson

BOGGS Armstead 21 S Laborer Acc Acc s/o Ibby to Betsy Bundick 18 S Acc Acc d/o Sarah on 30 Dec 1869 at Acc by A Joynes

BOGGS Calvin S 26 S Captain Acc Acc s/o Joseph & Susan to Manie Smith 22 S Acc Acc d/o John W & Ann on 9 Jun 1875 at Onancock by RC Jones

BOGGS Charles Col 19 S Dredger Acc Acc s/o Mary Martin to Emma Smith Col 21 S Acc Acc d/o Mary on 27 Dec 1876 at Savageville by JK Plato

BOGGS Charles Col 24 W Laborer Acc Acc s/o Mary to Margaret Wise Col 22 S Acc Acc d/o Matilda Ann Finney on 30 Mar 1882 near Drum'tn by PM Lewis

BOGGS Charles W Col 22 S Wage-earner Acc Acc s/o Southey & Sarah to Manie Johnson Col 18 S Acc Acc d/o Richard & Laura on 3 Sep 1893 at Acc by T Turlington

BOGGS Edwin M 27 S Merchant Acc Acc s/o Levi R & Hester A to Maggie D Custis 24 S Acc Acc d/o Edward R & Pamelia A on 22 Dec 1886 at bride's home by RA Compton

BOGGS Francis T 34 S Farmer Acc Acc s/o Jos P to A E Fosque 33 S Acc Acc d/o Jno M & Nancy on 2 Jan 1867 at Acc by AB Dolly

BOGGS George Col 21 S Wage-earner Acc Acc s/o Southey & Sarah to Annie Finney Col 19 S Acc Acc d/o Chas & Maria on 30 Jun 1895 at Acc by J Duckett

BOGGS Henry Col 23 S Farmer Acc Acc s/o Lewis & Lucy to Gracie [Bailey] Bayly Col 18 S Acc Acc d/o Lewis & Mary on 13 Mar 1889 at Acc by JA Haynes

BOGGS Henry R 21 S Merchant Acc Acc s/o Levi R & Hester to Kate A Rayfield 20 S Acc Acc d/o Jas T & Sally A on 22 Jan 1879 at Slugtkill Nk by SC Boston

BOGGS Henry W 20 S Farmer Acc Acc s/o Littleton T & Emma T to Margaret H [Bailey] Bayly 23 S Acc Acc d/o Thos S & Elizabeth on 24 Feb 1886 at Acc by WC Vaden

BOGGS James 24 S Sailor Acc Acc s/o Jos R & Susan to Anngeler Chandler 22 S Acc Acc d/o Jno W & Eliz on 30 Aug 1865 at Acc by JH Addison

BOGGS James A 26 S Carpenter & Farmer Acc Acc s/o Jas S & Elizabeth P to Annie E W Taylor 25 S Acc Acc d/o Joseph B & Elizabeth on 20 Feb 1861 at Andrew Chp by JH Addison

BOGGS John Col 22 S Wage-earner Acc Acc s/o Chas & Emma to Julia Ann Custis Col 21 S Acc Acc d/o

Marriages

Elizabeth on 22 Sep 1895 at Onley by JR West

BOGGS John W 25 S Sailor Acc Acc s/o Joseph P & Susan to Laura A Fosque 22 S Acc Acc d/o John M & Ann on 16 Oct 1861 at Acc by WG Coe

BOGGS Joseph C 26 S Sailor s/o Joseph P & Susan to Amelia Lofland 24 d/o Alfred & Cassa lic: 24 Jul 1864 marr: 24 Aug 1864 at Accomack

BOGGS Levi R s/o James to Hester A Mapp d/o Geo S on 5 Jan 1854 by JH Addison

BOGGS Lewis C 25 S Farmer Acc Acc s/o Jno R & Leah to Keturah James Chandler 23 S Acc Acc d/o Jno W & Elizth on 17 Nov 1869 at Acc by JH Addison

BOGGS Lewis J Col 21 S Farmer Acc Acc s/o Lewis & Lucy to Hester Ames Col 19 S Acc Acc d/o Peggie on 19 Jan 1890 at Acc by RW Nichols

BOGGS Littleton 25 S Farmer Acc Acc s/o Wm Boggs & E Sturgis to Emma T Boggs 18 S Acc Acc d/o Henry Boggs & E Roger on 16 Dec 1863 at Acc by LK LeCato

BOGGS Luther N 29 S Sailor Acc Acc s/o Joseph P & Susan to Mollie B Dunton 18 S Acc Acc d/o Custis M & Elizth on 24 Nov 1875 at Oak Grove Ch by E Hebard

BOGGS Luther N 45 W Merchant Acc Acc s/o Joseph P & Susan E to Maggie C Wescott 31 W Acc Acc d/o Wm C & Catharine on 10 Dec 1891 at Acc by JM Anderson

BOGGS Otho Col 20 S Laborer Acc Acc s/o Raymond & Ibby to Harriet Watson Col 23 S Acc Acc d/o Rosy Dix on 13 Feb 1871 near Drum'tn by WF Williams

BOGGS Samuel 25 S Farmer Acc Acc s/o Sarah to Margaret Custis 21 S Acc Acc on 22 Sep 1869 at Acc by JH Addison

BOGGS Southey 26 S Farmer Acc Acc s/o Sarah to Sarah Ann Becket 21 S Acc Acc d/o Saml & Sally on 26 Dec 1866 at Acc by JH Addison

BOGGS William F Col 22 S Farmer Acc Acc s/o Peter T & Grace to Sarah A Henderson Col 21 S Acc Acc d/o Edward & Ann on 24 Dec 1893 at Acc by AJ Wallace

BOGGS William H 30 S Farmer Acc Acc s/o Wm & Elizth to Esther Bull 21 S Acc Acc d/o Edward & Susan on 30 Jan 1867 at Acc by AB Dolly

BOND George M 30 S Farmer Harford Co MD Harford Co MD s/o Thos T & Mary A to Annie E Coard 21 S Acc Acc d/o Wm R & Elizth on 2 Jan 1868 at Acc by ES Grant

BONNEWELL Cornelius [Bonawell] 23 S Oysterman Acc Acc s/o William to Mollie Drummond 17 S Acc Acc d/o John T & Evelyn on 29 Dec 1892 at Temp'ville by JW Nicholson

BONNEWELL Elijah F 23 S Farmer Acc Acc s/o Clement & Sally to Elizabeth Small 17 S Acc Acc d/o Arsemous & Arminda on 1 Aug 1880 at Piney Forks by SC Boston

BONNEWELL Elmer T [Bonewell] 21 S Oysterman Baltimore City MD Acc s/o Peter W & Eliza to Mary C Corbin 17 S Acc Acc d/o Stephen & Missouri on 10 Mar 1895 at Sykes Isld by ML Williams

BONNEWELL George P 22 S Oysterman Acc Acc s/o George P & Margt Ann to Matilda L Hall 20 S Acc Acc d/o Anthony L & Jane on 20 Dec 1881 at Messongo by JE Bundick

BONNEWELL George T [Bonewell] 18 S Farmer Acc Acc s/o Clem & sallie to Emma Budd 23 S Acc Acc d/o McKeel & Hattie on 22 Aug 1867 at Acc by BT Ames

BONNEWELL John [Bonnwell] 19 S

Farmer Acc Acc s/o Robert & Nancy to Georgie A Kellam 23 S Acc Acc d/o Edward W & Ann on 28 Dec 1881 at Acc by CD Crawley

BONNEWELL John William [Bonowell] 20 S Farmer Acc Acc s/o Clement & Sarah to Emeline Edna Milliner 18 S Acc Acc d/o Thomas & Sally on 21 Jun 1874 near Locustville by LK LeCato

BONNEWELL John Wm [Boniwell] 35 W Carpenter Acc Acc s/o Clemons & Sally to Jane Simpson 19 S Acc Acc d/o William & Margaret on 8 Dec 1887 at Acc C H by W Chinn

BONNEWELL Peter William (Bonowell) 29 W Oysterman to Eliza Ellen Lewis 21 S d/o Revel J & Matilda lic: 24 Dec 1872 marr: at Sykes Isld

BONNEWELL Robert T [Bonewell] (Bonawell) 20 S Sailor Acc Acc s/o Nely & Elizth (Scott) to Nancy (wid/o Thomas) Gibbons 19 W Acc Acc d/o Wm & Fanny Watson on 17 Mar 1858 at Acc by M Oldham

BONNEWELL Robert W 22 S Fireman on Steamboat Acc Acc s/o Thos & Margaret to Ida V Corbin 18 S Acc Acc d/o Edward J & Ellen C on 18 Mar 1891 at Acc by JM Anderson

BONNEWELL Thomas 18 S Farmer Acc Acc s/o John T & Margaret to Kate C Guy 24 S Acc Acc d/o Major & Susan Ann on 23 Jun 1880 at Mr Bonnewell's by CC Wertenbaker

BONNEWELL Williamd H 20 S Farmer Acc Acc s/o Robt & Nancy to Cordelia B Drummond 17 S Acc Acc d/o Geo & Ada on 28 Jan 1880 at Garrisons Chp by CC Wertenbaker

BOOL Fisher 35 W Sailor N'hamp: Chinco: Isld s/o Daniel N & Sally to Johanna Fenrrick 24 S Sussex Co DE Chinco: Isld d/o Jno & Hester A on 2 Oct 1886 at Chinco: Isld by BF Jester

BOOL Patrick H 21 S Sailor N'hamp: N'hamp: s/o Danl & Sallie to Mary Ann Ward 18 S Acc Acc d/o James & Tabitha on 7 Apr 1869 at N'hamp: by JB Craighill

BOOTH Alfred 22 S Oysterman Acc Acc s/o John & Adeline to Lavinia E Jones 21 W MD Acc on 27 May 1884(?) at Chinco: Isld by JD Reese Certificate returned 12 Jan 1889

BOOTH Burton 21 S Oysterman Chinco: Isld Chinco: Isld s/o Covington & Mary to Euphamia Sharpley 20 Chinco: Isld Chinco: Isld d/o Parker & Mary A lic: 21 Oct 1864

BOOTH Daniel 22 S Mariner Chinco: Isld Chinco: Isld s/o Covington & Nancy to Nancy Sharpley 17 S Chinco: Isld Chinco: Isld d/o Parker & Mary on 27 Jan 1858 at Chinco: Isld by P Bowdin (John Wishart says he over 21)

BOOTH David W 22 S Sailor Acc Acc s/o William & Eliz'th to Eller Harrison 18 S N'hamp: Acc d/o William H & Fannie J on 30 Jul 1890 at Chinco: Isld by GE Wood

BOOTH George 30 S Dealer in Oysters Acc Acc s/o Daniel & Nancy to Rebecca J Andrews 19 S Acc Acc d/o William & Mary on 5 Apr 1892 at Chinco: Isld by JW Turner

BOOTH John 22 S Waterman Chinco: Isld Chinco: Isld s/o Coventon & Nancy to Adaline Mason 17 S Chinco: Isld Chinco: Isld d/o Randal & Anna on 5 Nov 1859 at Chinco: Isld by P Bowdin Sr (John A M Whealton acknowledge his signature)

BOOTH Levin 23 S Oysterman Acc Acc s/o John & Adeline to Jane Bowden 19 S Wor Co MD Acc d/o Henry & Hetty on 24 Dec 1888 at Chinco: Isld by SU Grimsley

BOOTH Thomas 20 S Oysterman Acc Acc s/o Covington & Nancy to

Marriages

Nancy [Dasey] Daisey 19 S Acc Acc d/o Wm & Margaret on 11 Dec 1869 at Acc by P Bowdin Jr

BOOTH Thomas 39 W Oysterman Acc Acc s/o Covington & Nancy to Martha Watson 39 S Wor Co MD Acc d/o William & Annie Bowden on 20 Oct 1889 at Thos Broughton's by BP Truitt

BOOTH Wm single Laborer Chinco: Isld Chinco: Isld s/o Covey & Nancy to Elizth [Bowdin] Bowden single Chinco: Isld Chinco: Isld d/o Elizth Carpenter on 4 Aug 1853 at r/o Sarah James by P Bowdin

BOSTON Henry 27 S Sailor Sussex Co DE Acc s/o Henry & Mary to Mary Booth 23 S Acc Acc d/o Covington & Nancy on 6 Apr 1867 at Acc by P Bowdin Sr

BOSTON W T 53 W Farmer Wor Co MD Wor Co MD s/o Isaac & Amelia to Zenie C Rowins 35 W Wor Co MD Acc d/o John P & Martha Marshall on 20 Dec 1882 at Chinco: Isld by OS Walton

BOWDEN A T 22 S US Life Saving Station Chinco: Isld Chinco: Isld s/o Parker & Maria to Mary C Chandler 22 S Sussex Co DE Chinco: Isld d/o Joshua J & Heater on 2 Jan 1883 at Chinco: Isld by WP Thornton

BOWDEN Burton J 19 S Oysterman Acc Acc s/o Ira & Mary to Lucy L [Reid] Read 16 S Acc Acc d/o William A & Ibba on 17 Aug 1890 at Chinco: Isld by GE Wood

BOWDEN Crippen 18 S Fisherman Chinco: Isld Chinco: Isld s/o Crippen & Nancy to Sarah Andrews 21 S Chinco: Isld Chinco: Isld d/o Mordica & Nancy on 6 Mar 1856 at Chinco: Isld by WP Thornton (John Thornton says she over 21)

BOWDEN Crippen J 23 S Oysterman Acc Acc s/o Crippen & Sarah to Lizzie A Barrett 20 S Acc Acc d/o Alfred P & Nancy C on 26 Oct 1892 at Chinco: Isld by RB Sanford

BOWDEN Daniel J 26 S Oysterman Acc Acc s/o Wm B & Margaret to Sarah A Williams 18 S Wor Co MD Acc d/o John A & Mary A on 22 May 1893 at Chinco: Isld by RB Sanford

BOWDEN Daniel W Col 21 S Oysterman Acc Acc s/o Parker & Maria to Malissa Bowden Col 18 S Acc Acc d/o Jesse on 13 Jun 1880 at Chinco: Isld by WP Thornton

BOWDEN Frank B 20 S Oysterman Acc Acc s/o Parker to Mary E Jones 16 S Wor Co MD Acc d/o George C on 26 Dec 1890 at Chinco: Isld by GE Wood

BOWDEN Frank B 21 W Oysterman Acc Acc s/o Parker & Mariah to Jennie E Merritt 21 S Acc Acc d/o George & Catharine on 24 Nov 1892 at Chinco: Isld by JF Wooden

BOWDEN George 25 S Oysterman Acc Acc s/o William & Margaret to Manie Bloxom 18 S Acc Acc d/o John W & Martha A on 5 Mar 1891 at Chinco: Isld by GE Wood

BOWDEN George H 20 S Oysterman Acc Acc s/o Mary to Mary E Benson 19 S Acc Acc d/o Wm J & Eliz'th on 21 May 1888 at Chinco: Isld by SU Grimsley

BOWDEN Ira 50 W Oysterman Acc Acc s/o Parker & Anna to Rebecca Jones 44 W Acc Acc d/o John & Margaret Birch on 7 Aug 1892 at Chinco: Isld by RB Sanford

BOWDEN J W 21 S Oysterman Acc Acc s/o Wm B & Marg't to Mary Snead 17 S Acc Acc d/o Thomas & Alice on 12 Mar 1892 at Chinco: Isld by JF Wooden

BOWDEN John 23 S Sailor Wor Co MD Chinco: Isld s/o Saml & Harriet to Mary Bowden 18 S Acc Chinco: Isld d/o Parker & Maria on 17 Dec

1875 at Chinco: Isld by P Bowdin Sr
BOWDEN John [Bowdin] 24 W Oysterman Chinco: Isld Chinco: Isld s/o Parker & Ann to Nancy Wilgus 23 W Sussex Co DE Sussex Co Del d/o Clarissa on 21 Jul 1877 at Chinco: Isld by WP Thornton
BOWDEN John J 21 S Waterman Acc Acc s/o Mary to Maggie A Elliott 21 S N'hamp: Acc on 3 Oct 1882 at Chinco: Isld by OS Walton
BOWDEN John P 19 S Oysterman Chinco: Isld Chinco: Isld s/o Crippen & Nancy to Comfort J Bowden 19 S Chinco: Isld Chinco: Isld d/o Wn B & Margaret on 25 Feb 1877 at Chinco: Isld by WP Thornton
BOWDEN John S 18 S Oysterman Acc Acc s/o Ira & Mary to Comfort Bloxom 23 S Acc Acc d/o Richard & Patience on 6 Aug 1877 at Chinco: Isld by P Bowdin Sr
BOWDEN Jorias 21 S Oysterman Acc Acc s/o Crippen & Sarah to Annie Steelman 15 S Acc Acc d/o David & Elizabeth on 3 Jan 1885(?) at Chinco: Isld by SU Grimsley Certificate returned 12 Jan 1889
BOWDEN Joshua J 20 S Oysterman Chinco: Isld Chinco: Isld s/o Wm & Margt to Nancy M Tarr 18 S Chinco: Isld Chinco: Isld d/o David & Mary A on 26 May 1872 at Chinco: Isld by P Bowdin Sr
BOWDEN Joshua P [Bowdin] 22 S Oysterman Chinco: Isld Chinco: Isld s/o Parker & Maria to Mary E Jones 17 S Chinco: Isld Chinco: Isld d/o John J & Louisa on 15 Dec 1885 at Chinco: Isld by SU Grimsley
BOWDEN Littleton [Bowdin] 22 S Mariner Wor Co MD Chinco: Isld s/o Henry & Margaret to Demeriah (D) Thornton 16 S Chinco: Isld Chinco: Isld d/o Wm P & Nancy on 7 Mar 1861 at Chinco: Isld by P Bowdin Jr

BOWDEN Parker Jr 22 S Oysterman Acc Acc s/o Wm & Margurett to Sarah Bell Merritt 16 S Wor Co MD Acc d/o E H & Sarah on 17 Aug 1884(?) at Chinco: Isld by JD Reese Certificate returned 12 Jan 1889
BOWDEN Parker Jr [Bowdin] 22 S Waterman Chinco: Isld Chinco: Isld s/o Parker & Mary to Mariah C [Burch] Birch 17 S Chinco: Isld Chinco: Isld d/o Thos & Mary on 5 Jun 1856 at r/o Parker Bowdin Jr by P Bowdin Sr (John A M Whealton says he over 21)
BOWDEN William [Bowdin] 23 S Oysterman Acc Acc s/o Caleb & Charity (John & Charity) to Lydia A Lewis 18 S Acc Acc d/o John & Sarah on 8 Jun 1868 at Acc by P Bowdin Jr (lic: 14 May 1868)
BOWDEN Wm T 21 S Chinco: Isld Chinco: Isld s/o Crippen & Nancy to Roxanna A Tarr 17 S Chinco: Isld Chinco: Isld d/o David & Mary on 4 May 1877 at Chinco: Isld by WP Thornton
BOWDOIN Frank 22 S Laborer Acc Acc s/o Ann to Sophy Anna Young 17 S Acc Acc d/o Laura Stran on 16 Dec 1878 at the Parsonage by A Handy
BOWDOIN John R 65 W Physician N'hamp: Acc to Elizabeth E White 45 S Acc Acc d/o Wm C & Nancy on 9 Dec 1885 at Mappsville by WA Street
BOWDOIN Parker Sr 69 W Clergyman Acc Acc s/o William & Anna to Patsy Jester 56 W Acc Acc d/o George & Patience Jane Burch on 20 Sep 1874 at Chinco: Isld by J Lewis
BOWDOIN Robt T Col 23 S Laborer Acc Acc s/o Candace to Margaret Webb Col 25 S Acc Acc d/o Margaret on 4 Dec 1878 at Locust Mount by A Handy
BOWEN Esau Col 19 S Sailor Acc Acc

Marriages

s/o James & Ann to Alice Broughton Col 21 S Acc Acc d/o Bennet & Laura on 9 Jun 1889 near Temp'ville by JC Cluff

BOWEN James Col 66 S Laborer Acc Acc s/o Levi & Zilla to Ann Lewis Col 35 S Acc Acc d/o Geo & Celia on 8 Aug 1872 at Acc by M Oldham

BOWEN Sidney A 28 S Merchant Wor Co MD Wor Co MD s/o Geo C & Hetty to Alice J Conquest 20 S Acc Acc d/o Edwd H & Mary Ann on 24 Feb 1881 near Temp'ville by LB Betty

BOWEN William M 26 S Carpenter Wor Co MD Acc to Ella N Scott 19 S Acc Acc d/o John T & Margaret on 29 Apr 1890 at Onancock by RA Compton

BOWLES George Col 40 S Laborer Petersburg VA Acc to Jane Kellam Col 45 S Acc Acc on 11 Apr 1887 at Acc C H by P Sheppard

BOWLES George H Col 20 S Farmer Acc Acc s/o George & Jane to Susan Bundick Col 17 S Acc Acc d/o George & Bell Sarah on 15 Jan 1893 at Acc C H by BJ Hargarves

BRADFORD Charles 32 W Waterman Chinco: Isld Chinco: Isld s/o Noah & Polly to Rachel Jester 20 S Chinco: Isld Chinco: Isld d/o Elijah & Patsey on 10 Nov 1859 at Chinco: Isld by P Bowdin Sr

BRADFORD Ezra to Rachel C Coleburn d/o Jno lic: 26 Mar 1855

BRADFORD Francis M 25 S Farming Acc Acc s/o Wm & Maria to Rachel A Poulson 24 W Acc Acc d/o Wm & Mary Miller on 2 Sep 1883 at Locust Mount by JWA Elliott

BRADFORD George W Col 22 S Laborer Acc Acc s/o Mariah to Hester Tankard Col 21 S Acc Acc d/o Susan on 3 Jan 1886 at Acc by JB Lewis

BRADFORD Jas W 32 S Sailor Acc Acc s/o Wm & Nancy to Susan Mears 33 S Acc Acc d/o Geo & Patsy on 11 Oct 1863 at Acc by JWA Elliott

BRADFORD Jno H 23 S Laborer Acc Acc s/o Nancy to Sally A (Sarah Ann) Watkinson 18 S Acc Acc d/o Wm & Mary on 3 Mar 1862 at Acc by BT Ames

BRADFORD John 45 W Farmer b: Bradford Nk s/o Abel & Sally to Jane Hyslop 25 S b: near Land Shift d/o James & Mary on 17 May 1855 at Acc by J Burton (Thorogood Mears says she over 21)

BRADFORD John E 29 S Merchant Acc Acc s/o Benj S & Catharine to Emma L Adams 17 S N'hamp: Acc d/o James & Mary on 14 Aug 1878 at Locust Mount by WH Carroll

BRADFORD John H 34 S Farmer Acc Acc s/o Nath & Peggy to Sarah Ann Turner 27 S Acc Acc d/o Jno R & Mary on 30 Sep 1865 at Acc by BT Ames

BRADFORD Noah 22 S Oysterman Acc Acc s/o Charles & Rachel to Annie Young 15 S Acc Acc d/o Theodore J & Mary on 25 May 1884(?) at Chinco: Isld by JD Reese Certificate returned 12 Jan 1889

BRADFORD William 43 W Carpenter b: Bradford Nk s/o Able & Sally to Mariah Johnson 38 W b: Matchapungo(?) d/o Anthony & Nancy Bell & (wid/o John Johnson dec'd) on 17 Jun 1855 at Match by A Wallace

BRADFORD William Thomas 22 S Farmer Acc Acc s/o Thomas J & Nancy to Sally A Kellam 25 S Acc Acc d/o Hulton & Susan on 28 May 1856 near Pungo: by M Oldham

BRADFORD Wm T 26 S Farmer Acc Acc s/o Emma to Annie M Milliner 19 S Acc Acc d/o Thos H & Sarah Ann on 8 Feb 1882 at Acc by SC

Boston

BRADSHAW Aaron B 40 W Merchant Smith Isld MD Smith Isld MD s/o Henry & Polly to Marcha Crockett 20 S Tangier Isld Tangier Isld d/o Alexander & Catharine on 26 May 1886 at Tangier Isld by WSP Bonen

BRADSHAW Elisha E 36 W Fisherman MD Acc s/o Nathaniel L to Bettie Crockett 18 S Acc Acc d/o John M & Emma on 7 Oct 1885 at Tangier Isld by CS Baker

BRADSHAW James 29 S Sailor Som Co MD Som Co MD s/o Richd & Rachel to Levinia S Turner 23 S Acc Acc d/o Jas & Margt on 28 Dec 1874 at Pungo: by JH Amiss

BRASURE Elijah D 22 S Oysterman Sussex Co DE Acc s/o Joshua & Eliz to Mary A Birch 22 S Wor Co MD Acc d/o Jno E & Eliz on 16 Jun 1881 at Chinco: Isld by OS Walton

BRASURE Jacob 21 S Farmer Sussex Co DE Acc s/o Alfred & Catharine to Laura Savage 17 S Acc Acc d/o Isaac J & Patience on 5 Aug 1892 at Acc by JB Workman

BRAXTON James Col 40 S Farmer Essex Co VA Acc s/o George & Ellen to Margaret [Bevans] Beavans Col 35 S Acc Acc d/o John on 24 Dec 1890 at Acc by JB Lewis

BRAXTON Samuel Col 22 S Wage-earner Acc Acc s/o James & Margaret to Sarah E Ames Col 16 S Acc Acc d/o Custis & Leah on 26 Dec 1888 at Acc by JA Haynes

BRICKHOUSE Jacob Col 50 S Carpenter Acc Acc s/o Seymorun Sandford to Arinthia Jacobs Col 35 S Acc Acc on 27 Oct 1877 at Belle Haven by JE Humphreys

BRIDDELL William S 23 S Book-keeper Wor Co MD Wor Co MD to Elizabeth Joyce Turlington 20 S Acc Acc d/o John W & Amanda on 20 Feb 1889 at Acc by WJ Twilley

BRIDDLE Orrison 24 S Waterman Som Co MD Acc to Laura F Bunting 20 S Acc Acc d/o Levin T & Sarah on 24 Jan 1894 at Sanford by JR Tillery

BRIMER Alfred F 21 S Farmer Acc Acc s/o Samuel & Eliza to Mary E Dryden 18 S Acc Acc d/o W E & Nancy E on 13 Aug 1891 at Oak Hall by JS Wallace

BRIMER Saml L 24 S Farmer Acc Acc s/o Saml S & Mary to Jane S Smith 23 S Acc Acc d/o Noah on 2 Feb 1859 at Acc by D Coulling (Raymond R Parks says both over 21)

BRIMER Wm H 24 S Sailing b: Acc s/o Saml Brimer & Anna Bishop to Martha Ann Ward 24 W b: Wor Co MD d/o Elijah Shepard & Dolla Tar on 17 Aug 1858 at New Church by T Waters (Raymond Parks says he over 21)

BRINNEY Alfred Col 23 S Oysterman Acc Acc s/o Edward & Elizth to Mary M Hudson Col 18 S Acc Acc d/o Mary on 5 Feb 1888 at Chinco: Isld by SU Grimsley

BRINNEY Edward Col 55 S Oysterman Acc Acc s/o Ocker & Peggy to Elizabeth George Col 50 S Acc Acc on 20 Jun 1880 at Chinco: Isld by JC Cluff

BRINNEY James E Col 26 S Laborer Acc Chinco: Isld s/o Edwd & Elizzia to Purcilla Riley Col 20 S Acc Chinco: Isld d/o Parker & Mary E on 30 Mar 1884 at Acc by JHB Hubbard

BRINNEY John Col 22 S Acc Acc s/o Edward to Mary Ewell Col 33 S Acc Acc d/o Elizabeth on 8 Mar 1880 at Chinco: Isld by JC Cluff

BRINNEY Joseph Col 28 S Oysterman Acc Chinco: Isld s/o Edwd & Elizth to Charlotte Taylor Col 18 S Chinco: Isld Chinco: Isld d/o Sallie on 31 Dec 1882 at Chinco: Isld by JC Cluff

BRINNEY Wesley FN 22 S Mariner b:

Chinco: Isld s/o Arthur & Louisa to Jane Ward FN 22 S b: Assawoman d/o Noah & Keziah on 15 Oct 1855 at Chinco: Isld by WP Thornton (John Thornton says both over 21)

BRITTINGHAM Frank Col 23 S Farmer Acc Acc s/o Alsie to Henrietta Long Col 21 S Acc Acc d/o Jno Long on 28 Dec 1875 at Modest Town by SP Whittington

BRITTINGHAM Hiram 36 S Farmer Acc Acc s/o John & Esther A to Florence M Johnson 24 S Acc Acc d/o Solomon T & Susan A on 29 Nov 1893 at Horntown by WW Wood

BRITTINGHAM John Col 26 S Wage-earner Acc Acc s/o Joseph & Mary to Henrietta Matthews Col 30 S Acc Acc d/o Caleb & Sarah on 16 Jun 1895 at Temp'ville by GHT Byrd

BRITTINGHAM John E 32 W Merchant Acc Acc s/o Elizth to Mary Dix 18 S Acc Acc d/o Thorgood & Julia on 29 Aug 1861 at Acc by T Waters (John W Taylor says all this correct)

BRITTINGHAM John H 29 S Farmer Acc Acc s/o James & Ann to Sallie Landing 23 S Som Co MD Som Co MD d/o Wm & Ann on 8 Oct 1860 at Acc by W Merrill (Henry Chesser says both over 21)

BRITTINGHAM John P 31 S Laborer Acc Acc s/o Thomas & Mary Ann to Margaret Taylor 24 S Acc Acc on 15 Dec 1874 near Horntown by IT Adkins

BRITTINGHAM John P 44 S Farmer Acc Acc s/o Thomas & Mary A to Gertrude Evans 20 S Acc Acc d/o James H on 17 Mar 1887 at Oak Hall by TG Pullen

BRITTINGHAM Lloyd 22 S Farmer Acc Acc s/o Jno & Esther to Ella J Conquest 22 S Acc Acc d/o Edwd & Ann on 13 Dec 1876 at Conquest Ch by M Oldham

BRITTINGHAM Wm Col 21 S Wage-earner MD Acc to Catherine Watson Col 22 S Acc Acc d/o Mary Godwin on 24 Dec 1891 at Acc by JE Bundick

BROADWATER Amos to Mary Taylor d/o William lic: 27 Nov 1854

BROADWATER Amos K [Brodwater] 25 S Oysterman Acc Acc s/o Amos K & Polly to Celicia F Hall 24 S Acc Acc d/o A & Cordelia on 29 Dec 1885 at Oak Hall by DM Wallace

BROADWATER George Col 27 S Laborer Acc Acc s/o James to Easter Fisher Col 28 S Acc Acc d/o Eliza on 5 Oct 1872 at Modest Town by A Joynes

BROADWATER Jacob FN 42 S Farmer Acc Acc s/o Canvass Godwin to Leah Ocher (FN) 35 S Acc Acc d/o (Briney) Osher & Mary Berry on 24 Jan 1864 at Acc by GW Burris (J Henderson of Horntown requested license)

BROADWATER James 42 W Farming Acc Acc s/o Betsy to Sally (Scott) Smith 25 W Acc Acc d/o Wm H & Ann M Corbin on 10 Mar 1872 at Acc by TM Poulson

BROADWATER James Henry [Brodwater] 29 S Farming Acc Acc s/o Elizth to Hester Taylor 29 W Acc Acc d/o Henry & Mary Showard on 19 May 1861 at Acc by T Waters (Samuel J Tindal says he over 21)

BROADWATER James Jr FN to Comfort Planter FN lic: 5 Apr 1854 John E Bundick says both over 21

BROADWATER John [Brodwater] Col 22 S Farmer Acc Acc s/o Samuel to Arinthia Nock Col 21 S Acc Acc d/o Ann on 31 May 1893 at Temp'ville by JC Cluff

BROADWATER Jos E [Brodwater] 23 S Physician Acc Acc s/o David & Mary A to Eliz A Justice 21 S Acc Acc d/o Jas & Sallie on 28 Nov 1860 at Acc by W Merrill (Wm H Feddeman says both over 21)

BROADWATER Joseph E [Brodwater] 31 S Physician Acc Acc s/o David to Mary E Oldham 28 S N'hamp: Acc d/o Montcalm & Claria on 30 Jul 1868 at Acc by M Oldham

BROADWATER Lloyd N [Brodwater] 26 S Oysterman Acc Acc s/o Amos & Polly to Marina F Stant 19 S Acc Acc d/o Edward T & Ieannette on 14 Jun 1882 at Acc by RB Beadles

BROADWATER Robert J [Brodwater] Col 24 S Sailor Acc Acc s/o Wesley & Mary to Tillie J Joynes Col 23 S Acc Acc d/o Dennis & Assice(?) on 4 Feb 1885 at Acc by AJ Satchell

BROADWATER Sam'l [Brodwater] Col 40 W Farmer Acc Acc s/o Brickey to Hester Ann Watson Col 30 S Acc Acc d/o Agariah & Patience on 17 Jan 1892 at Acc by JE Bundick

BROADWATER Samuel [Brodwater] Col 49 S Laborer Acc Acc to Airy Northam Col 48 S Acc Acc on 25 Dec 1879 at Modest Town by A Joynes

BROADWATER Wallace H Col 21 S Wage-earner Acc Acc s/o Lizzie to Hattie Watson Col 20 S Acc Acc d/o Charlotte Wimbough on 9 Dec 1888 at Mappsville by AJ Satchell

BROADWATER Walter 24 S Sailor Acc Acc s/o Walter & Polly to Hester Bull 22 S Acc Acc d/o James & Ritta on 21 Aug 1872 at Messongo by JC Reed

BROADWATER Wesley [Brodwater] Col 30 S Farmer Acc Acc s/o Annie to Mary Justice Col 35 S Acc Acc d/o Peggy on 19 Dec 1877 at News Town by A Joynes

BROADWATER William (Brodwater) (Col) 60 W Laborer Acc Acc s/o Brutchey to Eliza Mills (Col) 40 S Acc Acc on 22 Jan 1871 near Modest Town by WF Williams

BROUGHTON Arsemus Col 25 S Farmer Acc Acc s/o Caleb & Laura to Annie Harmon Col 18 S Acc Acc d/o John & Eliza on 20 Apr 1892 at Acc by JC Cluff

BROUGHTON George T Col 37 S Farming Acc Acc s/o Sarah to Elizabeth George Col 26 S Acc Acc d/o Joe & Peggy on 13 Mar 1884 near Atlantic P O by JC Cluff

BROUGHTON James W 23 S Insurance Agent Baltimore MD Acc s/o Jas & Eliza A to Eveline J Conquest 22 S Acc Acc d/o Richd & Harriet on 3 Feb 1869 at Acc by GW Matthews

BROUGHTON Upshur K 23 S Merchant MD Acc s/o Kellam & Mary to Elizabeth R Carmine 19 S VA Acc d/o Henry D & Rebecca on 19 Jan 1887 at bride's home by RA Compton

BROUGHTON William T 27 S Engineer Acc Acc s/o Wm J & Eliza A to Rebecca L McMath 18 S Acc Acc d/o Jno P & Kate A on 24 Feb 1881 at Onancock by JC Watson

BROWERS Joseph 38 W Steward Antwerp Belgium NY s/o Aeges & Collatta to Maggie A Sharpley 26 W Philadelphia PA Acc d/o Jas & Annie Lewis on 19 Oct 1879 at Chinco: Isld Par by IT Adkins

BROWN Calvin Col 25 S Oysterman Acc Acc s/o Arthur Miller & Mary Brown to Lizzie Fields Col 23 S Acc Acc d/o James Fields & Martha Roberts on 20 Feb 1889 at Horntown by N Morris

BROWN Charles 22 S Farmer b :NJ s/o Charles to Virginia Warren 24 S b: N'hamp: d/o John L & Tabitha lic: 12 Sep 1874 marr: 16 Sep 1874 at Holly Church

BROWN Edward T 20 S Farmer Acc Acc s/o Charles & Margt to Bettie A Richardson 23 S Acc Acc d/o Wm & Elizth on 5 Mar 1879 at Acc by SC

Marriages

Boston
BROWN George Col 28 S Laborer Wor Co MD Acc to Mary Smith Col 24 S Acc Acc d/o Abram & Amy on 14 Jun 1881 at Pungo: by TW Nettles

BROWN James 40 S Farmer Acc Acc to Margt [Brodwater] Broadwater 25 S Acc Acc on 11 Apr 1867 at Acc by GW Matthews

BROWN John 35 S Sailor Sussex Co DE Acc s/o Henry & Mary to Elizabeth Wimbrough 40 W Acc Acc d/o Wm & Mary Sharpley on 2 Apr 1867 at Acc by P Bowdin Sr

BROWN John Col 28 S Farmer Acc Acc s/o Mary to Elizth Croswell Col 23 S Acc Acc d/o Keziah on 10 Mar 1884 near Oak Hall by JC Cluff

BROWN John M 24 S Photographer Pittsville MD Pittsville MD s/o K J & Matilda M to Hellen M Powell 19 S Wor Co MD Acc d/o Edward Z & Catharine on 22 Jun 1892 at Chinco: Isld by JF Wooden

BROWN John P Col 40 S Wage-earner Acc Acc to Deliah Ann Harmon Col 16 S Acc Acc d/o Horace & Fanney on 8 Aug 1894 at Temp'ville by GHT Byrd

BROWN Joshua 23 S Laborer NJ Acc to Harriet Richardson 23 W Acc Acc d/o Clement Bonawell on 29 Jan 1871 at Acc by LK LeCato

BROWN Thomas Col 35 S Sailor Acc Acc s/o Samuel & Martah to Mary E Stevenson Col 21 S Acc Acc on 1 Oct 1890 at Acc by L Duncan

BROWNE James Henry Col 38 S Farmer Acc Acc to Isabella Taylor Col 28 S Acc Acc d/o Sarah Ann on 9 Oct 1881 near New Church by JC Cluff

BROWNE Thos H Bayly 27 S Attoney Acc Acc s/o Peter F & Sally to Anna D Fletcher 22 S Acc Acc d/o Jas H & Elizth on 5 Feb 1873 at Acc by M Oldham

BUCK William 50 S Blacksmith b :NJ to Elizabeth Justice 45 W lic: 30 Dec 1862

BUDD George W 23 S Farmer Acc Acc s/o Wm & Sallie to Missouri Indiana V Hopkins 18 S MD Acc d/o Jno & Sarah on 17 Mar 1870 at Acc by JB Converse

BUDD John 56 W Farmer Acc Acc s/o McKeel & Peggy to Polly Gladding 45 W Acc Acc d/o George Trader on 14 Dec 1881 at Lee Mont by WA Crouse

BUDD Laban J 29 S Farmer Acc Acc s/o Thos & Sally to Mattie S Dix 19 S Acc Acc d/o Wm T & Peggy on 6 Jan 1886 at Acc by WA Street

BUDD Robert 34 S Sailor Acc Acc s/o Mc Keel & Eliza to Mary Carmine 23 S Acc Acc d/o Smith on 12 Feb 1882 at Chesconessex by PA Leatherbury

BUDD Thomas 18 S Farmer Acc Acc s/o Wm & Sarah to Indiana Mears 17 S Acc Acc d/o Bagnell & Eliza on 22 Dec 1875 at Drum'tn by FR Boston

BUDD Thomas E 24 S Farmer Acc Acc s/o John & Polly to Ann Twiford 20 S Acc Acc d/o Juluis & Ann on 13 Oct 1875 at Julius Twiford's by RC Jones

BUDD Thomas H 28 W Farmer Acc Acc s/o Wm & Sally to Annie L Sturgis 17 S Acc Acc d/o Elijah W & Laura on 15 Nov 1885 at Acc by JW Hundley

BUDD Wm F 23 S Farmer Acc Acc s/o Thomas & Sally to Mary A Lewis 19 S Acc Acc d/o Wm P & Margt on 8 Dec 1875 at Acc by FR Boston

BUDD Wm H 19 S Farmer Acc Acc s/o Wm S & Sarah to Susan A Holland 17 S Acc Acc d/o Samuel H & Clasisa on 9 Jan 1861 at Reese Chp by ES Grant

BULL Alfred S 42 S Merchant Acc Acc s/o Joseph T & Harriet E to

Catharine S Turner 37 W Acc Acc d/o John & Margaret Lawrence on 17 Jul 1895 at Acc by JM Dunaway

BULL Andrew M 35 S Farmer Acc Acc s/o Edward T & Mary E to Annie L Mears 22 S Acc Acc d/o George T & Margaret S on 29 Dec 1891 at Locust Mount by JWA Elliott

BULL Arcemus 20 S Oysterman Acc Acc s/o Robert L & Jane to Mary A Marshall 19 S Acc Acc d/o John W & Amelia on 11 Oct 1893 at Temp'ville by JW Nicholson

BULL Bagwell 30 S Farmer s/o Wm & Susan to Jane C S Grinnalds 16 S d/o John & Mary lic: 13 Feb 1865 marr: 15 Feb 1865

BULL Benjamin F 18 S Gentleman Acc Acc s/o Thos S & Polly to Bettie J Parker 18 S Acc Acc d/o John M & Ellen on 3 Jun 1866 at Acc by AB Dolly

BULL Edward T 22 S Farmer b: Drum'tn s/o Elisha & Easter to Mary E Turner 18 S b: Belle Haven d/o Saml & Sally & (ward/o George K Turner who gave consent) on 28 Jan 1855 near Belle Haven by A Wallace

BULL Eli 23 S Merchant Acc Acc s/o Elisha to Susan S Fox 22 S Acc Acc d/o Golden T on 21 Feb 1868 at Acc by BT Ames

BULL Elijah 29 S Farmer Acc Acc s/o Elisha to Lousia Ayres 20 S Acc Acc d/o Edwd B & Elizabeth (W) who gave consent on 24 Feb 1864 at Acc by ES Grant (lic: 22 Feb 1864)

BULL Elijah E 20 S Farmer Acc Acc s/o Geo W & Elizth to Nellie S Hart 16 S Acc Acc d/o Wm D & Mary Cath on 6 Aug 1882 at Acc by SC Boston

BULL Floyd L 21 S Sailor Acc Acc s/o Robert L & Sarah J to Alice A Wilkerson 17 S Acc Acc d/o Jay F & Martha on 1 Jan 1890 at Acc by JS Wallace

BULL Francis A 36 S Farmer Acc Acc s/o Jno & Elizabeth to Ann S [Philips] Phillips 18 S Acc Acc d/o Smith & Elizabeth on 26 Feb 1862 at Acc by P Warren

BULL George 23 S Farmer b: Drum'tn s/o George & Hetty to Mary White 23 S b: Acc d/o Robert & Betsey on 26 Apr 1857 at r/o Calbe Broadwater by JF Chaplain

BULL George 22 S Sailor b: Acc s/o Suthy & Mary to Elizabeth [Bonewell] Bonnewell 17 S b: Acc d/o Clement & Sally on 20 Jul 1858 at r/o Clement Boniwell by LK LeCato (Major Bull says he over 21)

BULL George 40 W Farmer Acc Acc to Tabitha Whealton 38 W Acc Acc on 23 Oct 1875 at Acc by TM Poulson

BULL George E to Bettie R Turlington lic: 31 Jan 1859 John A Ayres says both over 21

BULL George E 22 S Farmer Acc Acc s/o Stephard T & Mary Ann to Sadie A LeCato 20 S Acc Acc d/o John M & Betsy Ann on 16 Jan 1895 at Acc by JR Griffith

BULL Henry (Col) 52 S Laborer Acc Acc s/o Isaac Bayly & Comfort Wescott to Bethany Case (Col) 35 S Acc Acc on 5 Sep 1870 at Acc by E Hebard

BULL Henry Col 32 S Farm Laborer Acc Acc s/o Susan Kellam to Sarah Bundick Col 33 S Acc Acc d/o Sarah on 29 Oct 1884 at Acc by R Davis

BULL Henry C 22 S Farmer Acc Acc s/o Benjamin F & Bettie to Willie E Nottingham 23 S N'hamp: Acc d/o Severn & Lacretia on 27 Oct 1892 at Pungo: by JM Anderson

BULL Henry Clay 18 S Farmer Acc Acc s/o Thos & Mary to Marietta M Mapp 17 S Acc Acc d/o Wm & Catharine on 20 Dec 1863 at Acc by LK LeCato

BULL Henry Francis 22 S Farmer Acc

Acc s/o Elijah F & Louisa to Henrietta Grinnalds 18 S Acc Acc d/o John Wm & Margaret T on 10 Aug 1887 at Drum'tn by J McNabb

BULL Henry Lee 28 S Mechanic Acc Acc s/o Edward T & Mary E to Amanda A Willis 28 W Acc Acc d/o John B & Margaret E Bundick on 3 Dec 1890 at Acc by JR Strugis

BULL Henry R 21 S Farmer Acc Acc s/o Eli W & Susan to Lula W Fitchett 20 S Acc Acc d/o Sam'l P & Elishea A on 28 Dec 1893 near Drum'tn by WF Hayes

BULL James 26 S Farmer Acc Acc s/o London & Virga to Rachel Sample 23 S Acc Acc d/o Shepard & Rachel on 26 Dec 1866 at Acc by D Titlow

BULL James D 36 S Farmer Acc Acc s/o James H & Mary A to Alicia R Daugherty 21 S Acc Acc d/o James A & Alicia on 10 Jul 1890 at Acc by WJ Twilley

BULL James H widr to Elizabeth B Bell lic: 1 Jun 1859 Alfred J Mears says she over 21

BULL James H 22 S Sailor Acc Acc s/o James & Harriet to Melvina C Simpson 21 S Acc Acc d/o John A on 18 May 1892 at Acc by JL King

BULL James R 22 S Farmer Acc Acc s/o James R & Susan R to Alice Lee Stockley 22 S Acc Acc d/o Sylvester & Margt on 20 Dec 1876 at Acc by E Hebard

BULL Jas H 20 S Farmer Acc Acc s/o Jas to Harriett Corbin 20 S Acc Acc on 18 Mar 1862 at Acc by GH Ewell

BULL John E 20 S Farmer Acc Acc s/o Elijah F & Larua to Arivenia E Milliner 20 S Acc Acc d/o John W & Margaret on 10 Jan 1895 at Acc C H by JM Dunaway

BULL John T s/o Thomas (of Caty) who gave consent to Tabitha Hancock lic: 23 Jan 1854 Thos H Bloxom says she over 21

BULL John T 23 S Farmer Acc Acc s/o Custis & Margt to Julia A James 18 S Acc Acc d/o John T & Susan on 8 Dec 1869 at Acc by JC Martin

BULL Joseph S 29 S Farmer Acc Acc s/o Edwd & Sauas to Fannie L [Rodgers] Rogers 17 S Acc Acc d/o Arthur & Elizth on 5 Nov 1879 at Bobtown by CC Wertenbaker

BULL Leroy J 20 S Farmer Acc Acc s/o Eli W & Susan to Kate R Mapp 18 S Acc Acc d/o George C & Rose on 23 Jan 1889 at Wachapreague by WJ Twilley

BULL Lorenzo D to Drusilla Mears lic: 2 May 1860 Raymond R Stant says both over 21

BULL Mirty W 24 S Merchant Acc Acc s/o Eli W & Susan to Mary Lynn Tunnell 19 S Acc Acc d/o Wm D & Eliz'th B on 13 Dec 1894 at Locustville by B Clark

BULL Robert 20 S Farmer Messongo Messongo s/o James & Sarah to Sarah J Smith 18 S Messongo Messongo d/o Valentine & Sally on 15 Jan 1865 at r/o James Bull by GH Ewell

BULL Shephard T 23 S Farmer Acc Acc s/o Edwd & Susan to Mary A Kellam 18 S Acc Acc d/o George A & Ann A on 20 Dec 1871 at Acc by JE Humphreys

BULL Southey B 18 S Gentleman Acc Acc s/o Thos J & Polly to Louisa F Ames 18 S Acc Acc d/o Richd T & Louisa on 16 Feb 1869 at Acc by JC Martin

BULL Stran Col 75 S Farmer Acc Acc to Mary Hyslop Col 75 S Acc Acc on 27 Oct 1885 near Craddockville by GHT Byrd

BULL Wesley 20 S Farmer Acc Acc s/o Wm & Sarah to Margaret Nelson 28 S Acc Acc on 5 Jan 1870 at Acc by JC Martin

BULL William 45 W Sailor b: Acc s/o

William & Nancy to Catharine Mears 18 S b: Acc d/o James Mears (who gave consent) & Mary Beloat on 9 Jan 1859 at r/o Jas Mears by LK LeCato

BULL William H 35 S Farmer Acc Acc s/o Custis & Margaret to Catherine Colonna 26 S Acc Acc d/o Alfred & Mary on 30 Dec 1888 at Nocks Br by JWA Elliott

BULL William L 21 S Farmer Acc Acc s/o John T & Julia A to Lola M Beloate 19 S Acc Acc d/o Julius D & Edna B on 6 Nov 1895 at Onley by EF Garner

BULL William S 20 S Farmer Acc Acc s/o William H & Kittie T to Alice W Bloxom 17 S Acc Acc d/o Alfred & Emma A V on 6 Nov 1889 at Mappsville by WA Street

BULL Wm H 22 S Farmer Acc Acc s/o Wm H & Sally to Sallie A Young 21 S Acc Acc d/o Richard & Nancy on 29 Dec 1859 at Downings Ch by W Merrill (Thorgood G Taylor says both over 21)

BULL Wm H 30 W Laborer Acc Acc s/o Wm & Sallie to Catharine Baker 18 S Acc Acc d/o Asa & Tabitha on 3 May 1868 at Acc by G Bradford

BULL Wm S 22 S Farmer Acc Acc s/o George & Mary S to Bertha L Wright 16 S Acc Acc d/o Edward & Virginia on 10 Jan 1894 at Lee Mont by JET Ewell

BULLOCK Harvey Kyle 29 S Electrician Spotsylvania Co Farmville PE Co s/o Alfred & Eliz'th R to Alaha Omega Doughty 19 S New York City NY Acc d/o Geo Lloyd & Margaret on 23 Oct 1895 at Acc C H by B Clark

BULMAN Muscoe R 30 S Merchant Acc Acc s/o Leroy C & Elizabeth to Theresa Swanger 25 S Acc Acc d/o Emanuel B & Rebecca on 1 Feb 1888 at Locustville by WJ Twilley

BUNDICK Abaham Col 19 S Laborer Acc Acc s/o Henry & Tabby to Hester A Hope Col 18 S Acc Acc d/o Jacob on 25 Nov 1885 at Drum'tn by LW Lee

BUNDICK Abbott FN s/o Elijah to Leah Wallop FN d/o Clarissa who gave consent lic: 13 Dec 1859 John J Laws says he is over 21

BUNDICK Alfred 24 S Farmer b: Acc s/o Joseph & Margt to Elizabeth S Small 16 S b: Acc d/o Stewart & Louisa on 5 Mar 1856 at Drummond Store by ES Grant

BUNDICK Asa J 26 S Carpenter Acc Acc s/o Wm J & Elizth S to Carrie L Lewis 19 S Acc Acc d/o Wm H & Arinthia on 5 Dec 1883 at Acc by AJ Walter

BUNDICK Asa T 27 S Carpenter Acc Acc s/o John E & Leah to Susie V Ewell 17 S Acc Acc d/o Charles & Susan on 3 Nov 1881 near Mappsville by JE Bundick

BUNDICK Columbus W 21 S Farmer Acc Acc s/o John & Lovie to Missouri E [Mathews] Matthews 17 S Acc Acc d/o Robert & Josephine on 26 Dec 1888 at Parksley by HS Dulany

BUNDICK David T 21 S Farmer Acc Acc s/o Wm P & Mary T to Manie W Savage 16 S Acc Acc d/o Edw'd & Letetia C on 27 Dec 1893 at Acc by JL King

BUNDICK Edward J 28 S Farmer Acc Acc s/o George T & Drucilla to Lizzie G Miles 20 S Acc Acc d/o Elijah J & Sally on 19 Nov 1890 at Modest Town by HS Dulany

BUNDICK Edward T 25 S Oysterman Acc Acc s/o John A & Mary to Nannie A Bundick 21 S Acc Acc d/o George T & Drucilla H on 5 Jun 1887 at Acc by JW Ward

BUNDICK Edward T 22 S Oysterman Acc Acc s/o Severn & Caroline to

Marriages

Dolly P Stant 16 S Acc Acc d/o Emily S on 15 Jun 1889 at Acc by JS Wallace

BUNDICK Elijah 25 S Farmer s/o Samuel & Sally to Margaret S Kellam 22 S d/o Thomas & Polly lic: 2 Oct 1864 marr: 2 Oct 1864 at Acc

BUNDICK George 24 S Farmer Acc Acc s/o George & Annie to Maggie Satchell 17 S Acc Acc d/o William & Eliza on 14 Dec 1871 at Onancock by J Carroll

BUNDICK George H Col 32 S Farmer Acc Acc s/o Virginia to Belle Ward Col 42 S Acc Acc d/o Mary on 5 Apr 1887 at Kelly Farm by P Sheppard

BUNDICK George H 73 S Farmer Acc Acc s/o William & Polly to Mary Dix 63 S Acc Acc d/o George & Sally on 12 Sep 1888 at Acc by JS Wharton

BUNDICK George Thos widr to Drucilla H Miles d/o Sally lic: 31 Oct 1854 John W Nock says she over 21

BUNDICK Horace N 23 S Oysterman Acc Acc s/o Severn & Caroline to Manie P Terry 20 S Acc Acc d/o James F & Mary on 4 Jun 1884 at Pocomoke by M Oldham

BUNDICK James E 25 S Farmer Acc Acc s/o Jno B & Margt E to Manie E Mears 18 S Acc Acc d/o Arthur T & Ellen M on 13 Dec 1883 at Powelton by JW Stiff

BUNDICK Jno 23 S Oysterman Acc Acc s/o Tabitha to Elizabeth Ewell 21 S Acc Acc d/o Gillet & Eliz on 28 Mar 1864 at Acc by GH Ewell

BUNDICK John 26 S Farming Acc Acc s/o Wm & Polly to Lovey Hickman 23 S Acc Acc d/o Robt & Amm on 26 Dec 1861 at Acc by ES Grant

BUNDICK John 35 W Oysterman Acc Acc s/o Matilda to Sally Taylor 18 S Acc Acc d/o Wm of T & Mary on 20 Aug 1876 at Acc by JE Bundick

BUNDICK John Col 31 S Wage-earner Acc Acc s/o Leah to Metosa Augusta Griffin Col 21 S Acc Acc d/o Harriet Mapp on 18 Sep 1892 at Acc by AJ Satchell

BUNDICK John A 43 W Merchant Acc Acc s/o George W to Annie W Hickman 22 S Acc Acc d/o Thomas on 31 Jan 1861 at Reese Chp by ES Grant (Richard Hickman says she over 21)

BUNDICK John A 29 S Attorney-at-Law Acc Acc s/o John A & Annie W to Willie C Wright 26 S Acc Acc d/o Wm T & Mary C on 30 Oct 1895 at Acc C H by HL Derby

BUNDICK John F 24 S Farmer Acc Acc s/o Jno & Margt E to Elizth L Ayres 24 S Acc Acc d/o Edwd E & Sarah on 6 May 1879 at Locust Mount by JWA Elliott

BUNDICK John S 77 W Farmer Acc Acc s/o John & Sarah to Mary West 64 W Acc Acc d/o Laban & Sally Gunter on 22 Mar 1857 at Cross Rd by BT Ames

BUNDICK John T 22 S Sailor Acc Acc s/o Mary E to Annie Simpson 15 S Acc Acc d/o Ruben & June on 5 May 1889 at Crowsontown by HS Dulany

BUNDICK John T J Col 30 W Wage-earner GA Acc to Mary Winder Col 23 S Acc Acc on 13 Aug 1890 at Savageville by JB Lewis

BUNDICK John W 25 S Farmer Acc Acc s/o John H & Mary to Emma [Shreves] Shrieves 19 S Acc Acc d/o Wn S & Tabitha on 24 Jan 1877 at Modest Town by DA Woodson

BUNDICK Lewis Col 27 S Laborer Acc Acc s/o Eliza Duffee to Leah Bundick Col 30 S Acc Acc d/o Patience on 20 Apr 1876 near New Town by A Joynes

BUNDICK Louis Col 25 S Wage-earner Acc Acc s/o Esther to Rose Ella Poulson Col 21 S Acc Acc d/o John

& Elianna on 3 Feb 1889 near Onancock by JH Offer

BUNDICK Muscoe Col 37 S Wage-earner Acc Acc s/o Leah to Lydia Dennis Col 25 S Acc Acc d/o Harriet on 19 Mar 1895 at Acc by AJ Satchell

BUNDICK Purnel Col 26 S Laborer Acc Acc to Lucy Bundick Col 18 S Acc Acc d/o Easter on 4 Jan 1874 at Acc by A Joynes

BUNDICK Richard J 24 S Farmer Acc Acc s/o Geo T & Sally to Dame A Onley 25 S Acc Acc d/o Edward T & Sally on 12 Jan 1871 at Acc by DA Woodson

BUNDICK Severn to Caroline Thornton d/o John lic: 14 Jan 1856 William Lucas says both over 21

BUNDICK Thomas 24 S Farmer Acc Acc s/o Wm & Polly to Mary E Sparrow 16 S Acc Acc d/o Jas W & Ann on 27 Dec 1860 at Ayres Chp by ES Grant (Wm Coston says he over 21)

BUNDICK Thomas 23 S Farmer Acc Acc s/o George & Anna to Mary Wessells 20 S Acc Acc d/o Ephriam & Mary on 21 Feb 1867 at Acc by ES Grant

BUNDICK Thomas 36 S Farmer Acc Acc s/o George T & Sallie to Mary Wigton 37 W Acc Acc d/o Wm S & Tabitha Shieaves on 30 Dec 1880 at Modest Town by JW Hundley

BUNDICK Thomas E to Mary A Lewis lic: 20 Dec 1858 Wm Fisher says both over 21

BUNDICK William 23 S Farmer Acc Acc s/o George & Anne to Anna Lewis 21 S Acc Acc d/o Levin on 10 Sep 1874 at Acc by PA Leatherbury

BUNDICK William Col 20 S Wage-earner Acc Acc s/o Henry & Tabbie to Betsey Bundick Col 18 S Acc Acc d/o Margaret Parks on 13 Oct 1889 near News Town by AJ Satchell

BUNDICK William H 22 S Oysterman Acc Acc s/o John H & Mary to Maggie Ross 19 S Acc Acc d/o John N & Mary on 4 Jan 1888 at Modest Town by JW Ward

BUNDICK William Lee 22 S Farmer Acc Acc s/o Wm P & Mary T to Bertha M Shield 19 S Acc Acc d/o Peter E & Virginia on 27 Nov 1895 at Mappsville by JL King

BUNDICK William T 20 S Farmer Acc Acc s/o John B & Margaret to Cath S Ames 18 S Acc Acc d/o E T & Sarah on 8 Jan 1868 at Acc by E Hebard

BUNDICK William T 21 S Farmer Acc Acc s/o George T & Sally to Mary T Shrieves 21 S Acc Acc d/o David M & Sarah A on 8 Dec 1870 at Zion Ch by DA Woodson

BUNDICK William T 22 S Farmer Acc Acc s/o Thos of Wm & Mary to Sallie D Wright 22 S Acc Acc d/o Charles & Margaret on 30 Oct 1889 at Parksley by HS Dulany

BUNDICK William T 25 S Farmer Acc Acc s/o Wm J & Seymour to Polly A Bundick 21 S Acc Acc d/o John on 6 Jun 1892 at Mappsville by JL King

BUNDICK Wm H 35 W Sailor Acc Acc s/o Tully & Molly to Sallie Justice 30 S Acc Acc d/o Wm & Sally on 25 Feb 1882 at Lee Mont by WA Crouse

BUNDICK Wm H Jr 28 S Merchant Brooklyn NY Acc s/o Wm H & Marg't to Estelle J Watts 28 S Acc Acc d/o John G & Adeline on 8 Sep 1892 at Acc by SU Grimsley

BUNDICK Wm W 21 S Farmer Acc Acc s/o Wm to Manie Kellam 23 S Acc Acc d/o Thos Arale & Mary Kellam on 1 Dec 1886 at Locust Mount by JWA Elliott

BUNTING Alfred C Col 22 S Sailor Acc Acc s/o Margaret to Sarah [Reed] Read Col 19 S Acc Acc d/o

Marriages

Mary on 24 Dec 1876 at Savageville by JK Plato

BUNTING Alonzo L 21 S Blacksmith Wor Co MD Acc s/o John J & Sallie S to Emma S Young 21 S Acc Acc d/o Louis & Mary on 10 Apr 1889 at Mappsville by WA Street

BUNTING Cardinal L 28 S Farmer Acc Acc s/o Thos C & Maria to Mary E Bell 16 S Acc Acc d/o John E & Esther on 19 Jul 1879 at Upshur Nk by JWA Elliott

BUNTING Charles L 25 S Waterman Acc Acc s/o Henry Clay & Susan J to Cora D Parkes 21 S Acc Acc d/o Charles & Margaret on 25 Dec 1889 at Temp'ville by WF Hayes

BUNTING Dewitt C 21 S Farmer Acc Acc s/o George C & Ellen E to Nellie E Gladding 19 S Acc Acc d/o George T & Georgianna on 11 Dec 1894 at Acc by GJ Hill

BUNTING Edw'd W 24 S Oyster Planter Acc Acc s/o Henry & Mary to Sallie C Truitt 19 S Acc Acc d/o William & Sarah on 16 Mar 1892 at Greenbackville by RS Williamson

BUNTING Ezekiel Col 45 S Laborer Acc Acc to Ann West Col 45 S Acc Acc on 16 Jun 1876 near Craddockville by WH Corbin

BUNTING George W 25 S Farmer Acc Acc s/o George & Rosy to Mary Ann West 23 S Acc Acc d/o Edward J & Margt A on 25 Dec 1872 at Bethel Ch by JE Bundick

BUNTING George W 35 W Farmer Acc Acc s/o George S & Rose A to Mary W Thornton 26 S Acc Acc d/o Thos & Elizabeth on 16 Dec 1885 at Mappsville by WA Street

BUNTING Gillet F 21 S Farmer Acc Acc to Ellen Chesser 20 S Acc Acc d/o Jas on 21 Jul 1868 at Acc by JO Moss

BUNTING Henry Clay 22 S Farmer s/o Shepherd & Amanda to Susan Jane Bunting 16 d/o Wm H & Mary A lic: 6 Jan 1865 marr: 10 Jan 1865

BUNTING Henry T 48 W Farmer Acc Acc s/o Sheppard to Emily J Colonna 39 W Acc Acc d/o Thos Brittingham on 22 May 1884 near Temp'ville by M Oldham

BUNTING Jacob to Mary Custis d/o Margaret who gave consent lic: 16 May 1856 John W Core says he over 21

BUNTING James Col 22 S Wage-earner Acc Acc s/o James & Margaret to Colline Ashby Col 21 S Acc Acc d/o Amanda Murphy on 28 Mar 1888 at Locust Mount by JWA Elliott

BUNTING James Sr Col 63 W Oysterman Acc Acc s/o Corilla Read to Ibby Jane [Parks] Parkes Col 58 W Acc Acc on 14 Feb 1892 at Locust Mount by RH Coleman

BUNTING John S 25 S Carpenter Acc Acc s/o Teackle & Evaline to Olivia Miles 21 S Acc Acc d/o Byrd & Jane on 6 Dec 1893 at Temp'ville by JW Nicholson

BUNTING Joshua Col 66 S Laborer Acc Acc s/o Comfort to Mary Finney Col 50 S Acc Acc on 24 Oct 1875 at Savageville by JK Plato

BUNTING Kendal 19 S Sailor Acc Acc s/o Jno W & Susan to Mary A Jones 16 S Acc Acc d/o Danl & Mary on 17 Jan 1880 at Chinco: Isld by R Williamson

BUNTING Peter Col 24 S Wage-earner Acc Acc s/o James & Harriet to Manie [Scarborogh] Scarborough Col 18 S Acc Acc d/o Peter on 30 Mar 1895 at Acc by L Duncan

BUNTING Robert E Col 24 S Farmer Acc Acc s/o Ezekiel & Queen Anna to Rachel Gaskins Col 22 S Acc Acc d/o John W T & Lizzie on 26 Jan 1887 at Craddockville by GHT Byrd

BUNTING Sylvester T 28 S Farmer Acc Acc s/o George to Susanna

Thornton 25 S Acc Acc d/o Wm & Elizth on 27 Mar 1867 at Acc by GW Matthews

BUNTING Teagle 25 S Farmer Acc Acc s/o Sheppard & Susan to Emeline Small 23 S Acc Acc d/o Handy & Mana on 30 May 1860 at Acc by W Merrill (Asa Taylor said both over 21)

BUNTING Thomas H 30 S Laborer Acc Acc s/o William H & Mary to Nannette Potts 28 S N'hamp: Acc d/o Jeau G W & Nancy on 3 May 1893 at Chinco: Isld by RB Sanford

BUNTING Thos widr to Harriet Kellam on 29 Nov 1853 by J Allen

BUNTING William H 21 S Farmer Acc Acc s/o Henry C & Susan J to Lidia H Onley 17 S Acc Acc d/o Smith & Eliz'th on 25 Jun 1890 at Acc by JS Wallace

BUNTING William R 62 W Farmer Acc Acc s/o Wm R & Mahala to Polly G Bull 52 W Acc Acc d/o William Haley on 19 Mar 1893 at Acc C H by DJ Traynham

BUNTING Wm C 20 S Merchant Chinco: Isld Chinco: Isld s/o Jno W & Susan to Hattie Mumford 21 S Wor Co MD Chinco: Isld d/o Saml J on 17 Feb 1886 at Chinco: Isld by JD Reese

BURKE Daniel J 33 S Engineer Boston MA Acc to Mary S Doughty 18 S Wor Co MD Acc d/o Abner on 21 Oct 1888 at Powelton by W Chinn

BURNSIDE Daniel Col 29 S Sailor Nassau West Indies Acc s/o Benj & Ophilia to Catharine Wise Col 18 S Washington DC Acc d/o Margaret Pew on 29 Jul 1884 at Onancock by R Davis

BURR Worhington L 20 S Farmer Long Isld NY Acc s/o Charles W & Mary to Ida C Ewell 17 S Acc Acc d/o Chas & Susan on 22 Nov 1876 at Modest Town by DA Woodson

BURROUGHS William C 27 S Farmer Mercer Co NJ Acc s/o Ralph & Caroline to Laura J Coryell 20 S Mercer Co NJ Acc d/o Cornelius & Sarah on 10 Oct 1888 at Greenbackville by BF Jester

BURTON Alexander B 30 S Waterman Acc Acc s/o William F & Margaret A to Hadda Kellam 20 S Acc Acc d/o Robert W T & Emma on 3 Nov 1895 at Locustville by EF Garner

BURTON Allen Col 30 S Farmer Acc Acc s/o Margaret to Leah Ames Col 28 S Acc Acc d/o Lucy on 22 Dec 1890 at Acc by JB Lewis

BURTON Beady FN 29 S s/o Mary to Mary Bunting FN 34 S d/o Esther lic: 29 May 1865 marr: 29 May 1865

BURTON Charles Col 23 S Farmer Acc Acc s/o Tinney to Mary Smith Col 16 S Acc Acc on 8 Mar 1887 at Acc by L Duncan

BURTON Charles S 26 S Life Saving Station Acc Acc s/o Wm F & Margaret to Mary Fox 24 S Acc Acc d/o Golden S & Elizth on 28 Dec 1884 near Locustville by WC Vaden

BURTON Edmond T Col 21 S Acc Acc s/o Sarah to Jennie Trower Col 17 S Acc Acc d/o Jane & Jesse on 24 Jun 1883 at Locust Mount by JWA Elliott

BURTON Edward T Col 30 W Wage-earner Acc Acc s/o Sarah to Mary Snead Col 24 S Acc Acc d/o Mary Murphy on 8 Jun 1890 at Savageville by JB Lewis

BURTON Ezekiel T Col 26 S Sailor Acc Acc s/o Sarah to Bridget Ashby Col 24 S Acc Acc d/o Mary on 4 Jan 1874 at Onancock by R Davis

BURTON James Col 28 S Sailor Acc Acc s/o Sary to Louisa Mapp Col 27 S Acc Acc d/o Martha on 30 Nov 1882 at Acc by GW Young

BURTON Jas S Col 37 S Fisherman Acc Acc s/o Harriet to Georgianna Miles Col 38 S Acc Acc d/o Annie

Marriages

on 25 Sep 1891 at Fair Oaks by RH Coleman

BURTON John Col 25 S Sailor Acc Acc s/o Harriet to Mary A [Bailey] Bayly Col 20 S Acc Acc d/o Martha on 23 Dec 1880 at Locust Mount by RJ Waters

BURTON John E 23 S Sailor Acc Acc s/o Wm F & Margt to Lucinda Williams 21 S Sussex Co DE Acc d/o E F & Sophia on 27 Aug 1879 at Chinco: Isld by IT Adkins

BURTON John E Col 22 S Laborer Acc Acc s/o Mary Hatiney to Rosie Davis Col 19 S Acc Acc d/o Richard & Julia on 23 Mar 1887 at Locust Mount by JWA Elliott

BURTON John W 34 S Farmer Acc Acc s/o Garrison & Sally to Elizabeth S Bradford 16 S Acc Acc d/o John of A on 24 Oct 1869 at Acc by JWA Elliott

BURTON John W 24 S Farmer Acc Acc s/o Jno & Maria to Melissa Hall 29 S Acc Acc d/o Thos & Sally on 6 Feb 1878 at Downings Ch by A Wiles

BURTON Joshua T 25 S Farmer Acc Acc s/o Wm T & Margt to Jannie M James 22 S Acc Acc d/o John T & Susan on 21 Dec 1876 near Locustville by LK LeCato

BURTON Joshua T B 21 S Farmer Acc Acc s/o Jno R & Sally to Arinthia S Kellam 18 S Acc Acc d/o Wm E & Susan on 27 Jul 1876 near Locustville by LK LeCato

BURTON Lloyd T Col 24 S Acc Acc s/o Obedience to Emma Susan Floyd Col 22 S Acc Acc on 1 Jun 1883 at Drum'tn by LW Lee

BURTON Louis S Col 24 S Farmer Acc Acc s/o Sarah to Mary E Bunting Col 17 S Acc Acc d/o Margaret on 14 Jan 1877 at Onancock by JK Plato

BURTON Thos Hy Col 30 S Acc Acc s/o Mary to Mary Susan Ashby Col 30 S Acc Acc d/o Charles & Mary on 2 Jan 1876 near Little Rest by HT Rich

BURTON William J 48 W Sailor Acc Acc s/o Wm H & Mary H to Mary F Babbitt 38 S Acc Acc d/o Chas E Sr & Susan on 28 Oct 1894 at Chinco: Isld by SU Grimsley

BURTON Wilson FN 27 S Sailor Acc Acc s/o Slaves to Sarah (Ann) [Bibbins] (Beavans) Bibbins (FN) 17 S Acc Acc d/o Henry Bibbins (Henry Beavens who gave consent) & Arah on 29 Dec 1858 at Acc by JWA Elliott

BURTON Wm A 22 S Merchant Acc Acc s/o Jno R & Sally M to Sadie P Swanger 21 S Acc Acc d/o Emanuel B & Ann R on 7 Dec 1881 at Locustville by JC Watson

BURTON Wolsey 22 S Seaman Sussex Co DE Sussex Co DE s/o John & Jansey to Mary E Collins 19 S Sussex Co DE Chinco: Isld d/o Charles & Hester on 31 Dec 1876 at Chinco: Isld by P Bowdin Sr

BYRD Abel James [Bird] 28 S Carpenter Acc Acc s/o Abel J & Sarah A to Emma Cora Mears 20 S Acc Acc d/o Benjamin W & Emma S on 29 May 1889 at bride's home by JH Riddick

BYRD Albert Franklin 22 S Merchant Acc Acc s/o Colmer S & Hetty to Charlotte Emory Matthews 24 S Acc Acc d/o Wm S & Susan on 29 Apr 1858 near Temp'ville by JF Chaplain (Wm S Byrd says both over 21)

BYRD Alonzo D 22 S Farmer Acc Acc s/o Wm S to Martha F Godwin 19 S Acc Acc d/o Marcellus F & Mollie on 6 Nov 1895 at Acc by JL King

BYRD Andrew W Col 21 S Wage-earner Acc Acc s/o Henry & Rachel to Louisa Ann Bayly Col 18 S Acc Acc d/o Daniel & Mary on 7 Jan 1891 near Savageville by JB Lewis

BYRD Arthur W 22 S Farmer Acc Acc s/o Wm W to Rebecca J Hall 22 S Acc Acc d/o Thos J & Esther on 27 Dec 1893 at Acc by TM Poulson

BYRD Colwell P s/o Johannas to Elizabeth A Trader d/o William lic: 16 Sep 1854

BYRD Cornelius J 23 S Farmer Acc Acc s/o Wm T & Hetty to Rebecca A Duncan 24 S Acc Acc d/o Jno R & Orrilulia A on 20 Dec 1883 at Acc by TM Poulson

BYRD Daniel H 35 W Waterman Acc Acc s/o Obed S & Hetty to Clara C Young 18 S Acc Acc d/o Levin R & Mary on 15 Dec 1895 at Mappsville by JL King

BYRD Ebern T 25 S Blacksmith Acc Acc s/o Ebern & Maria to Harriet A Parker 20 S Acc Acc d/o John M & Ellen on 18 Dec 1870 at Acc by LK LeCato

BYRD Edmund Col 60 W Farmer Acc Acc s/o Patience to Lucinda Hayward Col 35 S Wor Co MD Acc d/o Isaac & Pina Hack on 10 Dec 1890 at Acc by L Duncan

BYRD Edwd P 30 S Merchant Acc Acc s/o Richd P & Nancy A to Margt E S Bundick 30 S Acc Acc d/o Jno A & Margt B on 27 Nov 1878 at Zion Ch by DA Woodson

BYRD Geo Henry Col 21 S Day Laborer Acc Acc to Rachel Hack Col 21 S Acc Acc on 26 Dec 1886 at Acc by JWA Elliott

BYRD George Col 23 W Wage-earner Acc Acc s/o Henry & Rachel to Mary Mason Col 21 S Acc Acc d/o Jane on 2 Dec 1890 at Savageville by JB Lewis

BYRD George F 23 S Sailor Acc Acc s/o George W & Eliz'th to Julia A Mears 16 S Acc Acc d/o Zadock S & Julia on 25 Dec 1890 at Mappsville by WA Street

BYRD George H Col 21 S Wage-earner Acc Acc s/o George & Virginia to Phoebe Davis Col 20 S Acc Acc d/o Thorogood & Mary on 22 Jan 1888 at Acc by AJ Satchell

BYRD George T [Bird] 34 S Farmer Acc Acc s/o Geo P & Mary to Jane Trader 24 S Acc Acc d/o Saml T & Elizabeth on 15 Feb 1885 at Mappsville by WA Street

BYRD George T [Bird] 21 S Plasterer Acc Acc s/o Abel J & Sarah Ann to Carrie F Stiles 18 S Iowa Co IA Acc d/o Thomas W & Abigail on 27 Dec 1887 at Wachapreague by WJ Twilley

BYRD Harmonson [Bird] 25 S Farmer Acc Acc s/o Obed S & Hetty to Sallie Trader 20 S Acc Acc d/o Samuel on 7 Jan 1885 at Acc by WA Street

BYRD Henry 26 S Sailor Acc Acc to Kelsy Bundick 22 S Acc Acc d/o Leah on 13 Mar 1877 near Mappsville by JE Bundick

BYRD Henry Col 25 S Sailor Acc Acc to Ellen Conquest Col 17 S Acc Acc d/o Leah on 11 Sep 1879 at Mary Branch by A Joynes

BYRD Henry [Bird] Col 32 W Sailor Acc Acc to Martha Savage Col 28 S N'hamp: Acc d/o Agnes Thomas on 31 Dec 1884 at Onancock by GHT Byrd

BYRD Henry Parker 22 S Farmer Acc Acc s/o Alex W & Sally A to Lucy H Evans 19 S Acc Acc d/o John W & Matilda on 27 Nov 1895 at Horntown by JET Ewell

BYRD Isaac Col 30 S Laborer Acc Acc s/o Bill Twiford & Rachel Sommers to Elizabeth Downing Col 23 S Acc Acc d/o Wm & Sally on 3 Apr 1886 at Woodbury by AJ Satchell

BYRD James 21 S Sailor Acc Acc s/o James to Maggie J Gladding 17 S Acc Acc d/o Calvin R & Elizabeth on 25 Mar 1874 at Acc by M Oldham

BYRD Jno L 30 S Farmer Acc Acc s/o

Marriages

Geo & Elizth C to Bettie A Summers 22 S Acc Acc d/o Jno & Vienna on 17 Dec 1884 at Mappsville by JW Carroll

BYRD Jno Wm 22 S Farmer Acc Acc s/o Thos H & Mary Ann to Elizth M Byrd 23 S Acc Acc d/o Jacob & Susan on 15 Jan 1879 at Jacob Byrd's by TM Poulson

BYRD Johannas L 22 S Sailor Acc Acc s/o Travis & Polly to Lizzie E Parkes 20 S Acc Acc d/o John Y & Catharine on 20 Dec 1876 near Conquest Ch by M Oldham

BYRD John Col 45 S Farmer Acc Acc s/o Mary Crippen to Agnes Tyler Col 40 W Acc Acc d/o Judy Fisher on 7 Dec 1879 at Mappsville by A Joynes

BYRD John Col 24 S Farmer Acc Acc s/o Jno & Mary to Ellen Davis Col 22 S Acc Acc d/o Thorogood & Mary on 16 Dec 1883 at Acc by AJ Satchell

BYRD John Col 45 S Farmer Acc Acc to Josephine Broughton Col 17 S Acc Acc d/o George on 20 Nov 1889 at Atlantic by JC Cluff

BYRD John [Bird] Col 26 W Laborer Acc Acc s/o Mary to Peggy Bloxom Col 35 S Acc Acc d/o Alsie on 1 Mar 1876 at News Town by A Joynes

BYRD John H [Bird] 25 S Mechanic Acc Acc s/o Abel & Sarah to Mary S Phillips 19 S Acc Acc d/o Wesley L & Sarah on 14 May 1879 near Oak Grove Ch by JWA Elliott

BYRD John Henry Col 22 S Laborer Acc Acc s/o Egypt Savage & May Byrd to Polly Nock Col 19 S Acc Acc d/o Parker & Ann Nock on 4 Jun 1871 at Modest Town by A Joynes

BYRD John J [Bird] Col 39 S Blacksmith Acc Acc s/o Mary Crippen to Adah Matthews Col 26 S Acc Acc d/o Adah on 19 Dec 1872 at Acc by M Oldham

BYRD John O 27 S Sailor Acc Acc s/o John W & Nancy to Arinthia E Bloxom 22 S Acc Acc d/o George of J & Tabitha on 6 May 1874 at Guilford by JM Anderson

BYRD John T 29 S Merchant Acc Acc s/o Richd P & Nancy J to Maggie N Mason 20 S Acc Acc d/o Jas H & Mary on 28 Jan 1886 at Zion Ch by WA Street

BYRD John T Col 19 S Farmer Acc Acc s/o John C & Betsy to Sadie Custis Col 16 S Acc Acc d/o Levi & Rachel on 7 Jan 1894 at Acc by AJ Satchell

BYRD Jonannes F 24 S Farmer Acc Acc s/o Jacob K & Susan to Mary A Martin 17 S Acc Acc d/o Jas W & Louisa on 4 Sep 1873 at Conquest Ch by TM Poulson

BYRD Levin J 23 S Farmer Acc Acc s/o Parker & Mary to Anna Chase 19 S Acc Acc d/o Alsavada & Sallie A on 3 Aug 1887 at Mappsville by WA Street

BYRD Littleton J 23 S Sailor Acc Acc s/o Geo W & Elizth to Eliza S Mears 23 S Acc Acc d/o Julius & Susan on 25 Jun 1884 at Acc by TM Poulson

BYRD Mahlon F 21 S Blacksmith Acc Acc s/o Ebern T & Harriet A to Lela M Campbell 14 S Acc Acc d/o Archie C & Margaret on 4 Feb 1894 at Pungo: by JR Griffith

BYRD Manton L Col 23 S Farmer Acc Acc s/o Edward & Fanny to Catharine L Phillips Col 23 S Acc Acc d/o Edmond & Mary on 23 Dec 1885 near Pungo: by GHT Byrd

BYRD Nathaniel W 60 W Shoemaker Acc Acc s/o Major & Nancy to Sally Rayfield 62 W Acc Acc d/o Wm & Rosa Fitchett on 10 Jan 1869 at Acc by DA Woodson

BYRD Parker [Bird] 50 W Farmer Acc Acc s/o Johanna & Delany to

Margaret A Northam 45 W Acc Acc d/o Arthur & Peggy Wessells on 13 Jan 1876 at Acc by DA Woodson

BYRD Robert T Col 24 S Wage-earner Richmond City Acc s/o Robert & Maria to Maggie E West Col 19 S Acc Acc d/o Coston & Lizzie on 8 Jul 1894 at Acc by TW Nettles

BYRD Samuel Col 24 S Farmer Acc Acc s/o Ary Fosque to Katie Susan Kellam Col 21 S Acc Acc d/o Ann on 21 Jan 1877 at Savageville by JK Plato

BYRD Samuel Col 21 S Acc Acc s/o Ezekeil & Mary to Hannah Downing Col 19 S Acc Acc d/o Steward & Hannah on 2 Aug 1882 near Jenkins Bridge by JC Cluff

BYRD Sewell U 24 S Merchant Acc Acc s/o Sewell A & Ellen J to Lelia L Mason 20 S Acc Acc d/o Thorgood & Elizabeth A on 26 Jan 1887 at Guilford by JW Carroll

BYRD Solomon 24 S Carpenter Acc Acc s/o Eburn & Marie to Mary F Doughty 18 S Acc Acc d/o Major & Cath on 30 Nov 1867 at Acc by JWA Elliott

BYRD Southey [Bird] Col 22 S Laborer Acc Acc s/o Henry & Rachel to Margaret Sunket Col 22 S Acc Acc d/o Mark & Sarah on 4 Jan 1888 at Acc by JA Haynes

BYRD Staton F [Bird] 22 S Sailor Captain Acc Acc s/o Parker & Mary C to Clara Lucas 19 S Acc Acc d/o Saml & Tabitha on 27 Dec 1881 at Acc by JW Hundley

BYRD Teakle L 21 S Farmer Acc Acc s/o Parker & Mary Bird to Mary E Fisher 16 S Acc Acc d/o John D & Delia on 15 Apr 1874 at Oak Hall by TM Poulson

BYRD Thomas Col 21 S Farmer Acc Acc s/o Mary Major to Emma Beavans Col 21 S Acc Acc d/o Elizth on 15 Feb 1873 near Pungo: by C Burriss

BYRD Thomas S 24 S Sailor Acc Acc s/o Selby & Amanda to Annie W Kelly 18 S Acc Acc d/o Elijah B & Evaline on 12 Nov 1874 at bride's father's by DA Woodson

BYRD Thomas T [Bird] 18 S Farmer Acc Acc s/o Elizabeth to Bettie Turner 18 S Acc Acc d/o James & Tuny on 21 May 1871 at Acc by JE Humphreys

BYRD Thomas W 19 S Waterman Acc Acc s/o Obed S & Hetty C to Mary Fisher 18 S Acc Acc d/o Thorogood J & Tabitha on 24 Jun 1894 at Acc by C Clement

BYRD Walter 25 S Oysterman Acc Acc s/o Jas & Susan to Susan Gladding 20 S Acc Acc d/o Burnell B & Mary on 8 Dec 1875 at Modest Town by DA Woodson

BYRD Warren S 23 S Sailor Acc Acc s/o Obed S & Hettie C to Ida S Young 17 S Acc Acc d/o Benjamin F & Elizabeth on 8 Jan 1890 at Mappsville by JW Ward

BYRD William Col 35 S Farmer Acc Acc s/o Esther Bundick to Hester Laws Col 23 S Acc Acc d/o Rebecca on 26 Sep 1880 at First Bapt Ch by A Joynes

BYRD William C (A) 25 S Oysterman Acc Acc s/o Custis & Polly to Malvina Ross 22 W Acc Acc d/o Solomon & Sally Glading on 19 Nov 1860 at Acc by JC Mears (Elijah J Miles says he over 21)

BYRD William H 28 S Oysterman Crisfield MD Crisfield MD s/o Wm R & Sally J to Cora T Marshall 18 S Acc Acc d/o James W & Olivia on 8 Dec 1887 at Temp'ville by M Oldham

BYRD William S 21 S Farmer Acc Acc s/o Jacob K & Susan to Sallie Byrd 21 S Acc Acc d/o Eburn & Maria on 6 Oct 1869 at Acc by TM Poulson

Marriages

BYRD William Selby 36 W Merchant Acc Oak Hall s/o Colmore S & Hetty to Mary Jane Broughton 18 S Baltimore MD Acc d/o James & Eliza on 7 Apr 1859 at Acc by JF Chaplain

BYRD Winfield S 25 S Farmer Acc Acc s/o Richd P & Nancy J to Bettie M Mason 28 S Acc Acc d/o Chlr H & Mary A on 24 Oct 1872 at Acc by EM Bryan

BYRD Wm A 40 W Farmer Acc Acc s/o Custis & Polly to Mary Davis 26 S Acc Acc d/o Henry & Hetty on 16 Aug 1876 at Acc by JM Anderson

BYRD Wm R 21 S Farming Acc Acc s/o John W & Nancy to Margaret J Byrd 17 S Acc Acc d/o Selby & Amanda on 15 Dec 1870 at Guilford by JET Ewell

CABB J W [Cobb] 28 S Farmer Acc Acc s/o Jas & Leah to Jennie A Johnson 21 S Acc Acc d/o Alfd & Mary on 27 Oct 1886 at Acc by CA Grice

CAINE James J 40 W Engineer Philadelphia PA Philadelphia PA s/o John & Catherine to Mary Doughty 45 W NJ Acc d/o Salem & Rachel Applegate on 15 Jul 1890 at Acc by JWA Elliott

CALDWELL George R 25 S Lawyer Wheeling VA Wheeling VA s/o Alfred & Martha to Sue M Smith 22 S Acc Acc d/o Meare & Ann M on 28 Jun 1866 at Acc by C Collin

CAMACK J S 34 W Watchmaker Philadelphia PA Chinco: Isld s/o Saml & Margt to Hester A Thornton 20 S Chinco: Isld Chinco: Isld d/o Parker & Eliza on 2 Jun 1877 at Chinco: Isld by WP Thornton

CAMPBELL Archibald A 19 S Farming Acc Acc s/o Frances A & Sarah to Maggie Waterfield 18 S Acc Acc d/o Wm H & Margaret on 23 Dec 1874 at bride's father's by LK LeCato

CAMPBELL Francis A 20 S Teamster Acc Acc s/o Francis A & Sarah to Hennie E Bunting 18 S Acc Acc d/o J C & Mary on 13 Oct 1881 near Locustville by LK LeCato

CAMPBELL Francis A 32 W Farmer Acc Acc s/o Francis A & Sarah to Dora C Turner 22 W Acc Acc d/o John H & Bettie A Stevens on 7 Dec 1893 near Locust Mount by JWA Elliott

CANNON Joseph T 31 S Confectioner Norfolk City Norfolk City s/o Jos & Laura to Maggie S Kellam 20 S Acc Acc d/o Jas L & Solly on 19 Sep 1872 at Belle Haven by JE Humphreys

CAPEHART Armistead L 24 S Planter NC Kittrell NC s/o Baldy A & Meta to Lillian W Bagwell 22 S Acc Acc d/o Edmund R & Maggie D on 20 Jul 1892 at Onancock by HL Derby

CAREY James A 65 W Salesman DE Acc to Emeline Thornton 46 W Acc Acc d/o Delilah Christopher on 6 Nov 1887 at Temp'ville by M Oldham

CARMINE Charles 27 S Farmer Acc Acc s/o Smith Carmine to Mary E Watkinson 24 S Acc Acc d/o Evans & Alicia Watkinson on 22 Feb 1888 at Drum'tn by J McNabb

CARMINE George D [Carmines] 22 S Wheelwright Acc Acc s/o Jane to Phoebe E Henson 25 S Boston MA Acc d/o Thos & Cath on 15 Jul 1869 at Acc by WF Williams

CARMINE George E [Carmines] 21 S Farmer N'hamp: Acc s/o Wm & Lavirnia to Eliza Evans 16 S Acc Acc d/o George W & Nellie on 3 Apr 1878 at Onancock by WJ Duhadway

CARMINE Henry D 25 S Plaster b: Acc s/o James & Elizth to Rebecca A Watson 20 S b: Acc d/o Jno R & Cartharine on 12 Jan 1859 at Reese

Chp by ES Grant (Robert R White says he over 21)

CARMINE John J 25 S Sailor Acc Acc s/o Henry D & Rebecca to Mary H Melson 22 S Acc Acc d/o Henry & Louisa C on 26 Jun 1895 at Onancock by EF Garner

CARMINE Smith R 32 S Laborer b: Acc s/o Wm Carmine & Nancy Topin to Elizabeth Kelly 26 S b: Acc d/o Wm East & Mary Kelly on 28 Dec 1857 at Acc by P Warren (Bagwell C Mason says both over 21)

CARPENTER Charles 26 S Oysterman Acc Acc s/o Revel & Elizth to Susan Tatham 28 S Acc Acc on 15 Oct 1869 at Acc by WP Thornton

CARPENTER Charles H 25 W Oysterman s/o Revel & Elizabeth to Redemia A Jester 19 S d/o John & Annie lic: 11 May 1871 marr: 14 May 1871

CARPENTER John 21 S Oysterman Acc Acc s/o Revel & Elizth to Elizabeth [Chericks] Cherricks 21 S Acc Acc d/o Daniel & Betsy on 28 May 1867 at Acc by P Bowdin Sr

CARPENTER Leonard J s/o (John B) to Elizabeth Susan Richardson d/o (Mary J) on Mar 1856(?) by JG Councill Certificate returned 12 Jan 1859

CARPENTER Richard 47 W Oysterman Acc Acc s/o Revel & Elizth to Mary J Hill 47 W Acc Acc d/o Wm P & Nancy Thornton on 22 Nov 1883 at Chinco: Isld by WP Thornton

CARPENTER Wm 21 S Oysterman Acc Acc s/o Richard & Mary to Nancy Williams 21 S Acc Acc d/o Selby & Susan on 22 Nov 1882 at Chinco: Isld by WP Thornton

CARTER Geo 21 S Oysterman Chinco: Isld Chinco: Isld s/o Zadock & Polly to Margaret Hammonds 17 S Sussex Co DE Chinco: Isld d/o E English & Jane Reed on 4 May 1877 at Chinco: Isld by WP Thornton

CARTER Samuel L Col 28 S Wage-earner Richmond Acc s/o Robert & Martha Ann to Polly Bayly Col 22 S Acc Acc d/o Rose on 30 Sep 1894 at Acc by PW Lee

CARTER Zadock 35 W Oysterman Acc Acc s/o Joshua & Sally to Mary E Lofland 25 S Sussex Co DE Acc d/o Clement W & Mary on 5 Mar 1869 at Acc by WP Thornton

CARUTHERS George 30 S Farmer Acc Acc s/o James & Rose to Margaret Custis 22 S Acc Acc d/o George & Eveline on 17 Dec 1882 at Acc by SC Boston

CARUTHERS Robert 30 S Farmer Acc Acc s/o James & Rosie to Melvina Lewis 30 W Acc Acc d/o James & Mary Hart on 8 Jul 1874 near Slugtkill (Slutkill Neck) by O Littleton

CARUTHERS Wm 35 S Farmer Acc Acc s/o James & Rosa to Melissa W Lewis 25 S Acc Acc d/o Henderson & Nancy on 16 Nov 1881 at Joynes Br by LE Barrett

CASE Henry Col 23 S Wage-earner Acc Acc s/o Geo & Catharine to Rose Hatton 18 S Acc Acc d/o Lewis & Ida on 26 Dec 1895 at Acc by RE Lee

CATHELL John 35 W Sailor Wor Co MD Acc s/o Len & Nancy to Margt Thornton 22 S Acc Acc d/o Jno & susan on 11 Jul 1867 at Acc by P Bowdin Sr

CATHELL John S [Cathel] 56 W Sailor Wor Co MD Acc to Margaret Young 32 S Philadelphia PA Acc on 29 Apr 1882 at Chinco: Isld by WP Thornton

CATHELL John Showell 22 S Oysterman Acc Acc s/o John & Margaret to Mary A Sharpley 18 S Acc Acc d/o John A & Matilda on 30 Dec 1892 at Chinco: Isld by RB Sanford

Marriages

CATHELL Washington 22 S Sailor Acc Acc s/o John S & Margaret to Jane Claville 18 S Acc Acc d/o James & Eliz'th on 6 Jul 1890 at Chinco: Isld by GE Wood

CAUSAY Rich A 24 S Photographist MD Snow Hill MD s/o Jasiah & Sally to Margaret S Parkes 21 S Acc Acc d/o Parker W & Nancy on 21 Jan 1874 at Acc by IT Adkins

CHAMBERS David 21 S Oysterman Acc Acc s/o David & Janet to Georgianna [Willet] Willett 18 S Acc Acc d/o Wm Elizth on 27 Feb 1868 at Acc by LK LeCato

CHAMBERS Edward 24 S Farmer Philadelphia Acc s/o David C & Jane to Priscilla Turner 15 S Acc Acc d/o Richd & Mary on 3 Mar 1886 at Acc by JE Humphreys

CHAMBERS John B 25 S Waterman Philadelphia PA Acc s/o David & Jane to Lizzie Jane Turner 20 S Acc Acc d/o Richard & Mary on 25 Dec 1889 near Craddockville by JE Humphreys

CHAMBERS William 21 S Farmer Acc Acc s/o David & Gerogianna to Georgianna Hopkins 17 S Acc Acc d/o William H & Cornelia A on 3 Aug 1890 at Belle Haven by JE Humphreys

CHAMBERS Wm J 23 S Farmer Philadelphia PA Acc s/o David C & Jane to Otelia E Savage 28 S Acc Acc d/o Saml & Elizth on 12 Nov 1879 at Belle Haven by FA Davis

CHANCE David A 20 S Farmer Acc Acc s/o James W & Mary A to Emma J Crowson 18 S Acc Acc d/o James P & Sarah on 16 Jan 1884 at Locust Mount by JWA Elliott

CHANCE George 23 S Farmer Acc Acc s/o Jas & Mary Ann to Catharine A Mears 19 S Acc Acc d/o Jas & Mary on 1 Jan 1879 at John Cobb's by LK LeCato

CHANCE James 22 S Sailor Acc Acc s/o Wm & Ann to Mary Ann Haley 19 S Acc Acc d/o Benj & Betsy on 26 Dec 1853 at r/o Haley by J Burton

CHANCE John T 31 S Farmer Acc Acc s/o James & Mary Ann to Willianna A Savage 24 S Acc Acc d/o Edmond & Eliz'th on 27 Dec 1891 at Locust Mount by JWA Elliott

CHANCE Joseph 21 S Sailor Acc Acc s/o Wm & Ann to Emma L Haley 17 S Acc Acc d/o Benj & Elizth on 18 Apr 1861 at r/o Elizth Haley by LK LeCato

CHANCE Obed D 26 S Farmer Acc Acc s/o Joseph & Laura to Jospehine Kellam 23 S Acc Acc d/o Catharine on 17 Jan 1895 at Grangeville by JR Sturgis

CHANDLER Alfred Col 21 S Farmer Acc Acc s/o Irma to Susan Coleburn Col 18 S Acc Acc d/o Sabra on 29 Sep 1875 at Morris Chp by HT Rich

CHANDLER Bowdoin Col 40 S Farmer Acc Acc s/o Susan to Jane Scarborough Col 35 S Acc Acc d/o Harriet Carr on 20 Apr 1879 near Cross Rd by A Handy

CHANDLER Cornelius 26 S Farmer Acc Acc to Sally Ann Kellam 17 S Acc Acc d/o James E on 3 Nov 1881 at Acc by JWA Elliott

CHANDLER Eba T 18 S Oysterman Rosanna DE Chinco: Isld s/o Joshua L & Catharine M to Hetty J Bishop 18 S Rosanna DE Chinco: Isld d/o Henry & Jane on 15 Apr 1877 at Chinco: Isld by P Bowdin Sr

CHANDLER Edward 26 S Sailor Acc Acc to Sarah Riley 21 S Acc Acc d/o Adah on Dec 1869 at Acc by JH Addison

CHANDLER Edward Col 21 S Laborer Acc Acc s/o Betsy to Eliza Finney Col 17 S Acc Acc d/o Mary on 16 Jan 1883 at Savageville by F Wood

CHANDLER George Col 21 S Farmer

Acc Acc s/o Richd & Sabra to Mary Drummond Col 25 S Acc Acc d/o Cancies on 31 Jun 1872 near Mary Branch by N Morris

CHANDLER George T Col 23 S Farmer Acc Acc s/o Edward & Eliza to Maggie Glenn Col 23 S Acc Acc d/o John & Eliza on 19 Nov 1890 at Onancock by GHT Byrd

CHANDLER Henry Col 22 S Wage-earner Acc Acc s/o Jane to Rose Williams Col 18 S Acc Acc d/o James & Harriet on 19 Dec 1894 at Acc C H by AJ Satchell

CHANDLER James 22 S Laborer Acc Acc s/o Leah to Leah Snead 21 S Acc Acc d/o Abel & Nannie on 16 Jan 1868 at Acc by WT Tull

CHANDLER James F 23 S Sailor Acc Acc s/o James & Nancy to Arninida (Arminda) Taylor 22 S Acc Acc d/o Mathew H & Kessie on 17 Nov 1874 at Acc by DA Woodson

CHANDLER James F 42 W Sailor Acc Acc s/o James & Nancy to Cora Belle [Thornes] Thorns 25 S Acc Acc d/o Dennis & Eveline on 13 Oct 1895 at Acc by MF Sanford

CHANDLER James Henry Col 22 S Wage-earner Acc Acc s/o Tamer West to Patience Elenora Parker Col 25 S Acc Acc d/o Hannah on 6 Jan 1889 at bride's home by JK Adams

CHANDLER Jehue (Jehu) (Col) 21 S Sailor Acc Acc s/o Alfred Rew & Sarah Chandler to Ellen Custis Col 20 S Acc Acc d/o Lewis Custis & Cadace Rew on Dec 1869 at Acc by JH Addison

CHANDLER John 31 S Painter s/o Edward & Mary to Margaret S Ames 17 S d/o Wm C & Elizabeth lic: 23 Jan 1865 marr: 24 Jan 1865

CHANDLER John 25 S Farmer Acc Acc s/o John & Sally to Alice Lee West 19 S Acc Acc d/o George R & Jane S on 20 Dec 1876 at Zion Bapt Ch by DA Woodson

CHANDLER John Col 23 S Day Laborer Acc Acc s/o Elizabeth to Louisa Fosque Col 22 S Acc Acc d/o Adah on 8 Sep 1882 at Savageville by F Wood

CHANDLER John J 25 S Farmer Acc Acc s/o Thos J & Julia W to Catharine Showard 21 S Acc Acc d/o Southey & Susan on 27 Nov 1872 at Reese Chp by JET Ewell

CHANDLER John M 21 S Farmer Acc Acc s/o Thos B & Sarah to Cynthia A Lewis 21 S Acc Acc d/o Jas & Cassandra on 9 Oct 1872 at Reese Chp by O Littleton

CHANDLER John T 22 S Farmer Acc Acc s/o Sylvester R & Nancy to Martha Fitzgerald 23 S Elizabeth City Co Acc d/o Thomas & Ann on 16 Nov 1870 at Onancock by E Hebard

CHANDLER Littl 63 W Farmer b: Acc s/o Nathan & Ellenor to Lucretia Ayres 47 W b: Acc d/o Sol & Elizth Gray & wid/o Levin Ayres on 13 Apr 1854 at r/o Littl Chandler by ES Grant

CHANDLER Lybrand M 22 S Waterman Acc Acc s/o Thomas R & Emily S to Rebecca A White 22 S Acc Acc d/o Elijah J & Susan D on 19 Mar 1895 at Acc by AJ Reamy

CHANDLER Mitchell H 24 S Farmer Acc Acc s/o Randal & Mary to Margt V Doughty 22 S Acc Acc d/o Edwd & Margt on 18 Dec 1877 at Onancock by JH Amiss

CHANDLER Sylvester Randall 25 S Accountant Acc Baltimore MD s/o Sylvester R & Mary A to Amanda Louise Mason 23 S Acc Acc d/o Thorogood & Eliz'th A on 27 Apr 1892 at Acc by JW Nicholson

CHANDLER Thomas J 23 S Sailor Acc Acc s/o Thos R & Emily to Alice A Hickman 18 S Acc Acc d/o Joseph &

Jane on 11 May 1887 at bride's father's by RA Compton

CHANDLER Thomas M 40 W Mechanic Acc Acc s/o Edwd & Mary to Mary A Kellam 35 S Acc Acc d/o Wm H & Sarah on 24 Jan 1886 at Acc by JE Humphreys

CHANDLER Thomas R 50 W Farmer Acc Acc s/o Bagwell & Ann to Harriet E Scott 23 S Acc Acc d/o James & Mary on 18 Mar 1889 at Onancock by JW Hundley

CHANDLER William E Col 21 S Farmer Acc Acc s/o George & Mary to Annie Pitts Col 22 S Acc Acc d/o John & Ellen on 27 May 1894 at Acc by JC Young

CHANDLER Wm D 23 S Farmer Acc Acc s/o Jno W & Elizth to Agnes M Boggs 24 S Acc Acc d/o Jno R & Leah on 17 Jan 1872 at Acc by O Littleton

CHANDLER Wm J Jr 17 S Oysterman Sussex Co DE Acc s/o Wm J & Sarah E to Sadia Birch 16 S Acc Acc d/o James S & Martha S on 14 Jun 1891 at Chinco: Isld by JW Turner

CHARNOCK Charles W 19 S Oysterman Acc Acc s/o Edward & Fanny to Julia [Dyes] Dies 22 S Acc Acc d/o Stephen & Alsie on 22 May 1875 at Tangier Isld by RC Jones

CHARNOCK Chas W 22 W Oysterman Acc Acc s/o Edwd & Fanny to Delilah Pruitt 18 S Acc Acc d/o Geo & Elizth on 31 Aug 1879 at Tangier Isld by WJ Duhadway

CHARNOCK Geo W 22 S Landman Acc Acc s/o Edwd & Sally to Elenor Dalby 30 S Acc Acc d/o Saml & Ann on 17 Jun 1862 at Acc by JWA Elliott

CHARNOCK John A 30 W Sailor Acc Acc s/o Joseph & Eliza to Mary J Dies 19 S Acc Acc d/o John & Matilda on 16 Aug 1888 at Tangier by GL Hardesty

CHARNOCK John E 21 S Waterman Acc Acc s/o Joseph & Eliza A to Betsy Ann [Parks] Parkes 23 S Acc Acc d/o John & Rachel on 19 Jun 1880 at Tangier Isld by LE Barrett

CHARNOCK John E 27 S Mariner Acc Acc s/o Edward C & Euphamia to Hettie J Crockett 17 S Acc Acc d/o Edward & Margaret on 15 Jul 1888 at Tangier by GL Hardesty

CHARNOCK Joseph 23 S Waterman Acc Acc s/o Wm & Nancy to Eliza A Charnock 22 S Acc Acc d/o Edwd & Susan on 14 Jul 1858 at Pungo: by M Oldham (Thomas Hall Kellam says both over 21)

CHARNOCK Lewis A 24 S Waterman Acc Acc s/o Joseph & Eliza to Maggie B [Parks] Parkes 21 S Acc Acc d/o Severn M & Matilda on 1 May 1894 at Tangier by WR Gwinn

CHARNOCK William 27 Seaman Acc N'hamp: s/o Thos & Nancy to Charlotte Lilliston 21 Acc Acc d/o Jno & Sally on 5 Jan 1858 at Pungo: by M Oldham (Robert Gray says he over 21)

CHARNOCK Wm 23 S Waterman Acc Acc s/o Joseph & Eliza to Catharine Moore 30 S Acc Acc d/o James & Maria on 1 May 1882 at Onancock by IG Fosnocht

CHASE Alravader F 23 S Oysterman Acc Acc s/o Alravader & Sally Ann to Jane Miles 21 S Acc Acc d/o David B & Mary J on 31 Dec 1884 at Mappsville by WA Street

CHASE Alsavada J 21 S Sailor Acc Acc s/o Teackle R & Ann Eliza to Bettie S Byrd 21 S Acc Acc d/o Geo P & Mary on 10 Jan 1877 near Messongo by DA Woodson

CHASE Alsavder to Sarah Davis d/o Henry who gave consent lic: 29 Sep 1856 Edward Anderton says he over 21

CHASE Columbus 22 S Waterman Acc

Acc s/o Teagle R & Ann Eliza to Annie E Lankford 22 S Acc Acc d/o Jas F & Ann on 30 Jun 1886 at Acc by WA Street

CHASE Emory J 22 S Waterman Acc Acc s/o Teagle & Ann Eliza to Amelia F Poulson 19 S Acc Acc d/o Marion J & Sarah on 25 Dec 1884 at Acc by WA Street

CHASE Henry R 24 S Waterman Acc Acc s/o Alsavada & Sally to Marseally Gladding 18 S Acc Acc d/o Calvin R & Elizth on 29 Dec 1886 at Acc by WA Street

CHASE Robert J 24 S Oysterman Acc Acc s/o William K & Elizabeth to Lulie Byrd 17 S Acc Acc d/o James J & Maggie on 21 May 1893 at Mappsville by JL King

CHASE Teackle T 23 S Mariner Acc Acc s/o Teackle R & Ann Eliza to Manie K Lankford 21 S Acc Acc d/o Louis James & Hester A on 5 Jun 1889 at bride's home by WA Street

CHASE Webster 22 S Waterman Acc Acc s/o Alsavada & Sally A to Hannah R Smith 18 S Acc Acc d/o James & Sally F on 13 Apr 1887 at A Chase's by JS Wharton

CHERRICKS Chas H [Chericks] 19 S Oysterman Chinco: Isld Chinco: Isld s/o Jno T & Mary A to Ellen Daisey 18 S Chinco: Isld Chinco: Isld d/o Jas & Catharien on 2 Oct 1886 at Acc by BF Jester

CHERRICKS George 21 S Sailor Acc Acc s/o John & Margt to Gozelle (Goselle) Thornton 19 S Acc Acc d/o Ann on 15 Jan 1875 at Chinco: Isld by WP Thornton

CHERRICKS George 21 S Oysterman Acc Acc s/o James & Eliza to Mary E Watson 18 S Acc Acc d/o John P & Elizabeth on 1 Mar 1895 at Chinco: Isld by SU Grimsley

CHERRICKS James [Cherix] 24 S Mariner Wor Co MD Chinco: Isld s/o Wm & Mary to Susan [Ferguson] Ferguson 22 S Chinco: Isld Chinco: Isld d/o James & Mary on 9 Sep 1857 at Chinco: Isld by WP Thornton (John A M Whealton says both over 21)

CHERRICKS Jan H [Chericks] 17 S Oysterman Chinco: Isld Chinco: Isld s/o James & Eliza to Alice Russell 16 S Chinco: Isld Chinco: Isld d/o Elijah & Charlotte on 13 Nov 1886 at Chinco: Isld by SU Grimsley

CHERRICKS Jas [Cherrix] 35 S Farmer Acc Acc s/o Arthar & Nancy to Eliza Thornton 33 S Acc Acc d/o Jas & Susan on 12 Nov 1863 at Acc by WP Thornton

CHERRICKS John J [Chericks] 23 S Oysterman Chinco: Isld Chinco: Isld s/o Jno & Susan to Martha E Bowden 15 S Wor Co MD Chinco: Isld d/o Henry C on 7 Mar 1886 at Chinco: Isld by SU Grimsley

CHERRICKS John T [Cherix] 21 S Sailor Acc Acc s/o John & Margt to Mary A Sharpley 18 S Acc Acc d/o Teagle & Euphania on 13 Jul 1866 at Acc by P Bowdin Sr

CHERRICKS John T Jr 21 S Oysterman Acc Acc s/o John T & Mary A to Mary E Jones 18 S Acc Acc d/o Major & Lucy A on 22 Feb 1894 at Chinco: Isld by RB Sanford

CHERRICKS Joshua 21 S Sailor Chinco: Isld Chinco: Isld s/o DAniel & Elizabeth to Elizabeth Jester single Chinco: Isld Chinco: Isld d/o Elijah & Patsey on 30 Mar 1861 at Chinco: Isld by P Bowdin Sr (Joseph Hill says both over 21)

CHERRICKS Michael [Cherick] 22 S Waterman Chinco: Isld Chinco: Isld s/o Daniel & Elizabeth to Mary Booth 20 S Horntown Chinco: Isld d/o Crippen & Maria on 11 Dec 1859 at Chinco: Isld by WP Thornton

CHERRICKS Thomas [Chericks] 22 S

Oysterman Acc Acc s/o John J & Susan to Della Bowden 15 S Acc Acc d/o Mary Lewis on 18 Feb 1888 at Chinco: Isld by RI Watkins

CHERRICKS Wm 22 S Oysterman Acc Acc s/o James & Susan to Susan [Tindle] Tindall 16 S Acc Acc d/o Jas & Malinda on 31 Aug 1882 at Assateague Beach by WP Thornton

CHESSER Abbott 22 S Acc Acc s/o Jno & Susan to Emma Taylor 18 S Acc Acc d/o Thomas & Patsey on 16 Jan 1881 at Conquest Ch by M Oldham

CHESSER Albert J 46 S Oystering Acc Acc s/o Danuel & Elizabeth to Addie J Kellam 26 S Acc Acc d/o John W & Indianna on 11 Jul 1888 at Pungo: by JH Riddick

CHESSER Henry T 23 S Farmer Acc Acc s/o Henry & Mary to Ruth Bull 17 S Acc Acc d/o George & Mary on 2 Feb 1879 at Assawoman by JW Hundley

CHESSER John to Susan Northam d/o Elizabeth lic: 10 Feb 1858 John Mears of M says both over 21

CHESSER John 29 W Laborer Acc Acc s/o Eli & Lucinda to Zipporah Evans 31 W Acc Acc d/o David & Peggy Taylor on 9 Mar 1861 at Acc by JC Mears

CHESSER John C 32 W Laborer to Matilda Dix 23 W lic: 29 Aug 1864 marr: 29 Aug 1864 at Accomack

CHESSER Lambert H 31 S Mechanic Acc Acc s/o Robt & Betsy to Mary E Nock 20 S Acc Acc d/o Saml & Mary on 29 Dec 1875 at Temp'ville by JM Anderson

CHESSER Obed W 26 S Carpenter Acc Acc s/o Smith & Margt to Gertrude Taylor 23 S Acc Acc d/o Teagle & Sarah on 23 Jan 1884 at Acc by M Oldham

CHESSER Oliver 33 S Farmer Acc Acc s/o Robert & Betsy to Mary Frances Byrd 23 S Acc Acc d/o Thos & Ann on 28 Mar 1872 at Oak Hall by TM Poulson

CHESSER Purnell H 24 S Store Keeper Acc Acc s/o Eastus & Harriet to Theodosia Ayres 18 S Acc Acc d/o Robt & Emaline on 19 Dec 1883 at Temp'ville by M Oldham

CHESSER Robert W 27 S Farmer Acc Acc s/o Robt & Betsy to Mary Cath Taylor 19 S Acc Acc d/o Colmore L & Rosa Ann on 16 Mar 1873 at Wattsville by TM Poulson

CHESSER Sewell F 35 S Sailor Acc Acc s/o Robt & Betsy to Missouri Bayly 19 S Acc Acc d/o Lewis on 22 Dec 1878 at Temp'ville by M Oldham

CHESSER Thorogood 44 S Oysterman Acc Acc s/o Jas to Elizabeth Chesser 24 S Acc Acc on 30 Dec 1863 at Acc by GH Ewell

CHESSER Wm 22 S Farmer Acc Acc s/o Marcellus W & Caroline to Clara Winder 19 S Acc Acc d/o Jno A & Mary on 20 Jan 1886 at New Church by TM Poulson

CHESSER Wm P 25 S Oysterman Acc Acc s/o Henry & Mary to Bettie F Nock 17 S Acc Acc d/o George W & Delilah on 16 Dec 1885 at Temp'ville by M Oldham

CHRISTAN Rubert G 22 S Mason Acc Acc s/o Wm S & Sarah to Julia Savage 21 S Acc Acc d/o Edwd G & Elizth on 29 Nov 1883 near Onancock by WC Vaden

CHURCH Henry Col 48 S Farmer Acc Acc to Henrietta Snead Col 39 S Acc Acc d/o Peter on 16 Sep 1871 near Locustville by N Morris

CHURCH John Col 22 S Sailor Acc Acc s/o Sally Parker to Susan Bayly Col 22 S Acc Acc d/o Bridget on 29 Jul 1873 at Acc by JE Humphreys

CHURN Alances S 25 S Capenter Acc Acc s/o Edwd & Polly to Virginia Colonna 19 S Acc Acc d/o Alfred &

Mary on 28 Dec 1886 at Hallwood by AD Davis

CHURN Henry K widr to Rose Ann Justice d/o Saml Justice (of R) Senr lic: 19 Sep 1854 Wm Taylor of C says she over 21

CHURN Henry K widr to Eveline J Boggs lic: 24 Jul 1860 E J Gillispie says she was over 21

CHURN John E 25 S Teacher Acc Acc s/o Wm W & Sally to Cath T (Catharine) Lilliston 15 S Acc Acc d/o John S & Ann & (ward/o Edwd G Grant who gave consent) on 19 May 1859 at Jno W Cordgate's by ES Grant

CHURN John W L 23 S Bar Keeper Acc Acc s/o Jno E & Kate to Anna A Lewis 21 S Acc Acc d/o Wm J & Margt on 31 Dec 1884 at Acc by AJ Walter

CHURN Laban C 22 S Milling Acc Acc s/o Edward & Polly to Frances S Caruthers 17 S Acc Acc d/o James W & Eilz'th W on 20 Dec 1888 at Onancock by JW Hundley

CLARK Charles S 24 S Oysterman Acc Acc s/o Elias & Eliza to Mary Whealton 18 S Acc Acc d/o Margaret Bishop on 6 Jan 1895 at Chinco: Isld by SU Grimsley

CLARK Eilas 26 S Sailor NJ Acc s/o Thos & Elizabeth to Eliza Taylor 29 W Chinco: Isld Acc d/o Robt & Bridget Snead on 4 Jul 1863 at Acc by P Bowdin Jr

CLARK George H 20 S Oysterman Acc Acc s/o Leonard & Charlotte A to Mamie M Carter 15 S Acc Acc d/o George & Maggie on 31 Mar 1892 at Chinco: Isld by JW Turner

CLARK John S 18 S Oysterman Acc Acc s/o Samuel & Comfort to Lizzie J Birch 17 S Acc Acc d/o David H & Mary Frances on 31 Dec 1892 at Chinco: Isld by RB Sanford

CLARK Lenard 18 S Oysterman NJ Acc s/o Thos & Elizabeth to Charlotte A [Chericks] Cherricks 17 S Acc Acc d/o Arthur & Caroline on 20 Feb 1869 at Acc by P Bowdin Jr

CLARK Odell [Clock] 22 S Sailor Long Isld NY Long Isld NY s/o S W & Amand to Mary J O Lewis 18 S Acc Chinco: Isld d/o Jno & Sarah now Sarah Snead on 30 Mar 1884 at Chinco: Isld by SU Grimsley

CLARK Oliver 26 S Sailor Acc Acc s/o Elias & Eliza to Airy Porter 18 S Acc Acc d/o Wm J & Mary on 19 Jun 1890 at Chinco: Isld by GE Wood

CLARK Saml 31 S Mariner NJ Acc s/o Jas & Elizabeth to Elizabeth C Loun 21 S Chinco: Isld Acc d/o Jas & Elizabeth on 7 Apr 1863 at Acc by WP Thornton

CLARK Thomas 25 S Seafaring NJ Chinco: Isld s/o Thos & Eliz to Anna M Whealton 18 S Chinco: Isld Chinco: Isld d/o Dan & Mary A on 30 May 1877 at Chinco: Isld by R Williamson

CLARK Thomas 20 S Sailor Chinco: Isld Chinco: Isld s/o Samuel & Comfort to Mary E Rhodes 15 S NY Watchapreague d/o Washngton & Mary E on 29 Aug 1885 at Locust Mount by JWA Elliott

CLARK Thomas 41 W Sailor Atlantic Co NJ Acc s/o Thomas & Elizabeth to Susan Wimbrough 28 W N'hamp: Acc d/o William & Annie Harrison on 12 Oct 1892 at Chinco: Isld by RB Sanford

CLAVILLE George 22 S Sailor Acc Acc s/o Jas & Mary to Ellen Thornton 20 S Acc Acc d/o Ann Tarr on 9 May 1866 at Acc by WP Thornton

CLAVILLE James 19 S Oysterman Acc Acc s/o James & Mary to Elizabeth Bloxom 17 S Acc Acc d/o Richd & Patience on 20 Jan 1868 at Acc by P Bowdin Jr

Marriages

CLAVILLE John H 20 S Oysterman Acc Acc s/o George O & Ellen to Ellen Snead 15 S Acc Acc d/o Thomas & Alice on 14 May 1887 at Chinco: Isld by SU Grimsley

CLAVILLE William [Clavel] (Claville) 28 S Sailor Wor Co MD Chinco: Isld s/o James & Hester to Erista E B R (Vesta) Whealton 17 S Chinco: Isld Chinco: Isld d/o William & Tabitha on 20 Dec 1855 at r/o P Bowdin by P Bowdin (John A M Whealton says he over 21)

CLAYTON George Col 21 S Wage-earner Acc Acc s/o Harry & Jane to Mary Downing Col 22 S Acc Acc d/o Mary on 4 Sep 1888 at Acc by JK Adams

CLAYTON George T 32 S Gentleman Acc Acc s/o Thomas R & Hetty to Virginia L Mason 22 S Acc Acc d/o James & Sarah on 9 Dec 1874 at Woodstock by IT Adkins

CLAYTON Henry Col 43 S Laborer Acc Acc to Sally White Col 35 S Acc Acc d/o Sally on 13 Jun 1886 at Acc by AJ Satchell

CLAYTON John F Col 26 S Oysterman Acc Acc to Eve Sherwood Col 19 S Acc Acc d/o Mary on 15 Nov 1885 near Lee Mont by CA Horsey

CLAYTON John Hy Col 24 S Farm Laborer Acc Acc s/o Rosy Hickman to Kitty White Col 23 S Acc Acc d/o Sinah on 3 May 1885 at Metompkin Bapt Ch by AJ Satchell

CLAYTON Smith Col 30 S Farmer Acc Acc s/o Sallie Summers to Harriet Downing Col 22 S Acc Acc d/o Julia Ann on 7 Nov 1878 at the Parsonage by A Handy

CLAYTON Thos G 33 S Farmer Acc Acc s/o Geo & S R to Mary S Wessells 18 S Acc Acc d/o Russel & Polly on 24 Dec 1863 at Acc by ES Grant

CLEMENT Charles 29 S Minister Campbell Co Acc s/o Chas B J & Kate S to Clara T Churn 23 S Acc Acc d/o Edward T & Amret on 28 Nov 1894 at Acc by JL King

CLIFFORD George W Col 21 S Laborer Baltimore MD Acc to Oceanna Kellam Col 19 S Acc Acc d/o Mary on 11 Nov 1880 at Belle Haven by SMG Copeland

CLOWS Peter J (Claws) 50 W Steward b: Sussex Co DE s/o Isaac & Sarah to Sarah Jane Mears 42 W b: Acc d/o Benj & Ann Annis & (wid/o John B Mears) on 7 Nov 1855 at Pungo: by M Oldham

CLUFF George W 20 S Sailor Acc Acc s/o Littleton & Nancy to Mary A Taylor 19 S Sussex Co Acc d/o Chls & Hulda on 5 Apr 1872 at Chinco: Isld by P Bowdin Sr

CLUFF Hiram C 20 S Oysterman Acc Acc s/o James & Elizabeth to Sarah E Carpenter 15 S Acc Acc d/o John & Eliz'th on 1 Mar 1890 at Chinco: Isld by BP Truitt

CLUFF James 21 S Sailor Acc Chinco: Isld s/o Littl T & Nancy to Elizabeth [Dazy] Daisey 17 S Chinco: Isld Chinco: Isld d/o Parker & Elizabeth on 9 Feb 1860 at Chinco: Isld by P Bowdin Sr (Daniel Whealton says he over 21)

CLUFF James 21 S Farmer Acc Acc s/o Mollie Savage to Rachel Brown 18 S Acc Acc d/o James on 9 May 1869 at Acc by A Joynes

CLUFF James 40 W Sailor Horntown Chinco: Isld s/o Litton T & Nancy L to Nancy E Wharton 16 S Chinco: Isld Chinco: Isld d/o Henry & Nancy on 17 Dec 1881 at Chinco: Isld by WP Thornton

COARD Benjamin Thomas Col 24 S Farmer Acc Acc s/o Maria to Sabra Jane Parker Col 27 S Acc Acc d/o Major & Sabra on 20 Apr 1881 at Presby Manso by JG Anderson

COARD Calvin Col 21 S Laborer Acc Acc s/o Elizth to Milly Hargis Col 18 S Acc Acc d/o Charlotte on 26 Dec 1877 near New Church by JC Cluff

COARD Charles 21 S Farmer Acc Acc s/o Jno & Nancy to Maggie E Bishop 19 S Acc Acc d/o Geo & Susan on 11 Nov 1883 at Hunting Ck by AJ Walter

COARD Charles R 22 S Editor of Paper Acc Acc s/o Wm R & Betsie W to Nancy Rew 18 S Acc Acc d/o Richard S & Nancin N on 29 Nov 1860 at Rew School House by ES Grant (John W Coard says he over 21)

COARD Charles R 28 W Farmer Acc Acc s/o John W & Nancy B to Carrie S Gunter 22 S Acc Acc d/o Edward M & Melissa on 24 Mar 1889 at Acc by W Chinn

COARD Chas R 30 W Farming Acc Acc s/o Wm R & Elizabeth to Mary V Whittington 25 S Baltimore City Acc d/o Druscilla & Jno on 6 Sep 1870 at Acc by JET Ewell

COARD Eslie T Col 28 S Carpenter Acc Acc s/o Jno & Nancy to Lelia M Kellam Col single Acc Acc d/o Elijah L on 9 Dec 1875 at Drum'tn by FR Boston

COARD James to Maria Taylor wid lic: 24 Apr 1854 George Wallop says he over 21

COARD John R 24 S Farmer Acc Acc s/o John W & Nancy B to Arinthia Mason 18 S Acc Acc d/o William & Tabitha on 20 Dec 1876 near Wiseville by FH Mullineaux

COARD Levi Col 39 S Wage-earner Acc Acc s/o Levi to Harriet Ann [Douglas] Douglass Col 25 S Acc Acc on 3 Jan 1889 at Wattsville by N Morris

COARD Oliver H 22 S Carpenter Acc Acc s/o George S & Harriet to Cornelia Young 24 S Acc Acc d/o William & Susan on 26 Dec 1888 at Onancock by JW Hundley

COARD S R 48 W Carpenter Acc Chinco: Isld s/o William & Nancy to Elizabeth Thornton 35 W Acc Chinco: Isld d/o Jno & Elizth Russell on 27 May 1880 at Chinco: Isld by R Williamson

COARD Wellington 22 S Mechanic Acc Acc s/o George & Harriet to Williana Young 18 S Acc Acc d/o Wm & Susan on 2 Dec 1874 at Zion Ch by DA Woodson

COARD William M 23 S Farmer Acc Acc s/o Jno W & Nancy B to Annie A Grant 22 S Acc Acc d/o Edwd L & Tabitha J on 12 Nov 1873 at Wiseville by O Littleton

COARD Wm F 21 S Farmer Acc Acc s/o Geo & Harriet to Sarah K Wessells 18 S Acc Acc d/o Ephraim & Nancy on 12 Feb 1879 near Drum'tn by FH Mullineaux

COBB (also see CABB)

COBB James W 26 S Sailor Acc Acc s/o Wm T & Virginia to Sarah Ann Parker 24 S Acc Acc d/o Lewis & Ann on 6 Aug 1894 at Acc C H by JM Dunaway

COBB John 43 S Mechanic b: Acc s/o William & Mary to Alsie East 36 S b: Acc d/o Severn & Levenia on 25 Sep 1855 at r/o Littl K Lecato by LK LeCato (John P Walker says they over 21)

COBB John 40 W Carpenter to Margaret Bradford 28 S d/o Wm lic: 26 Dec 1864

COBB Leonidas J 21 S Farmer Acc Acc s/o William T to Mary S Savage 18 S Acc Acc d/o Robert F & Elizabeth on 30 Dec 1891 at Acc by AC Berryman

COBB Wm T 21 S Farming Acc Acc s/o Jas & Leah to Sarah Jane Willett 18 S Acc Acc d/o Wm & Eliz on 12 Aug 1865 at Acc by JWA Elliott

COBEY Joshua 30 W Farmer Carol Co

Talbert Co s/o Wm & Mary to Mary Watkinson 33 W Acc Acc d/o Wm & Susan Hall on 18 Dec 1862 at Acc by D Titlow

COLE Joseph Jr 27 S Carpenter Baltimore City MD Acc s/o Joseph & Rose A to Minnie G [Twyford] Twiford 21 S Acc Acc d/o Thomas W on 3 Jan 1881 at Onancock by GH Ray

COLEBURN Alfred A 33 S Acc Acc s/o Saml C & Dorinda to Margaret S Ayres 26 S Acc Acc d/o Jno & Margt on 27 Jan 1869 at Acc by OP Twiford

COLEBURN Edward Col 27 S Laborer Acc Acc s/o Matilda to Juliet Taylor Col 26 S Acc Acc d/o Betsy on 20 Jul 1881 at Locust Mount by JWA Elliott

COLEBURN George (C) single Shoemaker Acc Acc s/o George & Mary to Juliet (Julia) Downing single Acc Acc d/o Francis (dec'd) & Betsey on 19 Oct 1857 at r/o Francis Downing by JW Ewell (lic: 10 Apr 1854 J W Elliott says both over 21 & lic: 16 Oct 1857 Edward J Bull says both over 21)

COLEBURN George B Col 22 S Farmer Acc Acc s/o Matilda to Ella C Ames Col 23 S Acc Acc d/o Samuel & Margaret on 6 Aug 1882 at Acc by JE Humphreys

COLEBURN George R [Colbourn] 35 S Merchant Sussex Co DE Acc s/o Jeremiah & Eliz'th to Ida V Jones 19 S Acc Acc d/o John J & Louisa on 17 Jul 1890 at Chinco: Isld by GE Wood

COLEBURN George W 33 S Carpenter Acc Acc s/o John & Elizth to Margaret S Kellam 34 W Acc Acc on 31 Jul 1867 at Acc by JWA Elliott

COLEBURN Henry 31 S Sailor Acc Acc s/o Arina to Sarah Topping 23 S Acc Acc d/o Fanny on 23 Aug 1866 at Acc by D Titlow

COLEBURN James Col 20 S Farmer Acc Acc s/o Henry & Sarah to Recie Becket Col 21 S Acc Acc d/o Major & Janie on 13 Jan 1895 at Acc by J Duckett

COLEBURN Jefferson [Colbourn] Col 33 S Carpenter Acc Acc s/o Milly Melborun to Josephine Brown Col 17 S Acc Acc d/o Ida Copes on 26 Dec 1894 at Acc by JC Cluff

COLEBURN Jno F widr to Nervilla E Ames d/o Zadock on 7 Nov 1852 by J Allen

COLEBURN John W 24 S Farmer s/o John & Elizabeth to Annie C Twiford 16 S d/o Thomas W & Mary E lic: 17 Apr 1865 marr: 21 Apr 1865

COLEBURN Lewis Col 57 S Farmer Acc Acc s/o Bricka to Margaret Dix Col 32 W Acc Acc on 9 Dec 1875 near News Town by A Joynes

COLEBURN Lewis Col 70 W Farmer Acc Acc s/o Bricker to Sarah Ann [Connor] Conner Col 50 W Acc Acc d/o Rich & Tamay Stephens on 3 Oct 1894 at Acc by AJ Wallace

COLEBURN Louis Col 24 S Laborer Acc Acc s/o Bridget Turlington to Tabitha Allen Col 23 S Acc Acc d/o Esther on 16 Jun 1881 at Drum'tn by PM Lewis

COLEBURN Robert P 18 S Printer Acc Acc s/o William C & Sally A to Mary A Wharton 20 S Culpepper Co VA Acc d/o John S & Ella D on 25 Dec 1889 at Lee Mont by WA Street

COLEBURN William 25 S Laborer Acc Acc s/o Hannah to Martha W Matthews 18 S Acc Acc d/o Henry on 1 Sep 1867 at Acc by S Marshall

COLEBURN William C 25 S Merchant Acc Drum'tn s/o James & Sally to Sarah A Ross 19 W Acc Drum'tn d/o James P & Margaret Taylor & wid/o William H Ross on 23 Feb 1858 at Locustville by JF Chaplain (J W

Gillet says he over 21)

COLEBURN Wm J 24 S Merchant Acc Acc s/o Wm C & Sally to Cordie A Lewis 24 S Acc Acc d/o John E & Margt Susan on 20 May 1884 at Onancock by WC Vaden

COLICK William 24 S Laborer Sussex Co DE Acc s/o James & Nancy to Sarah A Lewis 20 S Acc Acc d/o John & Eliza on 24 Feb 1869 at Acc by P Bowdin Jr

COLLICK John Col (mulatto) 39 S Laborer Acc Acc s/o Littleton & Leah to Susan Justice Col (mulatto) 39 S Acc Acc d/o George & Rosy on 2 Aug 1872 at Sexes Isld by M Oldham

COLLINS Alex (Alexander) C FN 21 S Mechanic Acc Acc s/o Griffin (Tabby Mears) to Mary Sample FN 24 S Acc Acc d/o Litt & Mary on 3 Dec 1862 at Acc by JWA Elliott (lic: 24 Nov 1862)

COLLINS Burnis 25 S Oysterman Acc Egg Harbor NJ s/o Jno & Rebecca to Sarah E Jester 18 S Acc Acc d/o Wm & Emily on 31 May 1881 at Chinco: Isld by OS Walton

COLLINS Caleb Col 60 W Farmer N'hamp: N'hamp: s/o Major & Luky to Jane Outten Col 35 W Acc Acc d/o Arthur & Catharine Taylor on 2 Sep 1891 at Franktown by T Peeden

COLLINS David D 26 S Oysterman Sussex Co DE Acc s/o James & Marinda to Jane Holloway 17 S Sussex Co DE Acc Acc d/o Norris & Jane on 6 Sep 1873 at Chinco: Isld by P Bowdin Sr

COLLINS Eba W 28 W Waterman Acc Acc s/o Eli & Mary to Cornelia Collins 22 S Acc Acc d/o Richd & Mary on 14 Feb 1877 at Greenbackville by IT Adkins

COLLINS Eli Curtis 24 S Waterman Acc Acc s/o Eba W & Isabelle to Lelia G [Colburne] Coleburn 18 S Wor Co MD Acc d/o Thos F & Matilda E on 27 Jun 1895 at Greenbackville by AS Bean

COLLINS Frederick Col 22 S Wage-earner N'hamp: Acc s/o James Collins & Edith Savage to Adah Bayly Col 22 S N'hamp: Acc d/o Betsy on 30 Oct 1895 at Belle Haven by J Savage

COLLINS Irving Col 37 W Oysterman Wor Co MD Acc to Gallie Townsend Col 22 S Acc Acc d/o John H & Martha on 9 Jul 1888 at Horntown by N Morris

COLLINS James Col 50 W Farmer Acc Acc s/o Betsy Watson to Jane Dennis Col 30 S Acc Acc d/o Jno & Mary on 17 Nov 1885 at Shilo Bapt Ch by TW Nettles

COLLINS James Col 45 W Wage-earner MD Acc s/o James & Matilda to Mary H Hargis Col 24 S Acc Acc d/o Peter & Harriet on 25 Dec 1892 at New Church by TM Poulson

COLLINS James S 35 W Oysterman Acc Acc s/o Edwd & Harriet T to Sallie Dunton 30 S Acc Acc d/o John & Kessie on 4 Dec 1884 at Acc by TM Poulson

COLLINS John 21 S Oysterman Sussex Co DE Acc s/o Charles & Hester to Sarah Tarr 17 S Acc Acc d/o James E on 8 May 1887 at Chinco: Isld by SU Grimsley

COLLINS Levi FN 50 S Oysterman Acc Acc s/o Geo Hickman & Milla Wise to Esther (-----) FN 50 S Acc Acc d/o Ephrain James & Dinal Leamore on 12 Apr 1868 at Acc by P Bowdin Sr

COLLINS Mark Col 26 S Farmer Acc Acc s/o Gordon Kellam & Sally Gordon to Kitty West Col 26 S Acc Acc d/o Nellie on 10 Apr 1881 at New Boston by TW Nettles

COLLINS Nathaniel (Col) 32 W

Marriages

Mariner N'hamp: Acc s/o John Coston & Phoeba Collins to Margt [Scarbugh] Scarborough (Col) 28 S Acc Acc d/o Thomas Davis & Maria Scarbugh on 21 Sep 1870 at Savageville by WF Williams

COLLINS Peter W 26 S Waterman Sussex Co DE Acc s/o Eli & Mary to Leah L Peyton 21 S Wor Co MD Acc d/o William & Mary on 1 Feb 1871 at Greenback by JE Maloy

COLLINS Scarburgh Col 22 S Farmer Acc Acc s/o Sarah Walker to Emma Savage Col 17 S Acc Acc d/o Robert & Caroline on 10 Mar 1895 at Acc by TW Nettles

COLLINS Southey 21 S Farmer Acc Acc s/o Frances to Lottie (West) Ames 25 W Acc Acc on 27 Dec 1868 at Acc by WF Williams

COLLINS Thos J 28 S Oysterman Acc Acc s/o Littleton T & Eliz'th J to Laura E Pusey 22 S Som Co MD Acc d/o Wm H & Henrietta on 14 Jun 1891 at Oak Hall by JS Wallace

COLLINS William Col 21 S Laborer N'hamp: Acc s/o Wilcher & Mary to Ellen D Ewell Col 21 S Acc Acc d/o Jesse & Louisa on 27 Aug 1885 at Folly Land by LW Lee

COLLINS William T 22 S Waterman Acc Acc s/o Sarah to Willieanna Stant 23 S Acc Acc d/o John on 24 Dec 1889 at Acc by JE Bundick

COLLINS Wm J 20 S Oysterman Sussex Co DE Chinco: Isld s/o Chas & Hester to Maria Brasure 16 S Sussex Co DE Chinco: Isld d/o Joshua H & Elizth on 7 Feb 1886 at Chinco: Isld by JD Reese

COLONNA Alfred to Mary Dix d/o Wm H who gave consent lic: 11 Jan 1860 Richard Lewis said he over 21

COLONNA Allen Obed [Colona] 30 S Mechanic N'hamp: Acc s/o Wm & Louisa to Amelia Emma McMath 18 S Acc Acc d/o Saml & Elizth on 30 May 1877 near Pungo: by JE Humphreys

COLONNA Arthur B 25 S Farmer Acc Acc s/o Abel B & Margt to Annie T Ames 24 S Acc Acc d/o Richd T & Louisa on 7 Jan 1869 at Acc by JC Martin

COLONNA Arthur B [Colona] 24 S Carpenter N'hamp: N'hamp: s/o Wm & Louisa to Willie A [Mackmath] McMath 19 S Acc Acc d/o Saml & A E on 12 Dec 1877 at Middlesex Acc Co by JE Humphreys

COLONNA Chas F [Colona] 26 S Clerk Acc Acc s/o Wm C & Mary to Jennie C Bull 16 S Acc Acc d/o George W & Eliz'th on 15 Nov 1891 at Pastoria by GF Farring

COLONNA Edward T [Colona] 20 S Farmer Acc Acc s/o William & Charlotte to Manie E Hickman 17 S Acc Acc d/o Robert W & Elizabeth on 3 Nov 1889 at Lee Mont by JS Wharton

COLONNA Elijah 40 W Farmer & Carpenter Guilford Acc to Mary Bundick 21 S Acc Acc on 27 Dec 1860 at Richard Sparrow's by GH Ewell (A J Taylor says she over 21)

COLONNA Elijah James [Colona] 22 S Farmer Acc Acc s/o Elijah & Mary E to Miranda W Scott 18 S Acc Acc d/o Walter & Margaret on 1 Oct 1890 at Drum'tn by WJ Twilley

COLONNA Everett [Colona] 23 S Sailor Acc Acc s/o John to Annie Andrews 18 S Acc Acc d/o Wm & May on 6 Nov 1886 at Chinco: Isld by SU Grimsley

COLONNA George D H 34 W Farmer Acc Acc s/o Jno W & Susan to Sallie [Shepard] Shepherd 34 W Acc Acc d/o Joseph & Maier Henderson on 25 Jan 1867 at Acc by GW Matthews

COLONNA Henry W [Colona] 25 S Farmer Acc Acc s/o Edwd to Lillie A Birch 15 S Acc Acc d/o Wm P &

Sarah on 14 Feb 1886 at Chinco: Isld by SU Grimsley

COLONNA Jas 27 S Farmer Acc Acc s/o Wm & Sally to Mary F Tipton 21 S Acc Acc d/o Ephraine & Nancy on 20 Dec 1871 at Acc by JE Humphreys

COLONNA Jno W 21 S Farmer Acc Acc s/o Jno T & Susan to Sarah E Kellam 22 S Acc Acc d/o Richd & Missouri on 4 Feb 1882 at Pungo: by CD Crawley

COLONNA John Col 24 S Laborer Acc Acc s/o George & Sally to Mary S Bayly Col 21 S Acc Acc on 9 Nov 1881 at Pungo: by TW Nettles

COLONNA John [Colona] Col 21 S Wage-earner Acc Acc s/o George & Sarah to Josephine Sample Col 23 S Acc Acc d/o James & Caroline on 22 Dec 1889 at bride's home by TW Nettles

COLONNA John E 23 S Sailor Acc Acc s/o Thomas & Ann to Sarah J Wallace 22 S Acc Acc d/o James D & Elizth on 28 Dec 1871 at Acc by OP Twiford

COLONNA John Edward 23 S Farmer Acc Acc s/o Elijah & Mary E to Sally L Mason 26 W Acc Acc d/o Edward & Betsy Gray on 19 Dec 1894 at Acc by WF Hayes

COLONNA John R 47 W Farmer Acc Acc s/o Jno & Susan to Olivia Jane Merrill 30 W Acc Acc d/o Edward Thornton on 22 Jan 1871 at Acc by TM Poulson

COLONNA John T 21 S Harness Mkr Acc Acc s/o Edwd & Mary Ann to Susan E Chandler 19 S Acc Acc d/o Edwd & Mary on 18 Mar 1857 at Acc by M Oldham (Geo B Robbins says he over 21)

COLONNA John W 21 S Waterman Acc Acc s/o Wm C & Mary to Mary Virginia Parkes 15 S Acc Acc d/o Wm J & Sally on 2 Mar 1881 at Onancock by SC Boston

COLONNA John W [Colona] 28 S RR Agent Acc Acc s/o R W & Annie B to Rachel W Blackstone 26 S Acc Acc d/o Thos W & Sarah on 20 Nov 1895 at Pungo: by HL Derby

COLONNA Major Col 52 W Laborer Acc Acc s/o Manuel & Serrena to Sophia Outten Col 43 W Acc Acc d/o Parker & Mary West on 4 Dec 1883 at Acc by TW Nettles

COLONNA Robert [Colona] 37 W Oysterman Acc Acc s/o John R & Eliza to Winnoa Pruitt 18 S Acc Acc d/o John S & Mary Ann on 24 Jul 1895 at Chinco: Isld by SU Grimsley

COLONNA Robert L 24 S Plasterer Acc Acc s/o Elijah & Mary E to Susan L [Shreaves] Shrieves 19 S Acc Acc d/o Louis F & Susan on 11 Jan 1888 at Drum'tn by JW Hundley

COLONNA Thomas C Col 21 S Laborer Acc Acc to Leah J Wise Col 18 S Acc Acc d/o Sandy & Lydis on 19 Mar 1879 at Belle Haven by JE Humphreys

COLONNA Tully S 25 S Oysterman Acc Acc s/o Wm & Sally to Eleshea Ann Hart 25 S Acc Acc d/o John & Eleshea on 27 Dec 1876 at Leatherbury Chp by PA Leatherbury

COLONNA William to Mary Berry d/o Charles lic: 28 Jan 1856

COLONNA William 22 S Farmer Acc Chinco: Isld s/o J to Patience [Bloxsom] Bloxom 19 S Acc Chinco: Isld d/o Wm & Tabitha on 12 Sep 1875 at Chinco: Isld by WP Thornton

COLONNA William [Colona] Col 24 S Wage-earner Acc Acc s/o Harriet to Mary S Duncan Col 17 S Acc Acc d/o Hezekiah J on 19 Apr 1892 at Acc by TW Nettles

COLONNA Edwd B (Coleman) 36 W Farmer Acc Acc s/o Jno W & Susanna to Emily Jane Ross 25 W Acc Acc d/o Thos & Margt

Brittingham on 3 Feb 1864 at Acc by GC Burriss

COLONY William 20 S Farmer Acc Acc s/o Arthur & Mary to Mary S Bradford 18 S Acc Acc d/o Jno E & Sarah on 8 Feb 1883 at Acc by SC Boston

CONANT Wm 21 S Carpenter Lynchburg VA Chinco: Isld s/o A W & Mary to Sarah E Melvin 17 S Chinco: Isld Chinco: Isld d/o Thos & Lydia on 19 Nov 1877 at Chinco: Isld by WP Thornton

CONAWAY Columbus 21 S Sailor Gloucester Co VA Acc s/o Eli & Mayr to Mary S Sparrow 21 S Acc Acc d/o John R & Jane on 9 Oct 1890 at Acc by JM Anderson

CONNER Benj C 27 S Teacher Som Co MD Williamsburg PA s/o Nathan C & Sally to Bettie S Tyler 28 S Acc Acc d/o Jno D & Rebecca on 16 Aug 1877 at Onancock M E Ch by GT Tyler

CONNER Charles H [Connor] Col 24 S Farmer Acc Acc s/o Jesse & Sarah A to Mary Poulson Col 21 S Acc Acc d/o James H & Mary on 28 Dec 1890 at Acc by J Duckett

CONNER Geo W 21 S Oysterman Acc Acc s/o Martin & Charlotte to Margt Jane Tarr 16 S Acc Acc d/o David & Mary on 9 Feb 1879 at Chinco: Isld by WP Thornton

CONNER George FN 32 S Farmer b: Acc s/o Geo & Hannah to Mary Fisher FN 27 S b: Acc d/o Judy Fisher (FN) on 12 Jan 1855 at Edmd Fisher's by C Hill

CONNER George T Col 38 S Blacksmith Acc Acc s/o Jesse & Sarah to Rachel E Custis Col 22 S Acc Acc d/o Thomas & Sarah on 6 Sep 1882 at Drum'tn by LW Lee

CONNER Jesse FN 26 S Blacksmith New Church Drum'tn s/o Geo & Hannah to Sarah Ann Stevens FN 17 S Drum'tn Drum'tn d/o Rica & Tamer on 26 Jan 1854 at r/o Rica Stevens by C Hill (Wm H Massey says he over 21)

CONNER Jesse D Col 21 S Laborer Acc Acc s/o Jesse & Sarah to Mary Lewis Col 18 S Acc Acc d/o Margaret on 13 Nov 1881 at Acc by RJ Waters

CONNER Jesse F Col 27 S Farmer Acc Acc s/o Geo & Mary to M Ida Dickerson Col 22 S Acc Acc d/o Arthur & Eliza on 20 Jan 1886 near Oak Hall by JC Cluff

CONNER Levin 30 S Shoemaker Acc Acc s/o Samuel & Emaline M to Virginia W Taylor 24 S Acc Acc d/o Colmore & Rosey on 31 May 1881 at Greenbackville by HC Stern

CONNER Wilmore [Connor] Col 22 S Wage-earner Acc Acc s/o George & Mary to Elizabeth Williams Col 20 S Acc Acc d/o Drucilla on 11 Jan 1891 at Wattsville by AS Amos

CONQUEST Alfred to Delilah Thornton wid lic: 31 Mar 1856 Wm B Savage says both over 21

CONQUEST Alfred Col 26 S Sailor Acc Acc s/o Leah to Drucilla Bayly Col 21 S Acc Acc d/o Arthur & Mary on 19 Jun 1873 at Acc by R Davis

CONQUEST Edmond Col 23 S Laborer Acc Acc s/o Lukey Young to Kate Bagwell Col 18 S Acc Acc d/o Ephraim & Ann on 26 Nov 1876 at Savageville by JK Plato

CONQUEST Edmund Col 30 S Laborer Acc Acc s/o Sabra to Aynes Cropper 25 S Acc Acc d/o Peter & Mary on 3 Jan 1886 at Acc by LW Lee

CONQUEST Frank 33 S Farmer Acc Acc s/o Alfred E & Delila to Alice L Holland 18 S Acc Acc d/o Edward T B & Mary A on 7 Nov 1888 at Mappsville by WA Street

CONQUEST George Col 22 S Laborer

Acc Acc s/o Sally to Mary J Douglass Col 18 S Acc Acc d/o Jane on 5 Nov 1879 at Temp'ville by JC Cluff

CONQUEST George Col 21 S Farmer Acc Acc s/o Sabra Custis to Fannie Ashby Col 19 S Acc Acc d/o Louisa on 2 Apr 1884 near Savageville by LW Lee

CONQUEST George Col 25 S Wage-earner Acc Acc s/o Harriet to Mary Trader Col 28 S Acc Acc d/o Nancy on 16 Jun 1895 at Temp'ville by GHT Byrd

CONQUEST George W Col 30 W Sailor Acc Acc s/o Major & Sabra to Bettie Gray Col 24 S Acc Acc d/o John H & Hannah on 24 Dec 1891 at Acc by BJ Hargarves

CONQUEST Harry Col 40 S Farmer Acc Acc s/o Major & Sabra to Caroline Bayly Col 38 S Acc Acc d/o John & Betsy on 6 Sep 1894 at Acc by PW Lee

CONQUEST Henry Col 40 S Farmer Acc Acc s/o Abram Warmer & Grace Conquest to Ada Chandler Col 40 S Acc Acc d/o Thos & Leah Laylor on 15 Dec 1869 near Deep Ck by S Marshall

CONQUEST James Col 30 W Laborer Acc Acc s/o Eliza to Elizabeth Sample Col 25 S Acc Acc d/o Jesse Annis & Emphemia on 18 Nov 1869 at Acc by A Joynes

CONQUEST James H Col 26 S Farmer Acc Acc s/o Levi & Mary to Emma S Ewell Col 25 S Acc Acc d/o Jesse & Louisa on 1 Jan 1880 at Drum'tn by RH Govans

CONQUEST John 26 S Laborer Acc Acc s/o Leah Chandler to Mary Ann Parker 27 S Acc Acc d/o Mahala on 21 Dec 1866 at Acc by WT Tull

CONQUEST John Col 28 S Farmer Acc Acc s/o Littleton & Hester to Ella B Kellam Col 23 S Acc Acc d/o George C & Lucinda on 24 Jan 1892 near Pungo: by JH Offer

CONQUEST Levi Col 23 S Farmer Acc Acc s/o Esther to Hester Kellam Col 20 W Acc Acc d/o Lucinda on 10 Aug 1876 at Savageville by JK Plato

CONQUEST Levi Col 60 S Farmer Acc Acc s/o Sniah to Mary Bagwell Col 60 S Acc Acc d/o James & Ibby on 28 Jun 1894 at Acc by PW Lee

CONQUEST Littleton Col 40 S Farmer Acc Acc s/o Grace to Esther Ashby Col 39 S Acc Acc d/o Tamar on 17 Jul 1871 at Deep Ck by N Morris

CONQUEST Louis Col 29 S Laborer Acc Acc s/o Mary to Margt Ann Williams Col 21 S Acc Acc d/o Rachel on 2 Feb 1876 at Metompkin by JW Ruff

CONQUEST Major Col 24 S Farmer Acc Acc s/o Major & Sabra to Mary J Phillips Col 21 S Acc Acc d/o George & Leah on 9 Aug 1888 at Acc by AJ Satchell

CONQUEST Nathaniel B 22 S Farmer Acc Acc s/o Nathaniel F & Ann to Josephine H Shield 17 S Acc Acc d/o Asa & Elizabeth on 29 Jan 1873 at Temp'ville by JE Potts

CONQUEST Nathl F 57 W Farmer b: Acc s/o Joseph & Mary to Caroline W Matthews 29 S b: Acc d/o Wm J & Ann P on 6 Apr 1854 at Chinco: Isld by T Waters (John W Matthews said she over 21)

CONQUEST Parker Col 23 S Wage-earner Acc Acc s/o Kitty to Araminta Drummond Col 21 S Acc Acc d/o John on 5 Jun 1889 at Onancock by JH Offer

CONQUEST Wilber J Col 21 S Laborer Acc Acc s/o Sally to Mary E Matthews Col 15 S Acc Acc d/o Martha on 13 Nov 1878 at Temp'ville by JC Cluff

CONQUEST William H 26 W Farmer Acc Acc s/o Alfred & Delilah to Ida

Marriages

L Taylor 16 S Acc Acc d/o Revel P & Louisa on 7 Jan 1891 at Temp'ville by WF Hayes

CONQUEST Wm H 20 S Farmer Acc Acc s/o Alfred E & Delia to Maggie L Savage 23 S Acc Acc d/o J J & Mary on 7 Jun 1885 at Temp'ville by M Oldham

CONRADES William 30 W Tonsorial Artist Baltimore MD Acc to Effie M Hopkins 20 S Acc Acc d/o Joseph I & Keziah on 26 Jun 1895 at Acc by AJ Reamy

COOPER Charles 23 S Farmer Wic Co MD Acc s/o Thomas D to Sarah Matthews 17 S Acc Acc d/o George & Emma on 24 Jul 1889 at New Church by TM Poulson

COOPER John G 33 S Farmer Wor Co MD Acc to Rebecca E Lawson 16 S Acc Acc d/o Wm & Hester on 29 Oct 1879 at Locust Mount by JWA Elliott

COOPER John G 46 W Teamster Wor Co MD Acc to Margaret Sturgis 40 W Acc Acc d/o Catharine Savage on 12 Dec 1894 at Acc by JR Sturgis

COOPER Joseph L 53 W Fisherman Derbyshire England Acc s/o George & Martha to Melissa D Marshall 33 W Acc Acc d/o David & Jane Crockett on 3 May 1894 at Tangier by WR Gwinn

COOPER Joseph L (S) 30 S Oysterman Derby England Acc s/o George & Martha to Matilda A Pruitt 22 S Acc Acc d/o William & Ellen on 8 Sep 1874 at Acc by RC Jones

COOPER Joseph L Jr 21 S Waterman Acc Acc s/o Joseph L & Matilda to Annie Teaser 21 S Acc Acc d/o Ann on 4 Jul 1895 at Tangier Isld by CP Swain

COPES Alfred Col 30 S Laborer Acc Acc s/o Henry Conquest & Margt Copes to Elizabeth Johnson Col 24 S Acc Acc d/o Saml & Hannah on 19 Oct 1879 at Temp'ville by JC Cluff

COPES Alfred Col 34 D Sawyer Acc Acc s/o Margaret to Arra Hall Col 32 W Acc Acc d/o Harriet Godwin on 3 Sep 1893 at Temp'ville by GHT Byrd

COPES Clayton Col 25 S Farmer Acc Acc s/o John & Catharine to Maggie Feddeman Col 16 S Acc Acc d/o Abel & Sarah on 25 Jan 1894 at Acc by JC Cluff

COPES Francis Col 25 S Laborer Acc Acc to Ida Savage Col 22 S Acc Acc d/o Mollie on 6 Jul 1879 at Temp'ville by JC Cluff

COPES George Col 23 S Farmer Acc Acc s/o Margaret to Caroline Selby Col 21 S Acc Acc d/o Sarah on 5 Jan 1876 at Mt Zion Chh by SP Whittington (lic: 24 Dec 1872)

COPES George T Col 36 W Laborer Acc Acc s/o Thomas Downing & Margaret Copes to Leah Hinman Col 29 W Acc Acc d/o Stewart & Hannah Downing on 6 Jul 1887 at Chinch Town by N Morris

COPES James E 22 S Farmer Acc Acc s/o Wm of T & Sophia to Caroline Mason 21 S Acc Acc d/o Wm & Tabitha on 21 Dec 1865 at Acc by ES Grant

COPES John widr to Mary Andrews d/o Robert Andrews dec'd & Catherine Fisher who gave consent lic: 13 Dec 1854

COPES John Col 21 S Laborer Acc Acc to Catharine Conquest Col 21 S Acc Acc d/o Sally on 13 Aug 1871 at Acc by A Joynes

COPES John B 23 S Waterman Acc Acc s/o Thomas L & Elizabeth W to Otelia S [Shreaves] Shrieves 21 S Acc Acc d/o John T & Margaret A on 19 Aug 1888 at Lee Mont by JW Norris

COPES John H 22 S Farmer Acc Acc s/o John H & Mary K to Willianna Fitzgerald 16 S Acc Acc d/o Thomas

H & Henrietta P on 6 Nov 1889 at Drum'tn by WJ Twilley

COPES Thomas L (John L) 25 S Farmer Acc Acc s/o William & Sophia to Elizabeth W Blackstone 28 S Acc Acc d/o Thos W & Ann P on 1 Dec 1859 at Ayres Chp by ES Grant (Thomas D Lewis says both over 21)

COPES Wm (William) 57 W Shoemaker N'hamp: Acc s/o Thomas & Jane to Margaret Susan Blackstone 35 S Acc Acc d/o Thos & Ann on 25 Oct 1860 at Ayres M E Ch by JA Massey (Louis B Drummond says both over 21)

COPES Wm T 25 S Farmer Acc Acc s/o Thos P & Nancy to Leah J Turlington 21 S Acc Acc d/o Saml M & Betsy on 28 Jun 1865 at Acc by BT Ames

CORBETT Edward E 23 S Clerk Acc Acc s/o Richd & Meranda to Theressa Crockett 17 S Acc Acc d/o Elisha & Lucy on 25 Dec 1885 at Tangier Isld by CS Baker

CORBILL James H (Corbitt) 23 S Blacksmith NC Acc s/o Wm & Elizth to Elizth Sturgis 25 S Acc Acc d/o Kondal & Betsy on 2 Jan 1867 at Acc by ES Grant

CORBIN Ames C 27 S Oysterman Acc Acc s/o James & Ellen to Drucilla C Bull 26 S Acc Acc d/o James W & Henrietta on 16 Oct 1881 at Messongo by M Oldham

CORBIN Corbin F D 22 S Oysterman & Farmer Acc Acc s/o James & Ellen to Mamie M Bunting 18 S Acc Acc d/o Henry C & Susan J on 23 May 1888 at Downings Ch by TG Pullen

CORBIN Cornelius 42 S Merchant Acc Acc s/o Stephen & Mary to Arinthia D Warner 25 S Acc Acc d/o Solomon & Arinthia on 2 Jan 1890 at Atlantic by JW Ward

CORBIN Covington 22 S Oysterman Acc Acc s/o James H & Ellen to Annie Lee Hall 17 S Acc Acc d/o Thomas & Jane on 9 Jun 1881 at Oak Hall by RB Beadles

CORBIN Daniel D 37 S Oysterman Acc Acc s/o Littleton & Mary to Maria L Nock 20 S Acc Acc d/o Samuel & Polly on 21 Dec 1882 at Mappsville by JW Hundley

CORBIN Edward J Col 48 S Oysterman Acc Acc s/o Betsy to Lydia Holden Col 43 S Acc Acc d/o Eliz on 27 Nov 1872 at Pocomoke Nk by M Oldham

CORBIN George Col 45 S Oysterman Acc Acc s/o Anina Hannon to Dina Coard Col 35 S Acc Acc on 11 May 1879 at Drum'tn by RH Govans

CORBIN George Col 65 W Wage-earner DE Acc s/o John to Lucy Parramore Col 50 S Acc Acc d/o Agnes on 3 Aug 1893 at Acc by AJ Satchell

CORBIN Isariah FN 23 S Teamster Acc Acc s/o Wm Watts $ R Corbin to Sally Duffy FN 25 S Acc Acc d/o Isaac & Scarborough on 6 Apr 1862 at Acc by JE Maloy

CORBIN James Col 25 S Sailor Acc Acc s/o Harriet to Hester Collins Col 15 S Acc Acc d/o Susan on 11 Aug 1875 at Acc by JE Bundick

CORBIN James Col 40 W Sailor Acc Acc s/o Harriet to Henrietta Fletcher Col 18 S Acc Acc d/o Sam's & Barbara on 1 Jul 1883 at Temp'ville by M Oldham

CORBIN James Edward Col 20 S Oysterman Acc Acc s/o Lydia to Sarah Jane Fletcher Col 18 S Acc Acc d/o Julia on 18 May 1873 at Pocomoke Nk by S Johns

CORBIN John Col 28 S Oysterman Acc Acc s/o Harriet to Elizabeth Godwin Col 24 S Acc Acc d/o Obed & Harriet on 4 Sep 1888 at Marsh Market by JC Cluff

CORBIN John W 35 W Farmer Acc

Acc s/o Rachel to Mary [Parks] Parkes 38 W Acc Acc d/o Samuel & Ann Brimer on 18 Jun 1871 at Acc by WT Wilkerson

CORBIN Levin Col 40 S Laborer Acc Acc s/o John & Airy to Ann Duncan Col 22 S Acc Acc d/o Sarah on 24 Aug 1875 at Horntown by S Johns

CORBIN Levin 48 W Oysterman Acc Acc s/o Sarah to Sarah [Crippin] Crippen Col 44 S Acc Acc d/o Alsie on 18 Apr 1881 near Horntown by PJ Adams

CORBIN Littleton J 40 S Merchant Acc Acc s/o Littleton to Carrie C Massey 23 S Acc Acc d/o John & Louisa on 21 Oct 1891 at Horntown by JS Wallace

CORBIN Raymond Col 21 S Oysterman Acc Acc s/o Harriet to Mary Foreman Col 21 S Acc Acc d/o Sewell & Maria on 1 Jan 1893 at Acc by JC Cluff

CORBIN Robert J 21 S Farmer Som Co MD Acc s/o Robert J & Mary A to Hortense Hall 20 S Acc Acc d/o Robt T & Susan E on 12 Mar 1884 at Hall's Store by M Oldham

CORBIN Stephen 23 S Waterman Acc Acc s/o Robert & Betsy to Missouri Miles single Acc Acc d/o Jesse T & Missouri on 16 May 1878 at Flag Pond by A Wiles

CORBIN Sylvester R 21 S Oysterman Acc Acc s/o James & Ellen to Susan A Smith 18 S Acc Acc d/o Wm H C & Rosy Ann on 26 Dec 1877 at bride's parents' by A Wiles

CORBIN Thos H Bayly 35 S Farmer Acc Acc s/o Peter D & Charlotte to Peggie E Parker 35 S Acc Acc d/o Tully W & Peggie E on 29 Nov 1882(?) at Lee Mont by FM Birch Certificate returned 6 Jun 1883

CORE Ernest Col 23 S Laborer Acc Acc s/o Sabra to Hester Joynes Col 40 W Acc Acc d/o Isaac Broghton on 7 Aug 1887 near Temp'ville by JC Cluff

CORE Golden F 21 S Farmer Acc Acc s/o John W & Amy to Mary A Young 17 S Acc Acc d/o Richard W & Susan M on 15 Nov 1882 at Onancock by SC Boston

CORE Jno W 28 S Farmer Acc Acc s/o Levin J & Mary A to Mary E Budd 21 S Acc Acc d/o Thos & Sarah on 22 Jan 1879 at Onancock by SC Boston

CORE John R 19 S Farmer Acc Acc s/o John W & Amy to Mary E Parkes 19 S Acc Acc d/o Noah & Mary A on 31 Mar 1875 at Wiseville by FR Boston

CORE Levin E 25 S Blacksmith Acc Acc s/o Levin to Sarah A Milliner 23 S Acc Acc d/o Jas H & Elizth on 15 Aug 1883 at Onancock by SC Boston

CORE Oliver Col 22 S Farmer Acc Acc s/o Telpha to Sarah Dickerson Col 16 S Acc Acc d/o Eliza on 25 Jan 1877 near Modest Town by A Joynes

CORE Walter Col 21 S Laborer Acc Acc s/o Comfort Core now Parker to Bettie Dix Col 17 S Acc Acc d/o Mary on 25 Sep 1884 at Acc by AJ Satchell

CORE William S 23 S Plasterer Acc Acc s/o Levin J & Mary to Ruhamah Burniette Flick 17 S Acc Acc d/o Christian D & Emma on 12 Nov 1885 at Acc C H by W Chinn

CORE William T 16 S Farmer s/o John W & Amy to Frances Parker 17 S d/o George W & Margaret lic: 29 Jun 1874 marr: 1 Jul 1874 at Littleton LeCato's

CORYELL Eli C 34 W Farmer Mercer Co NJ Acc s/o Cornelius & Sarah to Sudie M Lewis 33 S Acc Acc on 27 Mar 1895 at Mappsville by JL King

CORYELL Eli C [Caryell] 26 S Farmer NJ Acc s/o Cornelius & Sarah to Emma J Burroughs 22 S Acc Acc d/o

Ralph & Caroline E on 3 Jun 1886 at Acc by JW Carroll

CORYELL William A 25 S Farmer Mercer Co NJ Acc s/o Cornelius & Sarah to Martha F Fisher 25 S Acc Acc d/o James P & Hettie on 20 Oct 1895 at Modest Town by WW Wood

COSTEN Severn Col 22 S Sailor N'hamp: Acc s/o Leah to Louisa Watson Col 21 S Acc Acc d/o Susan on 27 Sep 1875 at Onancock by PA Leatherbury

COULLING David to Annie Wharton Parker d/o Geo Parker lic: 7 Aug 1855 James H Parker says both over 21

COURTNEY John R 22 S Farmer Cecil Co MD Acc to Sarah W Scott 22 S Acc Acc d/o John & Eliza on 10 Jun 1873 at Deep Ck by EM Bryan

COURTNEY John R 29 W Sailor Cecil Co MD Acc s/o Wm & Eliz to Elizabeth Lewis 33 S Acc Acc d/o Dan'l & Eliz on 26 Jun 1881 at Deep Cr Nk by PA Leatherbury

COVINGTON George W 35 S Carriage Maker Acc Acc s/o Royston & Nancy to Bettie Coleburn 35 S Acc Acc d/o Wn H & Hetty C on 24 Jan 1884 at New Church by M Oldham

COXTON Edward 21 S Farmer Acc Acc s/o Thomas & Mary to Mary Henderson 32 W Acc Acc d/o Jesse & Jane Bayly on 1 Dec 1889 at Drum'tn by WJ Twilley

COXTON Thomas 47 W Farmer Acc Acc s/o Wm & Nancy to Margaret Simpson 43 W Acc Acc d/o Wm & Elishea on 16 Jan 1884 at Acc by AJ Walter

COXTON Thomas A 24 S Farmer Acc Acc s/o Wm & Virginia to Lelia L Lewis 19 S Acc Acc d/o Wm T & Elizth on 20 Dec 1883 at Onancock by IG Fosnocht

COXTON Thos 26 S Farmer Acc Acc s/o Wm & Nancy to Mary Lilliston 30 W Acc Acc d/o Jesse & Mary Hancock on 3 Dec 1862 at Acc by ES Grant

COXTON Wm 22 S Tailor b: Drum'tn s/o Wm & Nancy to Virga (Wid/o Edward) West 26 W b: Drum'tn d/o Nathal & Nancy Ling on 10 Dec 1854 at Locustville by A Wallace (Asa Lilleston said both over 21)

CRAMMER Abram W 38 W Ship Carpenter NJ Acc s/o Jno & Mary to Sarah F Ardis 22 S Acc Acc d/o Wm & Margt on 1 Aug 1872 at Modest Town by DA Woodson

CRANDELL Wesley 58 W Oysterman Acc Acc to Rose L Allen 28 W Acc Acc on 5 Nov 1890 at Sykes Isld by JS Wallace

CRANE Arthur B 24 S Telegraph Operator Richmond Chinco: Isld s/o A Judson & Sarah E Florence to Halcyone Caulk 18 S Acc Chinco: Isld d/o C J & Cornelia E on 31 Aug 1886 at Chinco: Isld by SU Grimsley

CRANE Thos H 24 S Soldier (Army of the Potomac) Acc (Queen Ann Co MD) Acc s/o (Stephen M & Mary) to Ann E Hickman 23 S Acc Acc d/o (Kendall & Henretta R) on 23 Mar 1864 at Acc by GH Ewell

CRIPPEN Ambrose Col 24 S Oysterman Acc Acc to Elizabeth Logan Col 22 S Acc Acc on 20 Feb 1876 near Horntown by SP Whittington

CRIPPEN Edward (Crippin) FN to Emeline Bayly FN d/o Hannah who gave consent lic: 18 Mar 1856 Meshack Fisher says he over 21

CRIPPEN Ernest Col 22 S Wage-earner Acc Acc s/o Vena to Ida Finney 22 S Acc Acc d/o Nathaniel & Lucy on 26 Dec 1895 at Modest Town by DB Savage

CRIPPEN George Col 27 S Laborer Acc Acc s/o Sally to Sally Ann Crippen Col 25 S Acc Acc d/o Mary on 29 Dec 1870 at Temp'ville by M Oldham

CRIPPEN George Col 22 S Sailor Acc Acc s/o Elizth to Emma Phillips Col 18 S Acc Acc d/o Liddy on 27 Dec 1876 near Poor House by A Joynes

CRIPPEN Henry C Col 38 S Oysterman Acc Acc s/o Alicia Selby to Jane Marshall Col 45 S Acc Acc d/o Sarah on 20 Jul 1873 at Acc by S Johns

CRIPPEN James 22 S Sailor Acc Acc s/o Savage & Eliza to Martha Smith 18 S Acc Acc d/o James & Henny on 4 Jun 1882 at Chinco: Isld by JC Cluff

CRIPPEN James [Crippin] Col 22 S Oysterman Acc Acc s/o John & Frances to Mary Logan Col 21 S Acc Acc d/o Isaac & Eliza on 5 Jan 1893 at Chinco: Isld by RB Sanford

CRIPPEN John Col 27 S Laborer Acc Acc s/o Elizabeth to Harriet Fox Col 33 S Acc Acc d/o Leah on 28 Jan 1800 near News Town by A Joynes

CRIPPEN Louis 36 S Farmer Acc Acc s/o Eliza to Mary Floyd 45 S Acc Acc d/o Leah on 10 Nov 1879 at Drum'tn by RH Govans

CRIPPEN Nathaniel Col 24 S Farmer Acc Acc s/o Anna to Maggie V Northam Col 22 S Acc Acc d/o Ary on 31 Dec 1890 at Acc by AJ Satchell

CRIPPEN Samuel Col 21 S Laborer Acc Acc s/o John & Frances to Jane Logan Col 18 S Acc Acc d/o Iriash & Eliza on 1 Nov 1894 at Chinco: Isld by RB Sanford

CRIPPEN Spencer Col 19 S Wage-earner Acc Acc s/o Edward & Emaline to Rosana Byrd Col 16 S Acc Acc d/o Kelcey on 21 Sep 1890 at Acc by AJ Satchell

CRIPPEN Thomas Col 25 S Laborer Acc Acc s/o Thos & Elizth to Rose Ann Hickman Col 25 S Acc Acc on 21 Sep 1872 at Acc by A Joynes

CRIPPEN Thomas Col 21 S Oysterman Acc Acc s/o Matilda to Susan [Baily] Bayly Col 20 S Acc Acc d/o Jno & Betsy on 26 Jan 1880 at St Luke Ch by RH Govans

CRIPPEN Thomas Col 36 W Laborer Acc Acc s/o Elizabeth to Lucy Moore Col 28 S Acc Acc d/o Sarah on 29 Apr 1883 at Acc by AJ Satchell

CROCKETT Allen 23 S Sailor Acc Acc s/o Henry & Annie to Missouri Hart 23 S Acc Acc d/o James & Mary on 7 Jan 1875 at Onancock by JH Amiss

CROCKETT Andrew 21 S Oysterman Acc Acc s/o Major & Zipporah to Triffie Evans 21 S Acc Acc d/o Thos E & Rhoda on 17 Jun 1883 at Tangier Isld by CS Baker

CROCKETT Asbury 19 S Waterman Acc Acc s/o Major & Zipporah to Margaret Crockett 19 S Acc Acc d/o Jesse & Charlotte on 17 Apr 1881 at Wise Point by LE Barrett

CROCKETT Benjamin 22 S Sea Captain Acc Acc s/o Asa & Susan to Elnora R Carmine 21 S Acc Acc d/o Henry D & Rebecca on 2 Feb 1881 at Onancock by JC Watson

CROCKETT Carey 22 S Sailor Acc Acc s/o John & Sally to Mary C Crockett 18 S Acc Acc d/o Dempsey & Matilda on 21 Oct 1884 at Acc by CS Baker

CROCKETT Charles A 24 S Oysterman Acc Acc s/o Major & Zipporah to Nellie A Thomas 18 S Acc Acc d/o Joshua & Julia on 15 May 1876 at Tangier Isld by RC Jones

CROCKETT Charles B 25 S Waterman Acc Acc s/o Jesse & Charlotte to Sarah Crockett 19 S Acc Acc d/o Don & Ellen on 28 Sep 1884 at Acc by CS Baker

CROCKETT David 21 S Oysterman Tangier Isld Tangier Isld s/o Josiah

& Elizabeth to Elizabeth Savage 20 S Acc Acc d/o Mary on 29 Mar 1857 at Acc by JH Addison (J P Thomas says both over 21)
CROCKETT Edward L 23 S Merchant Acc Acc s/o Elisha & Margaret to Julia F Thomas 18 S Acc Acc d/o George M & Mary on 8 Dec 1889 at Tangier Isld by J Connor
CROCKETT Elisha 24 S Oysterman Acc Acc s/o Severn & Henny to Ellen Dies 22 S Acc Acc d/o Sewell & Polly on 11 Nov 1873 at Chesconessex by PA Leatherbury
CROCKETT Elisha 24 W Oysterman Acc Acc s/o David & Elizabeth to Mary Crockett 22 S Acc Acc d/o Thos & Margaret on 23 Sep 1883 at Tangier Isld by CS Baker
CROCKETT Elisha 24 S Boatman Acc Acc s/o John & Sarah to Sarah Crockett 20 S Acc Acc d/o Wm & Alice on 10 Feb 1884 at Tangier Isld by CS Baker
CROCKETT Elisha T 21 S Waterman Acc Acc s/o Davy & Elizth to Elizabeth A Shears 18 S Acc Acc d/o Gabriel & Milissa on 3 Mar 1878 at Tangier Isld by WJ Duhadway
CROCKETT Ellit 24 S Sailor b: Tangier Isld s/o John & Sarah to Catharine Pruitt 18 S b: Tangier Isld d/o Wm & Rachel on 8 Sep 1857 at Tangier Isld by JF Chaplain (L H Thomas says he over 21)
CROCKETT George 30 S Sailor Acc Acc s/o Asa & Cassandra to Virginia F Davis 21 S Acc Acc d/o Savage & Leah on 14 Mar 1877 at Acc by JWA Elliott
CROCKETT George 23 S Oysterman Acc Acc s/o Risden & Margt to Ellen Crockett 21 S Acc Acc d/o Wm & Alcie on 27 Oct 1878 at Tangier Isld by WJ Duhadway
CROCKETT George R 42 W Farmer Acc Acc s/o George & Sinah to Sarah Martin 18 S Acc Acc d/o George & Elizth on 11 May 1876 at Acc by JM Anderson
CROCKETT George S 21 S Waterman Acc Acc s/o Southey & Rachel P to Margaret S Coxton 21 S Acc Acc d/o Wm & Jennie on 22 Dec 1886 at Cross Rd by RA Compton
CROCKETT Hanse 20 S Waterman Acc Acc s/o John & Jane to Evaline Gibbons 17 S Acc Acc d/o Jno & Jane on 17 Apr 1881 at Wise Point by LE Barrett
CROCKETT Henry 22 S Oysterman Acc Acc s/o John & Sally to Sarah F Dies 17 S Acc Acc d/o Joshua & Miranda on 15 Jul 1888 at Tangier by GL Hardesty
CROCKETT Henry 19 S Sailor Acc Acc s/o Severn & Hennie to Sarah Evans 18 S Acc Acc d/o William & Emily on 13 Apr 1890 at Tangier Isld by J Connor
CROCKETT James E 24 S Sailor Acc Acc s/o Asa J & Susan to Lena Evans 16 S Acc Acc d/o Elijah P & Margaret on 16 Apr 1890 at bride's father's by JM Anderson
CROCKETT Jesse 20 S Sailor b: Tangier Isld s/o Frances & Nelly & (ward/o Lewis Crockett) to Charlet [Dise] Dies 15 S b: Tangier Isld d/o Polly on 27 Mar 1856 at Acc by JH Addison
CROCKETT Jesse W 19 S Sailor Acc Acc s/o William H H & Arabella to Bettie L Thomas 17 S Acc Acc d/o William S & Mary on 30 Sep 1888 at Tangier by GL Hardesty
CROCKETT Jno A [Crocket] 31 S Sailor Acc Acc s/o Asa J & Susan to Bettie P Ayres 26 S Acc Acc d/o Jno & Margt on 1 Mar 1882 at Acc by CD Crawley
CROCKETT John to Ellen Crockett d/o Thomas lic: 29 Dec 1856 George Crockett says both over 21

CROCKETT John 22 S Waterman Tangier Isld Tangier Isld s/o Severn & Chloe to Jane (Dise) Dies 20 S Tangier Isld Tangier Isld d/o William & Elizabeth on 22 Mar 1857 at Acc by JH Addison (J P Thomas says he over 21)

CROCKETT John 19 S Waterman Tangier Isld Tangier Isld s/o Feris & Nelly to Sally Evans 19 S Tangier Isld Tangier Isld d/o Major & Shada on 17 Oct 1859 at Tangier Isld by AM Wiggins (John P Thomas said both over 21)

CROCKETT John 31 W Oysterman s/o George & Sinah to Rachel Ann Linton 18 S d/o Stephen & Mary who gave consent lic: 6 Oct 1864 James Miles says he over 21

CROCKETT John A 20 S Sailor Acc Acc s/o John W & Sarah to Lucy Crockett 20 S Acc Acc d/o John & Sally on 18 Dec 1887 at Tangier Isld by SJ Morris

CROCKETT John D 24 S Fisherman Acc Acc s/o Dorr & Ellen to Eveline Thomas 22 S Acc Acc d/o John P & Caroline on 11 Oct 1885 at Tangier Isld by CS Baker

CROCKETT John W 19 S Waterman Acc Acc s/o Charles A & Nellie to Sarah E Williams 17 S Acc Acc d/o Seth & Emily on 25 Aug 1895 at Tangier by CP Swain

CROCKETT Joseph S 24 S Sailor Acc Acc s/o Thomas W & Cordelia to Margaret S Guy 21 S Acc Acc d/o John W & Margaret on 14 Feb 1894 at Acc by AJ Reamy

CROCKETT Joshua 20 S Sailor Acc Acc s/o Major & Zipporah to Olivia [Parks] Parkes 16 S Acc Acc d/o William R & Amanda on 8 Nov 1889(?) at Tangier Isld by J Connor Certificate returned 16 Sep 1890

CROCKETT Lewis 25 S Sailor Acc Acc s/o Peter M & Ann to Olivia Crockett 18 S York Co VA Acc d/o Caney W & Elizabeth on 1 May 1889 at T A Crockett's by J Connor

CROCKETT Lewis D 21 S Sailor Acc Acc s/o Zachariah & Emeline to Mary R Brown 20 S Acc Acc d/o Britann on 10 Jun 1888 at Tangier by GL Hardesty

CROCKETT Lewis H 23 S Waterman Acc Acc s/o David & Emeline to Rachel Crockett 16 S Acc Acc d/o Peter & Mary on 27 Jul 1867 at Acc by WT Tull

CROCKETT Lewis Hill 22 S Waterman Acc Acc s/o Wm H H & Arabella to Jennie [Connor] Conner 22 S Acc Acc d/o James & Mary on 20 Mar 1892 at Onancock by JB Pruitt

CROCKETT Louis A 21 S Waterman Acc Acc s/o John & Sarah to Rhoda L Evans 17 S Acc Acc d/o Thos & Rhoda on 3 Mar 1878 at Tangier Isld by WJ Duhadway

CROCKETT Louis F 21 S Waterman Acc Acc s/o Risden & Margaret S to Ellen Flawbush 18 S Som Co MD Acc d/o Mary J on 1 May 1894 at Tangier by WR Gwinn

CROCKETT Louis H 21 S Merchant Acc Acc s/o Elisha to Frances P Thomas 20 S Acc Acc d/o Caroline on 3 May 1893 at Tangier Isld by ZH Webster

CROCKETT Noah 20 S Sailor Acc Acc s/o Resdon & Margt to Sallie Tyler 22 S Smith Isld MD Acc d/o Severn & Virginia on 4 Jun 1883 at Tangier Isld by CS Baker

CROCKETT Peter 18 S Waterman b: Tangier Isld s/o Trivace & Nelly & (ward/o Lewis Crockett) to Ann Crockett 15 S b: Tangier Isld d/o Lewis & Mary on 7 Apr 1856 at Acc by JH Addison

CROCKETT Riley 24 S Oysterman Acc Acc s/o Geo & Sinah to Margt (Margaret) Crockett 21 S Acc Acc d/o Thos & Mary on 6 Nov 1861 at Acc by GH Ewell

CROCKETT Risdon D 19 S Waterman Acc Acc s/o Risdon & Margaret to Sevenia [Dise] Dies 16 S Acc Acc d/o Gilbert M & Pottliana on 29 Sep 1895 at Tangier by CP Swain

CROCKETT Severn [Crocket] 30 S Oystering Acc Acc s/o George & Sinah to Rebecca Drewer 26 S Baltimore MD Acc d/o Susan on 10 Aug 1861 at Acc by GH Ewell (Parker Miles says above facts "are stated on my information given to the clerk")

CROCKETT Severn J 24 S Mariner Acc Acc s/o Severn & Rebeca to Agnes Myers 22 S Portsmouth Acc d/o Maria on 9 Nov 1890 at Sykes Isld by JS Wallace

CROCKETT Severn T 33 W Oysterman Acc Acc s/o Thomas & Mary to Mary C Linton 19 S Acc Acc d/o William & Louisa on 21 Nov 1880 at Sykes Isld by JW Hilldrup

CROCKETT Southy 40 W Waterman Acc Acc s/o Joseph & Zipporah to Rachel (A) Moore 21 S Acc Acc d/o Geo & Ann on 15 Oct 1857 at Acc by JH Addison (Henry C Drummond says both over 21)

CROCKETT Thomas L 20 S Merchant Acc Acc s/o Peter M & Ann to Maria Crockett 18 S Acc Acc d/o Elisha & Lucy on 9 Sep 1888 at Tangier by GL Hardesty

CROCKETT Thos [Crocket] 27 S Farmer b: Acc s/o Joseph & Zipporah to Susan [Pane] Payne 22 S b: Acc d/o Wm & Euphemia (who gave consent) on 20 Dec 1854 at Acc by JH Addison (lic: 19 Dec 1854)

CROCKETT Thos W 37 W Farmer Acc Acc s/o Jos & Zipporah to Cordelia Paul 30 S Acc Acc d/o Dennard & Henrietta on 10 Jan 1866 at Acc by JC Addison

CROCKETT Travis A 21 S Oysterman Acc Acc s/o John & Charlotte A to Mary Spence 17 S Acc Acc d/o Richd & Adaline on 22 Sep 1878 at Tangier Isld by WJ Duhadway

CROCKETT William 21 S Oysterman Acc Acc s/o John & Sarah to Elizabeth Burrse 22 S N'hamp: Acc d/o Joseph & Virginia on 23 May 1875 at Tangier Isld by RC Jones

CROCKETT William 22 S Sailor Acc Acc s/o John & Jane to Sarah [Parks] Parkes 19 S Acc Acc d/o John E & Eliza on 9 Mar 1890 at Tangier Isld by J Connor

CROCKETT William [Crocket] Col 25 S Oysterman Acc Acc s/o George & Sina to Rebecca [Crocket] Crockett Col 25 W Acc Acc d/o Susan Druer on 24 May 1873 at Sykes Isld by M Oldham (lic: 21 May 1873 does not show them as Col)

CROCKETT William H 21 S Sailor Acc Acc s/o Planner & Polly to Margaret J Stant 21 S Acc Acc d/o Samuel & Jane on 17 Feb 1875 near Onancock by RC Jones

CROCKETT William H 37 W Waterman Acc Acc s/o John W & Sarah to Sarah Crockett 30 W Acc Acc d/o Dow & Ellen on 29 Aug 1894 at Tangier Isld by WR Gwinn

CROCKETT William Hy 39 W Waterman Acc Acc s/o Jno Wm & Sarah to Mary Ellen Briscoe 35 W Middlesex Co Acc on 25 Dec 1895 at Tangier by CP Swain

CROCKETT William R 30 S Mariner Acc Acc s/o Zachariah & Emeline to Mary E Pruitt 24 S Acc Acc d/o Raymond & Margaret on 9 Jun 1889 at Tangier Isld by J Connor

CROCKETT Williams 21 S Waterman Acc Acc s/o Severn & Eleanor to Matilda J Spence 21 S Acc Acc d/o Richard & Adaline on 4 Jan 1878 at Wise Point by WJ Duhadway

Marriages

CROCKETT Wm H 25 S Sailor Acc Acc s/o Henry to Kate L Killman 20 S Acc Acc d/o Ezikiel H & Mollie on 26 Dec 1883 near Onancock by WC Vaden

CROCKETT Wm H 24 S Sailor Acc Acc s/o Risden & Margaret to Eliza J Pruitt 19 S Acc Acc d/o William & Ellen on 1 Apr 1891 at Tangier Isld by J Connor

CROCKETT Wm R 18 S Oysterman Acc Acc s/o Zachariah & Emeline to Nelly Crockett 22 S Acc Acc d/o Lewis & Mary on 15 May 1876 at Tangier Isld by RC Jones

CROCKETT Wm R 25 S Waterman Acc Acc s/o Zachariah & Emeline to Amanda D Thomas 21 S Acc Acc d/o Joshua & Julia A on 21 Sep 1884 at Acc by CS Baker

CROCKETT Zachariah H 29 S Sailor Acc Acc s/o Lorenzo Dow & Ellen to Emily Rally 33 W Acc Acc d/o Lewis & Mary Crockett on 19 Oct 1884 at Acc by CS Baker

CROPPER Aaron 60 S Farmer Acc Acc to Charlotte Brinney 55 S Acc Acc d/o Ocker on 1 Nov 1868 at Acc by S Marshall

CROPPER Abel Col 39 S Laborer Acc Horntown s/o Lucy to Mary Ann Ewell Col 29 W Acc Horntown d/o Alsye Logan on 4 Jan 1880 near Horntown by PJ Adams

CROPPER Henry W Col 32 S Laborer Acc Acc s/o Jenice to Mary Feddeman (black) 26 S Acc Acc d/o Leah on 4 Mar 1874 at Horntown by S Johns

CROPPER Isaac (FN) 58 W Farming b: Acc s/o Abel Leainer & Easter Croper to Mary (Milkey) Brittingham (FN) 36 Wor Co MD d/o George Corbin & Mary Robberts on 13 Feb 1861 at Acc by T Waters

CROPPER Isaac 25 S Farmer Acc Acc to Louisa Savage 20 S Acc Acc d/o Harry on 11 Aug 1870 at Acc by S Marshall

CROPPER James Col 46 S Oysterman Acc Acc s/o Lney to Louia Feddeman Col 35 S Acc Acc on 11 May 1873 at Horntown by S Johns

CROPPER James E 33 W Waterman Wor Co MD Acc s/o Samuel & Mary to Martha Birch 30 W Acc Acc d/o Major & Susan Jones on 18 Dec 1876 at Chinco: Isld by R Williamson

CROPPER John 62 W Farmer Acc Acc to Emma Chance 32 S Acc Acc d/o James & Mary A on 26 Dec 1889 at Oak Grove by JWA Elliott

CROPPER John W Col 29 S Oysterman Acc Acc s/o Levi & Emily to Mary C White Col 29 S Acc Acc d/o Ann on 4 May 1885 at Acc by JC Cluff

CROPPER John Wm 21 S Farmer Acc Acc s/o John H & Sarah to Margaret Susan Ward 20 S Acc Acc d/o John L & Malinda on 29 Dec 1869 at Acc by LK LeCato

CROPPER Joseph Col 38 S Farmer Acc Acc s/o Cratie to Elizabeth Smith Col 39 S Acc Acc d/o Sarah Parkes on 17 May 1885 at Acc by JC Cluff

CROPPER Joshua Col 25 S Farmer Acc Acc s/o Levi to Mary Williams Col 26 S Acc Acc d/o Geo & Drucilla on 30 Oct 1879 at Atlantic by JC Cluff

CROPPER Robert J 23 S Farmer Acc Acc s/o John H & Sarah A to Virginia C White 17 S Acc Acc d/o Geo T & Fanny A on 5 Dec 1877 near Locustville by LK LeCato

CROPPER Sewell Col 24 S Laborer Acc Acc s/o Eliza to Sarah Duffy Col 18 S Acc Acc d/o Sarah on 16 Jan 1895 at Temp'ville by GHT Byrd

CROPPER Solomon Col 21 S Acc Acc to Harriet Marshall Col 21 S Acc Acc on 1 Jan 1879 at New Church by TM Poulson

CROPPER Wm Col 21 S Laborer Acc Acc s/o Anena to Emaline Handy Col

18 S Acc Acc d/o Caroline on 18 Jan 1878 near New Church by JC Cluff

CROPPER Wm F R 38 S Mechanic Wor Co MD Acc s/o Joseph & Gertude to Mary E Birch 23 S Acc Acc d/o Thomas & Mary C on 28 Jun 1871 at Acc by EM Bryan

CROSBY Chas H 25 S Farmer Acc Acc s/o Thos F & Polly to Lou Emma Harrison 17 S Acc Acc d/o Thomas C & Sarah M on 30 Dec 1885 at Acc by WC Vaden

CROSLEY Augustus 29 S Farmer Acc Acc s/o Thos & Polly to Carolin A Evans 21 S Acc Acc d/o Wm & Jane on 29 Dec 1878 at Wm Evans' by JC Watson

CROSLEY James 20 S Waterman Acc Acc s/o Geo & Bridget to Sally Williams 23 S Acc Acc d/o Seth & Rosey on 4 Jun 1863 at Acc by D Titlow

CROSLEY Samuel 60 W Mariner Acc Acc to Tabitha S Carmine 26 S N'hamp: Acc d/o Wm & Lavinia on 4 Aug 1875 at Chesconessex by FR Boston

CROSLEY Thomas F 22 S Farmer Acc Acc s/o Thomas & Polly to Mary W Killman 21 S Acc Acc d/o Wm & Betty on 30 Dec 1875(?) at Slutkill Nk by JH Amiss Certificate returned 5 Apr 1877

CROSS George B 24 S Jefferson Co WV Jefferson Co WV s/o Reason & Ann to Lillie B Kearney 19 S Jefferson Co WV Acc d/o A P Northam Late Kearney on 22 Dec 1880 at Modest Town by EH Wellman

CROSWELL Frank black 23 S Waterman s/o Mary to Emma Jane Hall black 19 S d/o Malinda lic: 21 May 1873

CROSWELL Handy Col 21 S Oysterman Acc Acc s/o Annie Croswell (now Lewis) to Maggie Johnson Col 20 S Acc Acc d/o Samuel & Maria on 25 Nov 1894 at Acc by JC Cluff

CROSWELL John H to Arinthia Johnson ward/o Samuel C Johnson lic: 9 Jan 1854

CROWSON Charles Col 22 S Laborer Acc Acc s/o Peter & Fanny to Margaret E Satchell Col 17 S Acc Acc d/o Abel & Maria on 19 Dec 1883 at Metompkin Ch by LW Lee

CROWSON Isaac Col 23 S Farmer Acc Acc to Mary Seymour Col 19 S Acc Acc d/o Clarissa on 27 Mar 1884 at Drum'tn by LW Lee

CROWSON James to Sarah Melson d/o James dec'd lic: 8 Jan 1856 Henry Melson says both over 21

CROWSON Joseph 23 S Farmer Acc Acc s/o Levin & Demaria to Mary S Hall 16 S Acc Acc d/o John & Sally on 4 Mar 1874 near Onancock by O Littleton

CROWSON Lewis T 26 S Mechanic Acc Acc s/o Levin & Deimena to Sallie D Rew 20 S Acc Acc d/o George S & Margt S on 9 Feb 1876 at Hunting Ck by RC Jones

CROWSON Peter Col 56 S Farmer Acc Acc s/o James to Fanny Dix Col 50 S Acc Acc d/o Dinah on 4 Apr 1882 near Acc C H by AJ Satchell

CROWSON Thomas Col 22 S Laborer Acc Acc s/o Fanny to Indiana W Pitts Col 17 S Acc Acc d/o Rosy Lilliston on 27 Apr 1881 near Poor House by A Joynes

CUGLER Samuel 23 S Sailor NJ Acc s/o Saml & Elizabeth to Sally Lewis 19 S Acc Acc d/o Henry C & Charlotte on 14 Sep 1881 at Acc by LB Betty

CULERY John 18 S Sailor Acc Acc s/o Elizth Small formerly Culery to Nancy Emily Hart 14 S Acc Acc d/o Wm D & Catharine on 26 Dec 1883 at Acc by PA Leatherbury

CUSTIS (Thomas) E C to Margaret E Finney d/o Edward O on 17 Jun 1858 at bride's father's by C Colton (George D Wise says he over 21)

CUSTIS Adams Col 37 S Laborer Acc Acc s/o Agnes to Rachel West Col 36 W Acc Acc d/o Louis & Margt Dix on 1 Jan 1879 near News Town by A Joynes

CUSTIS Benjamin Col 32 S Acc Acc to Margaret Ames Col 21 S Acc Acc on 9 Jul 1871 near Pungo: by TM Cole

CUSTIS Coleburn E 22 S Waterman Acc Acc s/o Littleton H & Ellen to Minnie C Bennett 18 S Acc Acc d/o Thomas H & Georgianna on 25 Dec 1895 at Pungo: by JM Dunaway

CUSTIS Edmund Col 21 S Farmer Acc Acc s/o Louisa Kellam to Nannie LeCato Col 21 S Acc Acc d/o Minnie on 30 Dec 1874 at Locust Mount by HT Rich

CUSTIS Edward 38 S Farmer b: Acc s/o Henry & Tabitha to Pamilia Joynes 36 S b: Acc d/o Elias & Margaret on 6 Dec 1855 at Acc by JH Addison

CUSTIS Edward H 30 S Farmer Acc Acc s/o Wm Sanuel & Eleanor D Custis to Susan W Parker 26 S Acc Acc d/o Tully W & Margaret on 1 Nov 1871 near Onancock by TA Tidball

CUSTIS Edward R 44 S Merchant Acc Acc s/o Thomas & Mary to Alice M Bull 19 S Acc Acc d/o Benj F & Bettie on 30 Oct 1894 at Pungo: by JR Griffith

CUSTIS Elisha J 28 S Sailor NJ NJ s/o David N & Rebecca C to Ellen T Nock 21 S Acc Acc d/o Samuel & Polly on 21 Nov 1882 at Conquest Ch by JW Hundley

CUSTIS Francis B 23 S Carpenter Acc Acc s/o Wm H & Elizabeth to Elizabeth C Drummond 22 S Acc Acc d/o James & Harriet on 18 Dec 1856 at Acc by JH Addison (Henry C Drummond says both over 21

CUSTIS Francis T 22 S Farmer Acc Acc s/o Francis B & Elizth C to Laura S Harrison 16 S Acc Acc d/o Thos C & Sarah M on 3 Nov 1886 at Acc by WC Vaden

CUSTIS Frazier Col 23 S Wage-earner Acc Acc s/o Margaret Ann to Ibby Conquest Col 21 S Acc Acc d/o Electra Fitchett on 16 Sep 1894 at Acc by L Duncan

CUSTIS George 24 S Farmer Acc Acc s/o Geo & Emaline to Lillie J Davis 20 S Acc Acc d/o Edwd & Susan on 29 Dec 1886 at Pungo: by JW Hundley

CUSTIS Harry W 24 S Farmer Acc Acc s/o Wm Saml & Eleanor to Maggie V Custis 21 S Acc Acc d/o Wm Stran & Virginia on 29 Oct 1873 at Acc by EM Bryan

CUSTIS Henry Col 29 W Wage-earner Acc Acc s/o Louis & Mary to Ella Boggs Col 19 S Acc Acc d/o Southey & Sarah on 16 Mar 1894 at Acc by JH Offer

CUSTIS Henry Col 28 S Farmer Acc Acc s/o Louis & Mary to Laura Stran Col 17 S Acc Acc d/o Perry & Rosa on 4 Jan 1888 at Acc by JA Haynes

CUSTIS Henry Col 53 S Wage-earner Acc Acc to Emma [Reed] Read Col 57 S Acc Acc d/o Marilla Roberts on 26 Nov 1891 at Acc by L Duncan

CUSTIS Isaiah Col 24 S Farmer Acc Acc to Mary Cropper Col 26 S Acc Acc d/o Charlotte on 18 Dec 1873 near Acc C H by A Joynes

CUSTIS Jacob Col 45 S Farmer Acc Acc s/o Solomon to Eliz'th George Col 39 S Acc Acc d/o Spencer on 6 Sep 1891 at Acc by RH Coleman

CUSTIS James Col 27 W Laborer Acc Acc s/o Margaret to Annie Boggs Col 22 S Acc Acc on 31 Mar 1879 at Drum'tn by RH Govans

CUSTIS James Col 24 S Wage-earner Acc Acc s/o Mary Rogers to Sally Kerr Col 22 S Acc Acc d/o Margaret Becket on 28 Aug 1892 at Savageville by JH Offer

CUSTIS James H 21 S Waterman Acc Acc s/o Littleton H & Ellen to Lillie L Guy 20 S Acc Acc d/o Major & Susan A on 16 Mar 1892 at Acc by JM Anderson

CUSTIS James M 24 S Farmer Acc Acc s/o Luther W & Adah to McCreany J [Justis] Justice 17 S Acc Acc d/o Isaiah W & Margaret S on 25 Dec 1890 at Lee Mont by AJ Fristoe

CUSTIS James T Col 21 S Sailor Acc Acc s/o Laura to Elizabeth Griffin Col 21 S Acc Acc d/o Harriet on 28 Dec 1892 at Acc by JW Cook

CUSTIS James W Col 21 S Wage-earner Acc Acc s/o John R Custis & Alicia Sample to Annie Drummond Col 23 S Acc Acc d/o John & Susan on 27 Mar 1891 at Acc by LE Toulson

CUSTIS John Col 26 S Acc Acc s/o Wm & Tina Waters to Mary A Savage Col 20 S Acc Acc d/o Littleton & Dinah on 5 Mar 1881 at bride's home by TW Nettles

CUSTIS John H Col 22 S Wage-earner Acc Acc s/o Wesley & Martha to Henrietta Finney Col 31 S Acc Acc d/o Charles & Ellen on 9 Dec 1889 at Onancock by GHT Byrd

CUSTIS John R 22 S Farmer Acc Acc s/o Luther W & Ada to Mary Hinman 22 S Acc Acc d/o Samuel & Mary on 28 Dec 1881 at Guilford Ch by LB Betty

CUSTIS John W 21 S Farmer Acc Acc s/o Harry W & Maggie V to Elizabeth A [Parks] Parkes 22 S Acc Acc d/o George P & Elizabeth P on 2 Oct 1895 at Acc C H by B Clark

CUSTIS John W H Col 20 S Farm Laborer Acc Acc s/o Margaret Ann to Mary A Chandler Col 19 S Acc Acc d/o Mary Savage on 25 Feb 1885 at Drum'tn by LW Lee

CUSTIS Levi Col 45 W Laborer Acc Acc s/o Maria Dennis to Mary Lilliston Col 30 W Acc Acc d/o John & Agues Pepper on 1 Feb 1877 near News Town by A Joynes

CUSTIS Levin William 33 S Farmer Acc Acc s/o Jas & Leah to Jannie Savage 21 S Acc Acc d/o Emma Upshur on 24 Mar 1867 at Acc by G Bradford

CUSTIS Lewis Col 26 S Farmer Acc Acc s/o Agnes to Sally Finney Col 27 S Acc Acc d/o Susan on 26 Feb 1885 at Acc by AJ Satchell

CUSTIS Littl H 26 S Sailor Acc Acc s/o Wm & Eliz to Ellen T Kellam 27 S Acc Acc d/o Wm B & Harriet on 8 Jul 1863 at Acc by JWA Elliott

CUSTIS Louis Col 23 W Wage-earner Acc Acc s/o Agnes to Tabbie Finney Col 37 S Acc Acc d/o Henry & Tabbie on 28 Dec 1890 at Acc by AJ Satchell

CUSTIS Luther s/o John H to Adah (Grinalds) Grinnalds d/o Parker dec'd & ward/o Major Mason who gave consent lic: 31 Aug 1857 Major Mason says he over 21

CUSTIS Luther J 23 S Farmer Acc Acc s/o Luther & Adah to Nancy L Hinman 17 S Acc Acc d/o William S & Mary on 10 Dec 1890 at Parksley by HS Dulany

CUSTIS Luther W 41 W Farmer Acc Acc s/o John H & Sally to Hester Baker 25 S Acc Acc d/o Sheppard & Mary on 24 Feb 1876 near Modest Town by JE Bundick

CUSTIS Oswald F 20 S Farmer Acc Acc s/o Francis B & Eliz'th C to Berlie I Chandler 18 S Acc Acc d/o Thos R & Emma T on 27 Dec 1893 at Onancock by GE Booker

CUSTIS Peter Col 24 S Farmer Acc

Acc s/o Ellen to Betsy Boggs Col 29 W Acc Acc d/o Sarah Bundick on 4 Oct 1884 at Acc by CA Horsey

CUSTIS Revel 25 S Brick Layer b: Onancock s/o William & Malinda to Jane Northam 26 S b: Onancock d/o Custis & Nancy on 21 Jun 1855 at Onancock by J Allen

CUSTIS Robert L 24 S Farmer Acc Acc s/o Luther W & Adah to Mary E Hinman 19 S Acc Acc d/o William S & Mary on 12 Jan 1890 near Parksley by HS Dulany

CUSTIS Robert P 35 S Merchant Acc Acc s/o Wm Saml & Eleanor to Sarah S Parker 26 S Acc Acc d/o John W H & Sarah on 10 Nov 1881 near Mr Parker's Onancock by EH Wellman

CUSTIS Tankard J 20 S Farmer Acc Acc s/o Francis B & Eliz'th to Willianna Harrison 18 S Acc Acc d/o James E & Margaret on 5 Dec 1888 at bride's home by RA Compton

CUSTIS Tankard J 26 W Merchant Acc Acc s/o Francis Z & Elizabeth C to Sarah A Drummond 19 S Acc Acc d/o James C & Anna J on 10 Oct 1894 at Acc by GE Booker

CUSTIS Thomas Col 38 S Laborer Acc Acc s/o Rachel to Harriet White Col 30 S Acc Acc d/o Esther on 11 Jul 1871 at Acc by N Morris

CUSTIS Thomas Col 66 W Farmer Acc Acc s/o Lura to Rachel Ames Col 39 S Acc Acc d/o Mary on 9 Oct 1880 at Acc by PM Lewis

CUSTIS Thomas J 25 S Farmer Acc Acc s/o Edwd R & Pamelia to Mary E Nock 23 S Acc Acc d/o Edwd T & Caroline A on 6 Jan 1886 at Acc by JH Amiss

CUSTIS Tobie Col 23 S Wage-earner Acc N'hamp: s/o Mary to Tillie Ames Col 19 S Acc Acc d/o Margaret Beach on 15 Dec 1894 at Acc by ET Outen

CUSTIS William (Col) 25 S Laborer Acc Acc s/o Henry Carr & Rose Custis to Harriet Coleburn (Col) 21 S Acc Acc d/o Laura on 9 May 1870 at Drum'tn by WF Williams

CUSTIS William P 23 S Farmer Acc Acc s/o Wm Saml & Eleanor D to Eliza Susan Horsey 18 S Som Co MD Acc d/o John & Sarah Ann on 29 Jun 1859 at Acc by J Crosdale

CUSTIS William R 21 S Farmer Acc Acc s/o Francis B & Elizabeth to Amanda L Evans 22 S Acc Acc d/o William of Z & Jane on 5 Oct 1892 at Onancock by AC Berryman

CUSTIS Wm Col 28 S Acc Acc to Clara Tankard Col 25 S Acc Acc on 3 Oct 1877 at Burtons Chp by A Handy

CUSTIS Wm H B 22 S Sailor Acc Acc s/o Littleton & Ellen to Cordelia H Hundley 18 S Acc Acc d/o William & Margaret on 30 Dec 1891 at Acc by JM Anderson

CUTLER George H 20 S Farmer Acc Acc s/o George & Mary Ann to Fannie Gibbons 18 S Acc Acc d/o Thomas & Nancy on 27 Jan 1875 at Oak Grove Ch by JE Humphreys

CUTLER George T 30 S Carpenter Acc Acc s/o Geo & Deliah to Drucilla Trader 30 S Acc Acc d/o Henry & Mary on 2 Mar 1870 at Temp'ville by O Littleton

CUTLER James B 18 S Oysterman Acc Acc s/o Joseph C & Matilda to Ellen Maud Furniss 18 S Wor Co MD Acc d/o Isaac J & Mary W on 2 May 1894 at Oak Hall by DJ Traynham

CUTLER James P 29 S Brick Layer Acc Acc s/o George & Delilah to Elizabeth A Taylor 23 S Acc Acc d/o Wm & Annie on 9 Nov 1881 at Oak Hall by RB Beadles

CUTLER John R 33 S Farmer Acc Acc s/o George W & Mary Ann to Alice V Kellam 29 S Acc Acc d/o Judson & Cordelia A on 19 Jan 1887 at Mrs

C A Kellam's by JR Strugis

CUTLER John W 25 S Farmer Acc Acc s/o Geo & Delilah to Elizabeth A Johnson 23 S Acc Acc d/o Jas on 31 Dec 1868 at Acc by JO Moss

CUTLER Richard J 21 S Farmer b: Acc s/o Peter & Rosey to Virginia M Nock 20 S b: Acc d/o Elijah J & Margt on 7 Mar 1855 at Acc by M Oldham

CUTLER Richard J 45 W Farmer Acc Acc s/o Peter & Rosa to Mary T Nock 45 S Acc Acc d/o Elijah & Margt on 19 May 1878 at Camp Ground by LK LeCato

CUTLER Robert Col 21 S Wage-earner Acc Acc to Maggie White Col 17 S Acc Acc d/o Tabbie on 22 Jul 1891 at Lee Mont by LE Toulson

CUTLER Smith 45 W Carpenter b: Acc s/o Jno & Easter to Eliza Thomas 40 W b: Acc d/o Revel Lewis & Amelia Marshall on 30 Apr 1855 at Acc by T Waters

CUTLER Thomas Col 21 S Laborer Acc Acc to Ella Phillips Col 19 S Acc Acc d/o Richd & Arrna on 30 Dec 1886 at Acc by JK Adams

CUTLER William H 25 S Oysterman Acc Acc s/o Smith Cutler to Mary A Hall 20 S Acc Acc d/o Asa & Cordelia on 18 Dec 1873 at Acc by M Oldham

DAISEY Arden 24 S Merchant Acc Acc s/o William & Margaret to Lizzie Andrews 19 S Acc Acc d/o Mordican & Mary on 24 Oct 1892 at Chinco: Isld by RB Sanford

DAISEY Arden D 20 S Seaman Acc Acc s/o Parker & Elizabeth to Ann Thornton 19 S Acc Acc d/o Joseph & Eliza on 1 Dec 1870 at Chinco: Isld by WP Thornton

DAISEY Ardin 26 W Oysterman Acc Acc s/o Parker T & Elizth to Lydia A Daisey 18 S Acc Acc d/o Wm & Peggy on 27 May 1879 at Chinco: Isld by WP Thornton

DAISEY David [Daizy] 44 W Waterman Acc Acc s/o Wm & Polly to Elizabeth [Daizy] Daisey 45 w Wor Co MD Acc d/o Thos & Sophia Melvin on 2 Feb 1863 at Acc by P Bowdin Jr

DAISEY David Jr 19 S Oysterman Acc Acc s/o Wm H to Louesianna Thornton 18 S Acc Acc d/o Miles B & Eba on 25 Aug 1883 at Chinco: Isld by WP Thornton

DAISEY David T 60 W Oysterman Acc Acc s/o Wm & Mary to Mary [Burch] Birch 50 W Acc Acc d/o Eli & Elizth Matthews on 22 Jul 1879 at Chinco: Isld by WP Thornton

DAISEY Frazier 34 S Oysterman Acc Acc s/o Wm J & Peggy to Sarah Jones 34 W Acc Acc d/o John H & Jane Hill on 14 May 1895 at Chinco: Isld by SU Grimsley

DAISEY Isaac 21 S Oysterman Chinco: Isld Chinco: Isld s/o Isaac & Polly to Mary Nancy Smith 20 S Chinco: Isld Chinco: Isld d/o Wm & Elizth Booth on 23 Jul 1876 at Chinco: Isld by WP Thornton

DAISEY Isaac Jr 35 W Sailor Acc Acc s/o Isaac & Polly to Jane Taylor 34 W Acc Acc d/o Parker & Elizabeth Daisey on 8 Dec 1889 at Chinco: Isld by SU Grimsley

DAISEY James 37 W Oysterman Acc Acc s/o David & Polly to Polly Hopkins 16 S Acc Acc d/o Henry & Mary Hopkins now Daisey on 8 Nov 1884(?) at Chinco: Isld by SU Grimsley Certificate returned 12 Jan 1889

DAISEY James (Daizy) 22 S Acc Acc s/o James & Nelly to Mary Andrews 22 S Acc Acc d/o Mordeica lic: 12 Mar 1862

DAISEY James [Dasey] 56 W Farmer Acc Acc s/o Wm & Mary to Mary Hudson 22 S Wor Co MD Acc d/o

Wm & Betsy Wheeler on 24 Feb 1866 at Acc by WP Thornton

DAISEY James Jr [Daysey] 22 S Oysterman Acc Acc s/o David & Ann to Catharine Mason 22 S Acc Acc d/o Randall & Ann on 14 Sep 1867 at Acc by WP Thornton

DAISEY Jas 27 S Oysterman Acc Acc s/o Wm H & Mary to Matilda Ann Thornton 16 S Acc Acc d/o John J & Mary Ann on 17 Mar 1891 at Chinco: Isld by GE Wood

DAISEY John 62 W Oysterman Acc Acc s/o Wm & Polly to Mary Ann Mason 60 W Acc Acc d/o Wm & Elizth Sharpley on 4 Sep 1872 at Chinco: Isld by WP Thornton

DAISEY John (Jr) [Daysey] 24 S Mariner Chinco: Isld Chinco: Isld s/o James & Leah to Jane Caroline Sharpley 17 S Chinco: Isld Chinco: Isld d/o Parker & Mary on 1 Mar 1856 at Chinco: Isld by WP Thornton (John Thornton says he over 21)

DAISEY John D [Dasey] 22 S Sailor Acc Acc s/o David & Ann to Maria Thornton 21 S Acc Acc d/o Parker & Eliza on 30 Jan 1870 at Acc by WP Thornton

DAISEY Parker 23 S Oysterman Acc Acc s/o John Daisey & Elizabeth Kirtland to Elizabeth Booth 21 S Acc Acc d/o John & Adaline on 20 Nov 1886(?) at Chinco: Isld by SU Grimsley Certificate returned 12 Jan 1889

DAISEY Parker T 21 S Sailor Acc Acc s/o Issac & Mary to Elizth J Conner 18 S Acc Acc d/o Martin G on 19 Mar 1879 at Chinco: Isld by WP Thornton

DAISEY Philip P 20 S Oysterman Acc Acc s/o William P & Mary A to Demariah Hill 17 S Acc Acc d/o Joh A & Jane on 12 Dec 1890 at Chinco: Isld by JW Turner

DAISEY William [Dazsey] 17 S Sailor Acc Acc s/o Parker & Elizth to Mary A Steelman 17 S Acc Acc d/o David & Elizth on 11 Nov 1867 at Acc by P Bowdin Sr

DAISEY Wm H [Daysey] 22 S Waterman Acc Acc s/o David & Ann to Mary Melvin 20 S Acc Acc d/o Sanl & Elizabeth on 2 May 1862 at Acc by P Bowdin

DALBY William M B 35 S Farmer Acc Acc s/o Lemuel & Annie P to Rachel A Damlin 30 W Acc Acc on 17 Feb 1867 at Acc by JWA Elliott

DALY Joseph J 23 S Tonsorial Artist Harford Co MD Acc s/o Michael F & Alice F to Annie F Crockett 22 S Acc Acc d/o James Dumply & Matilda on 12 Dec 1893 at Tangier by ZH Webster

DAMBRICK Charles Godlove 34 S Farmer Germany Acc s/o John G & Henrietta to Lizzie Catherine Cutler 37 S Acc Acc d/o George & Delilah on 26 Oct 1887 at Temp'ville by JW Carroll

DARBY James L 21 S Farmer Acc Acc to Rebecca Tatham 17 S Acc Acc d/o Preson (dec'd) & (ward/o Wm J Thornton who gave consent) on 8 Aug 1861 at Acc by T Waters

DARBY William L 22 S Oysterman Acc Acc s/o James H & Rebecca to Martha Matthews 21 S Acc Acc d/o George W & Emma on 17 Aug 1890 at New Church by RS Williamson

DAUGHERTY James A [Dougherety] 31 S Shoemaker b: Baltimore MD s/o Patrick & Ruth to Elitia A White 26 S b: Acc d/o (Capt) Thos White & Mary Bloxom on 11 May 1856 at Locustville by BT Ames (Henry C White says both over 21)

DAUGHERTY James P 25 S Merchant Acc Acc s/o James A & Etitia to Ella Lee Watson 20 S Acc Acc d/o John E & Elizabeth on 19 Jan 1890 at Acc by W Chinn

DAUGHERTY Wm B [Dougherty] 22 S Farmer Acc Acc s/o James A & Elishea to Sudie L Fitchett 19 S Acc Acc d/o Saml P & Ann on 3 Jan 1884 near Acc C H by JG Anderson

DAVIS Benj C 61 W Farmer Acc Acc to Susan M Mason 34 S Acc Acc d/o Stephen & Harriet on 9 Oct 1872 at Acc by JE Humphreys

DAVIS Benjamin 60 W Farmer Acc Acc to Rosina M Fedford 39 W Norfolk VA Acc on 4 Mar 1869 at Acc by JC Martin

DAVIS Benjamin F 23 S Sailor MD Acc s/o Benj & Melcah A to Margaret R West 17 S Acc Acc d/o George J & Susan on 6 May 1869 at Acc by E Hebard

DAVIS Charles Col 24 S Laborer Acc Acc s/o Dennis & Bridget to Sarah Elizth Harmon Col 20 S Acc Acc d/o Wm Bunting & Sarah Hayman on 2 Dec 1884 at Acc by GW Young

DAVIS Cornelius Col 23 W Sailor Acc Acc s/o Jno & Eliza to Susan Boggs Col 17 S Acc Acc d/o Peter & Grace on 13 May 1883 at Savageville by F Wood

DAVIS Frank L Col 25 S Farmer Acc Acc s/o William & Rosa to Ellen Wise Col 22 S Acc Acc d/o Adam & Lizzie on 4 Sep 1887 at Temp'ville by JW Carroll

DAVIS George Col 23 S Laborer Acc Acc s/o Dennis & Bridges to Cordelia Wise Col 21 S Acc Acc d/o John & Annice on 4 May 1881 at Locust Mount by JWA Elliott

DAVIS George E 29 S Farmer & Wheel Wright Acc Acc s/o Henry S & Leah A to Maggie S Nock 23 S Acc Acc d/o Levin W & Sarah on 22 Dec 1880 near Locust Mount by JWA Elliott

DAVIS George E Col 27 S Sailor Acc Acc s/o Center to Bettie Custis Col 20 S Acc Acc d/o Louisa Ashby on 3 Jan 1886 at Red Hill by CA Horsey

DAVIS George R Col 21 S Laborer Acc Acc s/o Richard & Juliet to Victoria James Col 18 S Acc Acc d/o Lydia Glenn on 4 Dec 1887 at Locust Mount by JWA Elliott

DAVIS George W 22 S Waterman Acc Acc s/o Benjamin F & Maggie B to Anna M Brittingham 19 S Acc Acc d/o John A & Mary E on 27 Jun 1894 at Acc by JR Griffith

DAVIS George W 24 S Farmer Acc Acc s/o Napoleon B & Ann to Lola Powell 17 S Acc Acc d/o James H & Emma on 24 Dec 1895 at Acc by HS Dulany

DAVIS Gideon W 28 S Farmer Wor Co MD Acc s/o John & Mollie to Lavinia Frances Maddox 19 S Som Co MD Acc d/o William & Sarah on 27 Dec 1871 near Onancock by O Littleton

DAVIS Grant Col 24 S Wage-earner Acc Acc s/o Mary to Annie Rayfield Col 23 S Acc Acc d/o Rachel on 14 Nov 1895 at Acc by AJ Satchell

DAVIS Harrison Col 24 S Sailor Acc Acc s/o Cynthia to Anna White Col 17 S Acc Acc d/o White on 21 Aug 1879 at Acc by A Joynes

DAVIS Henry Col 24 S Farming Acc Acc s/o Mary to Hester A Griffin Col 19 S Acc Acc d/o Mary on 18 Sep 1873 near Guilford by A Joynes

DAVIS Henry 20 S Oysterman Acc Acc s/o Saml G to Airy E [Tindle] Tindall 16 S Acc Acc d/o Jno H & Elmira on 7 Oct 1883 at Chinco: Isld by WP Thornton

DAVIS Henry 73 W Farmer Acc Acc s/o James & Nancy to Sarah Chase 41 S Acc Acc d/o Robt & nancy on 4 Oct 1884 at Acc by JE Bundick

DAVIS Henry T 26 S Sailor Acc Acc s/o Henry & Hetty to Elizth J Gladding 17 S Acc Acc d/o Calvin R & Elizth on 4 Jan 1882 at Mr Calvin

Gladding's by JW Hundley

DAVIS Isaac Col 23 S Farmer Acc Acc s/o Harriet Nock to Martha Dickerson Col 22 S Acc Acc d/o Charles on 27 Jan 1884 at New Church by AJ Satchell

DAVIS Isaac J Col 24 S Sailor Acc Acc s/o Dennis & Bridget to Sudie Pitts Col 18 S Acc Acc d/o Juliet on 20 Jun 1883 at Locust Mount by JWA Elliott

DAVIS Isaac Jas 26 S Merchant Wor Co MD Pocomoke City MD s/o Littleton D & Charlotte J to Cornelia Jones 27 W Acc Acc d/o Thomas & Sallie E Hall on 17 Oct 1888 at Acc by TG Pullen

DAVIS James T 22 S Farmer Acc Acc s/o Wm P & Sallie to Susan Taylor 32 S Acc Acc d/o Matthew H & Kassandra C on 6 Jan 1875 at Acc by TM Poulson

DAVIS Jefferson 21 S Plasterer Wor Co MD Acc s/o Samuel G & Elizabeth to Mary G Bloxom 23 W Acc Acc d/o James W & Mary Birch on 1 Jun 1884(?) at Chinco: Isld by SU Grimsley Certificate returned 12 Jan 1889

DAVIS John Col 40 S Farmer Acc Acc s/o Mary to Harriet Wharton Col 35 S Acc Acc d/o Ibby on 23 Jan 1878 at Modest Town by A Joynes

DAVIS John Col 25 S Laborer Acc Acc s/o Wm & Rosa Ann Davis to Olevis Lang Col 22 S Acc Acc d/o Jno & Louisa on 19 Dec 1883 at Drum'tn by LW Lee

DAVIS John Col 32 S Oysterman Acc Acc s/o Dennis & Bridget to Elizabeth Doughty Col 28 S Acc Acc d/o Emma on 15 Apr 1892 at Acc by RH Coleman

DAVIS John Col 24 S Oysterman Acc Acc s/o George Davis & Caroline Scarborough to Maggie Ashby Col 21 S Acc Acc d/o Henry & Sarah on 8 Mar 1892 at Acc by RH Coleman

DAVIS John S 39 S Farmer Acc Acc s/o John W & Mana to Sarah E Holland 30 W MD Acc d/o Wm & Susan Tull on 13 Mar 1867 at Acc by M Oldham

DAVIS John S 26 S Farmer MD Acc s/o Benj & Mileah to Ella F Beach 24 S Acc Acc d/o Abel J & Sarah on 22 Dec 1878 at Craddockville by CC Wertenbaker

DAVIS John T Col 22 S Farmer Acc Acc s/o Isaac & Sarah to Mary E Gillespie Col 22 S Baltimore MD Acc d/o Isaac & Virginia on 31 Jan 1894 at Temp'ville by GHT Byrd

DAVIS John W 23 S Mail Driver Acc Acc s/o Wm P & Sallie E to Gertie F Poulson 23 S Acc Acc d/o Thos M & Mary E on 31 Jan 1878 near Wagram by M Oldham

DAVIS John W 23 S Oysterman Acc Acc s/o Robert W & Mary to Martha Tyler 15 S Acc Acc d/o John R & Mary on 26 Dec 1888 at Acc by WA Street

DAVIS Joseph Col 21 S Farmer Acc Acc s/o Isaac & Sarah to Sally Bundick Col 21 S Acc Acc d/o Wm & Elizth on 21 May 1882 near Temp'ville by JC Cluff

DAVIS L J 25 S Waterman Sussex Co DE Sussex Co DE s/o Elijah to Arinthia Killman 18 S Acc Acc d/o Thos & Laura on 11 Aug 1886 at Acc by WA Street

DAVIS Lee 21 S Merchant Acc Acc s/o Thos & Eva to Indie Floyd 19 S Acc Acc d/o Jno R & Lucy on 20 Nov 1895 at Belle Haven by REC Lawson

DAVIS Louis Col 25 S Farmer Acc Acc s/o Harriet to Leah Northam Col 24 S Acc Acc d/o Ann on 29 Oct 1882 near Poor House by AJ Satchell

DAVIS Louis Col 23 S Farmer Acc Acc s/o Sarah to Margaret A Davis Col 19 S Acc Acc d/o Jno & Harriet on

13 Jan 1886 at Acc by AJ Satchell
DAVIS Major T 43 S Carpenter Acc Acc s/o Jno W & Maria A to Annie E Selby 26 S Acc Acc d/o Wm W & Mary A P on 30 Jan 1877 at Acc by WT Wilkerson
DAVIS Napoleon B 21 S Laborer RI Acc s/o Peter A & Sarah to Ann Paul 27 S Acc Acc d/o Dennard & Hessy on 25 Dec 1862 at Acc by D Titlow
DAVIS Nathan 26 W Sailor PA Acc s/o Peter & Sarah to Emily C Young 23 S Acc Acc d/o Saml & Mary A on 15 Mar 1879 at Chesconessex by JC Watson
DAVIS Nathan 35 W Farmer Philadelphia PA Acc s/o Peter & Sarah Ann to Lovey Onley 17 S Acc Acc d/o William & Triphena on 12 Feb 1889 at Acc by JW Ward
DAVIS Neal Col 23 S Sailor Acc Acc to Emma C Custis Col 23 S Acc Acc d/o Mary on 26 Aug 1880 at Onancock by JW Diggs
DAVIS Noah 25 S Farmer & Oysterman Acc Acc s/o Henry & Hetty to Sarah A Matthews 21 S Acc Acc d/o Alred & Elizabeth on 3 Mar 1880 near Messongo by DA Woodson
DAVIS Peter 24 S Farmer Acc Acc to Annie Planter 21 S Acc Acc d/o Agnes on 3 Apr 1869 at Acc by JO Moss
DAVIS Peter Col 21 S Farmer Acc Acc s/o Isaac & Sarah to Jane Davis Col 21 S Acc Acc d/o Thorogood & Mary on 17 Jan 1886 at Acc by AJ Satchell
DAVIS Peter Col 40 W Farmer Acc Acc to Emma Holden Col 37 W Acc Acc d/o Isaiah & Patience on 5 Jan 1890 at Acc by AJ Satchell
DAVIS Peter H 33 S Leaman(?) MD Acc s/o Benj & Mitcha to Maggie E Ames 19 S Acc Acc d/o Richd T & Louisa on 17 Jan 1872 at Oak Grove Ch by O Littleton
DAVIS Robinson 23 S Farmer Acc Acc s/o Henry & Hetty to Mary S Taylor 17 S Acc Acc d/o Saml T & Critty on 30 Dec 1861 at Acc by T Waters
DAVIS Sam'l S Col 21 S Farmer Acc Acc s/o Samuel & Sarah to Elizabeth Mason Col 17 S Acc Acc d/o Heberd & Mary on 27 Dec 1891 at Acc by LE Toulson
DAVIS Samuel (black) 51 S Farmer MD Acc to Sarah Rayfield (black) 41 S Acc Acc d/o Sarah on 6 Jul 1871 at Acc by N Morris
DAVIS Samuel 32 W Artist Wor Co MD Chinco: Isld s/o David & Sarah to Elizabeth Watson 29 S Acc Chinco: Isld d/o David & Hetty on 2 Feb 1871 at Chinco: Isld by WP Thornton
DAVIS Samuel Col 24 S Laborer Acc Acc s/o Bridget to Henny Beach Col 20 S Acc Acc d/o Charles & Sylva on 10 Nov 1875 at Locust Mount by HT Rich
DAVIS Samuel J 30 S Merchant Acc Acc s/o Jones & Ann to Rowena F [Burten] Burton 18 S Acc Acc d/o Geo Burten & Ann Roley on 2 May 1860 at Acc by T Waters (George Wallops say he over 21)
DAVIS Savage Col 23 S Laborer Acc Acc s/o Isaac & Sarah to Ida Byrd Col 19 S Acc Acc d/o John & Ida on 13 Apr 1879 at Temp'ville by JC Cluff
DAVIS Solomon Col 26 S Farmer Acc Acc s/o John to Mary E Northam Col 22 S Acc Acc d/o Edward & Harriet on 26 Oct 1890 at Mappsville by AJ Satchell
DAVIS Stockton Col 21 S Farmer Acc Acc s/o Thoro & Mary to Sarah Laws Col 27 W Acc Acc d/o Esther Houten on 29 Sep 1879 at Modest Town by A Joynes
DAVIS Sydney 22 S Sailor Wor Co MD

Acc s/o Samuel Y to Mary J Stubbs 17 S Acc Acc d/o Andrew & Caroline on 12 Dec 1882 at Chinco: Isld by WP Thornton

DAVIS William H 23 S Farmer Acc Acc s/o Noah & Milky to Rebecca C Kelly 35 S Acc Acc d/o Wm & Rebecca on 28 Mar 1867 at Acc by GW Matthews

DAVIS Willie F 17 S Farmer Acc Acc s/o Littleton B & Hester A to Maggie S Mears 17 S Acc Acc d/o George T & Peggy on 10 Jan 1894 at Locust Mount by JWA Elliott

DAVIS Wm Col 35 S Laborer Acc Acc to Rosy Bloxom Col 40 S Acc Acc on 30 Mar 1878 at Guilford by A Joynes

DAVIS Wm H Col 23 S Farmer Acc Acc s/o Saml & Sarah to Susan Ann Parker Col 20 S Acc Acc d/o Major & Sabra on 25 Dec 1877 at Morris Chp by A Handy

DAVIS Wm J 24 S Oysterman London England Chinco: Isld s/o James L & Mary S to Louisa Connaway 17 S Wor Co MD Chinco: Isld d/o Isaac & Rosetta on 12 Aug 1877 at Chinco: Isld by R Williamson

DENNIS Charles T 28 S Farmer Acc Acc s/o Wm H & Mary to Lula O Coleburn 22 S Acc Acc d/o Jno W & Annie on 30 Mar 1892 at Acc by RB Scott

DENNIS Jno FN 24 S Oysterman Acc Acc s/o Geo Evans & Eliza Dennis to Mary Thompson FN 20 S Acc Acc d/o Elijah & Mana Poulson on 14 Jun 1855 at Acc by M Oldham (John J Hutchinson says both over 21)

DENNIS John Col 30 S Farmer Acc Acc s/o John & Mary to Cornelia Parker Col 30 S Acc Acc d/o George & Mary on 27 Dec 1894 at Belle Haven by REC Lawson

DENNIS John C 28 S Lumberman Wor Co MD Roanoke s/o Rufrin & Sallie A to Marion J Scott 21 S N'hamp: Acc d/o Thomas M & Hennie on 10 Nov 1892 at Onancock by WC Lindsay

DENNIS John Jr 20 S Oysterman Acc Acc s/o John Sr & Eliza to Oliva E Marshall 18 S Acc Acc d/o Saml Marshall & Armina Bonnewell on 20 Jun 1884 at Sykes Isld by RB Beadles

DENNIS Joshua Col 55 S Farmer Som Co MD Acc s/o Silvia to Harriet Drummond Col 46 S Acc Acc d/o Leah on 29 Jun 1882 near Woodbury by AJ Satchell

DENNIS Littleton Col 22 S Laborer Acc Acc s/o Harriet to Lura Emma Pruitt Col 20 S Acc Acc d/o Betsy Bloxom on 15 May 1879 near News Town by A Joynes

DENNIS Riley Col 37 S Fireman Acc Acc s/o Litha to Sally Ann Corbin Col 35 S Acc Acc d/o Betsy on 8 Jun 1873 at Pocomoke by S Johns

DENNIS Sewell 26 S Teamster Wic Co MD Acc s/o Ephraim W & Mary Anne to Lelia Pruitt 17 S Acc Acc d/o Wm H & Henretta on 19 Nov 1879 at Conquest Ch by M Oldham

DENNIS Wesley Col 29 S Oysterman Acc Acc s/o Levi Fletcher & Feny Dennis to Silvy Ann Jones Col 25 S Acc Acc d/o Simon & Susan on 2 Jun 1883 at Jenkins Bridge by JC Cluff

DENNIS Wm Col 22 S Acc Acc s/o Toby & Rachel to Mila Williams Col 20 S MD Acc d/o Joseph & Mary on 10 Oct 1878 near New Church by TM Poulson

DENNIS Wm H 45 W Farmer Wor Co MD Acc s/o Lemauel to Sarah Matthews 33 S Acc Acc d/o Edwd on 17 Nov 1878 at Atlantic P O by JW Hundley

DERICKSON Job 29 S Seafarer in US Life Station Wor Co MD Chinco: Isld s/o J W H & Arena to Annie

[Bowdin] Bowden 18 S Acc Chinco: Isld d/o Parker & Mariah on 8 May 1882 at Chinco: Isld by WP Thornton

DESHIELDS Frank J 26 S Mechanist Som Co MD Wor Co MD s/o Alfred J & Charlotte E to Sarah H Broughton 22 S Baltimore City Acc d/o James & Charlotte on 3 Jan 1871 at Emanul Ch by J Crosdale

DICKERSON Arthur Col 42 S Farmer Acc Acc s/o Leah to Eliza [Bird] Byrd Col 30 S Acc Acc d/o Eliza on 19 Dec 1877 at News Town by A Joynes

DICKERSON Bowman Col 23 S Laborer Acc Acc s/o Emeline to Rosa Bundick Col 21 S Acc Acc d/o Rosa on 24 Dec 1878 at News Town by A Joynes

DICKERSON Charles Col 39 W Farmer Acc Acc to Sally Laws Col 29 S Acc Acc d/o Rebecca on 28 Nov 1886 at Acc by JC Cluff

DICKERSON David Col 40 S Laborer Acc Acc s/o Virginia Crippin to Annie Gibbons Col 24 S Acc Acc d/o Hannah Bayly on 19 Nov 1879 near News Town by A Joynes

DICKERSON Douglas S Col 25 S Wage-earner Acc Acc s/o Arthur & Eliza to Tillie Wise Col 22 S Acc Acc d/o Wilson & Phoebe on 11 Oct 1895 at Acc by JC Cluff

DICKERSON Edmund Col 45 W Wage-earner Acc Acc s/o Virginia to Esther Griffin Col 40 W Acc Acc d/o Rose Hope on 16 Dec 1888 at Acc by AJ Satchell

DICKERSON George Col 25 S Wage-earner Acc Acc s/o David to Florence Savage Col 20 S Acc Acc d/o Dennis B & Ann on 9 Jan 1895 at Acc by AJ Satchell

DICKERSON George D Col 27 S Wage-earner Acc Acc s/o Edward & Emeline to Willianna Gunter Col 19 S Acc Acc d/o H Thomas & Anna on 16 Jan 1894 at Acc by AJ Satchell

DICKERSON James Col 21 S Farmer Acc Acc s/o Arthur to Ella Laws Col 18 S Acc Acc d/o Sarah on 26 Sep 1886 at Acc by AJ Satchell

DICKERSON Jesse Jr s/o Jesse to Susanna Byrd d/o John W who gave consent lic: 8 Apr 1856

DICKERSON John (Col) 22 S Farmer Acc Acc s/o Sarah Crippen to Sally Clayton (Col) 20 S Acc Acc d/o Edwd Crippen & Anna Clayton on 27 Feb 1870 at Modest Town by A Joynes

DICKERSON John Col 23 S Sailor Acc Acc s/o Eliza to Tamar Justice Col 22 S Acc Acc d/o Netty Conquest on 20 Apr 1884 at Mappsville by AJ Satchell

DICKERSON John Col 23 S Laborer Acc Acc s/o Emeline to Eliza Ann White Col 21 S Acc Acc d/o Kitty on 28 Dec 1887 at Acc by AJ Satchell

DICKERSON Spencer Col 23 S Laborer Acc Acc s/o Arthur & Eliza to Martha Kelly 25 W Acc Acc d/o Jno Griffin & Sabra Hinman on 4 Dec 1869 at Acc by A Joynes

DICKERSON Sylvester Col 25 S Day Laborer Acc Acc s/o Sarah to Nancy Davis Col 17 S Acc Acc d/o Wm & Rose A on 27 Dec 1883 at Metompkin Ch by AJ Satchell

DICKERSON Thomas 27 S Mariner b: Acc s/o Jesse Dickerson to Elenor D Russell 19 S b: Acc d/o Thos & Sally on 27 Mar 1855 at r/o Wm R Lewis by ES Grant

DICKERSON Thomas J 22 S Sailor Acc Acc s/o Thos & Eleanor D to Mary O Lewis 18 S Acc Acc d/o Absalom & Elizth on 13 Feb 1878 at Conquest Ch by JB Merritt

DICKERSON Wm D Col 22 S Wage-earner Acc Acc s/o Edmond & Emeline to Maggie Watts Col 15 S Acc Acc d/o Abbott & Hannah on 29

Marriages

Dec 1892 at Acc by AJ Satchell
DIES Andrew F 20 S Waterman Acc Acc s/o Gilbert M & Flora to Georgianna Gibbons 16 S Acc Acc d/o John & Jane on 31 Oct 1886 at Acc by AD Davis
DIES Gillet 21 S Oysterman Acc Acc s/o John & Christianna to Mary Parkes 21 S Acc Acc d/o Thomas & Sally on 8 Sep 1874 at Tangier Isld by RC Jones
DIES Jno W F 35 W Oysterman Acc Acc s/o Peter & Eliza to Julia Crockett 20 S Acc Acc d/o James D & Matilda on 5 Sep 1891 at Tangier Isld by J Connor
DIES John [Dize] 18 S Oysterman Acc Acc s/o John & Amy to Louisa Walter 16 S Matthews Co VA Acc d/o William L & Mary Ellen on 9 Dec 1888 at Tangier by GL Hardesty
DIES John T [Dize] 19 S Sailor Acc Acc s/o Gilbert T & Mary E to Bettie F Spence 19 S Acc Acc d/o Richard A & Adaline on 28 Oct 1894 at Tangier Isld by WR Gwinn
DIES John W 19 S Sailor Acc Acc s/o John L & Christina to Sallie J Parkes 22 S Acc Acc d/o Gabriel & Betsy on 22 Jun 1875 at Onancock by RC Jones
DIES John W 33 W Sailor Som Co MD Acc s/o Smith & Jane to Mary E Guy 18 S Acc Acc d/o Robt P & Margt T on 1 Sep 1886 at Acc by L Rosser
DIES John W [Dise] 36 W Sailor Som Co MD Acc s/o Smith & Jane to Elizabeth Scott 16 S Acc Acc d/o Wingfield A & Melinda on 17 Jun 1891 at Acc by JM Anderson
DIES Nathan 22 S Oysterman Acc Acc s/o John & Ann to Bettie Parkes 23 S Acc Acc d/o Gabrel on 27 Jan 1884 at Tangier Isld by CS Baker
DIES Peter [Dyes] 22 S Sailor Som Co MD Dorchester Co s/o Henry & Charlotte to Mary Washington Evans 17 S Som Co MD Acc d/o Wm & Sarah on 16 Jun 1869 at Acc by JH Addison
DIES Thomas [Dye] 21 S Oysterman Acc Acc s/o John & Ann to Floney Byrd 21 S Northumberland Co Acc on 15 Jun 1874 at Onancock by RC Jones
DIES Thomas D 33 W Sailor Som Co MD Acc s/o Henry & Charlotte to Minnie J Evans 23 S Acc Acc d/o John & Melinda on 26 Mar 1890 at Hoffman's Wharf by JM Anderson
DIES Thomas L 27 W Oystering Acc Acc s/o John & Ann to Sallie J Crockett 19 S Acc Acc d/o John & Sarah on 9 Dec 1883 at Tangier Isld by CS Baker
DIES Thomas L [Dize] 36 W Waterman Acc Acc to Mary J Thomas 37 W Acc Acc on 2 May 1893 at Tangier Isld by ZH Webster
DIES William [Dyes] 24 S Oysterman Acc Acc s/o William & Elizabeth to Neely Taws 22 S Acc Acc d/o Quincy & Mary on 8 Sep 1874 at Tangier Isld by RC Jones
DIGGS Richard Col 32 S Sailor Matthews Co VA Acc s/o George & Jane to Rose Brown Col 28 S Acc Acc d/o William Taylor & Sallie Brown on 25 May 1890 at Acc by L Duncan
DILLMAN James P 40 S Gentleman b: PA to Mary Blossomgale 30 W d/o (-----) Evans lic: 26 Aug 1865 marr: 27 Aug 1865
DISHAROON John F 20 S Electric Light Operator Acc Salisbury MD s/o James(?) & Anna E to Lillie C Collins 20 S Acc Acc d/o Charles & Hester A on 24 Jan 1895 at Chinco: Isld by CW Matthews
DISHAROON John S 25 S Millwright Wic Co MD Acc s/o James & Amelia to Mary Ann Mason 18 S Wic Co MD Acc d/o Edward E &

Elizth on 15 Apr 1874 at Acc by TM Poulson

DIX Asa T Dr widr to Lydia J Cave d/o Wm who gave consent lic: 19 May 1855

DIX Charles Col 22 S Laborer Acc Acc s/o Littleton & Mary to Elishia Finney Col 17 S Acc Acc d/o Emeline on 29 Dec 1881 at Acc by AJ Satchell

DIX Charles Col 27 W Farmer Acc Acc s/o Littleton Dix & Mary Wessells to Agnes Waters Col 22 S Acc Acc d/o Agnes on 6 Feb 1890 at Acc by AJ Satchell

DIX Charles C 29 S Farmer Acc Acc s/o Asa T & Lydis J to Maggie S Wright 22 S Acc Acc d/o Wm T & Mary S on 27 Oct 1886 at Woodbury by JW Carroll

DIX Clyde 25 S Farmer Acc Acc s/o Isaac & Virginia to Alice Nock 25 S Acc Acc d/o John W H & Mary A on 1 Jun 1892 at Acc by JL King

DIX Edward Col 21 S Hostler N'hamp: Acc s/o Edward to Lizzie Mason Col 20 S Acc Acc d/o Samuel Mason & Maria Coard on 31 Aug 1888 at Drum'tn by P Sheppard

DIX George 33 S Farmer Acc Acc s/o Samuel & Betsy to Margaret Sparrow 35 W Acc Acc d/o Edward & Susan Charnock on 6 Jan 1875 at Foxville by JE Bundick

DIX George Col 22 S Laborer Acc Acc s/o Lewis & Margt to Leah Coleburn Col 21 S Acc Acc d/o Louis on 18 Dec 1879 at Drum'tn by RH Govans

DIX George Col 23 S Farmer Acc Acc s/o Eliza to Ann Finney Col 22 S Acc Acc d/o Sinah on 24 Aug 1879 at Acc by A Joynes

DIX George M 50 W Farmer Acc Acc s/o George & Sally to Sinah [Only] Onley 25 S Acc Acc d/o William & Triphena on 18 Dec 1887 at Lee Mont by JW Norris

DIX Isaac 26 S Farmer Acc Acc s/o Thomas & Nancy to Virginia W Bloxom 24 S Acc Acc d/o Danil & Sarah on 28 Jan 1863 at Acc by OF Fletcher

DIX James to Matilda Small d/o Solomon & Sally who gave consent lic: 11 Jan 1859

DIX John Jr Col 23 S Laborer Acc Acc s/o Ann to Henriette Colonna Col 21 S Acc Acc d/o Sarah on 22 Jun 1881 at Bells Nk by JE Humphreys

DIX John of Thos 20 S Farmer Acc Acc s/o Thos & Peggy to Julianna A Barnes 16 S Acc Acc d/o James & Emaline on 9 Jan 1876 at Woodstock by IT Adkins

DIX John W 22 S Farmer Acc Acc s/o Jno W & Mary A to Arinthia T Dix 21 S Acc Acc d/o Revel & Nancy on 19 Jun 1881 at Lee Mont by WA Crouse

DIX John W 20 S Farmer Acc Acc s/o John to Genettie G Wessells 18 S Acc Acc d/o Arthur & Mary on 27 Dec 1893 at Acc by LE Spencer

DIX Levi 24 S Farmer b: Acc s/o George to Matilda Berry 28 S b: Acc d/o James on 23 Jan 1856 at r/o Geo H Ewell by GH Ewell (Geo M Dix says both over 21)

DIX Levi D 49 W Farmer Acc Acc s/o Jno & Rosy to Charlotte A Bayne 30 S Acc Acc d/o Walter D & Harriet on 25 Nov 1863 at Acc by J Atkinson

DIX Levin A 30 S Physician Acc Acc s/o Wm to Emily E Walters 28 W Acc Acc d/o Jno M & Eliz Coleburn on 2 May 1871 at Acc by O Littleton

DIX Littleton Col 24 S Farmer Acc Acc s/o Littleton & Mary to Ella Mason Col 19 S Acc Acc d/o Alice on 2 Feb 1882 near News Town by AJ Satchell

DIX Littleton Col 54 S Laborer Acc Acc s/o Easter Bagwell to Hester Wright Col 35 S Acc Acc on 20 Nov

Marriages

1882 at Drum'tn by LW Lee
DIX Louis F Col 19 S Wage-earner Acc Acc s/o Mary to Mary Bloxom Col 19 S Acc Acc d/o Alfred & Sabra on 6 Apr 1892 at Acc by AJ Satchell
DIX Peter 23 S Laborer Acc Acc s/o Ann to Elizabeth Nedab 22 S Acc Acc d/o Levin & Tarnar on 2 Aug 1868 at Acc by JH Offer
DIX Peter Col 37 W Laborer Acc Acc s/o Ann to Mary Turner Col 37 W N'hamp: Acc on 10 Jul 1878 at Drum'tn by RH Govans
DIX Peter Col 23 S Farm Laborer Acc Acc s/o Mary Wessells to Lizzie Savage Col 20 S Acc Acc d/o Mary Gibbons on 2 Jun 1884 at Acc by AJ Satchell
DIX Peter Col 42 S Laborer Acc Acc s/o George Searber & Ann Diets to Vernulia [Browne] Brown Col 45 W MD Acc d/o Jona & Rosey Poulson on 2 Apr 1884 at Acc by J Savage
DIX Revel to Nancy Taylor d/o Justice B who gave consent lic: 31 Dec 1855 Zorobabel Chandler says he over 21
DIX Revel Col 46 S Farmer Acc Acc s/o James to Nancy Custis Col 28 S Acc Acc d/o Basha on 15 Dec 1883 at News Town by AJ Satchell
DIX Samuel 25 S Farmer Acc Acc s/o Samuel & Nancy to Sally R Small 20 S Acc Acc d/o Marcellus & Sally on 17 Dec 1890 at Acc by WA Street
DIX Samuel (H) 22 S Farmer Acc Acc s/o Samuel H Dix & Elizabeth Simpson to Nancy Rayfield 16 S Acc Acc d/o Major & Sally on 31 Jan 1861 at Acc by JC Mears (John Y Bloxom says he over 21)
DIX Smith Col 23 S Farm Laborer Acc Acc s/o Clarissa White to Maggie Allen Col 18 S Acc Acc d/o James & Margaret on 8 Jul 1880 near Bull Run by PM Lewis
DIX Southly Col 50 W Laborer Acc Wor Co MD s/o John & Leah to Hetty Merrill Col 45 W Acc Acc d/o Peter & Sarah East on 8 Oct 1879 near New Church by JC Cluff
DIX Thorogood J 22 S Farmer Acc Acc s/o Revel & Nancy to Sarah B [Shreaves] Shrieves 19 S Acc Acc d/o Wm & Jane on 13 Feb 1884 at Drum'tn by JW Hundley
DIX William T 24 S Farmer Acc Acc s/o Wm H & Susan to Margt J Hope 21 S Acc Acc d/o Wm S & Jane on 20 Dec 1866 at Acc by P Warren
DIX William T 30 S Carpenter Acc Acc s/o Samuel & Nancy to Maggie E Bundick 19 S Acc Acc d/o John & Lovie on 28 Dec 1892 at Parksley by JL King
DIXON Gilbert H 27 S Farmer Wor Co MD Acc s/o John & Mattie to Mary Taylor 33 W Acc Acc on 10 Jan 1892 at Belinda by JW Nicholson
DIXON John W 45 S Teamster MD Acc to Mattie Perdie 40 S MD Acc on 8 Oct 1884 at Acc by JW Carroll
DIXON Major T 21 S Carpenter Acc Acc s/o George W & Elizabeth to Nettie J Taylor 23 S Acc Acc d/o Thomas T & Martha on 25 Dec 1887 at Temp'ville by M Oldham
DOBBS Joseph E 24 S Carpenter Portsmouth VA Baltimore City MD s/o Wm D to Maranda W Groton 23 S Acc Acc d/o Thos & Harriet on 20 Nov 1884 at Acc by M Oldham
DOBBS William Drury 55 W Carpenter Portsmouth City VA Baltimore City MD s/o Willoughty & Rachel to Elizabeth Bell 37 S Acc Acc on 1 May 1881 near Oak Hall by RB Beadles
DONAVAN Avery 20 S Telegraph Operator Sussex Co DE Acc s/o Robert J & Rachael to Ida Dawson 21 S Sussex Co DE Acc d/o Thomas W & Elizth (Decd) on 22 Feb 1882 at Franklin City by HC Stern
DORAN Wm Francis 29 S Oysterman

Providence RI Acc s/o Thos & Mary Ellen to Mary V Dies 30 W Acc Acc d/o Thos & Mary on 26 Jul 1886 at Onancock by CA Grice

DOREMUS Andrew D 27 S Carpenter NJ Acc to Courithea S Mears 27 W Acc Acc on 7 Feb 1878 at Belle Haven by JE Humphreys

DORSEY John Col 37 S Teamster Acc Acc to Mary Sample Col 27 S Acc Acc d/o Sally on 26 Jul 1882 at Acc by TW Nettles

DOUGHTY Abel T 26 S Merchant Acc Acc s/o Jno R & Mary to Susan E Fisher 21 S IL Acc d/o G S & Tabitha on 5 Feb 1880 at Garrisons Chp by CC Wertenbaker

DOUGHTY Augustus T 48 W Blacksmith Acc Acc s/o John R & Mary R to Mary S McLane 32 W Acc Acc d/o Lorenzo D & Sophia Mears on 22 May 1887 at Middlesex by JR Strugis

DOUGHTY Chas D Col 23 S Wage-earner N'hamp: Acc s/o Ann Brickhouse to Laura E West Col 16 S Acc Acc d/o Emmie on 9 Nov 1893 at Pungo: by JM Anderson

DOUGHTY Clarence Col 19 S Wage-earner Acc Acc s/o Susan to Margaret Gunter Col 18 S Acc Acc d/o Solomon & Arinthia on 29 May 1895 at Onancock by SW Watkins

DOUGHTY George L 33 W Bar Keeper Acc Acc s/o John O & Mary C to Elizabeth S Kellam 30 S Acc Acc d/o Lingcon & Tally on 19 Jan 1882 at Acc by RD Stimson

DOUGHTY James C Jr 18 S Farmer Acc Acc s/o James C & Margaret S T to Sarah F Guy 21 S Norfolk Co Acc d/o Robert & Caroline on 19 Sep 1880 at Acc by CC Wertenbaker

DOUGHTY Jno B 23 S Mechanic Acc Acc s/o Jno R & Mary to Rebecca A Ames 18 S Acc Acc d/o Richd T & Lousia on 11 May 1864 at Acc by JWA Elliott

DOUGHTY Jno T 27 S Farmer Acc Acc s/o Major & Kitty to Georgeana Bell 23 S Acc Acc d/o Robins & Sally on 12 Dec 1877 at Oak Grove Ch by JWA Elliott

DOUGHTY John 23 S Mechanic s/o John & Molly to Mary Ames 17 d/o Wm & Lizzy lic: 9 Jan 1865 marr: 11 Jan 1865

DOUGHTY Leonida R 27 S Wheelwright Acc Acc s/o James C & Margaret to Susan B Slocomb 27 S Acc Acc d/o Wm C & Susan on 23 Dec 1885 at Onancock by WC Vaden

DOUGHTY Major R 26 S Farmer Acc Acc s/o Major & Betty to Bettie V Mapp 18 S Acc Acc d/o Jas Mapp & Sophia E Richardson on 1 Dec 1880 at Oak Grove Ch by CC Wertenbaker

DOUGHTY Major R 28 W Farmer Acc Acc s/o Major & Kitty to Manie C Mapp 18 S Acc Acc d/o James & Sophionia on 29 Mar 1883 near Locustville by JWA Elliott

DOUGHTY Major R 39 W Farmer Acc Acc s/o Major & Kitty to Sallie A Read 23 S Acc Acc d/o Littleton & Henrietta on 4 Oct 1893 at Pungo: by JM Dunaway

DOUGHTY Oswald D 30 S Sewing Machine Agent Acc Acc s/o Jno O & Mary C to Yula B Kellam 24 S Acc Acc d/o Benj I & Cath A on 12 Dec 1883 at Acc by WC Vaden

DOUGHTY Richard T 24 S Carpenter Acc Acc s/o Major & Kitty to Hetty L Bradford 18 S Acc Acc d/o Abel & Tamey on 7 Feb 1875 near Collies Ch by FR Boston

DOUGHTY Richd Col 26 S Farmer Acc Acc s/o Jane to Elizth Smith Col 23 S Acc Acc d/o Esther on 19 Dec 1877 near Belle Haven by JE Humphreys

DOUGHTY Samuel Col 31 S Farmer

Acc Acc s/o Wm Satchel & Jane Docoty to Jennie Jarvis Col 31 S Acc Acc d/o Henry & Anna Smith on 11 Jul 1875 at Savageville by JK Plato

DOUGHTY Theodore Col 41 S Farmer Acc Acc s/o Wm West & Jane Doughty to Nancy Bunting Col 42 S Acc Acc d/o Ezekiel & Susan Anne on 28 Sep 1887 at Acc by L Duncan

DOUGHTY Wm H Col 22 S Farm Laborer Acc Acc s/o Jane to Margaret [Reed] Read Col 21 S Acc Acc d/o Mary on 10 Nov 1885 near Belle Haven by JE Humphreys

DOUGHTY Wm J 31 S Merchant Acc Acc s/o Jas A & Margt S to Maggie S Chandler 26 S Acc Acc d/o Sylvester R & Mary on 17 Mar 1878 at Onancock by JH Amiss

DOUGLASS Frederick [Doulgas] Col 22 S Wage-earner Acc Acc s/o Thos & Ellen to Clara [Douglas] Douglass Col 20 S Acc Acc d/o Jacob & Jane on 20 Dec 1893 at Temp'ville by GHT Byrd

DOUGLASS James L 24 S Soldier US Army b: PA to Susan E Bayly 19 lic: 25 Oct 1864 Eliz Bayly gave permission

DOUGLASS Louis 35 S Laborer Acc Acc s/o Betsy to Leah Downing 30 S Acc Acc d/o Virginia on 9 Jan 1868 at Acc by S Marshall

DOUGLASS Thomas of N (Douglas) 23 S s/o Wm to Harriet E Marshall 23 S d/o James & Harriet lic: 24 Jun 1864 Wm S Byrd says both are over 21

DOUGLASS William Col 23 S Farmer Acc Acc s/o Louis Conquest to Virginia Dickerson Col 19 S Acc Acc d/o Charles & Virginia on 16 Dec 1883 at Acc by AJ Satchell

DOWNING Asa Jas Col 27 S Farmer Acc Acc to Sarah Eliz'th Seymour 28 W Acc Acc d/o John & Catharine Floyd on 29 Dec 1895 at Acc by JN Waters

DOWNING Charles Col 22 S Sailor Acc Acc s/o Easter Mears to Virginia Doughty Col 18 S Acc Acc d/o Jane on 19 Jul 1874 at Pungo: by JK Plato

DOWNING Dan'l W Col 20 S Farmer N'hamp: N'hamp: s/o Mary Fitchett to Bettie Savage Col 18 S Acc Acc d/o Peter (of Patience) & Tann on 1 Nov 1893 at Acc by TW Nettles

DOWNING Edward T s/o John to Anna E Twiford d/o Obed P who gave consent lic: 20 Jul 1858 John W Sturgis says he over 21

DOWNING Francis (F) 32 S Farmer Acc Acc s/o Francis Downing & Elizabeth Beach to Elizabeth Harmon 31 S Acc Acc d/o John Narmon & Margaret Nock on 20 Mar 1861 at r/o Littl Lecato by LK LeCato (Levin J Hyslop says both over 21)

DOWNING Francis A 21 S Farmer Acc Acc s/o Francis A & Eliz'th J to Mamie E Wescott 21 S Acc Acc d/o Joseph J & Elizabeth on 25 Mar 1891 at Acc by JR Strugis

DOWNING Frank Col 29 S Acc Acc s/o Mary to Georgianna [Douglas] Douglass Col 20 S Acc Acc d/o Sarah on 7 Sep 1882 at Oak Hall by JC Cluff

DOWNING Geo 31 S Farmer b: Acc s/o Joshua & Nancy to Charlotte Drummond 26 S b: Acc d/o Philip & Patience Drummond on 10 Aug 1854 at New Church by T Waters

DOWNING George FN to Sarah Case FN d/o Chas FN who gave consent lic: 29 May 1854 Thos W Smith says Geo over 21

DOWNING George FN to Ann Armstrong FN lic: 30 Jan 1854

DOWNING George Col 45 W Farmer Acc Acc s/o Leah to Ayrie Smith Col 34 S Acc Acc d/o Dinah on 2 Dec 1874 near Belle Haven by R Davis

DOWNING George Col 47 W Farmer Acc Acc to Sarah Bell 37 S Acc Acc on 29 Dec 1875 at Garrisons Chp by RH Govans

DOWNING George Col 36 S Farmer Acc Acc s/o Hester to Sarah Byrd Col 32 S Acc Acc d/o Mary on 29 Mar 1882 near News Town by AJ Satchell

DOWNING George Col 23 S Sailor Acc Acc s/o Edmond & Emily to Virginia Nock Col 20 S Acc Acc d/o Wm & Harriet on 25 Jan 1882 at Acc by LW Lee

DOWNING George Col 30 W Farmer Acc Acc s/o Edmond & Emma to Laura Etta Ames Col 27 S Acc Acc d/o George on 27 Jun 1889 at Mappsburg by JB Lewis

DOWNING George M Col 28 S Laborer Acc Acc s/o Geo & Ann to Mary Bayly Col 25 S Acc Acc d/o Mary on 1 May 1884 near Horntown by JC Cluff

DOWNING George R Col 23 S Wage-earner Acc Acc s/o Joshua & Rosie to Gertrude Selby Col 22 S Acc Acc d/o Joseph & Hannah on 29 Dec 1889 at New Church by TM Poulson

DOWNING Henry P Col 20 S Farmer Acc Acc s/o Shepherd & Amy to Margaret Smith Col 22 S Acc Acc d/o Eliza on 1 Jan 1890 at Acc by N Morris

DOWNING James William 30 S Sailor Acc Acc s/o John & Mary to Elizabeth A Matthews 32 W Acc Acc d/o Major & Susan Savage on 7 Oct 1858 at Acc by JF Chaplain (Alfred J Mears says he over 21)

DOWNING Jno B 55 W Ship Carpenter b: Acc s/o Francis & Polly to Julia Ann Bloxom 28 S b: Acc d/o Wm W & Eliza E on 13 Aug 1856 at r/o Mrs Bloxom's by J Allen (Isaac Purnell says she over 21)

DOWNING Jno R 23 S Farmer b: Ames Ridge s/o Jno & Mary to Mariah Jane Bell 19 S b: Bradford Nk d/o Jas & Charlotte & (ward/o James R Garrison who gave consent) on 31 Jan 1855 near Bradford Nk by A Wallace

DOWNING John 28 S Farmer b: Acc s/o Jno Downing & Mary Mears to Anna Twiford 17 S b: Acc d/o Obed Twiford & Charlott Ailworth on 23 Jul 1858 at r/o David Mears by LK LeCato

DOWNING John (FN) 21 S Farm Hand Acc Acc s/o Geoge Nock & Leah Downing to Hester Jubilee (FN) 20 S Acc Acc d/o Shepard & Rachel on 2 Jan 1861 at Locust Mount by JWA Elliott (Rachel Case gives consent for Hester & Levin B Belote says he over 21)

DOWNING John Col 25 S Laborer Acc Acc s/o Henry & Susan to Mary Parkes Col 22 S Acc Acc d/o James W & Elizth on 23 Nov 1882 at Acc by GW Young

DOWNING John B 19 S Farmer Acc Acc s/o Francis & Lizzie to Polly W Trower 16 S Acc Acc d/o Thomas & Ann on 26 Oct 1881 at Hollies Ch by SC Boston

DOWNING John O 21 S Farmer Acc Acc s/o Edwd Harma A to Laura V Copes 21 S Acc Acc d/o Wm W on 22 Oct 1884 at Acc by RB Beadles

DOWNING John R 43 W Farmer Acc Acc s/o Jno & Mary to Alice E Smith 26 S Acc Acc d/o James G & Elizth S G on 11 Nov 1875 near Dunkirk by BW Dougherty

DOWNING John T Col 39 S Wage-earner Acc Acc s/o Geo to Emma Conquest Col 35 S Acc Acc on 31 Dec 1893 at Wattsville by EH Bean

DOWNING Joshua Col 49 W Farmer Acc Acc s/o Virginia Downing to Esther Bishop Col 24 S Som Co MD Acc d/o James & Sarah on 17 Apr

1895 at Acc by TM Poulson

DOWNING Joshua Wm Col 23 S Wage-earner Acc Acc s/o Joshua & Rosa to Annie Hargis Col 18 S Acc Acc d/o Peter & Harriet on 4 Mar 1893 at New Church by TM Poulson

DOWNING Orban W 22 S Farmer Acc N'hamp: s/o Jno B & Julia A to Hester A Hutchinson 18 S Acc Acc d/o E W & Caroline E on 10 Dec 1879 at Craddockville by E Hebard

DOWNING Robert W Col 24 S Farmer Acc Acc s/o Shepperd & Amy to Burlena Snead Col 22 S Acc Acc d/o Edmund & Sarah on 25 Jan 1888 at Acc by AJ Satchell

DOWNING Robert W Col 28 S Farmer Acc Acc s/o Shepherd & Amy to Georgianna Melvin Col 25 S Acc Acc d/o George & Jane on 14 Feb 1892 at Wattsville by AS Amos

DOWNING Samuel 38 S Laborer to Emma Webb 35 lic: 26 Dec 1864

DOWNING Shephard FN 24 S Farmer (Laborer) Acc Acc to Annie Lurton (Waters) FN 22 S Acc Acc on 4 Jan 1863 at Acc by GH Ewell

DOWNING Startton Bayly (Dr) 33 S Physician b: N'hamp: s/o Edwd W P & Margt to Camilla Major 17 S b: Acc d/o Wm (L) (dec'd) & Eliz'th & (ward/o James M Savage who gave consent) on 5 May 1858 at Acc by P Warren

DOWNING Thomas Col 31 S Laborer Acc Acc s/o Betsy jubilee to Cardilia E Shield Col 17 S Acc Acc d/o Sarah E on 13 Mar 1883 at Acc by GW Young

DOWNING Wesley Col 27 S Wage-earner Acc Acc s/o Mary to Eliza Wessells Col 22 S Acc Acc d/o Ann on 30 Mar 1890 at Acc by AJ Satchell

DOWNING William Col 58 W Farmer Acc Acc s/o Guy & Sally to Ann Sample Col 43 S Acc Acc d/o Lizzie Walker on 13 Nov 1889 at Acc by JB Lewis

DOWNING Wm FN 22 S Farmer Acc Acc s/o Leah to Margt S (Serah) Webb FN 19 S Acc Acc d/o Jno & Harriett on 12 Mar 1862 at Acc by JWA Elliott

DOWNS Daniel T 39 W Keeper of Mill b: Somerset ME s/o Gusham & Elizth Tipets to Laceretta [Brymer] (Brimer) Brimer 29 S b: Acc d/o Jos & Polly on 24 Sep 1858 at Acc by T Waters (Stephen Bloxom says she over 21)

DREWER John R 21 S Mariner Acc Acc s/o Jno W & Eliza to Kate E Griffin 21 S Norfolk Norfolk d/o Cornelius & Virginia A on 11 Jun 1886 at Temp'ville by M Oldham

DREWER Lloyd M 21 S Merchant Acc Acc s/o John W & Eliza J to Virginia Lee Grinnalds 21 S Acc Acc d/o James H & Tabitha Jane on 10 Jul 1892 at Oak Hall by RB Scott

DRUMMOND Alfred T Col 21 S Farmer Acc Acc s/o Handy & Louisa to Mary S West Col 19 S Acc Acc d/o Peggie on 23 Nov 1890 at Acc by TW Nettles

DRUMMOND Augustus 21 S Sailor Acc Acc s/o Wm & Mary R to Margaret S Sturgis 20 S Acc Acc d/o James & Margaret on 9 Apr 1861 at r/o Wm S Sturgis by LK LeCato

DRUMMOND Charles (FN) 24 S Farmer Acc Acc s/o Charles Drummond & Minley Wright to Marian Godfrey FN 23 S Acc Acc d/o Levin Godfrey (FN)& Marthy Guy on 6 Jan 1861 at r/o Littl Lecato by LK LeCato (Wm Hargis says both over 21)

DRUMMOND Charles Col 44 S Farmer Acc Acc s/o Charles & Aminta to Lucy Garrison Col 40 S Acc Acc d/o Esau & Nannie on 1 Sep 1875 at Acc by HT Rich

DRUMMOND Charles Col 22 S Farmer Acc Acc s/o Aninta to Annie Bayly Col 21 S Acc Acc d/o Barbara on 5 Oct 1884 at Acc by LW Lee

DRUMMOND Charles Col 22 S Laborer Acc Acc s/o George & Sarah Lewis to Ella Dix Col 21 S Acc Acc d/o Charlie Lewis & Farncis Dix on 1 Sep 1887 at Acc by AJ Satchell

DRUMMOND Charles Col 26 S Wage-earner Acc Acc s/o Charles & Mary to Martha White Col 21 S Acc Acc d/o Emma on 24 Sep 1888 at Acc by JK Adams

DRUMMOND Charles Col 26 S Wage-earner Acc Acc s/o Abel Drummond & Leah Riley to Eliza Savage Col 25 S Acc Acc d/o Peter & Rose Waples on 4 Jun 1891 at Acc by LE Toulson

DRUMMOND Charles Col 34 W Farmer Acc Acc s/o Chas & Lucy to Emma West Col 20 S Acc Acc d/o John R & Elsia on 3 Jul 1895 at Onancock by PW Lee

DRUMMOND Constantine to Susan Chesser d/o Polly who gave consent lic: 12 Jul 1857 James Tilor says he over 21

DRUMMOND Edmund Col 32 S Farmer Acc Acc s/o Charles & Amenta to Betsy Winder Col 23 S Acc Acc d/o George & Dina on 30 May 1875 near Bull Run by JW Ruff

DRUMMOND Edmund Col 45 S Farmer Acc Acc s/o Edmund & Mary to Margaret Sample Col 40 S Acc Acc d/o William Satchell & Eliza Sample on 13 Jan 1888 at Acc by JK Adams

DRUMMOND Francis R 30 S Farmer Acc Acc s/o James & Ruth to Annie J Bayly 20 S Acc Acc d/o Thos S & Elizth M on 22 Dec 1881 at Thos S Bailey's by JC Watson

DRUMMOND Geo FN 30 S Farmer b: Acc s/o Philip & Patience to Rachel [Stokely] (Stockley) Stokely (FN) 17 S b: Acc d/o Peter Custis & Mary Stokely on 7 Feb 1855 at Acc by T Waters

DRUMMOND Geo Col 22 S Laborer Acc Acc s/o Elzie Riley to Maria Bayly Col 21 S Acc Acc d/o Lydia Bull on 1 Jan 1879 at Onancock by PA Leatherbury

DRUMMOND Geo E 21 S Sailor b: Acc s/o Wm & Mary to Adah Kellam 18 S b: Acc d/o Argyle & Sally on 11 Jan 1855 near Pungo: by M Oldham

DRUMMOND George Col 25 S Wage-earner Acc Acc s/o Abe & Leah to Annie Wise Col 19 S Acc Acc d/o Abel & Carolina on 30 Dec 1894 at Acc by AJ Wallace

DRUMMOND George H Col 22 S Farmer Acc Acc s/o Annie to Sarah A Johnson Col 21 S Acc Acc d/o Isaac & Maria on 2 Mar 1891 at Acc by JS Wallace

DRUMMOND George W 21 S Carpenter Acc Acc s/o George E & Adah to Mary G Kellam 24 W N'hamp: Acc d/o Louis M Stewart on 15 Feb 1888 at Mappsburg by CD Crawley

DRUMMOND Harry Col 22 S Farmer Acc Acc s/o Alsie Riley to Rosa Edwards Col 18 S Acc Acc d/o Jno & Emaline on 29 Dec 1886 at Onancock by JC Williams

DRUMMOND Harry E 22 S Merchant Acc Acc s/o Henry C & Sallie A to Edith G Boggs 20 S Acc Acc d/o Lewis F & Catharine on 31 May 1893 at Acc by AC Berryman

DRUMMOND Harvey C 33 S Farmer s/o James & Harriet to Sarah A Joynes 26 d/o Elias & Sarah lic: 8 Aug 1864 marr: 8 Aug 1864 at Accomack

DRUMMOND Henry 53 W Farmer

Marriages

Acc Acc s/o Richard & Catharine to Margaret S Custis 38 S Acc Acc d/o Wm H & Elizth on 24 Dec 1859 at Acc by JH Addison (Robert T Drummond says both over 21)

DRUMMOND Herbert A 21 S Merchant Acc Acc s/o Kosciusko & Celia A to Malinda Drummond 25 S Acc Acc d/o William R & Malinda on 19 Jun 1894 at Acc by DJ Traynham

DRUMMOND Iraiah 32 W Farmer Acc Acc s/o Charlotte Custis to Sarah Drummond 20 S Acc Acc d/o Spencer & Marian on 5 Mar 1882 at Drum'tn by AJ Satchell

DRUMMOND Isaiah Col 26 S Farmer Acc Acc s/o Mary to Mary West Col 17 S Acc Acc d/o Mary on 6 Jan 1876 at Bapt Ch by A Joynes

DRUMMOND James (C) 24 S Ship Carpenter b: Acc s/o James & Harriet to Elizabeth S Moore 21 S b: Acc d/o William & Jane on 2 Jan 1856 at Acc by JH Addison

DRUMMOND James C 39 W Carpenter Acc Acc s/o James C & Harriet to Ann F Chandler 25 S Acc Acc d/o Jno W & Elizth on 2 Nov 1870 at M E Ch S by JH Addison

DRUMMOND James M 23 S Farmer Acc Acc s/o Henry & Margt to Tabitha S Mason 21 S Acc Acc d/o Stephen & Euphemia on 17 Nov 1886 at Acc by CA Grice

DRUMMOND Jesse 33 S Farmer Acc Acc s/o Patience to Esther Douglass 23 S Acc Acc d/o Wm & Eliza on 22 Jan 1868 at Acc by S Marshall

DRUMMOND Jesse Col 25 S Acc Acc to Hester Fields Col 25 S Acc Acc on 3 Oct 1877 near New Church by JC Cluff

DRUMMOND Jno R L 23 S Farmer Acc Acc s/o Jno H & Carissa A to Mary E Ames 18 S Acc Acc d/o Levin & Lottie E on 13 Oct 1886 at Acc by L Rosser

DRUMMOND John Col 32 S Farmer Acc Acc s/o Charles & Arninta to Susan Bagwell Col 28 S Acc Acc d/o James & Ibby on 28 Dec 1876 near Drum'tn by PM Only

DRUMMOND John Col 20 S Farm Laborer Acc Acc s/o Emma Doughty to Mary S Garrison Col 19 S Acc Acc d/o Jacob & Isabella on 31 May 1885 at Locustville by LW Lee

DRUMMOND John E Col 23 S Farmer Acc Acc s/o Edmond Drummond & Emma Doughty to Mary F West Col 24 S Acc Acc d/o Nathaniel & Bridget on 2 Oct 1889 at Onancock by JH Offer

DRUMMOND John E Col 28 W Farmer Acc Acc s/o Edmund & Emma to Cordelia F Ewell Col 19 S Acc Acc d/o John E & Ellen on 14 Jul 1894 at Drum'tn by R Davis

DRUMMOND John S 22 S Boatman Acc Acc s/o John T & Eveline to Mary O Dickerson 25 W Acc Acc d/o Absalom & Eliz Lewis on 14 Dec 1887 at Temp'ville by WF Hayes

DRUMMOND John T 22 S Sailor Acc Acc s/o Jas H & Harriet to Susan E Taylor 18 S Acc Acc d/o Joseph (B)& Elizth on 21 Jul 1859 at Acc by JH Addison (James A Boggs says he over 21)

DRUMMOND John T 23 S Oysterman Acc Acc s/o Wm H & Elizth to Comfort E [Brodwater] Broadwater 18 S Acc Acc d/o Walter & Polly on 4 Sep 1861 at Acc by GH Ewell (Julius D Godwin says above correct and both over 21)

DRUMMOND John T Col 23 S Laborer Acc Acc s/o George Alice to Emma Bayly Col 24 S Acc Acc on 4 Oct 1876 at Onancock by JK Plato

DRUMMOND Joseph 26 S Wheelwright Acc Acc to Rosa A Cutler 20 S Acc Acc d/o George &

Mary A Cutler on 27 Jan 1876 near Pungo: by JE Humphreys

DRUMMOND Kosciusko 23 S Oysterman Acc Acc s/o Wm & Elizth to Cecilia Taylor 21 S Acc Acc d/o Jas B & Nancy on 24 Dec 1867 at Acc by JO Moss

DRUMMOND Levi Col 21 S Laborer Acc Acc s/o Robt Drummond & Mary Cropper to Nellie Edwards Col 16 S Acc Acc d/o John & Emaline on 12 Apr 1883 at Onancock by SC Boston

DRUMMOND Levin (black) 21 S Farmer Acc Acc s/o Mary to Euphemia Ann Matthews (black) 18 S Acc Acc d/o Easter on 13 Jan 1875 at Acc by HT Rich

DRUMMOND Levin H Col 20 S Laborer Acc Acc s/o Louisa to Sarah Young Col 18 S Acc Acc d/o Louisa on 1 Nov 1882 at Drum'tn by LW Lee

DRUMMOND Lewis W 22 S Sailor Acc Acc s/o Constantine & Susan to Elizth McCready 18 S Acc Acc d/o Geo R & Elizth on 2 Feb 1882 at Acc by RB Beadles

DRUMMOND Louis D 39 W Carriage Maker Acc Acc s/o Savage H & Mahala Bell (error) to Mary A Bell 35 S Acc Acc d/o Savage H & Mahala Bell on 29 Sep 1881 at Cat's Bridge by JE Humphreys

DRUMMOND Millard F 22 S Oysterman Acc Acc s/o Wm R & Melinda to Emma F Smith 18 S Acc Acc d/o Custis & Rose on 25 Dec 1879 at Meth Par by JW Hilldrup

DRUMMOND Nelson D Col 33 S Farmer Acc Acc s/o Nelson Custis & Rachel Drummond to Betsey Kerr Col 37 S Acc Acc d/o Harriet on 13 Jan 1886 at Acc by CA Horsey

DRUMMOND Parker Col 27 S Laborer Acc Acc s/o Tabby to Margaret Seymour Col 18 S Acc Acc d/o Betsey on 16 Mar 1883 at Drum'tn by LW Lee

DRUMMOND Purnel Col 24 S Oysterman Acc Acc s/o Mary to Ann Griffin Col 22 S Acc Acc d/o Stephen Rayfield & Leah Griffin on 30 Dec 1869 at Hunting Ck by A Joynes

DRUMMOND Robert 45 W Farmer Acc Acc s/o James & Harriet to Emma Waters 30 W Acc Acc d/o Elias & Sally Joynes on 5 Dec 1877 at Sluytkill Nk by JH Amiss

DRUMMOND Robt Col 21 S Laborer Acc Acc s/o Robt & Mary to Nellie Finney Col 18 S Acc Acc d/o Virginia Bailey on 4 Nov 1877 at Drum'tn Ch by AJ Williams

DRUMMOND Robt J (T) 25 S Farmer & Calker Acc Acc s/o James & Harrit to Susan A (Ann) Boggs 21 S Acc Acc d/o William C & Elizabeth on 31 Dec 1856 at Acc by JH Addison

DRUMMOND Samuel Col 25 S Laborer Acc Acc s/o Mary to Martha S Ayres Col 17 S Acc Acc d/o Elizth on 8 Jan 1882 at Bay Side Par by RJ Waters

DRUMMOND Spencer FN s/o Charles to Miriam Godfrey FN d/o Levin lic: 5 Jan 1861 Wm Hargis says both over 21

DRUMMOND Spencer Col 25 S Wage-earner Acc Acc s/o Leah Riley to Mary H Fosque Col 18 S Acc Acc d/o Lewis & Ary on 11 Aug 1889 at Onancock by JH Offer

DRUMMOND Spencer J 28 S Merchant Acc Acc s/o Henry C & Sally A to Olivia W Lilliston 19 S Acc Acc d/o Alexander W & Bettie E on 6 Nov 1895 at Onancock by GE Booker

DRUMMOND Thomas 22 S Sailor Acc Acc s/o Richard & Susan to Jane Killman 19 S Acc Acc d/o Ezekiel &

Palunia on 21 Apr 1875 at Slugtkill Nk by JH Amiss

DRUMMOND Thomas Col 18 S Laborer Acc Acc s/o Polly to Annie Young Col 17 S Acc Acc d/o Margaret Holden on 7 Oct 1883 at Whitesville by JH Nutter

DRUMMOND Thomas Col 24 S Farmer Acc Acc s/o George & Ailey to Annie V Bayne Col 25 S Acc Acc d/o James H & Emma F on 23 May 1894 at Acc C H by AJ Satchell

DRUMMOND William Col 22 S Laborer Acc Acc s/o Mary Snead to Jannetta Ewell Col 15 S Acc Acc d/o Sarah on 10 Jan 1875 at Acc by HT Rich

DRUMMOND William L 26 S Farmer Acc Acc s/o John H & Clarissa A to Nannie Wescott 30 S N'hamp: Acc d/o Edward D & Virginia S on 29 Jan 1891 at Acc by JA Barker

DRUMMOND Wilson Col 38 S Wage-earner Acc Acc to Catharine Bagwell Col 27 S Acc Acc d/o Ephraim on 4 Jan 1891 near Savageville by JB Lewis

DRUMMOND Wm Col 45 S Farmer Acc Acc s/o Agnes to Maggie Crowson Col 22 S Acc Acc d/o Fannie on 21 Jul 1878 at Poor House by A Joynes

DRUMMOND Wm H 20 S Carpenter Acc Acc s/o Henry & Mary to Rose A Ames 22 S Acc Acc d/o Julius & Susan on 24 Dec 1879 at Acc by FA Davis

DRUMMOND Wm Thos (FN) 27 S Farming Acc Acc s/o Solomon Wallops & Jane Drummond Town to Margaret C (Caroline) Douglass (FN) 19 S Acc Acc d/o Wm & Eliza (who gave consent) on 14 Mar 1860 at Acc by T Waters (Samuel Q Davis says he over 21)

DRYDEN John E 24 S Merchant New Town MD New Town MD s/o Henry & Eleanor to Josephine Bohn 21 S Norfolk VA Acc d/o Henry & Elizth on 11 May 1875 at Onancock by FR Boston

DRYDEN Thomas 22 S Farmer Acc Wor Co MD s/o Littleton & Charlotte to Minnie C Powell 21 S Wor Co MD Acc d/o Edward & Catharine on 27 Oct 1892 at Chinco: Isld by RB Sanford

DUDLEY Cyrus (Col) 24 S Laborer Acc Acc s/o Henry & Caroline to Leah Slocomb (Col) 21 S Acc Acc d/o Mary on 30 Dec 1873 at Horntown by S Johns

DUER Abel C 20 S Farmer Acc Acc s/o Joshua R & Sarah A to Sarah C Kellam 21 S Acc Acc d/o Geo A & Ann A on 9 Feb 1876 at Garrisons Chp by JE Humphreys

DUFFY Alfred Col 23 S Laborer Acc Acc s/o Eliza to Jane Mason Col 20 S Acc Acc d/o Sabra on 7 Oct 1873 near New Town by A Joynes

DUFFY Alfred Col 22 S Farmer Acc Acc s/o George & Sarah to Melissa Trehearn Col 23 S Acc Acc d/o Edmund on 28 Dec 1892 at Acc by AJ Satchell

DUFFY George [Duffie] Col 25 S Laborer Acc Acc s/o Peter & Eliza to Sarah Mason Col 24 S Acc Acc d/o Jamie on 29 Sep 1873 at New Town by A Joynes

DUFFY Simon Col 30 S Farmer Acc Acc s/o Levin Duffy & Mary Bundick to Sarah Taylor Col 35 W Acc Acc d/o William Twyford & Rachel Bird on 18 Sep 1887 at News Town by AJ Satchell

DUFFY William [Duffie] Col 21 S Wage-earner Acc Acc s/o Alfred & Jane to Mary Finney Col 19 S Acc Acc d/o Abram & Clarissa on 5 Jan 1893 at Acc by AJ Satchell

DUKES Chas L 21 S Farmer Acc Acc s/o John & Eliza to Ida J Matthews

21 S Acc Acc d/o Alfred J & Linay A on 25 Oct 1893 at Lee Mont by JET Ewell

DUNCAN Griffin Col 21 S Farmer Acc Acc s/o Jane Kellam to Margaret Downing Col 21 S Acc Acc d/o Saml & Emma on 24 May 1874 at Belle Haven by JE Humphreys

DUNCAN Hezikiah Col 25 S Laborer Acc Acc s/o Lydia Satchall to Margaret Jacobs Col 21 S Acc Acc d/o Elizabeth Martin on 25 Oct 1871 at Acc by JE Humphreys

DUNCAN James W 21 S Farmer Acc Acc s/o William & Mary to Emma F Colonna 17 S Acc Acc d/o Wm & Charlotte on 27 Aug 1871 at Acc by O Littleton

DUNCAN John R s/o Meshack to Thealey Ann (Bird) Byrd d/o Eborn who gave consent lic: 23 Dec 1856 John Rew Jr says he over 21

DUNCAN John W 24 S Merchant Acc Acc s/o John H & Elizabeth to Elizabeth Kellam 21 S Acc Acc d/o Geo & Ann on 23 Feb 1880 at Craddockville by E Hebard

DUNCAN Levi Col s/o Kiah Kellam & Jane Kellam to Elizabeth (Bevans) Beavans Col d/o Severn Bivins & Elizabeth Bivans lic: 27 Dec 1869 marr: 29 Dec 1869 near Pungoteague

DUNCAN Louis Col 55 S Farmer Acc Acc s/o George & Lucinda Foskey to Mary West Col 50 S Acc Acc d/o William & Lucy on 4 Sep 1895 at Pungo: by CW Satchell

DUNCAN Meshack E 29 S Farmer Acc Acc s/o John R & Othelia to Martha L Fitchett 26 S Acc Acc d/o John G & Eliz'th on 28 Dec 1892 at Acc by JL King

DUNCAN Nathaniel Col 21 S Wage-earner Acc Acc s/o Griffin to Susan Carter Col 20 S Acc Acc d/o Susan on 12 Nov 1890 at Acc by L Duncan

DUNCAN Thomas 26 S Farmer Acc Acc s/o Wm T & Mary to Laura Sparrow 26 W Acc Acc d/o Henry P Lilliston on 14 Nov 1877 at Zion Ch by DA Woodson

DUNTON Custis M widr to Elizth C Willis d/o Littl on 9 Nov 1852 at Acc by M Oldham

DUNTON Frank S [Dunston] 23 S Farmer Acc Acc s/o Jno & Kerry to Anna Smith 17 S Acc Acc d/o Sally C on 4 Jan 1880 at Greenhill by CS Arnett

DUNTON George [Dunston] Col 24 S Laborer NC Acc s/o Rose Poole to Cordie Savage Col 22 S Acc Acc d/o Margaret on 18 Oct 1884 at Acc by CA Horsey

DUNTON Henry R 24 S Farmer N'hamp: Acc s/o Saml K & Margt to Mary F LeCato 19 S Acc Acc d/o Littleton K & Nancy on 25 Jan 1872 at Acc by O Littleton

DUNTON Jacob T Col 24 S Laborer Acc Acc s/o Rachel to Charlotte Kellam Col 28 S Acc Acc d/o Sally on 7 Aug 1881 at Locust Mount by RJ Waters

DUNTON Jesse R Col 28 S Farmer Acc Acc s/o Rachel to Mary Hateney Col 19 S Acc Acc d/o Thomas & Mary on 29 Oct 1890 at Oak Grove by JWA Elliott

DUNTON John T s/o James S dec'd to Margaret S Taylor d/o Henry W who gave consent & is from Temperanceville lic: 23 Jan 1854 Major T Davis says he over 21

DUNTON John T 38 W Farmer Acc Acc to Margaret J Mason 29 S Acc Acc on 5 Sep 1866 at Acc by M Oldham

DUNTON Rascusko 40 W Farmer N'hamp: N'hamp: s/o Jno R & Emily to Mary G Kellam 21 S Acc Acc d/o Augustus J F & Mary E on 13 Apr 1881 at Acc by GH Ray

DUSKEY George 22 S Farmer Wor Co MD Chinco: Isld s/o Stephend & Leah to Drucilla Jester 16 S Chinco: Isld Chinco: Isld d/o Wm & Elizth on 15 Oct 1882 at Chinco: Isld by OS Walton

EARLY John E Col 23 S Cooper Washington DC Acc s/o James & Cella to Amanda M Fisher Col 17 S Acc Acc d/o George E & Harriet on 3 Jan 1892 at Acc by AJ Satchell

EASON Samuel W 28 S Clergyman Norfolk Co N'hamp: s/o Isaac N & Narcissa C to Wessie E Nock 27 S Acc Acc d/o John O & Sarah A on 11 Jul 1894 at Acc by JR Sturgis

EAST Bayly B 19 S Farmer Acc Acc s/o Dial W & Henrietta to Maggie L Powell 22 S Acc Acc d/o James H & Emma on 10 Sep 1890 at Onancock by GW Burke

EAST Dial W 21 S Farmer Acc Acc s/o Peter T & Susan to Henrietta Martin 19 S Acc Acc d/o Jane on 7 Dec 1870 at Acc by LK LeCato

EAST George T 64 W Farmer Acc Acc s/o John & Susan to Elizabeth D Evans 62 W Acc Acc on 18 Sep 1878 near Chinch Town by TM Poulson

EAST George W 24 W Sailor s/o George T & Sarah to Elizabeth Bull 22 d/o James & Lulice lic: 24 Dec 1864 marr: 29 Dec 1864 at Accomack

EAST George W 20 S Farmer Acc Acc s/o Peter W & Mary J to Bettie S Lewis 20 S Acc Acc d/o William Thos & Elizabeth W on 4 Jun 1890 at Deep Ck by GF Farring

EAST Hugh G F 23 S Mariner Acc Acc s/o Mary to Amanda F [Culling] Cullen 24 S N'hamp: Acc d/o David on 22 Dec 1875 at Acc by RC Jones

EAST James 21 S Waterman b: Acc s/o Wm & Nancy to Eliz Gray single b: Acc d/o Thos & Nancy & (ward/o James Gray) on 12 Jun 1856 at r/o Jno D Taylor by ES Grant (James Crowson says he over 21)

EAST James H 28 S Sailor Acc Acc s/o James H & Eliz'th to Maggie L Crockett 21 S Acc Acc d/o Henry L & Eliza on 1 Dec 1890 at Onancock by GW Burke

EAST James S P 19 S Farmer Acc Acc s/o James T & Julia A to Ida Parker 22 S Acc Acc d/o Alicia on 16 Oct 1887 near Onancock by JW Hundley

EAST James Thomas 31 S House Carpenter Acc Onancock s/o Levin & Leah to Julia Ann East 18 S Acc Onancock d/o Peter & Susan on 25 Sep 1859 near Locustville by D Titlow (John S Gibb saus he over 21)

EAST Leroy G 25 S Farmer Acc Acc s/o George to Anna M Burton 17 S Acc Acc d/o Stewart & Rachel on 30 Nov 1881 at Downings Ch by RB Beadles

EAST Peter B 20 S Farmer Acc Acc s/o James T & Juliet to Rebecca L Guy 21 S Acc Acc d/o John W & Mary Susan on 4 Dec 1881 at Acc by SC Boston

EAST Peter T 75 W Farmer Acc Acc s/o James & Rachel to Susan Kelly 48 W Acc Acc d/o Edward & Eliz'th Watson on 23 Nov 1892 at Onancock by AJ Reamy

EAST Peter T 18 S Farmer Acc Acc s/o Peter W & Mary J to Jennie [Shreaves] Shrieves 21 S Acc Acc d/o Wm J & Polly on 20 Mar 1895 at Acc by MF Sanford

EAST Peter W 22 S Farmer Acc Acc s/o Peter T & Margaret to Mary J Kellam 22 S Acc Acc d/o Thos on 13 Oct 1869 at Acc by JC Martin

EAST Robert H 24 S Farmer Acc Acc s/o Wm S & Lucy to Mary Ida Walker 17 S Acc Acc d/o Wm & Kate on 3 Jan 1894 at Acc C H by JM Dunaway

EAST Samuel H. 18 S Farmer Acc Acc

s/o Peter & Susan to Otelia J Hayle 27 S Acc Acc d/o James & Rosetta on 19 Dec 1875 near Locustville by LK LeCato

EAST William 32 S Farmer s/o Wm & Nancy to Elizabeth Bundick 22 S d/o George & Ann lic: 21 Dec 1864 marr: 29 Dec 1864 at Accomack

EAST William 23 S Farmer Acc Acc s/o Wm to Willianna Beasley 17 S Acc Acc d/o Susan on 28 Feb 1883 at Acc by SC Boston

EAST William B 36 W Manufacturing Norfolk Co Norfolk City s/o John & Margaret A to Mary H Holt 19 S Acc Acc d/o Edward V & Margaret C on 12 Dec 1894 at Acc by GP Rutledge

EAST William T 26 S Farmer Acc Acc s/o William A & Eliz'th to Mary Ann Bradford 18 S Acc Acc d/o Benjamin T & Mary Ann on 27 Dec 1891 at Acc C H by VW Bargamin

EAST Peter T 70 W Farmer Acc Acc s/o James & Rachel to Susan Parker 27 S Acc Acc d/o Ailsie on 8 Jan 1888 at Onancock by RA Compton

EDLOR M Jerimah Col 43 S Evangelist Jamaica West Indies Norfolk Co s/o Lewis & Emma to Phoebe A Kellam Col 24 S Acc Acc d/o Sarah on 1 Aug 1894 at Onancock by JG Martin

EDMONDS George A [Edmunds] 33 S Farmer Acc Acc s/o Thos & Annie to Alexine M Davis 25 S Acc Acc d/o Shy S & Leah on 11 Dec 1867 at Acc by E Hebard

EDMONDS John W 42 S Editor Acc Acc s/o John W & Tabitha A to May Gunter 35 S Acc Acc d/o Benjamin T & Ellen on 8 Nov 1888 at bride's home by JW Hundley

EDMONDS Perry [Edmunds] 22 W Laborer Acc Acc s/o Mary Willis to Rachel Stevens 23 S Acc Acc d/o Milly Savage on 4 Mar 1868 at Acc by JH Hughes

EDMONDS Thomas C 27 S Farmer

Acc Acc to Annie M Broxton 23 S Richmond Co VA Acc d/o Thos & Mary on 16 Oct 1872 at Acc by JE Humphreys

EDWARDS Edward C 22 S Farmer Acc Acc to Susan Bull 19 S Acc Acc d/o Major & Sarah on 3 Jan 1872 at Acc by O Littleton

EDWARDS Elder N 19 S Farmer Acc Acc s/o John H & Hester A to Dora C Marsh 17 S Som Co MD Acc d/o David A & Matilda on 4 Sep 1895 at Acc by HS Dulany

EDWARDS Ezar W 44 W Farmer Acc Acc s/o John & Alice to Indiana Susan [Kilmon] Killman 46 S Acc Acc d/o Charles & Rosa on 16 Oct 1889 at Onancock by RA Compton

EDWARDS Ezra W 22 S Sailor Acc Acc s/o John & Ailsey to Martha W Poulson 31 S Acc Acc d/o John & Eliza on 14 Nov 1866 at Acc by WT Tull

EDWARDS James T 2(?) S Farmer Acc Acc s/o John & Alice to Josephine M Smith 18 S Acc Acc d/o Ezekiel Y & Margt on 7 Oct 1874 at Onancock by RC Jones

EDWARDS James T 22 S Farmer Acc Acc s/o Egar W & Martha to Daisy D Guy 18 S Acc Acc d/o James E & Jane on 3 Jan 1894 at Onancock by AJ Reamy

EDWARDS Jno H 24 S Waterman Acc Acc s/o Jno & Ailey to Hester A Williams 24 S N'hamp: Acc d/o Wm & Esther on 11 May 1864 at Acc by ES Grant

EDWARDS John W 21 S Farmer Acc Acc s/o Henry H & Hester to Lena J Northam 21 S Acc Acc d/o James & Pauline on 20 Dec 1893 at Acc by EC Atkins

EDWARDS Madison Col 31 S Farmer Acc Acc s/o John & Emeline to Esther [Gillet] Gillett Col 26 S Acc Acc d/o Maria on 30 Dec 1890 at

Acc by JB Lewis

EICHELBERGER Benjamin T [Eichilberger] 23 S Farmer Acc Acc s/o Wm F & Mary to Margaret E James 17 S Acc Acc d/o Geo W & Margt on 25 Jan 1877 at Acc by LK LeCato

EICHELBERGER Henry [Eichelbeger] Col 22 S Farmer Acc Acc s/o Isaac to Mary Savage Col 30 S Acc Acc d/o Lizzie Finney on 16 Feb 1887 at bride's home by TW Nettles

EICHELBERGER Isaac Col 22 S Wage-earner Acc Acc s/o Isaac to Fanney [Baily] Bayly Col 16 S Acc Acc d/o Wm T & Delia on 1 Apr 1894 at Chinco: Isld by JH Offer

EICHELBERGER John A 28 S Farmer Acc Acc s/o Wm & Mary to Susan A Bundick 22 S Acc Acc d/o John & Mary on 27 Oct 1875 at Bradford Nk by LK LeCato

EICHELBERGER Wm J 30 S Farmer Acc Acc s/o Wm & Mary to Charlotte A J Walker 25 S Acc Acc d/o James & Sally on 10 Apr 1873 at Acc by LK LeCato

ELLIOTT Geo W 21 S Farming Acc Acc s/o Abel & Louisa to Bettie S Kellam 21 S Acc Acc d/o Thos & Polly on 25 Jun 1865 at Acc by JWA Elliott

ELLIOTT Henry Col 44 S Wage-earner Acc Acc s/o Darkey to Leah Ross Col 38 S Acc Acc on 16 Sep 1894 at Acc by PW Lee

ELLIOTT John FN 34 S Laborer Acc Acc s/o Mary to Sarah Sample FN 23 S Acc Acc d/o Betsy on 7 Jul 1855 at r/o Levin Nedah by JWA Elliott (Chas T Sturgis says both over 21)

ELLIOTT John Col 21 S Farm Labor Acc Acc to Phebe Ward Col 21 S Acc Acc d/o Eliza on 14 Mar 1883 at Locustville by LW Lee

ELLIOTT John Abram Col 23 S Farmer Acc Acc s/o Sarah to Mary Ellen Smith Col 21 S Acc Acc d/o Elize Giddings on 29 Jul 1895 at Acc by JN Waters

ELLIOTT John Thomas s/o Thomas to Caroline Parker d/o Thomas lic: 6 Jan 1855 Geo Parker says both over 21

ELLIOTT John W 34 S Farmer Acc Acc s/o John & Nancy to Margaret Lewis 22 S N'hamp: Acc d/o Edwd & Eliza on 16 Jan 1868 at Acc by JWA Elliott

ELLIOTT Thos G 26 S Merchant Acc Acc s/o Jas & E G to Margt S Bell 17 S Acc Acc d/o Lorenzo D & Aliary on 30 Aug 1863 at Acc by ES Grant

ELLIS Avara 39 W Oysterman Wor Co MD Acc s/o Avara to Margaret E Marshall 19 S Acc Acc d/o Dennard & Elizth on 13 Feb 1867 at Acc by JE Bundick

ELLIS Avery A 48 W Sailor Acc Acc to Sophia Jones 48 W Acc Acc d/o John & Jemima Parrymore on 4 Nov 1888 at Chesconessex by JW Easley

ELLIS James M 23 S Oysterman Acc Acc s/o Avery J & Eliza to Matilda J Dennis 17 S Acc Acc d/o John & Elizar A on 6 Aug 1876 at Saxes Isld by JM Anderson

ELLIS John A 21 S Oysterman Acc Acc s/o Avara J & Eliza A to Margaret A Crockett 15 S Acc Acc d/o Severn J & Rebecca A on 7 Nov 1878 at Jenkins Bridge by A Wiles

ELMORE George W 35 S Painter MD Acc to Indiana S Kellam 35 W Acc Acc on 8 Jan 1866 at Acc by GS May

ELMORE Vincent H 30 S Painter N'hamp: Acc s/o Richd & Jane to Roberta H Colonna 21 S Acc Acc d/o Jno & Susan on 10 Dec 1879 at Acc by FA Davis

ENGLISH Alfred 39 W Oysterman b :NJ to Harriet Aydelotte 39 W d/o James Hargis lic: 19 Feb 1870 near

Horntown

ENNIS John Col 22 S Farmer Acc Acc s/o George & Emma to Maggie Sample Col 21 S Acc Acc d/o Leah on 28 Sep 1893 near Belle Haven by J Savage

ENSOR John B 29 S Carriage Maker Baltimore Co MD Baltimore City MD s/o Wm O & Eliz'th to Bertie B Nock 23 S Acc Acc d/o Levin W & Sarah C on 18 Feb 1891 near Wachapreague by WJ Twilley

ESKRIDGE John 25 S Waterman Spotsylvania Co Acc s/o Benjamin & Maria to Ann Lurton 21 S Acc Acc d/o James & Betsy on 27 Jun 1874 at Tangier Isld by RC Jones

ESKRIDGE Mayland [Eschridge] 21 S Oysterman Fredbry VA Tangier Isld s/o Benjamin & Maria to Jane [Dyes] Dies 23 S Tangier Isld Tangier Isld d/o Isaac S & Polly on 6 May 1874 at Tangier Isld by RC Jones

EVANS Alfred J 26 S Waterman Acc Acc s/o Solomon C & Maggie A to Kate A White 20 W Acc Acc d/o Lewis H & Mary on 15 Mar 1893 at Acc by AJ Reamy

EVANS Alma T 22 S Farmer Acc Acc s/o Wm & Sallie to Elizabeth T Custis 19 S Acc Acc d/o Littleton & Ellen on 18 Nov 1886 at Acc by JWA Elliott

EVANS Alonzo F 23 S Sailor Acc Acc s/o Solomon C & Margaret to Edith L [Twyford] Twiford 20 S Acc Acc d/o James H & Kate on 21 Apr 1891 at Acc by JB Pruitt

EVANS Caleb 23 S Waterman Smith Isld MD Acc to Amanda June [Crocket] Crockett 22 S Acc Acc d/o Major & Zippora on 28 Jun 1874 at Tangier Isld by RC Jones

EVANS Calvin Col 22 S Farmer Acc Acc s/o Harriet to Laura F [Justis] Justice Col 17 S Acc Acc d/o Sarah on 16 Nov 1884 at Acc by JC Cluff

EVANS Dennard W 20 S Sailor Acc Acc s/o Denard & Sarah to Mary S Evans 18 S Acc Acc d/o Wm S & Mary on 23 Apr 1879 at Mr Wm Jones' by JC Watson

EVANS Egbert G 20 S Sailor Acc Acc s/o Wm of Geo & Sally to Mary S Wise 20 S Acc Acc d/o Benj D & Louisa on 17 Sep 1879 at Pungo Meth Ch by CC Wertenbaker

EVANS Ellis 27 S Farmer Acc Acc s/o George W & Nellie to Rachel T Fitchett 17 S Acc Acc d/o Saml P & Alicia Ann on 5 Nov 1884 at Acc

EVANS Ethelbert 18 S Waterman Acc Acc s/o John H & Caroline to Maggie S [Parks] Parkes 17 S Acc Acc d/o John A & Juley on 26 Sep 1894 at Tangier Isld by WR Gwinn

EVANS Francis 60/70 W Farmer b: Acc s/o Elijah & Lovey to Elizabeth Lurton 30/40 S b: Acc d/o Jacob & Nancy (Abel) on 13 Aug 1856 at r/o E S Grant by ES Grant (Geo W Evans says both over 21)

EVANS Frank 20 S Oysterman Acc Acc s/o John & Triffie to Eliza Murphy 21 S Acc Acc d/o George & Jane on 28 Oct 1888 at Tangier by GL Hardesty

EVANS George (FN) 54 S Farmer b: Acc s/o Abram Bradford & Zilla Richarson to Esther Evans (FN) 57 S b: Acc d/o Joshus Sewell & Mary Savage on 18 Jan 1855 near Pungo: by M Oldham

EVANS George FN widr to Adah Nock FN lic: 8 Dec 1856 Thomas H Selby says she over 21

EVANS George Col 23 S Laborer Acc Acc s/o George & Esther Evans to Rosena Major Col 28 S Acc Acc d/o George & Rachel Major on 23 Jan 1876 near Pungo: by WH Corbin

EVANS George 23 S Waterman Acc Acc s/o Thos & Rhoda to Elizabeth Lord 21 S Acc Acc d/o John E &

Zipporah on 13 Jul 1893 at Tangier Isld by ZH Webster

EVANS George B 25 S Oysterman Acc Acc s/o Richard & Rhoda to Sadie U Hickman 19 S Acc Acc d/o Geo & Eliz'th on 27 Dec 1893 at Keller by JM Dunaway

EVANS George D 25 S Farmer Acc Acc s/o Wm P & Hester to Mary A Byrd 24 S Acc Acc d/o Colomore E on 6 Jun 1877 at Oak Grove Ch by CC Wertenbaker

EVANS George D 23 S Sailor Acc Acc s/o William & Jane to Jennie [Colona] Colonna 22 S Acc Acc on 11 Sep 1889 at Onancock by RA Compton

EVANS George E 24 S Sailor Acc Acc s/o George & Nellie to Sadie E Davis 18 S Acc Acc d/o Napoleon B & Anna on 28 May 1890 at Acc by GW Burke

EVANS George O 18 S Oysterman Acc Acc s/o Elizabeth A Spence to Eliza E Crockett 18 S Acc Acc d/o John & Rachel on 2 Mar 1882 at Sykes Isld by RB Beadles

EVANS George W (Charles H) 18 S Sailor Acc Acc s/o George W & Nellie to Sarah M Windsor 17 S Washington DC Acc d/o Samuel & Catharine on 20 Apr 1882 at Onancock by JC Watson

EVANS Isaac 35 S Laborer Acc Acc s/o Esther to Rosa Read 30 S Acc Acc d/o Rachel on 1 Jun 1868 at Acc by C Burriss

EVANS James E (H) 35 W Farmer Acc Acc s/o John E & Sally to Margaret Hope 19 S Acc Acc d/o Robert & Caroline on 29 Sep 1869 at Acc by JO Moss

EVANS Jesse 24 S Merchant Acc Acc s/o Wm & Esther to Virginia Chesser 21 S Acc Acc d/o Washington & Caroline on 9 Jul 1884 at Oak Hall by RB Beadles

EVANS John 64 W Farming b: Acc s/o Geo C Eavins & Leah Bell to Elizabeth Corbin 46 S b: Acc d/o Ralph Corbin & Elizth Dennis on 19 May 1859 at Acc by T Waters (Wm P Evans says she over 21)

EVANS John 23 S Waterman Acc Acc s/o Louis & Patty to Maria Pruitt 22 S Acc Acc d/o Raymond & Nelly on 8 Jun 1871 at Chesconessex by J Carroll

EVANS John C widr to Harriet A Wallop wid/o John S Wallop lic: 6 Mar 1856

EVANS John E 22 S Sailor Som Co MD Acc s/o Frances to Triphenia A Marsh 16 S Som Co MD Acc d/o Jno W & Margt on 15 May 1867 at Acc by WT Tull

EVANS John E 22 S Sailor Acc Acc s/o Elzy & Annie M to Lillian M Custis 20 S Acc Acc d/o Benj F & Mary A on 14 Mar 1894 at Savageville by GE Booker

EVANS John S 39 S Carriage Mkr MD Acc to Susan Evans 31 W Acc Acc d/o Elijah Russell on 27 Sep 1871 at Acc by J Crosdale

EVANS John T 43 W Sailor Acc Acc s/o Lewis & Pattie to Annie Pruitt 25 S Acc Acc d/o Thomas & Mary on 8 Nov 1890 at Tangier Isld by J Connor

EVANS John W 21 S Oysterman Acc Acc s/o Hamilton P & Zippor Ellen to Ann Riley Hall 18 S Acc Acc d/o Betsy on 29 Oct 1871 at Acc by DA Woodson

EVANS John W 18 S Sailor Smith Isld MD Acc s/o Geo W & Nellie to Jane Mister 19 S Acc Acc d/o Edward & Margaret on 1 Jan 1874 at Chesconessex by WF Talbott

EVANS John W 25 S Sailor Acc Acc s/o Dennard & Sarah to Kessy Budd 23 S Acc Acc d/o McKell & Eliza on 1 May 1878 at Chesconessex by JH

Amiss

EVANS Joseph F 23 S Sailor Acc Acc s/o Solomon C & Margaret S to Rose B Chandler 18 S Acc Acc d/o Thomas H & Emma T on 13 Mar 1894 at Hoffman's Wharf by JR Griffith

EVANS Lewis Col 25 S Wage-earner Acc Acc s/o Parker & Clarisa to Rowena Matthews Watson Col 16 S Acc Acc d/o Bettie Watson on 29 Aug 1894 at Temp'ville by GHT Byrd

EVANS Lloyd W 21 S Farmer Acc Acc s/o George W & Nellie to Mary E Riley 19 S Acc Acc d/o John F & Frances on 18 Dec 1889 at Jno F Riley's by JW Hundley

EVANS Noah 28 S Farmer Acc Acc s/o Peter & Triphenia to Tabitha T Williams 22 S Acc Acc d/o Seth & Rosey on 13 Sep 1866 at Acc by WT Tull

EVANS Noah T 29 S Sailor Acc Acc s/o William & Jane to Cordie L Crockett 18 S Acc Acc d/o Southey & Rachel on 23 Apr 1889 at White's Br by JW Hundley

EVANS Riley 20 S Laborer Acc Acc s/o Harriet to Adah Cluff 30 S Acc Acc on 7 May 1869 at Acc by A Joynes

EVANS Severn 21 S Oysterman Acc Acc s/o Thos & Rhoda to Leanah Crockett 19 S Acc Acc d/o Doro & Maggie on 27 Dec 1885 at Tangier Isld by CS Baker

EVANS Severn J 27 S Sailor Acc Acc s/o Hamilton & Zippie to Mollie J Trader 17 S Acc Acc d/o Raymond & Elizth on 20 Dec 1883 at Cattail Nk by M Oldham

EVANS Severn T 22 S Waterman Acc Acc s/o John & Nancy to Matilda F [Kelley] Kelly 18 S Acc Acc d/o Edw'd T & Sarah P on 26 Nov 1893 at Acc by JT Edmondson

EVANS Solomon J 21 S Sailor Som Co MD Acc s/o Elijah & Matilda to Margt Ann Kelso 17 S Som Co MD Acc d/o John & Ann on 18 Jul 1866 at Acc by W Evans

EVANS Teagle T 21 S Oysterman Acc Acc s/o Dennard & Sarah to Alexine Evans 16 S Acc Acc d/o George & Nellie on 1 Apr 1874 at Acc by O Littleton

EVANS Thomas 19 S Sailor Acc Acc s/o Geo & Eliz A to Arrella Linton 19 S Acc Acc d/o Wm & Louisa on 29 Jul 1883 at Sykes Isld by RB Beadles

EVANS Thomas 24 S Merchant Acc Acc s/o Wm & Hester to Annie F Otwell 21 S Acc Acc d/o Wm T & Virginia C on 25 Jul 1883 at Horntown by RB Beadles

EVANS Thomas 30 S Sailor Acc Acc s/o John & Mary to Sadie Lilliston 15 S Acc Acc d/o George D & Mary on 22 Oct 1890 at Onancock by GW Burke

EVANS Thomas W 21 S Farmer Acc Acc s/o Geo W & Nellie to Mary C Carmine 18 S Acc Acc d/o Wn & Laorina on 27 Nov 1872 at Chesconessex by PA Leatherbury

EVANS Wallace W 24 S Waterman Acc Acc s/o Soran & Mary C to Susan Johnson 32 W Acc Acc d/o Lewis J & Betsy Spence on 20 Dec 1894 at Acc by PA Leatherbury

EVANS William 21 S Waterman Smith Isld MD Smith Isld MD s/o Elijah & Rachel to Emeline Crockett 21 S Tangier Isld Tangier Isld d/o Peter & Mary on 27 Jun 1859 at Tangier Isld by G Cummins (Geo W Evans says both over 21)

EVANS William L 20 S Oysterman Acc Acc s/o Geo & Elizth to Sarah A Miles 19 S Acc Acc d/o Jesse T & Matilda on 26 Oct 1878 at Saxes Isld by A Wiles

EVANS William T 22 S Farmer Acc Acc s/o Noah & Tabitha to Ida M Ayres 25 S Acc Acc d/o Littleton T & Eliza on 10 Dec 1890 at Acc by GW Burke

EVANS Wm 22 S Sailor Acc Acc s/o Wm & Jane to Educy Crockett 18 S Acc Acc d/o Thos & Dely on 22 Jul 1877 near Onancock by JH Amiss

EWELL Alfred Col 41 W Oysterman Acc Acc s/o Edmund to Eliza Taylor Col 25 S Acc Acc d/o Elijah Selby on 23 Oct 1876 at Chinco: Isld by WP Thornton

EWELL Alfred Col 22 S Laborer Acc Acc to Elisha Davis Col 23 S Acc Acc d/o John & Harriet on 9 Oct 1884 at Acc by AJ Satchell

EWELL Alfred S 28 S Farmer Acc Acc s/o Thos to Indiana R Parkes 24 S Acc Acc d/o Mark & Elizth on 28 Dec 1881 at Lee Mont by WA Crouse

EWELL Augustus D F 41 S Physician Acc Acc s/o Parker & Elizabeth to Susan S Pate 38 W N'hamp: Acc d/o Edward & Sarah Thomas on 6 Oct 1880 at Acc by FH Mullineaux

EWELL Beauregard 28 S Sailor Acc Acc s/o Edward & Margaret to Sarah E Taylor 25 S Acc Acc d/o Samuel C (of C) & Sarah on 27 Mar 1895 at Lee Mont by JET Ewell

EWELL Burwell B 40 S Farmer Acc Acc s/o Geo H & Nancy to Eveline T [Grinnald] Grinnalds 21 W Acc Acc d/o Samul & Addius Mason on 13 Dec 1868 at Acc by JET Ewell

EWELL Charles B 22 S Farmer Acc Acc s/o Charles & Susan to Mollie A Abbott 18 S Acc Acc d/o David D & Mary A on 25 Dec 1884 at Acc by WA Street

EWELL Charles H Col 20 S Wage-earner Acc Acc s/o Samuel & Mary to Sarah G Kellam Col 18 S Acc Acc d/o George C & Lecundia on 16 Jan 1895 at Acc by L Duncan

EWELL David F 21 S Farmer Acc Acc s/o Jas & Sally to Mary Ellen Justice 21 S Acc Acc d/o Wm & Elisa on 13 Feb 1870 at Acc by JET Ewell

EWELL Edwd A 23 S Farmer Acc Acc s/o Charles & Susan to Elizabeth J Stevenson 31 S Acc Acc d/o Jno P & Euphrina S on 17 Sep 1884 at Acc by WA Street

EWELL Ezra Dingley 27 S Carpenter Marshfield MS Acc s/o Lyman & Charlotte to Melitha Ann (Melithea) [Dyer] Dies 22 S Provincetown MA Acc d/o William & Phoebo on 6 Jan 1858 near Modest Town by JF Chaplain (Thomas Mays says both over 21)

EWELL Henry W Col 23 S Farm Laborer Som Co MD Acc s/o Louisa to Susan Holden Col 27 S Acc Acc d/o Hester on 7 Nov 1883 at Jenkins Bridge by JC Cluff

EWELL Isaac Col 25 S Laborer Acc Acc s/o Maria to Louisa Taylor Col 20 S Acc Acc d/o William & Candice on 9 Mar 1876 near Poor House by A James

EWELL Isaac Col 67 S Laborer Acc Acc s/o Millie to Mary Wessells Col 48 S Acc Acc d/o Leah on 26 Nov 1885 at Acc by AJ Satchell

EWELL James 21 S Laborer Acc Acc s/o Maria to Mary E Slocomb 21 S Acc Acc d/o Mary on 23 Jan 1868 at Acc by S Marshall

EWELL James D 23 S Waterman Acc Acc s/o James E & Julia A to Julia C Justice 17 S Acc Acc d/o Revel J & Sallie on 1 Jun 1884 at Acc by JW Carroll

EWELL John 21 S Farmer Acc Acc s/o Jas to Margt A Littleton 19 S Acc Acc d/o Thos & Sallie on 4 Oct 1866 at Acc by JE Bundick

EWELL John E Col 23 S Oysterman Acc Acc s/o Peter & Mary to

Georgie Church Col 21 S Acc Acc d/o James & Mahala on 10 Nov 1895 at Horntown by L Duncan

EWELL John E T 21 S Teacher b: Acc s/o George H & Nancy to Arinthia S Russell 19 S b: Acc d/o George & Margaret on 24 Jan 1856 at r/o Geo Russel by ES Grant

EWELL John R 28 S Farmer Acc Acc s/o Charles & Susan to Susan J Silverthorn 27 S Acc Acc d/o Samuel & Mary on 29 Nov 1882 at Acc by JW Hundley

EWELL John R 27 S Sailor Acc Acc s/o James & Juliet A to Arinthia C L Barnes 23 S Acc Acc d/o John & Sally on 25 May 1884 at Acc by JW Carroll

EWELL John R 37 W Sailor Acc Acc s/o James & Julia A to Sallie P Lewis 28 S Acc Acc d/o Alfred J & Maria on 2 Oct 1895 at Acc by AJ Walter

EWELL John S 31 S Farmer Acc Acc s/o Gillet F & Elizabeth to Sarah A Lewis 24 S Acc Acc d/o Thomas P & Margaret on 7 Aug 1871 at Guilford by ST Ferguson

EWELL John T Col 21 S Laborer Chinco: Isld Horntown s/o Peter & Nancy to Martha Blake Col 21 S Chinco: Isld Chinco: Isld d/o Oak & Mary on 24 Mar 1879 at Chinco: Isld by R Williamson

EWELL Obediah J 22 S Farmer Acc Acc s/o Solomon F & Ellen to Emma Killman 21 S Acc Acc d/o Samuel & Emily on 31 Dec 1885 at Acc by HG Cowan

EWELL Peter Col 28 S Laborer Acc Acc s/o Mary to Mary Ann Logan Col 22 S Acc Acc d/o Alsey on 31 Dec 1874 at Horntown by S Johns

EWELL Richard J 22 S Sailor Acc Acc s/o Jane to Mary L Green 17 S Acc Acc d/o Charles A & Mary E on 29 Dec 1889 at Sanford by WF Hayes

EWELL Samuel 21 S Oystering Acc Acc s/o Liddy Chandler to Mary Seymour 18 S Acc Acc d/o Philis on 7 Feb 1869 at Acc by WF Williams

EWELL Samuel Col 42 W Farmer Acc Acc s/o William & Lydia to Emma J Booker Col 22 S Acc Acc d/o John & Peggy on 12 Dec 1888 at Acc by JA Haynes

EWELL Solomon E 27 S Farmer Acc Acc s/o Gilbert & Elizabeth to Elenor S [Parks] Parkes 27 S Acc Acc d/o John & Tabitha on 31 Aug 1859 at Reese Chp by ES Grant (A J Taylor says both over 21)

EWELL William H 25 S Farmer Acc Acc s/o Chas & Susan to Synthia J Silverthorn 18 S Acc Acc d/o Mary on 18 Dec 1878 at Modest Town by DA Woodson

EWELL William L 23 S Oysterman Acc Acc s/o James & Julia Ann to Bettie Rew 22 S Acc Acc d/o Revel & Jane on 25 May 1890 at Parksley by HS Dulany

EWELL William T Col 22 S Farmer Acc Acc s/o John & Ellen to Sarah A Roberts Col 21 S Acc Acc d/o Moses & Martha on 12 Nov 1890 at Acc by J Duckett

EWELL Wm Col 22 S Sailor Acc Acc s/o Nancy to Alice White Col 21 S Acc Acc d/o Rosa on 1 Mar 1877 at Bay Side Ch by A Handy

EWELL Wm L 27 S Oysterman Acc Acc s/o Edward E & Marg't to Virginia L Taylor 23 S Acc Acc d/o William & Mary on 11 Sep 1892 at Lee Mont by JET Ewell

FANTON Noah 21 S Farmer Acc Acc s/o James & Mary to Sally D Young 18 S Acc Acc d/o Samuel & Sally on 2 Jun 1875 at Guilford by JM Anderson

FARLOW William E 30 S Farmer Wic Co MD Acc s/o Billy F & Elizabeth to Mary E Hancock 25 S Wor Co MD Acc d/o Sidney & Sallie on 1

Feb 1888 at Atlantic by TG Pullen

FARMER John H 27 S Merchant Halifax Co VA Halifax Co VA s/o Archer H & Martha to Annie H Evans 25 S Pocomoke City MD Acc d/o Thomas A & Mary A on 24 Oct 1888 at Onancock by J McNabb

FAUNTLeROY Henry H to Catharine A (Reid) Read lic: 2 Mar 1861 B S Colonna says both over 21

FEDDEMAN Charles W [Fedderman] 21 S Merchant Acc Acc to Mary A Thomas 20 S Acc Acc d/o E R & Amanda on 1 Jun 1881 at Pocomoke by RB Beadles

FEDDEMAN George Col 21 S Acc Acc to Margt S Marshall Col single Acc Acc d/o Edward on 27 Sep 1882 near Oak Hall by JC Cluff

FEDDEMAN George Thomas (Fedderman) 25 S Farmer b: Acc s/o Joseph M & Betsey to Mary Elizabeth Massey 17 S b: Acc d/o John & Patsey & ward/o John Brittingham who gave consent) on 11 Nov 1857 at r/o Jno Brittingham by JF Chaplain (Wm M Fredderman says he over 21)

FEDDEMAN Suel 29 S US Rev Marine Service Wor Co MD Acc s/o John W & Hester to Ellen Thornton 18 S Acc Acc d/o James W & Delilah on 25 Jan 1884(?) at Chinco: Isld by SU Grimsley Certificate returned 12 Jan 1889

FEDDEMAN Wm H 24 S Merchant Acc Acc s/o Wm & Eliz to Mary E Johnson 18 S Acc Acc d/o Thos & Nancy on 22 Jan 1862 at Acc by W Cox

FENTRESS Walter 21 S Merchant Dorchester Co MD Baltimore MD s/o Bennet & Agnes to Ida LeCato 21 S Acc Wheeling WV d/o Edward & Mary H on 16 Jul 1878 near Oak Grove Ch by LK LeCato

FENWICK David L 22 S Sailor Sussex Co DE Acc s/o John & Hester A to Annie E Russell 16 S Acc Acc d/o Oliver & Drucilla on 10 Feb 1887(?) at Chinco: Isld by SU Grimsley Certificate returned 12 Jan 1889

FERGUSON Frank A 22 S Farmer Altoona PA Acc s/o Antoni B & Mary J to Annie East 30 W Acc Acc d/o Jane Martin on 4 Sep 1889 at Onancock by JW Hundley

FERGUSON Frank A 29 W Farmer Wilkesbarre Co PA Acc s/o Anthony B & Mary J to Susan V Johnson 25 S Acc Acc d/o Margaret Sarah on 30 Dec 1894 at Savageville by AJ Reamy

FIELDS Ayres Col 22 S Farmer Acc Acc s/o Caleb & Sarah Matthews to Emma Watson Col 18 S Acc Acc on 9 Oct 1878 near Temp'ville by JC Cluff

FIELDS Ayres Col 25 W Laborer Acc Acc s/o Caliph & Sarah Matthews to Louisa Drummond Col 16 S Acc Acc d/o John & Hester on 31 May 1882 near Jenkins Bridge by JC Cluff

FIELDS John FN 24 S Sailor Acc Acc s/o Gertrude to Margaret Armstrong FN 21 S Acc Acc d/o Mary on 10 Jun 1866 at Acc by GW Matthews

FIGGS Jas E W 24 S Clerk Wor Co MD Acc to Ida A [Harman] Harmon 30 W Wor Co MD Acc on 1 Dec 1886 at Acc by BF Jester

FINNEY Abram Col 46 S Farmer Acc Acc s/o Henry & Tabbie to Clarissa Conquest Col 36 S Acc Acc d/o Isaac & Mary on 15 Feb 1891 near Pastoria by AJ Satchell

FINNEY Alfred W 23 S Farmer Acc Acc s/o Alfred & Mary to Roberta West 17 S Acc Acc d/o Geo R & Jane S on 27 Dec 1883 at Acc by JG Anderson

FINNEY Andrew Col 19 S Wage-earner Acc Acc s/o Henry & Tabitha to Mary Ella Byrd Col 19 S Acc Acc d/o John H & Polly on 24 Apr 1889 at Acc by AJ Satchell

FINNEY Andrew J Col 19 S Wage-earner Acc Acc s/o Stephen Finney & Martha Hickman to Margaret Ann West Col 20 S Acc Acc d/o Peter & Rachel on 14 May 1894 at Acc C H by AJ Satchell

FINNEY Charles P 26 S Sailor Acc Acc s/o Thos W & Sallie to Emma S Boggs 21 S Acc Acc d/o Jos P & Susan on 29 Nov 1865 at Acc by JH Addison

FINNEY Charles P 37 W Merchant Acc Acc s/o Thos W & Sarah to Margaret Susan Ames 22 S Acc Acc d/o Jno E & Margt on 24 Mar 1875 near Cross Rd by JH Amiss

FINNEY Damon Col 54 S Laborer Acc Acc s/o Rachel to Mary Poulson Col 40 W Acc Acc d/o Lucy Ames on 9 Feb 1879 at Savageville by JW Diggs

FINNEY David B 26 S Farmer Acc Acc s/o Edwd O & Margt S to Virginia M Bunting 19 S Acc Acc d/o Thos C & Maria on 1 Nov 1866 at Acc by AB Dolly

FINNEY Edmund Col 21 S Laborer Acc Acc s/o Sarah to Emma Finney Col 21 S Acc Acc d/o Mary on 5 Apr 1874 at Savageville by R Davis

FINNEY Edmund (Edward) Col 22 S Sailor Acc Acc s/o Scarborugh to Mary Banks Col 23 S Acc Acc d/o Susan Custis on 18 Feb 1872 at Onancock by R David

FINNEY Edward Col 22 S Wage-earner Acc Acc to Nora Taylor Col 17 S Acc Acc d/o Henry Long on 1 Nov 1893 at Acc by AJ Satchell

FINNEY Geo FN 37 S Sailor Acc Acc s/o Jack Scarborah & Timpey Finsay to Judah Boggs FN 22 S Acc Acc d/o Peter Finney & Sarah Boggs on 30 Dec 1865 at Acc by JC Addison

FINNEY Geo Wash Col 62 W Wage-earner Acc Acc s/o Frank & Keziah to Rachel Ann Custis Col 45 W Acc Acc d/o Jesse & Virginia Nock on 15 Nov 1892 at Savageville by JH Offer

FINNEY George Col 23 S Wage-earner Acc Acc s/o George White & Lizzie Finney to Mary Clayton Col 17 S Acc Acc d/o Bowden & Hester on 23 Dec 1894 at Acc by AJ Satchell

FINNEY George B 23 S Mason Acc Acc s/o Alfred W & Mary to Mollie S Lang 21 S Acc Acc d/o Henry & Kitty on 23 Aug 1885 at Onancock by JW Hundley

FINNEY George T Col 18 S Wage-earner Acc Acc s/o George to Mary Northam Col 16 S Acc Acc d/o Charles on 10 Mar 1895 at Acc by AJ Satchell

FINNEY George W Col 24 S Farmer Acc Acc s/o Geo W Sr & Patsey to Missouri Gunter Col 30 S Acc Acc d/o Lucy on 17 Dec 1893 near Savageville by JH Offer

FINNEY Handy Col 33 S Teamster Acc Acc s/o Aaron & Sabra to Harriet Lewis Col 22 S Mecklenburg VA Acc d/o Thos & Sally on 1 Mar 1883 at Drum'tn by LW Lee

FINNEY Heber Col 21 S Laborer Acc Acc s/o Rose to Williana Phillips Col 16 S Acc Acc d/o Malinda on 1 Apr 1880 at Acc by A Joynes

FINNEY Henry Col 50 S Farmer Acc Acc s/o Matilda to Tabitha Bundick Col 45 S Acc Acc d/o Leah on 10 Apr 1873 at Wise Mill by A Joynes

FINNEY Henry Jr Col 26 S Laborer Acc Acc s/o Henry S & Tabitha to Mary Dickerson Col 22 S Acc Acc d/o Arthur & Eliza on 23 Jun 1881 near the Poor House by AJ Satchell

FINNEY Henry Sr Col 70 W Farmer Acc Acc s/o Matilda to Esther Dickerson Col 50 W Acc Acc d/o Rosa Hope on 21 Oct 1894 at Acc by AJ Satchell

Marriages

FINNEY Isaac Col 24 S Sailor Acc Acc s/o Jack to Virginia Boggs Col 19 S Acc Acc d/o Peter & Gracie on 20 Oct 1880 near Onancock by JW Diggs

FINNEY James Col 40 S Laborer Acc Acc s/o Sarah to Virginia A Leatherbury Col 20 S Acc Acc d/o Arena on 2 Jan 1878 at Savageville by JK Plato

FINNEY James Col 21 S Wage-earner Acc Acc s/o Moses & Evalilne to Fannie Wise Col 21 S Acc Acc d/o Sabra on 9 Jun 1889 at Mappsville by AJ Satchell

FINNEY John 21 S Laborer Acc Acc s/o Susan to Mary Duffy 23 S Acc Acc d/o Eliza on 17 Apr 1881 near News Town by A Joynes

FINNEY John Col 22 S Laborer Acc Acc s/o Susan to Emma [Bevans] Beavans Col 19 S Acc Acc d/o Robt on 3 Dec 1884 at Acc by GHT Byrd

FINNEY John Col 19 S Laborer Acc Acc s/o Sarah to Annie Watts Col 18 S Acc Acc d/o Hannah on 5 Aug 1885 at Acc by AJ Satchell

FINNEY John C 27 S Farmer Acc N'hamp: s/o John F & Bettie to Nannie S West 20 S Acc Acc d/o Thos M & Annie on 27 Apr 1892 at Craddockville by JM Anderson

FINNEY John T 30 S Carpenter Acc Acc s/o Thos W & Sally to Susan A Phillips 18 S Acc Acc d/o Solomon & Ann on 28 Nov 1860 at Acc by JH Addison (Franceis T Boggs says he over 21)

FINNEY Levi Col 36 S Sailor Acc Acc s/o Tinny to Sarah Smith Col 22 S Acc Acc d/o Juliet Ann on 2 Jan 1876 at White Marsh by JK Plato

FINNEY Louis Col 21 S Farm Laborer Acc Acc s/o Susan to Leah Dickerson Col 21 S Acc Acc d/o David on 21 Nov 1883 at Acc by AJ Satchell

FINNEY Louis Col 27 S Wage-earner Acc Acc s/o Ann to Hester Mears Col 25 S Acc Acc d/o Maria on 2 Nov 1890 at Savageville by JB Lewis

FINNEY Louis Col 56 S Wage-earner Acc Acc s/o Tinney to Mary S Kellam Col 45 W Acc Acc on 20 May 1894 at Acc by T Turlington

FINNEY Montesco Col 21 S Sailor Acc Acc s/o Henry & Tabby to Mary Hickman Col 19 S Acc Acc d/o Rose A on 7 Jan 1886 at Acc by AJ Satchell

FINNEY Moses Jr Col 30 S Wage-earner Acc Acc s/o Moses Sr & Emeline to Rosa Bagwell Col 22 S Acc Acc d/o Daniel & Rena on 14 Apr 1895 at Acc by AJ Satchell

FINNEY Nathan Col 44 S Farmer Acc Acc s/o Hetty to Lucy Warner Col 32 S Acc Acc d/o Betsy on 5 Jan 1879 at Abel Joynes by A Joynes

FINNEY Oswald T Col 21 S Laborer Acc Acc s/o Ann Snead to Leah J Conner Col 17 S Acc Acc d/o Jesse & Sarah on 25 Dec 1879 at Morris Chp by RJ Waters

FINNEY Parker Col 24 S Farmer Acc Acc s/o Lewis Finney & Sarah Taylor to Emma [Bivens] Beavans Col 22 S Acc Acc d/o Moses & Ressie on 3 Jun 1883 at Savageville by P Sheppard

FINNEY William Spencer 24 S Mechanic Acc Acc s/o William (of Wm) & Margart S to Pearl Elizabeth Boggs 20 S Acc Acc d/o Littleton T & Emma T on 9 Jan 1889 at bride's father's by RA Compton

FISH Charles H 23 S Oysterman Acc Acc s/o Wm H & Rosetta to Estella Carpenter 18 S Acc Acc d/o Charles & Denna Ann on 9 Jun 1893 at Chinco: Isld by RB Sanford

FISH William H 37 W Oysterman Atlantic Co NJ Chinco: Isld s/o Alexander & Amelia to Alice Savage

27 S Wor Co MD Chinco: Isld d/o Wesley & Jane on 14 Jun 1886 at Chinco: Isld by SU Grimsley

FISHER Abednago 23 S Farming Acc Acc s/o Kendal & Susan to Critty Tatham 21 S Acc Acc d/o Ezkl & Cornelia on 28 Mar 1867 at Acc by M Oldham

FISHER Andrew Col 22 S Wage-earner Acc Acc s/o Agnes to Vianna Williams Col 18 S Acc Acc d/o James & Harriet A on 31 Dec 1890 at Acc by AJ Satchell

FISHER Frank M 23 S Farmer Acc Acc s/o John T & Hester A to Mary E [Brodwater] Broadwater 21 S Acc Acc d/o Amos on 24 Dec 1879 at Temp'ville by JW Hilldrup

FISHER George E Col 21 S Laborer Acc Acc to Harriet Dickerson Col 18 S Acc Acc d/o Arthur & Eliza on 2 Jan 1873 at Acc by A Joynes

FISHER George M 22 S Farmer Acc Acc s/o Jas & Hetty to Mary Wessells 19 S Acc Acc d/o Wm & Caroline on 19 Dec 1883 at Acc by JW Hundley

FISHER George T Col 21 S Laborer Acc Acc s/o Eliza to Annie White Col 19 S Acc Acc d/o Arina on 28 Dec 1872 at Acc by A Joynes

FISHER Henry 24 S Oysterman NJ Acc s/o Elexander & Milla to Rosetta Munger 17 S Acc Acc d/o James & Martha Ann on 24 Feb 1869 at Chinco: Isld by P Bowdin Jr

FISHER Isaac 21 S Laborer Acc Acc s/o Eliza to Maggie Hinman 16 S Acc Acc d/o Saml & Sarah on 30 Dec 1886 at Acc by AJ Satchell

FISHER James Col 26 W Laborer MD Acc to Ann Lurton Col 25 S Acc Acc on 30 Sep 1877 at Belle Haven by JE Humphreys

FISHER James H Col 19 S Wage-earner Acc Acc s/o George T & Anice to Ida M Baker Col 19 S Acc Acc d/o Lizzie on 28 Apr 1895 at Mappsville by JL King

FISHER James P to Hetty Bloxom d/o Major dec'd lic: 29 Dec 1856 Sylvanus H Lucas says both over 21

FISHER John 44 W Florist s/o Nicholas & Margaret Ann to Sophia Young 41 W lic: 2 Jun 1865

FISHER John Col 23 S Mill Worker VA VA s/o George Fisher & Elizth Crippen to Leah Wise Col 22 S MD MD d/o George Wise & Esther Ward on 4 Oct 1876 at Line of Md by TM Poulson

FISHER John H 24 S Farmer Acc Acc s/o Kendall & Susan to Laura C Wessells 18 S Acc Acc d/o Thomas J & Catharine on 18 Mar 1874 near Modest Town by JE Bundick

FISHER Littleton Col (dark) 21 S Laborer Acc Acc s/o Isaac & Matilda to Margaret E Davis Col (dark) 16 S Acc Acc d/o Wm & Mary on 21 Jan 1872 near Modest Town by JE Bundick

FISHER Patrick M 21 S Farmer Acc Acc s/o Abednego T & Lucretia to Inda A Richardson 16 S Acc Acc d/o Joseph A & Nevilla on 27 Dec 1893 at Temp'ville by JR Tillery

FISHER Riley widr to Louisa Brown lic: 21 Aug 1855 Stephen Hinman says she over 21

FISHER Samuel 30 S Laborer Acc Acc s/o Meshack & Rachel to Mary Trader 18 S Acc Acc d/o Mary on 8 Dec 1869 at Acc by JE Bundick

FISHER Samuel Col 25 S Laborer Acc Acc to Clarissa Watson Col 17 S Acc Acc d/o Clarissa on 30 Oct 1873 at Modest Town by TM Poulson

FISHER Samuel 24 S Farmer Acc Acc s/o Meshack & Rachel to Rachael Chesser 22 S Acc Acc d/o James & Jane on 28 Dec 1875 near Conquest Ch by M Oldham

FISHER Sylvester F 21 S Farmer Acc

Acc s/o Jno D & Delilah P to Margaret C Nock 18 S Acc Acc d/o Samuel & Polly on 20 Mar 1878 at Conquest Ch by JB Merritt

FISHER Thorogood J 24 S Farmer s/o Kendal & Susan to Tabitha Kelly 22 d/o Richard & Elizabeth lic: 8 Nov 1865 marr: 10 Nov 1865

FISHER Wesley Col 25 S Oysterman Acc Chinco: Isld s/o George Fisher & Sallie Gillet to Nannie Savage Col 30 S Richmond VA Chinco: Isld d/o Isaac & Mary on 4 Mar 1883 at Chinco: Isld by JC Cluff

FISHER William W to Betsy Matthews d/o Samuel dec'd & Eliza who gave consent lic: 28 Jan 1861

FISHER Wm W 21 S Farmer Acc Acc s/o Jno T & Hester A to Julia D [Brodwater] Broadwater 22 S Acc Acc d/o Amos K & Polly on 24 Dec 1884 at Temp'ville by M Oldham

FITCHETT John Col 33 S Laborer Acc Acc s/o Susan Young to Electra Conquest Col 22 S Acc Acc d/o Mary on 12 Jun 1881 near Acc by PM Lewis

FITCHETT John L 28 S Harness Mkr N'hamp: Acc s/o Jacob & Mary to Susan A Lilliston 21 S Acc Acc d/o Jno S & Ann on 11 Jan 1862 at Acc by ES Grant

FITCHETT John Y widr to Mary E Byrd wid lic: 19 May 1859

FITCHETT Samuel 21 S Laborer b: N'hamp: s/o Jacob & Mary to Ann Bunting 17 S b: Acc d/o Thos & Lovey Bunting on 16 Dec 1858 at r/o James Gray by ES Grant (John L Fitchett says he over 21)

FITCHETT Stran Col 26 S Farmer Acc Acc s/o Abraham & Mary to Fannie Rogers Col 21 S Acc Acc d/o George & Susan on 4 Nov 1891 at Acc by TW Nettles

FITCHETT Thomas Col 22 S Farmer Acc Acc s/o Mary to Margaret Ellen [Bevans] Beavans Col 21 S Acc Acc d/o Severn & Eliz on 9 Feb 1881 at Onancock by JW Diggs

FITCHETT Wm L Col 26 S Farmer Acc Acc s/o Mary Gaskins to Mary Bayly Col 20 S Acc Acc d/o Frank & Jane on 18 Dec 1878 near Cross Rd by RH Govans

FITZGEARLD Thomas H 21 S Farmer Acc Acc s/o Samuel & Louisa to Henrietta P Milliner 16 S Acc Acc d/o Thomas & Sarah Ann on 3 Sep 1873 at Locustville by LK LeCato

FITZGERALD Hezekiah 30 W Merchant Acc Acc s/o Thos & Margaret to Annie W Lewis 20 S Acc Acc d/o Wm H & Arinthia on 30 Oct 1878 near Woodstock by FH Mullineaux

FITZGERALD James 23 S Brick Mason Acc Acc s/o Saml to Elizabeth Core 20 S Acc Acc d/o Jno C & Emma on 6 Nov 1872 at Miny Branch by EM Bryan

FITZGERALD Thomas 33 W Brick Mason Acc Acc s/o Sam'l & Louisa to Susan Ann Justice 23 S Acc Acc d/o Mary on 19 Aug 1883 at Acc by JG Anderson

FITZGERALD Thomas J 24 S Sailor Elizabeth City Co Acc s/o Thos E & Margt A to Cornelia D Lewis 20 S Acc Acc d/o Leoriedas & Sally on 7 Apr 1881 at Acc by LE Barrett

FLEMING Augustus 34 W Sailor Germany Acc s/o August & Maria to Venice Melvin 15 S Chinco: Isld Acc d/o Isaac J & Maria on 1 Mar 1883 at Chinco: Isld by WP Thornton

FLEMING Augustus [Flemings] 25 S Sailor NY NY s/o Adoff T & M to Mary E Townsend 18 S Acc Chinco: Isld d/o Wm L & Maria on 14 Aug 1875 at Chinco: Isld by P Bowdin Sr

FLEMING John [Flemming] Col 22 S Wage-earner Wor Co MD Acc s/o Levin & Ellen to Ann Davis Col 24 S

Acc Acc d/o Levi Davis & Mary Walker on 9 Nov 1891 at Acc by L Duncan

FLEMING Wm F 35 S Lumber & Farmer Som Co MD Acc s/o Wm T & Mary E to Mary Sue Smith 27 S Acc Acc d/o Thos W & Susan on 24 Dec 1877 at r/o Thos W Smith by CC Wertenbaker

FLETCHER Benjamin Col 43 S Farmer Acc Acc s/o Eupharie to Mary Elizth Whittington Col 34 S Acc Acc d/o Rachel on 22 May 1873 at Tunnell's Mill by S Johns

FLETCHER Corbin D Dr. 24 S Physician Acc Acc s/o Thomas & Betsey to Catherine Poulson 22 S Acc Acc d/o Robert J & Catharine on 27 Oct 1856 at Onancock by H Drunning (Wm R Parramore says both over 21)

FLETCHER Dennis Col 37 S Farmer Acc Acc s/o Mary Gillespie to Margt A Whittington Col 35 S Acc Acc d/o Rose Ann on 16 Mar 1873 at Pocomoke by S Johns

FLETCHER Douglas D 34 S Farmer Acc Acc s/o Jno T & Sarah to Sudes C Parker 29 S Acc Acc d/o Jno W H & Sarah on 24 Mar 1881 at Acc by EH Wellman

FLETCHER George Albert 26 S Sailor Acc Acc s/o Thomas & Sarah to Rathalia A Mears 24 S Acc Acc d/o Jno E & Eliz J on 20 Apr 1881 at Acc by JWA Elliott

FLETCHER Henry Col 25 S Laborer Acc Acc to Eleshea Fields Col 23 S Acc Acc d/o Sarah on 4 Apr 1883 at Oak Hall by JC Cluff

FLETCHER James E 20 S Oysterman Acc Acc s/o John W & Nancy to Maggie Virgina Birch 17 S Acc Acc d/o Decatur & Rebecca R on 8 Aug 1894 at Chinco: Isld by RB Sanford

FLETCHER James H 26 S Farmer Acc Acc s/o James J & Lizzie to Lizzie E Bloxom 31 W Acc Acc d/o Bennet & Polly Parkes on 21 Dec 1881 at Acc by LB Betty

FLETCHER John Col 26 S Oysterman Acc Acc s/o Mary to Mary A Drummond Col 22 S Acc Acc d/o Ann on 21 Nov 1872 at Acc by M Oldham

FLETCHER John Col 25 S Farmer Acc Acc s/o Benjamin & Louise to Ritie Tunnell Col 17 S Acc Acc d/o John & Sarah on 4 Feb 1894 at Acc by EH Bean

FLETCHER John R 22 S Farmer Acc Acc s/o John R & Louisa to Rose E Walker 22 S Acc Acc d/o Henry C & Margaret on 19 Feb 1889 at Pungo: by EH Wellman

FLETCHER John Wesley 22 S Oysterman N'hamp: Acc s/o Charles & Margaret to Nancy Claville 15 S Acc Acc d/o James & Mary on 31 Jan 1870 at Chinco: Isld by P Bowdin Jr

FLETCHER Peter Col 22 S Wage-earner Acc Acc s/o James & Louisa to Adaline F Wharton Col 21 S Acc Acc d/o Henry & Scarborough on 30 Nov 1893 at Temp'ville by JC Cluff

FLETCHER Robert Col 21 S Farmer Acc Acc s/o James & Louisa to Martha J Copes Col 18 S Acc Acc d/o John & Catherine on 23 Apr 1890 at Acc by JS Wallace

FLETCHER Samuel Col 35 S Oysterman Acc Acc s/o Isaac & Ann to Tamen Ann Whittington Col 35 S Acc Acc d/o David & Nancy on 10 May 1875 at r/o Grooms by S Johns (lic: 13 Mar 1874)

FLETCHER Spencer Col 39 S Sailor Acc Acc s/o Benj Holden & Fannie Fletcher to Mary Phillips Col 33 S Acc Acc d/o James Brown & Arie Brodwater on 25 Aug 1887 at Chinch Town by N Morris

Marriages

FLETCHER Thomas 42 S Speculator b: Acc s/o Thos & Elizth W to Mary Jane Collins 27 S b: Wor Co MD d/o Jas & Elizth on 16 Sep 1857 at r/o M Geo Fletcher by JM Dennis (George S Fletcher says both over 21)

FLETCHER Thomas 21 S Carpenter Acc Acc s/o Thomas to Emma E Smith 19 S Acc Acc d/o Thomas & Sally on 15 Sep 1880 near Temp'ville by JW Hundley

FLETCHER William Col 24 S Farmer Acc Acc to Margaret Hickman Col 22 S Acc Acc on 6 Jan 1872 at Wise Mill by A Joynes

FLETCHER William 23 S Farmer N'hamp: Acc s/o Sally to Mary Bundick 22 S Acc Acc d/o Alfred J & Elizth on 3 Mar 1880 at Onancock by SC Boston

FLETCHER William Col 23 S Oysterman Acc Acc s/o Benjamin to Mary Fletcher Col 18 S Acc Acc d/o John & Ann on 24 Dec 1890 at Temp'ville by JC Cluff

FLETCHER William T 27 S Farmer Acc Acc s/o James H & Elizabeth A to Sallie Seymour Parramore 21 S Acc Acc d/o Thomas C & Juliet A on 27 Nov 1889 at St James Ch by J McNabb

FLETCHER Wm Spencer 50 S Farmer Acc Acc s/o Hy & Mary J to Elizabeth S Fletcher 40 S Acc Acc d/o Thos & Elizth on 28 Nov 1867 at Acc by TG Houghton

FLICK Chrestian D 24 S Gentleman Brookville PA Brookville PA to Emma L Lilliston 23 S Acc Acc d/o John S & Ann on 31 Aug 1865 at Acc by D Titlow

FLOYD Edward Col 21 S Wage-earner Acc Acc s/o Henry & Peggie to Emma J Custis Col 19 S Acc Acc d/o Laura on 11 May 1892 at Acc by AJ Satchell

FLOYD George Col 40 S Wage-earner Acc Acc to Rhoda Stuart Col 30 S Acc Acc d/o Smith & Jane on 19 Aug 1889 at Acc by L Duncan

FLOYD George Col 23 S Wage-earner Acc Acc s/o Henry & Peggie to Sarah Holland Col 21 S Acc Acc d/o Grace on 22 Jun 1893 at Acc by AJ Satchell

FLOYD George Frederick 29 S Physician Acc Acc s/o Frederick & Catherine to Mary Swanger 23 S Acc Acc d/o Emanuel B & Elma Rebecca on 24 May 1888 at Locustville by WJ Twilley

FLOYD James Col 22 S Laborer Acc Acc s/o Charlotte to Belle S Wright Col 21 S Acc Acc d/o Jane on 7 Apr 1878 at Acc by LK LeCato

FLOYD James G 25 S Farmer Acc Acc s/o Elijah Floyd to Elizth M Sturgis 18 S Acc Acc d/o Thomas on 17 Nov 1853(?) at Acc by W Fisher Certificate returned 17 Apr 1858

FLOYD Jas B 23 S Shoemaker b: Acc s/o Benjn & Mary to Mary Callahan 19 S b: Acc d/o Griffin & Leah on 15 Feb 1855 at Locust Mount by JWA Elliott

FLOYD John Col 30 S Oysterman Acc Acc s/o John & Catherine to Frances Ayres Col 23 S Acc Acc d/o Edith on 29 Dec 1888 at Acc by JK Adams

FLOYD John Col 60 S Farmer Acc Acc to Catharine Harmon Col 55 S Acc Acc d/o Tabitha on 29 Oct 1893 at Locust Mount by JWA Elliott

FLOYD Louis J 28 S Carpenter Acc Acc s/o John to Sudie A Bradford 18 S Acc Acc d/o Wm T & Sally on 18 Feb 1879 at Pungo Meth Ch by CC Wertenbaker

FLOYD Louis L Col 22 S Wage-earner Acc Acc s/o Charlotte to Charlotte Jones Col 21 S Acc Acc d/o Elijah & Arinthia on 5 Jun 1895 at Locust Mount by JWA Elliott

FLOYD Obediah Col 27 S Wage-earner

Acc Acc s/o Mary to Lizzie Ewell Col 20 S Acc Acc d/o John & Ellen on 26 Dec 1889 at Acc by JH Thomas

FLOYD Thomas Col 21 S Wage-earner Acc Acc s/o Henry & Peggie to Sallie F White Col 16 S Acc Acc d/o Nancy on 4 Jan 1891 at Acc by LE Toulson

FLOYD Thomas Col 21 S Farmer Acc Acc s/o Peggie to Ella Bell Col 21 S Acc Acc d/o Virginia on 25 Dec 1892 at Acc by TW Nettles

FLOYD William Col 24 S Farmer Acc Acc s/o Mary Floyd to Henrietta Wharton Col 25 S Acc Acc d/o Adaline Fisher on 3 Jan 1895 at Acc by PW Lee

FLUHARTY Daniel A 23 S Farmer Caroline Co MD Acc s/o John N & Sarah A to Susan E Taylor 26 S Acc Acc d/o William & Ann on 8 Apr 1888 at Temp'ville by M Oldham

FLUHARTY John 18 S Waterman Acc Acc s/o William E to Virginia Ellis 18 S Acc Acc d/o James M & Matilda on 23 Jun 1895 at Sykes Isld by ML Williams

FOREMAN Douglas James Col 23 S Laborer Acc Acc s/o Sally to Mary Hall Col 25 S Acc Acc d/o Sarah on 29 Dec 1887 at Messongo by N Morris

FOREMAN Isaac Col 30 S Laborer Acc Acc to Comfort E Custis Col 23 S Acc Acc d/o Comfort E on 25 May 1882 near Jenkins Bridge by JC Cluff

FOREMAN Isaac Col 30 W Farmer Wagram Jenkins Bridge s/o Sallie to Susan Taylor Col 22 S Atlantic Oak Hall d/o Louisa on 14 Jan 1885 near Temp'ville by JC Cluff

FOREMAN Venus Col 27 W Wage-earner Acc Acc s/o Sally to Lucy Hope 25 S Acc Acc d/o Rosa on 8 Dec 1895 at Acc by AJ Satchell

FOSKEY George 21 S Laborer Acc Acc s/o George & Rebecca to Margaret Foskey 18 S Acc Acc d/o Solomon & Adah on 30 Mar 1870 at Acc by JH Addison

FOSKEY William T 45 W Farmer Acc Acc s/o Nathl & Sallie to Sarah J Lungren 38 S PA Acc on 19 Jun 1867 at N'hamp: by GS May

FOSQUE Alfred Col 22 S Laborer Acc Acc s/o Lara to Catharine M Finney Col 17 S Acc Acc d/o Henry & Tabitha on 27 Mar 1873 at Metompkin by A Joynes

FOSQUE Edward Col 33 S Farmer Acc Acc s/o Matilda to Burley Savage Col 35 S Acc Acc d/o Adah on 29 Dec 1886 at Acc by L Duncan

FOSQUE Frederick Col 24 S Laborer Acc Acc s/o Louisa to Ann Dix Col 28 W Acc Acc d/o Sina Finney on 11 Mar 1886 at Acc C H by AJ Satchell

FOSQUE George B 31 S Merchant Acc Acc s/o Jno M & Ann R to Alice L Drummond 25 S Acc Acc d/o Jno R & Elishia on 23 Jul 1874 at Drum'tn by O Littleton

FOSQUE Henry Col 20 S Sailor Acc Acc s/o George to Louisa Fosque Col 18 S Acc Acc d/o Thos on 27 Feb 1872 at Onancock by R David

FOSQUE Henry Col 20 S Laborer Acc Acc s/o Louisa to Hennie Gray Col 17 S Acc Acc d/o Isaac Gray & Clarissa Poolman on 24 Apr 1873 at Metompkin Township by A Joynes

FOSQUE Henry Col 24 S Farmer Acc Acc s/o Lucy to Rachel Smith Col 21 S Acc Acc d/o Amy on 2 Jan 1878 near Boston by TW Nettles

FOSQUE Henry K Col 34 W Brick Layer Acc Acc s/o George & Rebecca to Rebecca F Matthews Col 22 S Acc Acc d/o George A & Martha on 22 Dec 1889 at Onancock by JH Offer

FOSQUE James 19 S Acc Acc s/o James & Emma to Margaret Parker

22 S Acc Acc on 9 Dec 1883 near Onancock by WC Vaden

FOSQUE Jesse Col 23 S Farm Laborer Acc Acc s/o Solomon & Ada to Clara Ashby Col 21 S Acc Acc d/o Leah on 16 Jan 1884 at Drum'tn by LW Lee

FOSQUE John Thomas 26 S Carpenter b: Acc s/o Nathel & Margt to Virginia Elizth Oliver 19 S b: Acc d/o Wn W & Juliett on 23 Dec 1857 at Acc by P Warren (John H White says be over 21)

FOSQUE Lewis Col 22 S Farmer Acc Acc s/o Rececca to Ary Hope Col 24 S Acc Acc d/o Mary on 5 Jun 1873 at Onancock by R Davis

FOSQUE Nathaniel T 29 S Carpenter Onancock Onancock s/o Jno M & Ann R to Elizabeth L Bull 23 S Scarborough Nk Scarburgh Nk d/o Thos S & Mary on 3 Aug 1856 at r/o Jno R Watson by JH Harmonsley (Francis A Bull says both over 21)

FOSQUE Nathaniel T Jr 29 S Jeweller Acc Acc s/o Nath'l T & Eliz'th to Mildred Lee Mears 18 S Acc Acc d/o Christopher C & Margaret on 12 Dec 1894 at Acc by JR Sturgis

FOSQUE Perry Col 21 S Laborer Acc Acc s/o Solomon & Mary to Eliza Kellam Col 21 S Acc Acc d/o Arena Smith on 28 Sep 1887 at Onancock by GHT Byrd

FOSQUE Solomon Col 29 S Laborer Acc Acc s/o Rayner Addison to Mary Turner Col 41 S Acc Acc d/o Nellie on 8 Sep 1878 near Pungo: by JW Diggs

FOSQUE Stran Col 23 S Laborer Acc Acc s/o Henry & Airy to Rosy Sample Col 15 S Acc Acc d/o John & Mary on 13 Apr 1879 at St Luke Ch by RH Govans

FOSQUE William J 22 S Farmer Acc Acc s/o Wm T & Eliza to Susan M Smith 21 S Acc Acc d/o Hugh G & Margt on 7 May 1873 at Acc by JE Humphreys

FOSTER Thos F 23 S Seaman York Co Jersey City NJ s/o Jno & Lucy to Emma T Martin 18 S N'hamp: Acc d/o Thos & Malinda on 14 Jul 1863 at Acc by D Titlow

FOWLER Elmer M 22 S Telegraph Operator N'hamp: Acc s/o John & Susan to Hattie M Marshall 18 S Acc Acc d/o Littleton F & Esther A on 27 Nov 1889 at New Church by TM Poulson

FOWLER Jno T 26 S Farmer Acc Acc s/o Jno M & Mary to Sue F Roberts 23 S Acc Acc d/o Edwin S & Betsy on 19 Dec 1877 near Garrisons Chp by JE Humphreys

FOX Edward G 30 S Farmer Acc Acc s/o Zorobabel & Eliz'th to Elizabeth B James 24 S Acc Acc d/o John T & Susan on 13 Dec 1888 at Locustville by WJ Twilley

FOX Hezekiah 25 S Farmer Acc Acc s/o Golden T & Elizabeth to Bettie S Mears 18 S Acc Acc d/o Gilbert J & Elizabet P on 14 Dec 1887 at Drum'tn by WJ Twilley

FOX James G 38 S Merchant Acc Acc s/o James & Nancy to Jenetta S Wessells 18 S Acc Acc d/o Thomas & Elizth on 13 Feb 1870 at Acc by JET Ewell

FOX Jno 21 S Carpenter b: Acc s/o William & Mary to Margaret E PhilLips 18 S b: Acc d/o Levin W & Susan on 1 Feb 1857 at r/o Levin Philips by BT Ames

FOX Samuel M to Elizabeth A Gibbons lic: 14 Dec 1859 Thomas S White says both over 21

FOX Thomas A 27 S Farmer Acc Acc s/o Jas & Nellie to Sallie A Daugherty 26 S Acc Acc d/o Jas A & Eleshea on 6 Dec 1883 at Acc by AJ Walter

FOX William 24 S Farmer Acc Acc s/o

Jas & Nelly to Demeria Hall 24 S Acc Acc d/o Jno & Sally on 4 Jan 1872 near Onancock by J Carroll

FRANCIS Toby 41 S Laborer Acc Acc to Eliza Francis 26 S Acc Acc d/o Annie on 7 Feb 1877 near Belle Haven by RH Govans

FRANKLIN Edgar 26 S Secretary Board of Trade Lynchburg Lynchburg s/o Jacob H & M E to Margaret H Quinby 26 S Acc Acc d/o Upshur B & Georgie G on 3 Aug 1892 at Onancock by AC Berryman

FRANKLIN John A Col 28 S Wage-earner Wor Co MD Acc to Ida C Jacobs Col 18 S N'hamp: Acc d/o Tabitha Connor on 22 Oct 1888 at Belle Haven by JE Humphreys

FREEMAN Ishmael Indian 49 W Minister La Pass NM La Pass NM s/o Antonia David & Julia Ann to Georgianna [Colburn] Coleburn Col 31 S Acc Acc d/o Louis on 13 Mar 1894 at Onancock by FW Overton

FREEMAN Wm M 30 W Sailor Acc Acc s/o Isaac & Hannah to Elizabeth Whealton 23 W Acc Acc d/o Teackle & Emphama on 7 Sep 1861 at Acc by P Bowdin

FROSH Alexander 22 S Soldier b: PA to Gertrude A Bloxom 18 S sis/o S Bloxom lic: 25 May 1864 marr: 25 May 1864 at Accomack

FURNISS Chas S 27 S Farmer Som Co MD Som Co MD s/o Isaac J & Mary W to Triphemia A Linton 24 S Acc Acc d/o John A & Margaret on 22 Apr 1891 at Sykes Isld by DM Lenox

FURNISS Isaac W 21 S Blacksmith Som Co MD Acc s/o Jas Furniss to Isabella Linton 19 S Acc Acc d/o Wm & Louisa on 28 Jan 1883 at Sykes Isld by RB Beadles

FURNISS Isaac W 33 W Blacksmith Som Co MD Acc s/o Isaac J & Mary W to Malissa F Crockett 19 S Acc Acc d/o Edward & Margaret on 22 Mar 1893 at Sykes Isld by RB Scott

FURNISS Sidney O 22 S Farmer Wor Co MD Acc s/o James to Mary A Justice 15 S Acc Acc d/o John W & Mary on 12 Feb 1893 at Sykes Isld by RB Scott

GAINES Levin W Col 40 W Teacher Som Co MD Acc s/o Wm & Maria to Jane Bull Col 33 S Acc Acc d/o Jno & Mary on 9 Aug 1882 at Onancock by JC Ayler

GALL Charles 25 S Merchant Europe Acc to Elizabeth Booth 16 S Acc Acc d/o Covington & Nancy on 11 Nov 1870 at Chinco: Isld by P Bowdin Sr

GARDNER Benj 29 S Carpenter Acc Acc s/o Wm & Sarah to Elizabeth East 21 S Acc Acc d/o Peter & Susan on 21 Oct 1863 at Acc by D Titlow

GARDNER Benjamin F 20 S Farmer Acc Acc s/o Benj F & Eliz'th to Maggie T Savage 17 S Acc Acc d/o Robert T & Eliz'th on 25 Nov 1894 at Acc by AJ Reamy

GARDNER Charles 28 S Farmer Acc Acc s/o Wm T & Mary to Eva Johnson 18 S Acc Acc d/o Isaiah & Tabitha on 4 Dec 1878 at Acc by JG Anderson

GARDNER Charles D 18 S Sailor Acc Acc s/o James T & Eliza to Sallie L Scott 20 S Acc Acc d/o John W & Mary on 29 Jul 1894 at Acc by GE Booker

GARDNER George E 26 S Farmer Acc Acc s/o James T & Eliza to Harriet T Kellam 16 S Acc Acc d/o Thomas B & Margaret T on 28 Jan 1891 at Acc by AC Berryman

GARDNER Henry Edward 24 S Farmer Acc Acc s/o John & Juliet to Rebecca T Bull 20 S Acc Acc d/o Elijah F & Louisa on 2 Jan 1889 at Drum'tn by WJ Twilley

GARDNER James S 20 S Mariner Acc Acc s/o Jas T Susan L to Elizabeth S [Reed] Read 20 S Acc Acc d/o

Elizabeth on 23 Sep 1875 near Onancock by FR Boston

GARDNER John 33 S Farmer b: Acc s/o Wm & Sophia to Juliett Lilliston 19 S b: Acc d/o (Samuel E & Nattala who gave consent) on 2 Feb 1859 at Reese Chp by ES Grant (Samuel E Littiston says he over 21)

GARDNER John H 22 S Farmer Acc Acc s/o James & Eliza to Virginia G Cobb 20 S Acc Acc d/o Wm T & Virginia on 29 Jun 1887 near Onancock by JW Hundley

GARDNER John J 21 S Farmer Acc Acc s/o Charlotte to Lillian M [Colona] Colonna 16 S Acc Acc d/o William C & Mary on 1 Aug 1888 at Mappsville by WA Street

GARDNER John L 42 S Farmer Acc Acc s/o Wm & Sally to Rebecca D Rew 15 S Acc Acc d/o Susan on 5 Jan 1887 at Onley by CA Grice

GARDNER Peter FN 25 S Laborer b: Matchapungo to Betsey Case FN 21 S b: Ames Ridge d/o Charles on 26 Dec 1855 at Ames Ridge by J Burton (Charles Case says both over 21)

GARDNER Wm H 26 S Farmer Acc Acc s/o Wm T & Polly to Margaret Young 24 S Acc Acc on 24 Dec 1872 at Acc by LK LeCato

GARRETT George W 29 S Carriage Mkr N'hamp: Acc s/o Charles & Tabitha to Eliza F C Scott 29 S Acc Acc d/o Eliza on 23 Aug 1877 at Monie Camp Grove by JE Humphreys

GARRISON Berry F 25 S Farmer Acc Acc s/o Geo & Elizth to Romenia O Kellam 21 S Acc Acc d/o Aug J & Mary E on 23 Sep 1866 at Acc by AB Dolly

GARRISON George Col 65 W Laborer Acc Acc to Patience Parker Col 88 W Acc Acc on 4 Dec 1879 at Savageville by JW Diggs

GARRISON George Col 24 S Laborer Acc Acc s/o Maria to Mary Frances James Col 21 S Acc Acc on 18 Apr 1883 at Acc by LW Lee

GARRISON George Col 64 W Farm Laborer Acc Acc to Easter or Esther Custis Col 64 S Acc Acc on 10 Aug 1884 at Acc by P Sheppard

GARRISON George Col 20 S Wage-earner Acc Acc s/o Sally to Litia A Taylor Col 18 S Acc Acc d/o Tabitha on 29 Nov 1892 at Locust Mount by RH Coleman

GARRISON George A Col 21 S Wage-earner Acc Acc s/o Alfred Garrison & Eliz'th Taylor to Susan A Gunter Col 21 S Acc Acc d/o Alfred & Sarah on 28 Oct 1888 at Onancock by GHT Byrd

GARRISON George S 25 S Farmer Acc Acc s/o George to Juliet S Roberts 20 S Acc Acc d/o Edwin S & Betsy on 12 Jan 1860 at Locust Mount by JWA Elliott (George T Mapp says both over 21)

GARRISON George T 32 S Attorney Acc Acc s/o Jas R & Susan P to Charlotte E Ailworth 19 S Acc Acc d/o James J & Sallie on 19 Sep 1867 at Acc by JD Thomas

GARRISON James Col 25 S Farmer Acc Acc s/o Thomas to Emma Bell Col 28 S Acc Acc on 22 Oct 1890 at Onancock by GHT Byrd

GARRISON John Col 40 S Farmer Acc Acc s/o Keziah to Mary Allen Col 35 S Acc Acc d/o Robert & Janey on 2 Nov 1894 at Acc by PW Lee

GARRISON Richard FN 40 S Laborer Acc Acc to Clarissa Beloate FN 35 S Acc Acc on 8 Dec 1865 at Acc by TL Tomkinson

GARRISON William F [Garison] (Garrison) 22 S Farmer b: Acc s/o George S & Elizabeth to Emma Laura Mears 18 S b: Locustville d/o John W & Margaret on 6 Mar 1856 at Locustville by RB Hazzard

(Francis A Downing says he over 21)
GASKILL Charles H 21 S Sailor Canden Co NJ Acc s/o Jno T & Elizth N to Sarah L Smith 17 S Acc Acc d/o Jno & Susan on 29 Jan 1880 at Temp'ville by M Oldham
GASKILL James I 28 S Oysterman NJ Acc s/o John T & Eliz'th to Annie U Godwin 16 S Acc Acc d/o William C & Lucretia on 24 Feb 1892 at Mappsville by JL King
GASKINS Adolphus Col 23 S Farmer Acc Acc s/o Thomas Gaskins & Lizzie Kellam to Emma Church Col 16 S Acc Acc d/o Susan Rodgers on 9 Nov 1890 at Acc by TW Nettles
GASKINS Edward T Col 48 S Farmer Acc Acc s/o Rachel to Maggie S Collins Col 43 W Acc Acc d/o Maria Scarborough on 20 Oct 1886 at Onancock by GHT Byrd
GASKINS George Col 22 S Laborer Acc Acc s/o Straun & Sarah to Emma Susan Harmon Col 17 S Acc Acc d/o Caroline on 28 Oct 1877 at Belle Haven by JE Humphreys
GASKINS George Col 21 S Wage-earner Acc Acc s/o Emeline to Nellie Snead Col 21 S Acc Acc d/o Littleton & Maria on 14 Nov 1888 at Savageville by JA Haynes
GASKINS Isaac Col 28 S Sailor Acc Acc s/o John & Mary to Adeline Joynes Col 21 S Acc Acc d/o Susan on 30 Jul 1893 at Savageville by JH Offer
GASKINS James Hy Col 47 W Farmer Acc Acc s/o Philis to Sarah Walter Col 36 S Acc Acc on 28 Oct 1885 at Savageville Ch by P Sheppard
GASKINS John 33 S Laborer Acc Acc s/o Leah Harmon to Vinetta Joynes 33 S Acc Acc d/o Keziah on 30 Dec 1868 at Acc by WF Williams
GASKINS John S to Letita R B Broadwater d/o Walter who gave consent lic: 10 Feb 1857 Edward H Anderton says he over 21
GASKINS John S Jr 26 S Merchant Acc Acc s/o John S Jr & Letitia to Ida F Taylor 22 S Acc Acc d/o Alfred R & Mary on 26 Dec 1888 at Downings Ch by JS Wallace
GASKINS John W 26 S Farmer Acc Acc s/o Rachel to Harriet J Kerry 24 S Som Co MD Acc on 9 Jah 1878 near Jenkins Bridge by JB Butler
GASKINS Meshack 21 S Oysterman Acc Acc s/o Jno S & Letitia to Delia Taylor 19 S Acc Acc d/o Alfred R on 18 May 1881 at Oak Hall by RB Beadles
GASKINS Severn W Col 30 S Laborer Acc Acc s/o Rachel to Leah A Mears Col 25 S Acc Acc d/o Clarissa on 20 Apr 1875 at Acc by JK Plato
GASKINS Severn Wm Col 49 W Farmer Acc Acc s/o Rachel to Maggie S Fitchett Col 34 W Acc Acc d/o Severn & Elizabeth Bevans on 4 Jan 1894 at Onancock by FW Overton
GASKINS William H Col 28 S Farmer Acc Acc s/o James H & Eliz'th to Josephine F Phillips Col 26 S Acc Acc d/o Edmond & Mary on 23 Nov 1892 at Acc by TW Nettles
GEORGE Robert Col 45 S Farmer Acc Acc s/o Eliza to Eliza Scott Col 48 S Acc Acc d/o Mollie on 13 Aug 1894 at Acc by PW Lee
GEORGE William Col 25 S Sailor Acc Acc s/o Charlotte to Agnes Wise Col 24 S Acc Acc d/o Mahala on 10 Jun 1880 at Onancock by JW Diggs
GEORGE Zachariah 30 S Oysterman Acc Acc s/o Polly to Lena Blake 21 S Acc Acc d/o Rhoda Williams on 9 Jan 1868 at Acc by P Bowdin Sr
GEORGE Zachariah Col 56 S Laborer Acc Acc s/o Adder & Polly to Lizzie Leary Col 27 S Dover DE Acc d/o Robert & Louisa on 25 Dec 1889 at Acc by L Duncan

Marriages

GIBB Joseph Col 23 S Wage-earner NC Acc s/o Henry & Jane Farmer to Missouri Turner Col 24 S Acc Acc d/o Henry & Jane on 4 Jul 1893 at Onancock by FW Overton

GIBB William J 28 S Farming Acc Acc s/o Joseph W & Eliza to Susan L Henderson 32 W Acc Acc d/o Oliver & Mary Ann Logan on 30 Apr 1861 at Horntown by T Waters

GIBBONS Alfred J 25 S Farmer Acc Acc s/o James T & Mary to Susan S Wright 23 S Acc Acc d/o John & Louisa on 30 Dec 1888 at Parksley by HS Dulany

GIBBONS Alfred J 28 W Farmer Acc Acc s/o James T & Mary to Elizabeth Wright 24 S Acc Acc d/o John & Louisa on 27 Apr 1890 at Parksley by HS Dulany

GIBBONS Edward T Col 22 S Laborer Acc Acc s/o Edward & Ayres to Alice Downing Col 19 S Acc Acc d/o Amanda on 27 Apr 1887 at News Town by AJ Satchell

GIBBONS John Col 24 S Laborer Acc Acc s/o Mary to Tabitha Bundick Col 25 S Acc Acc d/o Patience on 14 Jan 1875 at Metompkin by A Joynes

GIBBONS John E to Sally Warner d/o Solomon dec'd lic: 21 Dec 1854 Thos F White says both over 21

GIBBONS William 21 S Waterman Acc Acc s/o John & Jane to Sarah C Sparrow 21 S Acc Acc d/o Edward & Catharine on 4 Jul 1894 at Tangier by WR Gwinn

GIBBONS William H s/o James to Matilda A White d/o James S lic: 30 Sep 1857 Thomas S White says both over 21

GIDDINGE Wm Col 26 S Laborer N'hamp: Acc s/o Spry & Margt Parkerson to Mary Shaw Col 22 S Acc Acc d/o Jno Stran & Harriet Gunter on 8 Jul 1884 at Acc by LW Lee

GIDDINGS John Col 20 S Farmer Acc Acc s/o Alfred & Rosina to Maggie Floyd Col 18 S Acc Acc d/o Peter & Eliz'th on 3 Dec 1890 at Acc by JB Lewis

GILDEN Edward to Mary Eliza (Belote) Beloate d/o Geo dec'd & ward/o James Kellam who gave consent lic: 24 Aug 1854 James Kellam says he over 21

GILDEN Joseph T 22 S Seaman N'hamp: Acc s/o Wm & Elizabeth to Jane [Starling] Sterling 18 S Acc Acc d/o Wm & Margaret on 15 Mar 1861 at Wm Starling's by AM Hall

GILDEN Obed J 30 S Steamboating Acc Acc s/o Edward & Eliza to Susan A Read 19 S Acc Acc d/o Littleton D & Hennie on 3 Dec 1890 at Acc by JM Anderson

GILDEN Wm E 25 S Farmer Acc Acc s/o Wm E & Mary to Judia A Mister 18 S Acc Acc d/o Lorenzo D on 11 Feb 1880 at Acc by SC Boston

GILL John R 23 S Minister Northumberland Co Acc s/o Zaccheus R & Nancy L to Ida M Russell 23 S Acc Acc d/o John W & Sallie T on 12 Jun 1893 at Bloxom by JW Nicholson

GILLESPIE Albert to Catherine A Dix ward/o Wm Pettitt who gave consent lic: 23 Dec 1857 Wm H Singleton says he over 21

GILLESPIE George 25 S Farmer Acc Acc s/o Peter & Susan to Annie Thornton 22 S Acc Acc d/o Wn & Emeline on 4 Jan 1883 at Mappsville by JW Hundley

GILLESPIE John W to Sally A White d/o Wm C who gave consent lic: 20 Dec 1856 Wm Fisher says he over 21

GILLESPIE Peter J 21 S Laborer Acc Acc s/o Peter & Susan to Emma J Northam 16 S Acc Acc d/o Wm & Margaret on 11 Nov 1874 at Bethel

Ch by DA Woodson

GILLESPIE Richard 23 S Sailor Acc Acc s/o Peter & Susan to Alberta Lewis 23 S Acc Acc d/o Parker & Betsy on 9 Apr 1884 at Temp'ville by M Oldham

GILLESPIE William C 21 S Farmer Acc Acc s/o Albert & Betsy to Manie S Fitchett 18 S Acc Acc d/o Jno Y & Mary E on 24 Feb 1881 at Mr Jno Y Fitchell's by JW Hundley

GILLETT Edward (Littleton) Col 26 S Laborer Acc Acc to Mary A Allen Col 28 S Acc Acc on 20 Dec 1871 at Horntown by W Phillips

GILLETT Gilbert G [Guillette] 44 W Farmer MD Acc s/o Elizth to Virginia [Shields] Shield 32 S Acc Acc d/o Asa on 15 Jan 1879 at Modest Town by JW Hundley

GLADDING Alfred 29 W Farming b: Acc s/o Henry & Mary to Lavania (C) Drummond 27 W b: Acc d/o Walter S & Rebeckar Slocomb on 11 Nov 1856 at Acc by T Waters

GLADDING Alfred M 22 S Carpenter Acc Acc s/o Geo W & Sally to Bettie A Corbin 20 S Acc Acc d/o Geo W & Missouri on 6 Jan 1886 at Temp'ville by M Oldham

GLADDING Burwell 22 S Farmer b: Muddy Ck s/o Sally Gladdon to Mary Hickman 21 S b: Muddy Ck d/o Polly on 10 Mar 1855 at r/o Polly Hickman by GH Ewell

GLADDING E Dawson 28 S Sailor Acc Acc s/o Saml & Elizth to Hetty Topping 40 W Acc Acc d/o Zedinck & Elizth Bayly on 11 Mar 1877 near Messongo by TM Poulson

GLADDING Edwd G 33 S Farming b: Acc s/o Susan to Polly Trader 23 S b: Acc d/o Wm & Nancy on 31 Dec 1857 at r/o Wm Trader by ES Grant (David Mason says both over 21)

GLADDING George W 23 S Shoemaker Acc Acc s/o Geo & Milcha to Anna Whealton 18 S Acc Acc d/o Erastus & Mary on 10 Jan 1872 at Acc by JC Reed

GLADDING James H 46 W Farmer Acc Acc to Susan J East 33 S Acc Acc d/o George T on 2 Jan 1878 near Jenkins Bridge by A Wiles

GLADDING Jas E 32 S Merchant Acc Acc s/o Jno W & Margt A to Mary A Silverthorn 29 W NJ Acc d/o Geo & Mary Meelham on 26 Dec 1886 at New Church by BF Jester

GLADDING John 40 S Farmer Acc Acc to Elizth Gardner 30 W Acc Acc d/o Peter T & Susan East on 28 Dec 1879 at Acc by JC Watson

GLADDING Lloyd S 25 S Sailor Acc Acc s/o Saml & Elizth P to Hetty Hurley 18 S Acc Acc d/o Robert & Ann on 5 Feb 1878 near Messongo by TM Poulson

GLADDING Octaveis 20 S Sailor Acc Acc s/o Calvin R & Elizth to Florence N [Bird] Byrd 24 S Acc Acc d/o Obed S & Hetty on 4 Jan 1882 at Mr Calvin Gladding's by JW Hundley

GLADDING Oliver J 32 W Sailor Acc Acc s/o Solomon & Sallie to Danverse Jane Marshall 22 S Acc Acc d/o Stephen & Patience on 25 Mar 1870 at Acc by JET Ewell

GLADDING Olvier J 23 S Oysterman s/o Solomon & Sally to Elizabeth Fisher 24 wid lic: 6 Feb 1865 marr: 8 Feb 1865

GLADDING Solomon J 20 S Farmer Acc Acc s/o Burwell B & Mary to Burnetta Trader 21 S Acc Acc d/o Wm P & Margaret on 3 May 1880 at Bethel Bapt Ch by DA Woodson

GLADDING William 23 S Oysterman Acc Acc s/o Burwell & Mary to Sally Lewis 27 S Acc Acc d/o Parker & Elizabeth on 29 Mar 1881 near Bethel by JE Bundick

GLADSON Thomas Col 25 S Farmer

N'hamp: Acc s/o Sarah Simpkins to Nancy A Webb Col 18 S Acc Acc d/o John & Emma on 2 Dec 1886 at Acc by JE Humphreys

GLENN Edmund T Col 41 S Fisherman Acc Acc to Betsey Glenn Col 45 S Acc Acc on 10 Dec 1891 at Acc by RH Coleman

GLENN George Col 32 S Farmer Acc Acc s/o Mary to Lydia Bunting Col 38 S Acc Acc d/o William on 2 Oct 1889 at Locust Mount by JWA Elliott

GLENN George T Col 23 S Farmer Acc Acc s/o Louis & Bettie to Mary A Burton Col 18 S Acc Acc d/o Thos H & Mary S on 17 Dec 1893 at Locust Mount by JWA Elliott

GLOVER Henry M 25 S Carpenter Philadelphia PA Philadelphia PA s/o John & Alice to Emma E Jester 19 S Acc Acc d/o Joseph V & Annie on 24 Aug 1893 at Chinco: Isld by RB Sanford

GODFREY Fredinand Col 20 S Laborer Acc Acc s/o John & Betsy to Leah A Dennis Col 17 S Acc Acc d/o Joshua & Harriet on 20 Sep 1885 at Acc by AJ Satchell

GODFREY John FN to Elizabeth Laws FN lic: 1 Nov 1856 George Allen says both over 21

GODWIN Adolphus 20 S Farmer Acc Acc s/o Samuel A & Clarinda S to Florence Martin 19 S Acc Acc d/o George W on 12 Jun 1895 at Acc by ML Williams

GODWIN Alfred Col 27 S Laborer Acc Acc s/o Betsy to Esther Crippen Col 25 S Acc Acc on 5 Jan 1879 at Temp'ville by JC Cluff

GODWIN Charles 28 S Farmer Sussex Co DE Chinco: Isld s/o David & Coppie to Matilda Birch 23 S Chinco: Isld Chinco: Isld d/o Jno & Margt on 12 Dec 1878 at Chinco: Isld by R Williamson

GODWIN Edmund Spencer 35 S Oysterman Acc Acc s/o Edwd G & Elizth to Bernetta Susan Hall 21 S Acc Acc d/o Geo E & Sally on 27 Nov 1872 at Pocomoke Nk by M Oldham

GODWIN Eugene M 23 S Farmer Acc Acc s/o Obadiah W & Eliz'th to Sally A Matthews 18 S Acc Acc d/o Wm H & Mary on 25 Nov 1891 at Acc by WW Wood

GODWIN George W 23 S Farmer Acc Acc s/o Wm & Elizth to Ella A Fletcher 18 S Acc Acc d/o Thos R & Seymorn on 26 Dec 1878 at Conquest Ch by M Oldham

GODWIN James E 23 S Railroading Acc Acc s/o James E & Eliz'th to Mary A [Bailey] Bayly 18 S Acc Acc d/o Richard & Sally on 31 Dec 1890 at Temp'ville by WF Hayes

GODWIN Julius D 25 S Oysterman Acc Acc s/o Edmund to Mary J Knight 18 S Acc Acc d/o Wm S & Charlotte on 15 Mar 1866 at Acc by GW Matthews

GODWIN Julius D 33 W Oysterman Acc Acc s/o Edwd & Elizabeth to Adaline F Mears 17 S Acc Acc d/o Zadoc & Juliet Ann on 9 Jul 1873 at Temp'ville by M Oldham

GODWIN Littleton C 21 S Farmer Acc Acc s/o Obadiah W & Elizth to Olivia A Martin 19 S Acc Acc d/o James W & Louisa on 24 Aug 1884 at Acc by JW Carroll

GODWIN Obediah Col 35 S Laborer Acc Acc s/o Betsy to Harriet A White Col 30 S Acc Acc d/o William on 21 Jun 1885 near Temp'ville by JC Cluff

GODWIN Samuel A 26 S Sailor Acc Acc s/o O W & Elizabeth to Clarinda S Chase 16 S Acc Acc d/o Teagle R & Eliza on 1 Jul 1874 at Acc by EM Bryan

GODWIN Samuel A 32 W Farmer Acc Acc s/o Obediah W & Elizabeth to

Damariah Davis 24 S Acc Acc d/o Alfred & Emaline Davis on 20 Oct 1880 at Conquest Ch by JW Hundley

GODWIN Sylvester B Col 29 S Sailor Acc Acc s/o Jacob & Leah to Rose Davis Col 33 W Wor Co MD Acc d/o George & Grace Manuel on 30 Dec 1894 at Acc by L Duncan

GODWIN William C 23 S Oysterman Acc Acc s/o Edward & Elizth to Critty Davis 24 S Acc Acc d/o Henry & Hetty on 6 Jan 1870 at Messongo by JET Ewell

GODWIN William J 28 S Milling Acc Acc s/o James & Eliz'th to Ella M Cutler 18 S Acc Acc d/o John W & Sarah E on 26 Dec 1888 at Temp'ville by WF Hayes

GODWIN William P 18 S Farmer Acc Acc s/o Samuel A & Alarmda S to Susan J Poulson 18 S Acc Acc d/o Marion J & Sarah S on 31 Oct 1894 at Acc by JL King

GOFFIGON John Almer 21 S Sailor Acc Acc s/o Wm P & Margaret S to Fluvanna J Bundick 18 S Acc Acc d/o John B & Margaret on 17 Nov 1880 at Bradford Nk by JWA Elliott

GOFFIGON Obediah (widr) to Elizabeth S Wescott (wid) on 13 Apr 1859 at Belle Haven by M Oldham

GOFFIGON Wm P 45 W Farmer N'hamp: Acc s/o Wm & Mary to Elizabeth Harrison 42 S Acc Acc d/o Jas Hainson & Polly Garrison on 5 Dec 1863 at Acc by LK LeCato

GORDY John 24 S Sailor Wor Co MD Chinco: Isld s/o Cyrus & Eliza to Mary Ann Brimer 22 S Acc Chinco: Isld d/o Woodson & Susan on 15 Mar 1884 at Chinco: Isld by SU Grimsley

GORN Stephen 37 S Sailor Morris Co NJ Acc s/o Patrick & Julia to Vienna Mason 28 S Acc Acc d/o Jeremiah & Elizabeth on 1 Jan 1890 at Temp'ville by WF Hayes

GOSWELLING Wm C 27 S Steam Milling Wor Co MD Acc s/o Stephen & Esther J to Alicia A Powell 23 S Acc Acc d/o Wm & Amanda on 21 Oct 1891 at Parksley by JF Anderson

GRANT Edward Col 28 S Laborer Acc Acc s/o Annie Snead to Mary Leatherbury Col 24 S N'hamp: Acc d/o Elnvira on 6 Jul 1871 at Acc by N Morris

GRANT John D 28 S Comm of Revenue Acc Acc s/o Edwd S & Tabitha J to Susan E Coard 27 S Acc Acc d/o Jno W & Nancy on 8 Dec 1875 near Wiseville by IT Adkins

GRANT William B Col 22 S Farmer Acc Acc s/o William H & Sarah to Mary M S Dickerson Col 19 S Acc Acc d/o John F & Sallie F on 25 Jan 1891 at Acc by AJ Satchell

GRAY Dennis W 39 S Farmer s/o Dennis & Polly to Amanda Taylor 29 d/o John & Catharine lic: 22 Nov 1864 marr: 26 Nov 1864 in Acc Co

GRAY George 23 S Sailor Acc Acc s/o Thomas & Nancy to Rockzanah T Bell 17 S Acc Acc d/o Thorogood & Catharine on 13 Feb 1868 at Acc by ES Grant

GRAY Henry (R) 37 W Farmer b: Acc s/o Unknown & Elizabeth Gray to Demeriah Scott 35 S b: Acc d/o John & Tabitha on 27 Dec 1855 at r/o Sally Russels by GH Ewell (Geo P Ewell says both over 21)

GRAY Isaac Col 42 S Farmer Acc Acc s/o Leah Gunter to Elzey Taylor Col 39 S Acc Acc d/o Peggy on 17 Jul 1873 near Acc C H by A Joynes

GRAY James T 22 S Farmer Acc Acc s/o James & Elizth to Laura Winger 27 S Acc Acc d/o Samuel & Kitty on 24 Dec 1884 at Acc by IG Fosnocht

GRAY Jas E 24 S Farmer Acc Acc s/o Jas & Mahala to Betsy Chandler 17 S Acc Acc d/o Jno B & Sally on 12 May 1864 at Acc by ES Grant

Marriages

GRAY John H Col 44 W Carpenter Acc Acc s/o Edmond Snead & Hannah Gunter to Annie Gray Col 29 W Acc Acc d/o Levi Custis on 31 Oct 1889 at Acc by JH Thomas

GRAY John H 24 S Farmer Acc Acc s/o Dennis W & Amanda to Ida S [Justis] Justice 22 S Acc Acc d/o John & Margaret A on 30 Dec 1891 at Acc by AJ Fristoe

GRAY John H Col 22 S Wage-earner Acc Acc s/o William & Tabitha to Mary Drummond Col 22 S Acc Acc d/o Abraham & Leah on 22 Mar 1891 at Acc by LE Toulson

GRAY Thomas J 27 S Sailor Acc Acc s/o Sheppard & Mary to Mary Rebecca Evans 16 S Acc Acc d/o John E & Triphenia on 15 Aug 1888 at Chesconessex by JW Easley

GRAY Thomas R 31 W Farmer Acc Acc s/o Thos & Nancy to Sally Mason 27 S Acc Acc d/o Stephen & Harriett on 26 Feb 1862 at Acc by ES Grant

GRAY Thos R 26 W Farmer b: Acc s/o Thos & Nancy to Kesiah S Chandler 37 S b: Acc d/o Elisha (Decd) & Anna on 31 Dec 1854 at Acc by ES Grant (Levin R Ayres says both over 21)

GRAY William [Grey] Col 26 S Hostler Wic Co MD Pocomoke City MD s/o Selby & Jane to Atty Winslow Col 25 W Acc Acc d/o Louis Douglas & Patsey Lambden on 21 Feb 1888 at Horntown by N Morris

GRAY William E 23 S Farmer Acc Acc s/o James & Elizabeth to Willie Insley 22 W Acc Acc d/o Edward & Sarah Tignal on 28 Mar 1893 at Acc by AJ Reamy

GRAY Wm Col 21 S Laborer Acc Acc s/o Maria Coard to Bettie Stevens Col 22 S Acc Acc d/o Rike & Mary on 2 Oct 1884 at Acc by LW Lee

GREEN Chas A 22 S Sailor Squan NJ Acc s/o Jas H & Maria to Bettie A Nelson 22 S Acc Acc d/o Geo & Eliz on 27 Dec 1882 at Acc by M Oldham

GREEN William H 38 W Farmer Baltimore MD Acc s/o Thos d & Nancy to Mary P Conquest 22 S Acc Acc d/o Edward H & Mary on 4 Oct 1866 at Acc by GW Matthews

GRIFFIN Douglas Col 20 S Waterman Acc Acc s/o Sarah to Maggie Joynes Col 19 S Acc Acc d/o Henry & Susan on 26 Dec 1894 at Acc by AJ Wallace

GRIFFIN James A 20 S Waterman Raleigh NC Acc s/o Dolphus & Sallie to Mollie B Young 15 S Acc Acc d/o Isaac W & Louisa on 19 Jun 1895 at Sykes Isld by ML Williams

GRIFFIN McComas Col 31 S Oysterman Acc Acc s/o William & Betsey to Tabitha Rachel Turner Col 20 S Acc Acc d/o Henry & Jane on 20 Mar 1892 at Acc by LE Toulson

GRIFFIN William Col 38 S Laborer Acc Acc s/o Nancy to Esther Pettitt Col 25 S Acc Acc d/o Rosa on 22 May 1873 at Metompkin Township by A Joynes

GRINNALDS James H 24 S Farming Acc Acc s/o John C & Mary to Tabitha J Parkes 22 S Acc Acc d/o John, Sr on 8 Jan 1862 at Acc by ES Grant

GRINNALDS Jas Earl [Grinnald] 20 S Farmer Acc Acc s/o James H & Tabitha J to Elizabeth Louden 22 S Portsmouth VA Acc on 21 Dec 1882 at Acc by WC Vaden

GRINNALDS Jefferson D 23 S Sailor Acc Acc s/o Thos J & Elizth to Roberta S [Twyford] Twiford 22 S Acc Acc d/o Geo D & Elizth on 16 Aug 1883 at Wise Point by CS Baker

GRINNALDS Jno Wm 57 W Farmer Acc Acc s/o John C & Mary A to Marg't Cath White 60 W Acc Acc d/o William & Elashia Lewis on 9

Aug 1893 at Acc by JET Ewell

GRINNALDS John W 28 S Farmer s/o John & Mary to Margaret T White 25 d/o Richard & Henrietta lic: 5 Dec 1864 marr: 7 Dec 1864 at Accomack

GRINNALDS Southey [Grinals] 22 S Farmer b: Acc s/o Parker to Polly Mason 25 S b: Acc d/o (Major) on 3 Nov 1855 at r/o Geo H Ewell by GH Ewell (William J Bundick says they over 21)

GRINNALDS Southey S 22 S Farmer Acc Acc s/o Jno C & Mary to Annie T Cropper 21 S Acc Acc d/o Jno H & Sarah Ann on 11 Dec 1878 near Locustville by LK LeCato

GRINNALDS Thos C 27 S Sailor Acc Acc s/o Thos J & Betsie to Bettie D Byrd 20 S Acc Acc d/o Geo W & Elizth on 26 Feb 1879 at Modest Town by M Oldham

GRINNALDS William Thos 21 S Farmer Acc Acc s/o John Wm & Margaret to Sudie W Bishop 19 S Acc Acc d/o George J & Susan on 3 Nov 1887 at Drum'tn by J McNabb

GROSS Hosea Thomas Col 21 S Barber Calvert Co MD Acc s/o Henry & Rebecca to Leah Susan Dix Col 18 S Acc Acc d/o Mary Bayly on 5 Sep 1878 near Drum'tn by A Joynes

GROTON Edward T 23 S Carpenter Acc Acc s/o Wm & Elizth to Mollie W Tull 18 S Acc Acc d/o Jno & Elizth on 24 Dec 1879 at Bethel Ch by JW Hundley

GROTON Emory D 28 S Milling Acc Acc s/o Thomas & Harriet to Susan J Fisher 18 S Acc Acc d/o John T & Hester A on 26 Dec 1887 at Temp'ville by M Oldham

GROTON Geo B 21 S Farmer Acc Acc s/o Wm & Margt to Adaline Landing 17 S Acc Acc d/o Jas & Mary on 17 Dec 1879 at Modest Town by JW Hundley

GROTON George H 22 S Farmer Acc Acc s/o Henry & Ann to Marie J Hope 16 S Acc Acc d/o John T F & Catharine on 15 Feb 1893 at Locust Mount by JWA Elliott

GROTON Henry [Groten] 19 S Farmer Acc Acc s/o Wm & Lovey to Sarah A Bundick 20 S Acc Acc d/o Saml & Sarah on 2 Jan 1867 at Acc

GROTON James P [Groten] 30 S Merchant Acc Acc s/o Wm D to Matilda Garrison 30 S Acc Acc on 19 Dec 1861 at Acc by BT Ames

GROTON James T 28 S Farmer Acc Acc s/o Thos & Harriet J to Girtie Brittingham 19 S Acc Acc d/o Wm & Charlotte on 10 Mar 1886 at Oak Hall by DM Wallace

GROTON John W [Groten] 23 S Farmer Acc Acc s/o William & Margaret to Mary A Northam 20 S Acc Acc d/o Wm C & Mary on 5 Jan 1870 at Conquest Ch by M Oldham

GROTON Robert [Groten] 20 S Carpenter Acc Acc s/o Robt & Sally to Charlotte Nock 18 S Acc Acc d/o Saml & Polly on 5 Nov 1884 at Acc by WA Street

GROTON Skinner O 20 S Farmer Acc Acc s/o Thomas & Harriet to Roseann T Drummond 21 S Acc Acc d/o John T & Cmfort on 25 Dec 1884 at Acc by DM Wallace

GROTON Thomas [Groten] 27 S Farmer Acc Acc s/o Wm D & Lovey to Mollie Hopkins 24 S Acc Acc d/o Joseph & Betsy on 31 Dec 1879 at Onancock by SC Boston

GROTON William s/o John to Sally A Northam d/o Henry B who gave consent lic: 27 Dec 1860

GROTON William L 21 S Farmer s/o Wm T & Mary to Mary M Watson 17 S d/o Joseph C & Elizabeth lic: 13 Feb 1871 marr: 15 Feb 1871 near Locustville

GROTON William T 21 S Farmer Acc

Marriages

Acc s/o Henry & Sarah A to Virginia C Johnson 17 S Acc Acc d/o John T & Rachel H on 6 Feb 1889 at Acc by W Chinn

GROTON William T 31 W Farmer Acc Acc s/o William D & Lovey to Theresa C Lilliston 18 S Acc Acc d/o Robert & Mary on 28 Dec 1890 at Acc by JT Moore

GUNTER Alfred Col 30 S Oysterman Acc Acc s/o Hennie to Margaret Johnson Col 21 S Acc Acc d/o Sarah Johnson on 19 Dec 1872 near Deep Ck by N Morris

GUNTER Benjamin C Col 32 S Farmer Acc Acc s/o Edward C & Lucy to Mary Susan Parker Col 23 S Acc Acc d/o Mary Ellen on 30 Mar 1893 at Acc by L Duncan

GUNTER Edmond Col 32 S Sailor Acc Acc s/o Leah Griffin to Martha Chandler Col 30 S Acc Acc d/o Labra Parker on 5 Apr 1876 at Buck Lot by HT Rich

GUNTER Ernest Col 21 S Wage-earner Acc Acc s/o Solomon & Arinthia to Sally Jane Holden Col 21 S Acc Acc d/o Mary Ann on 21 Jul 1895 at Onancock by SW Watkins

GUNTER Isaiah T Col 36 S Farmer Acc Acc s/o Martha Wharton to Annie White Col 28 S Acc Acc d/o Louis & Fannie on 30 Oct 1889 at Acc by AJ Satchell

GUNTER James H 25 S Farmer Acc Acc s/o James & Sally to Sarah Ann Bundick 17 S Acc Acc d/o Thomas & Mary on 29 Jan 1879 at Zion Ch by DA Woodson

GUNTER John Col 40 S Laborer Acc Acc s/o Henny to Emma White Col 27 S Acc Acc on 2 Mar 1876 at Deep Ck by HT Rich

GUNTER John J 26 S Lawyer Acc Acc s/o Benj T & Ellen F to Florence M Custis 21 S Acc Acc d/o Thos E C & Elizabeth on 2 Aug 1886 at Onancock by J McNabb

GUNTER Levin Col 65 S Farmer Acc Acc s/o Jsaac & Leah to Henny Jones Col 50 W Acc Acc d/o Hannah on 9 Nov 1870 at Deep Ck by N Morris

GUNTER Littleton Col 23 S Farmer Acc Acc s/o Tinsy to Racilia Laws Col 20 S Acc Acc d/o Joshua & Sylva on 4 Feb 1877 at Drum'tn by PM Only

GUNTER Parker (Col) 40 S Foreman Steam Mill Acc Acc s/o Isaac & Leah to Sarah Ewell (Col) 26 S Acc Acc d/o Thomas & Leah on 2 Apr 1870 at Acc by S Marshall

GUNTER Samuel W 21 S Farmer s/o Wm & Annie to Elizabeth Grinnalds 21 S d/o John & Mary lic: 26 Dec 1870

GUNTER Solomon 24 S Laborer Acc Acc s/o Hennie to Arinthia Nock 18 S Acc Acc d/o Leah on 26 Dec 1868 at Acc by WF Williams

GUNTER Thomas Col 45 W Laborer Acc Acc s/o Leah to Milca Miles Col 21 S Acc Acc d/o Alsie on 13 Jul 1876 at Deep Ck by JK Plato

GUNTER Thomas Col 27 S Laborer Acc Acc s/o Rosie to Margaret Custis Col 21 S Acc Acc d/o Ann on 29 Apr 1880 at Onancock by JW Diggs

GUY Benj F 22 S Farmer Acc Acc s/o Wm T & Sarah to Annie Stevens 18 S Acc Acc d/o John H & Bettie A on 22 Nov 1893 near Locust Mount by JWA Elliott

GUY Claude H 19 S Farmer Acc Acc s/o Selby & Mary Ann to Emma Jane Tipton 17 S Acc Acc d/o J Thos & Rachel on 5 Dec 1894 at Acc by JR Griffith

GUY Edward T 25 S Farmer Acc Acc s/o John W & Margaret to Lottie L Tipton 22 S Acc Acc d/o Thomas & Rachel on 21 Nov 1894 at Acc by

EC Atkins

GUY Ellison 22 S Farmer Acc Acc s/o William & Susan to Jane Read 19 S Acc Acc d/o Samuel & Elizabeth on 16 Nov 1870 at Andrew Chp by JH Addison

GUY George to Anna Metcalf d/o Jesse lic: 17 Jan 1860 Samuel Milliner said both over 21

GUY George B 30 S Sailor Acc Acc s/o George to Arinthia J Garrison 28 S Acc Acc d/o George & Elizth on 27 Feb 1867 at Acc by AB Dolly

GUY George W 22 S Farmer Acc Acc s/o Jno W & Mary to Carrie L Hargis 19 S Acc Acc d/o Geo F & Hester P on 24 Nov 1880 at Cross Rd by SC Boston

GUY John W 19 S Farmer Acc Acc s/o Wm T & Sarah J to Mary E Ward 16 S Acc Acc d/o Wm P & Margt S on 5 Nov 1879 at Acc by CC Wertenbaker

GUY John Wm 23 S Waterman b: Pungo: s/o John Wm & Suannna L to Mary Ann Rayfield 24 S b: Onancock d/o Samuel & Nancy A (Levi) on 25 Jul 1855 at Onancock by J Allen (John A Martin says both over 21)

GUY Joseph 21 S Farmer Acc Acc s/o William T & Susan to Nannie G Miller 22 S Portsmouth VA Acc d/o John & Mary E on 30 Oct 1889 at Pungo: by JH Riddick

GUY Louis F 20 S Farmer Acc Acc s/o John W & Mary to Mary S Powell 19 S Acc Acc d/o Nathl & Juliet on 21 Feb 1877 at Onancock Par by JH Amiss

GUY Otho S 21 S Farmer Acc Acc s/o John W & Margaret E to Ella Cora Barnes 17 S Acc Acc d/o George W & Isabella on 31 Mar 1895 at Locust Mount by JWA Elliott

GUY Robert 23 S Mechanic b: Acc s/o George & Margaret to Caroline Drummond 20 S b: Acc d/o Wm & Mary on 21 Feb 1855 near Pungo: by M Oldham

GUY Robert J 28 S Farmer Norfolk City Acc s/o Robert J & Caroline to Josephine Doughty 25 S N'hamp: Acc d/o Joseph & Sallie on 21 Dec 1892 at Acc by T Burton

GUY Robert L 26 S Sailor Acc Acc s/o Robert P & Margaret T to Maggie V Wise 26 S Acc Acc d/o Benjamin D & Louisa J on 31 May 1893 at Acc by JM Anderson

GUY Robert P 48 S Mariner Acc Acc to Margt T Mears 34 W Acc Acc on 6 Jun 1866 at Acc by LK LeCato

GUY Selby 21 S Sailor Acc Acc s/o Wm & Susan to Mary Anna Scott 18 S Acc Acc d/o Tully & Tabitha on 13 Sep 1865 at Acc by JH Addison

GUY Selby 33 S Sailor Acc Acc to Bernetta Hopkins 22 W Acc Acc on 5 May 1878 near Onancock by SC Boston

GUY Sidney C 24 S Engineer Acc Acc s/o James E & Maria J to Lula Lee Core 17 S Acc Acc d/o Wm T & Fannie E on 29 Dec 1895 at Onancock by AJ Reamy

GUY Thomas 24 S Sailor Acc Acc s/o Robert & Tabitha to Mary Crockett 25 S Acc Acc d/o Asa & Susan on 12 Jan 1873 at Acc by O Littleton

GUY William H 23 S Farmer Acc Acc s/o John W & Mary to Julia A Gardner 23 S Acc Acc d/o Benjamin & Eliz'th on 23 Jan 1889 at bride's mother's by RA Compton

GUY William Jr to Sarah E [Stephens] Stevens d/o (James) on 20 Jun 1860 at Acc by M Oldham (George S West said he over 21)

GUY William T 60 W Farmer Acc Acc to Carissa Ann Tipton 16 S Acc Acc d/o J Thos on 7 Jan 1891 at Acc by JM Anderson

HACK George W Col 23 S Farmer Acc

Acc s/o Stephen & Sabra to Lenn Parker Col 21 S Acc Acc d/o John G & Margaret on 9 Dec 1894 at Acc by TW Nettles

HACK John H Col 23 S Farmer Acc Acc s/o Stephen & Sabra to Mary A Simpkins Col 20 S Acc Acc d/o Isaac & Susan on 31 Dec 1890 at Acc by JB Lewis

HACK Kiah Col 47 S Farmer Acc Acc s/o Leah to Sally Savage Col 40 S Acc Acc d/o Sally on 22 Nov 1874 at Savageville by JK Plato

HACK Kiah Col 50 W Farmer Acc Acc to Mary Jane West Col 35 W Acc Acc d/o Emanuel & Caroline Harmon on 1 Jan 1891 at Acc by L Duncan

HACK Stephen 28 S Farmer Acc Acc s/o Tabitha to Sabra Savage 21 S Acc Acc d/o Emory on 28 Jan 1869 at Acc by OP Twiford

HACKETT Robert Col 52 S Farmer Acc Acc to Margaret Bayly Col 45 S Acc Acc d/o Adah on 14 Apr 1891 at Acc by JWA Elliott

HACKETT Sylvester Col 23 S School Teacher Acc Acc s/o Robert & Margaret to Hester C Nedab Col 19 S Acc Acc d/o William & Sarah on 25 May 1892 at Acc by PW Lee

HALEY John R 30 S Sailor b: Acc s/o William & Nancy to Margaret Parker 22 S b: Acc d/o Levin & Elizabeth on 31 Mar 1859 at r/o Wm Parker by LK LeCato (William Parker says both over 21)

HALEY John T 26 S Farmer Acc Acc s/o James P & Rosetta to Rebecca E Gladding 17 S Acc Acc d/o Jno & Margt on 28 Feb 1877 near Onancock by JH Amiss

HALL Allen J 24 S Oysterman Acc Acc s/o Asa & Cordelia to Amanda W Lewis 16 S Acc Acc d/o Wm T & Susan on 12 Nov 1879 at Acc by JW Hilldrup

HALL Amos J 31 S Waterman Acc Acc s/o Asa & Cordelia to Beatie Hurley 19 S Acc Acc d/o Robert J & Comfort A on 17 May 1893 at Temp'ville by JW Nicholson

HALL Anthony L 28 W Farmer Acc Acc s/o Thos & Sally E to Elizabeth Gladding 26 W Acc Acc d/o Geo & Milcah on 25 Jan 1871 at Acc by O Littleton

HALL Anthony L 35 W Farmer Acc Acc s/o Thos & Sally to Sallie E Byrd 25 S Acc Acc d/o Saml R & Mary E on 24 Oct 1877 at Atlantic Meth Parsonage by CC Wertenbaker

HALL Asa 23 S Oysterman Acc Acc s/o Asa & Cordalia to Mary E [Justis] Justice 18 S Acc Acc d/o Thomas & Mary on 11 Nov 1874 at Temp'ville by M Oldham

HALL Benj F 21 S Farmer Acc Acc s/o Thos S & Sally to Sarah A Andrews 20 S Acc Acc d/o Wm J & Emaline on 8 Jan 1882 near Messongo Ch by JW Hundley

HALL Calvin W 22 S Wage-earner Acc Acc s/o Santa to Catharine Dixon 21 S Wor Co MD Acc d/o John W on 26 Dec 1888 at Temp'ville by WF Hayes

HALL David Col 22 S Laborer Acc Acc s/o Harriet to Amy Godwin Col 19 S Acc Acc d/o Harriet on 23 Feb 1880 at Acc by A Joynes

HALL Frank C 20 S Oysterman Acc Acc s/o Asa & Cordelia to Oceanna Woods 17 S Acc Acc d/o John & Susan on 20 Dec 1876 at Messongo by M Oldham

HALL Geo 26 W Sailor Acc Acc s/o Jno & Nancy to Sarah Jester 21 S Acc Acc d/o Jas & Fanny on 26 May 1864 at (Chinco Isld) by P Bowdin

HALL George 20 S Mariner Chinco: Isld Chinco: Isld s/o Jno Hall & Nancy Russell to Frances [Reid] Read 18 S Chinco: Isld Chinco: Isld d/o Wm & Euphenny on 10 Jun 1856 at Chinco: Isld by WP Thornton

HALL George Col 52 S Farmer Acc Acc to Tamar Drummond Col 57 S Acc Acc d/o Sarah Rayfield on 6 Jul 1871 at Acc by N Morris

HALL George Col 21 S Farmer Acc Acc s/o Geoge & Tamar to Sarah Dorne Col 21 S Chester Co PA Acc on 12 Mar 1874 at Metompkin by A Joynes

HALL George Jr Col 28 W Farmer Acc Acc s/o Geo Sr & Tamar to Rachel Gainer Col 26 S Baltimore City MD Acc d/o Prudence on 2 Mar 1882 at Bay Side Par by RJ Waters

HALL George W 25 S Waterman Acc Acc s/o George E & Sallie D to Milcah A Hall 24 S Acc Acc d/o Robert T & Susan E on 4 Jul 1889 at Sykes Isld by JS Wallace

HALL Handy Col 23 S Sailor Acc Acc s/o Malinda to Georgianna Foreman Col 19 S Acc Acc d/o Sally on 12 Jun 1881 at Temp'ville by M Oldham

HALL Henry 58 W Farmer Acc Acc s/o Henry & Sally to Mary C [Brodwater] Broadwater 52 S Acc Acc d/o Savage & Nancy on 27 Feb 1873 at Temp'ville by M Oldham

HALL Henry X 27 S Merchant Acc Acc s/o Henry & Arnnet to Mamie E Smith 22 S Queens Co NY Acc d/o Zaphar & Mary T on 16 May 1878 at Guilford by JB Merritt

HALL Isaac Col 25 S Sailor Acc Acc s/o Harriet to Elizabeth Onley Col 18 S Acc Acc d/o Elizabeth on 17 Feb 1877 at Temp'ville by JB Merritt

HALL James Col 25 S Laborer Acc Acc to Rosey [Parks] Parkes Col 28 S Acc Acc d/o Violet on 28 Jun 1874 at Acc by HT Rich

HALL James A 50 W Merchant Acc Acc s/o Henry & Amert to Nellie Payne 25 S Wor Co MD Acc d/o George W & Maggie M on 5 Jun 1894 at Marsh Market by C Clement

HALL James A (Alfred) 28 S Merchant Acc Acc s/o Henry & Ambert to Lovey C Copes 25 S Acc Acc d/o Thomas S & Elizabeth on 26 Jul 1870 at Messongo by JET Ewell

HALL Jno F 23 S Farmer Acc Acc s/o Thos J & Elizth H to Virginia S Onions 19 S Acc Acc d/o Wesley & Eliza on 21 Dec 1884 at Guilford by JW Carroll

HALL John Col 21 S Wage-earner Acc Acc s/o Lucy to Mary E S White Col 18 S Acc Acc d/o Henry & Lucy on 22 Jun 1890 at Acc by LE Toulson

HALL John D 38 S Farmer Acc Acc s/o John (of R) & Sally to Arinthia J Lewis 28 W Acc Acc d/o Elizabeth Northam on 14 Oct 1894 at Acc by JR Tillery

HALL John H 23 S Oysterman Acc Acc s/o Robert T & Susan to Nina M Payne 18 S Wor Co MD Acc d/o George W & Maggie on 1 Nov 1893 at Acc by RB Scott

HALL Littleton Col 23 S Wage-earner Acc Acc s/o James & Caroline to Georgianna Warrington Col 17 S Acc Acc d/o Edward & Harriet on 11 Feb 1891 near Jenkins Bridge by JC Cluff

HALL Napoleon R 20 S Oysterman Acc Acc s/o Geo E & Sally to Mary W Lewis 15 S Acc Acc d/o Parker & Elizth on 13 Apr 1881 at Bethel Ch by M Oldham

HALL Robert J 26 S Farmer Acc Acc s/o Thos J & Elizth to Polly D Hickman 20 S Acc Acc d/o John E & Matilda D on 21 Jun 1885 at Lee Mont by HG Cowan

HALL Samuel 21 S Farmer Acc Acc s/o Harriet to Sarah Laws Col 18 S Acc Acc d/o Anina on 13 Feb 1881 at Acc by A Joynes

HALL Santa Ana (Santanna) 24 S Sailor Acc Acc to Elizabeth J Wessells 20 S Acc Acc d/o Richd & Polly (who gave consent) on 31 Dec 1863 at Acc by GH Ewell

HALL Santa Ann 23 S Farmer Acc Acc s/o Santa Anna & Betsy to Ella F Bunting 22 S Acc Acc d/o Geo W & Mary on 29 Dec 1895 at Mappsville by JL King

HALL Santanna 38 W Farmer Acc Acc s/o Robert & Jane to Emma J Taylor 23 S Acc Acc d/o Shaderack & nancy on 3 Mar 1880 at Modest Town by JW Hundley

HALL Seaford 23 S Oystering Acc Acc s/o Henry & Sally to Mary E Northam 23 S Acc Acc d/o John & Elizth on 29 Aug 1860 at r/o Elizth Northam by EW Stickney (Henry B Northam says both over 21)

HALL Siles 23 S Oysterman Acc Acc s/o Anthony E & Annie to Susan Marshall 19 S Acc Acc d/o Jno R & Annie E on 15 Jul 1883 at Sykes Isld by RB Beadles

HALL Silvarius C 21 S Merchant Acc Acc s/o Walter J & Mary E to Mary B Walden 18 S Middlesex Co VA Acc d/o Franklin & Mary S on 12 Jun 1889 at bride's home by WF Hayes & WJ Twilley

HALL Spencer D 19 S Sailor Acc Acc s/o Thomas S & Jane to Mary L Broadwater 17 S Acc Acc d/o Walter F & Hester A on 9 Jul 1890 at Sanford by WF Hayes

HALL Thomas single Laborer Chinco: Isld Chinco: Isld to Mahala Carpenter single Chinco: Isld Chinco: Isld d/o Richd & Nancy on 15 Mar 1853 at my house by P Bowdin

HALL Thomas J 33 S Oysterman Acc Acc s/o Robert T & Susan E to Ella L Tatman 24 S Acc Acc d/o Jesse & Mary on 12 Jun 1895 at Acc by DGC Butts

HALL Thomas S 21 S Farmer Acc Acc s/o Robert & Jane to Jane Duncan 19 S Acc Acc d/o Meshack & Critta on 10 Oct 1860 at Acc by W Merrill

HALL William C 36 S Merchant Acc Acc s/o William to Virginia D Milliner 20 S Acc Acc d/o Maria Milliner on 19 Aug 1880 near Woodstock by JG Anderson

HALL William T 32 S Farmer Acc Acc s/o Thomas J & Elizabeth H to Tabitha S Byrd 17 S Acc Acc d/o William T & Hetty W on 12 Jan 1887 at J W Byrd's by TM Poulson

HALL Wm E Col 20 S Farmer Acc Acc s/o Sarah to Sarah A Davis Col 19 S Acc Acc d/o Samuel & Leah A on 12 Jul 1885 at Whitesville Ch by CA Horsey

HALL Wm H 28 W Farmer Acc Acc s/o Thos H & Sally to Missouri E Tull 22 S Acc Acc d/o Jno S & Elizth on 1 Feb 1882 near Sea Side by JW Hundley

HALLAMON James to (-----) (-----) lic: May 1864

HALLMAN Phillip B 21 S Butcher Montgomery Co PA Philadelphia PA s/o Wm D & Maggie to Sally M Stiles 21 S Tuckerton NJ Acc d/o S D O Stiles on 2 Aug 1886 at Powelton by CD Crawley

HALLY William Col 36 S Farmer King & Queen Co Acc s/o Ona to Eliza Snead Col 18 S Acc Acc d/o Hannah on 31 Mar 1872 at Locust Mount by JWA Elliott

HAMMERSLEY Jas W 30 S Minister b: Tobages Stick s/o Jas & Sophia J to Rosa A (Ann) [Wescoat] Wescott 21 S b: Franktown d/o Hezekiah P (Decd) & Susan on 14 Mar 1855 at Onancock by C Hill (Chas Hill says both over 21)

HANCOCK Henry 23 S Oysterman Acc Wor Co MD s/o Peter to Sarah E Ellis 18 S Wor Co MD Acc d/o Wm H & Eliza on 18 Jan 1882 at Greenbackville by HC Stern

HANDY D Claude 29 S Physician MD Annapolis MD s/o Gordon & Anna C to Annie D Bagwell 21 S Acc Acc d/o Thos P & Sallie N on 18 Nov 1869 at Acc by JB Craighill

HANDY Frank Col 23 S Laborer Acc Acc s/o Richard Drummond & Elizabeth Handy to Elizabeth Custis Col 18 S Acc Acc d/o Adam & Rachel on 25 Dec 1887 at Acc by AJ Satchell

HANDY Grant G Col 21 S Farmer Acc Acc s/o R P & Mary to Emma S Wise Col 20 S Acc Acc d/o Adam & Elizabeth on 25 Nov 1894 at Acc by AJ Satchell

HANDY James Thomas Col 21 S Laborer Acc Acc s/o Comfort Ann to Lulie Wharton Col 17 S Acc Acc d/o Willianna Taylor on 24 Feb 1895 at Temp'ville by GHT Byrd

HANDY Levin J Col 23 S Laborer MD Acc to Louisa Conquest Col 21 S Acc Acc d/o Sallie on 16 Nov 1873 at Modest Town by A Joynes

HANDY Parker Col 32 S Oysterman Acc Acc s/o Mary to Arinthia Tunnell Col 24 S Acc Acc d/o Sarah on 6 Feb 1884 near Atlantic P O by JC Cluff

HANDY Stewart Col 22 S Laborer Acc Acc s/o Caroline to Harriet Mills Col 27 S Wor Co MD Acc d/o Isaac & Mary on 24 Sep 1877 near New Church by JC Cluff

HANDY Thomas black 37 S Farmer s/o Beky to Mary Jane Dennis black 25 S d/o Ann lic: 24 Dec 1872 marr: near Modest Town

HANDY William Col 23 S Farmer Acc Acc s/o Rosena Young to Mary Jane Bowles Col 19 S Acc Acc d/o George & Jane on 4 Oct 1888 at Drum'tn by P Sheppard

HARDING Rufus W 25 S Conductor Wellflach MA Boston MA s/o Joseph & Eliza to Maude M Rich 21 S Acc Acc d/o Benj S & Rachel S on 24 May 1881 at Onancock by JC Watson

HARGIS Albert S 21 S Farmer Acc Acc s/o Jas F & Missouri to Ruth Fitzgerald at Acc C H by JM Dunaway

HARGIS Bagwell C 21 S Farmer Acc Acc s/o George P & Hester to Essie Thomas Richardson 18 S Acc Acc d/o John T & Sophronia on 6 Nov 1889 at Acc by JER Riddick

HARGIS Beauregard 29 S Farmer Acc Acc s/o John to Susan Watkinson 25 D Acc Acc d/o George & Susan on 9 Dec 1891 near Onley by VW Bargamin

HARGIS Benjamin F 24 S Carpenter Acc Acc s/o Geo P & Hester P to Julia Doughty 18 S N'hamp: Acc d/o Thomas M on 7 Aug 1889 at Powelton by JWA Elliott

HARGIS Ezekiel 21 S Farmer Acc Acc s/o Belle Purnell to Arinthia A Lewis 15 S Acc Acc d/o Thomas L & Peggie on 19 Oct 1892 at Acc C H by VW Bargamin

HARGIS George widr to Charlotte Mears d/o Levin who gave consent lic: 25 Feb 1856

HARGIS George P 21 S Farmer Acc Acc s/o Geo & Ann to Hester A Mears 18 S Acc Acc d/o Jas & Mary on 24 Feb 1862 at Acc by BT Ames

HARGIS James F 23 S Farmer Acc Acc s/o Geo & Annie to Missouri Mears 18 S Acc Acc d/o Jsa & Mollie on 23 Dec 1867 at Acc by LK LeCato

HARGIS John H 22 S Capenter Acc Acc s/o James & Sarah to Maggie A [Shields] Shield 24 S Acc Acc d/o Asa & Elizth on 31 Dec 1877 at Assawoman Mill by JW Hundley

HARGIS John Wm 20 S Farmer Acc Acc s/o Belle Purnell to Mary V Bradford 19 S Acc Acc d/o Emory on 25 Jun 1878 at Onancock by JH

Amiss

HARGIS Joseph 22 S Sailor Acc Acc s/o Jno & Elizth to Triphenia Powell 17 S Acc Acc d/o Nathl & Juliet on 8 Jan 1879 near Locustville by LK LeCato

HARGIS Nathaniel 19 S Farmer Acc Acc s/o Elizabeth to Lovey Purnell 16 S Acc Acc d/o Belle on 29 Nov 1880 at Acc by JC Watson

HARGIS Nathaniel 24 W Farmer Acc Acc s/o Elizabeth to Mollie Gardner 18 S Acc Acc d/o WIlliam & Shady on 1 Jul 1891 at Acc by JT Moore

HARGIS Nora Col 24 S Wage-earner Acc Acc s/o Peter to Caroline Ward Col 21 S Acc Acc d/o Mary Brittingham on 30 Jul 1888 at New Church by TM Poulson

HARGIS Solomon 25 S Farmer Acc Acc s/o John & Elizabeth to Mary Watkinson 24 S Acc Acc d/o George & Margaret on 28 Jan 1874 at Locustville by LK LeCato

HARGIS Wm H 24 S Wheelwright Acc Acc s/o Thomas to Mary Ellen Mears 21 S Acc Acc d/o Gilbert & Elizth on 19 Jan 1876 at Drum'tn by JH Amiss

HARMANSON Chas L 28 S Physician Acc Acc s/o Jno L & Anna J to Ann Hay Battaile 21 S Acc Acc d/o Henry & Addie on 14 Apr 1886 at bride's home by J McNabb

HARMANSON James R to Tabitha Snead d/o Lewis L who gave consent lic: 10 Jun 1858 Geo F Wilkins says he over 21

HARMANSON John Col 23 S Farmer Acc Acc s/o Nellie to Emma Nock Col 20 S Acc Acc d/o Lorenzo & Louisa on 23 Dec 1891 at Grangeville by RH Coleman

HARMANSON William Col 37 S Wage-earner Acc Acc s/o Jacob & Adah to Ann Hack Col 35 S Acc Acc d/o Anthony on 7 Sep 1893 at Acc by L Duncan

HARMON Arthur FN to Elizabeth (Shepard) Shepherd FN lic: 29 May 1854 John W Elliott said both over 21

HARMON Benjamin Col 52 S Farmer Acc Acc s/o Lukey to Alice Doughty Col 46 S Acc Acc d/o Dina on 23 Oct 1894 at Wardtown by J Savage

HARMON Daniel Col 21 S Laborer Acc Acc s/o Betsy Seymores to Indianna Langedale Col 22 S Acc Acc d/o Elizth Waples on 25 May 1879 at Locustville by RH Govans

HARMON Daniel Col 38 W Farmer Acc Acc s/o Betsy to Ella Godfrey Col 18 S Acc Acc d/o Peter & Louisa on 22 Sep 1895 at Drum'tn by JH Offer

HARMON Emanael (Emanuel) Col 54 S Laborer Acc Acc s/o Elisha to Eliza Becket Col 45 S Acc Acc d/o Rachel on 23 Jun 1872 at Bruton Ch by N Morris

HARMON George Col 35 S Laborer Acc Acc s/o Manuel & Emeline to Harriet Crippen Col 30 W Acc Acc d/o Leah Fox on 15 Oct 1885 near Modest Town by AJ Satchell

HARMON Henry 21 S Laborer Acc Acc to Louisa Custis 21 S Acc Acc on 8 Apr 1869 at Acc by JE Humphreys

HARMON Horace Col 35 S Laborer Acc Acc s/o Phoebe Wise to Henrietta Fletcher Col 22 S Acc Acc d/o Sarah on 17 Apr 1895 at Acc by JC Cluff

HARMON James Col 59 W Wage-earner Acc Acc s/o James & Susie to Delilah [Milburn] Milbourn Col 42 W Acc Acc d/o Eliza on 20 Jan 1895 at Acc by JC Cluff

HARMON James H 26 S Farmer Acc Acc s/o Wm & Betsy to Margt R Willis 40 W Acc Acc d/o Joseph & Betsy Beach on 22 Dec 1856 at Wachapreague by JWA Elliott (John

W Harmon says he over 21)

HARMON Jesse H Col 20 S Farmer Acc. Acc s/o Tinnie to Jinnie Martin Col 22 S Acc Acc d/o Charlotte on 7 Apr 1886 at Locust Mount by JWA Elliott

HARMON Jno C (John E) 23 S Farmer Acc Acc s/o Leah to Anna S Crowson 15 S Acc Acc d/o Levin & Maria (who gave consent) on 17 Feb 1864 at Acc by D Titlow

HARMON John to Vinettae Joynes lic: 1 Feb 1864

HARMON John Col 22 S Laborer Acc Acc s/o Caroline to Susan Allen Col 22 S Acc Acc d/o Jennie on 14 Apr 1872 at Locust Mount by N Morris

HARMON John Col 22 S Laborer Acc Acc s/o Hester to Sally Watson Col 19 S Acc Acc d/o Clarissa on 30 May 1882 near Temp'ville by JC Cluff

HARMON John Col 25 S Acc Acc s/o Wm & Fanny to Eliza Taylor Col 25 S Acc Acc d/o Jacob & Margaret on 26 Apr 1882 near Oak Hall by JC Cluff

HARMON John Col 21 S Farmer Acc Acc s/o John to Sarah Drummond Col 16 S Acc Acc d/o John on 15 Oct 1885 near Temp'ville by JC Cluff

HARMON John Col 27 S Wage-earner Acc Acc s/o Isaac & Katie to Susan Turlington Col 28 S Acc Acc on 19 Dec 1888 at Locust Mount by JWA Elliott

HARMON John Col 52 S Wage-earner N'hamp: Acc s/o Margaret to Silvary [Shields] Shield Col 36 S Acc Acc d/o Littleon & Sarah Samples on 15 Nov 1893 at Acc by L Duncan

HARMON John B 31 S Farmer Acc Acc s/o James W & Melissa H to Maggie A Carmine 33 S Acc Acc d/o Tully & Sally on 24 Dec 1890 at Acc by JWA Elliott

HARMON John E 24 S Farmer Acc Acc s/o John H (W) & Peggy to Sarah A James 20 S Acc Acc d/o Thos & Molly & (ward/o Thomas H James who gave consent) on 24 Nov 1858 at Acc by P Warren

HARMON John H Col 19 S Farmer Acc Acc s/o John & Susan to Annie L Mears Col 15 S Acc Acc d/o Margaret on 4 Mar 1893 at Wachapreague by RH Coleman

HARMON John H Col 30 W Wage-earner Acc Acc s/o Isaac & Katie to Helen G Haley Col 16 S Acc Acc d/o Wm A & Alicia on 2 Dec 1894 at Acc by ET Outen

HARMON John W Col 19 S Oysterman Acc Acc s/o William & Jane to Rose Ann Fletcher Col 19 S Acc Acc d/o Dennis & Peggie on 24 Apr 1887 at Friendship M E Ch by RJ Waters

HARMON Leonard J 28 S Oysterman Acc Acc s/o John E & Sarah A to Sadie E Watson 18 S Acc Acc d/o David T & E F on 7 Mar 1892 at Belle Haven by T Burton

HARMON Lloyd Col 19 S Oysterman Acc Acc s/o Wm & Jane to Mary Foreman Col 16 S Acc Acc d/o Isaac on 25 Nov 1894 at Acc by JC Cluff

HARMON Moses Col 21 S Farmer Acc Acc s/o John & Matilda to Maggie James 20 S N'hamp: Acc d/o John & Margaret on 22 Dec 1895 at N'hamp: by J Savage

HARMON Otho F 20 S Farmer Acc Acc s/o Jno E & Sarah to Mattie Mears 17 S Acc Acc d/o Jno H & Tabitha on 1 Dec 1886 at Savageville by JW Hundley

HARMON Peter Col 21 S Wage-earner Acc Acc s/o Isaac & Katy to Emeline Haley Col 16 S Acc Acc d/o William & Alicia on 16 Aug 1892 near Keller by RH Coleman

HARMON Robt T 26 S Farmer Acc Acc s/o Jno C & Peggy to Sarah A

White 22 S Acc Acc d/o Geo F & Henny on 19 Nov 1862 at Acc by JWA Elliott

HARMON Thomas Col 21 S Farmer Acc Acc s/o Sylva to Sally Wise Col 18 S Acc Acc d/o John J & Mary on 21 Dec 1874 at Chesconessex by HT Rich

HARMON William Col 30 S Farmer Acc Acc s/o Emanual & Emaline to Ann Poulson Col 35 S Acc Acc d/o Henry & Rosey on 22 Sep 1881 at Locust Mount by JWA Elliott

HARMON William Col 35 S Farmer Acc Acc s/o Emanuel & Emeline to Elizabeth Downing Col 27 S Acc Acc d/o George & Sarah E on 2 Mar 1893 at Locust Mount by RH Coleman

HARMON William H 23 S Merchant Acc Acc s/o Levin & Caroline to Charlotte H Johnson 18 S Acc Acc d/o William & Margaret B on 22 Nov 1871 near New Church by WT Wilkerson

HARMON William H Col 29 S Oysterman Acc Acc s/o Nancy to Susan June Holden Col 30 S Acc Acc d/o Elzry on 19 Jan 1873 at Pocomoke by M Oldham

HARMON Williams (Col) 25 S Farmer Acc Acc s/o Wm Gardiner & Lukey Harman to Ann Smith (Col) 21 S Acc Acc d/o Abram & Sarah on 25 Sep 1870 at Acc by TM Cole

HARMON Wm 24 S Plasterer Acc Acc s/o Little. to Mamie Bell 16 S Acc Acc d/o Edwd & margt on 22 Oct 1879 at Mrs Bell's by SC Boston

HARMON Wm H (W) widr to Margt (wid/o Charles Decd) Kellam (wid) on 5 Jan 1854 by J Allen

HARMON Wm J Col 50 S Farmer Acc Acc s/o Adah Walker to Mary Susan Major Col 49 S Acc Acc d/o Leah on 14 Feb 1894 at Acc by ET Outen

HARRIS Douglas Col 26 W Cooper Richmond Acc s/o Henry & Henrietta to Virginia Drummond Col 18 S Acc Acc d/o Robert & Nellie on 7 Oct 1894 at Onancock by SA Brown

HARRIS Frank Col 24 S Wage-earner Acc Acc s/o Geo & Eliz'th to Ocia Matthews Col 30 W Acc Acc d/o George & Airy Hope on 6 Aug 1891 at Mappsville by AJ Satchell

HARRIS Isaac J 22 S Waterman Wor Co MD Acc to Susan R Colonna 19 S Acc Acc d/o John R & Eliza A on 12 Nov 1873 near Horntown by JE Potts

HARRIS Jno W 26 S Mechanic Acc Acc s/o Geo & Rachel to Mary J Savage 18 S Acc Acc d/o Littl on 3 Dec 1862 at Acc by JWA Elliott

HARRIS John F 22 S Farmer Acc Acc s/o John W & Mary to Eva Kimmerle 22 S Acc Acc d/o John & Emily on 4 Dec 1887 at Acc by WA Street

HARRIS John T 30 W Laborer NC Acc to Peggy Poulson 23 S Acc Acc d/o Jno & Elizabeth on 9 Jun 1867 at Acc by JL Taft

HARRIS John T 40 W Laborer NC Acc to Melissa D Cropper 22 S Acc Acc d/o Seymour & Sarah on 4 Nov 1875 at r/o Litt LeCato's by LK LeCato

HARRIS Lewis J 22 S Sewing Machine Agent MD Acc to Eliza Corbett 16 S Acc Acc d/o Richard & Miranda on 10 Oct 1893 at Tangier by ZH Webster

HARRIS Thomas 52 W Shoemaker N'hamp: Acc s/o William & Elizabeth to Nancy Chesser 42 S Acc Acc d/o Eli & Luanda on 6 Jul 1871 near New Church by TM Poulson

HARRIS Thomas G widr to Betsy Bayly wid lic: 13 Sep 1854

HARRIS William 20 S Laborer Prince Wm Co VA Acc s/o Jno & Elizth to Fanny Holt 30 W TX Acc on 11 May 1886 at Acc by L Rosser

HARRIS William T 20 S Farmer Acc Acc s/o John T & Peggie to Sudie Gardner 18 S Acc Acc d/o James T & Eliza on 26 Nov 1890 at Onancock by JB Pruitt

HARRISON Fred M 24 S Farmer Acc Acc s/o John & Margaret to Eveline [Kilmon] Killman 16 S Acc Acc d/o Frank & Indiana on 23 Nov 1892 at Locust Mount by JWA Elliott

HARRISON James E 24 S Waterman Acc Acc s/o Smith & Rachel to Margaret A Chandler 17 S Acc Acc d/o Bagwell & Ann on 12 May 1859 at Acc by JH Addison (Henry C Drummond says he over 21)

HARRISON James T 22 S Farmer Acc Acc s/o Thos & Sarah to Sudie V Gardner 20 S Acc Acc d/o Lizzie Gladding on 25 Dec 1895 at Acc by GE Booker

HARRISON John 23 S Farmer Acc Acc s/o Wm & Rachel to Laura Coard 17 S Acc Acc d/o Geo & Harriet on 11 Feb 1880 at Onancock by JC Watson

HARRISON Littleton C 30 S Farmer Acc Acc s/o Wm Smith & Mary Harrison to Clara L Nelson 18 S Acc Acc d/o Wm & Mary on 31 Oct 1883 at Acc by WC Vaden

HARRISON Thos 30 S Sailor Acc Acc s/o Jas & Cath to Sarah Hundley 23 S Acc Acc d/o Euphania on 23 Dec 1867 at Acc by JH Addison

HARRISON William 30 S Seaman Wor Co MD Acc s/o Edward & Mary A to Elizabeth [Clayville] Claville 21 S Acc Acc d/o Wm J & Vesta E B R on 9 Aug 1893 at Chinco: Isld by RB Sanford

HARRISON Wm H Col 24 S Laborer Acc Acc to Emma Fields Col 25 S Acc Acc d/o Sarah on 25 May 1882 near Jenkins Bridge by JC Cluff

HARRISON Wm S 60 W Sailor Acc Acc s/o Littleton Harrison to Susan Moore 44 S Acc Acc d/o Levi & Mary on 6 Jan 1867 at Acc by JH Addison

HART Aaron C 23 S Farmer NJ Acc s/o Mary Pettit to Ella F Green 22 S MD Acc d/o Wm on 31 Dec 1884 at Temp'ville by JW Carroll

HART Charles U 23 S Farmer Acc Acc s/o Robert P & Cath S to Lelia L Coxton 29 W Acc Acc d/o Wm T & Eliz'th S Lewis on 10 Jan 1894 at Acc by GE Booker

HART Dallis W 28 S Seaman Acc Acc s/o James & Mary E to Maggie H Crockett 16 S Acc Acc d/o Southey & Rachel P on 11 Feb 1884 near Onancock by WC Vaden

HART George W [Heart] 20 S Oysterman Acc Acc s/o John & Eleshea to Sally A Johnson 21 S Acc Acc d/o Joshua & Rachel on 15 Dec 1875 at Deep Ck by PA Leatherbury

HART Hezekiah 25 S Sailor Knox Co ME Acc s/o Ephraine H & Hannah to Susan Damlin 20 S Acc Acc d/o Wm & Rachel on 3 Dec 1865 at Acc by G Bradford

HART Hezekiah 27 W Sailor MA Acc to Margt E Damlin 18 S Acc Acc d/o Wm & Rachel A on 16 Aug 1868 at Acc by LK LeCato

HART Jas H 21 S Waterman & Farmer b: Acc s/o Jas & Mary to Susan Rayfield 19 S b: Acc d/o Levi & Anne & (ward/o John Arlington who gave consent) on 11 Jul 1855 at Acc by JH Addison

HART John A 20 S Wage-earner Acc Acc s/o John & Alicia to Alvertia Simpson 18 S Acc Acc d/o Revel J & Ellen on 19 Nov 1891 at Acc by JL King

HART John R 26 S Oysterman Acc Acc s/o Richd & Nancy to Elishea Hall 19 S Acc Acc d/o Robt & Elizth on 31 Jul 1868 at Acc by JE Bundick

HART John T 29 S Oysterman Acc Acc s/o John & Elishia to Nancy S Gray

Marriages

19 S Acc Acc d/o Thos & Nancy on 4 Feb 1869 at Acc by ES Grant

HART Major T 21 S Farmer Acc Acc s/o Dennis & Mary to Annie [Shreaves] Shrieves 18 S Acc Acc d/o Wm J & Polly on 13 Jun 1894 at Acc C H by JM Dunaway

HART Robert Dennis 23 S Sailor Acc Acc s/o James & Mary to Susan Killman 23 S Acc Acc d/o Ezekiel & Catharian on 5 Dec 1869 at Acc by JH Addison

HART Robert T 23 S Farmer Acc Acc s/o Robert D & Cath C to Clara M [Beloat] Beloate 17 S Acc Acc d/o John W & Joice M on 20 Dec 1893 at Keller by JM Dunaway

HART Selby 26 S Oysterman Acc Acc s/o Elizth to Jennie Bull 21 S Acc Acc d/o Ann on 26 Dec 1875 at Jas Martin's by TM Poulson

HART Thorogood D 24 S Oysterman s/o Richard & Nancy to Roney J Taylor 20 S d/o John & Susan lic: 7 Mar 1873 marr: 9 Mar 1873 near the Glebe

HART Thorogood D [Heart] 24 S Oysterman Acc Acc s/o Richard & Nancy to Nancy J Thorns 17 S Acc Acc d/o Elizabeth on 4 Feb 1874 near Mappsville by JE Bundick

HART William 25 W Oysterman Acc Acc s/o Betsy to Fanny Barnes 24 S Acc Acc d/o Archibald & Betsy on 21 Dec 1881 at Acc by JW Hundley

HART William C 22 S Farming Acc Acc to Sarah A (Wilkerson) Wilson 18 S Acc Acc d/o (Shadrack) on 29 Jan 1861 at Acc by T Waters (Samuel T Taylor says he over 21)

HART William T 22 S Farmer Acc Acc s/o Wm C & Sarah A to Vianna S Simpson 22 S Acc Acc d/o Alfred & Malvina on 20 Jan 1888 at Acc by JE Bundick

HART Wm S 21 S Oysterman Acc Acc s/o John T & Nancy to Mary E Gibbons 21 S Acc Acc d/o Benj B & Clara on 9 Dec 1891 at Chinco: Isld by GW Burke

HARTMAN Aaron R 27 S Farmer Acc Acc s/o Charles & Mary E to Emma A Hopkins 21 S Acc Acc d/o Jas & Betsy on 25 Feb 1883 at Locust Mount by JWA Elliott

HARTMAN Charles L 25 S Farmer Acc Acc s/o Charles H & Margaret to Mattie R Stevens 17 S Acc Acc d/o John H & Elizabeth A on 1 Oct 1885 at Locust Mount by JWA Elliott

HARTMAN Jacob M 27 S Conductor of RR Baltimore MD Baltimore MD to Sally C Northam 20 S Acc Acc d/o Wm of E & Drucilla on 15 Dec 1882 at Acc by MS Read

HARTMAN James J 21 S Farmer Acc Acc s/o Chas & Mary to Mary A Savage 20 S Acc Acc d/o Wm J & Margt on 26 Jan 1881 at Royal Oak by JWA Elliott

HARTMAN John H 24 S Farmer NJ Acc s/o Charles & Margt to Sarah A Haley 24 S Acc Acc d/o James & Rosetta on 23 Jun 1877 near Locustville by LK LeCato

HARTMAN Thomas L 23 S Farmer Acc Acc s/o Charles & Margaret to Mary E Bundick 19 S Acc Acc d/o Elijah T & Margaret on 22 Nov 1887 at Locust Mount by JWA Elliott

HARTY William E 33 W Oysterman Som Co MD Lancester Co VA s/o Levin W & Sarah to Margaret Ann Spence 21 S Acc Acc d/o Joshua & Rachel on 5 Aug 1872 at Acc by Myers & Talbott

HASTING Archelaus M 28 S Engineer Som Co MD Acc s/o Renalus T & Nancy to Martha A Rew 21 S Acc Acc d/o Wm & Julia on 17 Nov 1869 at Acc by E Hebard

HASTING Elijah 32 S Merchant Wor Co MD Acc s/o Winder & Lovia to Melissa Barger 32 W Acc Acc d/o

David & Margaret Collins on 19 Dec 1880 at Atlantic by JW Hundley

HATENEY George [Hatney] FN 28 S Farmer Acc Acc s/o Sarah A to Margt Ashby FN 25 S Acc Acc d/o Malinda on 31 Dec 1862 at Acc by JWA Elliott

HATENEY Henry (FN) 24 S Farming b: Wachapreague s/o Sarah to Caty Taylor (FN) 21 S b: Wachapreague d/o Ader on 21 Jun 1854 at Piggin Swamp by JWA Elliott (Arthur Medab said both over 21)

HATENEY Henry [Hatney] Col 60 S Wage-earner Acc Acc to Georgiann Heath Col 45 S Acc Acc on 12 Sep 1890 at Grangeville by N Morris

HATHWAY Jno W 23 S Farmer Acc Acc s/o Wm H & Louisa to Willie Russell 24 S Acc Acc on 19 Feb 1879 at J H Merril's by IT Adkins

HATHWAY John [Hathaway] 26 S Laborer Acc Acc to Elizabeth Taylor 35 W Wor Co MD Acc d/o Levin & Hester Henderson on 14 Dec 1858 at Acc by W Quinn (Levin Ayres says he over 21)

HATHWAY John W [Harthway] 30 W Farmer Acc Acc s/o Wm H & Louisa to Susan J Hudson 32 S Wor Co MD Acc d/o Jas & Nancy on 23 Dec 1885 at Oak Hall by DM Wallace

HATTEN James Jr Col 30 W Farmer Acc Acc s/o James & Lucinda to Missour Rogers Col 19 S Acc Acc d/o Grace Taylor on 27 Apr 1876 at Savageville by JK Plato

HATTON Benjamin (C) 26 S Brick Layer NY Acc s/o Wm P & Sarah to Euphemia Martin 26 S Acc Acc d/o Wm S & Rose on 15 Dec 1859 near Onancock by AM Wiggins (George W Mason says both over 21)

HATTON Geo E Col 22 S Farm Laborer Acc Acc s/o James & Peggy to Mary Elizth Dennis Col 21 S Acc Acc d/o John & Mary on 29 Dec 1880 at Belle Haven by SMG Copeland

HATTON George Col 42 S Farmer Acc Acc s/o Jas Sr & Lucinda to Mary Becket Col 26 S Acc Acc d/o Western & Emma on 31 Dec 1882 near Pungo: by F Wood

HATTON James Col 22 S Sailor Acc Acc s/o Eliza Sample to Sarah [Browne] Brown Col 25 S Acc Acc d/o Labra on 26 Dec 1878 at Acc by JG Anderson

HATTON James T Col 30 S Wage-earner Acc Acc s/o James & Rachel to Willianna Finney Col 24 W Acc Acc d/o William & Malinda Phillips on 25 Apr 1889 at Drum'tn by P Sheppard

HATTON William 19 S Farmer Acc Acc s/o Benj C & Euphemia to Ella B Winder 22 S Acc Acc d/o Caroline on 2 Feb 1881 at Onancock by CC Wertenbaker

HAYMAN Joseph K 23 S Carpenter Wic Co MD Philadelphia PA s/o Joseph J & Rebecca C to Abbie R Johnson 21 S Acc Acc d/o Geo W & Marg't J on 27 Dec 1893 at Onancock by GE Booker

HAYMAN Vaugham S 22 S Merchant MD Acc s/o Thos J & Margt to Sallie Dickerson 20 S Acc Acc d/o Thos & Eleanor on 11 Jan 1883 at Lee Mont by WA Crouse

HAYNES Augustus B 28 S School Teacher Richmond VA Marion Station MD s/o A B & C to Sadie M Wyatt 27 S Acc Acc on 24 Jan 1876 at Belle Haven by JE Humphreys

HAYNES Benjamin F 28 S Teacher Richmond Co VA Marion Som Co s/o Austin B & Cath to Nannie L Ward 18 S Acc Acc d/o A Jackson & Peggy E on 12 Sep 1872 at Belle Haven by EM Bryan

HAYNES James A Col 52 W Minister Westmoreland Co VA Acc s/o

Joseph & Mary to Annie Eliz'th Tankard Col 34 S N'hamp: Acc d/o Jacob & Harriet on 20 Sep 1888 at Pungo: by JEW Moore

HEATH Albert R 30 S Carpenter Acc Acc s/o George & Margaret to Cordelia J Beloate 22 S Acc Acc d/o Jas H of Levin & Elizabeth on 25 Dec 1887 at Hadlock by CD Crawley

HEATH Ashby Col 23 S Farmer Acc Acc s/o Wm & Emma to Dinah Bell Col 22 S Acc Acc d/o Ellen & John on 26 Nov 1885 near Belle Haven by J Savage

HEATH Bushard Col 31 S Laborer Acc Acc s/o Danl Jacob & Mary Heath (Col) to Rose (Nock) Heath Col 22 S Acc Acc d/o Jesse & Virg Nock (Col) on 26 Dec 1870 at Pungo: by TM Cole

HEATH James Col 20 S Farmer Acc Acc s/o Margt to Emaline Bell Col 20 S Acc Acc on 1 Jan 1873 at Savageville by R Davis

HEATH James Col 24 S Laborer N'hamp: Acc s/o James to Bettie Allen Col 18 S Acc Acc d/o Jiys Finney on 24 Nov 1881 at Onancock by SC Boston

HEATH James C 27 S Merchant Acc Acc s/o Cornelis to Lena T Chandler 19 S Acc Acc d/o Thos & Juliet W on 6 Dec 1877 at Reese Chp by JH Amiss

HEATH John Col 53 W Laborer N'hamp: Acc to Eliza Sample Col 42 S Acc Acc d/o George Major on 28 Aug 1887 at Acc by L Duncan

HEATH John W 24 S Sailor Acc Acc s/o Jno D & Peggy to Elizabeth S Chance 30 S Acc Acc d/o Wm on 1 Mar 1876 near Locustville by LK LeCato

HEATH Robert Thos 22 S Farmer Acc Acc s/o John D & Peggie to Susan East 20 S Acc Acc d/o William A & Eliz'th on 31 Dec 1890 at Acc by JWA Elliott

HEATH Samuel Col 22 S Laborer Acc Acc s/o Ann to Ada Burton Col 21 S Acc Acc d/o Sarah on 1 Dec 1878 at Locust Mount by A Handy

HENDERSON Robt S 52 W Farmer Som Co MD Acc s/o Jacob & Hetty to Mary E Bayly 27 S NY Acc d/o Jesse & Jane on 13 Feb 1884 at Onancock by JW Hundley

HENDERSON Sabastian C 43 W Farmer Acc Assawoman s/o Joseph & Maria to Esther A Parkes 34 S Acc Assawoman d/o John G & Catharine H on 2 Sep 1874 at Assawoman by JM Anderson

HENDERSON Sebastian 39 S Oysterman Acc Acc s/o Joseph & Mary to Sally Mears 21 S Acc Acc d/o Thos & Elizth on 2 Jul 1873 at Acc by M Oldham

HENRY Lloyd Col 22 S Farmer N'hamp: Acc s/o Charles & Sally Henry to Arinthia Coleburn Col 20 S Acc Acc d/o Henry & Sarah on 5 Sep 1894 at Drum'tn by R Davis

HENRY Zadock Col 24 S Wage-earner MD Acc to Hester Johnson Col 24 S Acc Acc d/o James H on 17 Dec 1890 at Acc by AS Amos

HERBERT Chester 22 S Sailor Baltimore City MD Acc s/o John & Mary to Lillie R Payne 15 S Acc Acc d/o Peter T & Mary on 12 Jan 1894 at Onancock by AJ Reamy

HEWES John 21 S Sailor r: Muddy Ck to Vianna McCready 19 S Muddy Ck Muddy Ck d/o James McCready on 14 Feb 1861 at r/o James McCready by GH Ewell (Samuel L Justice says he over 21)

HICKMAN Charles D 22 S Farmer Acc Acc s/o Edward & Ann to Malinda Charnock 23 S Acc Acc d/o Sol & Sarah on 2 Feb 1887 at Evergreen Ch by JR Strugis

HICKMAN Edward 43 W Farmer b:

Acc s/o Edward & Susan to Ann [Stephens] Stevens 20 S b: Acc d/o Thos & Betsy on 30 Jul 1856 at r/o B T Ames by BT Ames (Wm J Beloat says both over 21)

HICKMAN Edward T 24 S Farmer Acc Acc s/o Asa T & Jane C to Emma C Nelson 24 S Acc Acc d/o John on 13 Jan 1870 at Guilford by JET Ewell

HICKMAN Edward T 22 S Farmer Acc Acc s/o William & Nancy to Sarah E Holland 25 S Acc Acc d/o Samuel & Clarissa on 13 Jan 1875 near Locustville by LK LeCato

HICKMAN Edward T 36 S Farmer Acc Acc s/o Asa & Jane to Annie Bunting 28 S Acc Acc d/o Henry & Mary on 18 Jan 1882 at Atlantic Bapt Ch by JW Hundley

HICKMAN Elijah W 23 S Blacksmith Acc Acc s/o Edward & Sally to Viola J Wessells 20 S Acc Acc d/o John (C dec'd) & Nancy & ward/o Thorogood Mason who gave consent on 6 Feb 1861 at r/o Thorogood Mason by ES Grant (Thorogood Mason said he over 21)

HICKMAN Elijah W 20 S Farmer Acc Acc s/o Elijah & Rachel to Mary J [Wessells] Wessells 18 S Acc Acc d/o Arthur & Mary J on 23 Dec 1888 at Crowsontown by HS Dulany

HICKMAN Geo R 28 S Acc Acc s/o Asa & Jane to Mary [Aydelott] Aydelotte 25 S Wor Co MD Acc d/o Benj F on 21 Dec 1881 at Atlantic Bapt Ch by JW Hundley

HICKMAN George 23 S Waterman b: Acc s/o Robt & Rachel to Lucretia Olive 23 S b: King George Co d/o John & Margaret on 16 Jul 1856 at Acc by JH Addison (Henry C Summers says both over 21)

HICKMAN George 22 S Sailor Acc Acc s/o Edwd & Nancy to Elizabeth Hundley 19 S Acc Acc d/o Fanny on 31 Jan 1866 at Acc by JH Addison

HICKMAN George 22 S Wage-earner Acc Acc s/o Ephraim to Susan Northam 21 S Acc Acc d/o George & Annie on 10 Jan 1889 at Acc by AJ Satchell

HICKMAN George H 28 S Merchant Acc Acc s/o Richard & Sarah Ann to Eudie S Bundick 20 S Acc Acc d/o Alfred J & Eizabeth on 29 May 1889 near Locustville by WJ Twilley

HICKMAN Henry Col 25 S Farm Laborer Acc Acc s/o Lotty to Betty Annis Col 23 S Acc Acc d/o Betty on 24 May 1885 at Acc by AJ Satchell

HICKMAN Jacob 60 W Laborer Acc Acc to Rhoda Watson 52 S Acc Acc on 6 Oct 1870 at Acc by A Joynes

HICKMAN Jeff L 24 S Farmer Acc Acc s/o George L & Lucretia E to Indie A Poulson 23 S Acc Acc d/o John W & Eliz'th on 30 Mar 1892 near Onancock by JB Pruitt

HICKMAN Jno Cornelius 20 S Farmer Acc Acc s/o John E & Matilda to Sarah A Russell 16 S Acc Acc d/o Geo T & Mary on 14 Nov 1880 at Reese Chp by FH Mullineaux

HICKMAN John 22 S Waterman Acc Acc s/o Richd (A)& Polly to Matilda Ewell 20 S Acc Acc d/o Gilbert & Eliz on 30 Jun 1859 at Reese Chp by ES Grant

HICKMAN John T 24 S Farmer Acc Acc s/o George & Lucretia to Carrie J Hickman 21 S Acc Acc d/o Joseph & Jane on 30 Oct 1881 at Acc by JC Watson

HICKMAN Joseph 21 S Sailor Acc Acc s/o Robt & Rachel to Jane Parker 21 S Acc Acc d/o George & Mary on 5 Feb 1860 at Acc by P Warren

HICKMAN Judson C 19 S Farmer Acc Acc s/o Robt W & Betsy to Annie L Baker 17 S Acc Acc d/o Geo W & Alica on 28 Dec 1884 at Acc by WA Street

HICKMAN Levin Col 21 S

Wage-earner Acc Acc s/o Martha to Harriet Wise Col 19 S Acc Acc d/o Louisa on 26 Apr 1891 near Mappsville by AJ Satchell

HICKMAN Richard 30 W Farmer Acc Acc s/o Thos & Zeporah to Ella West 16 S Acc Acc d/o George R & Jane on 11 Feb 1869 at Acc by JET Ewell

HICKMAN Richard 21 S Farmer Acc Acc s/o Wm & Nancy to Elethea Bull 20 S Acc Acc on 8 Mar 1877 near Locustville by LK LeCato

HICKMAN Richd 30 W Farmer Acc Acc s/o Thomas to Evelin T Wessells 19 S Acc Acc d/o Ephraim & Nancy on 4 Apr 1867 at Acc by ES Grant

HICKMAN Robert 22 S Farmer Acc Acc s/o Robt & Ann to Elizabeth Coxton 22 S Acc Acc d/o Wm & Nancy on 25 Feb 1864 at Acc by ES Grant

HICKMAN Robert Jr 24 S Farmer Acc Acc s/o Robt & Betsey to Mollie [Somers] Summers 24 S Acc Acc d/o George & Eveline on 27 Dec 1893 at Modest Town by WW Wood

HICKMAN Samuel E 19 S Farmer Acc Acc s/o John E & Matilda to Laura E [Justis] Justice 17 S Acc Acc d/o William S & Mary on 8 Jul 1891 at Parksley by JF Anderson

HICKMAN Shephard G 22 S Farmer Acc Acc s/o Lovey to Annie M Barnes 18 S Acc Acc d/o Alfred & Mary on 28 Aug 1882 at Acc by JW Hundley

HICKMAN Thos S 23 S Farmer Acc Acc s/o Wm & Mary to Anne J Killman 30 S Acc Acc d/o Edwd & Margt on 3 Jan 1884 at Onancock Bapt Par by JW Hundley

HICKMAN William 28 S Farmer Acc Acc s/o Asa & Elizabeth to Mary Nelson 17 S Acc Acc d/o James & Nancy on 24 Jun 1860 at r/o E S Grant by ES Grant (Wm H Hickman Sen said he over 21)

HICKMAN William H 29 S Farmer Acc Acc s/o Asa & Jane to Lea Justice 21 S Acc Acc d/o James E & Elizabeth on 22 Apr 1891 at Acc by RS Williamson

HICKMAN William H 21 S Farmer Acc Acc s/o Wm C Jr & Mary to Hennie A Lawrence 22 S Acc Acc d/o John & Margaret on 9 Jan 1895 at Acc by JR Sturgis

HICKMAN Wm Thos 21 S Farmer Acc Acc s/o Richd & Sarah to M Virginia Lilliston 25 S Acc Acc d/o Natalie on 8 Jun 1879 at Modest Town by DA Woodson

HICKS Chas Col 25 S Wage-earner Henrico Co Acc to Louisa Ward Col 18 S Acc Acc d/o Asa & Mary on 11 Nov 1891 at Acc by JH Offer

HICKS Essex Col 25 S Wage-earner Henrico Co Acc s/o Essex & Cordelia to Arinthia Major Col 30 S Acc Acc d/o Emaline on 7 Sep 1893 at Acc by L Duncan

HIDEN Joseph H 25 S Minister Fluvanna Co VA Seale AL s/o James C & Bessie C to Ellen Z Battails 22 S Acc Acc d/o Henry & Aleliaida M on 30 Mar 1891 at Acc by JA Barker

HIGGINS Nathaniel B 26 S Laborer Acc Acc s/o Michael H & Marianna to Seneth Bateman 24 S NC Acc on 18 Sep 1878 at Onancock by JH Amiss

HILL Andrew 22 S Waterman Acc Acc s/o Thimothy & Zipporah to Mary A Daisey 18 S Acc Acc d/o Jno & Caroline Daisey on 29 Nov 1879 at Chinco: Isld by TAH O'Brien

HILL Basil Col 30 S Farmer Harford Co MD Acc s/o Peter & Juliet to Tinny A Stewart Col 23 S Acc Acc d/o Smith & Jane on 27 Oct 1886 at Pungo: by L Rosser

HILL Daniel 22 S Acc Acc s/o Thimothy & Zipporah to Mary A Hill 22 W Acc Acc d/o John & Caroline

Daisey on 10 Aug 1882 at Chinco: Isld by OS Walton

HILL Jno A 21 S Seaman MD Chinco: Isld s/o Jno & Molly to Mary Jane Thornton 18 S Chinco: Isld Chinco: Isld d/o Wm (P)& Nancy on 11 May 1854 at r/o Robt Watson by P Bowdin

HILL John 21 S Oysterman Acc Acc s/o Thimothy & Zipporah to Sarah Ann Whealton 17 S Acc Acc d/o Eba & Betsey Whealton on 18 Apr 1868 at Acc by P Bowdin Sr

HILL John F 24 S Farmer Acc Acc s/o John & Emily to Mary Jane Drummond 23 S Acc Acc d/o Wm & Mary Dencan on 6 Jan 1876 at Temp'ville by M Oldham

HILL John Fred 25 S RR Agent Wor Co MD Acc s/o George H & Eliz'th M to Sarah E Beloate 35 S Acc Acc d/o Joseph G & Betsy on 25 Nov 1893 at Onancock by AJ Reamy

HILL John M 25 W Sailor Acc Acc s/o J A & Jane to Mary Williams 16 S Acc Acc d/o Wm & Henrietta on 19 Dec 1882 at Chinco: Isld by WP Thornton

HILL John Miles 21 S Sailor Chinco: Isld Chinco: Isld s/o John A & Jane to Elizabeth Claville 16 S Chinco: Isld Chinco: Isld d/o Geo & Lydia A on 22 Oct 1878 at Chinco: Isld by WP Thornton

HILL John P 36 W b: Wor Co MD s/o Purnerl & Tabither to Mary Davis 35 W b: Acc d/o Henry & Fanny Sterling on 9 Dec 1857 at Acc by T Waters

HILL John P 45 W Farmer MD Acc to Jane Taylor 24 S Acc Acc d/o Nath & Maria on 1 Nov 1865 at Acc by M Oldham

HILL Joseph single Laborer Chinco: Isld Chinco: Isld s/o Rebecca & Thimothy to Anna Payne single main land Chinco: Isld on 8 Jul 1852 at my house by P Bowdin

HILL Joseph L 22 S Oysterman Acc Acc s/o John T & Sarah A to Lillie Russell 18 S Acc Acc d/o Oliver & Drucilla on 6 Jun 1894 at Chinco: Isld by SU Grimsley

HILL Joseph T 19 S Sailor Acc Acc s/o Timothy & Zipporah to Louisa J Smith 26 S Acc Acc d/o John & Sarah on 12 Mar 1872 at Acc by P Bowdin Sr

HILL Julius T 27 S Farmer Acc Acc s/o Jno P & Emma J to Emma E Bunting 21 S Acc Acc d/o Henry & Mary M on 13 Mar 1878 at Wattsville Ch by JW Hundley

HILL Littleton (R B) 20 S Waterman Wor Co MD Chinco: Isld s/o John & Mary & (ward/o Wm P Thornton who gave consent) to Mary (Maria) Bloxom 19 S Chinco: Isld Chinco: Isld d/o Wm P (Decd)& Tabitha on 8 Feb 1860 at Chinco: Isld by WP Thornton

HILL Lloyd 21 S Farmer Acc Acc to Susan Rew 20 S Acc Acc d/o Jno & Tabitha on 22 Dec 1880 at Acc by RB Beadles

HILL Lloyd P 24 W Merchant Acc Acc to Eveline Lewis 20 S Acc Acc d/o John T Lewis & Sarah on 18 Feb 1885 at Temp'ville by JW Carroll

HILL Timothy 67 W Dealer in Oysters Acc Acc s/o Timothy & Rebecca to Mary Blades 65 W Acc Acc d/o Daniel & Nancy Sharpley on 11 May 1893 at Acc by GP Jones

HILL Walter 20 S Oysterman Chinco: Isld Chinco: Isld s/o Jno A & Jane to Josephine Cluff 15 S Chinco: Isld Chinco: Isld d/o James & Elizth on 15 Jan 1884 at Chinco: Isld by WP Thornton

HILL William J Col 31 S Wage-earner Cambridge Acc s/o John & Lavinia to Hester Dennis Col 35 W Acc Acc d/o Isaac & Ann Horsey on 2 Aug

Marriages

HILL William T 19 S Sailor Chinco: Isld Acc s/o John A & Jane to Mary A Jester 18 S Acc Acc d/o Charles S & Drlilah J on 14 Dec 1874 at Chinco: Isld by P Bowdin Sr

HILL William T 23 S Oysterman Acc Acc s/o Joseph T & Louisa to Molly Hill 18 S Acc Acc d/o John A & Jane on 3 Jul 1895 at Chinco: Isld by SU Grimsley

HILL Wm A 23 S Farmer Acc Acc s/o John P & Emaline to Hetty Conquest 18 S Acc Acc d/o Alfred & Delila on 1 Mar 1877 near New Church by TM Poulson

HILL Wm H 22 S Oysterman Acc Acc s/o Henry to Emma Powell 21 S Wor Co MD Chinco: Isld d/o Levin & Mary on 14 Dec 1881 at Chinco: Isld by WP Thornton

HINMAN Arsesnus Col 24 S Laborer Acc Acc s/o George & Ann to Leah Downing Col 22 S Acc Acc d/o Stewart & Hannah on 30 Oct 1880 at Temp'ville by JC Cluff

HINMAN Emory 19 S Farmer Acc Acc s/o Nancy to Martha Middleton 18 S Acc Acc d/o Jno & Julia on 24 Dec 1882 at Acc by WP Wright

HINMAN George W [Hinmon] 27 S Oysterman b: Messongo s/o Perry to Julia A Stant 17 S b: Pig Point d/o Gilbert & Mary who gave consent on 21 Jun 1855 at r/o Gilbrt Stant by GH Ewell (Edward Anderton says he over 21)

HINMAN George W [Hinmon] 24 S Farmer Acc Acc s/o Thomas & Mary to Elizabeth W Nock 19 S Acc Acc d/o Littleton W on 3 Feb 1875 at Temp'ville by JM Anderson

HINMAN James Col 22 S Day Laborer Acc Acc s/o Ann to Emma [Justis] Justice Col 17 S Acc Acc d/o Louisa on 4 Jan 1885 at Temp'ville by JC Cluff

HINMAN John S 22 S Boating Acc Acc s/o John R & Susan to Carrie J Thornton 23 S Acc Acc d/o James & Mary on 7 Aug 1887 at Parksley by JW Norris

HINMAN Lewis F 20 S Oysterman Acc Acc s/o John R & Elizabeth to Elizabeth Justice 22 S Acc Acc d/o Revel & Nancy on 24 Dec 1871 near Woodstock by J Carroll

HINMAN Lorenzo Col 26 S Laborer Acc Acc s/o Ann to Celia Ann (Celie) Lewis Col 21 S Acc Acc d/o Ann Lewis on 21 Nov 1872 at Acc by M Oldham

HINMAN Lorenzo D Col 39 W Fireman Acc Acc s/o Ann to Mary Lizzie Anderson Col 38 S Som Co MD Acc d/o Louisa Logan on 28 Dec 1887 at Messongo by N Morris

HINMAN Samuel [Hinmon] (dark) 20 S Farmer Acc Acc s/o Labin to Sarah Matthews Col 22 S Acc Acc d/o Rachel on 18 Jun 1871 at Acc by A Joynes

HINMAN Samuel S widr to Mary Watson d/o Mitchell lic: 15 Feb 1856 James H Pettit says both over 21

HINMAN Sewell Col 39 W Farmer Acc Acc s/o Ann to Othelia Matthews Col 32 W Acc Acc d/o Claricsa on 17 Feb 1892 at Acc by JC Cluff

HINMAN Sewell [Hinmon] Col 23 S Laborer Acc Acc s/o Ann to Alice Downing Col single Acc Acc d/o Hannah on 31 Dec 1875 at Mt Zion Chh by SP Whittington

HINMAN Walter F Col 21 S Wage-earner Acc Acc s/o Sarah C to Mary Wise Col 22 S Acc Acc d/o Mahala on 28 Dec 1890 at Acc by AJ Satchell

HINMAN William Col 21 S Wage-earner Acc Acc s/o Lorenzo & Henrietta to Mary Holden Col 16 S Acc Acc d/o Drucilla on 11 Feb 1891 near Jenkins Bridge by JC Cluff

HINMAN Wm [Hinmon] 49 S Farmer b: Messongo to Sally White 34 S b: Messongo d/o John on 22 Dec 1856 at r/o Wm Hinmon by GH Ewell (Savage Copes says both over 21)

HITCHENS George T 30 S Sawyer Wor Co MD Acc to Mary F Nock 21 S Acc Acc d/o Edward & Mary on 10 Jul 1892 at Temp'ville by JW Nicholson

HITCHENS William H 26 S Milling Sussex Co DE Acc s/o Joseph H & Mary A to Georgie A Marshall 20 S Acc Acc d/o Richard & Nancy on 5 Feb 1888 at Temp'ville by M Oldham

HOFFMAN George B 24 S Merchant Acc Acc s/o William G & Mary E to Mamie J Kellam 20 S Acc Acc d/o Thomas C & Julia A on 27 Nov 1889 at Locustville by RA Compton

HOFFMAN Jas W 19 S Sailor Acc Acc s/o James W & Annie to Maggie Killman 15 S Acc Acc d/o Ezekiel H & Mollie on 21 Nov 1883 at Onancock by SC Boston

HOFFMAN Noah S 41 W Merchant's Clerk Acc Acc s/o Jas H & Sarah to Margaret C Jones 36 S Acc Acc d/o William & Jane on 26 Jan 1887 at Pungo: by JR Strugis

HOGAN Wm Jos 40 S Merchant r: Natchez MS to M Birditta Rayfield 21 S Canada Acc d/o Mary on 16 Sep 1891 at Hallwood by E Mickle

HOLDEN Alfred J Col 22 S Wage-earner Acc Acc s/o John Thos to Mary A Fletcher Col 18 S Acc Acc d/o James & Louisa on 28 Dec 1890 at Oak Hall by JS Wallace

HOLDEN George H Col 25 S Wage-earner Acc Acc s/o George W to Mehaleh Taylor Col 22 S Acc Acc d/o Scott Matthews & Lizzie Taylor on 27 Nov 1890 at Wattsville by AS Amos

HOLDEN George W Col 23 S Acc Acc s/o George & Mary to Grace Lang Col 25 S Acc Acc d/o Margaret Downing on 15 Dec 1881 near Oak Hall by JC Cluff

HOLDEN Gillet [Houlding] Col 35 W Farmer Acc Acc s/o Sally Dennis to Darkey [Crippin] Crippen Col 37 W Acc Acc d/o Juliet Ann Young on 9 Oct 1884 at Acc by CA Horsey

HOLDEN Isaac Col 25 S Sailor Acc Acc s/o Henry to Ellen Nock Col 22 S Acc Acc d/o Jane on 17 Mar 1878 at Modest Town by A Joynes

HOLDEN James [Holding] (Holden) (FN) 26 S Farming Acc Acc s/o James Harmon & Susan Holden to Harriet Walters (Wharton) (FN) 29 S Acc Acc d/o Nathan & Leac Selby on 29 Dec 1859 at Acc by T Waters (John W Hickman says both are 21)

HOLDEN James H [Holding] Col 32 S Oysterman Acc Acc s/o Henry & Malinda to Emory J Watson Col 21 S Acc Acc d/o Azariah & Patience on 21 Feb 1882 near Jenkins Bridge by JC Cluff

HOLDEN John Col 35 S Acc Acc s/o Geo & Lydia to Missouri Blake Col 36 S Acc Acc d/o Joshua & Maria on 16 Sep 1879 at Horntown by PJ Adams

HOLDEN Major L Col 25 S Sailor Acc Acc s/o Leah to Mary Brittingham Col 18 S Acc Acc d/o Joseph & Mary on 28 Dec 1890 at Oak Hall by JS Wallace

HOLDEN William Henry Col 21 S Wage-earner Acc Acc s/o Lovey Ann to Eliza Drummond Col 19 S Acc Acc d/o John & Susan Ann on 5 Jun 1895 at Onancock by SW Watkins

HOLLAND Frank 24 S Farmer Acc Acc to Bertie Ann Duncan 17 S Acc Acc d/o John R on 23 Mar 1875 at Line of Va by TM Poulson

HOLLAND George 26 S Farmer Acc Acc s/o Samuel & Clarissa to

Hannah Young 21 S Acc Acc d/o John & Mary on 7 Apr 1880 at Onancock by SC Boston

HOLLAND John W 33 S Carpenter Acc Acc s/o Saml & Clarissa to Sarah E Budd 30 S Acc Acc d/o Thomas & Sally on 10 Jan 1877 near Locustville by LK LeCato

HOLLAND Sewell 24 S Oysterman Acc Acc s/o Edw'd T B & Mary Ann to Mary E Matthews 18 S Acc Acc d/o John K & Eliza Jane on 30 Oct 1895 at Acc by DGC Butts

HOLLAND Thos M 23 S Oysterman Wor Co MD Acc s/o William & Mary to Mary E Watson 16 S Acc Acc d/o Jesse R & Catharine on 15 Nov 1891 at Chinco: Isld by JW Turner

HOLLAND William J 23 S Oysterman Acc Acc s/o Edward & Mary to Clara V Hall 16 S Acc Acc d/o Santanna & Elizth on 25 Feb 1880 at Temp'ville by M Oldham

HOLLAND Wm S (Sewell) 24 S Gentleman New Church Horntown s/o John S D & Sallie W to Alice B (Barbara) Cropper 20 S Horntown Horntown d/o Wm D & Rebecca W on 25 Nov 1874 at Horntown by IT Adkins

HOLLY Benjamin 17 S Farmer Acc Acc s/o Abel W & Elizabeth to Charlotte Mears 19 S Acc Acc d/o Jno & Sally on 27 Sep 1865 at Acc by JH Addison

HOLMES Levin Col 42 S Laborer Acc Acc s/o Jacob & Eliza to Ann Downing Col 35 S Acc Acc d/o Thomas & Mary on 10 May 1874 at Horntown by S Johns

HOLMES Spady Col 24 S Wage-earner PA Acc s/o Spaty & Esther to Martha Read Col 21 S Acc Acc d/o Thos & Emma on 22 Nov 1893 at Onancock by GHT Byrd

HOLMES Winder Col 23 S Farmer Acc Acc s/o James & Emma to Mollie Parker Col 17 S Acc Acc d/o Joseph & Amy on 16 Jan 1890 at Acc by JH Thomas

HOLSTEIN Asher 22 S Barber Acc Acc s/o Josiah & Comfort to Lizzie A Melvin 21 S Acc Acc d/o Thomas & Elizabeth on 20 Oct 1891 at Chinco: Isld by JW Turner

HOLSTEIN Charles 17 S Sail Maker Acc Acc s/o Josiah & Comfort to Mary J Jester 16 S Acc Acc d/o Eba & Mary on 29 Oct 1883 at Chinco: Isld by EH Miller

HOLSTEIN Wm 22 S Sailor Acc Acc s/o Jonah & Comfort to Elizabeth J Bowden 20 S Acc Acc d/o Littleton & Daninah on 2 Dec 1882 at Chinco: Isld by WP Thornton

HOLT Joseph 32 S Merchant N'hamp: Acc s/o George & Ann to Susan Robins 24 S N'hamp: Acc d/o Edward & Margaret on 21 Dec 1871 at Belle Haven by JE Humphreys

HOOPMAN Wesley 22 S Sailor Acc Acc s/o Jas & Sarah to Anna Scott 19 S Acc Acc d/o Geo & Betsy on 17 Aug 1863 at Acc by JWA Elliott

HOPE Benjamin T 23 S Farmer Acc Acc s/o Geo W & Sally to Mary [Shreaves] Shrieves 20 S Acc Acc d/o Wm & Jane on 8 Nov 1876 near Zion Bapt Ch by CV Waugh

HOPE Calie 21 S Farmer Acc Acc s/o John T F & Catharine to Minnie F Hope 17 S Acc Acc d/o John T & Rachel E on 26 Dec 1893 at Locust Mount by JWA Elliott

HOPE Edward Col 22 S Wage-earner Acc Acc s/o George & Jane to Laura [Justis] Justice Col 21 S Acc Acc d/o Moses & Mary on 20 Jan 1889 at Acc by AJ Satchell

HOPE Edward T 22 S Farmer Acc Acc s/o John T F & Catherine A to Susan B Bundick 20 S Acc Acc d/o Wm S & Martha A on 7 Jan 1891 at Acc by

JA Barker
HOPE Eli Col 24 S Oysterman Acc Acc s/o Eli & Adah to Mary M Wallop Col 21 S Acc Acc d/o John & Ann on 13 May 1891 at Wattsville by AS Amos
HOPE Elias 22 S Laborer Acc Acc s/o Noah to Rachael Davis 21 S Acc Acc d/o Sarah on 26 Dec 1867 at Acc by M Oldham
HOPE Elias Col 27 W Oysterman Acc Acc s/o Elias & Ada to Clarissa Justice Col 25 W Acc Acc d/o Edmund & Mary on 22 Jun 1871 at Conquest Ch by M Oldham
HOPE George W 23 S Farmer Acc Acc s/o Wm S & Jane to Susan J Gillespie 21 S Acc Acc d/o Edward J & Catharine on 26 Oct 1871 near Modest Town by DA Woodson
HOPE Henry Col 24 S Laborer Acc Acc s/o Rose to Mary Dennis Col 18 S Acc Acc d/o Joshus & Harriet on 24 Sep 1884 at Acc by AJ Satchell
HOPE Henry Col 28 S Farmer Acc Acc s/o George & Jane to Lucy A White Col 20 S Acc Acc d/o Wm & Rachel on 27 Oct 1895 at Acc by AJ Satchell
HOPE James F 22 S Farmer Acc Acc s/o Wm S to Maggie A Mapp 16 S Acc Acc d/o Jas T & Bettie C on 18 Dec 1878 at Pungo Bapt Ch by SC Boston
HOPE John F 25 S Mechanic Acc Acc s/o Geo S & Laura to Mary E Justice 18 S Acc Acc d/o Revel of J & Nancy on 14 Feb 1877 at Zion Bapt Ch by DA Woodson
HOPE John F 19 S Farmer Acc Acc s/o Wm T & Marg't A to Sadie G Colonna 18 S Acc Acc d/o Wm C & Mary on 3 Apr 1892 at Woodbury by HJ Wilson
HOPE John T F 22 S Farmer Acc Acc s/o Wm H & Margt S to Catharine Lewis 23 S Acc Acc d/o Richd & Cath on 25 Mar 1863 at Acc by ES Grant
HOPE Sylvester H 22 S Farmer Acc Acc s/o Geo S to Arinthia C Barnes 18 S Acc Acc d/o Alfred & Mary on 26 Dec 1877 at Zion Ch by DA Woodson
HOPE Wm L 24 S Farmer Acc Acc s/o Geo S & Sally to Mary M Watts 16 S Acc Acc d/o Jno L & Adaline on 28 Nov 1878 at Zion Ch by DA Woodson
HOPE Wm Thomas 23 S Farming Acc Acc s/o Geo & Laura to Margaret Ann Mason 23 S Acc Acc d/o Zorobabel & Polly on 19 Sep 1872 at Z Mason's by DA Woodson
HOPKINS Charles 23 S Farmer Acc Acc s/o Henry T & Margt to Minerva Crosley 19 S Acc Acc d/o Saml on 16 Apr 1873 at Acc by O Littleton
HOPKINS Charles W 45 W Sailor Acc Acc s/o Henry & Margaret to Julia A Lewis 48 S Acc Acc d/o Revel & Polly on 1 Aug 1894 at Acc by JET Ewell
HOPKINS Emerson Col 24 S Wage-earner Acc Acc s/o Henry to Cora Edwards Col 23 S Acc Acc on 21 Jan 1891 at Acc by L Duncan
HOPKINS Francis 22 S Farmer Acc Acc s/o Henry & Margt to Josephine Bull 20 S Acc Acc d/o George & Elizth on 31 Mar 1880 at Acc by SC Boston
HOPKINS Fred W 21 S Clerk Acc Baltimore City MD s/o John J & Adeline to Evelina S Milliner 21 S Acc Acc d/o Robert S & Susan on 23 Oct 1893 at Locustville by DJ Traynham
HOPKINS George 21 S Oysterman Chinco: Isld Acc s/o Henry & mary to Jane Birch 17 S Assateague Isld Acc d/o Thos L & Annie on 31 Jul 1879 at Chinco: Isld by WP Thornton
HOPKINS George J 23 S Mechanic Acc

Acc s/o Joseph & Betsy to Ella N Sturgis 15 S Acc Acc d/o Maggie on 30 Dec 1885 at Acc by WJ Twilley

HOPKINS Isaac P (P) 24 S Farmer Acc Acc s/o Jno & Sarah to Arinthia A Budd 21 S Acc Acc d/o Wm & Sarah on 19 Dec 1872 at Reese Chp by JET Ewell

HOPKINS John 25 S Oysterman Acc Acc s/o Henry & Mary to Lydia A Daisey 26 W Acc Acc d/o William & Peggy on 12 Sep 1888 at Chinco: Isld by SU Grimsley

HOPKINS John H 24 S Farmer Acc Acc s/o Joseph & Betsy to Adaline Bundick 23 S Acc Acc d/o Margaret on 10 Oct 1867 at Acc by M Oldham

HOPKINS John H 28 S Farmer Wor Co MD Acc s/o John & Sarah to Elizabeth L East 17 S Acc Acc d/o William L & Elizabeth on 20 May 1874 at Onancock by O Littleton

HOPKINS John H 21 S Merchant Acc Acc s/o John P L & Susan C to Ursula T Lewis 21 S Acc Acc d/o Alfred J & Maria on 30 Jun 1880 at Lee Mont by FH Mullineaux

HOPKINS John J 50 W Farmer Acc Acc s/o Joseph F & Elizabeth to Amanda A Gladding 31 S Acc Acc d/o John on 17 Jul 1895 at Acc by JM Dunaway

HOPKINS John P L 27 S Merchant Acc Acc s/o Stephen & Jane to Susan C Finney 25 S Acc Acc d/o Thomas W & Sallie on 9 Dec 1857 at Acc by JH Addison (Wm H A Hopkins says both over 21)

HOPKINS John R 22 S Farmer Acc Acc s/o John J & Adaline to Bettie S Bull 20 S Acc Acc d/o John T & Julia on 26 Nov 1890 at Locustville by JA Barker

HOPKINS Joseph J 24 S Farmer Acc Acc s/o Joseph & Mary to Keziah (Elizabeth) Fox 19 S Acc Acc d/o Golden T & Elizth on 24 Dec 1873 near Locustville by LK LeCato

HOPKINS Levin L 26 S Carpenter Acc Acc s/o Joseph & Betsy to Mary E Shield 18 S Acc Acc d/o Jesse J & Amelia on 8 Jan 1884 near Locustville by JWA Elliott

HOPKINS Spencer D 23 S Merchant Acc Acc s/o John P L & Susan to Georgie E Powell 26 S Acc Acc d/o George W & Margaret on 21 Dec 1887 at Onancock by RA Compton

HOPKINS Stephen 35 S Merchant s/o Stephen to Eleshea A C West 25 S d/o Revel & Elizabeth P lic: 15 Mar 1871 marr: 16 Mar 1871 at Onancock

HOPKINS Sydney T 24 S Farmer Acc Acc s/o Jno L & Susan to Marcelleus Littleton 19 S Acc Acc d/o Henry P & Elizabeth on 25 Nov 1885 at Acc by JW Hundley

HOPKINS William H 25 S Farmer Acc Acc s/o Joseph & Betsey to Cornelia E [Shreaves] Shrieves 19 S Acc Acc d/o Geo & Hetty on 6 Aug 1868 at Acc by M Oldham

HOPKINS William H A 45 W Merchant Acc Acc s/o Stephen & Jane to Mary E Feddeman 26 W Acc Acc d/o Thomas & Ann Johnson on 19 Jan 1870 at Onancock by JC Martin

HOPKINS Windred E 27 S Assistant Light Keeper Sussex Co DE Acc s/o D R & Mary C to Ida Taylor 17 S Acc Acc d/o Joshua J & Ellen on 27 Nov 1889 at Acc by BP Truitt

HOPKINS Wm Col 24 S Sailor Sussex Co DE Acc s/o Jno & Leah Jane to Caroline S Parker Col 16 S Acc Acc d/o Edward & Sarah E on 29 Nov 1885 near Cross Rd by GHT Byrd

HOPKINS Wm E 22 S Farmer Acc Acc s/o Jno W & Laura H to Sally Virginia Ayres 21 S Acc Acc d/o James K & Sally U on 9 Apr 1884 at Acc by RW Anderson

HORNSBY Geo W 24 S Laborer Acc

Acc s/o Jas & Eliz to Leah Ann Russell 18 S Acc Acc d/o Jno & Hannah on 10 Feb 1881 at Acc by JE Humphreys

HORNSBY James 25 S Farmer Acc Acc s/o Jas & Ellen to Hester Williams 23 W Acc Acc d/o Tabitha Collins on 12 Feb 1879 at Pungo Meth Ch by CC Wertenbaker

HORNSBY John 21 S Farmer Acc Acc s/o James & Elizabeth to Clara Wallace 17 S Acc Acc d/o John & Susan on 19 Oct 1881 at Bells Nk by JE Humphreys

HORSEY Francis 22 S Laborer Wor Co MD Acc s/o George to Minie (Minnie) Purnell 24 S Som Co MD Acc d/o George Hope & Charlotte Horsey on 30 Dec 1869 at Oak Hall by S Marshall

HORSEY Frank Col 20 S Farmer Acc Acc s/o Wm & Sarah to Mary A Whealton Col 18 S Acc Acc d/o Henry & Mary on 19 Jul 1880 near Line of Md by JC Cluff

HORSEY Henry C Col 40 S Laborer Som Co MD Oak Hall s/o Geo & Cecilia to Harriet Matthews Col 35 S Acc Temp'ville on 1 Apr 1883 at Oak Hall by JC Cluff

HORSEY John L Col 32 S Farmer Acc Acc s/o Henry & June to Eliza Nock Col 28 W Acc Acc d/o Wm T & Caroline Drummond on 4 Jan 1893 at Wattsville by ML McKenry

HORSEY Keusey C 37 S Merchant Acc Acc s/o Custis & Eglantine to Nellie F Witham 27 S Acc Acc d/o James & Harriet on 21 Nov 1889 at Jenkins Bridge by J McNabb

HORSEY Samuel Col 23 S Oysterman Pocomoke City MD Acc to Harriet White Col 24 S Acc Acc d/o Tabby on 6 Jan 1885 at Lee Mont by CA Horsey

HORSEY Shepherd Col 30 S Laborer Salisbury MD Acc s/o Temperance Jones to Ida Chandler Col 18 S Acc Acc d/o Martha on 26 Nov 1882 at Ohancock by JC Ayler

HOWARD James 30 S Waterman MD Acc s/o Ezekiel & Bettie to Florence Watson 21 S MD Acc d/o Mitchel & Rosetta on 3 Jan 1886(?) at Acc by BF Jester Certificate returned 31 Dec 1886

HOWARD Louis D 20 S Sailor Acc Acc s/o William H & Mary E to Ella N Lewis 22 S Acc Acc d/o William Wesley & Virginia Lewis on 19 Aug 1888 at bride's home by JW Norris

HOWARD William H 31 S Sailor Acc Acc to Mary E Mason 21 S Acc Acc d/o Danil & Cath on 10 Oct 1866 at Acc by ES Grant

HOWARD William H Jr 20 S Sailor Acc Acc s/o William H & Mary E to Eveline R Taylor 18 S Acc Acc d/o Augustin C & Elizabeth on 18 May 1890 at Guilford by WF Hayes

HOWELL John 22 S Oysterman Acc Acc s/o William & Adaline to Mary J Daisey 16 S Acc Acc d/o James & Mary on 28 Apr 1888 at Chinco: Isld by SU Grimsley

HOWELL Wm 30 S Waterman b: Germany s/o Henry & Elizabeth to Adeline Watson 26 S b: Acc d/o David & Betsy on 19 Feb 1860 at Horntown by W Merrill (W M Feddeman says both over 21)

HUDSON Alfred 24 S Merchant Sussex Co DE Acc s/o Walter & Sarah to Mary A Whealton 16 S Acc Acc d/o Wm Tibatha on 27 Apr 1867 at Acc by P Bowdin Sr

HUDSON James A 57 W Physician Georgetown DE Chinco: Isld s/o Daniel & Mary to Mary Ann Wheeler 19 S Newtown MD Chinco: Isld d/o Wm M & Eliza on 7 Feb 1860 at Chinco: Isld by P Bowdin Sr (Wm M Feddeman said she over 21)

HUDSON James R 25 S Oysterman

Wor Co MD Acc s/o Anania & Mary A to Mary L Bishop 16 S Acc Acc d/o R W & Nancy W on 23 Apr 1891 at Chinco: Isld by EH Derrickson

HUDSON John R 22 S Oysterman Sussex Co DE Acc s/o Annanias & Mary A to Nancy M Powell 18 S Wor Co MD Acc d/o Isaiah & Susan on 27 Sep 1890 at Chinco: Isld by GE Wood

HUDSON Joseph 45 W Mariner Wor Co MD Acc s/o Phillip & Mary to Mary J Hamons 40 S Wor Co MD Acc d/o Wm & Hester on 30 May 1869 at Acc by WP Thornton

HUDSON Joshua E 20 S Oysterman Acc Acc s/o Joshua B & Leah C to Drucilla Jones 16 S Acc Acc d/o Daniel & Mary on 4 Mar 1883 at Chinco: Isld by WP Thornton

HUDSON Nath'l Col 22 S Farmer Acc Acc s/o George & Leah to Sally F Bayly Col 18 S Acc Acc d/o Wm & Alice on 16 Sep 1891 at Onancock by J Duckett

HUDSON Robert 21 W House Carpenter Acc Acc s/o Wm M & Mary to Annie M Birch 19 S Acc Acc d/o Henry & Rosey on 17 May 1881 at Chinco: Isld by WP Thornton

HUGHES Obediah 21 S Sailor Acc Acc s/o Jno & Vienna to Permelia S Poulson 17 S Acc Acc d/o Jno E & Mary E on 30 Dec 1886 at Acc by WA Street

HUMPHERYS James 23 S Farmer Acc Acc s/o Joshua & Elizabeth to Bettie Fowler 22 S Acc Acc d/o John & Mary on 9 Feb 1876 at Garrisons Chp by JE Humphreys

HUMPHREYS Fontaine B 35 S Engineer Salisbury MD Acc s/o Jno & Margaret to Carrie F Bayly 30 S Acc Acc d/o Thos & Elizth E on 17 May 1883 at Mappsville by JW Hundley

HUMPHREYS Wm L 25 S Farmer Acc Acc s/o Joshua E & Elizth to Bettie H Abdell 19 S Acc Acc d/o Geo D & Mary L on 6 Mar 1884 at Belle Haven by JE Humphreys

HUNDLEY John T 23 S Farmer Acc Acc s/o William & Margaret to Racelia S Chambers 21 S Acc Acc d/o John A & Rachel on 9 Aug 1893 at Tangier Isld by AJ Reamy

HUNDLEY Wm 22 S Seaman Som Co MD Acc s/o Mary to Margt Evans 16 S Som Co MD Acc d/o Lewis & Sally on 13 Aug 1863 at Acc by D Titlow

HURLEY Horace 28 S Sailor Som Co MD Acc s/o Jno & Sally to Arinthia Marshall 18 S Acc Acc d/o Rich'd & Nancy on 25 Jul 1883 at Conquest Ch by WP Wright

HURLEY Hy S 23 S Oysterman Acc Acc s/o Robt & Comfort to Julia Ann Hall 22 S Acc Acc d/o Thos & Easter on 1 Aug 1877 at Downings Ch by JB Merritt

HURLEY William A 26 S Farmer Acc Acc s/o Chas A & Harriet A to Lula M Watson 21 S Acc Acc d/o Joseph H & Ocie E on 15 Jun 1892 at Horntown by WW Wood

HURST Emory B 20 S Waterman Acc Acc s/o Oliver & Elisha to Mary L Dix 22 S Acc Acc d/o George & Maggie on 11 Sep 1895 at Acc by HS Dulany

HURST James H 22 S Farmer Acc Acc s/o Wm & Margt to Harriet A Russell 21 S Acc Acc d/o Thos & Sally on 24 Dec 1862 at Acc by JE Maloy

HURST John T 35 S Sailor Acc Acc s/o James to Ellen Scott 30 W Acc Acc d/o Joshua & Rachel Johnson on 18 Jun 1890 at Acc by PA Leatherbury

HURST John Wesley 22 S Farmer Acc Acc s/o John & Mary to Annie J Chandler 19 S Acc Acc d/o Thomas

J & Julia M on 23 Dec 1874 at Reese Chp by RC Jones

HURST Martin Luther 25 S Farmer Acc Acc s/o John & Mary to Maggie Chandler 20 S Acc Acc d/o Thos & Juliet W on 8 Feb 1882 at Lee Mont by WA Crouse

HURST Oliver 27 S Oysterman Acc Acc s/o James & Susan to Melissa A Evans 21 S Acc Acc d/o John & Mary on 2 Jan 1873 at Acc by PA Leatherbury

HURST Oswald 40 S Oysterman Acc Acc s/o James & Susan to Elisha E Hart 16 S Acc Acc d/o George H & Sarah A on 10 Oct 1894 at Acc by EC Atkins

HURST Tully E 26 S Farmer Acc Acc s/o Wm & Polly to Susan Hurst 19 S Acc Acc d/o James & Susan on 30 Dec 1874 at Leatherbury Chp by RC Jones

HURST Wm 47 W Farmer Acc Acc s/o Thos & Susan to Mary Johnson 37 S Acc Acc d/o Issac & Abigale on 6 Aug 1862 at Acc by ES Grant

HUSSEY John Col 20 S Oysterman Acc Acc s/o Harriet Harman to Lucy Davis Col 30 S Acc Acc d/o Edward & Mary Savage on 9 Mar 1890 at Chinco: Isld by SU Grimsley

HUSSEY Peleg 55 W Blacksmith Lincoln Co ME Acc s/o Lamuel & Rebecca to Drucilla Bell 40 W Acc Acc d/o Robt & Nancy Mears on 25 Feb 1875 at Messongo by WJ Twilley

HUSSEY William D 24 S Laborer Acc Acc s/o Peleg & Caroline to Harriet A [Tindal] Tindall 24 S Acc Acc d/o George & Hetty on 20 Feb 1873 near New Church by JL Polk

HUTCHINSON Edmd W to Caroline E Bloxom d/o William on 11 Jan 1854 by J Allen (James B Poulson says both over 21)

HUTCHINSON Edwd W 28 S Acc Acc s/o Edward W to Jennie W Davis 24 S Acc Acc d/o Wm D & Sally on 14 Nov 1883 at Acc by JW Hundley

HUTCHINSON George Col 20 S Wage-earner Acc Acc s/o Geo Sr & Leah to Ella Susan Read 21 S Acc Acc d/o James & Ellen on 25 Dec 1895 at Onancock by SW Watkins

HUTCHINSON George O 28 S Merchant Acc N'hamp: s/o Edward W & Caroline S to Cynthia Anna Johnson 26 S Acc Acc d/o John W & Anna on 6 Nov 1895 at Wardtown by JR Sturgis

HUTCHINSON John T 33 S Farming Acc Acc s/o John W & Harriet to Catharine Ann Coleburn 32 S Acc Acc d/o Thos A & Maria Susan on 11 Jan 1860 at Acc by P Warren (Mitchell W West said both over 21)

HUTCHINSON Joseph R 22 S Carpenter Acc Acc s/o James H & Dorinda W to Harriet E Marsh 18 S Som Co MD Acc d/o William Walter Marsh & Alice on 28 Dec 1887 at Acc by JH Riddick

HUTCHINSON Oswald L 26 W Carpenter Acc Acc s/o James H & Dorinda to Florence F Christian 23 S Acc Acc d/o William Seymour & Sarah on 17 Jan 1889 at Locustville by RA Compton

HUTCHINSON Raymond R 49 S Merchant Acc Acc s/o Jno & Harriet T to Susan B Coleburn 32 S Acc Acc d/o Thos A & Manie S on 31 Jan 1878 near Locustville by JH Amiss

HUTCHINSON Thos M 21 S Farmer Acc Acc s/o John T & Kate A to Loretta Lee Core 24 S Acc Acc d/o Levin J & Mary A on 18 Feb 1891 at Acc C H by JA Barker

HUTCHINSON William Col 21 S Wage-earner Acc Acc s/o Louis & Harriet to Ella Doughty Col 17 S Acc Acc d/o Dory & Nancy on 1 Jan 1895 at Acc by L Duncan

Marriages

HYSLOP George W 33 S Farmer Acc Acc s/o James & Mary to Maggie S Turner 19 S Acc Acc d/o James & Catharine on 14 Jan 1875 at Acc by JE Humphreys

HYSLOP Levin J 27 S Cabinet Maker Acc Acc s/o Jas & Mary to Elizth J Sturgis 20 S Acc Acc d/o Chas T & Mary J on 13 Jan 1867 at Acc by AB Dolly

HYSLOP Levin J [Hyslup] 50 W Farmer Acc Acc s/o James & Mary to Mary B Mears 38 W Acc Acc d/o Silvester & Margaret Stockley on 20 Nov 1889 at Geo W Stockley's by JWA Elliott

HYSLOP Ward K 26 S Farmer Acc Acc s/o Smith & Julia to Maggie S Finney 21 S Acc Acc d/o John T & Bettie on 29 Jan 1890 at Craddockville by JM Anderson

HYSLOP William H 20 S Farmer Acc Acc s/o John W & Mary to Sadie M Mason 18 S Acc Acc d/o George B & Sallie on 12 Mar 1889 at Geo B Mears' by JH Riddick

JACKSON Geo Col 21 S Livery Stableman Acc Acc s/o Lucinda Bayly to Sudie Mapp Col 18 S Acc Acc d/o Hannah Parkes on 2 Jul 1879 at Onancock by JW Diggs

JACKSON George Col 27 D Blacksmith Acc Acc s/o Andrew & Lucinda to Sarah Kellam Col 21 S Acc Acc d/o Margaret on 6 Oct 1889 at Onancock by JH Offer

JACKSON Levin 23 S Acc Acc to Sarah Miller 16 S Acc Acc on 23 Dec 1882 at Chinco: Isld by OS Walton

JACOBS Acum Col 56 S Farmer Acc Acc s/o Custis & Alsie to Polly Becket Col 53 W Acc Acc d/o Samuel & Charity on 1 Oct 1870 at New Boston by C Burriss

JACOBS Alfred Col 26 S Farmer Acc Acc s/o Edwd & Lucy to Mary Major Col 22 S Acc Acc d/o George & Margt on 27 Sep 1876 at Belle Haven by RH Govans

JACOBS Arthur James [Jacob] 29 S Mechanic N'hamp: Acc s/o Arthur & Sarah to Sabra C Hack 23 S Acc Acc d/o John W & Sabra on 23 Jul 1856 at Acc by M Oldham (T W Blackstone says both over 21)

JACOBS Arthur T 24 S Farmer Acc Acc s/o Wm E & Charlotte to Laura A Ames 19 S Acc Acc d/o Thos W & Susan on 29 Jan 1873 at Acc by O Littleton

JACOBS Clifford E [Jacob] 23 S Mechanic Acc Jersey City NJ s/o Wm B & Sarah W to Christie Poole 22 S Princess Anne MD Acc d/o Wm W & Mary L on 8 Jan 1890 at Modest Town by JW Ward

JACOBS Edmond FN 45 S Laborer to Liney Sample FN 35 lic: 4 Jan 1865

JACOBS Edmond Col 32 S Farmer Acc Acc s/o Elizth Martin to Annie Bayly Col 18 S Acc Acc d/o Alfred & Maria on 24 Aug 1881 at Belle Haven by LW Lee

JACOBS Everett C 23 S Carpenter Acc Acc s/o Wm B & Sarah to Ella J Wessells 20 S Acc Acc d/o David B & Nancy on 4 Feb 1885 at Nelsomia by JW Carroll

JACOBS Henry Col 23 S Wage-earner Acc Acc s/o Sarah Gaskins to Josephine [Rodgers] Rogers Col 21 S Acc Acc d/o Lewis & Susan on 4 Oct 1893 at Onancock by JC Williams

JACOBS John 31 S Carriage Mkr Prin Anne Co Baltimore MD s/o John & Mary to Margaret E Churn 30 S Acc Acc d/o John & Eliza on 31 Dec 1869 near Belle Haven by JE Humphreys

JACOBS Robert Col 23 S Laborer Acc Acc s/o Acornb & Polly to Mary S [Bevans] Beavans Col 16 S Acc Acc d/o Peter & Jane on 2 Aug 1882 at

Pungo: by TW Nettles

JACOBS Severn Col 24 S Laborer Acc Acc s/o Edmond & Lucy to Emma B Dennis Col 18 S Acc Acc d/o Jno & Mary on 14 Jun 1881 at New Boston by TW Nettles

JACOBS William D [Jacob] Col 29 S Farmer Acc Acc s/o Edmond & Lucy to Peggie S Dennis Col 21 S Acc Acc d/o John & Mary on 25 Jan 1889 at Acc by L Duncan

JACOBS William L 27 S Dentist Acc Acc s/o Wm B & Sarah W to Missouri Smith 27 S Acc Acc on 2 Sep 1874 at Acc by JL Lodge

JAMES Abel T 26 S Farmer Acc Acc s/o Thomas H & Tabitha to Susan C Hopkins 18 S Acc Acc d/o Wm H A & Ketty on 12 Apr 1875 at Onancock by JH Amiss

JAMES Alfred W 25 S Farmer Acc Acc s/o Jno T & Elizth S to Levania F Savage 24 S Acc Acc d/o Bagwell & Margt on 19 Dec 1883 at Acc by WC Vaden

JAMES Asa D Col 26 W Wage-earner N'hamp: Acc s/o Ann Kellam to Marg't Sarah Collins Col 18 S Acc Acc d/o Sarah Walker on 12 Nov 1893 at Acc by TW Nettles

JAMES Dennis Col 21 S Laborer Acc Acc s/o Mary Logan to Ida Bayly Col 21 S Acc Acc d/o Lydia on 18 Jan 1879 at Onancock by JW Diggs

JAMES George T 21 S Farmer Acc Acc s/o Geo W & Margt to Viola S Parker 20 S Acc Acc d/o Jno E & Mary on 4 Jan 1883 at Acc by SC Boston

JAMES Jeffry Col 21 S Acc Acc s/o Henry & Mary Darby to Martha Boggs Col 17 S Acc Acc d/o Raymond & Ibby on 24 Oct 1885 at Acc C H by LW Lee

JAMES Jesse K to Virga A Lane wid on 19 Oct 1852 by J Allen

JAMES John H 25 S Farmer Acc Acc s/o Jno T & Susan to Llewellyn Phillips 22 S Acc Acc d/o Levin & Susan on 1 Feb 1882 at Mr Levin Phillips' by JC Watson

JAMES John T Col 40 S Farm Laborer GA Acc to Caroline Gibbons Col 39 S Acc Acc d/o Hannah on 6 Jul 1882 at Drum'tn by LW Lee

JAMES John T 58 W Farmer Acc Acc s/o Thos & Mary to Cordelia S Kellam 40 S Acc Acc d/o Thos H on 21 Mar 1883 at Locustville by CD Crawley

JAMES Peter 22 S Laborer Acc Acc s/o Margaret to Sarah Scarborough 21 S Acc Acc d/o Maria on 30 Dec 1867 at Acc by LK LeCato

JAMES Peter Col 40 W Farmer Acc Acc s/o Peter Mears & Margaret Harmon to Louisa Ewell Col 35 W Acc Acc d/o Levi & Mary Conquest on 16 Feb 1888 at St Luke Ch by P Sheppard

JAMES William L 21 S Farmer Acc Acc s/o Levin T & Eliz'th to Fanney H Crosley 18 S Acc Acc d/o James E & Sallie on 13 Feb 1889 at Onancock by JW Easley

JAMES Wilmer T 21 S Farmer Acc Acc s/o Jesse & Virga to Annie L Mapp 21 S Acc Acc d/o Geo C & Rose on 22 Oct 1879 at Oak Grove Ch by CC Wertenbaker

JAMES Wilson Col 24 S Sailor Acc Acc s/o Mary Jane to Sallie Clayton Col 16 S Acc Acc d/o Smith & Harriet on 29 Aug 1882 at Acc by LW Lee

JAMES Wm T 21 S Farmer Acc Acc s/o John T & Susan to Mary Fox 19 S Acc Acc d/o Zorobabel & Elizabeth on 23 Dec 1870 at Acc by LK LeCato

JARMAN Thos A 23 S Farmer Acc Acc s/o Wm & Elizth to Olivia A Baker 19 S Acc Acc d/o Oliver & nancy on 5 Nov 1879 at Modest Town by DA Woodson

JEFFRIES Charles 19 S Oysterman Acc Acc s/o Somers & Henrietta to Cornelia Cherricks 17 S Acc Acc d/o John T & Mary Ann on 19 May 1892 at Chinco: Isld by JF Wooden

JEFFRIES Elmer 19 S Oysterman Atlantic Co NJ Chinco: Isld s/o William & Rebecca to Mary A Russell 17 S Chinco: Isld Chinco: Isld d/o Elijah & Charlotte on 9 Sep 1876 at Chinco: Isld by P Bowdin Sr

JEFFRIES Elvy A [Jeffreys] 21 S Oysterman NJ Acc s/o Wm & Rebecca to Mary Ann Snead 17 S Acc Acc d/o Jno & Charity on 7 Mar 1869 at Acc by P Bowdin Sr

JEFFRIES Summers [Jeffers] 25 S Mariner NJ Chinco: Isld s/o Evin & Hannah to Henrietta [Wimbro] Wimbrough 18 S Chinco: Isld Chinco: Isld d/o Griffin & Elizth on 4 Sep 1869 at Acc by P Bowdin Jr

JEFFRIES Wm R 21 S Oysterman Acc Acc s/o E A & Mary A to Laura V Lewis 18 S Acc Acc d/o Daniel W & Drucilla J on 20 Dec 1894 at Chinco: Isld by JF Wooden

JENKINS Dan'l [Jenkin] FN 35 S Laborer Acc Acc s/o Esther to Elizth Wharton FN 22 S Acc Acc d/o Milly on 5 Mar 1866 at Acc by GW Matthews

JENKINS Henry F 22 S Oysterman Matthews Co VA Acc s/o James & Eliz'th to Emma C Evans 17 S Acc Acc d/o Wm Sarin & Mary C Evans on 15 Feb 1891 at Onancock by GW Burke

JENKINS John H 25 S Sailor Gloucester Co Acc s/o James J & Georgianna to Mary Susan Roberts 50 W Acc Acc d/o Charles & Mahala Taylor on 16 Apr 1893 at Acc by AC Berryman

JENKINS Littleton D 23 S Waterman Acc Acc s/o William & Susan to Maggie C [Twyford] Twiford 23 W Acc Acc d/o Susan Rew on 18 Aug 1895 at Lee Mont by RB Sanford

JENKINS William J 27 S Farming Som Co MD Acc s/o Littleton & sarah to Emily Susan Mason 24 S Acc Acc d/o David & Cath on 12 May 1872 at Acc by JET Ewell

JESTER Charles T 20 S Sailor Acc Acc s/o Charles & Dollie J to Mary E Whealton 18 S Acc Acc d/o Daniel Whealton & Emma Downing on 20 May 1874 at Chinco: Isld by P Bowdin Sr

JESTER Daniel J 27 W Sailor Acc Acc s/o Charles S & Delilah J to Lizzie Daisey 16 S Acc Acc d/o Wm P & Mary A on 13 Dec 1882 at Chinco: Isld by WP Thornton

JESTER Ebey 26 S Waterman Chinco: Isld Chinco: Isld s/o Elijah & Nancy to Mary Savage 21 S Sussex Co DE Chinco: Isld d/o Elisha & Nelly on 24 Jan 1858 at Chinco: Isld by P Bowdin (Joshna Wishart says both over 21)

JESTER Elias H 26 S Laborer Sussex Co DE Acc s/o Daniel to Alabama Moore 24 S Acc Acc d/o Thos & Susan on 19 Jan 1871 at Pocomoke by O Littleton

JESTER Elias J Col 24 S Blacksmith Acc Acc s/o Elias H & Alabama to Oshie E Summers Col 16 S Acc Acc d/o George & Eveline on 2 Jun 1895 at Mappsville by JL King

JESTER Elijah 21 S Light Ship Keeper Acc Acc s/o Eba & Mary to Lizzie A White 16 S Acc Acc d/o Francis A Keohlock on 24 Jul 1888 at Chinco: Isld by SU Grimsley

JESTER George H 21 S Oysterman Acc Acc s/o Charles S & Delilah J to Julia Whealton 17 S Acc Acc d/o Danl Wheaton & Mary A Mason(Wheaton) on 12 Nov 1882 at Chinco: Isld by WP Thornton

JESTER Henry 20 S Oysterman Acc

Acc s/o Eba & Mary to Annie Carpenter 16 S Acc Acc d/o John & Polly on 8 Nov 1884(?) at Chinco: Isld by SU Grimsley Certificate returned 12 Jan 1889

JESTER James 21 S Sailor Chinco: Isld Chinco: Isld s/o Charles & D J to Sarah E Steelman 16 S Chinco: Isld Chinco: Isld d/o David & Elizabeth on 9 Jun 1878 at Chinco: Isld by WP Thornton

JESTER John 57 W to Elizabeth (Burch) Birch 40 W lic: Apr/May 1865 John A M Whealton of Chincoteague applied between 17 Apr & 4 May 1865

JESTER John 46 W Oysterman Acc Acc s/o Jas & Rebecca to Rebecca Hill 53 W Acc Acc d/o John & Ruth Russell on 17 Jul 1866 at Acc by P Bowdin Sr

JESTER John 35 W Oysterman Chinco: Isld Chinco: Isld s/o John & Ann to Susan Birch 17 S Chinco: Isld Chinco: Isld d/o Jas S & Martha on 10 Jun 1883 at Chinco: Isld by WP Thornton

JESTER John B 23 S Oysterman Acc Acc s/o Wm & Elizabeth to Mary C [Kelley] Kelly 21 S Wor Co MD Acc d/o James & Mary on 5 Jan 1892 at Chinco: Isld by JF Wooden

JESTER John Jr 20 S Oysterman Acc Acc s/o Jno & Ann to Sarah Claville 14 S Acc Acc d/o James & Mary on 7 Nov 1866 at Acc by P Bowdin Sr

JESTER Joseph V 21 S Waterman Chinco: Isld Chinco: Isld s/o Chls & Delilah to Ann S Melvin 21 S Chinco: Isld Chinco: Isld d/o Saml & Elizth on 2 May 1872 at Chinco: Isld by P Bowdin Sr

JESTER Kendal Jr 21 S Merchant Acc Acc s/o Ruben & Catharine to Manie F Hill 18 S Acc Acc d/o John T & Sarah Ann on 12 Apr 1893 at Acc by GP Jones

JESTER Lambert 21 S Oysterman Acc Acc s/o Kendal & Eliza to Nancy Amelia Shelly 17 S DE Acc d/o Zacariah & Mary on 13 Feb 1870 at Acc by P Bowdin Jr

JESTER Mills T 21 S Waterman Acc Acc s/o Elias H & Alabama to Maggie L Young 16 S Acc Acc d/o Alfred D & Susan J on 22 Dec 1895 at Guilford by JR Sturgis

JESTER Selby 22 S Mariner Chinco: Isld Chinco: Isld s/o Kendal & Eliza to Maria [Daysey] (Daisey) Daisey 21 S Chinco: Isld Chinco: Isld d/o John & Margaret on 19 Mar 1857 at Chinco: Isld by P Bowdin (Randel Mason says both over 21)

JESTER William 24 S Shoemaking Acc Acc to Mary J Matthews 24 S Acc Acc d/o Edwd & Jane on 18 Jan 1865 at r/o George H Ewell by GH Ewell

JESTER William 22 S Oysterman Acc Acc s/o Chls S & Deliah to Elizabeth Jones 19 S Acc Acc d/o Edwd & Sarah on 28 Jan 1872 at Chinco: Isld by P Bowdin Sr

JESTER William J 32 W Carpenter Acc Acc s/o Chas S & Delilah to Elizabeth Russell 36 W Acc Acc d/o James & Mary Claielle on 8 Jun 1881 at Chinco: Isld by OS Walton

JESTER William T 21 S Oysterman Acc Acc s/o Joseph V & Ann to Laura A Fleming 18 S Acc Acc d/o August & Elizabeth on 5 Mar 1895 at Chinco: Isld by CW Matthews

JOHNSON Alfred B 35 S Farmer Acc Acc s/o Isaiah & Tabitha to Mary A Grinnalds 21 S Acc Acc d/o Jno Wm & Margaret on 2 Nov 1892 at Acc by JET Ewell

JOHNSON Alfred F single Mariner b: Acc s/o Jno R & Eliz to Mary A Lewis 16 S b: Acc d/o Samuel K (Decd) & ·Sally on 3 Jan 1857 near Reese Chp by ES Grant

JOHNSON Arthur 22 S Laborer Acc Acc s/o Ann to Charity Williams 23 S Acc Acc d/o Lelelia Williams on 5 Jan 1867 at Acc by M Oldham

JOHNSON Augustus W 24 S Farmer Acc Acc s/o Samuel & Caroline to Arinthia S Lewis 18 S Acc Acc d/o Leonidas & Sally on 24 Dec 1882 at Acc by WP Wright

JOHNSON Columbus M 23 S Merchant Acc Acc s/o John R Elizabeth to Virginia B Bowdoin 21 S Acc Acc d/o John R & Anamda on 6 Jul 1871 at Acc by O Littleton

JOHNSON Dearborn H 23 S Acc Acc s/o Jno R & Eliz to Caroline W Bloxom 22 S Acc Acc d/o Darius & H on 9 Jul 1863 at Acc by ES Grant

JOHNSON Elliott [Johnston] 59 D Gentleman Baltimore City MD Acc s/o Thomas D & Elizth E to Alice M [Langford] Lankford 22 S Baltimore City Acc d/o John & Maria on 9 Sep 1885 at Locust Mount by JWA Elliott

JOHNSON Erastus J 23 S Farmer Acc Acc s/o Jas T & Mary S to Louisa Copes 22 S Acc Acc d/o Solomon & Henrietta D on 9 Mar 1856 at Acc by J Allen

JOHNSON Erastus J 40 W Farmer Acc Acc s/o James T & Mary to Elizabeth H Mason 28 W Acc Acc d/o Thomas & Mary Scott on 13 Jan 1874 at Horntown by M Oldham

JOHNSON Ezekiel Col 37 S Farmer N'hamp: Acc s/o Sarah Bayly to Matilda A Finney 36 S Acc Acc d/o Mitlada A on 7 May 1879 at Locustville by RH Govans

JOHNSON George Col 40 S Farmer Acc Acc s/o Leah to Elizabeth [Brodwater] Broadwater Col 40 S Acc Acc d/o Ann on 23 Jan 1878 at Modest Town by A Joynes

JOHNSON George W 22 S Seaman Acc Acc s/o Thomas & Ann to Margaret J Fitzgerald 26 S Acc Acc d/o Thos E & Margaret on 2 Nov 1869 at Acc

JOHNSON Henry 21 S Farmer Acc Acc s/o Elizabeth to Elizabeth Bayly 23 S Acc Acc d/o Edward & Lovey on 2 Nov 1879 at Warrenton's Br by SC Boston

JOHNSON Isaac Col 40 W Farmer Acc Acc s/o Mary to Harriet Poole Col 39 W Acc Acc d/o Harriet Gladding on 14 Jan 1892 at New Church by TM Poulson

JOHNSON Isiah T 25 S Merchant Acc Acc s/o Jno R & Elizth to Mary W Core 19 S Acc Acc d/o William T & Mary on 31 Jan 1867 at Acc by P Warren

JOHNSON James 32 W Mariner b: Acc s/o Sah & Abigail to Maria Bell 24 S b: Acc d/o Elias & Polly on 16 Aug 1856 at Onancock by BT Ames (John T Johnson says she over 21)

JOHNSON James 56 S Laborer Acc Acc s/o Peggy to Harriet Mears 50 S Acc Acc d/o Esther on 1 Jan 1867 at Acc by JWA Elliott

JOHNSON James Col 26 S Teamster Acc Acc s/o Julia Ann to Rebecca Stockley Col 25 S Acc Acc d/o Mary on 27 Nov 1872 at Acc by M Oldham

JOHNSON James 21 S Laborer Acc Acc s/o James & Sally to Ocia Sterling 19 S Acc Acc d/o Mary Ann Taylor on 8 Jan 1873 at Temp'ville by JE Potts

JOHNSON James Col 68 W Laborer Acc Acc s/o Peggy to Lukie Becket Col 66 W Acc Acc d/o Rachel on 10 Feb 1879 near Locust Mount by JWA Elliott

JOHNSON James Edward 21 S by Water Matchapungo Matchapungo s/o John (Decd) & Maria to Peggy Bradford 22 S near Land Shift near Land Shift d/o Labin & Leah on 12 Feb 1857 at Burton Ch by J Burton

JOHNSON James H Col 43 S Laborer

Acc Acc s/o James & Mary to Sarah Fletcher Col 43 S Acc Acc d/o Maria on 16 Nov 1887 at Acc by N Morris

JOHNSON James T widr to Margaret Sterling d/o Samuel lic: 14 Jan 1857 James H(?) Sterling says she over 21

JOHNSON James T 68 W Farmer Acc Acc s/o William & Margaret to Elizabeth Ling 56 W Acc Acc d/o George & Polly Window on 15 Jan 1873 near Temp'ville by WT Wilkerson

JOHNSON James T 21 S Farmer Acc Acc s/o Edward & Margaret to Mary C Mears 21 S Acc Acc d/o James & Mary on 4 Mar 1880 at Locustville by LK LeCato

JOHNSON John Col 23 S Laborer Acc Acc s/o Silvia to Rachel Mapp Col 21 S Acc Acc d/o Jane on 28 Nov 1875 at Burtons Ch by HT Rich

JOHNSON John S widr to Mary Ann Tatham wid lic: 25 Jun 1855

JOHNSON John T 22 S Mariner b: Acc s/o Thos & Nancy to Kate M [Scarburg] (Scarburgh) Scarborough 23 S b: Acc d/o Americus (Decd) & Mary on 9 Dec 1856 at Reese Chp by ES Grant (George W Beloat says both over 21)

JOHNSON John T (Thomas) 23 S Farmer Acc Acc s/o Jno & Maria to Rachel H Bradford 20 S Acc Acc d/o Labin & Lach on 25 Aug 1862 at Acc by JWA Elliott

JOHNSON John W 23 S Farmer b: Acc s/o John & Ann to Tabitha Milliner 19 S b: Acc d/o Southy S & Nancy Milliner on 9 Feb 1859 at r/o Jas Sparrow by ES Grant

JOHNSON John W 24 S Oysterman Montgomery Co MD Acc s/o Jno & Susan A to Elsie Landing 19 S Acc Acc d/o A C & Margaret on 21 Feb 1886 at Tangier Isld by CS Baker

JOHNSON John W 29 S Farmer Acc Acc s/o Wm J & Margaret B to Fannie E Burton 26 S Acc Acc d/o Stewart & Rachel on 3 Jan 1894 at Oak Hall by JR Tillery

JOHNSON John Wm 29 S Sailor NJ NJ s/o Jas & Ourega to Nancy Carpenter 28 S Acc Acc d/o Revel & Elizth on 24 Jun 1866 at Acc by WP Thornton

JOHNSON Joseph S 22 S Farmer Acc Acc s/o James T & Margaret to Annie May Tindall 18 S Acc Acc d/o John H & Elizabeth J on 7 Jul 1889 at Acc by JW Ward

JOHNSON Joshua T 57 W Oysterman Northumberland Co Acc s/o Thos & Betsey to Annie Dies 55 W Acc Acc d/o Thomas & Sally Crockett on 8 Oct 1893 at Tangier by ZH Webster

JOHNSON Laban P 23 S Farmer Acc Acc s/o Jno W & Tabitha to Alice P Adams 19 S Acc Acc d/o James C & Mary A on 31 Oct 1885 at Zion Ch by WA Street

JOHNSON Marcellus A 19 S Oysterman Acc Acc s/o Joshua T & Rachal to Martha J Lewis 17 S Acc Acc d/o Thomas J & Elizabeth on 8 Dec 1880 at Leatherbury Ch by PA Leatherbury

JOHNSON Moses Col 41 S Painter Acc Acc s/o Chloe Mason to Maggie Finney Col 23 S Acc Acc d/o Annie on 9 Jun 1880 at Onancock by JW Diggs

JOHNSON Peter Col 60 S Laborer Acc Acc to Sarah Griffin Col 45 S Acc Acc on 27 Dec 1874 at Acc by HT Rich

JOHNSON Richard Col 25 S Farming Acc Acc to Loretta Fosque Col 20 S Acc Acc d/o Solomon & Ada on 21 Jun 1874 at Savageville by JK Plato

JOHNSON Samuel Col 22 S Laborer Acc Acc s/o Harriet to Sarah Custis Col 23 S Acc Acc d/o Sarah on 8 Dec 1878 at Temp'ville by JC Cluff

JOHNSON Solomon T 26 S Merchant Acc Acc s/o John A & Charlotte to

Susan A Marshall 30 S MD Acc d/o John D & Hester on 29 Jan 1868 at Acc by GW Matthews

JOHNSON Sylvester S to Sally A Northam d/o Gillet who gave consent lic: 6 Aug 1860 Thomas Groton says he over 21

JOHNSON T F 25 S Sailor Christana Norway NY s/o Christina & Mary Brandht to Catharine Young 20 S Chinco: Isld Chinco: Isld d/o F J & Mary on 27 Aug 1880 at Chinco: Isld by R Williamson

JOHNSON Thomas 58 W Mariner Acc Acc s/o Isaiah & abigal to Elizabeth S Kellam 40 S Acc Acc d/o Stockley & Comfort on 8 Dec 1869 at Acc by JC Martin

JOHNSON Thomas F 27 D U S Service Norway Chinco: Isld s/o Chrestian & Maria to Mary E Collins 25 D Chinco: Isld Chinco: Isld d/o David & Mary Tarr on 5 Jun 1883 at Chinco: Isld by WP Thornton

JOHNSON Thomas H 26 S Farmer Acc Acc s/o Jno W & Ann to Lucretia A White 20 S Acc Acc d/o Geo W & Charlotte on 21 Sep 1865 at Acc by ES Grant

JOHNSON Warren 21 S Farmer Acc Acc s/o Severn P & Mary E to Nora Corbin 24 S Acc Acc d/o George & Missouri on 20 Nov 1895 at Acc by GD Edmonston

JOHNSON Washington 21 S Farmer Acc Acc s/o James T to Annie Smith 18 S Acc Acc d/o Edwd & Cath on 2 Feb 1881 at Oak Hall by RB Beadles

JOHNSON William 20 S Sailor Acc Acc s/o Joshua & Rachel to Susan J Spence 18 S Acc Acc d/o Lewis & Elizth on 30 Jan 1878 at Chesconessex by PA Leatherbury

JOHNSON William Col 22 S Laborer Acc Acc s/o Peter to Sarah Gunter Col 21 S Acc Acc on 18 Apr 1881 at Acc by JC Watson

JOHNSON William 30 S Farmer Acc Acc s/o Ann to Nannie Copes 20 S Acc Acc d/o Thos & Bettie on 28 Dec 1882 at Temp'ville by M Oldham

JOHNSON William A 33 S Farmer Acc Acc s/o John & Maria to Matilda Ann Turner 35 W Acc Acc on 30 Jan 1867 at Acc by AB Dolly

JONES Abraham Col 21 S Farmer Acc Acc s/o Alice to Maggie Sample Col 21 S Acc Acc d/o Mary on 5 Dec 1886 at Acc by L Duncan

JONES Alex P 39 W Laborer DE Acc to Elizabeth (Thornton) Hart 17 S Acc Acc d/o Wm Thornton on 25 Dec 1862 at Acc by GH Ewell

JONES Alfred (Col) 22 S Oysterman Acc Acc s/o Abram & Elsy to Ann Downing 21 S Acc Acc d/o Juliet on 1 Jun 1870 at Acc by E Hebard

JONES Archie 31 S Merchant Acc Acc s/o E T & M J to Gertrude Whealton 22 S Acc Acc d/o John B & Mary A on 6 Mar 1889 at Chinco: Isld by RI Watkins

JONES Benjamin S 30 S Salesman Wor Co MD Acc s/o Benjamin I & Harriet to Kate E Barnes 18 S Acc Acc d/o George W & Eveline T on 3 Jan 1894 at Parksley by JET Ewell

JONES Daniel 21 S Mariner b: Chinco: Isld s/o James & Sarah to Mary [Furguson] Ferguson 22 S b: Chinco: Isld d/o James & Mary on 30 Dec 1855 at Chinco: Isld by WP Thornton (Wm T Watson says she over 21)

JONES Daniel 48 W Oysterman Acc Acc s/o James & Sallie to Elizabeth [Chericks] Cherricks 40 W Acc Acc d/o Elijah & Patsey Jester on 5 Mar 1883 at Chinco: Isld by WP Thornton

JONES Daniel Jr 19 S Oysterman Acc Acc s/o Daniel Sr & Mary to Annie Jones 17 S Acc Acc d/o James S Sr & Rebecca on 24 Apr 1894 at Chinco: Isld by RB Sanford

JONES David W 28 S Mason & Farmer Acc Acc s/o Smith & Mary to Zenette Slocomb 19 S Acc Acc d/o Wm C & Susan on 28 Apr 1870 at Temp'ville by O Littleton

JONES Elijah Col 21 S Farmer Acc Acc s/o Abel & Esther to Arinthia J Jubilee Col 24 S Acc Acc d/o William & Henny on 3 Jan 1874 at Belle Haven by JE Humphreys

JONES Francis T 31 S Carpenter Wor Co MD Wor Co MD s/o Thos & Cordelia to Annie O Hayman 24 S Acc Acc d/o James on 26 Nov 1884 at Acc by TM Poulson

JONES Geo E 21 S Farmer Acc Acc s/o George T & Arinthia S to Lena S Bell 19 S Acc Acc d/o John E & Mary E on 14 Oct 1891 at Wachapreague by JR Strugis

JONES George 30 S Merchant Norfolk City Norfolk City to Elizabeth E Holt 26 W Acc Acc d/o John W & Margaret Colonna on 27 Feb 1872 at Pungo: by O Littleton

JONES George P 30 S Clergyman Som Co MD Selbyville DE s/o Refus P & Mary E to Ida Matthews 27 S Acc Acc d/o James E & Martha S on 5 Jun 1894 at Acc by EH Derrickson

JONES George T 44 W Shoemaker MD Acc to Arinthia S Joynes 35 S Acc Acc d/o Jas on 23 Jan 1867 at Acc by AB Dolly

JONES George W 25 S Oysterman Acc Acc s/o Jno A & Amy to Elizabeth E Birch 17 S Acc Acc d/o Henry on 21 Feb 1886 at Chinco: Isld by SU Grimsley

JONES George W Col 30 S Wage-earner Acc Acc s/o Samuel & Susan to Henrietta Holden Col 27 S Acc Acc d/o Rhoda on 21 Feb 1894 at Temp'ville by JC Cluff

JONES Howard F 27 S Oysterman Acc Acc s/o John A & Airy to Ida V Watson 17 S Acc Acc d/o Thomas W & Lovey on 9 Jun 1889 at Chinco: Isld by SU Grimsley

JONES Iassc 21 S Mariner Acc Chinco: Isld s/o John & Anna to Phebe (Pheby) Sharpley 20 S Chinco: Isld Chinco: Isld d/o Henry (dec'd) & Sally & (ward/o John A M Whealton who gave consent) on 1 May 1857 at Chinco: Isld by WP Thornton

JONES Isaac D 23 S Oysterman Acc Acc s/o Jno A & Airy to Malinda Birch 16 S Acc Acc d/o Thos L & Ann on 20 Jul 1887 at Chinco: Isld by SU Grimsley

JONES Isaac J 26 W s/o John & Ann to Mary (Tindal) Tindall 16 S d/o John lic: 27 Mar 1865

JONES James single Seaman Chinco: Isld Chinco: Isld s/o Jas & Sarah to Anna [Cherix] Cherricks single Chinco: Isld Chinco: Isld d/o Danl & Betsy on 4 Aug 1853 at r/o Sarah James by P Bowdin

JONES James H 34 S Carpenter MD Baltimore City to Maggie Burton 27 S Acc Acc d/o Wm F & Margaret on 15 Oct 1871 near Locustville by LK LeCato

JONES James S 21 S Oysterman Acc Acc s/o Major & Susan to Rebecca Birch 22 S Acc Acc d/o John & Margt on 19 May 1869 at Acc by P Bowdin Jr

JONES James Sr 43 W Oysterman Acc Acc s/o Jas & Sally to Martha Pruitt 18 S MD Acc d/o Leonard P & Nancy on 7 Mar 1869 at Acc by WP Thornton

JONES John 28 S Farmer Chinco: Isld Assateague Isld s/o Daniel & Comfort to Ara Lewis 27 S Assateague Isld Assateague Isd d/o Isaac & Zesty on 9 Sep 1857 at Assateague Isld by WP Thornton (John A M Whealton says both over 21)

JONES John 21 S Mariner Acc Acc s/o

Marriages 185

James & Sally to Nancy [Reed] Read 19 S Acc Acc d/o Revel & Susan on 14 May 1859 at Acc by WP Thornton (John A M Whealton acknowledge her signature)

JONES John A 50 W Oysterman Chinco: Isld Chinco: Isld s/o Danl & Comfort to Hettie F Birch 15 S Chinco: Isld Chinco: Isld d/o Thos L & Ann on 12 Aug 1879 at Chinco: Isld by WP Thornton

JONES John D 20 S Oysterman Acc Acc s/o John A & Airy to Annie Pruitt 17 S Acc Acc d/o John S & Mary on 31 Aug 1890 at Chinco: Isld by GE Wood

JONES John E 24 S Oysterman Acc Acc s/o Jonh & Ann to Elizabeth Carpenter 21 S Acc Acc d/o Richard & Nancy on 22 Dec 1868 at Acc by P Bowdin Jr

JONES John W 23 W Oysterman Chinco: Isld Chinco: Isld s/o E & Sarah to Mary Mallett 18 S Wor Co MD Chinco: Isld d/o Edward on 5 Apr 1879 at Chinco: Isld by IT Adkins

JONES John W Col 25 S Wage-earner Som Co MD Acc s/o Elzey & Sarah E to Lydia Waples Col 35 S Acc Acc d/o Stephen & Rachel Drummond on 30 Jun 1888 at Onancock by GHT Byrd

JONES Joseph 21 S Oysterman Acc Acc s/o James S & Rebecca to Adelaide Daisey 19 S Acc Acc d/o David & Elizabeth on 28 Aug 1892 at Chinco: Isld by RB Sanford

JONES Joseph H 23 S Miller Wor Co MD Acc s/o H C & Annie to Minnie Dennis 22 S Salisbury MD Acc d/o D H & Ellen on 25 Jun 1884 at Conquest Ch by JW Carroll

JONES Lloyd 27 S Farmer Wor Co MD Acc s/o Geo T & Cora to Mary F Bull 23 S Acc Acc d/o Joseph T & Harriet E on 18 Dec 1879 near Hollies Ch by CC Wertenbaker

JONES Smith Col 20 S Laborer Acc Acc s/o Elsy to Margt H Jubilee Col 16 S Acc Acc d/o Jane on 11 Jan 1882 near Garret Lons Chp by JE Humphreys

JONES Thomas B 22 S U S Surfman Acc Acc s/o Burton & Sarah E to Maggie E Merritt 18 S Wor Co MD Acc d/o George & Catharine on 17 Apr 1895 at Chinco: Isld by CW Matthews

JOSEPH John Albert 29 S Fireman on RR Engine Sussex Co DE Wilmington DE s/o Gideon W & Elizabeth to Mary Elizabeth [Law] Laws 22 S Acc Acc d/o Walter & Mary Jane on 24 Dec 1889 at Franklin City by BP Truitt

JOYCE John 22 S Oysterman St Marys Co MD Acc to Nellie Crockett 17 S Acc Acc d/o Peter M & Sally A on 25 Dec 1893 at Tangier by ZH Webster

JOYNES Charles Col 27 S Farmer Acc Acc s/o Wilson & Amy to Susan Chandler Col 38 S Acc Acc d/o Sarah on 23 Jun 1895 at Acc by J Duckett

JOYNES Dennis Col 26 S Laborer Acc Acc s/o Dennis Sr & Alice S to Hester Selby Col 30 S Acc Acc on 5 Feb 1882 near Modest Town by JE Bundick

JOYNES Edward Col 56 S Teamster Acc Acc s/o Labra to Leah Drummond Col 30 S Acc Acc d/o Louisa on 22 Jan 1880 at Drum'tn by RH Govans

JOYNES Edward D 63 W Farmer Acc Acc s/o William R & Hetty to Margaret T Dunton 56 W Acc Acc d/o Elias & Margaret Ames on 3 Nov 1875 at Sluytkill Nk by JH Amiss

JOYNES Edward T 27 S Merchant Acc Acc s/o Edwd D & Ann C to Mary Ward 30 S Acc Acc d/o Wm on 12

Dec 1872 at Mt Oregon by EM Bryan

JOYNES Geo Savage Col 21 S Farmer Acc Acc s/o Smith & Harriet to Alicia Anna West Col 18 S Acc Acc d/o John R & Elia on 7 Jan 1886 at Drum'tn by LW Lee

JOYNES George Goodwin 24 S Teacher Acc Acc s/o Tully A T & Labra P to Sarah W Northam 21 S Acc Acc d/o Thomas A Vignetta A on 25 Nov 1880 at Onancock by SC Boston

JOYNES Henry Col 26 S Laborer Acc Acc s/o Kesiah Chandler to Mary J Young Col 19 S Acc Acc d/o Mary on 20 May 1880 near Acc C H by A Joynes

JOYNES Henry Col 25 S Farmer Acc Acc s/o Levin & Hester to Emma Ewell Col 23 S Acc Acc d/o Sarah on 16 Apr 1884 at Wiseville Ch by JH Nutter

JOYNES Henry C Col 22 S Farmer Acc Acc s/o Smith & Harriet to Mary Drummond Col 19 S Acc Acc d/o Spencer & Mariam on 24 Dec 1893 at Acc by PW Lee

JOYNES Hezekiah Col 28 S Wage-earner Acc Acc s/o John & Peggy to Ella Parker Col 22 S Acc Acc d/o Samuel & Mary on 26 May 1895 at Acc by J Duckett

JOYNES Isaac Col 24 S Laborer Acc Acc s/o Harriet to Amanda Seymour Col 24 S Acc Acc d/o Wm & Rose on 31 Dec 1878 at Acc by JW Diggs

JOYNES James FN 24 S Laborer Acc Acc s/o Arsena to Emma Joynes FN 26 S Acc Acc d/o Rebecca on 11 Mar 1866 at Acc by H Long

JOYNES John W 22 S Farmer Acc Acc s/o Edward D & Ann C to Ellen P Parker 18 S Acc Acc d/o John M & Ellen on 15 Dec 1870 at Onancock by E Hebard

JOYNES Joshua Col 44 S Laborer Acc Acc s/o Rhoda Davis to Sarah Ailworth Col 28 S Acc Acc d/o Kitty Allen on 1 Aug 1880 at St Luke Ch by PM Lewis

JOYNES Riley Smith Col 22 S Laborer Acc Acc s/o Harriet to Ida Seymour Col 21 S Acc Acc d/o Wm & Rose on 31 Dec 1878 at Acc by JW Diggs

JOYNES Seymour T Col 24 S Farmer Acc Acc s/o Smith & Harriet to Florence [Parks] Parkes Col 19 S Acc Acc d/o Michael & Arena on 9 Jun 1892 at Acc by PW Lee

JOYNES Southey Col 21 S Laborer Acc Acc s/o Isaac & Sarah to Susan A Kellam Col 20 S Acc Acc d/o Geo & Lucinda on 26 Dec 1872 at Onancock by R Davis

JOYNES Tho R Jr 26 S Farmer b: Drum'tn s/o Tho P & Ann B to Sally W Bagwell 25 S b: Acc d/o Tho P & Sally H on 12 Dec 1855 at Onancock by JM Cheveis(?) (John J Blackstone says both over 21)

JOYNES Thomas R 43 W Farmer Acc Acc to Mary A Smith 37 W Acc Acc on 31 Dec 1874 near Belle Haven by JE Humphreys

JOYNES Thomas R 40 S Farmer N'hamp: N'hamp: s/o Edwd & Sallie to Mary A Scarborough 24 S Acc Acc d/o Mitchell T & Hannah on 16 May 1883 at Powelton by JW Stiff

JOYNES Thomas S 24 S Carpenter s/o Elias & Sally to Sarah T Moore 26 S d/o Wm & Ginny lic: 14 Dec 1864 marr: 14 Dec 1864 at Accomack

JOYNES Thos S 34 W Carpenter Acc Acc s/o Elias D & Sally S to Harriet A Drummond 25 S Acc Acc d/o James & Ruth on 12 Dec 1877 at Anderson's Chp by JH Amiss

JOYNES William F 23 S Farmer N'hamp: Acc s/o Tully A T & Tabia P to Leah Gennie Hopkins 18 S Acc Acc d/o Wm H A on 19 May 1870 at Onancock by DA Woodson

JOYNES William J 31 S Farmer North Co VA Acc s/o John & Elishia to Mary J Doughty 25 S Acc Acc d/o Jno R & Mary R on 12 Jan 1869 at Acc by OP Twiford

JOYNES Wm 27 S Laborer Acc Acc s/o Sarah to Margaret Dix 16 S Acc Acc d/o Louis & Mary on 25 Dec 1869 at Acc by S Marshall

JUBILEE Custis Col 23 S Farmer Acc Acc s/o George & Jane to Ella Scarborough Col 21 S Acc Acc d/o Samuel & Louisa on 4 Mar 1893 at Acc by TW Nettles

JUBILEE Custis [Jublie] (Jubliee) (FN) 54 (widr) Laborer Acc Acc to Leah Elliott FN 52 Acc Acc d/o Eastes Elliott on 21 Nov 1858(?) at Upshur Nk by JW Ewell (Louis P Roberts says she over 21) Certificate returned 9 Apr 1858

JUBILEE John W Col 26 S Farmer Acc Acc s/o Wm & Henny to Isabella Roberts Col 18 S Acc Acc on 9 Feb 1876 at Garrisons Chp by JE Humphreys

JUBILEE Lewis Col 28 S Laborer Acc Acc s/o Custis to Mary Parramore Col 27 S Acc Acc d/o Abram & Lellie on 19 Dec 1883 at Acc by GW Young

JUBILEE Lloyd Col 23 S Farm Laborer Acc Acc s/o Mary to Melissa Mapp Col 19 S Acc Acc d/o Mary on 23 Dec 1883 at Acc by GW Young

JUBILEE William [Jubliee] Col 23 S Wage-earner Acc Acc s/o Geo & Jane to Harriet Bayly Col 24 S Acc Acc d/o Felix & Lina on 20 Dec 1893 at Acc by L Duncan

JUSTICE Alfred Col 21 S Laborer Acc Acc s/o Reelly to Elizabeth Twiford Col 23 S Acc Acc d/o Ritta on 6 Sep 1873 at Acc by A Joynes

JUSTICE Alfred [Justis] Col 20 S Farmer Acc Acc s/o Esther Wessels to Maggie Griffin Col 14 S Acc Acc d/o Hester on 6 Sep 1888 at Acc by AJ Satchell

JUSTICE Andrew R [Justis] 20 S Farmer Acc Acc s/o John & Melissa to Lelia E [Killmon] Killman 17 S Acc Acc d/o Alfred J & Margaret on 29 Dec 1889 at Parksley by HS Dulany

JUSTICE Anearus 19 S Farmer Acc Acc s/o Wm & Susan to Susan Ann Corbin 22 W Acc Acc d/o Wm C & Rose Ann Smith on 28 Dec 1881 at Downings Ch by RB Beadles

JUSTICE Arthur F 22 S Farmer & Mechanic Acc Acc s/o Thomas & Mary to Serena Drummond 23 S Acc Acc d/o Robinson & Malinda on 15 Dec 1875 at Messongo by M Oldham

JUSTICE Asa T 20 S Farmer Acc Acc s/o John & Malinda to Caroline Bundick 20 S Acc Acc d/o John & Mary on 26 Mar 1877 at Acc by M Oldham

JUSTICE Benjamin 23 S Oysterman DE Acc s/o Benj & Betsey to Polly Snead 22 W Acc Acc d/o Danl & Betsy Charnock on 15 May 1869 at Acc by P Bowdin Jr

JUSTICE Bennet [Justis] 24 S Waterman Acc Acc s/o Wm & Elishea to Julia Kelly 22 S Acc Acc d/o James on 29 Oct 1884 at Acc by AJ Walter

JUSTICE Charles 21 S Waterman Acc Acc s/o Wm & Sally to Melisa Barnes 21 S Acc Acc d/o Jas & Emeline on 23 Jun 1864 at r/o Jno Shrieves by ES Grant

JUSTICE Charles Col 24 S Laborer Acc Acc s/o Ibby Gibbons to Kitty Mason Col 23 S Acc Acc d/o Ann on 3 Oct 1874 at News Town by A Joynes

JUSTICE Charles Col 22 S Laborer Acc Acc s/o Easter to Jane Wessells Col 19 S Acc Acc d/o Anna on 5 Oct 1881 near Foxville by JE Bundick

JUSTICE Charles Col 23 S

Wage-earner Acc Acc s/o Sarah Poulson to Betsy Crippen Col 19 S Acc Acc d/o Martha A on 26 Apr 1891 near Mappsville by AJ Satchell

JUSTICE Charles J [Justis] 25 S Farmer Acc Acc s/o Revel (of I) & Nancy to Lacy M Bundick 20 S Acc Acc d/o Wm J & Seymour on 1 Dec 1889 at Mappsville by WA Street

JUSTICE Cornas 23 S Waterman Acc Acc s/o John & Catharine to Martha Parkes 23 S Acc Acc d/o Edwd & Nancy on 4 Jan 1880 at Guilford by FH Mullineaux

JUSTICE Daniel B (T) 24 S Farmer Acc Acc s/o Teackle & Tabitha to Emma Northam 25 S Acc Acc d/o Elijah & Comfort on 21 Oct 1874 at Bethel Ch by DA Woodson

JUSTICE Dennis Col 22 S Wage-earner Acc Acc to Sarah Nock Col 20 S Acc Acc d/o Burnetta on 10 Feb 1890 near Mappsville by JE Bundick

JUSTICE Edward [Justis] 24 S Carpenter Acc Acc s/o Thos & Mary to Elizabeth Hall 28 S Acc Acc d/o Hy & Sally on 31 Jan 1872 at Messongo by JC Reed

JUSTICE Edward B 19 S Grocer Acc Acc s/o Revel of J & Nancy to Alice L Bundick 19 S Acc Acc d/o Thos & Mary E on 9 Dec 1885 at Mappsville by WA Street

JUSTICE Edward T [Justis] 44 W Oysterman Acc Acc s/o Thomas & Mary to Cynthia [Parks] Parkes 28 S Acc Acc d/o Mark & Eliz'th on 2 Dec 1894 at Acc by DGC Butts

JUSTICE Francis 26 S Farmer Acc Acc s/o Wm & Susan to Annie L Warner 22 S Acc Acc d/o Solomon & Arinthia on 26 Dec 1883 at Oak Hall by RB Beadles

JUSTICE Frank P [Justis] 24 S Sailor Acc Acc s/o Saml & Lovey to Carrie S [Justis] Justice 19 S Acc Acc d/o Revel & Nancy on 29 Dec 1880 at Lee Mont by EG Chandler

JUSTICE Franklin [Jestis] 20 S Farmer Acc Acc s/o Jno & Malinda to Henrietta M Custis 20 S Acc Acc d/o Luther W & Ada on 9 Jan 1878 at Modest Town by DA Woodson

JUSTICE Geo T Col 21 S Farmer Acc Acc s/o Henry & Susan to Sarah Savage Col 20 S Acc Acc d/o Harry & Elizth on 4 Mar 1884 near Temp'ville by JC Cluff

JUSTICE George [Justis] Col 23 S Wage-earner Acc Acc s/o Ellen to Rachel Ann Byrd Col 22 S Acc Acc d/o Jane on 10 Oct 1895 near Mappsville by JC Cluff

JUSTICE George H 20 S Sailor Acc Acc s/o Teagle & Tabitha to Susan C Kelly 16 S Acc Acc d/o Richd & Elizabeth on 15 Mar 1876 at Bethel Ch by DA Woodson

JUSTICE George R [Justis] 20 S Farmer Acc Acc s/o Revel & Nancy to Elizabeth C Middleton 17 S Acc Acc d/o Geo & Eveline on 18 Jan 1872 at Hunting Ck by JC Reed

JUSTICE Isaac Col 43 S Farmer Acc Acc s/o Jeriah Hope to Mary Harmon Col 35 S Acc Acc d/o Peter on 9 Nov 1879 at Temp'ville by JC Cluff

JUSTICE Isaac Col 47 W Farmer Acc Acc s/o Isaiah Hope & Sarah Justice to Virginia Nock Col 30 S Acc Acc d/o Dennis & Sallie on 30 Jan 1887 at Temp'ville by JC Cluff

JUSTICE Isaiah 25 S Farmer Acc Acc s/o Wm & Sarah to Margt S Taylor 18 S Acc Acc d/o John & Cath on 20 Dec 1866 at Acc by ES Grant

JUSTICE Isaiah F 22 S Sailor Acc Acc s/o Jno & Cath to Cynthiana [Shreaves] Shrieves 18 S Acc Acc d/o Jno & Elizth on 26 Dec 1875 at Acc by RC Jones

JUSTICE Isaiah P 26 S Sailor Acc Acc s/o Revel & Nancy to Adaline W

Wessells 24 S Acc Acc d/o David B & Nancy on 21 May 1876 at Woodstock by RC Jones

JUSTICE James 21 S Laborer Acc Acc s/o Sarah to Hester Johnson 22 S MD Acc on 25 Apr 1869 at Acc by A Joynes

JUSTICE James [Justis] 21 S Merchant b: Acc s/o James to Elizabeth Small 23 S b: Acc d/o Solomon & Sally on 2 Apr 1855 at r/o Geo H Ewell by GH Ewell

JUSTICE James Edward 22 S Farmer Acc Acc s/o Teackle & Tabitha to Betty Satchell 22 S Acc Acc d/o Henry on 4 Nov 1869 at Acc by M Oldham

JUSTICE James H ward/o Southy T Lucas who gave consent to Eliz Small d/o Solomon lic: 26 Mar 1855 Richard P Byrd says she over 21

JUSTICE James Lee 21 S Farmer Acc Acc s/o Revel of S & Nancy to Eva S Shrieves 18 S Acc Acc d/o Jno & Virginia on 16 Mar 1884 at Acc by JW Carroll

JUSTICE James Thos 27 S Sailor Acc Acc s/o Wm & Eliza to Jane Lewis 26 S Acc Acc d/o Thos P & Margt on 9 Mar 1872 at Guilford by JET Ewell

JUSTICE Jno Wesley 23 S Oysterman Acc Acc s/o John H & Adaline to Mary C Wilkerson 18 S Acc Acc d/o Margaret on 15 Jul 1876 at Saxes Isld by JM Anderson

JUSTICE John to Malinda Wright d/o Catherine who gave consent lic: 30 Aug 1854

JUSTICE John 24 S Oysterman Acc Acc s/o Wm (of J) & Elizabeth to Margaret Wessells 14 S Acc Acc d/o Sarah on 3 Aug 1865 at Acc by ES Grant

JUSTICE John Col 24 S Farm Laborer Acc Acc s/o Hetty Conquest to Ellen Dickerson Col 21 S Acc Acc on 18 Jul 1880 at First Bapt Ch by A Joynes

JUSTICE John C 27 S Merchant Acc Acc s/o Revel of J & Nancy to Marcella A Lewis 21 S Acc Acc d/o Wm R & Sally on 9 Apr 1873 at Hunting Ck by JET Ewell

JUSTICE John H 52 S Oysterman Acc Acc s/o Richd & Esther to Mary Miles 45 S Acc Acc d/o Geo Crockett on 27 Feb 1881 at Sykes Isld by RB Beadles

JUSTICE John P 24 S Sailor Acc Acc s/o Jno & Catharine to Elizabeth S Parkes 22 S Acc Acc d/o Edwd & Ann on 12 Dec 1875 near Guilford by IT Adkins

JUSTICE John W [Justis] 22 S Sailor Acc Acc s/o Isaiah W & Margaret to Lew E Killman 17 S Acc Acc d/o Thomas S of C & Larua on 24 May 1893 at Lee Mont by JET Ewell

JUSTICE Joseph 22 S Farmer Acc Acc s/o Thomas & Mary to Mary A Miles 21 S Acc Acc d/o David D B & Mary on 24 May 1882 at Acc by RB Beadles

JUSTICE Joseph C ward/o Richard Conquest who gave consent to Mary R Nock wid/o Albert lic: 21 Jun 1856

JUSTICE Judson L 24 S Farmer Acc Acc s/o John & Malinda to Maggie C Shrieves 22 S Acc Acc d/o Jno Thomas & Margaret on 2 Jan 1889 at Parksley by HS Dulany

JUSTICE Lewis Col 21 S Sailor Acc Acc s/o Betsy Griffin to Margaret Young Col 15 S Acc Acc d/o Laura on 31 Dec 1878 at the Parsonage by A Handy

JUSTICE Maurice 25 S Farmer Acc Acc to Sarah Ann Bundick 18 S Acc Acc d/o Thomas & Mary on 1 Jan 1888 at bride's home by JW Norris

JUSTICE Parker 30 S Farming Acc Acc s/o Polly to Comfort [Killmon]

Killman 34 S Acc Acc d/o John & Nancy on 6 Jun 1861 at Acc by GH Ewell (William Taylor says both over 21)

JUSTICE Raymond 25 S Sailor Acc Acc s/o Wm & Elizth to Virginia J Middleton 17 S Acc Acc d/o Geo & Eveline on 28 Dec 1879 at Acc by FH Mullineaux

JUSTICE Revel J 26 S Oysterman Acc Acc s/o Revel & Nancy to Nancy R Middleton 16 S Acc Acc d/o Geo & Eveline C on 26 Jan 1873 at Acc by JET Ewell

JUSTICE Revel J (James) 23 S Waterman Acc Acc s/o Jno & Catharine to Sally Mason 20 S Acc Acc d/o Wm & Tabatha on 17 Dec 1863 at Acc by ES Grant

JUSTICE Robert L [Justis] 23 S Sailor Acc Acc s/o Revel J & Sallie to Lena T Annis 14 S Acc Acc d/o Maggie S on 30 Dec 1888 at Crowsontown by HS Dulany

JUSTICE Samuel 45 W Farmer Acc Acc s/o Ismiah & Sally to Mary A White 35 S Acc Acc d/o Henry B & Hetty on 28 Feb 1872 near Woodstock by DA Woodson

JUSTICE Samuel Col 25 S Laborer Acc Acc s/o Ibby Gibbons to Rosy Parkes Col 19 S Acc Acc d/o Major & Elsie Duffee on 31 Dec 1873 near News Town by A Joynes

JUSTICE Samuel 30 S Waterman Acc Acc s/o William & Eliza to Missouri E Hickman 19 S Acc Acc d/o Jno S & Matilda on 6 Feb 1881 at Mr Hickman's by LB Betty

JUSTICE Samuel (of B) 27 S Sailor Acc Acc s/o Revel of B & Nancy to Vienna Silverthorn 22 S Acc Acc d/o Saml C & Mary on 15 Dec 1870 at Acc by JET Ewell

JUSTICE Samuel G [Justis] 37 S Wage-earner Acc Acc s/o John & Malinda to Sallie V Simpson 16 S Acc Acc d/o Reuben & Jane on 31 Dec 1893 at Woodbury by WF Hayes

JUSTICE Samuel R Col 67 W Farmer Acc Acc s/o Richard & Tabitha to Ann Townsend Col 34 S Acc Acc d/o Littleton & Tabitha on 1 May 1874 at Hell Town by JE Bundick

JUSTICE William 25 S Acc Acc s/o William & Susan to Sally Dix 23 S Acc Acc d/o William & Susan on 22 Oct 1873 at Temp'ville by M Oldham

JUSTICE William T 22 S Farmer Acc Acc s/o Jno of J & Catharine to Arinthia S Taylor 16 S Acc Acc d/o Jno W & Elizth on 21 Jan 1883 at Acc by WA Crouse

JUSTICE Wm F 25 S Farmer Acc Acc s/o Revel & Nancy to Elizth S Barnes 19 S Acc Acc d/o Parker & Jane S on 17 Sep 1882 at Acc by LB Betty

JUSTICE Wm H Col 21 S Laborer Acc Acc s/o Henry & Louisa to Matilda [Staten] Staton Col 17 S Acc Acc d/o Ann on 7 Oct 1884 at Acc by JC Cluff

KAMBARN John D 25 S employed on Winter Quarter US Lt Ship Easton PA Acc s/o Criss to Mary E Fletcher 18 S Acc Acc d/o John W & Nancy on 22 Jan 1890 at Chinco: Isld by SU Grimsley

KAY Edward L 21 S Barrel Cooper Norfolk Co Norfolk Co s/o Mary to Maggie S Gardner 21 S Acc Acc d/o William T & Marg't S on 5 Sep 1893 at Onancock by AJ Reamy

KEER Robert Col 21 S Sailor Acc Acc s/o John & Susannah to Charity Parker Col 18 S Acc Acc d/o Isaac & Susan on 19 May 1871 at Savageville by WF Williams

KEESER John 22 S Wage-earner Acc Acc s/o Ann to Sophia M Evans 23 S Acc Acc d/o Denard & Sallie on 7 May 1890 at Onancock by GW Burke

KELLAM Alfred Col 21 S Laborer Acc Acc s/o Mary to Mary Alice Susan Fitchett Col 20 S Acc Acc d/o Mary on 15 Nov 1874 at Savageville by JK Plato

KELLAM Alfred S 22 S Farmer Acc Acc s/o Jno R & Mary E to Eliza B James 19 S Acc Acc d/o Thomas H & Tabitha A B on 4 Sep 1872 at Oak Grove Chp by O Littleton

KELLAM Andrew J Col 31 S Farmer Acc Acc s/o Thos H & Margt to Maggie S Burton Col 20 S Acc Acc d/o Jno R & Sally M on 22 Oct 1884 at Acc by WC Vaden

KELLAM Benjamin J 29 S Farmer Acc Acc s/o Stockly & Comfort to Catharine Young 20 S N'hamp: Acc d/o Ezekiel & Elizth on 18 Apr 1857 at Slutkill Nk by M Oldham (Thos W Blackstone says he over 21)

KELLAM Delaware Col 30 S Laborer Acc Acc to Mary Ann Taylor Col 40 S Acc Acc d/o Ann on 9 Dec 1880 at Belle Haven by SMG Copeland

KELLAM Douglas Col 21 S Farmer Acc Acc s/o Samuel & Emma to Sarah Frances Seymour Col 20 S Acc Acc d/o Mary S on 6 Dec 1888 at Acc by JA Haynes

KELLAM Edmund Col 50 S Farmer Acc Acc s/o Peggy Bird to Ann Walker Col 35 S Acc Acc d/o Adah on 16 Aug 1873 at Bay Side Ch by N Morris

KELLAM Edward Col 37 S Farmer Acc Acc s/o Mary Floyd to Adeline Mears Col 25 S Acc Acc d/o Lanetta on 26 Nov 1878 near Locustville by LK LeCato

KELLAM Edward Col 22 S Blacksmith N'hamp: Acc to Florence Phillips Col 24 W Acc Acc d/o Sarah on 14 Dec 1882 at Onancock by JC Ayler

KELLAM Edward L 27 S Farmer Acc Acc s/o John W & Indiana A to Fannie A Mears 16 S Acc Acc d/o Geo S G & Marianna on 18 Feb 1891 at Pungo: by JM Anderson

KELLAM Edward O 28 W Farmer Acc Acc s/o Revel & Jane to Manie E Bull 21 S Acc Acc d/o Benjamin F & Bettie on 4 Apr 1888 at Drum'tn by WJ Twilley

KELLAM Edward W s/o Agryle to Rosa Ann Hyslop d/o James lic: 1 Apr 1854 James Ed Kellam said both over 21

KELLAM Edwin E 34 S Physician Acc Acc s/o Jas (of A) to Bettie U Savage 24 S Acc Acc d/o Jas M on 7 Feb 1867 at Acc by JD Thomas

KELLAM Erastus A to Mary M Nottingham d/o Severn E lic: 28 Jan 1861 Thomas U Falio says both over 21

KELLAM Esau C 36 S Teacher Acc Acc s/o Jno & Betsy to Mary E Linton 19 S Acc Acc d/o Geo & Nancy on 17 Sep 1879 at Pocomoke by JE Bundick

KELLAM Frederick S Col 22 S Wage-earner Acc Acc s/o John L & Eve to Mary Eliz'th Duncan Col 21 S Acc Acc d/o Fannie Bunting on 14 Oct 1894 at Acc by TW Nettles

KELLAM Fredrick C A Jr 30 S Physician Acc Acc s/o Frederick C A Sr & Eliza to Bettie B Ames 30 W Acc Acc d/o John R & Mary Doughty on 20 Aug 1875 near Belle Haven by HM Anderson

KELLAM George 24 S Sailor Acc Acc s/o Leah to Mary Read 24 S Acc Acc d/o Sarah on 4 Apr 1869 at Acc by JH Addison

KELLAM George Col 35 S Farmer Acc Acc to Emma Parker Col 40 S Acc Acc on 24 Nov 1875 at Acc by HT Rich

KELLAM George C Col 47 S Farmer Acc Acc s/o Rose to Lucinda Bayly Col 44 S Acc Acc d/o Hetty on 11 Apr 1878 at Onancock by JK Plato

KELLAM George C Col 23 S Farmer Acc Acc s/o George & Lucinda to Mary Jane Watson Col 18 S Acc Acc d/o Sally on 25 Dec 1881 at Onancock by JC Ayler

KELLAM George C Col 32 W Farmer Acc Acc s/o George C & Lucinda to Sarah E Grant Col 26 S Acc Acc d/o Edward & Mary on 13 Jul 1892 at Savageville by JH Offer

KELLAM George E Col 20 S Farmer Acc Acc s/o Edmund & Adelaide to Mary E Snead Col 21 S Acc Acc d/o Mary on 24 Dec 1890 at Acc by N Morris

KELLAM George E G Col 20 S Barber Acc Acc s/o Samuel S & Emma S to Annie Walker Col 18 S Acc Acc d/o Nellie on 21 Dec 1892 near Savageville by JH Offer

KELLAM Henry Col 21 S Laborer Acc Acc s/o Margt to Delilah Collins Col 21 S Acc Acc on 13 Feb 1879 at Onancock by PA Leatherbury

KELLAM Henry 24 S Sailor Acc Acc to Mary E Jubilee Col 23 S Acc Acc d/o Mary on 21 Jul 1881 at Locust Mount by JWA Elliott

KELLAM Henry Col 51 S Laborer Acc Acc s/o Milly to Easter Johnson Col 60 S N'hamp: Acc d/o Juda on 18 Oct 1881 at Locust Mount by JWA Elliott

KELLAM Horace Col 38 S Laborer Acc Acc s/o Jno & Milly to Charlotte Poulson Col 23 S Acc Acc d/o Jno & Eleanna on 8 Nov 1882 at Onancock by JC Ayler

KELLAM Isaac Col 24 S Sailor Acc Acc s/o Sarah to Maggie Ashby Col 21 S Acc Acc d/o Caroline on 13 Feb 1879 at Acc by RH Govans

KELLAM James 37 S Farmer Acc Acc s/o Sally to Elizabeth Turner 22 S Acc Acc d/o Saml & Sally on 12 Sep 1862 at Acc by JWA Elliott

KELLAM James 45 W Farmer Acc Acc s/o Sally to Sarah W [Rodgers] Rogers 19 S Acc Acc d/o Susan on 1 Jun 1870 at Acc by E Hebard

KELLAM James C 28 S Farmer N'hamp: N'hamp: s/o Saml E D & Louisa to Virginia C Sturgis 24 S Acc Acc d/o Francis m & Polly on 17 Dec 1885 at Franktown M E Ch by EH Pritchell

KELLAM James F 23 S Farmer Acc Acc s/o M Judson & Cordelia to Flora A King 21 S Reidsville NC Acc on 10 Jan 1894 at Keller by JM Dunaway

KELLAM James Hy 26 S Farmer Acc Acc s/o Edward W & Annie to Georgie E Garrison 17 S Acc Acc d/o George & Juliet on 28 Dec 1881 at Acc by CD Crawley

KELLAM James Isaac Col 30 W Farmer Acc Acc s/o Peter & Sarah to Anne Harmon Col 19 S Acc Acc d/o Caroline Ashby on 17 Sep 1885 at Drum'tn by LW Lee

KELLAM James Thomas (Col) 20 S Acc Acc s/o Henry & Rosey to Harriet Wise (Col) 20 S Acc Acc d/o Lietago Wise & Leah Rodgers on 18 Apr 1870 at Onancock by WF Williams

KELLAM John 21 S Farmer Acc Acc s/o Nanny to Georgianna Snead 16 S Acc Acc d/o Abel & Nanny on 16 Jan 1868 at Acc by WT Tull

KELLAM John Col 45 S Farmer Acc Acc s/o Eli Teackle & Sarah to Eve Satchell Col 45 S Acc Acc d/o Adam & Bridget on 6 Jan 1870 near Pungo: by OP Twiford

KELLAM John Col 21 W Laborer Acc Acc s/o Nannie to Nice Smith Col 21 S Acc Acc d/o Nat Parker & Nice on 21 May 1871 at Acc by JH Addison

KELLAM John E Col 22 S Laborer Acc Acc to Susan Downing Col 19 S Acc Acc d/o Henry & Susan on 1 Sep 1881 at Acc by RJ Waters

KELLAM John H 24 S Farmer Acc Acc s/o Revel R & June to Cecilia M Chandler 20 S Acc Acc d/o Thomas M & Mary S on 30 Jan 1889 at Davis Wharf by JH Riddick

KELLAM John M Col 32 S Wage-earner Acc Acc s/o Louisa to Susan Martin Col 21 S Acc Acc d/o Mary Boggs on 4 Apr 1893 at Acc by LW Lee

KELLAM John R 47 W Farmer Acc Acc s/o Custis to Bettie W Kellam 21 S Acc Acc d/o Thos J & Margt on 31 Dec 1866 at Acc by JWA Elliott

KELLAM John W 20 S Physician Acc Acc s/o Jno R & Mary F to Mary E Ashby 21 S Acc Acc d/o Albert G & Belle on 18 Dec 1879 at Jn Bell's Nk by CC Wertenbaker

KELLAM John W 25 S Farmer Acc Acc s/o Wm H & Sarah C to Mary J Jones 20 S Acc Acc d/o Wm & Jane on 21 Dec 1879 at Craddockville by E Hebard

KELLAM Lee G Col 21 S Farmer Laborer Acc Acc s/o Adah to Rachel Nock Col 21 S Acc Acc d/o Eliza on 5 Jul 1882 near Locust Mount by JWA Elliott

KELLAM Lorenzo Col 25 S Farmer Acc Acc s/o John L Kellam & Emma Bayly to Cornelia Bayly Col 25 W Acc Acc d/o George & Eliza Sample on 30 Mar 1890 at Acc by L Duncan

KELLAM Nathanjel J 23 S Farmer Acc Acc s/o James & Patience S to Cordelia A Bell 22 S Acc Acc d/o Lorenzo D & Aley A on 15 Nov 1866 at Acc by LK LeCato

KELLAM Peter Col 45 S Laborer Acc Acc s/o Mary to Sarah Kellam Col 40 S Acc Acc d/o Sarah Phillips on 1 Apr 1886 at Drum'tn by LW Lee

KELLAM Richard W to Missouria A Kellam d/o (George A & ward/o Richard W Kellam who gave consent) on 14 Nov 1860 at N'hamp:

by M Oldham (Thomas H G Poulson says he over 21)

KELLAM Robert W T 22 S Farmer Acc Acc s/o Thomas & Tabitha to Emma S James 18 S Acc Acc d/o Jno T & Susan on 28 Dec 1871 at Locustville by JWA Elliott

KELLAM S E 22 S Farmer N'hamp: N'hamp: s/o Samuel E & Louisa H to Maggie A Sturgis 19 S N'hamp: Acc d/o F M & Dolly on 24 Nov 1885 at Franktown by JW Stiff

KELLAM Severn A 28 S Farmer Acc N'hamp: s/o Augustus & Mary Kellam to Susan M Ames 18 S Acc Acc d/o James S. & Susan Ames on 24 Jan 1876 at Acc by FR Boston

KELLAM Shaderick T 28 S Shoemaker Acc Acc s/o Thos & Eliza to Mary E Martin 19 S Baltimore City Acc d/o Isaac S & Jane on 28 Nov 1866 at Acc by AB Dolly

KELLAM Shelton Col 29 S Laborer Acc Acc to Jennie Turlington Col 18 S Acc Acc d/o Isaac & Betsy on 15 Dec 1886 at Locust Mount by JWA Elliott

KELLAM Shephard (S) 29 S Farmer Acc Acc s/o Stockly & Mary to Mary M Stringer 25 S Acc Acc d/o Benj & Caroline on 28 Jan 1864 at Acc by LK LeCato

KELLAM Sidney Thos 32 S Mechanic Acc Acc s/o Benj J & Catharine to Minnie G Ames 19 S Acc Acc d/o John H & Mary F on 30 Mar 1892 at Locustville by VW Bargamin

KELLAM Tankard G 18 S Farmer Acc Acc s/o John R & Bettie to Bertie Pennewell 17 S Pocomoke City MD Acc d/o Robert H & Martha on 15 Jan 1890 at Locustville by RA Compton

KELLAM Teackle Col 45 S Farmer Acc Acc s/o Mille to Rachel Hatton Col 30 S Acc Acc d/o Cassandra on 24 Nov 1881 at Locust Mount by JWA

KELLAM Thomas Col 22 S Wage-earner N'hamp: Acc s/o Samuel & Sarah to Hennie Jones Col 21 S Acc Acc d/o Elijah & Arinthia on 14 Nov 1888 at Acc by L Duncan

KELLAM Thomas C 21 S Merchant Acc Acc s/o John R & Mary to Julia A Ames 21 S Acc Acc d/o Benj T & Julia on 13 Jan 1869 at Acc by JC Martin

KELLAM Thomas of P 40 W Farmer to Leah Cobb 40 W lic: 11 Jan 1865 marr: 11 Jan 1865

KELLAM Thomas S 21 S Farmer Acc Acc s/o Thos & Polly to Mary S White 17 S Acc Acc d/o Elijah A J & Susan on 24 Dec 1876 at Peter East's by JH Amiss

KELLAM Thomas T (widr) to Margaret S Cropper on 18 Jul 1860 at N'hamp: by M Oldham (Charles K Taylor says she over 21)

KELLAM Thos 25 W Farmer Acc Acc s/o Thos of Thos to Elishua Rayfield 16 S Acc Acc d/o Major & Elizabeth on 8 Oct 1882 at Onancock by SC Boston

KELLAM Thos H 27 S Gentleman Acc Acc s/o Thos Hatton & Susan C to Sudie L Higgins 30 S Acc Acc d/o Michael H & Mary Anna on 13 Sep 1877 near Onancock by WJ Duhadway

KELLAM Walter Col 29 S Farmer Acc Acc s/o Jane to Cordelia Bayly Col 21 S Acc Acc d/o Harriet on 2 Sep 1880 at Belle Haven by SMG Copeland

KELLAM William Col 27 S Farmer Acc Acc s/o Teagle & Rachel to Rosetta Bayly Col 21 S Acc Acc d/o John & Rose Ann on 21 Jan 1891 at Acc by L Duncan

KELLAM William 20 S Farmer Acc Acc s/o Margaret to Ella Mears 21 S Acc Acc d/o Lorenzo & Sally on 25 Dec 1895 at Acc by JWA Elliott

KELLAM William B 62 W Sailor Acc Acc s/o Jane & Easter to Margaret Smith 24 S Acc Acc d/o John W & Malinda on 15 Jun 1874 at Onancock by LK LeCato

KELLAM William E 27 W Farmer Wash DC Acc s/o Charles & Margt to Susan Knock 37 W Acc Acc d/o Wm & Nancy Phillips on 15 Oct 1856 at r/o W Thos Bell by RB Hazzard

KELLAM William T 23 S Sailor Acc Acc s/o Revil R & Elizth to Emily J Mister 20 S Acc Acc d/o Edward C on 20 Sep 1874 at Acc by JWA Elliott

KELLAM Wm C Col 29 S Farmer Acc Acc s/o Thos A & Mary A to Matilda S Bundick 23 S Acc Acc d/o Wm & Nancy on 2 Jul 1884 at Locust Mount by JWA Elliott

KELLAM Wm E s/o Chas to Elizth S Bloxom wid on 5 Aug 1852 by J Allen

KELLAM Wm Hy Col 22 S Wage-earner Acc Acc s/o Charles Kellam to Maggie Ward Col 21 S Acc Acc d/o Anna Ward on 12 Nov 1892 at Savageville by JH Offer

KELLAM Zorobabel Col 23 S Farmer Acc Acc s/o Jane to Elizabeth Savage Col 17 S Acc Acc d/o John & Annie on 13 Jan 1887 at A J Satchell's by AJ Satchell

KELLY Able G 25 S Farmer b: Acc s/o Wescoat & Elizabeth to Mary A Beloate 20 S b: Acc d/o Joseph & Elizabeth on 11 Sep 1856 at r/o J Beloat by BT Ames

KELLY Alexander 27 S Farmer Acc Acc s/o James to Edna [Parks] Parkes 19 S Acc Acc d/o Albert S & Emma on 18 Jan 1888 at Acc by TG Pullen

KELLY Arzila F 23 S Farmer Acc Acc s/o Elijah E & Hetty Ann to Laura T

Johnson 16 S Acc Acc d/o Sylvester & Sally on 25 Dec 1878 at Temp'ville by JE McSparran

KELLY Augustus C 28 S Farmer Acc Acc s/o Elijah & Hetty to Mary E Conquest 19 S Acc Acc d/o Alfred & Delila on 21 Dec 1881 at Atlantic by LB Betty

KELLY Clyde 20 S Farmer Acc Acc s/o William & Susan to Susan E Edwards 21 S Acc Acc d/o Esan & Martha on 23 Jan 1889 at Onancock by JW Easley

KELLY Daniel 24 S Farmer Acc Acc s/o George W & Elizth to Melinda Churn 23 S Acc Acc d/o Edward & Mary on 7 Jan 1875 at Temp'ville by JM Anderson

KELLY Daniel John (Kelley) widr to Betsy Spence wid lic: 3 Oct 1855

KELLY Edward F 22 S Farming Acc Acc s/o Edwd Kelly & Rosey Bradford to Sarah A Hart 18 S Acc Acc d/o Richd Hart & Nancy Simson on 28 Nov 1858 at Acc by T Waters (Benjamin T W Byrd say he over 21)

KELLY Elijah B s/o James dec'd to Eveline Byrd d/o John W who gave consent lic: 5 Jan 1854 Martin K Kelly says he over 21

KELLY Fennick W 41 S Farmer Acc Acc to Matt L M Duer 18 S Acc Acc d/o Joshua & Sally on 7 Dec 1869 at Acc by JE Humphreys

KELLY George W 38 S Farmer Acc Acc s/o Wescoat to Elizabeth C Ward 28 S Acc Acc d/o William & Susan on 24 Apr 1870 at Acc by JC Martin

KELLY George W Col 26 S Wage-earner Acc Acc to Sarah A Drummond Col 28 S Acc Acc d/o William Tull on 16 Oct 1889 at Pitts Wharf by N Morris

KELLY Henry 21 S Oysterman Acc Acc s/o Edward H & Sarah to Eva Trader 14 S Acc Acc d/o Osborne J & Sarah A on 3 May 1893 at Acc by JL King

KELLY James to Critty Lang lic: 30 May 1859 Henry Chesser says both over 21

KELLY James 28 W Laborer Acc Acc s/o Geo to Mary F (Frances) Dix 21 S Middlesex Co VA Acc d/o Asa & Mary Ann on 5 Mar 1868 at Acc by ES Grant

KELLY James J 22 S Farmer St Geo Parish Back Ck s/o Thomas Kelley to Mary J Bundick 24 S Acc Back Ck d/o George & Ann on 22 Mar 1861 at Zorobable Mason's by GH Ewell (George Thomas Russell says both over 21)

KELLY James T 38 W Laborer Acc Acc s/o Thomas & Souphey to Emma Taylor 30 W Acc Acc d/o Justice B & Eliza on 24 Sep 1874 at Zion Chp by EM Bryan

KELLY Jas F 59 W b: Som Co MD to Emily Lewis 29 S b: Acc d/o Jas & Kessy on 6 Dec 1854 at r/o Jas Lewis by ES Grant

KELLY Jesse 24 S Farmer Acc Acc s/o George W & Elizabeth to Lizzie J Trader 18 S Acc Acc d/o Thomas & Sarah J on 26 Dec 1888 at Acc by WA Street

KELLY John [Kelley] 21 S Oysterman Wor Co MD Acc s/o Bowman & Sally to Phoebe E Young 18 S Acc Acc d/o Theodore J & Mary on 1 Nov 1892 at Chinco: Isld by RB Sanford

KELLY John W 20 S Photographie Artist N'hamp: N'hamp: s/o Thimothy to Emaline [Houston alis Holston] Houston 17 S Acc Acc d/o Joseph & Comfort on 3 Apr 1880 at bride's home by TAH O'Brien

KELLY John W 22 S Farmer Acc Acc s/o Elijah B & Evaline to Eveline C Wessells 17 S Acc Acc d/o Richard on 3 Jan 1894 at Acc by JR Tillery

KELLY Joseph Custis 24 S Engineer Tuckerton NJ Acc s/o James W & Hannah L to Bettie Eva Bonnewell 22 S Acc Acc d/o Thomas & Margaret on 26 Dec 1888 at Acc by JH Riddick

KELLY Martin K 21 S Farmer Acc Acc s/o John W & Margaret to Clara V Johnson 18 S Acc Acc d/o Wm J (of S) & Sarah W on 25 Dec 1894 at Acc by GJ Hill

KELLY Oscar A 24 S Farmer Acc Acc s/o Abel G & Mary A to Lillie E Hart 21 S Acc Acc d/o Robert D & Catherine on 18 Dec 1895 at Onley by LJ Hitt

KELLY Parker 23 S Farmer Acc Acc s/o Edward to Pamelia Prescott 18 S Acc Acc d/o John & Hetty on 26 Jan 1859 at r/o Davis Taylor (David R Taylor says both over 21)

KELLY Parker S 26 S Farmer Acc Acc s/o Geo W & Eliz to Annie Susan Byrd 22 S Acc Acc d/o Jacob & Susan on 7 Feb 1883 at Acc by WP Wright

KELLY Peter 22 S Farmer Acc Acc s/o Sarah to Eliza Justice 16 S Acc Acc d/o Sarah on 7 Mar 1869 at Acc by A Joynes

KELLY Richard W 27 S Farmer Acc Acc s/o Richard E & Elizth to Susan Ross 24 S Acc Acc d/o Silvester & Melinda on 4 Apr 1880 at Conquest Ch by JW Hundley

KELLY Riley L 32 S Shoemaker Acc Acc s/o Elijah to Mary E Gladding 18 S Acc Acc d/o Bagwell B & Mary A on 22 Jul 1879 at Bethel Ch by JE Bundick

KELLY Thomas [Kelley] 22 S Oysterman Acc Acc s/o Edward F & Sarah to Ocia Chesser 16 S Acc Acc d/o Thorogood & Elizabeth on 30 Dec 1885 at Acc by WA Street

KELLY Thos C 26 S Farmer Acc Acc s/o Elijah & Hetty to Sally C Nock 16 S Acc Acc d/o Edward & Mary on 22 Nov 1866 at Acc by M Oldham

KELLY Wescoat 78 W Farmer Acc Acc s/o Wm & Margt to Mary R Watson 59 W Acc Acc on 25 Feb 1869 at Acc by JC Martin

KELLY William H 49 W Farmer Acc Som Co MD s/o Thomas & Sophia to Nancy Adams 45 W Acc Acc d/o Thomas & Margaret West on 24 Feb 1895 at Acc by MF Sanford

KELLY William Morris 19 S Farmer Acc Acc s/o William P & Susan A to Mary E Knight 17 S Acc Acc d/o William R & Peggie on 12 Apr 1893 at Temp'ville by JW Nicholson

KELLY Wm D 35 W Farmer Acc Acc to Susan A Wyatt 25 W Acc Acc d/o Edwd Watson on 9 Apr 1868 at Acc by BT Ames

KELSO John 45 W Mariner Scotland Acc to Susan J Mason 30 S Acc Acc d/o Geo W & Ann on 9 Sep 1875 near Savageville by RC Jones

KEMERLE John 37 S Shoemaker Garland Switzerland Acc s/o John & Barbara to Margaret Jane Ames 25 W Acc Acc d/o Eliza Elliott (Wm) & (wid/o Wm) on 15 Jan 1860 at Acc by P Warren (Littleton Savage says he over 21)

KEMMERLE John 30 W Shoemaker Switzerland Acc to Emma J Savage 25 S Acc Acc d/o James K & Margt A on 16 Dec 1866 at Acc by JH Addison

KEMMERLY Jno 52 W Cordwainer Switzerland Acc to Catharine Richardson 40 W Acc Acc d/o Lancelott Ward on 24 Dec 1879 at Locustville by JWA Elliott

KENNARD George W 30 S Painter Kent Co MD Wilmington DE s/o Moses to Emma L [Shields] Shield 25 W Acc Acc d/o Solomon & Arinthia Warner on 2 May 1894 at Oak Hall

by DJ Traynham
KENNARD Philips 51 W Merchant Acc Acc to Emma Laura Garrison 29 W Acc Acc d/o Jno & Margt Mears on 26 Dec 1866 at Acc by LK LeCato
KENT Thomas Irving 36 W Merchant Wic Co MD Acc s/o James & Leah to Mary Susan Melson 26 W Acc Acc d/o William T & Susan M Lewis on 22 May 1889 at Parksley by HS Dulany
KERR George Col 29 S Farmer Acc Acc s/o Rose Wright to Lucy Jane [Beckett] Becket Col 25 S Acc Acc d/o Ann on 15 Oct 1881 at Drum'tn by PM Lewis
KILLMAN Adolphus A [Killmon] 19 S Farmer Acc Acc s/o Ezekiel H & Mary to Lillie C Scott 17 S Acc Acc d/o Thomas C & Patience on 14 Dec 1892 at Acc by AC Berryman
KILLMAN Alfred J [Kilmon] 21 S Mariner Acc Acc s/o John & Virginia to Margaret S Justice single Acc Acc d/o Revel & Nancy on 6 Jan 1870 at Guilford by JET Ewell
KILLMAN Alonzo M 22 S Sailor Acc Acc s/o Ezekiel H & Mary W to Olivia B Scott 18 S Acc Acc d/o William W & Panlina(?) on 11 Apr 1894 at Acc by AJ Reamy
KILLMAN Andrew J 20 S Sailor Acc Acc s/o John W & Elizth to Elizth A Crockett 17 S Acc Acc d/o Southey & Rachel on 29 Mar 1876 at Slutkill Nk by JH Amiss
KILLMAN Arthur 23 S Sailor Acc Acc s/o Saml & Katy to Annie D [Bennet] Bennett 16 S Acc Acc d/o James H & Margt on 7 Jan 1880 near Pungo: by E Hebard
KILLMAN Augustus 21 S Farmer Acc Acc s/o Saml & Kittie to Elizabeth Mears 27 S Acc Acc d/o Robert & Sally on 11 Jan 1874 near r/o Dora Mears by JE Humphreys
KILLMAN Charles Thomas 22 S Oysterman Acc Acc s/o Thomas & Laura W to Marceline E Ewell 21 S Acc Acc d/o Solomon & Eleanor on 10 Oct 1888 at Acc by HS Dulany
KILLMAN Clarence Snow [Killmon] 20 S Farmer Acc Acc s/o John H & Maggie S to Ethel Thomas 17 S Acc Acc d/o Joshua P & Susan on 9 Jan 1895 at Acc by EC Atkins
KILLMAN Edward 80 W Farmer Acc Acc to Elizth Moore 60 S Acc Acc d/o Levi on 14 Mar 1877 at Cashville by JH Amiss
KILLMAN Ellis 57 W Farmer Acc Acc s/o John & Nancy to Sarah E [William] Williams 35 S Acc Acc on 2 Apr 1882 at Guilford Ch by M Oldham
KILLMAN Ezekiel H (Hy) [Killmon] 18 S Waterman b: Slutkill Nk s/o Ezekiel & Catharian to Mary Crockett 21 S b: Slutkill Nk d/o Joseph & Zippy on 2 Jul 1855 at Onancock by J Allen
KILLMAN Ezekiel J 37 S Farmer Acc Acc s/o Chas & Rose to Harriet E Poulson 33 S Acc Acc d/o John on 5 Jan 1881 at Onancock by JC Watson
KILLMAN Ezekiel T 26 S Farmer Acc Acc s/o James W & Emaline to Seml Ann Bayly 20 S Acc Acc d/o Lewis & Lehlia on 18 Dec 1884 at Acc by JW Carroll
KILLMAN Francis G 25 S Farmer Acc Acc s/o Saml & Catharine to Indiannia D Bennett 20 S Acc Acc d/o James H & Mary on 4 Oct 1874 near Pungo: by L Moore
KILLMAN George W [Killmon] 19 S Farmer Acc Acc s/o Lorenzo D & Ruth to Emma Susan Hickman 25 S Acc Acc d/o George & Lucretia on 30 Oct 1889 at Acc by RA Compton
KILLMAN George W [Kilmon] 27 S Farmer Acc Acc s/o Wm & Keziah to Maggie A Wright 21 S Acc Acc d/o Elijah & Margt on 11 Dec 1867

at Acc by JH Addison

KILLMAN Henry L [Killmon] 28 W Farmer Acc Acc s/o Thomas & Caroline to Maggie H Evans 22 S Acc Acc d/o William & Jane on 29 Jan 1890 at Acc by RA Compton

KILLMAN Henry T 23 S Sailor Acc Acc s/o Samuel & Nancy to George Anna Gladding 17 S Acc Acc d/o Calvin & Elizabeth on 23 Feb 1871 at Muddy Ck by JET Ewell

KILLMAN Henry W 21 S Farmer Acc Acc s/o Lorenzo D & Ruth to Mame Gardner 16 S Acc Acc d/o Benjamin & Elizabeth on 29 Aug 1888 at Hollies Ch by JW Hundley

KILLMAN Howard F [Killmon] 20 S Farmer Acc Acc s/o John H & Susan to Ida F Brown 19 S Acc Acc d/o Chas T & Margt on 28 Nov 1875 at r/o Litt LeCato's by LK LeCato

KILLMAN James 24 S Waterman b: Acc s/o James & Elizth to Elizabeth A Killman 17 S b: Acc d/o Saml & Kesiah on 20 Mar 1856 at Acc by JH Addison

KILLMAN James E [Kilmon] 22 S Farmer Acc Acc s/o James (of Jas) to Lula F Parker 18 S Acc Acc d/o Thos H & Sarah on 5 Feb 1891 at Acc by JM Anderson

KILLMAN Jas W [Killmon] 28 S Mariner b: Acc s/o Jas H & Mary to Emeline Trader 23 S b: Acc d/o Parker (dec'd) & Nancy on 9 Feb 1855 at Messongo by T Waters (Samuel T Taylor says both over 21)

KILLMAN Jno H 40 W Carpenter Acc Acc s/o Wm & Keziah to Maggie S Mears 22 S Acc Acc d/o Edwd & Mary on 4 Aug 1869 at Acc by DA Woodson

KILLMAN John A 22 S Waterman Acc Acc s/o Ellis & Emeline to Mary B Bull 17 S Acc Acc d/o Danl & Alicia on 4 Feb 1877 at Modest Town by DA Woodson

KILLMAN John D [Kilmon] 26 S Farmer Acc Acc s/o James (of Jas) & Elizabeth to Margaret L Nock 17 S Acc Acc d/o James K & Mary Ann on 16 Jan 1890 at Acc by JM Anderson

KILLMAN John E 27 S Sailor Acc Acc s/o Thos & Caroline to Margt Jane Barnes 24 S Acc Acc d/o Arthur & Annie on 24 Jul 1878 near Cashville by JH Amiss

KILLMAN John H 21 S Farmer Acc Acc s/o Jno H & Margt S to Annie A Lawrence 20 S Acc Acc d/o Jno & Margt on 15 Dec 1880 near Savageville by SC Boston

KILLMAN John H 20 S Farmer Acc Acc s/o John W & Betsy to Manie J Hickman 23 S Acc Acc d/o Joseph & Jane on 13 Apr 1887 at Onancock by JW Hundley

KILLMAN John Henry s/o Wm to Margaret Susan Savage d/o Littleton who gave consent lic: 19 Jul 1854

KILLMAN John Henry widr to Elizabeth Shield d/o Asa lic: 3 Nov 1858 Wm Fisher says she over 21

KILLMAN John I [Killmon] 22 S Oysterman Acc Acc s/o Thos & Laura to Laura Young 18 S Acc Acc d/o George H & Susan on 31 Dec 1893 at Lee Mont by JET Ewell

KILLMAN John R 21 S Farmer Acc Acc s/o Alfred & Margaret to Corinthia Beasley 17 S Acc Acc d/o Mary J P on 15 May 1892 at Acc by HJ Wilson

KILLMAN John W 22 S Oysterman Acc Acc s/o Samuel & Emily to Manie J Hickman 21 S Acc Acc d/o Elijah & Rachel on 28 Feb 1888 at Lee Mont by JS Wharton

KILLMAN Jos A 25 S Sailor Acc Acc s/o Thos & Caroline to Sarah C Evans 31 S Acc Acc d/o Wm & Jane on 27 Dec 1882 at Acc by WC Vaden

KILLMAN Leroy J 22 S Farmer Acc Acc s/o John H & Maggie L to Cora L Beloate 18 S Acc Acc d/o George W & Jane S on 8 Feb 1893 at Acc by AC Berryman

KILLMAN Littleton H 22 S Farmer Acc Acc s/o Thomas & Caroline to Arinthia F Barnes 25 S Acc Acc d/o Arthur & Annie on 4 Jun 1884 near Onancock by WC Vaden

KILLMAN Lorenzo 20 S Farmer Acc Acc s/o Saml & Cath to Ruth Hickman 22 S Acc Acc d/o Robt & Rachel on 27 Jan 1859 at Acc by JH Addison

KILLMAN Lorenzo J 22 S Farmer Acc Acc s/o Lorenzo D & Ruth to Tabitha S Scott 16 S Acc Acc d/o Jno W & Laura S on 2 Dec 1885 at Acc by JW Hundley

KILLMAN Lybrand [Kilmon] 22 S Sailor Acc Acc s/o Ezekiel & Cath to Susan E Chandler 23 S Acc Acc d/o Bagwell & Nancy on 21 Feb 1869 at Acc by JH Addison

KILLMAN Oswald F 22 S Sailor Acc Acc s/o Esekiel H & Mary A to Juliet A Barnes 21 S Acc Acc d/o Archur & Ann on 11 May 1881 at Acc by JC Watson

KILLMAN Patrick W 20 S Farmer Acc Acc s/o Wm & Kesiah to Lavinia Scott 18 S Acc Acc d/o John & Maria on 25 Jan 1871 at Acc by E Hebard

KILLMAN Patrick W 33 W Farmer Acc Acc s/o Wm & Kariah to Margaret F Lawrence 21 S Acc Acc d/o Jno E & Margaret on 30 Sep 1883 at Acc by SC Boston

KILLMAN Samuel 24 S Fish & Shoe Mk Acc Acc s/o Saml & Caty to Sarah Ann [Shreaves] Shrieves 24 S Acc Acc d/o Abraham & Laura (Lavenia) on 14 Sep 1865 at Acc by JH Addison

KILLMAN Samuel T 21 S Sailor Acc Acc s/o Samuel & Emily to Burnetta J Parkes 23 S Acc Acc d/o Chas & Margt on 26 Dec 1882 at Lee Mont by WA Crouse

KILLMAN Thomas 32 S Farmer s/o Charles & Abby to Laura Parkes 22 d/o Mark & Elizabeth lic: 1 Dec 1864

KILLMAN Thorogood O 24 S Farmer Acc Acc s/o Samuel & Nancy to Indianna F Byrd 23 S Acc Acc d/o George W & Elizabeth C on 30 Jun 1880 at Modest Town by DA Woodson

KILLMAN Tiberius G 20 S Farmer Acc Acc s/o Wm & Elizth to Alice [Browne] Brown 17 S Acc Acc d/o Charles T & Margaret on 2 Nov 1873 near Pungo: by EM Bryan

KILLMAN William T [Kilmon] 53 W Farmer Acc Acc s/o William & Keziah to Annie L Hickman 24 S Acc Acc d/o George E & Elizabeth on 26 Nov 1890 at Acc by JM Anderson

KILLMAN Wm T [Kilmon] 36 S Farmer Acc Acc s/o Wm & Keziah to Malinda A Byrd 28 S Acc Acc d/o Eborn & Maria on 19 Apr 1868 at Acc by JH Addison

KING Addison S 21 S Oysterman Newtown MD Acc to Zipporah Crockett 18 S Acc Acc d/o Peter & Mary on 18 Aug 1878 at Tangier Isld by WJ Duhadway

KING Jacob Col 32 S Farmer MD Acc to Violet Poulson Col 21 S Acc Acc d/o Elijah & Mary on 12 Jan 1882 at Onancock by JC Ayler

KING John C 31 S Teacher Elizabeth City Co James City Co s/o John C & Eliza F to Eleanor L Adams 25 S Baltimore MD Acc d/o Geo F & Sarah L on 6 Sep 1866 at Onancock by GF Adams

KING Nathan Col 41 S Physician Windsor Canada Norfolk VA s/o

Framl & Hammah to Amy Parkes Col 37 S Acc Acc d/o Lucy Read on 27 Sep 1882 at Onancock by JC Ayler

KING W P Moore 23 S Pharmacist Eastville Washington DC s/o Randolph & Bettie W to Mollie M Smith 19 S Acc Acc d/o Nath'l S & Juliet on 21 Feb 1893 at Chinco: Isld by OS Walton

KNIGHT Dawson 21 S Oysterman Acc Acc s/o Dunseath & Elizth to Elizth Hall 20 S Acc Acc d/o Robert & Elizth on 27 Dec 1865 at Acc by GW Matthews

KNIGHT Henry 22 S Farmer b: Messongo to Arcnea [Marshall] Marshall 20 S b: Messongo d/o Nancy on 7 Apr 1855 at r/o Wm Marshel by GH Ewell

KNIGHT Henry W 54 W Farmer Acc Acc to Nancy Stant 49 S Acc Acc on 18 Jul 1886 at Acc by JE Bundick

KNIGHT John 23 S Waterman Acc Acc s/o Dawson & Eliz'th to Elizabeth A Andrews 20 S Acc Acc d/o John & Rachel on 26 Dec 1894 at Marsh Market by C Clement

KNIGHT William H 30 S Oysterman Acc Acc s/o Henry & Rena to Sally C Hall 20 S Acc Acc d/o George E & Sally D on 30 Mar 1892 near Belinda by JW Nicholson

KNIGHT William R 22 S Merchant Acc Acc s/o William & Sally to Peggy M Cullen 19 S Acc Acc d/o Jacob & Sally on 1 Feb 1872 at Messongo by JC Reed

KNODE Clinton 25 S Merchant Wash Co MD Wash Co MD s/o Severn G & Louisa to Ella T Rayfield 19 S Acc Acc d/o Thos J & Emily on 10 Sep 1874 at Acc C H by M Oldham

KNOX George D Col 21 S Sailor Acc Acc s/o John & Susan to Eva Finney Col 16 S Acc Acc d/o Mary on 16 Feb 1893 at Onancock by FW Overton

KOEING Ernest 20 S Tonsorial Artist Saxony Germany Acc to Ella T Flick 18 S Acc Acc d/o Chrisian D & Emma on 30 Dec 1886 at Acc by JW Carroll

KOLLOCK James 21 S Oysterman Acc Acc s/o Wm J & Sarah A to Nancy M Birch 20 S Acc Acc d/o Joseph F & Mary A on 1 May 1895 at Chinco: Isld by SU Grimsley

KOLLOCK John T 24 S Oysterman Acc Acc s/o Wm J & Sarah A to Janie Booth 23 S Acc Acc d/o Daniel & Nancy on 23 May 1895 at Acc by CW Matthews

KOLLOCK Wm J widr Acc Acc to Frances A White wid Acc Acc on 18 Nov 1877 at Chinco: Isld by R Williamson

LAIRD Josiah 22 S Waterman Acc Acc s/o John T & Zipporah to Emma [Parks] Parkes 16 S Acc Acc d/o Lewis B & Margaret on 27 Sep 1890 at Tangier Isld by J Connor

LAIRD Thomas S 20 S Sailor Acc Acc s/o John T & Zipporah to Mary [Parks] Parkes 19 S Acc Acc d/o Severn M & Martha J on 8 Apr 1891 at Tangier Isld by J Connor

LAKE Abel A 21 S Waterman Atlantic Co NJ Acc s/o Enoch & Eliza Ann to Mary P Burroughs 17 S Mercer Co NJ Acc d/o Ralph & Caroline on 25 Jan 1871 at Acc by O Littleton

LANDEN Arthur C 22 S to Margaret J Thomas single d/o Joshua who gave consent lic: 4 May 1865

LANDES Harvey E 21 S Farmer Rockingham Co Acc s/o Warrington & Maggie to Katie N Parker 22 S Acc Acc d/o Lewis & Agnes on 19 Aug 1894 at Acc by WP Wright

LANDING Custis 30 S Fisherman Acc Acc s/o Arthur C to Fanton J Crockett 16 S Acc Acc d/o Elisha of Severn & Ellen on 10 Aug 1892 at

LANDING James 35 W Milling MD Acc to Mary Alice Parker 22 S Acc Acc d/o George S & Rachael on 14 Mar 1870 at Acc by DA Woodson

LANDING James H to Mary Jane Ayres d/o James who gave consent lic: 15 Nov 1859 James M Northam says he over 21

LANDING John S 21 S Oysterman Acc Acc s/o Arthur C & Marg't to Amelia J Shores 17 S Acc Acc d/o Potty F & Mary A on 6 Dec 1893 at Tangier by ZH Webster

LANDING John W 23 S Farmer Acc Acc s/o William & Alice to Laura Scott 18 S Acc Acc d/o John W & Mary on 27 Dec 1893 at Acc by GE Booker

LANDING Joshua T 23 S Oysterman Acc Acc s/o Arthur C & Marg't to Esther [Parks] Parkes 21 S Acc Acc d/o John (of Irving) on 8 Nov 1893 at Tangier by ZH Webster

LANDING Wm T 26 S Shoemaker Acc Acc s/o James & Sallie to Sallie A Tatham 26 W Acc Acc d/o Edward & Polly Hickman on 12 Apr 1876 at Zion Bapt Ch by DA Woodson

LANE Alpheus 34 S Farmer Acc Acc s/o Sewell & Virga A to Olivia Heath 24 W Acc Acc d/o Geo G & Susan Fox on 21 Nov 1878 at Locustville by LK LeCato

LANE Horace S 23 S Farmer Acc Acc s/o Swell F & Virginia to Henrietta W Kellam 24 S Acc Acc d/o Elijah S on 15 Dec 1869 at Acc by JC Martin

LANG Frederick J 36 W Wage-earner Williamsburg NY Acc s/o Charles & Margaret to Ella N Scott 18 S Acc Acc d/o Winfield A & Malinda on 11 Dec 1894 at Harborton by JR Griffith

LANG Henry 25 S Farmer Acc Acc s/o Nathaniel & Nancy to Caty (F) Lewis 22 S Acc Acc d/o Henderson & Nancy on 1 Jan 1858 at Acc by JH Addison (Edward Lewis says he 21)

LANG James C 21 S Farmer Acc Acc s/o James & Lizzie to Ida D Warner 21 S Acc Acc d/o Solomon & Arinthia on 27 Jun 1888 at Mappsville by JW Ward

LANG James E 24 S Farmer Acc Acc s/o Henry & Catherine to Sallie W Finney 21 S Acc Acc d/o Alfred W & Mary on 23 Aug 1888 at Onancock by J McNabb

LANG Nathaniel J 25 S Farmer Acc Acc s/o Henry & Kitty to Virginia S Parkes 24 S Acc Acc d/o Thomas S & Sarah on 15 Jan 1890 at Acc by WJ Twilley

LANG Willman H 26 S Sailor Acc Acc s/o Henry & Catharine to Nannie J Milliner 22 S Acc Acc d/o James H & Elizabeth on 27 Dec 1885 at Lee Mont by HG Cowran

LANKFORD Charles C C 29 W Carpenter Som Co MD Acc s/o Clay & Sallie to Rebecca Jester 28 S Acc Acc d/o William & Eliz'th on 16 Oct 1890 at Chinco: Isld by GE Wood

LANKFORD George Col 20 S Oysterman Acc Acc to Sarah Ann Davis Col 18 S Acc Acc on 31 Dec 1871 at Modest Town by A Joynes

LANKFORD Henry T 25 S Waterman Acc Acc s/o James & Annie to Mary E Summers 18 S Acc Acc d/o Richd & Mary on 28 Nov 1877 at Modest Town by DA Woodson

LANKFORD Hiran W 21 S Painter Som Co MD Princess Anne s/o Joshua J & Mary A to Annie C Carmine 21 S Acc Acc d/o Thos C on 20 Aug 1874 at Acc by RC Jones

LANKFORD James F 21 S Oystering Acc Acc s/o Jas & Hester to Sarah E Wessells 20 S Acc Acc d/o Jno W & Caroline on 19 Dec 1877 at Conquest Ch by DA Woodson

LANKFORD James F 30 W Boatman Acc Acc s/o James & Hester A to

Anna E Chase 19 S Acc Acc d/o Teagle R & Eliza on 15 Dec 1887 at Bethel Ch by WA Street

LANKFORD John W 27 S Sailor Acc Acc s/o Levie J & Hester Ann to Willianna Trader 20 S Acc Acc d/o Alfred & Elizth on 21 May 1879 at Modest Town by DA Woodson

LANKFORD Saml T 24 S Waterman Acc Acc s/o Selby P & Margt J to Mary E Barnes 22 S Acc Acc d/o Jno & Sarah on 4 Jan 1878 at Temp'ville by JB Merritt

LAPETERS Jacob 24 S Farmer Russia VA Acc s/o Frank & Sarah to Ella Baker 19 S Sussex Co DE Acc d/o Peter & Nancy on 3 Dec 1884 near Belle Haven by JE Humphreys

LATHBURY Arthur 34 W Sailor Piny Isld Chinco: Isld s/o John & Nancy to Sarah Thornton 28 W Chinco: Isld Chinco: Isld d/o George & Hester Bird on 23 Feb 1859 at Chinco: Isld by P Bowdin

LAWRENCE John C 27 S Physician Murfreesboro NC Murfreesboro NC s/o John & Hannah to Tabbie M S Joynes 19 S Acc Acc d/o Tully A T & Sabre P on 12 Nov 1874 at Onancock by O Littleton

LAWRENCE John H 23 S Laborer b: Acc s/o Kendal Lawrence & Elizth Scott to Margaret S Guy 17 S b: Acc d/o John Wm Guy & Susan Lawrence on 9 Jan 1856 at Acc by P Warren (Edward J Savage says he over 21)

LAWS Custis Col 22 S Wage-earner Acc Acc s/o Martha Bayly to Willianna Kellam Col 18 S Acc Acc d/o Isaac & Sallie on 25 Dec 1892 at Acc by TW Nettles

LAWS Elijah F 24 S Merchant Som Co MD Acc s/o John W & Jane to Annie Claville 24 S Acc Acc d/o Wm J & Vesta E B R on 27 Jul 1887 at Chinco: Isld by Rl Watkins

LAWS Frank Col (dark) 20 S Laborer Acc Acc s/o Rebecca to Sarah A Abbott Col (mulatto) 17 S Acc Acc d/o Esther Outen on 28 Jan 1872 at Modest Town by A Joynes

LAWS James Col 22 S Laborer Acc Acc s/o Arelia Justices to Mary A Matthews Col 23 S Acc Acc d/o Clacissa Hope on 8 Jun 1879 at Modest Town by A Joynes

LAWS James Col 60 S Laborer Acc Acc to Zilla [Justis] Justice Col 55 S Acc Acc on 29 Dec 1886 at Acc by JC Cluff

LAWS James H Col 69 W Laborer Acc Acc s/o Edward & Leah to Sallie Handy Col 65 W Acc Acc on 31 Dec 1890 at Acc by JC Cluff

LAWS James Jr Col 21 S Laborer Acc Acc to Henny Taylor 21 S Acc Acc d/o Delah on 21 Nov 1869 at Acc by A Joynes

LAWS Jno Wm Col 23 S Laborer Acc Acc s/o Beckie to Sally A West Col 18 S Acc Acc d/o Leah on 5 Apr 1879 at Acc by A Joynes

LAWS John Col 22 S Laborer Acc Acc s/o Amelia to Fannie Mapp Col 18 S Acc Acc d/o Peter & Margaret on 30 Jan 1881 at Modest Town by A Joynes

LAWS John Col 27 S Farmer Acc Acc s/o James & Sarah to Maggie [Trehurn] Trehearn Col 26 S Acc Acc d/o Edmund & Lousia on 24 Jan 1894 at Acc by AJ Satchell

LAWS John Martin FN 21 S Farmer Acc Acc s/o Joshua & Sylvia to Maria Mears FN 21 S Acc Acc d/o Chas & Henrietta on 31 Dec 1865 at Acc by BT Ames

LAWS John W 33 W Laborer to Elizabeth M Fitzgerald 37 S lic: 28 Nov 1864

LAWS Joshua W Col 30 S Farmer Acc Acc s/o Joshua & Sylva to Hester Sample Col 25 S Acc Acc on 29 Dec

LAWS Joshua Wm FN 23 S Laborer Acc Acc s/o Joshua & Sylvia to Betsy Carter FN 21 S Acc Acc d/o Susan on 31 Dec 1865 at Acc by BT Ames

LAWS Lewis Col 22 S Farmer Acc Acc s/o Dorah to Leah Rew Col 16 S Acc Acc d/o Fanny on 2 Mar 1876 at Jno E Bundick's by JE Bundick

LAWS Lewis Col 34 S Laborer Acc Acc s/o Esther to Lucy Watson Col 22 S Acc Acc d/o Patience on 3 Jul 1880 at Modest Town by A Joynes

LAWS Martin Col 27 S Laborer Acc Acc s/o Joshua & Sylvia to Martha Goffigon Col 23 S Acc Acc on 21 Apr 1877 at Joshua Laws' by A Handy

LAWS Martin Z 23 S Student Acc Acc s/o Wm & Mary Ann to Virginia A Lucas 22 S Acc Acc d/o Southey T & Ann on 31 Jan 1866 at Acc by P Warren

LAWS Theodore Col 24 S Carpenter Acc Acc s/o Dora to Mary Northam Col 23 S Acc Acc d/o Ayrie Northam on 27 Dec 1885 near Mappsville by AJ Satchell

LAWS William Col 24 S Farmer Acc Acc s/o Frank & Sarah to Middie Davis Col 21 S Acc Acc d/o Thorogood & Mary on 13 Dec 1894 at Acc by AJ Satchell

LAWS William R 27 S Physician Acc Mt Plesant NJ s/o Wm & Sally to Alicia C Long 23 S Acc Acc d/o Thomas & Mary E on 7 Sep 1866 at Acc by GW Matthews

LAWSON George W 24 S Oysterman Acc Acc s/o William & Hettie to Ella F Bundick 21 S Acc Acc d/o William & Annie on 15 Apr 1891 at Acc by JR Strugis

LAWSON Wm 28 S Laborer Acc Acc s/o Wm & Lucraita to Elizabeth H [Philips] Phillips 25 S Acc Acc d/o Labin & Martin on 20 Sep 1863 at Acc by JWA Elliott

LEATHERBURY Alonzo T 30 W Farmer N'hamp: N'hamp: s/o Wm J & Virginia to Annie C Feddeman 20 S Acc Acc d/o Wm H & Mary on 8 Nov 1883 at St James Ch by RW Anderson

LEATHERBURY Edward R 30 S Physician b: N'hamp: s/o Jno W & Sally C to Bettie M (Elizabeth) Bagwell 21 S b: Acc d/o Dr Tho P & Sally H on 12 Dec 1855 at Onancock by JM Cheveis(?) (John J Wise says both over 21)

LEATHERBURY Edward W 23 S Merchant N'hamp: Acc s/o Thomas E & Janie to Margaret R Bagwell 22 S Acc Acc d/o Edmund R & Maggie D on 2 Jul 1894 at Onancock by HL Derby

LEATHERBURY Perry A 47 W Merchant Acc Acc s/o Thos & Nancy to Leah Ann Nelson 35 S Acc Acc d/o Geo on 5 Jul 1866 at Acc by TL Tomkinson

LEATHERBURY Thomas E 25 S Farmer North Co VA N'hamp: s/o Jno W & Sienna G to Joanna T West 20 S N'hamp: Acc d/o Chas J D & Elizth on 21 Jan 1869 at N'hamp: by JB Craighill

LeCATO Abram Col 50 W Farmer Acc Acc s/o Solomon Taylor & Rachel LeCato to Nellie West Col 25 S Acc Acc d/o Alfred & Keziah on 6 Nov 1889 at Savageville by JB Lewis

LeCATO Abram Col 50 S Farmer Acc Acc s/o Rachel to Mary Fitchett Col 45 W Acc Acc d/o Rhina Gaskins on 4 Nov 1886 at Acc by JA Haynes

LeCATO Alfred B 24 S Seaman Acc Acc s/o Edwin W & Mary H to Jennie Fox 18 S Acc Acc d/o George G & Susan E on 13 Oct 1881 at Locustville by JC Watson

LeCATO Arthur W 24 S Farmer Acc

Acc s/o John & Elizth L to Mary Susan Turner 17 S Acc Acc d/o George E & Elizth L on 23 Dec 1875 at Ganetsons Chp by JE Humphreys

LeCATO Benjamin Col 21 S Laborer Acc Acc s/o Hannah to Sophia Smith Col 19 S Acc Acc d/o Dinah on 12 Mar 1874 at Hank's Nest by WA Clayton

LeCATO Charles Col 24 S Farmer Acc Acc s/o Mima to Clarissa Poulson Col 22 S Acc Acc d/o Eleainro on 20 Sep 1876 at Savageville by JK Plato

LeCATO George 25 S Laborer Acc Acc s/o Hannah to Arena Copes 22 S Acc Acc d/o Bettie Ames on 30 Dec 1867 at Acc by JWA Elliott

LeCATO George 25 S Farmer Acc Acc s/o Annie to Ann Hatton 21 S Acc Acc d/o Mary on 3 Mar 1869 at Acc by WF Williams

LeCATO George T Col 25 S Farmer Acc Acc s/o Sarah Ashby to Caroline Byrd Col 22 S Acc Acc d/o Maria on 27 Jan 1892 at Acc by N Morris

LeCATO James E 22 S Farmer Acc Acc s/o John M & Bettie A to Lillian L Boggs 21 S Acc Acc d/o William H & Esther E on 10 Jan 1894 at Acc by JR Griffith

LeCATO John Col 25 S Farmer Acc Acc s/o Jno & Minnie(?) to Sarah Custis Col 24 S Acc Acc d/o Elizabeth on 29 Jan 1880 at Deep Ck by RJ Waters

LeCATO John M 21 S Farmer Acc Acc s/o Jno & Elizabeth to Elizabeth A Thompson 20 S Acc Acc d/o William & Catharine on 10 Jul 1870 at Belle Haven by JE Humphreys

LeCATO Lee Col 21 S Laborer Acc Acc s/o Leah to Louisa Turlington Col 17 S Acc Acc d/o Isaac on 3 Jun 1883 at Acc by GW Young

LeCATO Littleton K (widr) to Lavenia Badger on 11 Oct 1860 at Acc by M Oldham (Philip Kennard says she over 21)

LeCATO Littleton T 25 S Merchant Acc Acc s/o Nathl B & Elizabeth to Cordie E Smith 18 S Acc Acc d/o Hugh G & Margt on 8 Mar 1857 at Acc by M Oldham (Thos C Bunting says be over 21)

LeCATO Nathl J 20 S Clerk b: Acc s/o Nathl B & Elizth to Elizth S Eichelberger 17 S b: Acc d/o Wm (F) & Mary on 21 Mar 1855 at r/o Wm Eichelberger by JWA Elliott

LeCATO Riley Col 39 S Farmer Acc Acc to Susan Mears Col 19 S Acc Acc d/o Margaret S on 4 Apr 1895 at Locust Mount by JWA Elliott

LeCATO Robert Col 67 S Mail Carrier Acc Acc to Jemina LeCato Col 60 S Acc Acc on 4 Mar 1893 at Locust Mount by RH Coleman

LEE Robert E Col 28 S Wage-earner Cousie Co AL Acc s/o Edward Lee & Margaret to Elizabeth West Col 32 S Acc Acc d/o James T & Caroline on 16 Jan 1890 at Acc by L Duncan

LEGER George F 35 S Merchant MD IN s/o Resdon & Susan to Sallie E Melson 28 S Acc Acc d/o Jno D & Margt on 11 Apr 1878 at Onancock by JH Amiss

LESCALLETTE C A [Lescalitte] 23 S Jeweller Acc Acc s/o Benj A & Mary A to Clara F [Parks] Parkes 18 S Acc Acc d/o Jno P & Margt C on 13 Feb 1884 at Acc by JW Carroll

LESCALLETTE H W 30 W Mechanic Acc Acc s/o Burgiss & Mary Ann to Alice B Thornton 21 S Acc Acc on 27 Jun 1883 near Guilford Ch by JW Hundley

LEWIS Albert P 27 S Oysterman Acc Acc s/o Thomas P & Margaret to Mary F Ewell 27 S Acc Acc d/o Nancy Ewell on 23 May 1888 at Guilford by WF Hayes

LEWIS Alexander M 35 S Farmer Acc Acc s/o Wm K & Polly to Margt R

Lewis 21 S Acc Acc d/o Saml (of Jno) & Susan on 9 Oct 1867 at Acc by ES Grant

LEWIS Alfred 21 S Oysterman Red Wing MN Acc s/o Alfred & Rebecca to Lydia A Claville 16 S Acc Acc d/o George O & Ellen on 14 Jan 1884(?) at Chinco: Isld by SU Grimsley Certificate returned 12 Jan 1889

LEWIS Alfred J 22 S Mariner b: Acc s/o Saml K & Sally to Maria A Adams 18 S b: Acc d/o James C & Susan on 20 Dec 1855 at r/o Jas C Adams by ES Grant (Thomas S Lewis said he over 21)

LEWIS Alfred L 25 S Sailor Acc Acc s/o Alfred J & Maria A to Cora E Lewis 18 S Acc Acc d/o Wm T & Susan on 16 Jul 1885 at Onancock by CA Grice

LEWIS Burwell R 24 S Sailor Acc Acc s/o Thos P & Margt to Narcissa M Bagwell 21 S Acc Acc d/o Nancy G on 27 Dec 1882 at Acc by WA Crouse

LEWIS Charles 28 S Farmer Acc Acc s/o Edward & Frances to Catharine Simpson 25 S Acc Acc d/o Chas & Betsy on 21 Feb 1876 at Modest Town by DA Woodson

LEWIS Charles 24 S Oysterman Acc Acc s/o Revel J & Matilda to Charlotte Wessells 20 S Acc Acc d/o Albert F & Kessy B on 21 Dec 1878 at Sykes Isld by JW Hilldrup

LEWIS Daniel W 25 S Sailor s/o John & Sarah A to Lydia A Claville 30 W d/o Timothy & Rebecca Hill lic: 9 May 1865 marr: 13 May 1865

LEWIS Daniel W 35 S Oysterman Acc Acc s/o John & Sarah M to Drucilla J Sharpley 28 S Acc Acc d/o Wm & Elizth on 7 Feb 1875 at Chinco: Isld by P Bowdin Sr

LEWIS David 40 W Oysterman Chinco: Isld Chinco: Isld s/o Eba & Nancy to Sarah Jones 32 W Chinco: Isld Chinco: Isld d/o Wm Whealton on 12 Dec 1869 at Acc by P Bowdin Jr

LEWIS David 23 S Sailor Acc Acc s/o David & Rebecca to Sarah C Mason 18 S Acc Acc d/o James & Tabitha on 12 Sep 1882 at Chinco: Isld by WP Thornton

LEWIS Eba 25 S Oysterman Acc Acc s/o David & Rebecca to Sarah I (J) Collins 19 S Acc Acc d/o Charles & Hester I on 15 Jan 1874 at Chinco: Isld by J Lewis

LEWIS Edward widr Farming b: Acc s/o Zedock & Betsy to Emma (Emily) Kellam single b: Acc d/o Robt (Decd) & Leah on 29 Sep 1854 at Acc by JWA Elliott (Walter Scott says she is over 21)

LEWIS Edward C W 25 S Oysterman Acc Acc s/o Absalom & Elizabeth to Ida Stant 21 S Acc Acc d/o Thomas & Nettie on 4 Jul 1893 at Acc by RB Scott

LEWIS Edward R 26 S Waterman Acc Acc s/o Wesley W & Virginia to Emily L Ewell 23 S Acc Acc d/o Thomas & Laura on 14 Aug 1895 at Acc by DGC Butts

LEWIS Edwd F 24 S Oysterman Acc Acc s/o Jno T & Sally E to Augusta Nelson 21 W Acc Acc d/o Wm R & Belinda Drummond on 25 Sep 1877 at Temp'ville by M Oldham

LEWIS Emory J 23 S Dealer in Oysters Acc Acc s/o Wm T & Rebecca to Annie Jester 19 S Acc Acc d/o Lamber & Annie on 28 Dec 1892 at Chinco: Isld by GE Wood

LEWIS Frank C 21 S Trader Acc Acc s/o Wm R & Sarah C to Emma C Lewis 20 S Acc Acc d/o Jas S & Rachel J on 16 Sep 1877 at Doe Ck by FH Mullineaux

LEWIS George Col 23 S Laborer Acc Acc to Betsy Fletcher Col 24 S Acc Acc on 29 Aug 1872 at Temp'ville by M Oldham

LEWIS George Col 25 S Oysterman Acc Acc s/o Tabitha to Agnes Davis Col 16 S Acc Acc d/o Mary White on 17 Jan 1875 at Log Chp by A Joynes

LEWIS George 28 S Sailor Acc Acc s/o Levin D & Nancy to Comfort Melson 18 S Acc Acc d/o Jno H & Susan on 7 Feb 1878 near Reese Chp by FH Mullineaux

LEWIS George 22 S Sailor Acc Acc s/o Jno & Elizth to Charlotte A Lewis 24 S Acc Acc d/o David & Rebecca on 24 Mar 1880 at Chinco: Isld by IT Adkins

LEWIS George 30 W Oysterman & House Carpenter Acc Acc s/o Wm & Nancy to Elizabeth Daisey 33 W Acc Acc d/o Arthur & Caroline Cherricks now Caroline Stubbs on 1 Jun 1884(?) at Chinco: Isld by SU Grimsley Certificate returned 12 Jan 1889

LEWIS George W 23 S None b: Acc s/o Walter D & Elizth to Margaret Ann Mears 18 S b: Acc d/o Arthur & Ann on 2 Dec 1857 at r/o Arthur Mears by ES Grant

LEWIS George W 30 W Merchant Acc Acc s/o Walter & Betsy to Sally Hurst 22 S Acc Acc d/o John & Sally on 20 Dec 1871 at Hunting Ck by DA Woodson

LEWIS George W 20 S Oysterman Acc Acc s/o Wm & Nancy to Mary E Cherricks 18 S Acc Acc d/o John J & Susan on 13 Apr 1877 at Chinco: Isld by WP Thornton

LEWIS Green W 24 S Farmer Acc Acc s/o Edwd to Maggie R Berry 24 S Acc Acc d/o Chas P on 26 Dec 1879 at Modest Town by DA Woodson

LEWIS Hance J 25 S Farmer Acc Acc s/o Absalom & Elizth to Florence Marshall 16 S Acc Acc d/o Sylvester J & Polly on 27 Feb 1884 at Temp'ville by M Oldham

LEWIS Haram Col 23 S Fireman Acc Acc s/o Tabby to Emma Jane Webb Col 22 S Acc Acc d/o Margaret on 12 Jan 1876 at Locust Mount by JW Ruff

LEWIS Harrison H Col 31 S Farmer Acc Acc s/o Nancy Wise to Bridget J Booker Col 28 S N'hamp: Acc d/o Edith Borker on 3 Aug 1872 at Acc by JH Offer

LEWIS Harry 22 S Sailor Acc Acc s/o Alfred J & Margaret to Amanda S Martin 21 S Acc Acc d/o James W on 10 May 1893 at Lee Mont by AJ Walter

LEWIS Henderson 60 W Farmer Acc Acc s/o Zadock & Betsy to Betsy Smith 50 S Acc Acc d/o James on 7 Apr 1870 at Acc by LK LeCato

LEWIS Henry to Charlotte Phillips lic: 27 Aug 1857 Parker Lewis says both over 21

LEWIS Henry J 35 S Farmer Acc Acc s/o Revel & Polly to Sally A Ayres 25 S Acc Acc d/o Levin R & Susan on 14 Dec 1887 at Ayres Chp by JW Easley

LEWIS Hezekiah Col 23 S Farmer Acc Acc to Bernetta Bayly Col 21 S Acc Acc on 13 Nov 1881 at Acc by PM Lewis

LEWIS Homer 22 S Sailor Acc Acc s/o William P & Margaret to Ella [Justis] Justice 16 S Acc Acc d/o Charles & Melissa on 20 Aug 1890 at Parksley by HS Dulany

LEWIS James 23 S Waterman b: Acc s/o Rachael to Cassandra [Shreaves] Shrieves 22 S b: Acc d/o Wm & Polly on 13 Nov 1858 at r/o Henry Hill by ES Grant (Thomas S Lewis says both over 21)

LEWIS James 21 S Farmer Acc Acc s/o Henderson & Nancy to Nelvira Hart 21 S Acc Acc d/o James & Mary on 13 Feb 1861 at Andrew Chp by JH Addison (Wm Jones says she over

21)
LEWIS James A 22 S Oysterman Acc Acc s/o Major & Betsy to Indianna Lewis 22 S Acc Acc d/o Saml & Susan R on 21 Oct 1874 at Deep Ck Mill by RC Jones
LEWIS James E 20 S Farmer Acc Acc s/o Melvina Caruthers to Mattie A White 23 S Acc Acc d/o Elijah & Susan on 12 Dec 1886 at Savageville by JW Hundley
LEWIS James E 22 S Oysterman Acc Acc s/o Alfred J & Maria A to Sarah A Churn 22 S Acc Acc d/o John E & Catharien T on 21 Jul 1886 at Lee Mont by AJ Walter
LEWIS James H 20 S Carpenter Acc Acc s/o Henry C & Charlotte to Margt S Bradford 18 S Acc Acc d/o Emma A on 26 Mar 1884 at Onancock by JW Hundley
LEWIS James H 21 S Farmer Acc Acc s/o Wm & Nancy to Mary Lewis 20 S Acc Acc d/o Levin T & Mary on 15 Jan 1885 at Acc by W Chinn
LEWIS James R 24 S Carpenter Acc Acc s/o Raymond R & Sarah to Ethel Young 20 S Acc Acc d/o William & Susan on 16 Jun 1892 at Mappsville by JL King
LEWIS Jas J 20 S Farmer Acc Acc s/o Jas S & Elizth to Rose A Gray 20 S Acc Acc d/o Sallie S on 22 Dec 1886 at Onancock by CA Grice
LEWIS Jas S 19 S Waterman b: Acc s/o Jas & Kessy to Rachel Rew 17 S b: Acc d/o Jas & Elizth on 10 Aug 1854 near Ayres Chp by ES Grant
LEWIS Jas S 28 W Waterman Acc Acc s/o Jas & Casaider to Elizabeth A Shrieves 16 S Acc Acc d/o Jno & Eliz on 2 Jun 1864 at Acc by ES Grant
LEWIS Jefferson D 24 S Waterman Acc Acc s/o James T & Mary to Emma L Justice 21 S Acc Acc d/o Charles & Malissa on 2 Jan 1887 at John Barnes' by JW Norris
LEWIS John 21 S Farming Acc Acc s/o Leven & Mary to Alice [Witkinson] Watkinson 21 S Acc Acc d/o Leven & Sally on 21 Nov 1883 at Acc by SC Boston
LEWIS John D 24 S s/o Thomas & Sarah to Henrietta S Nicholson 22 S d/o John & Elizabeth lic: Feb/Mar 1865 lic: between 23 Feb and 22 Mar 1865
LEWIS John E 31 S Mariner b: Chinco: Isld s/o Isaac & Maria to Elizth Whealton 18 S b: Chinco: Isld d/o Wm & Mary & (ward/o Wm P Thornton who gave consent) on 12 Dec 1854 at Chinco: Isld by WP Thornton
LEWIS John F 25 S Farmer Acc Acc s/o Absalom & Elizabeth to Fanny J Ellett 21 S Farmville Prince Edward Co VA Acc on 14 May 1891 at Acc by JS Wallace
LEWIS John J 46 S Merchant Acc Acc s/o James & Ann to Sophia S Baker 42 S Acc Acc d/o Speppard & Mary on 10 Jun 1883 at Conquest Ch by M Oldham
LEWIS John T Col 25 S Sailor Acc Acc s/o Ann to Louisa Johnson Col 19 S Acc Acc d/o Maria on 30 Aug 1876 at Temp'ville by M Oldham
LEWIS John T 50 W Merchant Acc Acc s/o Revel & Permelia to Emily F Taylor 40 W Acc Acc d/o Wm B & Ann W Claville on 12 Jun 1880 at Sexes Isld by JE Bundick
LEWIS John T 24 S Telegraphist Acc Acc s/o Wm H & Arinthia J to Lula K [Parks] Parkes 23 S Acc Acc d/o John P & Manie on 10 Oct 1894 at Acc by RT Waterfield
LEWIS John W 23 S Sailor Acc Acc s/o Wm & Virginia A to Arinthia J Northam 22 S Acc Acc d/o Elizabeth on 10 Jul 1886 at Lee Mont by WA Street

LEWIS Joseph 24 S Sailor Acc Acc s/o Henderson & Nancy to Edna Bull 23 S Acc Acc d/o Nancy on 9 Dec 1869 at Acc by JH Addison

LEWIS Joseph 55 W Clergyman Sussex Co DE Acc s/o Stephen & Rachel to Sarah Lewis 40 W Acc Acc d/o Williams & Mary Whealton on 6 Apr 1874 at Chinco: Isld by P Bowdin Sr

LEWIS Joseph 45 W Sailor Acc Acc s/o Henderson to Hester Lewis 40 S Acc Acc d/o Edward on 20 Aug 1890 at Acc by AJ Fristoe

LEWIS Joshua Col 30 S Farmer Acc Acc s/o Joshua & Harriet to Lucy Jane Webb Col 24 S Acc Acc on 9 Dec 1894 at Acc by AJ Satchell

LEWIS Julious (Julius) 25 S Sailor Acc Acc s/o Edwd & Susan to Margaret Lingo 21 S Acc Acc d/o Robert & Mariah on 23 Feb 1859 at Acc by JWA Elliott (James Lingo says both over 21)

LEWIS Julius 44 S Sailor Acc Acc to Catharine Kelly 28 S Acc Acc d/o Jno & Nancy on 6 Feb 1876 at Garrisons Chp by JE Humphreys

LEWIS Leonidas 19 S Waterman b: Acc s/o Saml K (decd)& Sally to Sally Barnes 17 S b: Acc d/o John & Sally on 24 Feb 1859 at r/o Jno Barnes by ES Grant

Lewis Leroy 19 S Oysterman Acc Acc s/o John T & Sally to Amanda Marshall 17 S Acc Acc d/o Samuel & Amanda on 2 Jul 1890 at Acc by JS Wallace

LEWIS Levin R 30 S Mariner Acc Acc s/o Revel & Polly to Bernettie S [Shreaves] Shrieves 17 S Acc Acc d/o John & Elizabeth on 31 Feb 1861(?) at Doe Ck Nk by ES Grant (Edward S Grant says he over 21) Certificate returned 13 Feb 1861

LEWIS Levin T widr to Mary Bishop ward/o the said Levin T Lewis lic: 26 Mar 1855

LEWIS Levin T Col 21 S Farmer Acc Acc s/o Ann Bowen to Ann Croswell Col 21 S Acc Acc d/o Mary on 23 May 1873 at Temp'ville by M Oldham

LEWIS Lodey H 24 S Oysterman Acc Acc s/o James & Rachel to Julia J Melson 17 S Acc Acc d/o Jno H & Susan E on 25 Dec 1884 at Acc by AJ Walter

LEWIS Luther J 24 S Captain Som Co MD Som Co MD s/o Asa & Susan to Rebecca A Lewis 18 S Acc Acc d/o Jas & Rachel on 31 Dec 1879 at Capt J Lewis' by FH Mullineaux

LEWIS Major T 23 S Farmer Acc Acc s/o Spencer & Nancy to Mary A Annis 19 S Acc Acc d/o William & Elizth on 19 Aug 1869 at Acc by JET Ewell

LEWIS Maurice L 23 S Merchant Acc Acc s/o Levin D & Mary Ann to Libbie D Johnson 23 S Acc Acc d/o Durbin H & Caroline on 5 Oct 1887 at Lee Mont by JS Wharton

LEWIS Orris H 18 S Farmer Acc Acc s/o Raymond R & Sarah to Eva A [Shreves] Shrieves 16 S Acc Acc d/o James T & Mary on 17 Oct 1894 at Acc C H by JM Dunaway

LEWIS Orris L 21 S Oysterman Acc Acc s/o Susan to Ella M Lewis 15 S Acc Acc d/o Docie E on 1 Oct 1891 at Masonville by GF Farring

LEWIS Oswald T 21 S Oysterman Acc Acc s/o Raymond & Sarah to Susan [Shreaves] Shrieves 19 S Acc Acc d/o Wm of Wm & Caroline on 7 Mar 1872 at Acc by ST Ferguson

LEWIS R W 19 S Mechanic Acc Acc s/o Raymond R & Sarah to Laura T Mears 16 S Acc Acc d/o Joseph W & Sarah on 31 Jan 1884 at Onancock by JW Hundley

LEWIS Raymond R 38 W Oysterman Acc Acc s/o Absalom to Susan Parkes 31 S Acc Acc d/o Mark &

Marriages

Elizth on 11 Nov 1876 at Guilford by JM Anderson

LEWIS Revel J 22 S Oysterman Acc Acc s/o Revel J & Virginia to Edith M Nelson 18 S Som Co MD Acc d/o Robert & Gussie on 3 Aug 1890 at Sykes Isld by JS Wallace

LEWIS Revel S 35 W Oysterman Sexes Isld Sexes Isld s/o Revel & Milley to Virginia Miles 17 S Sexes Isld Sexes Isld d/o Parker (who gave consent) on 17 Feb 1859 at r/o Samuel Stant by GH Ewell

LEWIS Revil Thomas 22 S Waterman Acc Acc s/o Absalom & Elizabeth to Mary Indianna Collins 21 S Acc Acc d/o Litt T & Elizth on 1 Aug 1877 at Temp'ville by M Oldham

LEWIS Richard 75 W Farmer Acc Acc s/o Thomas & Sally to Mary Barnes 28 S Acc Acc d/o Samuel & Lydia on 12 Oct 1871 at r/o Saml Barnes by DA Woodson

LEWIS Robert J 20 S Farmer Acc Acc s/o William T & Elizabeth W to Ethel V Budd 17 S Acc Acc d/o William H & Susan on 16 May 1888 at Onancock by JW Easley

LEWIS Robert L 22 S Sailor Acc Acc s/o William P & Margaret to Rebecca S Watkinson 20 S Acc Acc d/o John T & Ann Eliza on 15 Apr 1888 at Acc C H by JS Wharton

LEWIS Robert L 26 S Sailor Acc Acc s/o Wm Wesley & Virginia A to Ella L Taylor 22 S Acc Acc d/o A C Hill Taylor & Virginia on 23 Aug 1893 at Lee Mont by JET Ewell

LEWIS Robert T 23 S Farmer Acc Acc s/o Walter D & Elizabeth to Margaret A Doughty 21 S Acc Acc d/o James A & Margaret on 9 Jan 1860 at Acc by P Warren (John E Lewis says both over 21)

LEWIS Robt E 25 S Farmer Acc Acc s/o Edwd & Emma to Emma L West 19 S Acc Acc d/o Edwd J & Margt on 21 Oct 1883 at Modest Town by JW Hundley

LEWIS Salathiel 21 S Oysterman Acc Acc s/o Absalom & Ann to Jennie Ellen Marshall 20 S Acc Acc d/o Gilbert & Henny on 5 Aug 1865 at Acc by GH Ewell

LEWIS Salathiel 23 S Oysterman Acc Acc s/o Hy & Pamelia to Dolly Miles 16 S Acc Acc d/o Severn P & Hester Ann on 7 Feb 1877 at Temp'ville by M Oldham

LEWIS Salathiel 40 D Mariner Acc Acc s/o Absalom to Anna Thomas 16 S Acc Acc d/o Corbin & Sarah on 5 Jul 1884 at Sykes Isld by RB Beadles

LEWIS Saml J 23 S Sailor Acc Acc s/o Al J & Maria A to Mary Emily Lewis 22 S Acc Acc d/o Jas & Mary on 18 Jun 1879 at Reese Chp by FH Mullineaux

LEWIS Sam'l J 49 S Oysterman Acc Acc s/o John & Polly to Sally Roberts 45 D Acc Acc d/o Michael Budd on 15 Nov 1893 at Acc by LE Spencer

LEWIS Samuel 35 S Farmer Acc Acc s/o James & Sarah to Annie Hickman 21 S Acc Acc d/o Elijah & Rachel on 17 Dec 1879 at Modest Town by DA Woodson

LEWIS Sebastian 52 S Farmer Acc Acc s/o Richd & Hessy to Permelia Waterhouse 36 W Acc Acc d/o Chas & Margt Berry on 24 Sep 1879 at Modest Town by DA Woodson

LEWIS Sebastian 52 W Farmer Acc Acc s/o Richd & Hessy to Mary Bowden 40 W Acc Acc d/o Zadock & Frances Watson on 4 Jan 1882 near Modest Town by JE Bundick

LEWIS Spencer of Jno 60 W Farmer Acc Acc s/o Jno & Melvina to Rachel Ann Marshall 45 S Acc Acc d/o Wm & Elizth on 20 Nov 1872 near Mason's Mill by JET Ewell

LEWIS Stanley J 22 S Merchant Acc

Acc s/o Levin D & Anna to Jeralean F Melson 19 S Acc Acc d/o Henry & Eveline on 26 Dec 1872 at Acc by JET Ewell

LEWIS Thomas 21 S Laborer Acc Acc s/o Thos Smith & Hannah Lewis to Ann Burton 21 S Acc Acc d/o Lewis & Sarah Garrison on 4 Jul 1869 at Acc by D Titlow

LEWIS Thomas 24 S Teamster Acc Acc s/o Levin to Margaret Hargis 16 S Acc Acc d/o John & Elizath on 13 Jan 1875 near Locustville by LK LeCato

LEWIS Thomas Col 35 S Laborer Acc Acc s/o Hannah to Margaret Bull Col 37 S Acc Acc on 25 Jun 1880 at Drum'tn by JW Diggs

LEWIS Thomas F 23 S Oysterman Acc Acc s/o Revel J & Matilda to Mary E Corbin 14 S Acc Acc d/o Robt & Eliza on 9 Aug 1872 at Acc by M Oldham

LEWIS Thomas F 30 W Waterman Acc Acc s/o Revel to Mary E Crockett 18 S Acc Acc d/o John & Rachel on 10 Aug 1882 at Temp'ville by M Oldham

LEWIS Thomas J 24 S Oysterman Acc Acc s/o Danl & Eliz to Elizabeth C Colonna 21 S Acc Acc d/o Wm & Sally on 29 Oct 1862 at Acc by ES Grant

LEWIS Tully J 20 S Waterman Acc Acc s/o Thomas J & Eliz'th to Lena E Hopkins 17 S Acc Acc d/o Chas W & Minerva on 3 Jun 1891 at Acc by GW Burke

LEWIS Tully M 21 S Merchant Acc Hunting Ck s/o James & Keziah to Elizabeth Mason 20 S Acc Acc d/o Wm & Tabitha on 20 Dec 1860 at bride's father's by JA Massey (Revel Justice of J says he over 21)

LEWIS Tully M 25 S Sailor Acc Acc s/o Tully M & Elizabeth to Leonra S Williams 21 S Acc Acc d/o Thomas H & Margaret on 31 Jul 1889 at Parksley by HS Dulany

LEWIS Walter D 25 S Merchant Acc Acc s/o Walter D & Elizth to Amanda E Ward 18 S Acc Acc d/o Wm & Susan on 28 Nov 1865 at Acc by P Warren

LEWIS Wesley 21 S Mariner Acc Acc s/o Wm K & Polly to Virginia Barnes 18 S Acc Acc d/o John & Sally on 4 Jun 1863 at Acc by ES Grant

LEWIS William 21 S Sailor b: Acc s/o John & Peggy to Margaret Taylor 23 S b: Acc d/o Southey on 24 Jan 1856 at r/o Julius Twiford by ES Grant (John Thos Powell says both over 21)

LEWIS William 31 S Oysterman Acc Acc s/o Sally to Mary A Lewis 22 S Philadelphia Acc d/o James on 19 Apr 1867 at Acc by WP Thornton

LEWIS William Col 28 S Oysterman Acc Acc s/o Mary to Georgianna Brown Col 25 S Acc Acc d/o Sarah Horsey on 16 Jul 1884 at Acc by JC Cluff

LEWIS William E 24 S House Carpenter Acc Acc s/o Willam W & Sarah E to Bettie B Bloxom 18 S Acc Acc d/o Wesley A & Peggy on 15 Jun 1887 at Locustville by JW Carroll

LEWIS William H 34 S Waterman Acc Acc s/o Raymond R & Catharine to Florence Wilkerson 19 S Acc Acc d/o Samuel W & Clara on 15 Aug 1895 at Acc by JC Watson

LEWIS William J 29 W Farmer Acc Acc s/o Major & Eliz'th to Nancy J Hinman 24 S Acc Acc d/o Jno R & Eliz'th on 18 May 1869 at Acc by JET Ewell

LEWIS William J 22 S Waterman Acc Acc s/o James T & Mary to Maggie A Twiford 22 S Acc Acc d/o George D & Eliz'th on 28 Dec 1890 at Parksley by HS Dulany

LEWIS William R 60 W Merchant Acc

Acc s/o James & Cassandria to Sudie E Melson 24 W Acc Acc d/o Thomas W & Frances Shrieves on 9 Jun 1889 at Ayres Chp by PA Leatherbury

LEWIS William S 19 S Farmer Acc Acc s/o Wm & Susan to Ella D Gray 19 S Acc Acc d/o James & Elizabeth on 3 Jun 1885 at Onancock by CA Grice

LEWIS William W 20 S Oysterman Acc Acc s/o Wm L & Margaret to Sarah E Clayton 16 S Acc Acc d/o George T & Virginia on 5 Feb 1893 at Acc by HJ Wilson

LEWIS Wm widr Laborer Chinco: Isld Chinco: Isld s/o Evens & Polly to Nancy Parker wid Chinco: Isld Chinco: Isld on 18 Sep 1852 at his house by P Bowdin

LEWIS Wm Chesnut 20 S Acc Acc s/o Jno T & Sarah to Mary E Marshall 16 S Acc Acc d/o Jno R & Eliza on 16 May 1878 at Flag Pond by A Wiles

LEWIS Wm Henry 20 S No Particular b: Acc s/o Samuel K (Decd) & Sally to Arinthia J Barnes 19 S b: Acc d/o John & Sally on 6 Aug 1857 at r/o Jno Barnes by ES Grant

LEWIS Wm T 22 S Sailor Acc Acc s/o Jno & Sarah to Rebecca Hill 17 S Acc Acc d/o Timothy & Rebecca on 10 Mar 1864 at Acc by P Bowdin Jr

LEWIS Wm T 44 W Oysterman Acc Acc s/o John & Sarah to Eliza J Williams 17 S Acc Acc d/o Selby & Susan on 30 Jul 1885 at Chinco: Isld by SU Grimsley

LEWIS Wm W 22 S Farmer/Paintor b: Acc s/o Wm & Elishea to Sarah E Churn 15 S b: Acc d/o Wm W & Sally on 18 Mar 1854 near Dan'l Lewis' by ES Grant

LEWIS Zadock 25 S Oysterman Acc Acc s/o Revel J & Virginia to Rachel Linton 18 S Acc Acc d/o William & Louisa on 27 Dec 1890 at Sykes Isld by JS Wallace

LEWIS Zadock W 22 W Oysterman Acc Acc s/o Selathiel to Ettie J Evans 18 S Acc Acc d/o Severn J & Eliza on 13 Dec 1888 at Hallwood by GE Wood

LEWIS Zadok 24 W Oysterman Acc Acc s/o Revel J & Virginia to Rennie Miles 19 S Acc Acc d/o Jesse T & Susan on 5 Apr 1893 at Acc by RB Scott

LIGHTEL William 30 S Tailor MD Acc s/o Thomas & amelia Lytle to Alice M Walker 26 S Acc Acc d/o Wm B & Mary A on 11 Aug 1875 at Onancock by FR Boston

LILLISTON Alexander W 27 S Farmer Acc Acc s/o Edmund & Rosy to Bettie S Fox 22 S Acc Acc d/o Golden F & Elizabeth on 20 Dec 1871 near Locustville by LK LeCato

LILLISTON Alfred J 24 S Carpenter Acc Acc s/o Henry P & Mary to Ellen F Melson 17 S Acc Acc d/o Jno D & Margt on 11 Mar 1869 at Acc by JC Martin

LILLISTON Edward 24 S Farmer Acc Acc s/o Isaac & Nancy to Elizabeth Wessells 19 S Acc Acc d/o Ephraim on 18 Mar 1869 at Acc by G Bradford

LILLISTON George D 25 S Farmer Acc Acc s/o Bowman & Cassgndia to Sarah Nock 19 S Acc Acc d/o Samuel & Margaret on 8 Jun 1870 at Onancock by D Titlow

LILLISTON Henry Lee 21 S Undertaker Acc Acc s/o Henry P & Elizth to Junie W Fitchett 16 S Acc Acc d/o Jno F & Susan on 19 Aug 1884 at Drum'tn by WC Vaden

LILLISTON James 20 S Farmer Drum'tn Drum'tn s/o James & Margt to Elizabeth Ann Davis 18 S Horntown Onancock d/o Thos S & Sarah (Sally A) on 23 Nov 1859 at Ayres Chp by D Titlow

LILLISTON John J 32 S Painter Acc

Acc s/o Natallie to Caroline T Justice 27 S Acc Acc d/o Susan on 27 Aug 1879 at Modest Town by DA Woodson

LILLISTON Levin Col 40 W Laborer Acc Acc s/o Rosie to Emma Holmes Col 35 W Acc Acc on 27 Sep 1875 at Acc by JW Ruff

LILLISTON Levin T 25 S Farmer Acc Acc s/o Natalia to Jane T Rew 22 S Acc Acc d/o Revel & Jane on 4 Jan 1880 near Craddockville by DA Woodson

LILLISTON Peter Col 32 S Laborer Acc Acc s/o Maria White to Mary Pepper Col 24 S Acc Acc on 17 Jul 1872 at Acc by A Joynes

LILLISTON Robert 23 S Farmer Acc Acc s/o Robert & Mary E to Roxanna Hargis 18 S Acc Acc d/o James F & Missouri on 27 Dec 1888 at Drum'tn by WJ Twilley

LILLISTON Samuel 23 S Farmer Acc Acc s/o Robert & Mary to Harriet Bull 20 S Acc Acc d/o Wesley W & Margaret on 29 Jan 1891 at Acc C H by JT Moore

LILLISTON Washington 26 S Farmer Acc Acc to Mary V Bradford 24 D Acc Acc on 9 Dec 1883 at Locustville by JG Anderson

LILLISTON William Col 24 S Wage-earner Acc Acc s/o Eldred & Mary to Mary L Ewell Col 22 S Acc Acc d/o John & Ellen on 5 Jul 1893 at Acc by AJ Satchell

LILLISTON William J 25 S Painter Acc Acc s/o James P & Eliz'th A to Kate E Baum 18 S Washington DC Acc d/o Edward & Martha on 20 Mar 1895 at Lee Mont by B Clark

LILLISTON Wm 24 S Farmer Acc Acc s/o Edwd & Rosy to Rebecca E Scott 17 S Acc Acc d/o Walter & Malinda on 18 Oct 1876 near Locustville by LK LeCato

LIND Richard 28 S Sail Maker Stockholm Sweden NY s/o Richd & Ann to Josephine Melvin 17 S Acc Chinco: Isld d/o Thos & Lydia A on 15 Sep 1875 at Chinco: Isld by WP Thornton

LING Alexander 60 W Farmer Acc Acc s/o Alex & Fanny to Elizabeth Taylor 50 W Acc Acc d/o Geo Window on 26 Feb 1868 at Acc by JO Moss

LING Alexander to Mary Jones lic: 3 Feb 1868

LING James C 22 S Farmer Acc Acc s/o Alexander & Rosana to Elizabeth D Taylor 21 S Acc Acc d/o Nathaniel & Maria on 2 Jan 1861 at Temp'ville by W Merrill (George W Wyatt says both over 21)

LING Meshack 22 S Acc Acc s/o Edwd & Hester to Anna M Blackwell 21 S Mercer Co NJ Acc d/o Jas M & Emma on 30 Dec 1879 at Acc by M Oldham

LING Wm W 25 S Farmer Acc Acc s/o Edwd T & Hester to Hester B Bull 19 S Acc Acc d/o George E & Mary on 9 Jul 1879 near Sea Side P O by JW Hundley

LINGO Benjamin F 29 S Merchant Acc Acc s/o Robert & Meria to Mary A Justice 18 S Acc Acc d/o Wm L on 8 Mar 1882 near Belle Haven by JE Humphreys

LINGO George 32 S Farmer Acc Acc to Caroline Matthews 21 S N'hamp: Acc on 18 Apr 1869 at Acc by JE Humphreys

LINGO James 24 S Mechanic b: Acc s/o Robert Lingo & Mariah Downing to Susan Lewis 18 S b: Acc d/o Edward Lewis & Lizer Bonwell on 16 Jan 1861 at Nath'l Turlington's by LK LeCato (Edward Johnson says both over 21)

LINGO John 23 S Laborer Sussex Co DE Acc s/o Wm H & Mary E to Ary L Hill 21 S Acc Acc d/o Littleton & Mary on 26 Nov 1886(?) at Chinco:

Isld by SU Grimsley Certificate returned 12 Jan 1889

LINGO John W 29 S Farmer Acc Acc s/o Robert & Margt to Eliza Lewis 38 W Acc Acc d/o Henry & Kessy Holly on 14 May 1856 at Acc by M Oldham (Thomas Hall Kellam says both over 21)

LINGO John W 31 W Farmer Acc Acc s/o Robt & Margt to Elizabeth Mason 30 W Acc Acc d/o Charles Smith & Sally Mears on 26 May 1858 at Acc by M Oldham

LINGO John W 43 W Farmer Acc Acc s/o Robert & Margaret to Patience P LeCato 26 S Acc Acc d/o John & Sally on 1 Sep 1870 at Acc by JE Humphreys

LINGO Robert (Linger) 26 S Brick Mason b: Acc s/o Robt & Marich to Hester Jane (Ann) Lewis 19 S b: Acc d/o Eliza on 20 May 1856 at Acc by JWA Elliott (W L Bell says he over 21)

LINTON Aaron 21 S Oysterman Acc Acc s/o George & Nancy to Melissa Thomas 15 S Acc Acc d/o Alonzo & Martha on 26 Mar 1882 at Sykes Isld by RB Beadles

LINTON George T 17 S Waterman Acc Acc s/o George W & Nancy to Lelia A Martin 16 S Acc Acc d/o William & Elizabeth on 12 Mar 1893 at Sykes Isld by RB Scott

LINTON George Wash 21 S Oysterman Acc Acc s/o George & Nancy to Mahala Jane Marshall 19 S Acc Acc d/o Robert & Mahala on 26 Sep 1874 at Sexes Isld by M Oldham

LINTON James 23 S Oysterman Acc Acc s/o William Lewis & Sally Linton to Arinthia V Justice 20 S Acc Acc d/o John H & Adaline on 26 Jan 1870 at Sexes Isld by M Oldham

LINTON John 22 S Oysterman b: Acc s/o William to Margt Wessells 20 S b: Acc d/o Betsey Wessells on 5 Jan 1855 at Sally Corbin's by GH Ewell

LINTON John W 25 S Oysterman Acc Acc s/o John & Margt to Laura C Fisher 28 D Acc Acc d/o Thomas & Ann C Wessells on 18 Oct 1885 at Guilford by JW Carroll

LINTON Sewell J 17 S Oysterman Acc Acc s/o John W & Margaret A to Virginia Lewis 17 S Acc Acc d/o Revel J & Virginia on 20 Jul 1890 at Acc by JS Wallace

LINTON Stephen Decatur 25 S Oysterman Acc Acc s/o Stephen & Mary to Mary Ann Ewell 23 S Acc Acc d/o Saml & Sally on 6 Aug 1876 at Saxes Isld by JM Anderson

LINTON Thomas H 21 S Oysterman Acc Acc s/o Stephen W & Mary to Ellen Marshall 23 S Acc Acc d/o Dennard & Eliath J on 12 Sep 1875 at Saxis Isld by WJ Twilley

LINTON Wm H 21 S Oysterman Acc Acc s/o Henry C & Rachel to Sarah Jane Darby 17 S Som Co MD Acc d/o Saml & Leah Jane on 10 Jan 1877 at Pocomoke Nk by M Oldham

LITTLE James M 35 S Ship Joiner Cecil Co MD Wilmington DE s/o Christopher A & Isabella B to Laura E Floyd 16 S Acc Acc d/o John M & Sarah F on 3 Jun 1888 at Acc by JW Ward

LITTLETON Frank D 25 S Mechanic Acc Acc s/o Richd & Mary to Jane Tatham 22 S Acc Acc d/o Ezeekiel & Elishea on 8 Mar 1876 at Bethel Ch by DA Woodson

LITTLETON Geo T 30 S Mechanic Acc Acc s/o Richard & Mary to Emma S Singleton 22 S Acc Acc d/o Wm & Elizth on 29 Dec 1875 at Bethel Ch by DA Woodson

LITTLETON George T 23 S Farmer Acc Acc s/o Saml & Adaline to Mary E Phillips 20 S Acc Acc d/o Saml on 26 Dec 1878 at Revel Justice Lee Mount by FH Mullineaux

LITTLETON George T 32 W Woodworker Acc Acc s/o Richard & Mary to Sally J Parkes 24 S Acc Acc d/o James & Polly on 28 Apr 1880 at David Bloxom's by DA Woodson

LITTLETON James 23 S Carpenter Acc Acc to Amanda P Ackley 26 S Philadelphia PA Acc d/o Jno T & Marretta on 2 Apr 1882 near Bethel Bapt Ch by JW Hundley

LITTLETON James G 23 S Undertaker Acc Acc s/o Thomas & Sallie to Anna Mears 22 S Acc Acc d/o Meshack & Betsey on 23 Feb 1890 at Modest Town by JW Ward

LITTLETON Richard 28 W Farmer Guilford Guilford s/o Geo to Catharine E Annis 36 W Guilford Guilford d/o Thos R & Hester Clayton on 23 Apr 1860 at r/o G H Ewell by GH Ewell

LITTLETON Robert T 23 S Farmer Acc Acc s/o Thos & Sally to Clara T Bloxom 18 S Acc Acc d/o Wm H & Mary on 19 Dec 1883 at Guilford Ch by JW Carroll

LITTLETON Thos G 23 S Farmer Wic Co MD Acc s/o Edwd L & Annie to Georgianna Groton 17 S Acc Acc d/o Wm & Sally Ann on 19 Dec 1879 at Acc by JW Hundley

LLOYD Ballvin F 21 S Sailor Matthews Co Matthews Co s/o Jeremiah & Ann to Martha A Twiford 18 S Acc Acc d/o Julius & Annie on 3 Jul 1879 at Lee Mont by FH Mullineaux

LLOYD Reuben 21 S Dredging Matthews Co VA Acc s/o Jeremiah & Fanny to Mary E Twiford 21 S Acc Acc d/o Julius R & Annie on 7 Jun 1886 at Onancock by CA Grice

LOFLAND Baxter Col 21 S Farmer Acc Acc s/o Stran Lofland & Ann Poulson to Mary Read Col 21 S Acc Acc d/o James & Ellen on 27 Dec 1885 at Drum'tn by LW Lee

LOFLAND Burnis FN 27 S Sailor Acc Acc s/o Severn Lofland & Hart Scharbough to Sarah Taylor FN 25 S Acc Acc d/o Jennie Taylor & Caleb Topping on 27 Dec 1865 at Acc by JC Addison

LOFLAND Charles H Col 23 S Hostler Acc Acc s/o Stran & Ann to Georgianna Lewis Col 22 S Acc Acc d/o George on 25 Nov 1890 at Onancock by J Duckett

LOFLAND Clement W 42 W Teacher DE Chinco: Isld s/o Wm & Elenor to Sarah Ann Jester 27 W Chinco: Isld Chinco: Isld d/o Elijah & Nancy on 25 Jan 1855 at r/o Parker Bowdin by P Bowdin

LOFLAND Clement W 50 W Clerk DE Acc s/o William & Elenor to Nancy Jester 21 S Acc Acc d/o Elijah & Martha (Kendall & Martha) on 24 Jun 1865 at Acc by P Bowdin

LOFLAND Clement W 45 W Teacher MD Acc s/o Wm & Elenor to Mary Ann Sharpley 45 W Acc Acc d/o Michael & Ann Reed on 15 Sep 1867 at Acc by P Bowdin Sr

LOFLAND Jas H A 30 S Physician Acc Acc s/o Alfred & Cassie to Catharine R Waters 28 W Acc Acc d/o Wm & Margt Finney on 2 Oct 1879 at Geo S Mapp's by JC Watson

LOFLAND Wm S D Col 22 S Farmer Acc Acc s/o Stran & Anna to Anna L Sample Col 18 S Acc Acc d/o Ambrose & Mary on 9 Dec 1891 at Acc by J Duckett

LOGAN Edward Col 23 S Laborer Acc Acc to Louisa Miller Col 22 S Acc Acc on 1 Jan 1871 near Horntown by O Littleton

LOGAN General Col 23 S Oysterman Acc Acc s/o Alicia to Mary Miller Col 22 S Acc Acc on 16 Sep 1875 at Horntown by IT Adkins

LOGAN Harry Col 21 S Sailor Acc Acc s/o Lewis & Mary to Ella Conquest Col 17 S Acc Acc d/o James &

Betsey on 26 Jun 1894 at Acc by JC Young

LOGAN Henry Col 42 S Shoemaker Acc Acc to Betsy Griffin Col 40 S Acc Acc d/o Susan on 25 Sep 1878 at Drum'tn by RH Govans

LOGAN Henry Col 24 S Wage-earner Acc Acc s/o Arthur Miller & Mary Logan to Mary A Crippen Col 21 S Acc Acc d/o John & Frances on 29 Oct 1888 at Chinco: Isld by RI Watkins

LOGAN John Col 40 W Farmer Acc Acc s/o Peter to Harriet Conquest Col 45 W Acc Acc on 29 Jul 1885 near Atlantic by JC Cluff

LOGAN Lewis N 28 S Oysterman Ireland Acc s/o David & Fannie to Lizzie E Bell 21 S Wor Co MD Acc d/o James & Jane on 29 Dec 1891 at Greenbackville by RS Williamson

LOGAN Nathan Col 21 S Laborer Acc Acc to Mary Chandler Col 21 S Acc Acc on 26 Dec 1871 at Savageville by R Davis

LOGAN Peter Col 52 S Farmer Acc Acc s/o Sarah Gillet to Sally A Church Col 43 S Acc Acc d/o Esther Henderson on 6 Jul 1873 at Horntown by S Johns

LOGAN Shadrach 40 S Farmer Acc Acc s/o Asloy to Sarah Davis 23 S Acc Acc d/o Tabitha on 9 Jan 1868 at Acc by P Bowdin Sr

LOGAN Simon Col 45 S Oysterman Acc Acc to Harriet [Milburn] Milbourn Col 40 S Acc Acc on 6 Mar 1882 near Jenkins Bridge by JC Cluff

LOGAN Thomas Col 22 S Farmer Acc Acc s/o Lewis & Mary to Emma Byrd Col 23 S Acc Acc d/o Henry on 27 Dec 1894 at Acc by AJ Satchell

LOGAN Wade H Col 23 S Oysterman Acc Acc s/o Isaac & Eliza to Leah Roberts Col 24 S Acc Acc d/o Priest H & Ellen on 19 Nov 1893 at Chinco: Isld by RB Sanford

LOGAN William [Logen] (Login) 22 S Laborer Acc Acc to Adeline Armstrong 27 S Acc Acc on 17 Jul 1870 near Horntown by S Marshall

LONG Wm L 30 S Farmer Acc Acc s/o Thomas & Mary to Nannie C West 21 S Acc Acc d/o Francis & Lizzie on 12 Jan 1876 at Modest Town by CV Waugh

LORD John T 25 W Sailor Som Co MD Acc s/o Brittianna to Sippora Crockett 22 S Acc Acc d/o Josiah & Betsy on 22 Jul 1867 at Acc by WT Tull

LUCAS Oliver (J) 26 S Farmer Acc Acc s/o Southy S & Nancy to Annie N Shrieves 19 S Acc Acc d/o David M & Sarah on 30 Dec 1863 at Acc by ES Grant

LUCAS Oliver J 35 W Merchant Acc Acc s/o Southey T & Nancy to Emma W Matthews 19 S Acc Acc d/o Wm H & Margaret on 12 Nov 1873 near Modest Town by WF Talbott

LUCAS Samuel s/o Catherine Andrews who gave consent to Tabitha White d/o Sofian who gave consent lic: 25 Jan 1858

LUCAS Solomon J 23 S Sailor Acc Acc s/o Sam'l & Tabitha to Annie Poulson 19 S Acc Acc d/o Jno E & Mary on 9 Aug 1883 at Acc by JW Hundley

LUCAS Sylvanus H to Esther E White lic: 15 Mar 1859 Samuel W Powell says both over 21

LUN James 23 S Oysterman Acc Acc s/o James & Betsy to Mary Nancy Bowden 18 S Acc Acc d/o Crippen & Mary on 8 Feb 1879 at Chinco: Isld by WP Thornton

LUND John P 24 S Oysterman Chinco: Isld Acc s/o Jas & Elizth to Rachel E McGee 23 S Sussex Co DE Acc d/o Jesse & Lydia on 6 May 1875 at

Chinco: Isld by WP Thornton

LYNCH Levin 22 S Oysterman Sussex Co DE Acc s/o Joseph B & Charlotte to Rebecca Bowden 17 S Acc Acc d/o Joshua J & Nancy M on 18 Dec 1890 at Chinco: Isld by GE Wood

MACKS James E 24 S Sailor N'hamp: Acc s/o Padsorne R & Anna to Ellen L Corbin 17 S Acc Acc d/o James H & Ellen on 10 Aug 1881 at Acc by RB Beadles

MAGEE George 24 S Sailor Wor Co MD Acc s/o Jesse & Sudia to Eliza Andrews 17 S Acc Acc d/o Mordicar & Mary on 28 Apr 1888 at Chinco: Isld by SU Grimsley

MAGEE John E 28 S Sailor Sessex Co DE Acc s/o Jesse & Lydia to Drucilla Jester 19 S Acc Acc d/o Isaac & Margt on 20 Oct 1879 at Chinco: Isld by WP Thornton

MAJOR Alexander Col 26 S Wage-earner Acc Acc s/o Thomas & Louisa to Nannie Eichelberger Col 27 S Acc Acc d/o Isaac on 12 Jan 1890 at Acc by TW Nettles

MAJOR Alfred T Col 37 S Farmer Acc Acc s/o Leah to Susan C Burton Col 27 S Acc Acc d/o Thos H & Mary S on 27 Sep 1893 at Locust Mount by JWA Elliott

MAJOR George (FN) 35 W Farmer Acc Acc s/o John & Zippie to Phoebe Martin (FN) 29 W Acc Acc d/o Seppy & Lavina Phillips on 23 Aug 1866 at Acc by LK LeCato

MAJOR George L Col 60 W Farmer Acc Acc s/o Joshua & Zipporah to Mary Sample Col 45 S Acc Acc on 17 Oct 1894 at Acc by JC Young

MAJOR Jesse Col 28 S Laborer Acc Acc to Charlotte Hatton Col 21 S Acc Acc on 24 Nov 1871 at Onancock by R Davis

MAJOR John FN to Louisa Thompson FN lic: 13 Aug 1858 Thomas M Folio says both over 21

MAJOR John S Col 48 S Farmer Acc Acc s/o Tinny Wright to Ellen Revell Col 31 S Acc Acc d/o Ellen on 4 Oct 1883 at Belle Haven by JE Humphreys

MAJOR Joshua Col 23 S Sailor Acc Acc s/o Geo & Rachel to Cordie Rosell Col 21 S Acc Acc d/o James & Jane on 19 Jan 1879 at bride's home by TW Nettles

MAJOR Lewis Col 26 S Sailor Acc Acc to Elizabeth (Major) Webb Col 19 S Acc Acc d/o Jno & Harriet Webb on 27 Mar 1872 near Belle Haven by JE Humphreys

MAJOR Perry 22 S Farmer Acc Acc s/o Margaret to Sarah Ames 21 S Acc Acc d/o Lucy on 24 Apr 1867 at Acc by WT Tull

MAJOR Perry Col 51 W Farmer Acc Acc s/o Margaret West to Ellen Watson Col 37 S Acc Acc d/o Mary on 31 Jul 1895 at Acc by RE Lee

MAJOR Thomas Col 56 S Farmer Acc Acc s/o Comfort to Lydia Bayly Col 47 S Acc Acc d/o Nicey Ch on 13 Feb 1873 at Acc by JE Humphreys

MAJOR William Thomas Col 26 S Wage-earner Acc Acc s/o Thomas & Louisa to Sarah Sample Col 21 S Acc Acc d/o Charles & Betsey on 2 Jan 1889 at Acc by L Duncan

MAJOR Wm Hy Col 24 S Wage-earner Acc Acc s/o John & Ellen to Laura E S Scarborough Col 22 S Acc Acc d/o David & Rachel on 15 Mar 1891 near Pungo: by L Duncan

MALLET Edward H 40 W Oysterman Acc Wor Co MD s/o Jno & Sally to Margaret Jester 40 S Acc Acc d/o Parker & Anna Bowden on 4 Jun 1881 at Chinco: Isld by WP Thornton

MANNEL John L Col 39 W Oysterman Acc Acc s/o Robert & Gracy to Sarah [Bailey] Bayly Col 31 S Acc Acc d/o Henry & Mary on 26 Mar 1891 at Wattsville by AS Amos

MANUEL John Col 30 S Oysterman Acc Acc s/o Robt & Grace to Mary C Selby Col 23 S Acc Acc d/o Esther Aydeotte on 2 Jul 1879 near Horntown by PJ Adams

MANUEL Robert W [Manuell] Col 22 S Laborer Acc Acc s/o Grace to Effie Roberts 21 S Acc Acc d/o Mary on 15 Jul 1875 at r/o Pastor by S Johns

MANUEL Samuel black 27 S Laborer s/o Robert & Grace to Arinthia Read black 24 S d/o John & Elizabeth lic: 11 Dec 1874 marr:13 Dec 1874

MANUEL Samuel Col 27 S Laborer Acc Acc s/o Robert & Grace to Arinthia Read Col 24 S Acc Acc d/o John & Elizth on 22 Dec 1877 at Acc by S Johns

MAPP Appie Col 51 S Wage-earner Acc Acc s/o Leah to Mary Harmon Col 42 S Acc Acc d/o Sarah on 4 Aug 1892 at Acc by RH Coleman

MAPP Caleb Col 60 W Wage-earner Acc Acc to Tittie Crippen Col 23 S Acc Acc on 8 Dec 1889 at Temp'ville by JC Cluff

MAPP Columbus 21 S Farmer Acc Acc s/o Geo S & Cath to Rose Ann Finney 24 S Acc Acc d/o William & Rosa on 17 Dec 1856 at Acc by JH Addison

MAPP Edward P 21 S Farmer N'hamp: N'hamp: s/o Jno & Cassandria to Catharine S Roberts 18 S Acc Acc d/o Louis S (Lewis) & Sarah on 2 Apr 1856 at Acc by M Oldham

MAPP Edward W 21 S Farmer Acc Acc s/o Jas & Bettie C to Sadie Annie Hope 20 S Acc Acc d/o Jno T F & Catharine on 13 Jan 1886 at Locust Mount by JWA Elliott

MAPP Francis B 22 S Farmer/Laborer N'hamp: N'hamp: s/o Jno C & Kessy to Sarah Frances Hatton 17 S Acc Acc d/o Wm P & Sarah Caroline Hatton on 31 May 1854 at N'hamp: by M Oldham (Wm A Joynes said Mapp over 21)

MAPP Fred G 23 S Farmer N'hamp: N'hamp: s/o Wm W & Margt A to Sally L Henderson 18 S Acc Acc d/o Amelius G & Susan R on 27 Dec 1875 at Belle Haven by JE Humphreys

MAPP George Col 26 S Farmer Acc Acc s/o Saml & Mary to Larretta [Bevans] Beavans Col 22 S Acc Acc d/o Severn & Elizth on 26 Dec 1886 at Acc by L Duncan

MAPP George Scarburgh 22 S Farmer Acc Acc s/o George L & Susan to Sarah S Walker 22 S Acc Acc d/o James K & Margaret L on 9 Jun 1870 at Pungo: by DA Woodson

MAPP George T 20 S Farmer Acc Acc s/o William E & Kate to Annie D Trower 20 S Acc Acc d/o Thomas L & Ann on 28 May 1890 at Oak Grove Ch by WJ Twilley

MAPP George T Jr to Victoria C Roberts d/o Edwin S who gave consent lic: 14 Jan 1861 Joseph G Savage says he over 21

MAPP James 25 S Farmer Acc Acc s/o Geo S & Elizth to Margt F Nottingham 22 S Acc Acc d/o David B & Leah G on 14 Sep 1853 at N'hamp: by P Warren

MAPP James B 21 S Farmer Acc Acc s/o James B & Bettie C to Sarah F Ward 26 S Acc Acc d/o Wm & Susan on 2 May 1880 near Locustville by LK LeCato

MAPP James B 26 W Farmer Acc Acc s/o James T & Betty C to Fanny P Lang 21 S Acc Acc d/o James C & Elizth D on 23 Dec 1885 at Conquest Ch by JW Carroll

MAPP James C 27 S Farming Acc Acc s/o Robin B & Sarah to Sophronia Mears 16 S Acc Acc d/o John S & Sarah on 12 Dec 1861 at Acc by JWA Elliott

MAPP John Col 22 S Wage-earner Acc

Acc s/o Appie to Susan Hargis Col 21 S Acc Acc d/o Caroline on 15 Feb 1891 at Belle Haven by T Peeden

MAPP John E 23 S Carpenter Acc Acc s/o Jas T & Elizth C to Mary C Richardson 22 S Acc Acc d/o Wm & Rachel on 19 Dec 1883 at Acc by WC Vaden

MAPP John H Col 30 S Farmer Acc Acc s/o Bridget Dregas to Cordie Parramore Col 24 S Acc Acc d/o Mary Ann on 31 Jul 1894 at Belle Haven by JG Lennon

MAPP Lewis H Col 25 S Laborer Acc Acc s/o Aaron to Ann Bull Col 26 S Acc Acc on 16 Jan 1876 near Burtons Ch by HT Rich

MAPP Lloyd T 18 S Farmer Acc Acc s/o Wm C & Cath K to Lanetta Roberts 21 S Acc Acc d/o Wm J & Ann on 24 Feb 1869 at Acc by JE Humphreys

MAPP Smith Col 21 S Seaman Acc Acc s/o Jane to Willie Burton Col 18 S Acc Acc d/o Sarah on 10 Jun 1885 at Locust Mount by JWA Elliott

MAPP Southey S 27 S Farmer Acc Acc s/o George C & Rosa to Olivia E Turner 19 S Acc Acc d/o John T & Virginia on 11 Apr 1894 at Acc by JG Lennon

MAPP William B 24 S Farmer Acc Acc s/o Wm C & Catharine to Mary R Smith 18 S Acc Acc d/o Francis S & Emma S on 22 Aug 1893 at Pungo: by JM Anderson

MAPP William R Col 60 W Wage-earner Acc Acc s/o Tabitha to Mary Mears Col 45 W Acc Acc d/o Joshua & Sylvia Laws on 10 Mar 1889 at Locustville by P Sheppard

MAPP Wm E 21 S Farmer Acc Acc s/o Fredrick & Catharine Floyd to Mary S Mapp 17 S Acc Acc d/o Wm E & Kate S on 26 Jan 1881 at Old Ch Rd by GH Ray

MAPP Wm W Col 21 S Sailor Acc Acc s/o Hannah Parkes to Dora Matthews Col 21 S Acc Acc d/o Sally on 15 Jun 1879 at Onancock by JW Diggs

MARINER George T 24 S Acc Acc s/o Geo T & Elizabeth to Melissa E East 24 S Acc Acc d/o Geo T & Sarah on 9 Dec 1873 at Temp'ville by M Oldham

MARINER Oliver [Marriner] 23 S Farmer Acc Acc s/o George & Elizth to Amanda Ailworth 21 S Acc Acc d/o Lewis & Ann on 30 Oct 1878 at Recom Taylor's by TM Poulson

MARINER William 23 S Miller b: Acc s/o Levin & Polly to Mary Ann Henderson 18 S b: Acc d/o Edwd & Margt on 30 Apr 1856 at Sign Post by JF Chaplain (John E Wise says he over 21)

MARINER William [Marriner] 25 S Sailor Acc Acc s/o George & Elizth to Charlotte Ailworth 22 S Acc Acc d/o Lenox & Ann on 31 Jul 1878 at Capt Green's Gate by JW Hundley

MARSH Benjamin F 18 S Farmer Acc Acc s/o John R & Arinthia to Maggie S Northam 21 S Acc Acc d/o James C & Pauline on 27 Jun 1894 at Acc by EC Atkins

MARSH Charles W 19 S Sailor Som Co MD Acc s/o Wm H & Alice A to Malissa Mister 23 S Acc Acc d/o Edward C & Sarah J on 21 Apr 1880 at W W Marsh's by GH Ray

MARSH Edward W 18 S Merchant Acc Acc s/o John W & Margaret to Nellie W Crockett 17 S Acc Acc d/o Henry L & Eliza J on 21 Dec 1885 at Onancock by CA Grice

MARSH Elijah W 23 S Sailor Acc Acc s/o Walter W & Alicia to Annie B Chandler 18 S Acc Acc d/o Thomas R & Emily S on 21 Apr 1887 at bride's father's by RA Compton

MARSH Geo F 23 S Sailor Acc Acc s/o Walter & Ailsia to Gertrude Hornsby 16 S Acc Acc d/o James H & Eliz'th on 17 Jun 1891 at Acc by JM Anderson

MARSH George F 21 S Sailor Acc Acc s/o Jno W & Margaret A to Mary Jane Crockett 21 S Acc Acc d/o Henry & Ann on 29 Apr 1880 at Chesconessex by PA Leatherbury

MARSH Jas Ranford 20 S Sailor Som Co MD Acc s/o David A & Matilda to Lena E Edwards 17 S Acc Acc d/o John H & Hester on 25 Dec 1895 at Acc by HS Dulany

MARSH John R 19 S Sailor Acc Acc s/o Jno W & Mary H to Arinthia T Mears 21 S Acc Acc d/o Arthur & Margt on 31 Dec 1873 at Chesconessex by WF Talbott

MARSH Walter H 20 S Farmer Acc Acc s/o John W & Margaret to Virginia Lewis 21 S Acc Acc d/o Thomas & Elizabeth on 20 Oct 1881 at Onancock by LE Barrett

MARSH William C 20 S Farmer Acc Acc s/o John W & Margaret A to Bettie B Mears 21 S Acc Acc d/o Thomas (of A) & Frances on 10 Dec 1890 at Acc by GW Burke

MARSH Wm W 21 S Waterman Smith Isld MD Smith Isld MD s/o Benj F & Shady to Sally A Fitchett 17 S Acc Acc d/o Samuel on 4 Aug 1886 at Onancock by CA Grice

MARSHALL Aaron 21 S Oysterman Acc Acc s/o Aaron & Malinda to Mary A Wessells 15 S Acc Acc d/o Thos & Cathr on 8 Jan 1863 at Acc by ES Grant

MARSHALL Alfred Col 26 S Farmer Acc Acc s/o Azariah & Ann to Mary Coard Col 24 S Acc Acc d/o Levi & Elizabeth on 26 Jan 1887 at Lina Coard's by RJ Waters

MARSHALL Alfred K 22 S Waterman Acc Acc s/o Parker H & Comfort Jane to Minnie L Byrd 17 S Acc Acc d/o Walter & Irene on 21 Feb 1894 at Temp'ville by JR Tillery

MARSHALL Alger W P 23 S Farmer Acc Acc s/o Pasrker H & Comfort to Julia A Shrieves 17 S Acc Acc d/o Louis on 22 Jun 1887 at Mappsville by WA Street

MARSHALL Benj C Col 23 S Wage-earner Acc Acc s/o James & Annie to Lovie A Conquest Col 21 S Acc Acc d/o Emma on 12 Apr 1891 near Temp'ville by JC Cluff

MARSHALL Bracey T 22 S Sailor Acc Acc s/o Mary Ann to Matilda J Marshall 25 S Acc Acc d/o Cornelia A on 4 Jul 1880 at Messongo by JE Bundick

MARSHALL Chas William 25 S Sailor Acc Acc s/o Robt J & Eliza J to Susan Bell 22 S Acc Acc d/o Elizabeth on 3 Nov 1878 at Messongo by JE Bundick

MARSHALL Daniel B 24 S Oysterman Acc Acc s/o Wm & Amelia to Mary T Bell 18 S Acc Acc d/o Lorenzo & Drucilla on 25 Dec 1878 at Messongo by JE Bundick

MARSHALL David 22 S Waterman Acc Acc s/o Robert & Maria to Laura Martin 19 S Acc Acc d/o Wm & Georgianna on 23 Feb 1890 at Acc by JS Wallace

MARSHALL Dennard Thos 19 S Sailor Acc Acc s/o James B & Sinah to Sadie E Moore 17 S York Co VA Acc d/o Edward B & Mary E on 28 Aug 1895 at Sykes Isld by ML Williams

MARSHALL Edward 36 S Oysterman Acc Acc s/o Tabitha to Esther Henderson 22 S Acc Acc d/o Esther on 16 Feb 1868 at Acc by S Marshall

MARSHALL Edward Col 24 S Laborer Acc Acc s/o Ann Slaton to Elizabeth Tunnell Col 18 S Acc Acc d/o Sarah Holland on 1 Aug 1877 near Wattsville by JC Cluff

MARSHALL Elterdge J 25 S Farmer Acc Acc s/o Sylvester J & Polly to

Mary R Taylor 24 S Acc Acc d/o David & Susan on 30 Dec 1885 at Temp'ville by M Oldham

MARSHALL George Col 28 S Laborer Acc Acc s/o Ann to Frances Conner Col 24 S Acc Acc d/o Harriet on 30 Dec 1874 at Horntown by S Johns

MARSHALL George W 21 S Oysterman Acc Acc s/o Robert & Maria to Ann E Hall 19 S Acc Acc d/o Anthony L & Sarah on 26 Mar 1882 at Sykes Isld by RB Beadles

MARSHALL Gilbert 23 S Oysterman b: Acc to Pamalia Miles 22 S b: Acc on 5 Oct 1854 at Saml Jester by GH Ewell

MARSHALL Henry Col 27 S Laborer Acc Acc s/o Ann to Charlotte Logan Col 21 S Acc Acc d/o Alice on 5 Jan 1879 at Horntown by JC Cluff

MARSHALL Herbert S 22 S Oysterman Acc Acc s/o Stringer & Narcissus to Annie Elizth Merrill 15 S Acc Acc d/o James H & Esther on 7 Sep 1884 at Temp'ville by JW Carroll

MARSHALL Isaac S Col 24 S Oysterman Acc Acc s/o George & Esther to Victoria Townsend Col 18 S Acc Acc d/o John H & Martha on 17 Jan 1892 near Horntown by AS Amos

MARSHALL James W 23 S Oysterman b: Acc s/o Aaron to Olevia Thomas 21 S b: Acc d/o John (dec'd) & (Eliza Cutler who gave consent) on 26 Feb 1856 at road to Saxes Isld by GH Ewell

MARSHALL Jas 23 S Farmer b: Acc to Hetty Bayly 22 S b: Acc d/o Betsy Bayly on 9 Nov 1854 at Mr Harris's by GH Ewell (Thos G Harris says both over 21)

MARSHALL Jas M 26 S Sailor King William Co VA Acc to Jennie Shores 19 S Acc Acc d/o Gabriel & Amelia on 28 Feb 1891 at Tangier Isld by J Connor

MARSHALL Jefferson B 19 S Oysterman Acc Acc s/o Richd & Nancy to Indiana Hurley 17 S Acc Acc d/o Robt & Ann on 16 May 1883 at Conquest Ch by JW Hundley

MARSHALL Jefferson D 30 W Waterman Acc Acc s/o Richard & Nancy to Alice L Smith 18 S Acc Acc d/o Wm S & Margaret on 17 May 1893 at Temp'ville by JW Nicholson

MARSHALL Jno (FN) 33 S Farmer b: Acc s/o Ephraim & Kesiah to Jane Piper (FN) 18 S b: Acc d/o Philip & Patience on 2 Aug 1854 near Wattsville by T Waters

MARSHALL John H 27 S Acc Acc s/o Thos E & Charlotte to Sarah A Gunter 23 W Acc Acc on 31 Dec 1885 at Chinco: Isld by TM Poulson

MARSHALL John R 27 W Oysterman Acc Acc s/o Robert & Mahala to Susan Miles 16 S Acc Acc d/o Parker & Ann on 24 Jan 1867 at Acc by M Oldham

MARSHALL John Scott 23 S Farmer s/o James & Harriet to Elizabeth Marshall 23 S d/o Samuel & Caroline lic: 23 Feb 1865

MARSHALL John W 42 S Waterman Acc Acc s/o Stephen & Patience to Elishea Ann Landing 30 S Acc Acc d/o James & Mary on 19 May 1892 at Temp'ville by JW Nicholson

MARSHALL Kendal 21 S Boatman Acc Acc s/o Stephen & Patience to Marianna Burton 24 S Acc Acc d/o William & Nancy on 27 Jan 1875 at Modest Town by DA Woodson

MARSHALL Levin Col 60 S Farmer Acc Acc s/o Chanty to Amy Marshall Col 50 S Acc Acc d/o Leah on 19 Sep 1877 near New Church by JC Cluff

MARSHALL Levin T 38 W Farmer Acc Acc s/o Shadrack D & Mahala to Margaret A [Hinmon] Hinman 39

S Acc Acc d/o Elijah & Nancy on 13 Sep 1865 at Acc by M Oldham

MARSHALL Oscar R 20 S Waterman Acc Acc s/o Oscar to Clarinda Wilkerson 17 S Acc Acc d/o Sewell & Sally J on 14 Feb 1894 at Oak Hall by DJ Traynham

MARSHALL Oscoe (Oscar) 23 S Oysterman Messongo Messongo s/o Persil A (Ann) to Priscilla Tyler 22 S Messongo Messongo d/o Molly Marshall on 9 Nov 1864 at r/o Wm Stants by GH Ewell

MARSHALL Oswald 22 S Acc Acc s/o Thos & Emaline to Jane Linton 21 S Acc Acc d/o Geo on 18 Jan 1880 at Sexes Isld by JW Hilldrup

MARSHALL Parker H 21 S Farmer Cattail Cattail s/o Stephen & Martha to Comfort J Chase 19 S Cattail Cattail on 8 Mar 1860 at r/o Stephen Marshall by GH Ewell (James D Byrd says both over 21)

MARSHALL Richard ward/o Henry B Northam who gave consent to Nancy Shay d/o Nancy lic: 28 Dec 1857 Henry B Northam says she over 21

MARSHALL Richard 22 S Oysterman Messongo Messongo s/o Anna Marshall to Belinda White 18 S Messongo Messongo d/o William on 5 Jan 1865 at r/o Anna Marshall by GH Ewell

MARSHALL Robert 54 W Oysterman Acc Acc s/o Jno & Hessy Marshall to Maria Spence 26 S Som Co MD Som Co MD d/o Jno & Leah Ann on 28 Sep 1858 at r/o Jno Spence by ES Grant (Raymond R Lewis says both over 21)

MARSHALL Robert 78 W Fisherman Acc Acc to Elizabeth Martin 50 W Acc Acc on 26 Aug 1884 at Acc by RB Beadles

MARSHALL Robert A 30 S Oysterman Acc Acc s/o Robert & Mahaly to Rachel Jones 30 W Acc Acc d/o Planner & Polly Crockett on 5 Nov 1882 at Sykes Isld by RB Beadles

MARSHALL Robert A 30 W Waterman Acc Som Co MD s/o Robert to Kate Nelson 18 S Acc Acc d/o Robert & Augusta on 14 Jan 1893 at Sykes Isld by RB Scott

MARSHALL Saml J 19 S Oysterman Sexes Isld Sexes Isld s/o Gillet & Molly to Amanda Lewis 19 S Sexes Isld Sexes Isld d/o Mary Lewis (Revel & Matilda) on 10 Nov 1864 at r/o Stephen Corbins by GH Ewell

MARSHALL Samuel 24 S Sailor Acc Acc s/o George & Catharine to Margaret Thornton 26 S Acc Acc d/o Edward & Elizabeth on 1 Feb 1874 at Temp'ville by M Oldham

MARSHALL Samuel 32 S Farmer Acc Acc s/o George to Cecelia Chesser 21 S Acc Acc d/o James on 12 Nov 1879 at Atlantic Ch by JW Hundley

MARSHALL Samuel H 38 S Sailor Acc Acc s/o Wm A & Mollie to Mary E Smart 21 S Acc Acc d/o Nath & Sallie on 22 Jul 1866 at Acc by JH Ellegood

MARSHALL Samuel H 20 S Sailor Acc Acc s/o Mary A to Sarah A Marshall 19 S Acc Acc d/o Wm H & Permelia on 8 Feb 1870 at Acc by JET Ewell

MARSHALL Samuel W 20 S Waterman Acc Acc s/o Samuel H & Sarah A to Willie A Mears 22 S Acc Acc d/o Wm T on 11 Oct 1894 at Mappsville by JL King

MARSHALL Solomon widr to Ann Marshall wid/o Thomas W lic: 16 Jun 1856

MARSHALL Stephen J Col 26 S Farmer Acc Acc s/o James & Sarah to Mary J Taylor Col 21 S Acc Acc d/o Sarah on 18 May 1887 at Temp'ville by JC Cluff

MARSHALL Stephen R 25 S Oysterman Acc Acc s/o Stephen & Patience to Mary E Byrd 35 W Acc

Acc d/o Thos & Cath Mears on 21 Feb 1867 at Acc by JE Bundick

MARSHALL Stringer A s/o Stringer dec'd to Narcissa Taylor d/o Southy lic: 16 Jan 1854 Wm J Johnson says both over 21

MARSHALL Thomas 21 S Waterman Acc Acc s/o Wm & Pamelia to Sallie Bell 21 S Acc Acc d/o Lorenzo & Drucilla on 28 Jun 1885 at Temp'ville by M Oldham

MARSHALL Thomas T 25 S Sailor Acc Acc s/o Sylvester J & Mary I to Henrietta J Tunnell 24 S Acc Acc d/o John J & Sinah on 24 Jul 1887 at Acc by M Oldham

MARSHALL Wilbur Col 24 S Laborer Acc Acc to Annie Savage Col 16 S Acc Acc d/o Hannah on 2 Aug 1882 near Oak Hall by JC Cluff

MARSHALL William 33 W Oysterman Acc Acc s/o Zacariah & Zipporah to Ellen H Lewis 25 S Acc Acc d/o Henry & Amelia on 29 Jul 1883 at Sykes Isld by RB Beadles

MARSHALL William 58 W Farmer Acc Acc s/o Hennie to Mary A Smith 42 W Acc Acc d/o James B Taylor on 27 Apr 1887 at Temp'ville by M Oldham

MARSHALL William G Col 60 S Laborer Acc Acc to Mary Roberts Col 60 S Acc Acc on 20 Nov 1887 at Acc by N Morris

MARSHALL William W s/o George D to Jane Broadwater d/o Savage lic: 22 Nov 1858 George Wallop says both over 21

MARSHALL William W 42 W Farmer Acc Acc s/o George E to Narcissa Marshall 38 W Acc Acc d/o Southey & Wisa Taylor on 29 Dec 1869 near Horntown by TM Poulson (lic: 21 Apr 1869)

MARSHALL Wm [Marshal] 30 S Farmer b: Chinch Town s/o Geo E to Jane [Brodwater] Broadwater 37 S b: Oak Hall d/o Savage on 24 Nov 1858 at Acc by RT Boyd

MARSHALL Wm Fletcher 20 S Oysterman Acc Acc s/o Zachariah & Zipporah to Emily Dennis 17 S Acc Acc d/o John & Eliza on 7 Dec 1873 at Sykes Isld by M Oldham

MARSHALL Wm H Col 21 S Lumberman Acc Acc s/o James Douglas to Henrietta Holland Col 21 S Acc Acc d/o Irving on 9 Dec 1883 at Horntown by JC Cluff

MARSHALL Wm J 42 W Sailor Acc N'hamp: s/o Washington & Susan to Elizth A Lewis 22 S Acc Acc d/o Absalom & Elizth on 11 Apr 1872 at Acc by M Oldham

MARSHALL Wm W 50 D Farmer Acc Acc s/o Geo E & Margt to Sarah M Truitt 32 W Wor Co MD Acc d/o John & Elizth Davis on 30 Oct 1878 at Atlantic by JW Hundley

MARSHALL Woodston 23 S Waterman Acc Acc s/o Rich'd R & Nancy to Annie J Rew 20 S Acc Acc d/o John & Tabitha on 25 Dec 1895 at Temp'ville by EF Garner

MARSTON Francis A (Marsten) 23 S Mechanic Richmond VA Williamsburg s/o Geo W (Wm) & Sarah to Margaret W Garrison 22 S Acc Acc d/o William & Susan on 2 Oct 1856 at Acc by M Oldham

MARSTON Harvey 32 S Merchant Acc Acc s/o Frank & Maggie to Missouri E Bell 26 S Acc Acc d/o Thomas H & Margaret A on 15 May 1889 at Oak Grove Ch by JWA Elliott

MARTIN Alfred 23 S Farmer Acc Acc s/o Maria to Elizabeth Williams 18 S Acc Acc d/o Geo & Drucilla on 25 Dec 1867 at Acc by S Marshall

MARTIN Arthur P 24 S Farmer Acc Acc s/o Wm H & Mary A to Sudie E West 17 S Acc Acc d/o Geo S & Susan on 23 Dec 1885 at Acc by L Rosser

Marriages

MARTIN Charles T 22 S Farmer Acc Acc s/o Susan J to Esther A Hopkins 19 S Acc Acc d/o Sarah A on 22 Dec 1881 at Acc by SC Boston

MARTIN Douglas A 27 S Waterman Acc Acc s/o Saml & Elizth to Margt H Johnson 19 S Acc Acc d/o Jas E & M S on 20 Nov 1878 at Oak Grove Ch by LK LeCato

MARTIN Edmund 30 S Laborer Acc Acc to Lucy Custis 22 S Acc Acc d/o Joshua & Jacdbon on 22 Jul 1869 at Acc by WF Williams

MARTIN Edmund Col 22 S Laborer Acc Acc s/o Charlotte to Mary E Drummond Col 19 S Acc Acc d/o Chas & Lucy on 28 Nov 1877 at Charles Drummonds' by A Handy

MARTIN Edmund Col 25 S Laborer Acc Acc s/o Caroline Drummond to Mary Miles Col 24 S Acc Acc on 21 Mar 1887 at Acc by JA Haynes

MARTIN Edward 24 S Oysterman Acc Acc s/o George & Elizath to Missouri D Marshall 20 S Acc Acc d/o James W & Olina on 21 Dec 1881 at Acc by RB Beadles

MARTIN Edward 29 W Oysterman Acc Acc s/o Geo & Elizth to Roxanna Wilkerson 18 S Acc Acc d/o Sewell R & Sally Jane on 2 Jan 1884 at Acc by RB Beadles

MARTIN Edward Col 25 S Wage-earner Acc Acc s/o Thomas to Mary Turlington Col 18 S Acc Acc d/o Rose on 17 Mar 1895 at Acc by J Duckett

MARTIN Edward B 23 S Farmer Acc Acc s/o Smith W & Elizabeth to Sally A Kidd 42 W Acc Acc d/o George & Amelia Christopher on 25 Nov 1885 at Pungo: by J McNabb

MARTIN Geo Thos Col 22 S Wage-earner Acc Acc s/o Edmund & Lucy to Virginia Kellam Col 22 S Acc Acc d/o John & Betsey on 5 Oct 1890 at Acc by LE Toulson

MARTIN George E L 24 S Farmer Som Co MD Som Co MD s/o Wm & Emaline to Zipporah A Crockett 18 S Acc Acc d/o Henry & Anna on 21 Apr 1881 at Onancock by JC Watson

MARTIN J W 30 S Mercantile Clerk James City Co VA Jamse City Co VA s/o Jno T & Sarah to Henrietta V West 20 S Acc Acc d/o Francis & Henrietta on 31 Aug 1881 at Modest Town by JW Hundley

MARTIN James Col 39 S Farmer Acc Acc s/o Samuel Harmon & Sarah Martin to Laura Phillips Col 35 S Acc Acc d/o Isaac & Maria on 13 May 1891 at Acc by RH Coleman

MARTIN James (Marten) FN to Ann Major FN d/o Annis Major FN who gave consent lic: 9 Jan 1854 Wm Charnock says he over 21

MARTIN James Alfred Col 23 S Farmer Acc Acc s/o James & Laura to Florence Susan Turlington Col 17 S Acc Acc d/o Fanny on 18 Dec 1889 at Onancock by GHT Byrd

MARTIN James P 30 S Farmer Acc Acc s/o Smith K & Rose W to Lizzie S Turlington 19 S Acc Acc d/o Samuel Z & Emma H on 27 Nov 1890 at Acc by RA Compton

MARTIN Jesse 20 S Oysterman Acc Acc s/o George & Elizth to Brunitta Linton 14 S Acc Acc d/o John & Margaret on 2 Mar 1882 at Sykes Isld by RB Beadles

MARTIN Jno 25 S Sailor b: N'hamp: s/o (Thomas) Mary Martin to Margt (C) Warrington 35 W b: N'hamp: d/o Levi & Sarah Ames on 22 Feb 1855 at Acc by JH Addison (Richard B Ames says he over 21)

MARTIN John 21 S Mariner Acc Acc s/o Elizabeth to Henrietta Lewis 17 S Acc Acc d/o Salathiel & Jennie E on 1 Nov 1884 at Acc by RB Beadles

MARTIN John Thomas Col 27 S Farmer Acc Acc s/o Southey &

Phoebe to Victoria Parker Col 21 S Acc Acc d/o George & Mary on 2 Jan 1889 at Acc by L Duncan

MARTIN Lewis 20 S Laborer Acc Acc s/o Mary to Fannie [Reed] Read 15 S Acc Acc d/o Emma on 16 May 1875 at Pungo: by JK Plato

MARTIN Lloyd Col 20 S Sailor Acc Acc s/o Anena to Arinthia Webb Col 18 S Acc Acc d/o Emma Downing on 29 Dec 1875 at Savageville

MARTIN Robert James Col 24 S Wage-earner Acc Acc s/o Southey & Phoebe to Rose Colonna Col 24 S Acc Acc d/o Harriet on 28 Nov 1888 at Acc by L Duncan

MARTIN Saml S 24 S Farmer Acc Acc s/o Isaac S & Jane J to Bettie E L Ames 16 S Acc Acc d/o Levin & Lettie E on 7 Sep 1886 at Craddockville by JW Hundley

MARTIN Shepherd Col 50 S Farmer Acc Acc s/o James & Fanny to Hannah Thompson Col 45 S Acc Acc d/o Abraham & Harriet on 1 Jan 1890 at Acc by L Duncan

MARTIN Smith K 41 W Farmer Acc Acc s/o Saml & Sophia to Rosina Wilson 25 S N'hamp: Acc d/o James S & Mary on 2 Mar 1859 at Acc by P Warren

MARTIN Smith T 23 S Farmer Acc Acc s/o Smith W & Elizth to Sallie T Johnson 17 S Acc Acc d/o John T & Rchel on 12 Jul 1882 at Oak Grove Chp by JWA Elliott

MARTIN Suthey [Marting] (Southey Martin) FN 21 S Sailor Acc Acc s/o James & Fanny to Pheby (Phebe) Phillips (FN) 21 S Acc Acc d/o Mathey Winney Phillips on 17 Dec 1857 at Locust Mount by JW Ewell (John C Watson says both over 21)

MARTIN Thomas D 20 S Farmer Acc Acc s/o James W & Louisa to Emma M Parkes 16 S Acc Acc d/o James (of B) & Peggie D on 19 Nov 1890 at Acc by TM Poulson

MARTIN Thos A 53 W Tailor Norfolk City Acc s/o Jas S & Mary to Virginia Ann [Browne] Brown 35 S Baltimore MD Acc d/o Wm D & Ann on 6 Mar 1862 at Acc by P Warren

MARTIN William 20 S Oysterman Acc Acc s/o Geo & Elizabeth to Georgianna Miles 19 S Acc Acc d/o Severn P & Hester Ann on 31 May 1873 at Acc by M Oldham

MARTIN William 41 W Laborer Acc Acc to Mary Ann Hart 41 S Acc Acc d/o James & Mary on 5 Sep 1875 at Sluytkill Nk by JH Amiss

MARTIN William H 25 S Farmer Acc Acc s/o Thos & Sally to Elizth Amanda Phillips 24 S Acc Acc d/o Jacob & Mary on 18 Dec 1861 at Acc by BT Ames

MARTIN William S 43 S Farmer Acc Acc s/o Wm & Rosa to Susan Harmon 27 S Acc Acc d/o Jno & Peggie on 11 Jun 1866 at Acc by BT Ames

MARTIN Wm H 53 W Farmer Acc Acc s/o Peter & Rosa to Sally A Doughty 40 S N'hamp: Acc d/o John & Sally Wescott on 18 Mar 1891 near Middlesex by WJ Twilley

MARVEL Nathaniel P 21 S Teacher b: Sussex Co DE s/o Burton & Elizth to Caroline K Clayton single b: Acc d/o George (Decd) & Ann on 6 Dec 1856 at Reese Chp by ES Grant (Calvin Taylor says both over 21)

MASON Alfred Col 23 S Laborer Acc Acc s/o Clarissa to Mary A Wharton Col 18 S Acc Acc d/o Martha on 22 Oct 1885 at Acc by AJ Satchell

MASON Alfred M 23 S Farmer Acc Acc s/o William P & Caroline S to Sallie L Gray 21 S Acc Acc d/o James E & Elizabeth on 26 Sep 1888 at Woodbury by WF Hayes

MASON Alvin to Margaret C Johnson

lic: 17 Oct 1871
MASON Alvin 26 S Farmer Acc Acc s/o William & Betsy to Willianna M Kellam 19 S Acc Acc d/o Wm E on 17 Apr 1873 near Locustville by LK LeCato
MASON Charles Col 36 D Wage-earner Acc Acc s/o Virginia to Sarah Nock Col 22 S Acc Acc d/o Hennie on 6 Jul 1892 at Acc by T Turlington
MASON Charles B 18 S Farmer Acc Acc s/o Charles H & Mary A to Nannie Milliner 19 S Acc Acc d/o John & Eliza on 20 Nov 1873 near Oak Grove Ch by LK LeCato
MASON Charles H 30 S Farmer Acc Acc s/o Richd & Betsy to Susan [Kilman] Killman 20 S Acc Acc d/o Daml & Emily on 7 May 1869 at Acc by JET Ewell
MASON David F 19 S Farmer Acc Acc s/o Zorobable W & Henrietta to Martha A Ewell 24 S Acc Acc d/o Solomon T & Laura on 25 May 1890 at Mappsville by WA Street
MASON Edward Col 23 S Farmer Acc Acc s/o Harry & Esther to Mary Griffin Col 17 S Acc Acc d/o Elizth Ayres on 26 Dec 1875 at Eater Mason's by HT Rich
MASON Edward Col 23 S Wage-earner Acc Acc s/o Clarissa Poulson to Florence E Mason Col 18 S Acc Acc d/o Alice on 28 Sep 1892 at Modest Town by AJ Satchell
MASON Edward P 27 S Farmer Acc Acc s/o David & Cath to Elizth Susan Barnes 21 S Acc Acc d/o Lewis & Margt M on 27 Jun 1878 at Woodstock by WJ Duhadway
MASON Edward T Col 44 W Farmer Acc Acc s/o Harry & Esther to Sarah Eliz'th Griffin Col 39 S Acc Acc d/o Mary on 17 Nov 1895 at Acc by AJ Satchell
MASON Eugene Robins 25 S Farmer Acc Acc s/o Thorogood & Elizabeth to Ida Grace Byrd 21 S Acc Acc d/o Sewell A & Ellen J S on 22 Dec 1880 at Mappsville by GH Ray
MASON Frank Col 22 S Farmer Acc Acc s/o Clarissa Poolenan to Eliza Seymour Col 22 S Acc Acc d/o Betsey on 30 Oct 1889 at Acc by JH Thomas
MASON Geo B 21 S Farmer Acc Acc s/o Geo & Nancy to Sarah A Parker 17 S Acc Acc d/o Jas & Henny on 18 Feb 1864 at Acc by D Titlow
MASON Geo H 20 S Sailor Acc Chinco: Isld s/o William & Amy to Charlotte A Andrews 19 S Acc Chinco: Isld d/o Isaac & Sarah on 15 May 1880 at Chinco: Isld by WP Thornton
MASON George black 46 S Farmer s/o Hetty to Nancy Harmon black 55 S d/o Millie lic: 13 Dec 1872 marr: at Pocomoke
MASON George Col 24 S Oysterman Acc Acc s/o Wm & Janie to Isabella Holden Col 22 S Acc Acc d/o Martha on 17 Dec 1893 at Temp'ville by JC Cluff
MASON George W 74 W Farmer Acc Acc s/o Edmund C & Elizabeth to Virginia Susan Mears 45 W Acc Acc d/o Joseph G & Virginia Beloate on 27 Oct 1892 near Onley Sta by EC Atkins & VW Bargamin
MASON Gillet 21 S Farmer Acc Acc s/o Zadock & Leah to Adaline [Shreaves] Shrieves 21 S Acc Acc d/o Wm S & Tabitha on 26 Oct 1865 at Acc by JE Bundick
MASON Gillet 34 W Farmer Acc Acc s/o Zadock & Leah to Sally [Shreaves] Shrieves 23 S Acc Acc d/o Wm S & Tabitha on 13 Feb 1878 at Modest Town by DA Woodson
MASON Harry 48 S Farmer Acc Acc s/o Henry Charnock & Lela Lewis to Esther [Strann] Stran 35 S Acc Acc d/o Henry Riley & Louisa Shann on

18 May 1869 at Acc by A Joynes
MASON Hebert Col 21 S Farmer Acc Acc s/o Henry & Eader to Mary Conquest Col 21 S Acc Acc d/o Henry & Adah on 9 Apr 1874 at Deep Ck by A Joynes
MASON Henry Col 22 S Laborer Acc Acc s/o Ann to Agnes [Duffee] Duffy Col 17 S Acc Acc d/o Eliza on 19 Jan 1876 near News Town by A Joynes
MASON Henry P to Sally A Colonna lic: 6 Dec 1859 Thomas Powell says both over 21
MASON Henry P 21 S Farmer Acc Acc s/o Zoro & Polly to Jane E White 22 S Acc Acc d/o Henry B & Hetty on 6 Jan 1869 at Acc by GW Matthews
MASON Henry T. 18 S Farmer Acc Acc s/o Major & Aet. to Mary A Parkes 18 S Acc Acc d/o Wm & Maude on 22 Dec 1875 at Acc by JM Anderson
MASON James 62 W Farmer Acc Acc s/o Major Sr & Rachel to Pamelia Mary Lewis 42 W Acc Acc d/o Saml & Lydia Barnes on 23 Jan 1884 at Guilford Ch by JW Carroll
MASON James Col 31 W Teamster Acc Acc s/o Clarissa Poolman to Anna Mason Col 17 S Acc Acc d/o Rachel on 6 Jan 1884 near News Town by AJ Satchell
MASON James 65 W Farmer Acc Acc s/o Major & Rachel to Mary E Poulson 50 W Acc Acc d/o Samuel & Nancy Killman on 17 Apr 1895 at Acc by DGC Butts
MASON James O 31 S Farmer Acc Acc s/o Saml & Elizth to Lottie C Sturgis 20 S Acc Acc d/o Jno W & Charlotte on 7 Apr 1880 at Craddockville by E Hebard
MASON James S 35 S Sailor Acc Acc s/o David & Catharine to Betty Killman 21 S Acc Acc d/o Samuel & Emma on 30 May 1880 at Lee Mont by FH Mullineaux
MASON Jas Franklin Col 23 S Farmer Acc Acc s/o Zorobable & Polly to Ida Susan Parkes 19 S Acc Acc d/o Wm & amanda S on 12 Feb 1879 at Conquest Ch by JE McSparran
MASON Jas H 22 S Farmer Acc Acc s/o Zadock & Leah to Mary E Hope 17 S Acc Acc d/o Wm S & Margt H on 2 Jun 1864 at Acc by ES Grant
MASON Jeremiah 21 S Farmer Acc Acc s/o Major & Nancy to Elizabeth H Bell 17 S Acc Acc d/o William (Decd)& Ann on 10 Jan 1861 at r/o Ann Bell by GH Ewell
MASON Jesse L 22 S Farmer Acc Acc s/o Southey & Sally to Blanche L Cullen 19 S Acc Acc d/o John S & Eliz'th on 3 Jan 1894 at Acc by JR Tillery
MASON John 21 S Farmer Acc Acc s/o Samuel & Eliza to Catharine Lingo 21 S Acc Acc d/o Robert & Maria on 15 Dec 1870 at Acc by LK LeCato
MASON John W 48 S Farmer Acc Acc s/o Wm & Eliz to Louisa A Coleburn 36 S Acc Acc d/o Saml & Dorinda on 13 Oct 1880 at Pungo: by CC Wertenbaker
MASON John William Col 23 S Laborer Acc Acc to Tamer Eliz Wharton Col 21 S N'hamp: Acc on 6 May 1883 at Drum'tn by LW Lee
MASON Judson Col 23 S Farmer Acc Acc s/o Peter & Ailsie to Amy Riley Col 22 S Acc Acc d/o Louis on 6 Jan 1895 at Acc by AJ Satchell
MASON Levin M 23 S Farmer Acc Acc s/o Stephen & Ann to Elizabeth L Trader 22 S Acc Acc d/o John on 30 Dec 1874 at Onancock by JH Amiss
MASON Lorenzo D 20 S Farmer Acc Acc s/o Edward P & Mary J to Hetty T Clayton 16 S Acc Acc d/o George T & Virginia on 28 Dec 1890 at Parksley by HS Dulany
MASON Louis Col 25 S Teamster Acc

Acc s/o Levi & Virginia to Missouri Heath Col 25 S Acc Acc d/o Jno & Adaline on 10 Aug 1881 at Pungo: by TW Nettles

MASON Major widr to Bernetta Justice d/o Samuel R lic: 3 Jan 1856 Robert Ayres says both over 21

MASON Major 20 S Acc Acc s/o Major & Ann to Elizabeth C Clayton 19 S Acc Acc d/o John & Ann on 12 Jan 1871 at Acc by O Littleton

MASON Middleton 32 S Farmer Acc Acc s/o Zadock & Leah to Ellen E Shrieves 19 S Acc Acc d/o William & Tabitha on 30 Nov 1871 near Modest Town by DA Woodson

MASON Middleton 38 W Farmer Acc Acc s/o Zadock & Leah to Sarah J Townsend 34 W Acc Acc d/o Meshack & Elizabeth Mears on 27 Feb 1878 at Modest Town by JW Hundley

MASON Orwell F 23 S Farmer Acc Acc s/o Jas & Sarah to Mary V Bunting 21 S Acc Acc d/o Geo & Rose Ann on 17 Dec 1879 at Conquest Ch by WW Royall

MASON Oswald C 22 S Farmer Acc Acc s/o Stephen & Annie to Sadie E Gardner 17 S Acc Acc d/o Benjamin & Elizabeth on 17 Oct 1888 at bride's home by RA Compton

MASON Otho E 23 S Farmer Acc Acc s/o Thorogood & Elizabeth A to Eulalia S Parkes 21 S Acc Acc d/o John & Mary on 26 Jan 1887 at Guilford by JW Carroll

MASON Peter H C widr to Sarah Logan d/o Oliver dec'd lic: 11 Nov 1856 John S Davis says she over 21

MASON Peter H C 40 W Farmer Wor Co MD Acc s/o Peter to Levinia C Gladding 40 W Acc Acc d/o Walter Slocomb on 16 Nov 1870 at Acc by M Oldham

MASON Peter H C 46 W Farmer Wor Co MD Acc s/o Peter & Eleinor to Annie R Corbin 33 S Acc Acc d/o Edwd T & Ann on 24 Jan 1877 at Acc by CC Wertenbaker

MASON Preson L 24 S Oysterman Acc Acc s/o Preson & Margt to Henrietta E Scott 21 S Acc Acc d/o Thos & Mary on 25 Apr 1867 at Acc by GW Matthews

MASON Robert J 25 S Merchant Acc Acc s/o Southy & Sally to Sally E Ewell 20 S Acc Acc d/o John O & Margaret on 30 Nov 1887 at Temp'ville by JW Carroll

MASON Samuel Col 20 S Laborer Acc Acc s/o Jannie to Emma White Col 22 S Acc Acc d/o Maria on 29 Jan 1874 at News Town by A Joynes

MASON Samuel H 56 S Blacksmith Acc Acc s/o Rose Bagwell to Polly Drummond Col 56 S Acc Acc on 1 May 1881 at Acc by RJ Waters

MASON Samuel P 22 S Farmer Acc Acc s/o Stephen & Annie to Fannie E Wallace 22 S Acc Acc d/o Margaret on 7 Dec 1887 at Pungo: by JR Strugis

MASON Southey 23 S Farmer b: Acc s/o Major & Nancy to Salley Nelson 17 S b: Acc d/o John on 6 Mar 1856 at r/o Geo H Ewell by GH Ewell (Southey Grinnalds says both over 21)

MASON Stephen E 21 S Acc Acc s/o Stephen & Harriet to Euphernia Trader 32 S Acc Acc d/o Ann Chandler on 5 Aug 1863 at Acc by JWA Elliott

MASON William 17 S Oysterman Acc Chinco: Isld s/o Wm & Amy to Mary A Whealton 35 W Acc Acc d/o Parker & Elizabeth Daisey on 4 Oct 1874 at my house by P Bowdin Sr

MASON William Col 21 S Laborer Acc Acc s/o Harry & Easter to Sarah Wise Col 16 S Acc Acc d/o Elizabeth Riley on 1 Oct 1878 at Morris Ch by A Handy

MASON William D 28 S Farmer Acc Acc s/o Jeremiah & Eliz'th to Mary T Bloxom 22 S Acc Acc d/o Thomas & Eliz'th on 26 Dec 1894 at Acc by DGC Butts

MASON William E T Col 19 S Wage-earner Acc Acc s/o Edward & Mary to Rachel Hinman Col 17 S Acc Acc d/o Samuel & Sarah on 22 May 1895 at Acc by AJ Satchell

MASON William H 25 S Farmer Acc Acc s/o Southey & Sally to Gertrude Taylor 18 S Acc Acc d/o Oliver H & Mary W on 14 Mar 1888 at Downings Ch by TG Pullen

MASON William T 24 S Farmer Acc Acc s/o Stephen E & Catherine C to Maggie T Edwards 20 S Acc Acc d/o Ezar W & Martha on 18 Sep 1889 at Finneys Wharf by GW Burke

MASON William T 20 S Farmer Acc Acc s/o Thorogood of Wm & Milcah Ann to Gertrude F Parkes 20 S Acc Acc d/o Elward (of J) & Nancy on 12 Oct 1892 at Lee Mont by JET Ewell

MASON William T [Mayson] (Mason) 19 S Mariner Chinco: Isld Chinco: Isld s/o Randal & Ann to Amy Lewis 22 W Chinco: Isld Chinco: Isld d/o Timothy Sr & Rebecca Hill on 3 Dec 1856 at Chinco: Isld by WP Thornton

MASON Wm B 24 S Farming Acc Acc to Henrietta Wessells 17 S Acc Acc d/o David B & Nancy on 8 Dec 1870 at Acc by JET Ewell

MASON Wm Hy 25 S Oysterman Acc Acc s/o Jas & Sarah to Malissa S Summers 22 S Acc Acc d/o Richd & Susan on 6 Nov 1878 at Guilford by JB Merritt

MASON Wm P 26 S Farmer Acc Acc s/o Zadock & Leah to Caroline Sparrow 28 S Acc Acc d/o Robt & Tibatha on 17 Dec 1863 at Acc by ES Grant

MASON Zadok O 25 S Farmer Acc Acc s/o James H & Mary to Edna E Taylor 24 S Acc Acc d/o A Jackson & Hettie on 27 Dec 1893 at Acc by LE Spencer

MASON Zorobabel W 29 S Farmer Acc Acc s/o Zorobabel & Polly to Elizabeth Young 19 S Acc Acc d/o Samuel T & Margt on 29 Oct 1876 at Guilford Ch by M Oldham

MASSEY Ayres Col 48 S Farmer Acc Acc to Margaret Selby Col 46 S Acc Acc d/o Leah Medad on 9 Apr 1879 at Acc by JC Cluff

MASSEY John 21 S Farmer b: Acc s/o John Massey & Martha Willis to Maria L V Tull 17 S b: Som Co MD d/o Wm M Tull & Elizth S Whitney & (ward/o Frederick A Tull who gave consent) on 22 Sep 1857 at Acc by P Warren (Fredrick A Tull said he over 21)

MASSEY John E 22 S Merchant's Clerk Wor Co MD Acc s/o John & Elizabeth to Sadie W Hudson 17 S Acc Acc d/o Alfred & Mary A on 1 Nov 1887 at Chinco: Isld by RI Watkins

MASSEY John E 24 W Hotel Keeper Wor Co MD Acc s/o S J & Hetty J to Bertie Hudson 17 S Acc Acc d/o Alfred & Mary A on 26 Feb 1890 at Chinco: Isld by EH Miller

MASSEY Otho D 18 S Telegraph Operator Acc Acc s/o James D & Mary E to Ida Nock 17 S Acc Acc d/o Virginia on 25 Sep 1891 at Mappsville by JL King

MATTHEWS A F 30 S Sailor & Oysterman Acc Acc to Mary Montgomery Babbitt 24 S New York City Acc d/o Charles E & Susan on 3 Mar 1880 at Chinco: Isld by TAH O'Brien

MATTHEWS Albert Col 20 S Farmer Acc Acc s/o Adrian & Martha to Ella Warren Col 21 S Acc Acc d/o Henrietta West on 6 Apr 1890 at Onancock by GHT Byrd

MATTHEWS Alfred E to Elizabeth Hinman d/o Perry dec'd lic: 26 Feb 1856 Wm J Bayly says both over 21

MATTHEWS Alfred J 22 S Farmer s/o Jacob & Seymour to Liney A Justice 20 S d/o John & Caty lic: 9 Jan 1865 marr: 12 Jan 1865

MATTHEWS Alfred T 19 S Farmer Acc Acc s/o A J & Lincie to Elizabeth P Young 19 S Acc Acc d/o Samuel & Rachel on 1 May 1887 at Frank Barnes' by JW Norris

MATTHEWS Asa W 32 S Sailor Acc Acc s/o Alfred E & Eliz'th to Sallie A Chase 23 S Acc Acc d/o Alsavada & Sallie A on 6 Aug 1893 at Acc by WA Street

MATTHEWS Caleb [Mathews] Col 53 S Farmer Acc Acc s/o Isaac & Peggy to Sarah Fields Col 53 S Acc Acc d/o Benjamin & Sarah on 18 Oct 1874 at Pocomoke by S Johns

MATTHEWS Ezikiel Col 20 S Laborer Acc Acc s/o Harriet Northam to Dosia Trader Col 22 S Acc Acc d/o George on 16 Sep 1880 near News Town by A Joynes

MATTHEWS Franklin T 18 S Farmer Acc Acc s/o Levin T & Virginia T to Susan W Young 27 S Acc Acc d/o John W & Laura T on 22 Jul 1888 at Lee Mont by JW Norris

MATTHEWS George A 26 S Farmer Acc Acc s/o Alfred & Elizabeth to Mileah Ann Davis 22 S Acc Acc d/o Alfred & Emaline on 21 Mar 1883 at Conquest Ch by JW Hundley

MATTHEWS George H Col 21 S Farmer Acc Acc s/o Adam & Martha to Charlotte Major Col 18 S Acc Acc d/o Jesse & Charlotte on 7 Feb 1894 at Onancock by FW Overton

MATTHEWS George S 21 S Farmer Acc Acc s/o Samuel H & Margaret A to Bettie J Gray 19 S Acc Acc d/o Jas Edward & Bettie on 9 Oct 1889 at Temp'ville by WF Hayes

MATTHEWS George W 63 W Minister Acc AR s/o Geo P & Pattie to Virginia A Rowley 52 S Acc Acc d/o John S & Drucilla B Robins on 14 Jul 1892 at Pungo: by JM Anderson

MATTHEWS George W s/o Thomas R to Emma Mears d/o Henry lic: 9 Jan 1860 James T Taylor(?) says both over 21

MATTHEWS Isaac Alias Sample Col 24 S Farmer Acc Acc s/o Sally Ames to Ann Smith Col 32 S MD Acc on 17 Dec 1876 near Pungo: by JK Plato

MATTHEWS James Col 24 S Farmer Acc Acc s/o Deborah to Mary F [Browne] Brown Col 17 S Acc Acc d/o Jane on 22 Oct 1876 at Atlantic P O by M Oldham

MATTHEWS James Col 22 S Farmer Acc Acc to Fannie E Wise Col 17 S Acc Acc d/o John & Mary on 2 Jun 1893 at Acc by J Duckett

MATTHEWS James E widr to Martha S (Fedderman) Feddeman wid lic: 15 Nov 1855

MATTHEWS James H Col 23 S Laborer Acc Acc s/o Henry & Susan to Alberta Mears Col 21 S Acc Acc d/o Jas & Ann on 4 Mar 1883 near Locust Mount by JWA Elliott

MATTHEWS John 38 W Mariner Acc Chinco: Isld s/o Wm & Sarah to Susan Hopkins 45 S Acc Chinco: Isld d/o Hy & Elizabeth on 2 Mar 1856 at Chinco: Isld by WP Thornton (John W Bloxom says both over 21)

MATTHEWS John 20 S Oysterman Acc Acc s/o Saml & Eliza to Ida Taylor 20 S Acc Acc d/o Saml C & Sally on 13 Jan 1877 at Guilford by JB Merritt

MATTHEWS John [Mathews] Col 47 S Farmer Acc Acc s/o Sarah to Harriet Conner Col 40 S Acc Acc d/o George & Hannah on 13 Dec 1874 at Friendship Ch by S Johns

MATTHEWS John E Col 35 S Farmer

Acc Acc to Mary Floyd Col 35 S Acc Acc d/o Sarah on 4 Oct 1888 at Acc by JK Adams

MATTHEWS John Jr Col 21 S Wage-earner Jackson NC Acc s/o John & Maria to Elizabeth Parker Col 21 S Acc Acc d/o David & Mary Ellen on 15 Jun 1892 at Acc by L Duncan

MATTHEWS John W (J) [Mathews] (Matthews) 30 S Farming Acc Acc s/o Wm J Mathews & Ann Abbland to Mary A P Selby 32 S Acc Acc d/o George Barnes & Eliza Givins on 7 Feb 1861 at Acc by T Waters (Levin Ayres says he over 21)

MATTHEWS Joseph W 54 W Farmer Acc Acc s/o William S & Susan to Emma Q Conquest 40 S Acc Acc d/o Edward H & Ann on 6 Aug 1890 at Acc by WF Hayes

MATTHEWS Julius G [Mathews] 29 S Mercantile Clerk VA Acc s/o William H & Margaret to Clara W Lucas 18 S Acc Acc d/o Southey T & Harriet on 16 Dec 1874 at Southey T Lucas' by DA Woodson

MATTHEWS Levin T 25 S Farmer Acc Acc s/o Jacob & Seymour to Virginia T Mason 21 S Acc Acc d/o David & Cath on 23 Dec 1868 at Acc by JET Ewell

MATTHEWS Major W 23 S Farmer Acc Acc s/o Wm H & Mary to Sallie S [Shreaves] Shrieves 18 S Acc Acc d/o William of Wm & Caroline on 22 Dec 1880 at Hunting Ck by LE Barrett

MATTHEWS Melly 47 W Carpenter N'hamp: N'hamp: s/o Alexander W & Anne to Henny Ward 23 S N'hamp: Acc d/o Wm & Betsy on 8 Feb 1885 near Craddockville by JE Humphreys

MATTHEWS Noah T 28 S Farmer Acc Acc s/o Wn H & Mary to Margt D Copes 21 S Acc Acc d/o Jno & Lovey on 17 Dec 1879 at Zion Bapt Ch by DA Woodson

MATTHEWS Oliver Col 60 S Laborer Acc Acc to Louisa Taylor Col 45 S Acc Acc on 24 Aug 1887 at Chinch Town by N Morris

MATTHEWS Peter H Col 24 S Farming Acc Acc s/o Margaret Logan to Georgianna White Col 23 S Acc Acc d/o Nicy on 1 Feb 1885 near Temp'ville by JC Cluff

MATTHEWS Riley Col 21 S Farm Hand Acc Acc s/o Clarissa Watson to Jane [Davis alias Only] Davis Col 24 S Acc Acc d/o Jane Davis alisa Only on 17 Mar 1878 at Sea Side Ch by A Joynes

MATTHEWS Robt 22 S Farmer Acc Acc s/o Jacob to Josephine Parkes 19 S Acc Acc d/o Noah & Mary J on 9 Jan 1868 at Acc by ES Grant

MATTHEWS Sam'l J S 24 S Farmer Acc Acc s/o John K & Eliza to Laura Ailworth 18 S Acc Acc d/o James & Emaline on 17 Jan 1892 near New Church by RS Williamson

MATTHEWS Sam'l W 30 S Merchant Acc Silverton CO s/o Wm L & Susan to Emma Taylor 26 S Acc Acc d/o Edward W & Mary on 10 Jan 1883 at Temp'ville by M Oldham

MATTHEWS Samuel 23 S Farmer Acc Acc s/o Thos & Sallie to Elizabeth Collins 23 S Acc Acc d/o Edwd & Harriet on 5 Jan 1868 at Acc by GW Matthews

MATTHEWS Samuel 20 S Oysterman Acc Acc s/o Samuel & Eliza to Laura E Lankford 18 S Acc Acc d/o Selby & Margt on 29 Dec 1874 near Guilford by JM Anderson

MATTHEWS Samuel H 22 S Farmer b: Acc s/o Jacob & Seymour to Margaret Mason 23 S b: Acc d/o Wm & Mary J on 7 Jan 1858 at r/o Wm Mason by ES Grant

MATTHEWS Samuel J 35 W Farmer

Acc Acc to Elizabeth Kelly 20 S Acc Acc d/o Richd & Eliz A on 23 Feb 1881 at Temp'ville by JW Hundley

MATTHEWS Scott Col 21 S Farming Acc Acc s/o Martha to Anna Wise Col 21 S Acc Acc d/o Eliza on 22 Feb 1873 at Savageville by R Davis

MATTHEWS Scott Col 33 W Farmer Acc Acc s/o Martha to Elizabeth Custis Col 25 S Acc Acc d/o Margaret on 19 Aug 1890 at Acc by BJ Hargarves

MATTHEWS Scott Jr Col 21 S Wage-earner Acc Acc s/o Scott Sr & Anna to Mary Jr James Col 21 S Acc Acc d/o Mary on 7 Jul 1895 at Acc by JR West

MATTHEWS Sewel Col 23 S Acc Acc s/o Jno & Eliath to Cornelia Ann Annis Col 16 S Acc Acc d/o Sarah on 20 May 1877 at Big Free School Farm by ET Banning

MATTHEWS Shadrac (Shadarac) [Mathews] Col 45 S Stevedore Acc Acc s/o Eaphernia to Ada Riley Col 44 S Acc Acc d/o Letty on 20 Aug 1873 at Warrington Br by A Joynes

MATTHEWS Sylvanus 24 S Farmer Acc Acc s/o Wm H & Mary to Clara Russell 17 W Acc Acc d/o Wm & Caroline Shreaves on 28 Dec 1884 at Acc by AJ Walter

MATTHEWS Sylvester Col 35 S Farmer Acc Acc s/o Ezekiel Hope & Ada Matthews to Emma Wilkerson Col 25 S Acc Acc d/o Levi & Sally on 16 Oct 1872 at Acc by M Oldham

MATTHEWS Thomas Col 25 S Laborer Acc Acc s/o Mary to Betsy (Beky) Brown Col 35 S Acc Acc d/o Mary on 1 Mar 1873 at Temp'ville by M Oldham

MATTHEWS Thomas R widr to Elizabeth Whealton wid lic: 5 Dec 1854

MATTHEWS Thos H 25 S Farmer Acc Acc s/o Geo & Emma to Lee [Shepperd] Shepherd 25 S Acc Acc d/o Irvin on 22 Dec 1886 at Oak Hall by TG Pullen

MATTHEWS Tully 30 S Farmer Acc Acc s/o Wm H & Mary E to Evaline T Ewell 36 S Acc Acc d/o Wm Thos & Elizth on 10 Feb 1884 at R W Matthews' by AJ Walter

MATTHEWS William H 20 S Farmer Acc Acc s/o Samuel & Eliza to Mary E Bundick single Acc Acc d/o John H on 14 Feb 1867 at Acc by G Bradford

MATTHEWS William H 43 W Farmer Acc Acc s/o Samuel to Mary J Pettitt 52 W NJ Acc on 4 Jun 1890 at Assawoman by WF Hayes

MATTHEWS Wm Col 21 S Laborer Acc Acc s/o Adam & Martha to Maggie L Wise Col 16 S N'hamp: Acc d/o Saml & Susan on 29 Dec 1886 at Onancock by GHT Byrd

MATTHEWS Wm S 21 S Farmer Acc Acc s/o Saml H & Margt A to Mary A Mears 18 S Acc Acc d/o Edwd & Nancy on 12 Dec 1883 at Guilford Ch by JW Carroll

MATTHEWS Wm T Col 37 W Wage-earner Acc Acc s/o Clarissa Hope to Adah Tunnell Col 23 S Acc Acc d/o Harriet Harmon on 21 Feb 1894 at Acc by AJ Satchell

MATTHEWS Zorobabel 25 S Mariner b: Acc s/o Jacob & Seymour to Sally A E Twiford 24 S b: Acc d/o George W (Decd) & Margt on 31 Dec 1857 at r/o Julius Twiford by ES Grant (George T Rew & Samuel H Matthews both say both over 21)

MATTHIAS John S (Sturat) 20 S Milling Wyoming Co NY Acc s/o John & Mary S to Emma S Scott 19 S Acc Acc d/o John T & Margaret S on 11 Jun 1891 at Onancock by AC Berryman

MAURIS Isaac FN to Peggy (Bailey) Bayly FN d/o Custis who gave consent lic: 3 Jan 1861 Alfred J Mears says he over 21

McCLARY Calvin W 37 W Engineer Delaware Co PA Acc s/o John T & Martha to Mary G Young 23 S Acc Acc d/o John & Maria on 20 Apr 1891 at Greenback by RS Williamson

McCONNELL Franklin P 30 S Farmer Philadelphia PA Acc s/o Thomas & Isabella to Elizabeth B Twiford 21 S Acc Acc d/o Obed P & Margaret on 10 Dec 1888 at Acc by JH Riddick

McCONNELL Harry C 29 S Merchant Acc Acc s/o Thos to V Lee Weaver 24 S Acc Acc d/o James C & Sallie P on 15 Jun 1892 at Onancock by JB Pruitt

McCREADY Geo R 23 S Sailor Acc Acc s/o Geo R & Sarah to Mary E Walter 17 S Acc Acc d/o William on 25 Dec 1892 at Tangier by ZH Webster

McCREADY George R 22 S Oysterman Messongo Muddy Ck s/o James to Ann Bell 27 S Messongo Muddy Ck on Feb 1860 at r/o James McCready by GH Ewell (George W Bird says both over 21)

McCREADY Jodiah 22 S Oysterman Acc Acc s/o Geo R & Elizth to Carrie L Drummond 18 S Acc Acc d/o Constantine & Susan on 21 Nov 1886 at Acc by M Oldham

McCREADY John 35 S Laborer Acc Acc s/o James & Sally to Matilda Chesser 30 W Acc Acc d/o Solomon & Sally Small on 7 Sep 1870 at Acc by JET Ewell

McCREADY John 25 S Sailor Pocomoke City MD Acc to Sallie Crockett 22 S Acc Acc d/o Severn & Hennie on 3 Jun 1883 at Tangier Isld by CS Baker

McCREADY John Barney 22 S Blacksmith Acc Acc s/o Andrew J & Amanda to Emma P Johnson 19 S Acc Acc d/o John W & Tabithia on 19 Oct 1892 at Acc by VW Bargamin

McCREADY Obediah 25 S Oysterman Acc Acc s/o Jas & Sally to Polly A Bundick 20 S Acc Acc d/o Severn & Caroline on 28 Aug 1879 at Conquest Ch by DA Woodson

McCREADY Robert Col 27 W Laborer Acc Acc s/o Jno & Betsy to Sarah D Crippen 19 S Acc Acc d/o Matilda on 9 Sep 1880 at Locustville by PM Lewis

McCREADY Solomon J 22 S Farmer Acc Acc s/o Thomas & Eliz'th to Josephine Marshall 22 S Acc Acc d/o Samuel & Sarah on 20 Jan 1895 at Mappsville by JL King

McCREADY Thomas [McKeady] 26 S Farmer Acc Acc s/o James & Sally to Elizth P Justice 30 D Acc Acc d/o Solomon & Sally Small on 21 Mar 1866 at Acc by JE Bundick

McCREADY Wm H 36 W Oysterman Acc Acc s/o Wm & Critty to Annie F B P Morgan 18 S Som Co MD Acc d/o Thos W & Harriet H on 20 Feb 1876 at Pocomoke Nk by JE Bundick

McKINSTREY Levi Col 36 W Wage-earner Acc Acc to Ella Parramore Col 29 S Acc Acc d/o Mary on 21 Oct 1889 at Locust Mount by JWA Elliott

McLANE John 36 S Carriage Mkr Acc Acc s/o Elizth M to Ellen Byrd 23 S Acc Acc d/o Ebren on 19 Jan 1870 at Acc by JE Humphreys

McLANE John 44 W Carriage Maker Acc Acc s/o Robert & Elizth to Mary S Mears 23 S Acc Acc d/o Lorenzo D & Soplara on 13 Feb 1878 near Pungo: by CC Wertenbaker

McMAHON Albert 24 S Lawyer New York City Brooklyn NY s/o Dennis & Lucy A to Maria Saunders 21 S NJ Acc d/o Wm S & Marianna J on 10 Jan 1893 at Onancock by LA McLean

McMATH Geo W 22 S Farmer Acc

Acc s/o Jno & Keziah to Margt D Beloate 22 S Acc Acc d/o James H & Eliza on 23 Oct 1878 at Onancock by JH Amiss

McMATH Jno P widr to Keziah A Kelly d/o Westcot on 11 Aug 1853 by J Allen

McMATH Saml T s/o Jno to Ann Elizth J Kelly d/o Wm on 22 Jan 1854 by J Allen

McNABB John 46 W Minister Ireland Acc s/o Henry & Elion to Kate A Harmanson 34 S Acc Acc d/o John L & Ann C on 30 Jul 1889 at Pungo: by GW Easter

MEARS Abel Thos 33 S Waterman Acc Acc s/o Abel & Elizth to Maggie S Phillips 22 S Acc Acc d/o Isaac S & Alsey on 4 Sep 1884 at Acc by JWA Elliott

MEARS Adam Col 50 S Day Laborer Acc Acc s/o Tabby to Mary Hatton Col 33 W Acc Acc d/o Emma Beckett on 15 Feb 1887 at bride's home by TW Nettles

MEARS Alfred J 23 S Wheelwright b: Ames Ridge s/o David & Juliet to Leah Ann Mapp 17 S b: Locust Mount d/o Geo B & Ann on 27 Sep 1854 at Locustville by A Wallace

MEARS Alfred J 25 S Farmer Acc Acc s/o Abel & Elizth to Cordelia C Kellam 17 S Acc Acc d/o Thomas P & Mary on 29 Nov 1876 at Hollies Ch by JWA Elliott

MEARS Alfred J 22 S Farmer & Oysterman Acc Acc s/o Luther J & Mary to Julia P Taylor 20 S Acc Acc d/o Jno H & Lucy C on 28 Dec 1880 near Locust Mount by JWA Elliott

MEARS Alfred S 23 S Farmer Acc Acc s/o Meshack & Elizabeth to Mary E Brimer 19 S Acc Acc d/o John H & Martha on 18 Sep 1888 at Chinco: Isld by JW Ward

MEARS Allie W 20 S Farmer Acc Acc s/o Alfred J & Leah W to Mary E Downing Col 19 S Acc Acc d/o Jno R & Jane on 10 Dec 1879 near J Downing's by LK LeCato

MEARS Andrew D Col 20 S Wage-earner Acc Acc s/o Charles D & Sarah to Patience L Allen Col 16 S Acc Acc d/o John on 21 Apr 1889 at Locust Mount by JWA Elliott

MEARS Andrew J 26 S Farmer Acc Acc s/o Luther J & Susan to Amanda F Ward 18 S Acc Acc d/o John T & Catharine on 23 Dec 1891 at Acc by JWA Elliott

MEARS Arlington B 25 S Farmer Acc Acc s/o Lorenzo D & Sophia to Belle S Mapp 21 S Acc Acc d/o Jas S & Margt on 19 Mar 1879 at bride's mother's by CC Wertenbaker

MEARS Arthur t 23 S Sailor Acc Acc s/o Edward S to Laura Hinman 21 S Acc Acc d/o John R & Susan on 1 Jan 1885 at Onancock by WC Vaden

MEARS Asbury 24 S Farmer s/o James & Molly to Vernetta Mears 22 d/o Edward & Molly lic: 24 Aug 1864 marr: 28 Aug 1864 at Accomack

MEARS Bagwell 40 W Carpenter & Farmer Acc Acc s/o Arthur & Margaret to Elizth A Rayfield 23 S Acc Acc d/o Jno & Nancy on 24 Mar 1858 at r/o Jsa Mears by BT Ames (Jas Mears says she over 21)

MEARS Benj J 25 S Farmer Acc Acc s/o Lorenzo & Sally to Roberta Kellam 18 S Acc Acc d/o Sallie B on 6 Jan 1886 at Acc by JH Amiss

MEARS Benjamin F 26 S Farmer Acc Acc s/o Edwd & Fanny to Patience Beloate 21 S Acc Acc d/o Levin B & Sally on 9 Dec 1883 near Garrisons Ch by JE Humphreys

MEARS Benjamin T 21 S Farmer Acc Acc s/o Bagwell C & Eliza A to Margie Kimmerle 19 S Acc Acc d/o John & Margaret E on 28 Dec 1887 at Acc by JW Hundley

MEARS Benjamin W 23 S Farming b:

Acc s/o John B & Jane to Emma S Mapp 17 S b: Acc d/o Geo B & Ann on 28 Jan 1857 at r/o Geo Mapps by BT Ames (Alfred J Mears says he over 21)

MEARS Berkely B 20 S Farmer Acc Acc s/o Alfred J & Leah A to Jannie F Downing 18 S Acc Acc d/o John R & Jane on 7 Dec 1875 near Oak Grove Ch by BW Dougherty

MEARS Calvin T 26 S Sailor Acc Acc s/o Levin & Tabitha to Susan F Mears 22 S Acc Acc d/o Bagwell & Eliz'th on 28 Jan 1869 at Acc by JC Martin

MEARS Charles D black 29 S Farmer s/o Ritter to Sarah Beach black 22 S d/o Sylva lic: 10 Jul 1873 marr: 13 Jul 1873 at Acc Co

MEARS Charles E Col 45 W Farmer Acc Acc s/o Charles & Ritta to Phillis Mears Col 35 S Acc Acc d/o George & Malinda on 12 Dec 1888 at Locust Mount by JWA Elliott

MEARS Charles Jr Col 20 S Wage-earner Acc Acc s/o Charles Sr & Sarah to Mary Davis Col 20 S Acc Acc d/o Centa on 26 Nov 1890 at Acc by JWA Elliott

MEARS Christopher C 23 S Farmer Acc Acc s/o Edward & Fanny to Margaret S Ward 22 S Acc Acc d/o Golden & Margt A on 19 Jan 1876 at Acc by JE Humphreys

MEARS Columbus 24 S Farmer Acc Acc s/o James & Molly to Emma C Bell 17 S Acc Acc d/o James & Elizabeth on 20 Aug 1871 at Acc by LK LeCato

MEARS Douglas 21 S Farmer Acc Acc s/o Edward & Mary to Arinthia J Wessells 19 S Acc Acc d/o Alfred J & Georgianna on 12 May 1889 at Acc by HS Dulany

MEARS Edmon J 23 S Farmer Acc Acc s/o Barsha & Abel to Nancy Mason 23 S Acc Acc d/o Zerobabel & Polly on 13 Nov 1859 at r/o Geo H Ewell by GH Ewell (Stephen Young said both over 21)

MEARS Edward 36 S Farmer Acc Acc s/o Arthur & Ann to Sally Sparrow 17 S Acc Acc d/o West & Margaret on 21 Oct 1875 at Onancock by PA Leatherbury

MEARS Edward 21 S Cooper Acc Acc s/o George & Eliz'th to Manie Kelly 32 S Acc Acc d/o James Kelly & Mary Dix on 10 Mar 1895 at Lee Mont by JET Ewell

MEARS Edward J 18 S Farmer Acc Acc s/o Edward & Nancy to Elizabeth Mason 16 S Acc Acc d/o Jeremiah & Betsy on 2 Dec 1880 at Acc by LB Betty

MEARS Edward T 21 S Farmer b: Acc s/o Arthur & Ann to Mary W Lewis 17 S b: Acc d/o Edward & Francis on 29 Dec 1858 at Reese Chp by ES Grant (Geo H Lewis says he over 21)

MEARS Edward T 23 S Sailor Acc Acc s/o Jno E & Elizth J to Gabillia E Beloate 22 S Acc Acc d/o Levin & Sally on 30 Mar 1882 at Hollies Ch by SC Boston

MEARS Eugene 39 S Mechanic Acc Acc s/o Abel & Eliz'th to Georgie A Showard 23 S Acc Acc d/o Kessie K on 23 Dec 1894 at Grangeville by JR Sturgis

MEARS Fletcher 21 S Farmer Acc Acc s/o Edward & Mary to Ella Lee Lewis 15 S Acc Acc d/o Thomas & Margaret on 13 May 1894 at Acc C H by JM Dunaway

MEARS Franklin P 25 S Farmer Acc Acc s/o David & Mary to Mary A T Bloxom 25 S Acc Acc d/o John J & Mary on 25 Aug 1875 at Modest Town by DA Woodson

MEARS Geo E 22 S Farmer Acc Acc s/o Philis to Margt Davis Col 19 S Acc Acc d/o Georgianna on 24 Dec 1884 at Locust Mount by JWA Elliott

MEARS Geo T 25 S Farmer Acc Acc s/o Jas (Geo T) & Eliza to Margt S (Sarah) Beloate 17 S Acc Acc d/o Levin & Sally (Sarah) on 12 Nov 1862 at Acc by JWA Elliott

MEARS George to Elizabeth S Turlington d/o Peter S who gave consent lic: 19 May 1860 Peter S Turlington says he over 21

MEARS George Col 25 S Wage-earner Acc Acc s/o Ann to Kate Mapp Col 21 S Acc Acc d/o Appie & Mary on 17 Apr 1889 at Acc by JA Haynes

MEARS George R 24 S Farmer Acc Acc s/o Gilbert J & Elizabeth to Laura F Watson 17 S Acc Acc d/o John E & Elizabeth S on 16 Jan 1889 at Nocks Br by WJ Twilley

MEARS George S G 23 S Farmer Acc Acc s/o Jno S & Sarah D to Marianna Roberts 19 S Acc Acc d/o Edum S & Betsy S on 13 Mar 1867 at Acc by JWA Elliott

MEARS George T 28 S Sailor Acc Acc s/o Lutha J & Mary K to Mary A Beloate 28 S Acc Acc d/o Levin B & Sally on 9 Dec 1883 near Garrisons Ch by JE Humphreys

MEARS George T 32 S Fisherman Acc Acc s/o James & Mollie to Hattie Rhodes 23 S VA Acc on 21 Jul 1889 at Powelton by JWA Elliott

MEARS George W 28 S Farmer Acc Acc s/o Abel & Bearsheba to Elizabeth Lewis 16 S Acc Acc d/o Spencer & Rachel on 22 Jun 1868 at Acc by JET Ewell

MEARS George W 22 S Farmer Acc Acc s/o Jas & Mary to Elizabeth Sarah Mears 24 S Acc Acc d/o Abel & Elizth on 15 Aug 1872 near Oak Grove Chp by JWA Elliott

MEARS George W 19 S Farmer Acc Acc s/o Meshack & Betsey to Sarah J Small 17 S Acc Acc d/o John S & Susan on 21 Jul 1889 at Mappsville by WA Street

MEARS George Washington 24 S Farmer Acc Acc s/o Abel to Annie Badger 22 S Acc Acc d/o Levin T & Elizabeth on 11 Dec 1889 at Oak Grove Ch by JWA Elliott

MEARS Gilbert Thomas 21 S Farmer Acc Acc s/o Gilbert J & Elizabeth P to Susan Ann Watkinson 21 S Acc Acc d/o Levin & Sally on 26 Oct 1887 near Drum'tn by WJ Twilley

MEARS Howard S 23 S Farmer Acc Acc s/o James H & Patience to Mary B Stockley 22 S Acc Acc d/o Syslvester & Margt on 3 Jan 1877 near Oak Grove Ch by LK LeCato

MEARS Hugh C 25 S Merchant Acc Acc s/o John S & Sarah D to Bettie L Mapp 21 S Acc Acc d/o James L & Margt on 23 Feb 1876 near Belle Haven by JWA Elliott

MEARS Isma W 25 S Carpenter Acc Acc s/o Robt & Elizth to Virginia F Kellam 25 S Acc Acc d/o Hulton on 19 Dec 1866 at Acc by G Bradford

MEARS James A 20 S Farmer Acc Acc s/o Gilbert J & Elizth P to Mary E Crosley 20 S Acc Acc d/o Thos & Sally on 22 Mar 1883 at Acc by SC Boston

MEARS James A Col 30 S Laborer Acc Acc s/o Malinda to Bettie Floyd Col 25 S Acc Acc d/o Maria on 10 Apr 1887 at Locust Mount by JWA Elliott

MEARS James B 20 S Farmer Acc Acc s/o Wm & Mary to Sallie A Ling 19 S Acc Acc d/o Edward T & Hetty on 10 May 1876 near Temp'ville by CV Waugh

MEARS James E 24 S Farmer Acc Acc s/o Jas to Virginia S Ames 18 S Acc Acc d/o Wm & Margt on 10 Nov 1867 at Acc by JWA Elliott

MEARS James H 21 S Sailor Acc Acc s/o Jno D & Margt to Rose Wise 19 S Acc Acc d/o Benj D & Louisa on 2 Feb 1881 at Hacks Nk by CC Wertenbaker

MEARS James H Col 21 S Wage-earner Acc Acc s/o George & Maria to Pearl Lena West Col 15 S Acc Acc d/o John R & Eliza on 9 Nov 1892 at Acc by BJ Hargarves

MEARS James O 22 S Farmer Acc Acc s/o Henry & Patience to Mary E Wright 19 S Acc Acc d/o Elizal & Margaret on 16 Nov 1869 at Acc by DA Woodson

MEARS James T 24 S Farmer Acc Acc s/o Zadock & Julia A to Caroline M Lewis 18 S Acc Acc d/o Absalom & Elizabeth on 1 Jun 1881 at Sykes Isld Ch by RB Beadles

MEARS Jefferson D 21 S Sailor Acc Acc s/o Zadock & Juliet to Jennie E Bowers 19 S Acc Acc d/o Wm J & Nancy on 19 Jul 1882 at Acc by RB Beadles

MEARS Jefferson D 22 S Oysterman Acc Acc s/o Zadock & Julia to Luzetts Woods 19 S Acc Acc d/o Alfred & Mary on 24 Dec 1884 at Acc by DM Wallace

MEARS John A 24 S Collector Acc Acc s/o Jno W A & Hester to Eliza C Powell 19 S Acc Acc d/o George L & Sally on 28 Feb 1873 at Acc by JE Humphreys

MEARS John E 21 S Sailor b: St Geo Parish s/o John B & Nancy to Elizabeth J Hutchinson 27 S b: St Geo Parish d/o John & Betsey (Edward) on 27 Mar 1856 at r/o Jno Mears by JWA Elliott (J W Elliott says both over 21)

MEARS John H 22 S Farmer Acc Acc s/o Jas N & Patience C to Tabitha S [Killmon] Killman 18 S Acc Acc d/o Wm & Kaziah on 31 Oct 1866 at Acc by LK LeCato

MEARS John R 20 S Farmer Acc Acc s/o James O & Mary to Nancy C Guy 18 S Acc Acc d/o George B & Arinthia on 24 Dec 1890 at Acc by JM Anderson

MEARS John T Col 24 S Sailor Acc Acc s/o Thorogood Webb & Polly Mears to Henrietta Elliott Col 17 S Acc Acc d/o George Bayly & Ann Elliott on 11 Feb 1892 at Acc by RH Coleman

MEARS John W 22 S Farmer Acc Acc s/o Jno R & Betsy to Susan A Pitts 26 S Acc Acc d/o Wm C & Ann on 23 Dec 1868 at Acc by DA Woodson

MEARS John W 23 S Farmer Acc Acc s/o Bagwell C & Elizabeth to Margaret S Rogers 19 S Acc Acc d/o John K & Elizar on 30 Nov 1870 at Acc by E Hebard

MEARS John W 27 W Farmer Acc Acc s/o John & Betsy to Emma Sicker 23 S Baltimore MD Acc d/o Edward J & Anna on 17 Mar 1875 at Belle Haven by JE Humphreys

MEARS John W 27 S Farmer Acc Acc s/o John S & Sally to Tabitha A Ward 17 S Acc Acc d/o Golden & Margt Ann on 14 Feb 1877 near Harrison Chp by JWA Elliott

MEARS Joseph Col 22 S Laborer Acc Acc s/o Abel & Elizth to Louilla Richardson Col 19 S Acc Acc d/o John T & Margt on 17 Jul 1878 near Locustville by LK LeCato

MEARS Joseph T 25 S Carpenter Acc Acc to Ellen T Budd 22 S Acc Acc d/o Wm S & Sarah Ann on 26 Nov 1868 at Acc by JH Addison

MEARS Laban J 30 S Laborer Acc Acc s/o James & Mary to Mary A Davis 25 S Acc Acc d/o Litt B & Hester Ann on 2 May 1886 near Locust Mount by JWA Elliott

MEARS Leonard C 26 S Merchant Acc Acc s/o Benjamin W & Emma S to Jennie M Custis 26 S Acc Acc d/o John W & Rose E on 26 Jan 1888 at Onancock by RD Stimson

MEARS Littleton W 28 S Farmer Acc Acc s/o Thos H Sr & Triphemia A to Julia E Nock 19 S Acc Acc d/o

George T & Herbanna on 25 Dec 1895 at Mappsville by JL King

MEARS Lloyd 23 S Sailor Acc Acc s/o Mahack & Elizabeth to Lisman (Louann) Littleton 19 S Acc Acc d/o Samuel & Adaline C on 29 Nov 1871 at Conquest Ch by M Oldham

MEARS Lloyd K 23 S Farmer Acc Acc s/o John & Margaret to Mahala Jane Taylor 25 S Acc Acc d/o Charles & Mahala on 4 Nov 1871 near Morrison Hill by LK LeCato

MEARS Lloyd W 25 S Sailor Acc Acc s/o Arthur & Margt to Manie E James 22 S Acc Acc d/o Levin on 27 Nov 1878 at Mr James' by SC Boston

MEARS Lorenzo D 30 S Farmer Acc Acc s/o Lorenzo Dow & Sopia A B Mears to Julia Mason 21 S Acc Acc d/o Geo B & Sally on 20 Mar 1888 at bride's father's by JH Riddick

MEARS Lorenzo T s/o Jesse to Sarah Beloate d/o George lic: 31 Oct 1855 Geo W Bell says both over 21

MEARS Meshack 38 W Farmer Acc Acc s/o Meshack & Margt to Betsy A West 17 S Acc Acc d/o Sol & Margt on 23 Jul 1862 at Acc by ES Grant

MEARS Michael 60 W Farmer Acc Acc s/o Kendal & Catharine to Margaret Susan [Stephens] Stevens 19 S Acc Acc d/o Thomas & Elizabeth on 15 Jun 1859 at Acc by JH Addison (Mitchell W West witnessed her signature)

MEARS Michael 72 W Farmer Acc Acc s/o Kendal & Katy to Mary Phillips 60 W Acc Acc on 1 Mar 1871 near Bobtown by E Hebard

MEARS Mitchel 27 S Farmer Acc Acc s/o Mitchel to Eveline C Stevens 30 S Acc Acc d/o Elizabeth C on 6 Feb 1878 at Onancock by SC Boston

MEARS Mitchell 24 W Farmer Acc Acc s/o Michael & Nancy to Elizabeth Parker 25 S Acc Acc d/o Fredrieck & Sally on 7 Jul 1880 near Bobtown by E Hebard

MEARS Oscar M 19 S Farmer Acc Acc s/o John W & Margaret to Annie L Carmine 16 S Acc Acc d/o George & Eliza on 26 Dec 1894 at Acc by JET Ewell

MEARS Oswald C 28 S Farmer Acc Acc s/o John to Margaret S Savage 17 S Acc Acc d/o Edward & Elizabeth on 7 Nov 1876 near Locustville by LK LeCato

MEARS Patrick 27 S Farmer Acc Acc s/o Richad W & Susan M to Rose Emma Young 14 S Acc Acc on 6 Feb 1884 at Onancock by WC Vaden

MEARS Peter Col 67 S Farmer Acc Acc s/o Easter to Mary Laws Col 30 S Acc Acc d/o Joshua & Sylvia on 12 Apr 1873 near Locustville by N Morris

MEARS Richard W 21 S Farmer Acc Acc s/o Abel & Elizabeth to Indie Mears 21 S Acc Acc d/o Michael on 15 May 1889 at Hollies Ch by JWA Elliott

MEARS Riley Col 20 S Sailor Acc Acc s/o Phillis A to Mary Davis Col 18 S Acc Acc d/o Bridget on 11 Apr 1883 at Locust Mount by JWA Elliott

MEARS Robert widr to Margt Boone on 8 Jan 1854 by J Allen (Elisha Bull says she over 21)

MEARS Samuel H Col 24 S Laborer Acc Acc s/o Ada to Jane Garrison Col 16 S Acc Acc d/o Louisa on 8 Nov 1882 at Pungo: by GHT Byrd

MEARS Sewell W 20 S Farmer Acc Acc s/o Thomas A & Francis to Marie Fitchett 22 S Acc Acc d/o Samuel & Mary on 27 Sep 1882 at Onancock by JC Watson

MEARS Thomas widr to Emma Mears wid on 13 Nov 1853 by J Allen

MEARS Thomas F 23 S Farmer Acc Acc s/o Meshac ((Meshack) &

Elizabeth to Coraline F Taylor 21 S Acc Acc d/o Thorogood S & Caroline S on 4 Feb 1874 at Zion Ch by EM Bryan

MEARS Thomas H 23 S Farmer Acc Acc s/o Henry & Sarah Mears to Trifany A S Taylor 18 S Acc Acc d/o Zadoc & Rachel on 29 Dec 1860 at Acc by JC Mears

MEARS Thomas R 21 S Farmer Acc Acc s/o Thos A & Frances A to Emma C Hurst 19 S Acc Acc d/o Wm & Polly E on 11 Jan 1883 at Acc by SC Boston

MEARS Thos 33 S Farmer b: Acc s/o Arthur & Margt to Frances Ann Riley 23 S b: Acc d/o Wm M & Betsy on 1 Mar 1853 at Ayres Chp by ES Grant

MEARS Walter 26 S Farmer Acc Acc s/o Geo & Patty to Ann Mears 15 S Acc Acc d/o Abel & Elizth on 13 Dec 1865 at Acc by WG Coe

MEARS William Col 25 W Farmer Acc Acc s/o Ann to Mary Mapp Col 16 S Acc Acc d/o Appie & Mary on 6 Jun 1894 at Locust Mount by JWA Elliott

MEARS William Col 22 S Farmer Acc Acc s/o Ann to Sarah Turlington Col 21 S Acc Acc d/o George & Malinda on 31 Dec 1890 at Onancock by GHT Byrd

MEARS William F 26 S Farmer Acc Acc s/o Jas H & Patiance to Mary F Dunton 26 W Acc Acc d/o Littleton & Mary LeCato on 6 Mar 1879 at Oak Grove by CC Wertenbaker

MEARS William H 22 S Farmer Acc Acc s/o James Oswald & Mary to Mollie L Chandler 18 S Acc Acc d/o Thomas M & Mary S on 10 Apr 1894 at Chinco: Isld by JR Griffith

MEARS William H P 23 S Farmer Acc Acc s/o Bagwell & Elizth to Virginia S Beloate 18 S Acc Acc d/o Jas G & Betsy on 19 Dec 1866 at Acc by P Warren

MEARS William T 26 S Farmer Acc Acc s/o John & Nancy to Leah Townsend 22 S Acc Acc d/o Littleton & Tabitha on 2 Jan 1868 at Acc by JE Bundick

MEARS Zadock 23 S Sailor b: Messongo s/o George (Sen) to Julia Ann Chesser 17 S b: Messongo d/o Polly on 12 Jul 1855 at r/o Arfaxes Bayly by GH Ewell (Jesse Dickerson says he over 21)

MEDAB Golden Col 23 S Laborer Acc Acc s/o Hetty to Martha Finney Col 46 S Acc Acc d/o Nellie on 1 Nov 1883 at Drum'tn by LW Lee

MEDAB Hezekiah Col 26 S Waterman Acc Acc s/o James to Elizabeth Creak Col 24 S Acc Acc d/o Elizabeth Parkes on 4 Mar 1883 at Chinco: Isld by JC Cluff

MEELHAM Joseph A 25 S Oysterman NJ Acc s/o George & Jane to Virginia A Hickman 20 S Acc Acc d/o Asa & Jane on 20 Dec 1871 near Horntown by M Oldham

MEILHARIN George 63 W Farmer French Dominiano Acc s/o Jno & Catharine to Elizth Farrow 36 S Great Britain Acc d/o Jas Martin & Mary Farrow on 27 Dec 1882 at Horntown by RB Beadles

MELSON Algermon J 22 S Livery Acc Acc s/o Henry & Emma to Eva L Barnes 21 S Acc Acc d/o George W & Eveline on 22 Feb 1893 at Lee Mont by JET Ewell

MELSON Benj T 25 S Painter Acc Acc s/o Thos & Sophia to Lizzie S Adams 24 S Acc Acc d/o Jas C & Mary A on 4 Apr 1877 at Makemie Ch by JG Hammer

MELSON Benjamin T 42 W Merchant Acc Acc s/o James T & Margaret S to Marceline C Parkes 23 S Acc Acc d/o George P & Elizabeth P on 23 Feb 1894 at Lee Mont by JET Ewell

MELSON Daniel 55 S Farmer b:

Muddy Ck s/o Jermiak to Ester Russell 57 S b: Guilford d/o Benjamin & Rachel on 4 Jul 1856 at a pine tree by GH Ewell (Isaac Russell says both over 21)

MELSON David to Susan Turner d/o John lic: 21 Dec 1855 Charles T Sturgis says both over 21

MELSON Edward 35 S Mariner Acc Acc to Mary S Lewis 15 S Acc Acc d/o Wm T & Susan S on 16 May 1877 near Deep Ck by FH Mullineaux

MELSON George T 25 S Farmer Acc Acc s/o Jno W & Eliath to Sallie Moore 24 S Acc Acc d/o Thos & Susan on 29 Dec 1868 at Acc by JO Moss

MELSON George T 31 W Farmer Acc Acc to Bunetta Smith 23 S Acc Acc d/o Henry & Mary on 21 Jan 1880 at Downings Ch by JW Hilldrup

MELSON Henry 27 S Mariner Acc Acc s/o Henry & Bridget to Louisa Mears 19 S Acc Acc d/o Edwd & Mary on 19 Mar 1863 at Acc by ES Grant

MELSON James S 23 S Farmer Acc Acc s/o Henry & Bridget to Margaret Satchell 16 S Acc Acc d/o Geo S & Lucretia on 24 Feb 1870 at Acc by JB Converse

MELSON John 28 S Waterman Acc Acc s/o Scarborough to Susan Bunting 23 S Acc Acc d/o Thos & Lovey on 29 Dec 1859 at Thos Bunting's by ES Grant (James Gray/Gracy(?) says both over 21)

MELSON John H 24 S Oysterman Acc Acc s/o John & Susan to Maggie A Rew 18 S Acc Acc d/o Jesse R & Sarah on 16 May 1888 at Onancock by JW Easley

MELSON John R 42 W Farmer b: Acc s/o Polly to Catharine Wise 33 W b: Acc d/o Jno & Elizth Watson on 18 Dec 1858 at r/o E S Grant by ES Grant

MELSON John T 21 S Farmer Acc Acc s/o Levin J & Sarah J to Leigh V Grinnalds 16 S Acc Acc d/o Jno Wm & Marg't on 7 Dec 1892 at Lee Mont by JET Ewell

MELSON John T 24 W Farmer Acc Acc s/o Levin J & Sarah J to Margaret S Matthews 23 S Acc Acc d/o Robert W on 25 Dec 1895 at Parksley by JM Dunaway

MELSON Levin J 22 S Farmer Acc Acc s/o John of B & Cath to Sarah Jane Parkes 21 S Acc Acc d/o Thos L & Sarah on 17 Nov 1870 at Reese Chp by JET Ewell

MELSON Levin T 22 S Sailor Acc Acc s/o Henry & Bridget to Sallie A Core 21 S Acc Acc d/o Levin J & Mary A on 30 Dec 1874 near Locustville by LK LeCato

MELSON Saml C 29 S Painter Acc Acc s/o Jas T & Margaret S to Ida V Coard 25 S Acc Acc d/o John W on 11 Aug 1886 at Woodbury by JW Carroll

MELSON Thomas J 28 S Farmer Acc Acc s/o Henry & Emeline to Arinthia A Hurst 23 S Acc Acc d/o James & Susan on 3 Jul 1889 near Onancock by PA Leatherbury

MELSON Thos H 24 S Sailor Acc Acc to Catharine Melson 22 S Acc Acc d/o James T & Sophia on 24 Apr 1867 at Acc by BT Ames

MELSON Wesley T 21 S Farmer Acc Acc s/o Jno R & Catharine to Sallie M [Shreaves] Shrieves 17 S Acc Acc d/o Jno & Elizth A on 16 Dec 1874 at Reese Chp by RC Jones

MELSON Wm J 26 S Farmer N'hamp: N'hamp: s/o Wm & Margt to Euginia Drummond 17 S Acc Acc d/o Robt A & Margt on 24 Sep 1879 at N'hamp: by A Broaddus Jr

MELVIN Avery 28 S Mariner b: Chinco: Isld s/o Thos & Sophia to Margaret [Cherics] (Chericks)

Cherricks 33 W b: Chinco: Isld d/o Henry & Mary Showard on 21 Jun 1856 at Chinco: Isld by WP Thornton (John Trornton says he over 21)

MELVIN David 20 S Oysterman Acc Acc s/o Thos & Lydis A to Hester Ann Bowden 18 S Acc Acc d/o Littleton & Deurinah on 12 Nov 1882 at Chinco: Isld by WP Thornton

MELVIN David L 33 W Farmer MD MD s/o Avery & Cath to Virginia S Bayly 21 S Acc Acc d/o Jno T & Elizth on 27 May 1869 at Acc by JE Maloy

MELVIN Isaac 23 S Sailor Acc Acc s/o Saml & Elizh to Maria C Townsend 27 W Acc Acc d/o Wm & Betsy Sharply on 1 May 1866 at Acc by P Bowdin Sr

MELVIN Isaac Col 25 S Sailor Acc Acc s/o Levin & Emma to Susan Matthews Col 22 S Acc Acc d/o Mary on 6 Jan 1887 at his parents' by JK Adams

MELVIN James D Col 21 S Wage-earner Acc Acc s/o Levin & Emma to Mary E Matthews Col 18 S Acc Acc d/o Susan on 23 Sep 1891 at Lee Mont by LE Toulson

MELVIN Thomas W (James W) 22 S Oysterman Acc Acc s/o Saml & Eliz'th to Drucilla J [Read] (Reed) Read 18 S Acc Acc d/o Jno & Eliz'th on 23 May 1869 at Acc by P Bowdin Jr

MELVIN Thos 35 W Oysterman Acc Acc s/o Thos & Sophia to Mahala Hall 25 W Acc Acc d/o Richd & Nancy Carpenter on 13 Apr 1869 at Acc by P Bowdin

MERRILL Henry T C widr to Elizabeth A Burton d/o John lic: 28 Dec 1857 James H Ball says she over 21

MERRILL Isaac L 22 S Oysterman Wor Co MD Acc s/o Isaac L & Sarah to Sarah J Bowden 18 S Acc Acc d/o Ira & Mary on 16 Nov 1889 at Chinco: Isld by EH Miller

MERRILL James to Esther Mariner lic: 19 Nov 1858 Kendal B Baylis says both over 21

MERRILL John 34 S Farming Acc Acc s/o Wm & Sallie to Olivia Jane Thornton 20 S Acc Acc d/o Edwd & Elizth on 1 Oct 1861 at Acc by T Waters

MERRILL John T 28 S Farmer Wor Co MD Wor Co MD s/o Thos H & Eliz'th to Florence V Smith 21 S Acc Acc d/o Wm H C & Eliz'th on 28 Dec 1892 at Acc by RB Scott

MERRILL William Henry 22 S Oysterman Acc Acc s/o James H & Esther to Charlotte A Taylor 16 S Acc Acc d/o Oliver L & Mary on 30 Apr 1890 at Greenbackville by RS Williamson

MERRITT Eba C 22 S Oysterman Wor Co MD Acc s/o Edward & Sarah to Ida A Gray 16 S Acc Acc d/o J A & Sarah E on 24 Jun 1890 at Chinco: Isld by SU Grimsley

MERRITT George E [Marriett] 29 W US Life Saving Service Wor Co MD Assateague Isld s/o Jas & Harriet to Mary C Birch 16 S Acc Chinco: Isld d/o David H & Mary F on 22 Jul 1886 at Chinco: Isld by SU Grimsley

MERRITT John E 25 S Sailor Wor Co MD Acc s/o Edward & Sarah to Ida Daisey 22 S Acc Acc d/o William & Peggy on 24 Dec 1891 at Chinco: Isld by JF Wooden

MESSICK William J 37 W Blacksmith Sussex Co DE Acc s/o George R & Leah to Lizzie E Mason 29 W Wic Co MD Acc on 9 Oct 1895 at Chinco: Isld by SU Grimsley

MESSICK Wm J 25 S Lewis DE Acc s/o George R & Leah to Mary D Bloxom 20 S Acc Acc d/o Leglamore & Iervinna on 7 Jun 1882 at Chinco: Isld by OS Walton

METCALF John widr to Ann Fosque

METCALF John W 24 S Farmer Acc Acc s/o Jesse & Keriah to Georganna Heath 21 S Acc Acc d/o George & Margaret on 13 Dec 1871 at Oak Grove Ch by JWA Elliott wid lic: 17 Aug 1859

METCALF Richard 23 S Farmer NY Acc s/o Jno & Jane to Ida C Burr 22 W Acc Acc d/o Charles & Susan Ewell on 26 Mar 1884 at Acc by A Woodyard

MIDDLETON Alexander T 28 S Sailor Acc Acc s/o John & Julia to Sarah E Lewis 20 S Acc Acc d/o James & Mary on 20 Mar 1889 at Onancock by JW Hundley

MIDDLETON Edward 40 S Teamster Acc Acc to Maria Townsend 31 S Acc Acc d/o Littleton & Tabitha on 7 Dec 1879 at Modest Town by DA Woodson

MIDDLETON George G 21 S Farmer Acc Acc s/o George & Eveline to Carvilla T Taylor 19 S Acc Acc d/o George T & Catherine on 28 Dec 1887 at Lee Mont by JW Norris

MIDDLETON John E 25 S Sailor Acc Acc s/o John & Julia to Emma Collins 25 S Acc Acc d/o Littleton & Elizabeth on 23 Jun 1880 at Oak Hall by JW Hilldrup

MIDDLETON Revel P 23 S Sailor Acc Acc s/o John & Betsy to Eliza Ellen Gaskins 22 S Acc Acc d/o William on 13 May 1871 at Temp'ville by M Oldham

MIDDLETON Wm 24 S Oysterman Acc Acc s/o Jno & Juliet to Laura M C [Paunell] Purnell 19 S Acc Acc d/o Wm M & annie on 29 Dec 1878 at Wm Middleton's by JE McSparran

MILBOURN Burrough [Melburn] 22 S Laborer Acc Acc s/o Harriet to Violet Hall Col 16 S Acc Acc d/o Harriet on 19 Apr 1881 at Temp'ville by M Oldham

MILBOURN Elijah [Milbourne] Col 25 S Oysterman Acc Acc s/o Harriet to Adaline [Milborune] Milbourn Col 22 S Acc Acc d/o Maria on 18 Dec 1884 at Acc by JW Carroll

MILBOURN Ellis [Milburn] Col 25 S Sailor Acc Acc to Sarah Hall Col 25 S Acc Acc on 29 Dec 1878 at Temp'ville by JC Cluff

MILBOURN Langley Col 28 S Oysterman Acc Acc s/o Millie to Elzey Harmon Col 17 S Acc Acc d/o William & Ailsie on 16 Jul 1890 at Temp'ville by JC Cluff

MILBOURN Louis [Milburne] Col 23 S Oysterman Acc Acc s/o Delilah to Mollie Corbin Col 21 S Acc Acc d/o James on 11 Feb 1894 at Acc by JC Cluff

MILBOURN Peaze Col 24 S Oysterman Acc Acc to Margaret Fletcher Col 19 S Acc Acc d/o Judy on 2 Jan 1889 near Temp'ville by JC Cluff

MILES Albert 19 S Oysterman Acc Acc s/o Severn & Hester to Missouri Spence 18 S Acc Acc d/o Thomas & Polly on 4 Nov 1894 at Acc by DJ Traynham

MILES Alfred 27 S Farmer Acc Acc s/o James & Betsey to Bettie [Bird] Byrd 20 S Acc Acc d/o William & Hetty on 16 Sep 1874 at Oak Hall by TM Poulson

MILES Ambros B 25 S Farmer Acc Acc s/o Jas P & Margt to Sarah East 26 S Acc Acc d/o Geo T & Sarah on 12 Feb 1868 at Acc by GW Matthews

MILES David D to Mary J Taylor d/o Asa who gave consent lic: 8 Feb 1860 Martin K Kelly says he over 21

MILES Edward E 26 S Druggist MD Acc s/o Robert H & Mollie M to Susan E Pitts 21 S Acc Acc d/o Thos C & Elizth on 25 Nov 1886 at Onley by JW Hundley

MILES Elijah J 34 W Farming Acc Acc s/o Elijah & Leah to Sally Matthews 19 S Acc Acc d/o Saml & Eliza on 2

Oct 1861 at Acc by JC Mears

MILES George Parker 23 S Oysterman Acc Acc s/o James & Mary to Amelia A Lewis 16 S Acc Acc d/o John T & Sally on 3 Jun 1876 at Saxes Isld Ch by JM Anderson

MILES James H 23 S Farmer Acc Acc s/o Elijah J & Sally to Mary J Onley 21 S Acc Acc d/o John H & Mary on 28 Jan 1891 at Modest Town by HS Dulany

MILES James P 60 W Farmer to Nancy Taylor 40 W lic: 13 Apr 1864 marr: 13 Apr 1864 at Accomack

MILES Jas E 21 S Mariner Acc Acc s/o Severn & Hester A to Oshia A McCready 16 S Acc Acc d/o Geo R & Sarah E on 23 Apr 1886 at Pocomoke by JW Carroll

MILES Jesse 30 W Oysterman Acc Acc s/o Parker & Ann to Susan Wessells 22 S Acc Acc d/o Betsy on 2 Jan 1868 at Acc by JE Bundick

MILES John 19 S Oysterman Acc Acc s/o Severn P & Hester A to Sarah Linton 17 S Acc Acc d/o John & Margaret J on Oct 1876 at Saxes Isld by JM Anderson

MILES John Col 22 S Wage-earner Acc Acc s/o Levi & Sarah to Betsy Drummond 22 S Acc Acc d/o George & Alsie on 29 Dec 1895 at Onancock by SW Watkins

MILES John P 23 S Oysterman Acc Acc s/o John H & Hannah to Elizth J Stant 19 S Acc Acc d/o Edwd & Milcah on 4 Feb 1869 at Acc by JO Moss

MILES John W 22 S Farmer Acc Acc s/o Wm & Hetty to Julia A Hopkins 20 S Acc Acc d/o Henry T & Margt on 18 Aug 1872 at Acc by WF Talbott

MILES Lawson J 22 S Farmer Acc Acc s/o James to Anna Walker 18 S Acc Acc d/o Saml & Mary on 24 Jan 1877 at Modest Town by DA Woodson

MILES Levi Col 22 S Laborer s/o Leah Drummond to Louisa Dickerson Col 17 S d/o Traney lic: 30 Jan 1865 marr: 4 Feb 1865

MILES Noah 20 S Oysterman Sexes Isld Sexes Isld s/o Parker & Mary to Mary A Linton 24 S Sexes Isld Sexes Isld d/o Molly on 29 Dec 1864 at r/o Betsy Youngs by GH Ewell

MILES Severn 21 S Oysterman Acc Acc s/o Severn & Hester to Julia E Charnock 18 S Acc Acc d/o Joseph & Eliza on 19 Mar 1890 at Chesconessex by GW Burke

MILES Severn J 20 S Oysterman Acc Acc s/o James of P & Mary to Miranda J Spence 18 S Acc Acc d/o Maria on 18 Oct 1874 at Pocomoke by M Oldham

MILES Severn Parker 22 W Oysterman b: Acc to Hester Ann Melson 23 S b: Acc on 28 Dec 1854 at Ja Corbin's by GH Ewell (Gillet Marshall says both over 21)

MILES William 23 S Farmer Acc Acc s/o Wm & Sally to Nancy Guy 27 S Acc Acc d/o Jonathan & Elizth on 2 Apr 1856 at Acc by M Oldham (Edward T Wise says both over 21)

MILES William M 24 S Farmer Acc Acc s/o Elijah J & Sally to Lacy M [Justis] Justice 24 W Acc Acc d/o Wm J & Seymour Bundick on 21 Mar 1894 at Hallwood by JL King

MILES Wm S 40 S Farmer Acc Acc s/o J P & Peggy to Annie E Taylor 21 S Acc Acc d/o Southey & Sally on 27 Oct 1886 at New Church by BF Jester

MILLER Alfred Col 23 S Farmer Acc Acc s/o Mary to Virginia Hickman Col 22 S Acc Acc d/o Tamar on 20 Nov 1890 at Newstown VA by AJ Satchell

MILLER Arthur 23 S Oysterman Acc Acc s/o Jacob & Clarissa to Juliet

Brinney 18 S Acc Acc d/o Edwd & Elizabeth on 17 Dec 1866 at Acc by P Bowdin Sr

MILLER Elijah H 44 S Minister Kent Co DE Newark MD s/o Elijah & Louisa to Bertie Caulk 25 S Baltimore MD Acc d/o Columbus & Cornelia on 23 Apr 1890 at Chinco: Isld by TO Ayres assisted by AS Morely & BP Truitt

MILLER Ethal Col 28 S Farmer Acc Acc s/o Sarah to Sarah Marshall Col 22 S Acc Acc d/o Elizabeth Cropper on 1 Jun 1881 at Horntown by PJ Adams

MILLER Fitzhugh J 23 S Farmer Acc Acc s/o Wm E & Mary to Virginia S Davis 18 S Acc Acc d/o Littleton B & Hester Ann on 5 Oct 1887 at Garrisons Chp by CD Crawley

MILLER Wm R 25 S Farmer Acc Acc s/o Wm E & Mary to Margaret Watkinson 23 S Acc Acc d/o Wm on 3 Oct 1883 at Acc by SC Boston

MILLINER Edmond F 34 S Farmer Acc Acc s/o Southey & Susan to Mary Parker 25 S Acc Acc d/o John M on 10 Dec 1885 at Woodbury by JW Carroll

MILLINER Elijah P 22 S Farmer Acc Acc s/o John & Eliza to Birdie Amanda Bull 17 S Acc Acc d/o Henry & Polly on 4 Jan 1885 at Drum'tn by JW Carroll

MILLINER George L 24 S Farmer Acc Acc s/o John & Eliza to Virginia Coxton 20 S Acc Acc d/o Wm H & Virginia on 22 Dec 1881 at W H Coxton's by SC Boston

MILLINER George W 25 S Farmer Acc Acc s/o James H & Elizabeth to Laura Lang 21 S Acc Acc d/o Henry & Catharine on 28 Dec 1892 at Acc C H by SU Grimsley

MILLINER George W 29 S Surfman Acc Acc s/o Sam'l S & Catharine to Addie E Hopkins 17 S Acc Acc d/o John J & Adeline on 9 Jan 1894 at Acc C H by JM Dunaway

MILLINER James H 24 S Sailor Acc Acc s/o Suthy & Nancy to Elizabeth S Ayres 18 S Acc Acc d/o Edmon & Elizabeth (W) on 3 Jan 1858 at Locust Mount by JWA Elliott (Wm H Harrison says he over 21)

MILLINER James H 59 W Sailor Acc Acc s/o Southey & Nancy to Mary Catharine Walker 38 W Acc Acc d/o John H & Mary Copes on 3 Jun 1894 at Drum'tn by WF Hayes

MILLINER Jesse James 20 S Farmer Acc Acc s/o John & Eliza to Dorothy A Bell 16 S Acc Acc d/o John E & Lucretia on 11 Dec 1889 at Drum'tn by WJ Twilley

MILLINER John R 22 S Farmer Acc Acc s/o William H & Sarah to Eveline Wessells 21 S Acc Acc d/o Alfred J & Gerogieanna on 8 Dec 1889 at Drum'tn by WJ Twilley

MILLINER John W 22 S Farmer Acc Acc s/o John & Eliza to Maggie A Gray 18 S Acc Acc d/o Levin & Ann on 18 Mar 1874 near Acc C H by EM Bryan

MILLINER Lee 22 S Carpenter Acc Acc s/o Samuel to Oceana Bundick 23 S Acc Acc d/o Alfred J & Elizabeth on 4 Mar 1885 at Woodbury by JW Carroll

MILLINER Robert S 27 S Coach Maker Acc Acc s/o Thos & Harriet to Mary Susan James 21 S Acc Acc d/o John Thos & Susan on 21 Dec 1870 at Acc by E Hebard

MILLINER Robert S Jr 26 S Farmer Acc Acc s/o John & Eliza to Ida N Harmon 20 S Acc Acc d/o Robert T & Sally A on 11 Dec 1889 at Drum'tn by WJ Twilley

MILLINER Samuel S 23 S Sailor Acc Acc s/o Southy (S)& Nancy to Catherine (S) Fosque 24 S Acc Acc d/o James Fosque & Polly Guy on 9

Jan 1861 at r/o Littl Lecato by LK LeCato (Jacob M Ross says both over 21)

MILLINER Thomas 23 S Mechanic s/o Maria to Jane Lilliston 22 S d/o Asa & Ann lic: 9 Mar 1871 marr: 9 Mar 1871 at Rev L LeCato's

MILLINER Thomas F 21 S Seaman Acc Acc s/o Thomas & Sarah Ann to Hester Ann Powell 28 S Acc Acc d/o Nathaniel on 5 Sep 1880 near Locustville by JC Watson

MILLINER William C 33 S Farmer Acc Acc s/o Thos & Harriet to Virginia West 18 S Acc Acc d/o George R & Jane S on 23 Dec 1880 at Acc C H by JG Anderson

MILLINER Wm 23 S Farmer Acc Acc s/o Caty to Sarah Small 21 S Acc Acc d/o Steward & Louisa on 11 Jan 1866 at Acc by ES Grant

MILLINER Wm T 23 S Life Saving Station Acc Acc s/o James H & Elizabeth to Ida Copes 17 S Acc Acc d/o John H & Mary on 18 Aug 1885 near Acc C H by A Woodyard

MILLS Alexander Col 27 S Farm Laborer Wor Co MD Acc s/o John & Martha to Mary S Parker Col 21 S Acc Acc d/o John & Sarah on 12 Jun 1884 at Acc by P Sheppard

MILLS Daniel J Col 28 S Laborer Pocomoke City Acc to Elizabeth Poulson Col 21 S Acc Acc d/o Lucinda on 6 Jan 1886 near Lee Mont by CA Horsey

MILLS Ira J 28 S Farmer Wor Co MD Acc s/o Levin & Mary to Virginia Payne 21 S Wor Co MD Acc d/o Ira & Emily on 7 Jan 1880 at Greenbackville by CS Arnett

MILLS Moses Col 24 S Wage-earner Pocomoke City MD Acc s/o John & Martha to Virginia Laws Col 34 S Acc Acc d/o Joshua & Sylvia on 20 Dec 1888 at St Luke Ch by P Sheppard

MILLS Moses Col 32 W Wage-earner Wor Co MD Acc s/o John & Martha to Rose Ann Stratton Col 35 W Acc Acc on 13 Nov 1895 at Acc by JH Robins

MILLS Thomas 22 S RR Employee Wor Co MD Acc s/o Samuel to Susan Rew 21 S Acc Acc d/o Henry & Margaret Ann on 27 Oct 1886 at Acc by JW Carroll

MILLS William S 35 W Engineer MD Acc to Margt C Roberts 26 S Acc Acc on 9 Oct 1867 at Acc by GS Battersby

MISTER Arthur David 24 S Farmer Acc Acc s/o Edward & Sarah to Maggie L Evans 17 S Acc Acc d/o John E & Triphemia on 9 Nov 1893 at Acc by EC Atkins

MISTER David R 40 S Merchant Acc Acc to Maggie E Roberts 20 S Acc Acc d/o Clinton & Sarah Jane on 12 Apr 1882 at Acc by CD Crawley

MISTER George T 18 S Oysterman Acc Acc s/o Wm W & Rachel J to Drusilla Martin 16 S Acc Acc d/o Wm & Georgianna on 23 Oct 1895 at Sykes Isld by ML Williams

MISTER Gilbert H 60 W Farmer Acc N'hamp: s/o Jas & Rachel to Anna J Ward 28 S Acc Acc d/o Southey & Ann on 31 Aug 1865 at Acc by D Titlow

MISTER Jefferson D 21 S Farmer Acc Acc s/o Lorenzo D & Susan E to Alice L Core 17 S Acc Acc d/o John W & Any on 29 Dec 1882 at Acc by SC Boston

MISTER Severn J 21 S Waterman Acc Acc s/o Edward C & Sarah J to Lula C Stant 19 S Acc Acc d/o John & Emily on 6 Feb 1895 at Acc by JET Ewell

MISTER William 24 S Mariner b: Acc s/o Jno & Lovy to Sally Bull 25 W b: Acc d/o Asa & Elizth Hickman on 29 Dec 1853 at r/o Wm Hickman by ES

Grant

MISTER William W 42 W Wage-earner Acc Acc s/o Jane to Mary Ann Linton 35 W Acc Acc d/o Samuel & Sallie Ewell on 10 Dec 1890 at Acc by JS Wallace

MITCHELL Geo W 25 S Sailor Acc Acc s/o Mary to Susan J Smith 22 S Acc Acc d/o Edward & Mahala on 10 Aug 1865 at Acc by JE Bundick

MITCHELL John 24 S Farmer Acc Acc s/o Tabbie to Ann Downing 20 S Acc Acc d/o Hessey on 6 Sep 1868 at Acc by A Joynes

MITCHELL Warren J 21 S Farmer Acc Acc s/o Geo W & Susan to Evelyn E Wessells 19 S Acc Acc d/o Sam'l & Georgianna on 20 Nov 1895 at Acc by RB Sanford

MOFFITT Emery 22 S Sailor Cecil Co MD Chinco: Isld s/o Thomas & Arinsintia to Tabitha Sharpley 19 S Chinco: Isld Chinco: Isld d/o Henry & Sarah (ward/o John A M Whealton who gave consent) on 1 Nov 1860 at Chinco: Isld by P Bowdin Sr (John A M Wheaton says he over 21)

MOFFITT Emory [Moffett] 42 D Merchant North East ME Chinco: Isld s/o Thos & Aramints to Mary [Chericks] Cherricks Col 42 S Acc Chinco: Isld d/o Jas & Mariah Booth on 16 Jul 1883 at Chinco: Isld by EH Miller

MOFFITT William H 40 S Tailor Talbot Co Temp'ville s/o William to Mary M K Burton 25 S Acc Temp'ville d/o Geo & Ann on 21 Nov 1860 at Temp'ville by W Merrill (James C Ling says both over 21)

MONGER George 21 S Acc Acc s/o James & Marthy to Sarah E Thornton 16 S Acc Acc d/o William & Elizabeth T on 9 Nov 1881 at Chinco: Isld by WP Thornton

MONGER Kendal single Laborer Chinco: Isld Chinco: Isld s/o Fanney to Patsy Jester wid Chinco: Isld Chinco: Isld d/o Geo & Patience Burch on 29 Jun 1854 at r/o Parker Bowdin by P Bowdin

MONTAGUE Henry Philip 41 W Daguerreoty b: Middlesex Co s/o Abraham & Jane Elizabeth to Mary Ann Evans 30 W b: Acc d/o Thomas & Leah Waters on 10 Dec 1856 at Horntown by JF Chaplain

MOORE Alfred Col 21 S Sailor Acc Acc s/o Sarah to Lucy Savage Col 19 S Acc Acc d/o Sarah on 15 Oct 1884 at Acc by AJ Satchell

MOORE Alfred Col 22 S Wage-earner Acc Acc s/o Edmund & Nellie to Emma Kate Stran Col 16 S Acc Acc d/o Perry & Rosa on 24 Dec 1890 at Acc by JB Lewis

MOORE Edward 22 S Sailor Acc Acc s/o Dinah to Nellie Hack 22 S Acc Acc d/o Harriet Turford on 30 Dec 1866 at Acc by WT Tull

MOORE George Col 22 S Laborer Acc Acc s/o Emaline Neely to Margaret Outten Col 18 S Acc Acc d/o Edmond & Sophronia on 16 Feb 1881 at Craddockville by TW Nettles

MOORE George Jr 23 S Sailor Acc Acc s/o James & Mary to Susan S Crockett 16 S Acc Acc d/o Southey & Rachel on 14 Jan 1880 at Mr Crockett's by JC Watson

MOORE George L 31 S Merchant Som Co MD Som Co MD s/o John H & Sally to Mary A Adams 21 S Acc Acc d/o James C & Mary on 9 Dec 1880 at Drum'tn by JG Anderson

MOORE George M Col 66 W Ship Carpenter Acc Acc s/o Levi to Elizabeth [Wallis] Wallace Col 42 S Acc Acc d/o Danl & Elizth on 17 Sep 1881 at Acc by SC Boston

MOORE Henry Col 61 W Farmer Acc Acc s/o Rachel to Emma Dix Col 55 W Acc Acc d/o Esther on 15 Mar 1893 at Acc by AJ Satchell

MOORE Jno D 36 W Farmer Lewis City DE Sussex Co DE s/o Elijah & Mary to Elizabeth Richardson 23 S Acc Acc d/o Isaiah & Margt on 20 Nov 1862 at Acc by D Titlow

MOORE John T 25 S Sailor Acc Acc s/o James & Maria to Maria Rayfield 27 S Acc Acc d/o Major & Betsey on 11 Oct 1890 at Tangier Isld by J Connor

MOORE Laban 28 S Farming Acc Acc s/o Thos & Susan to Mary Jane Thomas 23 S Acc Acc d/o James B & Pamela on 4 Jan 1871 at Downings Ch by O Littleton

MOORE Littleton P 45 S Farmer Acc Acc s/o Wm & Rebecca to Kitty C Blackstone 35 S Acc Acc d/o Thos & Ann on 24 Nov 1870 at Zion Ch by DA Woodson

MOORE Lloyd 23 S Waterman Acc Acc s/o Jas & Maria to Elizabeth Rayfield 18 S Acc Acc on 4 Oct 1886 at Onancock by CA Grice

MOORE Louis Col 22 S Sailor Acc Acc s/o Sarah to Patsy C Henderson Col 22 S Richmond City Acc d/o Maria on 19 Dec 1883 at Metompkin Ch by LW Lee

MOORE Moses 28 S Laborer Acc Acc s/o Dinah to Martha Perkins 17 S N'hamp: Acc d/o Mary J on 26 Aug 1869 at Acc by WF Williams

MOORE Perry Col 23 S Laborer Acc Acc s/o Emaline to Rose [Harmonson] Harmanson Col 18 S Acc Acc d/o Ada on 11 Mar 1882 at Pungo: by TW Nettles

MOORE Richard 22 S Sailor Acc Acc s/o James & Maria to Margaret Crockett 29 W Acc Acc d/o John & Hetty Evans on 19 Feb 1882 at Tangier Isld by LE Barrett

MOORE William 60 W Mechanic Acc Acc s/o John & Elizth to Caroline W Harrison 31 S Acc Acc d/o Jas H & Catharine A on 2 Apr 1873 at Acc by LK LeCato

MOORE Wm B 28 W Sailor Sussex Co DE Chinco: Isld s/o Shepard P & Nancy to Airylanta [Tindle] Tindall 22 W Acc Chinco: Isld d/o Thos L & Ann Birch on 1 Apr 1877 at Assateague Isld by R Williamson

MOREHEAD Samuel 45 S Veterinary Surgeon PA Acc to Mary Harmon 35 S Acc Acc d/o Leah on 5 Jan 1878 near Onancock by WJ Duhadway

MORRIS George W 30 S Milling Salisbury MD Acc s/o Peter T & Martha to Annie W Nock 19 S Acc Acc d/o Samuel & Polly on 29 Dec 1889 at Messongo Ch by WA Street

MORRIS James A 22 S Farmer NJ Acc s/o John & Catharine to Maggie E Thornton 23 S Acc Acc d/o William & Sally on 6 Apr 1882 near Conquest Ch by M Oldham

MORRIS Jas C 30 W Carpenter Wic Co MD Salisbury MD s/o Isaac & Nancy to Seney A Hart 16 S Acc Acc d/o Selby & Jenny on 23 Dec 1891 at Acc by JL King

MORRIS John to Harriet Bayly d/o Custis who gave consent lic: 31 Dec 1857 Alfred J Mears says he over 21

MORRIS John F 20 S Teamster NJ Acc s/o John to Mary E Bunting 19 S Acc Acc d/o Solomon & Mary on 24 Apr 1878 at Conquest Ch by JB Merritt

MORRIS Levin Col 21 S Laborer Acc Acc s/o John & Harriet to Sarah Collins Col 18 S Acc Acc d/o Alexander & Mary on 20 Apr 1881 at Bells Nk by JE Humphreys

MORRIS Wm 23 S Farmer York Co Acc s/o Edwd & Elizth to Elizabeth Taylor 22 S Acc Acc d/o Jas & Eliza on 5 Jul 1862 at Acc by TL Poulson

MUMFORD Henry 24 S Mariner Wor Co MD Acc s/o Wm M & Mary M to Hetty Catharine Justice 20 S Wor Co MD Acc d/o Jon & Elizabeth on 27 May 1869 at Acc by WP

Thornton
MUMFORD James F 25 S Oysterman Acc Acc to Susan A Chesser 17 S Acc Acc d/o Erastus P & Harriet H on 26 Feb 1879 at Temp'ville by M Oldham
MURPHY Break Col 33 S Sailor NC Acc s/o Isaac & Annie to Amanda Ashby Col 34 S Acc Acc d/o Malinda on 29 Apr 1882 at Locust Mount by RJ Waters
MURPHY Chas S 23 S Sailor Acc Acc s/o George & Jane to Hettie Charnock 21 W Acc Acc d/o Edmond & Margaret on 8 Apr 1891 at Tangier Isld by J Connor
MURPHY Isaac 25 S Soldier Som Co MD Acc to Nancy Trader 24 S Acc Acc d/o Wm Trader on 1 Feb 1864 at Acc by GH Ewell
MURPHY John Hymbirck Col 40 S Farmer Elizabeth City Co VA Acc to Rachel Snead Col 35 S Acc Acc d/o Tabbie Harmon on 16 Dec 1888 at bride's home by JK Adams
MURPHY William F 20 S Waterman Acc Acc s/o George W & Mary to Maggie L Bradshaw 18 S Acc Acc d/o Elisha T & Bettie on 5 May 1895 at Tangier Isld by CP Snow
MYERS James S 31 S Oysterman MA Acc s/o Amara & Annie to Matilda E Jackson 25 W Baltimore Hund DE Acc d/o Eli & Mary Collins on 19 Dec 1866 at Acc by P Bowdin Sr
NEDAB George H Col 24 S Laborer Acc Acc s/o Margaret to Alice C Glenn Col 18 S Acc Acc d/o Mary on 5 Jan 1873 at Acc by JWA Elliott
NEDAB Horace black 25 S Farmer to Ann Glenn black 23 S d/o Mary lic: 30 Dec 1872 marr: 5 Jan 1873 at Harpers Ferry
NEDAB John Col 29 S Laborer Acc Acc s/o Harriet to Sarah [Strame] Stran Col 21 S Acc Acc d/o Harriet on 26 Oct 1875 at Burton Chp by HT Rich
NEDAB Moses FN 24 S Oysterman b: Acc s/o Abraham & Lura to Nelly Beavans FN 18 S b: Acc d/o Henry (FN) & Alla on 19 Aug 1857 near Onancock by JF Chaplain
NEDAB Moses [Needab] Col 22 S Laborer Acc Acc s/o William Needab & Lizzie Bundick to Sarah F Doughty Col 18 S Acc Acc d/o Edmund Drummond Town & Emma Doughty on 6 Jan 1886 at Drum'tn by LW Lee
NEDAB Sewell C Col 26 S Farmer Acc Acc s/o Wm & Sally to Ibby Wharton Col 22 S Acc Acc d/o Sophia on 17 Dec 1891 at Acc C H by BJ Hargarves
NEELY Henry Col 45 S Laborer Acc Acc to Lucy Read Col 30 S Acc Acc d/o Amy on 31 Dec 1882 at Savageville by F Wood
NEELY Henry Col 47 W Wage-earner Acc Acc s/o Aaron Finney & Fannie Neely to Mary Custis Col 23 S Acc Acc d/o Margaret on 4 Sep 1890 at Acc by BJ Hargarves
NEELY John 24 S Attorney Montgomery Co MD Acc s/o John & Amelia to Manie V Rayfield 20 S Acc Acc d/o Thomas J & Emily on 13 Dec 1866 at Acc by P Warren
NELSON David Col 45 S Waiter Charleston SC Acc s/o David & Dolly to Maria Ames Col 30 S Acc Acc on 22 Aug 1881 at Acc by RJ Waters
NELSON James H 58 W Farmer Acc Acc s/o Spencer & Elkana to Sallie J Rayfield 34 S Acc Acc d/o George on 28 Dec 1893 near Assawoman by JL King
NELSON Jas H 28 S Farmer Acc Acc s/o Spencer & Elkana to Elizabeth Warner 21 S Acc Acc d/o Crittin on 3 Mar 1862 at Acc by ES Grant
NELSON John F 21 S Farming Acc

Acc s/o Spencer & Elkana to Mary J W [Shreaves] Shrieves 19 S Acc Acc d/o James on 2 Jan 1862 at Acc by ES Grant

NELSON John of Geo widr to Anne Hickman wid/o Robert lic: 14 Apr 1854

NELSON John T widr to Polly Northam d/o William lic: 26 Dec 1860 John Mears of M says she over 21

NELSON John T 29 W Farming Acc Acc s/o John & Gaily to Emma Taylor 18 S Acc Acc d/o Justice B on 8 Jan 1862 at Acc by ES Grant

NELSON Spencer 60 W Farmer Acc Acc s/o George & Elizth to Rosa Hardis 42 W MD Acc on 18 Jan 1872 at Modest Town by DA Woodson

NELSON Spencer R 25 S Farmer Acc Acc s/o Spencer & Elkanah to Lovey H Shrieves 26 S Acc Acc d/o David M & Sarah A on 9 Jan 1867 at Acc by G Bradford

NELSON Thomas s/o John to Sally A Lucas ward/o Southy T Lucas lic: 1 Feb 1854

NELSON Thomas A 23 S Farming Acc Acc s/o Spencer & Elhanah to Mariah R Lewis 20 S Acc Acc d/o Samuel & Susan on 15 Aug 1861 at Acc by ES Grant

NELSON William 25 S Farmer Acc Acc s/o John & Ann to Margaret [Shreaves] Shrieves 17 S Acc Acc d/o Wm & Jane on 7 Mar 1867 at Acc by ES Grant

NELSON William S 20 S Farmer Acc Acc s/o Spencer R & Lovey H to Ora V Bloxom 19 S Acc Acc d/o Wm H & Mary A on 19 Sep 1888 at Acc by WF Hayes

NEUMAN James F 27 S Physician NC Acc s/o Amasa J & Mary E to Maggie L Charnock 18 S Acc Acc d/o Edwe C & Euphernia on 16 Mar 1886 at Tangier Isld by CS Baker

NEVILLE William J Jr 29 S Farmer Acc Acc s/o William J & Mary H to Maggie E Mister 20 S Acc Acc d/o Lorenzo D & Susan on 12 Jun 1889 at bride's father's by RA Compton

NIBLETT Walter Clarence 21 S Farmer Lunenburg Co Lunenburg Co s/o Wm J & Ann E to Mary Inez [Brodwater] Broadwater 23 S Acc Acc d/o Joseph E & Mary E on 30 Nov 1893 at Temp'ville by WF Hayes

NICKOLSON Stephen W 30 S Farmer Wor Co MD Wor Co MD s/o Jos B & Sarah A to Amanda R Rhuark 30 S Wor Co MD Acc d/o Jno & Mary Ann on 23 Oct 1878 at Reese Chp by FH Mullineaux

NOCK Abram Col 23 S Farmer Acc Acc s/o Kitty Ailworth to Lizzie [Nock or Carr] Nock Col 33 S Acc Acc d/o Isaac & Catharine Parker on 1 Jun 1884 at Acc by P Sheppard

NOCK Albert W 22 S Farmer Acc Acc s/o Geo W & Delilah to Mary M Savage 17 S Acc Acc d/o Wm B & Rebecca on 21 Sep 1881 near Atlantic Ch by JW Hundley

NOCK Arthur 23 S Farmer Acc Acc s/o Leah to Sally Taylor 17 S Acc Acc d/o Comfort on 22 Apr 1867 at Acc by WT Tull

NOCK Charles Col 24 S Farmer Acc Acc s/o Maria to Lizzie Becket Col 24 S Acc Acc d/o Ann on 29 Dec 1884 at Acc by GW Young

NOCK Dennis Col 23 S Farm Laborer Acc Acc to Amanda Laws Col 22 S Acc Acc d/o Betsy Abbott on 14 Dec 1884 at Acc by AJ Satchell

NOCK Dennis Col 27 W Farmer Acc Acc s/o Parker & Ann to Mary Finney Col 19 S Acc Acc d/o Nathaniel & Elitia on 24 Dec 1893 near Mappsville by AJ Satchell

NOCK Douglas Col 25 S Steamboating Acc Acc to Annie Ballard Col 15 S

Marriages

Acc Acc d/o Sarah Walker on 11 Mar 1895 at Acc by TW Nettles

NOCK Edward E 26 S Farmer Acc Acc s/o Edward & Mary to Martha F Byrd 22 S Acc Acc d/o Wm T & Hetty on 16 Feb 1888 at Acc by WA Street

NOCK Edward T 22 S Merchant Acc Acc s/o Elijah W & Margt to Caroline A Boggs 20 S Acc Acc d/o John R & Leah M on 20 Oct 1858 at Acc by JH Addison (John W Chandler says he over 21)

NOCK Edwd Saml 22 S Farming Acc Acc s/o James E & Rachel to Malinda Scott 15 S Acc Acc d/o Walter & Malinda on 15 Aug 1878 at Zion Ch by DA Woodson

NOCK Enock Col 22 S Farmer Acc Acc s/o Mahala to Henny [Sheild] Shield Col 23 S Acc Acc on 6 Jun 1875 at Pungo: by JK Plato

NOCK Frank Col 22 S Farmer Acc Acc s/o Burnetta to Sarah Copes Col 28 S Acc Acc on 31 Mar 1890 at Acc by JE Bundick

NOCK George Col 36 S Farmer Acc Acc s/o Peter & Frances to Bettie Garrison Col 26 S Acc Acc d/o Thomas & Easter on 21 Jan 1891 near Savageville by JB Lewis

NOCK George Robert 27 S Carpenter Acc Acc s/o Jno W & Mary to Caroline Bunting 23 S Acc Acc d/o Henry & Mary on 15 Dec 1874 at Acc by TM Poulson

NOCK George S 27 S Merchant Acc Acc s/o Eliza & Margaret to Mary E Boggs 27 S Acc Acc d/o John & Leah on 24 Nov 1869 at Acc by JH Addison

NOCK George Thos Col 23 S Laborer Acc Acc s/o Arthur & Leah to Eliza Ann Drummond Col 21 S Acc Acc d/o Thos & Margt on 31 Dec 1882 at Onancock by JC Ayler

NOCK George W s/o Sally to Julila F Duncan d/o Meshack lic: 2 Jan 1854 Thos Groton says he over 21 & Wm T Duncan says she over 21

NOCK George W 25 S Farmer Acc Acc s/o Levin W & Polly W to Mary E Walter 19 S Acc Acc d/o John S & Annie on 6 Jan 1869 at Acc by JC Martin

NOCK Henry Col 22 S Farmer Acc Acc s/o Leah to Charlotte White Col 17 S Acc Acc d/o Mary Parkes on 29 Dec 1878 at Onancock by JW Diggs

NOCK Henry Col 23 S Farmer Acc Acc s/o Eliza to Eliza Laws Col 16 S Acc Acc d/o Aurella on 14 Dec 1884 at Acc by AJ Satchell

NOCK Horace P 23 S Farmer Acc Acc s/o Jas & Rachel to Armenia Gardner 16 S Acc Acc d/o Jno & Julia R on 2 Jan 1881 at Onancock by SC Boston

NOCK Isaac 40 S Farmer Acc Acc s/o Leah Chance to Harriet Elliott 28 S Acc Acc d/o Silvy on 31 Dec 1867 at Acc by JWA Elliott

NOCK Isaac Col 23 S Farmer Acc Acc s/o William & Harriet to Mary Shepherd Col 18 S N'hamp: Acc d/o Esther on 12 Oct 1894 at Acc by J Duckett

NOCK Isaac Col 21 S Farmer Acc Acc s/o Parker & Ann to Lida Hickman Col 21 S Acc Acc d/o Gilbert & Hester on 21 Jan 1894 at Acc by GHT Byrd

NOCK James 23 S Farmer Acc Acc s/o Betsy Snead to Mary A Gibbons 18 S Acc Acc d/o Hy & Levinia B on 2 Jan 1868 at Acc by E Hebard

NOCK James Col 45 S Laborer Acc Acc s/o Sarah to Amy [Bivens] Beavans Col 30 S Acc Acc d/o Obhelia on 25 Nov 1877 at Modest Town by A Joynes

NOCK James S 36 W Merchant Acc Acc s/o Jno W & Mary to Virginia Bunting 22 S Acc Acc d/o Henry T & Mary on 12 Jan 1882 near

Mappsville by JW Hundley

NOCK James W 25 S Farmer Acc Acc s/o Saml & Polly to Margt Ann Bayly 24 S Acc Acc d/o Thos & Elizth on 26 Feb 1879 near Mappsville by DA Woodson

NOCK John Col 50 S Laborer Acc Acc to Sarah Snead Col 45 S Acc Acc on 1 Mar 1874 at Onancock by R Davis

NOCK John Col 30 S Day Laborer Acc Acc s/o Leah to Susan Gunter Col 29 S Acc Acc d/o Hennie on 4 Apr 1886 at Onancock by GHT Byrd

NOCK John Col 28 S Wage-earner Acc Acc s/o Ibby Bevans to Julia Ann Badger Col 25 S Acc Acc d/o Ann Finney on 11 Nov 1888 at bride's home by TW Nettles

NOCK John Col 21 S Farmer Acc Acc s/o Ibby Nock to Peggy Beavans Col 18 S Acc Acc d/o Moses & Kessy on 27 Aug 1879 at New Boston by TW Nettles

NOCK John Alfred Col 23 S Farmer Acc Acc s/o Ann Sturgis to Mary E Rogers Col 21 S Acc Acc d/o Louis & Susan on 21 Dec 1892 at Acc by JH Offer

NOCK John E 29 S Farmer Acc Acc s/o Levin & Mary to Sarah A Elliott 26 S Acc Acc d/o Jno W A & Elizth on 3 Dec 1865 at Acc by WG Coe

NOCK John H Col 25 S Wage-earner Acc Acc s/o Alfred & Rachel to Susan Pitts Col 21 S Acc Acc d/o John & Ellen on 21 Jun 1891 at Onancock by J Duckett

NOCK John T 26 S Engineer Acc Brooklyn NY s/o Edward T & Caroline A to Kate M Evans 22 S Acc Acc d/o Elzy & Ann on 4 Jan 1893 at Acc by AC Berryman

NOCK John T Col 24 S Sailor Acc Acc s/o John L & Susan to Louisa E Fosque Col 16 S Acc Acc d/o Henry & Louisa on 26 May 1895 at Onancock by SW Watkins

NOCK John W 21 S Carpenter Acc Acc s/o James S to Mary A Showard 19 S Acc Acc d/o Alfred W on 11 Jan 1891 at Assawoman by WF Hayes

NOCK John W H 30 W Carpenter Acc Acc s/o John W & Mary to Mary E Kelly 18 S Acc Acc d/o Elijah & Hetty A on 29 Dec 1870 at Temp'ville by M Oldham

NOCK Levi 24 S Farmer Acc Acc s/o Mary to Sarah Custis 22 S Acc Acc d/o Ann on 6 Jan 1869 at Acc by JWA Elliott

NOCK Levin Col 45 W Farmer Acc Acc s/o Naria to Rhoda Northam Col 27 S Acc Acc d/o Ann on 24 Oct 1886 at Acc by AJ Satchell

NOCK Levin Floyd 33 S Attorney-at-Law Acc Acc s/o Levin H & Sarah C to Ellen James Brittingham 19 S Acc Acc d/o John & Hester N on 11 Jan 1888 at New Church by JH Amiss

NOCK Lorenzo Col 45 S Farmer Acc Acc s/o Mary to Louisa Ashby Col 35 S Acc Acc d/o Malinda on 11 Apr 1883 at Acc by GW Young

NOCK Peter Col 22 S Farmer Acc Acc s/o Leah Savage to Mary Riley Col 19 S Acc Acc d/o Elizie on 2 May 1875 at Onancock by JK Plato

NOCK Peter Col 32 W Laborer Acc Acc s/o Leah to Annie Savage Col 28 S Acc Acc d/o Susan on 25 Jan 1885 at Onancock by WC Vaden

NOCK Richard Col 23 S Laborer Acc Acc s/o Henry & Margaret to Margaret Gladding Col 22 S Acc Acc d/o Chas Ellis & Harriet Gladding on 25 May 1883 at Downings Ch by RB Beadles

NOCK Robert T Col 26 S Farmer Acc Acc s/o Rachel to Annie Kellam Col 22 S Acc Acc d/o Rachel on 26 Nov 1884 at Acc by P Sheppard

NOCK Samuel (FN) 25 S Farmer Acc Acc s/o Thos & Eliza to Rachel

Marriages 251

Sample (FN) 24 S Acc Acc d/o Isaac & Sabra on 27 Dec 1865 at Acc by JWA Elliott

NOCK Samuel W 35 S Farmer Acc Acc s/o Elijah W & Margt A to Susan B Colonna 24 S Acc Acc d/o Abel B & Margt on 23 Dec 1873 at Pungo: by LK LeCato

NOCK Samuel W 22 S Farmer Acc Acc s/o Edwd & Mary to Elizabeth A Trader 20 S Acc Acc d/o Alfred & Elizth on 29 Dec 1875 at Bethel Ch by DA Woodson

NOCK Thomas G 25 S Farmer Acc Acc s/o Littleton & Lizzie to Mary Marshall 20 S Acc Acc d/o Sylvester J & Polly on 20 Dec 1885 at Acc by M Oldham

NOCK William 25 S Gentleman Acc Acc s/o Mahala to Harriet Morris 25 W Acc Acc d/o Custis & Susan Bayly on 8 May 1867 at Acc by E Hebard

NOCK William Col 53 W Farmer Acc Acc s/o Mahola to Harriet Downing Col 37 S Acc Acc d/o Juliet on 26 Dec 1885 at Pungo Ch by P Sheppard

NOCK William Col 22 S Wage-earner Acc Acc s/o Jane to Virginia Watson Col 22 S Acc Acc d/o Agnes on 4 Jan 1891 near Mappsville by AJ Satchell

NOCK William L 21 S Merchant Acc Acc s/o Littleton & Elizth W to Mary Ida Justice 17 S Acc Acc d/o Joseph C & Mary Rachel on 27 Jan 1875 at Temp'ville by JM Anderson

NOCK Wm L 29 W Constable Acc Acc s/o Littleton & Elizth to Blanche Matthews 24 S Acc Acc d/o Joseph W & Sally on 1 Mar 1882 near Temp'ville by M Oldham

NORBECK George 65 W Retired Merchant Chambersbugh PA Washington DC s/o William & Polly to Julia Taylor 30 S Worcestershire England Acc d/o John & Frances on 17 Jun 1889 at Onancock by J McNabb

NORTHAM Alfred T 21 S Farmer Acc Acc s/o James M & Sarah A to Polly B Scott 22 S Acc Acc d/o Jas E & Eliz on 16 Jan 1881 at Reese Chp by EG Chandler

NORTHAM Armstrong 21 S Farmer Acc Acc s/o Airy to Margaret Joynes Col 22 S Acc Acc d/o Jno E Bundick on 19 Jul 1881 at Mappsville by JE Bundick

NORTHAM Arthur H 20 S Farmer Acc Acc s/o James M & Sarah A to Olivia Russell 17 S Acc Acc d/o Geo T & Mary on 4 Jan 1883 at Lee Mont by WA Crouse

NORTHAM Bowman Col 60 S Farmer Acc Acc to Susan Hickman Col 55 S Acc Acc on 25 Dec 1872 at Acc by A Joynes

NORTHAM Bruce L 21 S Farmer Acc Acc s/o George J & Mary A to Mary Barnes 22 S Acc Acc d/o William Barnes & Julia on 30 Dec 1894 at Mappsville by JL King

NORTHAM Charles W 27 S Farmer Acc Acc s/o David & Juliet to Catharine S Doughty 28 S Acc Acc d/o Edwd & Sarah on 3 Feb 1881 at Onancock by JC Watson

NORTHAM Custis W 26 S Farmer Acc Acc s/o Hy B & Milcab to Elizth Northam 24 S Acc Acc d/o John C & Elizth on 5 Nov 1867 at Acc by M Oldham

NORTHAM Custis W 52 W Farmer Acc Acc s/o Henry B & Micha to Elizabeth Mason 38 W Acc Acc on 28 Jan 1894 at Guilford by JR Tillery

NORTHAM David B 20 S Farmer Acc Acc s/o James C & Pauline to Mollie H Evans 18 S Acc Acc d/o Noah & Tabitha on 19 Nov 1890 at Acc by GW Burke

NORTHAM David J 34 S Farmer Acc

Acc s/o Gillet & Betsy to Eugenia C Godwin 23 S Acc Acc d/o James D & Elizabeth A on 4 Mar 1874 at Temp'ville by M Oldham

NORTHAM George Col 45 S Farmer Acc Acc s/o Danl & Rhoda to Anna Northam Col 45 S Acc Acc d/o Levi & Leah on 11 Oct 1872 at Acc by M Oldham

NORTHAM George Col 21 S Laborer Acc Acc s/o Ann to Emma Hope Col 21 S Acc Acc d/o Adah on 20 Jan 1878 at Modest Town by A Joynes

NORTHAM George (T) 35 S Farming b: Acc s/o Wm Northam & Susan Chistesser to Elizabeth (C) Byrd 32 S b: Acc d/o Johanas Byrd & Lany Coke on 28 Nov 1859 at Acc by T Waters

NORTHAM George W s/o Henry B who gave consent to Elizabeth Landing d/o James who gave consent lic: 20 May 1859

NORTHAM Grant Col 28 S Wage-earner Acc Acc s/o George & Annie to Florence Joynes Col 22 S Acc Acc d/o Harriet on 22 Sep 1895 near Mappsville by AJ Satchell

NORTHAM Henry B Jr to Hester Prescott d/o Hester who gave consent lic: 26 Apr 1858 Riley Fisher says he over 21

NORTHAM Henry C 30 S Merchant Acc Acc s/o William C & Marg't C to Sally A Hancock 23 S Wor Co MD Acc d/o Sidney M & Sally on 13 Apr 1892 at Acc by WW Wood

NORTHAM Henry R Col 30 W Farmer Acc Acc s/o Eliz'th Warrington to Elizabeth Watson Col 25 S Acc Acc d/o Virginia Drummond on 2 Mar 1891 near Temp'ville by JC Cluff

NORTHAM Isaiah D 28 S Farmer Acc Acc s/o David & Juliet to Lena Y Kellam 22 S Acc Acc d/o Benj J & Cath' A on 16 Nov 1892 at Pungo: by EC Atkins

NORTHAM James 33 S Farmer Acc Acc s/o John T & Adaline to Annie Hall 33 S Acc Acc d/o Thomas & Sallie on 1 Feb 1891 at Temp'ville by WF Hayes

NORTHAM James E 23 S Farmer Acc Acc s/o David A & Julia to Caroline East 19 S Acc Acc d/o Mary Morehead on 4 Nov 1869 at Acc by EG Irvin

NORTHAM James M s/o Henry B to Sarah A Landing d/o James lic: 26 Jul 1858 Henry B Northam says both over 21

NORTHAM Jno W 24 S Farmer Acc Acc s/o Jno T & Adaline to Mollie A Jarman 24 S Acc Acc d/o Wm & Rachel on 5 Nov 1879 at Modest Town by DA Woodson

NORTHAM John s/o William to Adeline Trader d/o Ishmeal lic: 2 Jun 1854 Valentine Trader said both over 21

NORTHAM John H 19 S Wage-earner Acc Acc s/o Henry B & Mary H to Margaret Lewis 22 S Acc Acc d/o Henry & Charlotte on 13 Jul 1890 at Mappsville by HS Dulany

NORTHAM John W 28 S House Carpenter Acc Acc s/o John & Elizabeth to Kissey Spence 20 S Acc Acc d/o John & Ann on 11 Feb 1860 at Sexes Isld by EW Stickney (John H Justice says he over 21)

NORTHAM John W 51 W Carpenter Acc Acc to Belle B Williams 23 S Acc Acc d/o Henry & Rosa on 1 Apr 1888 at Sykes Isld by TG Pullen

NORTHAM John W 24 S Oysterman Acc Acc s/o John W to Mary Spence 17 S Acc Acc d/o Lemos J & Lizzie B on 19 Mar 1890 at Onancock by GW Burke

NORTHAM Levi Col 21 S Day Laborer Acc New Church s/o Eastus & Elisa to Lizzie B Marshall Col 21 S Acc New Church d/o William & Eda on 7

Mar 1883 at Acc by JC Cluff

NORTHAM Levi Jacob 22 S Merchant Acc Acc s/o James & Rosa to Mary Grace Leppincott Long 19 S Acc Acc d/o Thos & Mary Elizth on 12 Jan 1859 at Conquest Ch by JF Chaplain (Thomas Ling gave concent)

NORTHAM Levin 24 S Laborer Acc Acc to Sarah Williams 18 S Acc Acc d/o Lettia on 3 May 1868 at Acc by G Bradford

NORTHAM Mosby 24 W Farmer Acc Acc s/o George J & Annie to Pollie Dix 18 S Acc Acc d/o Samuel H & Nancy on 28 Dec 1893 near Assawoman by JL King

NORTHAM Spencer Col 43 W Farmer Acc Acc s/o Arthur Dickerson to Elizabeth Smith Col 26 S NC Acc on 27 Feb 1890 at Acc by AJ Satchell

NORTHAM Thomas 21 S Farmer Acc Acc s/o John L & Adaline to Elizabeth Young 22 S Acc Acc d/o Sheppard & Sally on 11 Nov 1885 at Temp'ville by M Oldham

NORTHAM Thomas L 22 S Farmer Acc Acc s/o William C & Elizabeth to Adeline J Gladding 20 S Acc Acc d/o Oliver & Danvers J on 11 Jan 1891 near Nelsonia by JE Bundick

NORTHAM Watson F 23 S Farmer Acc Acc s/o Jno & Adaline to Margaret A Ewell 21 S Acc Acc d/o Jas & Julia A on 17 Aug 1881 at Temp'ville by JW Hundley

NORTHAM William s/o Elijah to Drucilla Bayly d/o Elizabeth Harris who gave consent lic: 6 Jan 1858 John Mears of M says he over 21

NORTHAM William R 22 S Farmer Acc Acc s/o George James & Marianna Northam to Olive E Ayres 18 S Acc Acc d/o Robert & Eveline on 8 Jun 1887 at Temp'ville by M Oldham

NORTHAMER Augustus single Farm Laborer Germany Acc to Rebecca Taylor 25 W N'hamp: Acc d/o Sarah Allen on 16 Jul 1882 at Bradford Nk by JW Stiff

NOTTINGHAM Benjamin S 36 S Merchant N'hamp: N'hamp: s/o Edward T to Cornelia Page Parker 35 S Acc Acc d/o Wm N & Sarah M on 25 Jan 1888 at Pungo: by J McNabb

NOTTINGHAM John E 38 S Merchant N'hamp: N'hamp: s/o Thos & Mary Ann to Malinda C Fisher 25 S Acc Acc d/o Frederick B & Rose on 8 Aug 1876 at Drum'tn Bapt Ch by WT Hundley

OLDHAM Edward S 27 S Merchant's Clerk Acc Acc s/o Montcalm Oldham & maria A to Sallie F Turner 23 S Amherst Co VA Acc d/o Louis E & Julia on 9 Sep 1886 at Temp'ville by M Oldham

OLDHAM Montcalm Jr 26 S Deputy Clerk Acc Acc s/o Montcalm Sr & Maria to Nannie A Rayfield 25 S Acc Acc d/o Thomas & Eliath on 19 Feb 1874 at Drum'tn by M Oldham

OLIVE Stephen 39 S Sailor b: King George Co s/o Jno D & Margt to Cath Jane Moore 25 S b: Acc d/o Levi & Susan on 1 Mar 1854 at Meth Ch, S Nk by JH Addison

OLIVER Wm H 18 S Farmer Baltimore MD Acc s/o Wm H & Margt to Caddie S Mapp 19 S Acc Acc d/o Edwin T & Indiana on 28 Jun 1877 at Oak Grove Ch by JWA Elliott

ONIONS R James [Onion] 22 S Farmer Acc Acc s/o Wesley & Eliza to Dora Taylor 18 S Acc Acc d/o Jas P A & malinda on 23 Nov 1884 at Acc by AJ Walter

ONIONS Wesley 23 S Oysterman Acc Acc s/o Wesley & Eliza to Bettie J Middleton 20 S Acc Acc d/o Jno & Julia A on 27 Dec 1882 at Lee Mont by WA Crouse

ONLEY Isaac [Only] Col 22 S Laborer Acc Acc s/o Elizabeth to Frances

Watson Col 23 S Acc Acc on 28 May 1882 at Acc by JE Bundick

ONLEY John 28 S Farmer Acc Acc s/o John to Mary A Watson 24 S Acc Acc d/o Wm C & Fannie on 28 Oct 1868 at Acc by OP Twiford

ONLEY John 23 S Farmer Acc Acc s/o Wm H & Trephenia to Henrietta Northam 22 S Acc Acc d/o George & Elizabeth on 7 Jan 1885 at Onancock by WC Vaden

ONLEY John E [Only] 29 S Box Maker Acc Camden NJ s/o Edward T & Sally P to Mary T Parkes 21 S Acc Acc d/o Bennet & Emily on 20 Jul 1887 at Acc by JW Ward

ONLEY John L 30 S Farmer Acc Acc s/o John H & Mary Ann to Geneva F Mears 19 S Acc Acc d/o Thos T & Cornelia on 25 Dec 1893 at Acc by WW Wood

ONLEY John R 24 S Farmer Acc Acc to Sarah Ann Ailworth 20 S Acc Acc d/o Levin Elizth on 17 Jan 1867 at Acc by GW Matthews

ONLEY John W 21 S Sailor Acc Acc s/o Smith & Elizabeth to Lavinia S Trader 17 S Acc Acc d/o Littleton P & Sarah on 8 Apr 1891 at Sanford by WF Hayes

ONLEY Julius F 23 S House Carpenter Acc Acc s/o John R & Sarah to Azie S Scott 16 S Acc Acc d/o John T & Margaret S on 8 Nov 1892 at Lee Mont by JET Ewell

ONLEY Major H 26 S Farmer Acc Acc s/o Jno H & Mary A to Emma F Ardis 22 S Acc Acc d/o Rosa Nelson on 29 Dec 1886 at Acc by AD Davis

ONLEY Thomas Col 22 S Wage-earner Acc Acc to Martha Hope Col 21 S Acc Acc d/o Margaret on 5 May 1895 at Acc by JE Bundick

ONLEY Thomas H 27 S Farmer Acc Acc s/o John & Lucy to Anna W Powell 21 S Acc Acc d/o Littleton & Belle E on 1 Jun 1881 at Acc by WC Tuelley

ONLEY William s/o John to Tiffany Hickman d/o Thomas lic: 6 Nov 1854 Geo T Satchell says both over 21

OTWELL William T 27 S Merchant Acc Acc s/o William T & Virginia C to Susan J Gibb 24 S Acc Acc d/o William J & Susan on 29 Dec 1892 at Horntown by RB Scott

OUTTEN Edward (Outen) FN to Sopha West FN d/o Mary who gave consent lic: 28 Jul 1856 Levin J White says he over 21

OUTTEN James Col 23 S Farmer Acc Acc s/o William & Tenney to Jane Taylor Col 21 S Acc Acc d/o Arthur on 29 Jan 1879 at Pungo: by JW Diggs

OUTTEN James [Outen] Col 65 S Wage-earner Acc Acc s/o James Outen & Rachel Drummond to Adah Beach Col 63 S Acc Acc d/o Adah Dunton on 14 Mar 1889 at Acc by JA Haynes

OUTTEN John E Col 35 S Farmer Acc Acc s/o William & Tinnie to Annie Smith Col 25 S Acc Acc d/o William & Polly on 29 Apr 1895 at Acc by L Duncan

OUTTEN John H 19 S Farmer N'hamp: Acc s/o Jacob & Mary to Sarah M Young 15 S Acc Acc d/o Richard W & Susan M on 6 Dec 1882 at Onancock by SC Boston

OVERTON Wm Henry 28 S Soldier NC Acc s/o Paul & Peggy to Anna M Lilliston 45 W Acc Acc d/o Thomas Hurst on 12 Jul 1865 at Acc by ES Grant

OWENS James P 36 S Sailor Acc Acc s/o Geo C & Catharine to Annie E Hargis 28 W Acc Acc d/o John T & Maggie Harrison on 27 Nov 1895 at Acc by JR Griffith

PADDY Williard D 21 S Laborer Warrenton VA Acc s/o Kesiah

Stratton to Viola Wise Col 18 S Acc Acc d/o Jno A & Eliza on 25 May 1881 at Onancock by PA Leatherbury

PAIN Nathaniel 23 S Fisherman Richmond VA Acc s/o Thomas & Mariah to Malinda Evans 19 S Acc Acc d/o George E & Annie on 4 Oct 1885 at Tangier Isld by CS Baker

PALMATARY George H to Irene Bagwell lic: 2 Sep 1858 John E Wise & Geo W Widgen both say both over 21

PALMER George Col 23 S Dredger Acc Acc s/o Mary Tunnell to Leah Watson Col 26 S Acc Acc d/o Clarissa on 9 Apr 1876 near Modest Town by JE Bundick

PALMER Jacob Col 28 S Farmer Acc Acc s/o John & Arzilla to Mary Baker 18 S Acc Acc d/o Lizzie on 25 Dec 1895 at Modest Town by DB Savage

PARKER Alfred Col 21 S Laborer Acc Acc s/o Isaac & Catharine to Frances Walter Col 21 S Acc Acc d/o Annie on 29 May 1883 at Shilo Bapt Ch by TW Nettles

PARKER Augustus 38 S Merchant Acc Acc s/o John R & Ann L to Sally R West 22 S Acc Acc d/o Revel & Margt C on 19 Mar 1879 at Onancock by JC Watson

PARKER Benjamin 22 S Farmer Acc Acc s/o Benj & Polly to Emma Baker 21 S Acc Acc d/o Asa & Tabitha on 22 Nov 1864 at Acc by GH Ewell

PARKER Benjamin T 35 S Mechanic Acc Acc s/o John R & Ann to Amanda Taylor 23 S Acc Acc d/o Joseph B & Elizabeth on 20 Dec 1871 at Cashville by O Littleton

PARKER Benjamin T 41 W Hotel Keeper Acc Acc s/o Jno R & Ann to Mary E Phillips 25 S Acc Acc d/o Solomon & Ann S on 12 Dec 1877 at Acc by JH Amiss

PARKER Benjamin T 54 W Hotel Keeper Acc Acc s/o John R & Ann to Leah S Boggs 40 S Acc Acc d/o John R & Leah M on 15 Jul 1891 at Acc by AC Berryman

PARKER Benjamin W 22 S Farmer Acc Acc s/o John E & Emma S to Elizabeth S Drummond 18 S Acc Acc d/o James C & Anna on 23 Jul 1890 at Acc by JB Pruitt

PARKER David Col 27 S Farm Laborer Acc Acc s/o Catharien to Mary E Stevens Col 28 S Acc Acc d/o Elizth Blackstone on 29 Oct 1883 at Acc by TW Nettles

PARKER Edward Col 22 S Laborer Acc Acc s/o Jno & Margt to Eliza Jane Anthony Col 18 S Acc Acc d/o Margaret on 2 Jun 1878 near Boston Ch by TW Nettles

PARKER Edward 33 S Sailor Acc Acc s/o Geo & Rachel to Elizth Cobb 25 S Acc Acc d/o Leah on 15 Mar 1879 at Onancock by SC Boston

PARKER Edward 48 S Laborer Acc Acc s/o Agnes to Sarah Phillips 40 S Acc Acc d/o Abby on 28 Dec 1881 at Cross Rd by GHT Byrd

PARKER Frank Col 22 S Waterman Acc Acc s/o Susan to Mary [Revel] Revell Col 18 S Acc Acc d/o Sarah on 8 Jul 1874 at Savageville by JK Plato

PARKER Gabriel 21 S Waterman Acc Acc s/o Gabriel to Eliza J [Striggle] Strigle 17 S Smith Isld MD Acc d/o Jas & Flora on 4 Oct 1886 at Onancock by CA Grice

PARKER Geo T 22 S Farmer Acc Acc s/o Saml & Mary to Tabitha [Killmon] Killman 21 S Acc Acc d/o Saml & Cath on 11 Jan 1866 at Acc by JH Addison

PARKER George F 44 S Merchant Acc Acc s/o John R & Ann L to Emma S Phillips 30 S Acc Acc d/o Solomon & Susan A on 14 Dec 1887 at

Drum'tn by WJ Twilley

PARKER George H Col 21 S Blacksmith Acc Acc s/o Lucy to Julia Wise Col 19 S Acc Acc d/o Purnell T & Peggie S on 19 Jan 1894 at Onancock by FW Overton

PARKER George T 23 S Farmer Acc Acc s/o William & Mary H to Nettie F Wallace 17 S Acc Acc d/o George B & Elizabeth A on 21 Dec 1887 at Pungo: by JH Riddick

PARKER George W 22 S Farmer Acc Acc s/o Matilda Bundick to Rose Ella M Crosley 19 S Acc Acc d/o Jas E & Sarah on 31 Jan 1883 at Onancock by WC Vaden

PARKER George W 28 S Farmer Acc Acc s/o Geo & Margt to Ella J Core 19 S Acc Acc d/o John W & Amy on 17 Jan 1883 at Onancock by SC Boston

PARKER George Washington 23 S Laborer r: Acc to Elizabeth Wharton 22 S Acc Acc on 16 Sep 1869 at Acc by A Joynes

PARKER Henry 43 W Oysterman Acc Acc s/o John to Elizabeth P Gladding 45 W Acc Acc d/o Bennett M & Henny Bird on 7 Jan 1867 at Acc by GW Matthews

PARKER Henry Col 23 S Steam Mill Snow Hill MD Acc s/o Clarissa to Olivia Copes Col 25 S Acc Acc on 24 Jun 1875 at Temp'ville by M Oldham

PARKER Henry Col 27 S Oysterman Acc Acc s/o Louis & Mary to Annie Milbourn Col 19 S Acc Acc d/o Delda on 27 Apr 1887 at Messongo Bridge by JC Cluff

PARKER Henry R 22 S Merchant Acc Acc s/o Jno M & Ellen to Margaret E Lingo 18 S Acc Acc d/o Jno W & Eliza on 23 Feb 1881 at Acc by GH Ray

PARKER James E 23 S Farmer Acc Acc s/o Saml & Sally to Elizth A Wallace 18 S Acc Acc d/o Geo B & Elizth on 16 Jul 1879 at Hollies Ch by CC Wertenbaker

PARKER James H 39 W Surgeon Dentist Acc Acc s/o George & Sarah A to Annie S [Gillet] Gillett 33 S Acc Acc d/o Wm & Henrietta on 28 Oct 1869 at Acc by P Warren

PARKER James L Col 21 S Farmer Acc Acc s/o Katharine to Lucy Wise Col 22 S Acc Acc d/o Wm & Charlotte on 1 Jun 1884 at Acc by P Sheppard

PARKER James Walter Col 56 S Farmer Acc Acc s/o Jane Hatton to Elizabeth Harmon Col 50 S Acc Acc d/o Margaret on 3 Oct 1880 at Acc by RJ Waters

PARKER John (FN) single Laborer Acc Acc s/o Geo & Fanny to Margaret Major (FN) single Acc Acc d/o Joahua Major & Zippy West on Jun 1855(?) near Pungo: by M Oldham (lic: 25 Jun 1855 & Aug K Kellam says both over 21)

PARKER John FN to Mary Jane West FN d/o Mary White who gave consent lic: 29 Dec 1856

PARKER John 21 S Laborer Acc Acc s/o Leah to Mary Kellam 20 S Acc Acc d/o Mary on 7 Feb 1869 at Acc by WF Williams

PARKER John Col 21 S Laborer Acc Acc s/o Jane Topping (Col) to Mary Snead Col 20 S Acc Acc d/o Margaret (Col) on 1 Jan 1871 at Onancock by WF Williams

PARKER John Col 62 W Farmer Acc Acc s/o Peggy to Annie Kellam Col 50 W Acc Acc d/o Ada Phillips on 24 Jan 1878 at Acc by A Handy

PARKER John Col 50 W Farmer Acc Acc s/o Littleton & Sarah to Elexine Savage Col 27 S Acc Acc d/o George Savage & Peggy Godwin on 27 Nov 1889 at Acc by L Duncan

PARKER John E 28 S Farmer Acc Acc s/o John R & Ann to Mary A Mears

17 S Acc Acc d/o John S & Sarah T (who gave consent) on 1 Dec 1859 at r/o John S Mears by JWA Elliott (John E White says he over 21)

PARKER John E 32 W Farmer Acc Acc s/o Jno R & Ann to Emma Walter 20 S Acc Acc d/o Geo & Matilda on 23 Dec 1863 at Acc by LK LeCato

PARKER John M 40 W Farmer Acc Acc s/o Revell & Betsy to Ann Bull 24 S Acc Acc d/o Custis Jr & Margt on 31 Dec 1865 at Acc by ES Grant

PARKER John T Col 21 S Laborer Acc Acc to Maggie [Beckett] Becket Col 21 S Acc Acc d/o Sarah on 27 Apr 1884 at Onancock by R Davis

PARKER John W Col 25 S Farmer Acc Acc s/o Lizzie to Cordelia Conquest Col 22 S Acc Acc d/o Levi & Mary on 12 Mar 1885 at Acc by GW Young

PARKER John W Col 22 S Wage-earner Acc Acc s/o John & Juliet to Onie Haley Col 18 S Acc Acc d/o William & Letia on 20 Nov 1892 at Locust Mount by RH Coleburn

PARKER Joseph Col 25 S Laborer Acc Acc s/o Tabby Poulson to Amy Snead Col 25 S Acc Acc d/o Peter & Amy on 1 May 1879 at Drum'tn by RH Govans

PARKER Joseph T 24 S Carpenter Acc Acc s/o George & Nancy to Susan P Parker 22 S Acc Acc d/o John & Margt on 19 Nov 1856 at Acc by JH Addison (Robert L Drummond says both over 21)

PARKER Levin 35 W Farmer Acc Acc s/o Geo to Annie R Smith 19 S Acc Acc d/o John W & Malinda W on 14 Oct 1869 at Acc by JH Addison

PARKER Levin T 30 S Farmer Acc Acc s/o Wm H & Margt to L Medora Colonna 18 S Acc Acc d/o Geo D & Sally E on 2 Jun 1886 at Oak Hall by DM Wallace

PARKER Lewis 24 S Farming Acc Acc s/o James to Jennie Lewis 18 S Acc Acc d/o James & Melvina on 11 Apr 1880 at Onancock by JC Watson

PARKER Lloyd Col 21 S Wage-earner Acc Acc s/o Leah Winder to Julia Ann Poulson 16 S Acc Acc d/o Laura Bundick on 22 Dec 1895 at Acc by J Duckett

PARKER Louis Col 49 W Acc Acc s/o Henry Samples & Sallie Parker to Jane [Douglas] Douglass Col 48 W Acc Acc d/o Daniel Abbott & Ann Watson on 29 Jul 1887 near Temp'ville by JC Cluff

PARKER Major Col 21 S Wage-earner Acc Acc s/o John & Kesiah to Annie Snead Col 16 S Acc Acc d/o Jane on 17 Jun 1891 at Savageville by JH Offer

PARKER Noah Col 30 S Farmer Acc Acc s/o George & Mary to Susan Sample Col 25 S Acc Acc d/o Charles & Betsy on 9 Feb 1887 at bride's father's by L Duncan

PARKER Obed Col 24 S Wage-earner Acc Acc s/o John & Jane to Maggie West Col 22 S Acc Acc d/o George & Peggie on 21 Apr 1889 at Acc by L Duncan

PARKER Oswald 26 S Sailor Acc Acc s/o James & Susan to Catharine [Bailey] Bayly 16 S Acc Acc d/o Edward & Lovey on 8 Dec 1880 near Savageville by SC Boston

PARKER Richard 22 S Farmer Acc Acc s/o Sallie to Mary A Wallace 23 S Acc Acc d/o Danl & Betsy on 8 May 1867 at Acc by JH Addison

PARKER Rike D Col 23 S Farmer Acc Acc s/o Major & Labra to Mary Ann Snead Col 21 S Acc Acc d/o George & Betsy on 8 Jan 1885 at Acc by AJ Satchell

PARKER Robert J 22 S Harness Mkr Som Co MD Acc s/o Levin & Susan to Kitty West 19 S Acc Acc d/o John

& Jane on 16 Feb 1868 at Acc by ES Grant

PARKER Samuel 24 S Laborer Acc Acc s/o Dinah to Mary Topping 18 S Acc Acc d/o Hy & Fannie on 24 Feb 1869 at Acc by WF Williams

PARKER Samuel Col 49 W Wage-earner Acc Acc s/o Diana to Rebecca Bayly Col 32 S Acc Acc d/o Jane Chandler on 10 Oct 1894 at Acc by J Duckett

PARKER Samuel B 19 S Farmer Acc Acc s/o Richard & Mary A to Ruth Parker 17 S Acc Acc d/o William & Mary A on 2 Nov 1887 at Cypress Br by JR Strugis

PARKER Severn Col 60 W Wage-earner Acc Acc to Emeline Brickhouse Col 35 S Acc Acc on 31 Aug 1895 at Belle Haven by REC Lawson

PARKER Severn Col 45 S Farmer s/o Samuel & Agnes to Elizabeth Crowns Col 28 S b: Baltimore lic: 21 Mar 1871 marr: 23 Mar 1871

PARKER Spencer 28 S Laborer & Seaman Acc Acc s/o Levin & Alice to Joanna Downes 25 S Acc Acc d/o Laura on 4 Oct 1885 at Acc by HG Cowan

PARKER Thomas H 27 S Farmer s/o James & Susan to Sarah F East 16 S d/o Peter T & Susan lic: 7 Nov 1871 marr: 8 Nov 1871

PARKER Tully Col 22 S Wage-earner Acc Acc s/o Samuel & Mary V to Martha Drummond Col 23 S Acc Acc d/o Spencer & Miriam on 8 Apr 1894 at Onley by R Davis

PARKER Walter 22 S Oysterman Acc Acc s/o Josiah & Matilda to Mary A Taylor 20 S Acc Acc d/o Willian of J & Mary on 21 Jun 1876 near Guilford by JE Bundick

PARKER Walter W 23 S Blacksmith WV Baltimore MD s/o Dryden & Mary to Amanda M Allen 19 S Jackson Co WI Acc d/o Ira B & Mary A on 27 Sep 1881 at Acc by SC Boston

PARKER Washington FN 21 S Laborer Acc Acc s/o Mahala to Harriet Smith FN 22 S Acc Acc d/o Lewis Garrison on 29 Dec 1865 at Acc by TL Tomkinson

PARKER William 30 S Canou Builder Acc Acc s/o George & Nancy to Mary H Parker 18 S Acc Acc d/o Thomas & Mary & (ward/o John T Elliott) on 2 Apr 1857 at Acc by JH Addison (Napoleon O White says he over 21)

PARKER William Col 21 S Light House Keeper Acc Chinco: Isld s/o Major J & Sabra to Venice Nedab Col 16 S Acc Chinco: Isld d/o Jos & Elizth on 24 Dec 1880 at Chinco: Isld by TAH O'Brien

PARKES Albert 21 S Farmer Acc Acc s/o John & Catharine to Sarah Emma Massey 21 S Acc Acc d/o Luther & Sallie on 3 Jan 1867 at Acc by GW Matthews

PARKES Alexander B 26 S Oysterman Acc Acc s/o Mark & Elizth to Virginia S Wessells 19 S Acc Acc d/o Thos & Ann on 28 Jan 1800 at Guilford Ch by WW Royall

PARKES Alfred 18 S Farmer Acc Acc s/o Ann Mason to Lizzie Downing 16 S Acc Acc d/o Hester on 6 Jan 1867 at Acc by ES Grant

PARKES Andrew C [Parks] 22 S Sailor Acc Acc s/o Louis B & Margaret to Margaret E Crockett 22 S Acc Acc d/o John & Jane on 9 Sep 1888 at Tangier by GL Hardesty

PARKES Arthur 22 S Farmer Acc Acc s/o Wm J & sally to Laura Holland 22 S Acc Acc d/o Samuel & Clarissa on 1 Apr 1880 at Modest Town by DA Woodson

PARKES Arthur F 35 S Farmer Acc Acc s/o Jno Y & Catharine to Sallie

A Godwin 24 S Acc Acc d/o Jas & Elizabeth on 6 Mar 1883 at Conquest Ch by M Oldham

PARKES Asbury 23 S Waterman Acc Acc s/o Trevis & Margaret to Virginia Evans 17 S Acc Acc d/o Wm L & Mary C on 30 May 1882 at Deep Ck by PA Leatherbury

PARKES Augustus [Parks] 22 S Oysterman Acc Acc s/o Mark & Elizth to Virginia Justice 18 S Acc Acc d/o Saml & Mary Ann on 26 Aug 1866 at Acc by JH Ellegood

PARKES Benj F 34 S Farmer Acc Acc s/o Robt C & Elizth to Ellen S Watts 23 S Acc Acc d/o Jno D & Adaline on 5 Dec 1878 at Modest Town by DA Woodson

PARKES Benjamin F 26 S Farmer Acc Acc s/o Jas B & Polly to Annie E Summers 22 S Acc Acc d/o Wm & Serena on 30 Sep 1883 at Mappsville by JW Hundley

PARKES Bennett 55 W Farmer Acc Acc s/o Benjamin & Mary to Mary A Bundick 50 W Acc Acc d/o Wm S & Tabbie Shrieves on 26 Jul 1894 at Modest Town by WW Wood

PARKES Charles W [Parks] 24 S Sailor Acc Acc s/o Travis E & Margaret to Dona Crockett 24 S Acc Acc d/o Peter M & Sally A on 13 May 1890 at Tangier Isld by J Connor

PARKES Charlie B [Parks] 22 S Sailor Acc Acc s/o John E & Eliza to Scany [Dize] Dies 18 S Acc Acc d/o John & Christianna on 9 May 1888 at Tangier Isld by GL Hardesty

PARKES Cornelius N 25 S Waterman Acc Acc s/o Noah & Mary Jane to Missouri Barnes 22 S Acc Acc d/o James & Emeline on 4 Sep 1884 at Acc by AJ Walter

PARKES Covington 23 S Farmer Acc Acc s/o Noah & Mary Jane to Jeanette F Taylor 25 S Acc Acc d/o Saml C & Sarah Ann on 7 Dec 1881 at Acc by WA Crouse

PARKES Edward C (Parks) s/o Robert C to Martha Moore d/o Wm S dec'd lic: 6 Feb 1861 Robert Alexander says both over 21

PARKES Edward T 33 S Merchant Acc Acc s/o Parker W & Nancy L to Jeanette M Dix 19 S Acc Acc d/o Asa T & Jeanetta on 18 Sep 1881 at Masonville by WA Crouse

PARKES Elijah 23 S Oysterman Acc Acc s/o John Edwd & Mary to Laura Crockett 22 S Acc Acc d/o Elliott & Catharine on 1 Sep 1884 at Tangier Isld by CS Baker

PARKES Francis D 40 S Gentleman Acc Acc s/o Jno D & Sarah to Bettie Parkes 26 S Acc Acc d/o Wm L & Mary on 7 May 1876 at Downings Ch by M Oldham

PARKES Francis D 55 W Farmer & Capitalist Acc Acc s/o John D & Sally S to Sudie S Kelly 22 S Acc Acc d/o Abel G & Mary on 7 Mar 1888 at Onancock by RA Compton

PARKES Francis O 22 S U S Light Ship Employee Acc Acc s/o Wm & Sally to Julia C [Reid] Read 16 S Acc Acc d/o Joshua W & Charity on 20 Jul 1885 at Chinco: Isld by JD Reese

PARKES Gabriel [Parks] 31 W Waterman Tangier Isld Tangier Isld s/o Stephen & Elizabeth to Jane Pruitt 28 S Tangier Isld Tangier Isld d/o Elijah & Catharine on 20 Feb 1861 at Acc by JH Addison (John Gibbons says she over 21)

PARKES George 22 S Oysterman Acc Acc s/o Gabriel & Betsy to Zipporah Parkes 20 S Acc Acc d/o Parker & Polly on 26 Apr 1875 at Chesconessex by PA Leatherbury

PARKES George E 22 S Farmer Acc Acc s/o Charles & Margt to Mary R Barnes 24 S Acc Acc d/o Thos & Nancy on 8 Oct 1884 at Acc by JW Carroll

PARKES George L [Parks] 34 W Sailor Acc Acc s/o Thomas & Margaret to Ellen Crockett 21 S Acc Acc d/o J Dumpsey & Emily on 7 Aug 1893 at Tangier Isld by ZH Webster

PARKES George M 25 W Farmer Acc Acc s/o George & Mary to Lena J Mason 17 S Acc Acc d/o James H & Mary on 5 Oct 1887 at Zion Ch by WA Street

PARKES George of B 23 S Farmer Acc Acc s/o George & Mary E to Soulie E [Shreaves] Shrieves 18 S Acc Acc d/o Wm & Jane M on 28 Dec 1881 at Bapt Ch by SC Boston

PARKES George P 23 S Farmer Acc Acc s/o Parker W & Nancy to Elizabeth P Grinnalds 23 S Acc Acc d/o Parker & Elizth on 12 Jun 1867 at Acc by ES Grant

PARKES Handy Col 30 W Farmer Acc Acc s/o Maria to Sarah Rayfield Col 34 S Acc Acc d/o Esther Poulson on 11 Dec 1878 at News Town by A Joynes

PARKES Handy [Parks] Col 25 S Laborer Acc Acc s/o Sukey to Rosa Gunter Col 26 S Acc Acc on 5 Feb 1885 near Lee Mont by CA Horsey

PARKES Harry [Parks] 19 S Sailor Acc Acc s/o John E & Eliza J to Polly J Pruitt 19 S Acc Acc d/o Raymond & Margaret A on 23 Oct 1894 at Tangier by WR Gwinn

PARKES Henry [Parks] 19 S Sailor Acc Acc s/o Parker & Polly to Bettie Evans 17 S Acc Acc d/o Danl & Margt on 17 Sug 1881 at Tangier Isld by LE Barrett

PARKES Henry F [Parks] 20 S Farmer Acc Acc s/o George P & Elizabeth P to Carrie O Bloxom 18 S Acc Acc d/o Custis W & Marg't on 8 Jun 1887 at Lee Mont by JW Norris

PARKES Henry L 22 S Oysterman Acc Acc s/o Trevis to Mary L Dies 21 S Acc Acc d/o Severn on 22 May 1875 at Tangier Isld by RC Jones

PARKES Isaac Col 25 S Farmer Acc Acc s/o Anena White to Esther Dix Col 21 S Acc Acc d/o Mary Wessells on 7 Nov 1883 at Acc by AJ Satchell

PARKES James 48 W Farmer Acc Acc s/o Benjamin to Margaret Russell 30 W Acc Acc d/o John H Custis on 31 Dec 1873 at Modest Town by JL Lodge

PARKES James E 22 S Farmer Acc Acc s/o Wm J & Sallie to Anna [Colona] Colonna 20 S Acc Acc d/o Wm & Mary on 15 Nov 1876 at Zion Ch by CV Waugh

PARKES James F 24 S Cabinet Maker Acc Acc s/o George & Mary E to Elizabeth M Scott 20 S Acc Acc d/o John T & Margaret on 7 Nov 1888 at Zion Ch by JS Wharton

PARKES James H W 23 S Farmer Acc Acc s/o Noah & Mary to Sarah A Barnes 19 S Acc Acc d/o Jno & Sally on 26 Dec 1883 at Hunting Ck by AJ Walter

PARKES James R [Parks] 62 S Farmer Acc Acc s/o Robt C & Eliz'th to Eliz'th S [Justis] Justice 38 W Acc Acc d/o Edward & Nancy Parks on 14 Sep 1893 at Acc by JET Ewell

PARKES Jas Col 22 S Farmer Acc Acc to Sally V S Finney Col 21 S Acc Acc d/o Henry & Tabitha on 11 Jun 1882 near Poor House by AJ Satchell

PARKES Jas of B 67 W Farmer Acc Acc to Maria Middleton 43 S Acc Acc d/o Littleton & Tabitha Townsend on 11 Nov 1891 near Parksley by GF Farring

PARKES Jesse Col 25 S Farmer Acc Acc s/o Eddie Coard to Ann Turlington Col 26 S Acc Acc d/o Mary on 5 Jul 1884 at Acc by GW Young

PARKES John [Parks] 64 W Carpenter Acc Acc s/o Benjamin to Bernetta Mason 60 W Acc Acc d/o Samuel

Justis on 26 Feb 1890 at Parksley by HS Dulany

PARKES John A 19 S Boatman Acc Acc s/o Thomas & Sally to Julia Thomas 18 S Acc Acc d/o John & Caroline on 9 Jul 1876 at Tangier Isld by RC Jones

PARKES John E 23 S Farmer Acc Acc s/o Geo & Mary to Mary A Johnson 22 S Acc Acc d/o Jno W & Labirta on 19 Dec 1883 at Acc by JW Hundley

PARKES John P 24 S Waterman Acc Acc s/o John W & Rachel to Catharine Crockett 23 S Acc Acc d/o Severn & Henry on 24 May 1880 at Tangier Sound by WJ Duhadway

PARKES John P [Parks] 24 S Carpenter Acc Acc s/o John Y & Catharine to Mareitta Waterfield 17 S Acc Acc d/o William & Margaret on 18 Nov 1869 at r/o Parents by JET Ewell

PARKES John T 32 W Sailor Acc Acc to Alexine D Lewis 21 S Acc Acc d/o Robt T & Margt A on 21 May 1884 at Onancock by WC Vaden

PARKES John W [Parks] 19 S Oysterman Acc Acc s/o John E & Eliza to Nellie Dies 18 S Acc Acc d/o Peter R & Ellen on 16 Sep 1891 at Tangier Isld by J Connor

PARKES John W [Parks] 23 S Farmer Acc Acc s/o Alfred S & Sarah E to Mary F Bunting 17 S Acc Acc d/o George W & Mary A on 13 Oct 1895 at Acc by GD Edmonston

PARKES Jona 23 S Carpenter Acc Acc s/o Wm J & Sally to Louisa Bundick 24 S Acc Acc d/o Alfred & Lizzie on 28 Aug 1884 at Acc by JW Hundley

PARKES Joshua S [Parks] 22 S Merchant Acc Acc s/o Thos & Sally to Clara E Crockett 18 S Acc Acc d/o Travis A & Mary E on 25 Dec 1895 at Tangier by CP Swain

PARKES Lewis 20 S Waterman Acc Acc s/o Thos & Sally to Eliza Crockett 18 S Acc Acc d/o David & Lizzie on 4 Jan 1878 at Wise Point by WJ Duhadway

PARKES Lewis Col 22 S Farm Labor Acc Acc s/o Michael & Arcena to Margaret Fosque Col 23 S Acc Acc d/o Lena on 8 Feb 1883 at News Town by AJ Satchell

PARKES Major [Parks] 18 S Oysterman Acc Acc s/o Parker & Polly to Adaline Evans 18 S Acc Acc d/o Lewis & Patsy on 3 Mar 1877 at Chesconessex by RC Jones

PARKES Michael Col 45 S Farmer Acc Acc s/o Dinah to Arrena White Col 40 S Acc Acc d/o Easter on 9 Feb 1882 at Drum'tn by PM Lewis

PARKES Michael Col 51 W Farmer Acc Acc s/o Dinah to Bettie Coleburn Col 40 S Acc Acc on 15 Sep 1892 at Acc by BJ Hargarves

PARKES Raymon [Parks] 40 W Farming b: Acc s/o Raymond & Nancy to Mary [Brimore] Brimer 24 S b: Acc d/o Saml Brimer & Anna Bishop on 31 Oct 1855 at New Church by T Waters (Wm B Savage says both over 21)

PARKES Robert L 27 S Merchant Acc Acc s/o Edward C & Martha to Annie E Fox 22 S Acc Acc d/o James G & Jeannette on 19 Dec 1893 at Norfolk by MB Wharton

PARKES Robt C 57 W Farmer Acc Acc s/o Edmund Sr to Margt Ann Wessells 48 S Acc Acc d/o Ephrain & Shady on 19 Sep 1861 at Acc by ES Grant (George S Hope says above correct and both over 21)

PARKES Sewel D 22 S Farner Acc Acc s/o Noah & Mary J to Arinthia L Justice 17 S Acc Acc d/o Samuel & Mary Ann on 14 Nov 1875 at Masonville by DA Woodson

PARKES Solomon S 22 S Sailor Acc Acc s/o Thomas E & Sally to Susan E Crockett 18 S Acc Acc d/o Major

& Zipporah on 9 Oct 1887 at Tangier Isld by SJ Morris

PARKES Sylvanius 23 S Farmer Acc Acc s/o Charles & Margt to Ella P Johnson 17 S Acc Acc d/o Saml & Caroline on 21 Jan 1878 at Guilford by JB Merritt

PARKES Sylvanus W 21 S Farmer Acc Acc s/o Parker W & Nancy to Mary J Coard 21 S Acc Acc d/o John W & Nancy B on 20 Jan 1875 at Woodstock by IT Adkins

PARKES Thomas E 20 S Oysterman Acc Acc s/o Thos & Sally to Polly J Crockett 20 S Acc Acc d/o Jesse W & Charlotte on 27 Dec 1885 at Tangier Isld by CS Baker

PARKES Thomas F [Parks] 21 S Sailor Acc Acc s/o Charles & Margaret D to Arinthia S Hinman 18 S Acc Acc d/o John R & Susan on 30 Dec 1891 at Acc by AJ Fristoe

PARKES Thomas S [Parks] 22 S Farmer Acc Acc s/o Thos S & Sarah R to Susan E Small 15 S Acc Acc d/o John S & Susan A on 10 Jun 1877 at Acc by FH Mullineaux

PARKES Wilbur J 25 S Farmer Acc Acc s/o Chas & Margaret to Reina Hall 25 S Acc Acc d/o Robt & Susan on 27 Dec 1885 at Marsh Market by DM Wallace

PARKES William to Amanda Wessells d/o John dec'd lic: 17 Dec 1856 John Parkes says both over 21

PARKES William B [Parks] 23 S Farmer Acc Acc s/o Bennett & Emma to Lula A Mears 18 S Acc Acc d/o Lloyd C & Lee Ann on 28 Nov 1893 at Modest Town by WW Wood

PARKES William E 21 S Sailor Acc Acc s/o Wm R to Lucy Ellen Crockett 21 S Acc Acc d/o Dow & Margaret on 4 Dec 1887 at Tangier Isld by SJ Morris

PARKES William R 40 W Sailor Acc Acc s/o Stephen & Betsey to Helen Pruitt 35 W Fredericksburg VA Acc d/o John B & Maria E Estridge on 11 Aug 1888 at Tangier by GL Hardesty

PARKES William S [Parks] 23 S Sailor Acc Acc s/o Parker & Polly A to Mary [Connor] Conner 21 S Lincoln City DE Acc d/o James & Mary on 2 Sep 1893 at Tangier by ZH Webster

PARKES William W [Parks] 22 S Farmer Acc Acc s/o George & Mary to Cordie E Bloxom 17 S Acc Acc d/o Custis W & Maggie on 5 Jun 1889 at Zion Ch by JS Wharton

PARKES Wm Col 60 W Watchman Steam Mill Acc Acc to Mary Bagwell Col 55 S Acc Acc on 12 Jul 1882 at Onancock by JC Ayler

PARKES Wm D 30 S Farmer Acc Acc s/o Wm J & Elizth C to Elizth F W Bundick 17 S Acc Acc d/o Wm & Seymour on 11 Feb 1880 near Foxville by DA Woodson

PARKES Wm T 22 S Farmer Acc Acc s/o Edwd C & Martha to Alice Core 23 S Acc Acc d/o Wm S & Mary E on 16 Jan 1884 at Zion Ch by JW Hundley

PARLOR Marshall Col 30 S Laborer Culpepper Co VA Acc to Sinah Coleburn Col 35 S Acc Acc d/o Rebecca on 30 Sep 1873 at Drum'tn by A Joynes

PARLOR Marshall Col 35 W Laborer Culpepper Co VA Acc s/o Mary to Comfort Core Col 30 S Acc Acc d/o Zilpah on 19 Apr 1882 near Drum'tn by AJ Satchell

PARRAMORE Benjamin Col 35 S Laborer Acc Acc s/o Mary to Margaret Garrison Col 17 S Acc Acc d/o Easter on 23 Dec 1875 at White Marsh by JW Ruff

PARRAMORE George Col 25 S Wage-earner Acc Acc s/o Abram to Sarah Nock Col 18 S Acc Acc d/o Levi & Sarah on 26 Nov 1890 at Acc

by JWA Elliott
PARRAMORE George F 24 S Attorney-at-Law N'hamp: Acc s/o Thomas C & Juliet S to Linnie S Powell 22 S Acc Acc d/o John T on 12 Mar 1885 at St James Ch by W Chinn
PARRAMORE Jacob B Col 27 S Farmer Acc Acc s/o Mary Bsound to Ellen Drummond Col 28 S Acc Acc d/o Charlotte on 11 Feb 1883 at Drum'tn by LW Lee
PARRAMORE Jno Col 21 S Laborer Acc Acc s/o Emma to Emma Custis Col 25 S Acc Acc d/o Lottie on 20 Mar 1884 at Drum'tn by LW Lee
PARRAMORE Stran Col 62 W Laborer Acc Acc s/o Chloe to Ann Becket Col 46 S Acc Acc d/o Lukey on 7 Nov 1877 at C Ashby's by A Handy
PARRAMORE William H Col 21 S Laborer Acc Acc s/o Edwd Sample & Mary Parramore to Leah Neely Col 20 S Acc Acc d/o Henry Healy & Mary Finney on 27 May 1883 at Acc by GW Young
PARSON Jefferson L 23 S Engineer Som Co MD Acc s/o Geo G & Millie to Clara A Matthews 22 S Acc Acc d/o Wm H & Mary E on 17 Aug 1892 at Acc by HJ Wilson
PATO Edward C 29 S Merchant VA Acc s/o Henry C & Susan S to Etta E Johnson 22 S Acc Acc d/o Durbin H & Carrie W on 10 Sep 1890 at Lee Mont by AJ Fristoe
PATTERSON John Col 24 S Farmer N'hamp: Acc s/o Thos & Eliza to Leah S White Col 23 S Acc Acc d/o Sinah on 21 Aug 1879 at Acc by A Joynes
PAYNE Bertie Lee 20 S Mechanic Wor Co MD Acc s/o Re(?)enda T & Elizabeth C to Bertha L Godwin 17 S Acc Acc d/o Marcellas F & Mary E on 8 Sep 1895 at Acc by JL King
PAYNE Edward L 19 S Wor Co MD Wor Co MD s/o E S & Betsey to Mary L Lilliston 16 S Acc Acc d/o Robt & Mary on 9 Mar 1881 at Acc C H by JG Anderson
PAYNE Edward O 22 S Waterman Acc Acc s/o Pete T & Mary to Florence A Gardner 16 S Acc Acc d/o Wm F & Missouri on 30 Dec 1894 at Acc by AJ Reamy
PAYNE James 34 S Waterman Wor Co MD Chinco: Isld s/o Moses & Sarah to Tabitha Whealton 40 W Assateague Isld Chinco: Isld d/o Isaac & Elizabeth Lewis on 15 Mar 1859 at Chinco: Isld by P Bowdin
PAYNE Moses J 45 W Farmer Wor Co MD Chinco: Isld s/o Moses & Sadie to Mary A Adkins 22 S Sussex Co DE Chinco: Isld d/o Jno & Mary on 4 Sep 1872 at Chinco: Isld by WP Thornton
PAYNE Peter T 27 S Sailor Acc Acc s/o Wm & Ephenna to Mary J East 20 S Richmond VA Acc d/o William S on 1 Jan 1867 at Acc by JH Addison
PEARCE David N 25 S Sailor Monmouth Co NJ Sgnan NJ s/o Joseph & Sarah Ann to Polly Hargis 22 S Acc Acc d/o Thos & Mary on 19 Nov 1873 at Acc by LK LeCato
PECOR Edwd 53 S Farming Canada Acc s/o Custis & Mary to Emeline [Killmon] Killman 30 W Acc Acc d/o Parker & Nancy Trader on 6 Jul 1865 at Acc by GH Ewell
PENDLETON Thos B Col 30 S Waiter at Hotel King & Queen Co Baltimore City MD s/o Wm & Catharine to Rachel A Gaskins Col 22 S Acc Acc d/o James H & Eliz'th on 17 Aug 1893 at Acc by JH Offer
PENNEY Benj 23 S Sailor England Acc to Alexius Hornsby 22 S Acc Acc d/o James & Eliz'th on 14 Oct 1891 at Acc by JM Anderson
PENY Vandalia 29 S Miller MD Acc

s/o Geo & Mary E to Rosey M Dennis 19 S MD Acc d/o Danl H & M E on 12 Jan 1881 at Conquest Ch by M Oldham

PEPPLER Harry A 21 S Engineer Salem NJ Philadelphia PA s/o Peter & Asenath to Effie Parker 16 S Acc Acc d/o Richard & Mary A on 11 Dec 1895 at Acc by JM Dunaway

PERKINS George FN to Leah Bundick FN lic: 18 Jun 1855 Thomas M Davis says both over 21

PERRIE Thomas H 22 S Farmer Prince Geo Co Prince Geo Co to Charlotte E C Ames 25 S Acc Acc d/o Jno A & Adelida on 19 Oct 1860 at Acc by J Crosdale (James H Parker says both over 21)

PETERS Clayton R 30 W Waterman Burlington Co NJ Acc s/o Wriale G & Catharin S A to Arinthia Mears 24 S Acc Acc d/o Lorenzo D & Sally on 26 Dec 1882 at Locust Mount by JWA Elliott

PETERSON Andrew 28 S Sailor Denmark New York NY s/o Loramoon & Joana to Hester A Whealton 20 S Chinco: Isld Chinco: Isld d/o Joshua & Nancy on 29 Sep 1874 at bride's father's by P Bowdin Sr

PETTITT Charles Col 21 S Laborer Acc Acc s/o Harriet to Emma Griffin Col 21 S Acc Acc d/o Peggy Byrd on 24 Sep 1882 near News Town by AJ Satchell

PETTITT Edwin [Pettit] 21 S Farmer Acc Acc s/o Jas H & Elizth to Sarah W Mills 21 S Acc Acc d/o Levin & Mary on 17 Sep 1879 at Temp'ville by JE McSparran

PETTITT James 50 W Acc Acc to Elizabeth Truitt 30 S Acc Acc on 17 Jan 1856 by W Quinn (Samuel H Hinman says both over 21)

PETTITT Levin widr to Sarah Ann Fisher d/o William lic: 5 Oct 1858 Meshack Mears says she over 21

PETTITT Wesley [Pettit] Col 35 S Wage-earner Acc Acc s/o Frank Ewell & Rachel Pettit to Comfort Ann Taylor Col 25 S Acc Acc d/o William & Jane on 4 Mar 1893 at New Church by ML McKenry

PETTITT William 63 W Farmer Acc Acc s/o Thos & Nancy to Mary Jane Hart 32 W NJ Acc d/o Aaron H & Mary R Cook on 27 Nov 1869 at Acc by M Oldham

PETTITT William T 26 S Farmer Acc Acc s/o Levin & Sarah to Henrietta Fisher 27 S Acc Acc d/o James & Hetty on 6 Jan 1889 at Acc by JW Ward

PETTITT Wm (William) 53 W Farmer Acc Acc s/o Thos & Nancy to Elizabeth (D) Feddeman 46 W Acc Acc d/o James & Elizabeth White on 1 May 1860 at Acc by W Merrill

PHILLIPS Alfred Col 24 S Farmer Acc Acc s/o George & Leah to Cora Parker Col 17 S Acc Acc d/o Hannah on 3 Jul 1889 at Acc by JH Thomas

PHILLIPS Augustus 23 S Farmer Acc Acc to Maggie S Drummond 17 S Acc Acc d/o Geo E on 13 Dec 1876 at Hollies Bap Ch by FR Boston

PHILLIPS David H to Betsy (Willet) Willett lic: 14 Feb 1867

PHILLIPS David H 61 W Farmer Acc Acc s/o Thos & Susan to Mary Phillips 54 W Acc Acc on 9 Dec 1868 at Acc by JH Addison

PHILLIPS Edward B 30 S Farmer Acc Acc s/o Jesse Phillips & Mahaly Bell to Mary (A) Badger 21 S Acc Acc d/o James Badger (dec'd) & Charlott James & (ward/o John S Martin who gave consent) on 25 Nov 1860 at r/o Zorobable Mears by LK LeCato (J E Byrd says he over 21)

PHILLIPS Edwd F 30 S Farmer Acc Acc s/o Benj & Katy to Leah V Wallace 17 S Acc Acc d/o Geo B &

Elizth on 16 Jul 1879 at Hollies Ch by CC Wertenbaker

PHILLIPS George 21 S Farmer Acc Acc s/o Geo C & Harriet to Sadie A Mapp 20 S Acc Acc d/o Geo C & Rose on 27 Oct 1881 at Acc by JWA Elliott

PHILLIPS George (C) 31 S Farmer b: Acc s/o Wm Nock & Kesy Phillips to Harriet Nelson 26 S b: Acc d/o James & Ann on 26 Jan 1859 at Acc by LK LeCato (Littleton B Davis says both over 21)

PHILLIPS George C 25 S Farmer Acc Acc s/o Levin W & Susan to Maggie A Martin 23 S Acc Acc d/o John S & Susan on 29 Nov 1876 at Acc by JWA Elliott

PHILLIPS George E 27 S RR Agent Acc Acc s/o Edward B & Mary A to Maggie L Bradford 26 S Acc Acc d/o Ezra & Rachel on 15 Feb 1893 at Norfolk by EB McCluer

PHILLIPS Hampton Col 24 S Farmer/Sailor Acc Acc s/o Elishea to Florence Mapp Col 24 S Acc Acc d/o Hannah on 18 May 1879 at Onancock by JW Diggs

PHILLIPS Isaac Col 30 S Merchant Acc Acc s/o Edmond & Mary to Cordelia Downing Col 26 S Acc Acc d/o George E & Sarah on 7 Mar 1883 at Pungo: by TW Nettles

PHILLIPS Isaac (Philips) to Alsey (Philip) Phillips d/o Kessey lic: 26 Mar 1855

PHILLIPS Isaac G 25 S Seaman Acc Acc s/o Isaac S & Slice Ann to Mary Jane Wallace 17 S Acc Acc d/o Jno C & Susan J on 6 Feb 1884 near Locust Mount by JWA Elliott

PHILLIPS Isaac S 43 W Waterman Acc Acc s/o Laban & Hester to Tabitha A Mears 25 W Acc Acc d/o Abel & Elizabeth on 29 Jan 1874 at Locust Mount by LK LeCato

PHILLIPS Isaack 28 S Sailor b: Acc s/o Labin & Hossy to Eley Phillips 21 S b: Acc d/o Kessea on 1 Apr 1855 at r/o Jno Richardson by JWA Elliott

PHILLIPS James W 19 S Farmer Acc Acc s/o L Thos & Margaret to Anna Lewis 22 S Acc Acc d/o James & Cassandra on 17 Jul 1892 at Mappsville by JW Nicholson

PHILLIPS Jesse 61 W Sea Captain Acc Locust Mount s/o John & Nancy to Juliet Bell 37 S Acc Locust Mount d/o William & Rachel on 8 Sep 1859 at r/o George H Bell by JWA Elliott (Geo W Bell said she over 21)

PHILLIPS Jesse Lee 28 S Carpenter Acc Acc s/o Wesley S to Ida Lee Johnson 21 S Acc Acc d/o John W on 2 Jun 1892 at Wachapreague by JR Strugis

PHILLIPS John E 34 S Farmer Acc Acc s/o Solomon & Ann S to Malinda Hall 24 S Acc Acc d/o John & Sally on 14 Oct 1874 at Acc by O Littleton

PHILLIPS John E 22 S Farmer N'hamp: N'hamp: s/o John B & Tabitha to Mary Eliz'th Bell 19 S Acc Acc d/o Abel A & Emma E on 25 Dec 1895 at Keller by EE Harrell

PHILLIPS John S 21 S Farmer Acc Acc s/o Sam'l & Mary to Emma Lewis 21 S Acc Acc d/o Tully M & Elizth on 27 Dec 1882 at Acc by WA Crouse

PHILLIPS John T 27 S Sailor Acc Acc s/o Isaac & Alice to Maria Booth 19 S Acc Acc d/o Wm & Elizth on 16 May 1884 at Chinco: Isld by WP Thornton

PHILLIPS John W 21 S Farmer Acc Acc s/o Lavinia to Sarah [Bevans] Beavans 18 S Acc Acc d/o Severn & Elizth on 22 Jan 1868 at Acc by JH Offer

PHILLIPS John W 23 S Farmer Acc Acc s/o John & Rose to Tabitha Ames 18 S Acc Acc d/o Wm C & Elizabeth on 21 Dec 1871 at Acc by JE Humphreys

PHILLIPS John W 39 S Farmer Acc Acc s/o Levin W & Susan to Susan E Ayres 30 S Acc Acc d/o Thomas R & Sallie on 18 Jan 1893 at Acc by EC Atkins

PHILLIPS Joshua Col 36 S Farmer Acc Acc s/o Sarah to Esther Allen Col 34 S Acc Acc d/o Esther on 19 Nov 1877 at Acc by A Handy

PHILLIPS Lee R 26 S Farmer Acc Acc s/o Levin W & Susan to Alice L Martin 25 S Acc Acc d/o John S & Susan on 8 Jun 1892 at Acc by VW Bargamin

PHILLIPS Levin T 22 S Carpenter Acc Acc s/o Levin & Charlotte to Margaret J Groton 19 S Acc Acc d/o Wm & Margaret on 4 Jan 1871 at Onancock by AC Bledsoe

PHILLIPS Louis J 35 S Merchant Acc Acc s/o Jesse & Mahala to Olivia S Goffigon 30 S Acc Acc d/o Wm P & Margt on 24 Mar 1878 near Locust Mount by JWA Elliott

PHILLIPS Richard 24 S Oysterman s/o Lydia to Arrena J Lewis 18 S d/o Eliza lic: 27 Feb 1867

PHILLIPS Robert FN Waterman Acc Acc s/o Southey Colonna & Winney Phillips to Juliet Martin FN Acc Acc d/o Jas & Fanny on 2 Jan 1856 at Pungo: by M Oldham (John W Colonna says both over 21)

PHILLIPS Robert (Col) 22 S Laborer Acc Acc s/o Raymond Boggs & Lydia Phillips to Millie Davis (Col) 23 S Acc Acc d/o Edmund Steinghin & Cynthia Davis on 25 Jan 1870 at Wiseville by A Joynes

PHILLIPS Samuel T 23 S Sailor Acc Acc s/o Saml & Mary to Vernetta S Littleton 19 S Acc Acc d/o Saml & Adaline C on 17 Jul 1881 at Guilford by LB Betty

PHILLIPS Thomas 22 S Farmer Acc Acc s/o Ann to Georgie C Wyatt 17 S Acc Acc d/o George W & Susan A on 25 Jan 1882 at Onancock by JC Watson

PHILLIPS Thos 52 W Shoemaker Acc Acc s/o Geo to Margaret Matthews 29 S Acc Acc d/o Saml & Eliza on 9 Oct 1878 near Modest Town by JE Bundick

PHILLIPS William Col 34 S Sailor Acc Acc s/o Scipio & Lavinia to Tinny [Bevans] Beavans Col 20 S Acc Acc d/o Severn & Elizabeth on 17 Sep 1873 near Pungo: by R Davis

PHILLIPS William H 24 S Farmer s/o Solomon & Ann to Susan Milliner 23 S d/o Southey & Susan lic: 8 Feb 1871 marr: 9 Feb 1871 near Locustville

PHILLIPS William J 30 S Farmer Acc Acc s/o Levin W & Susan E to Margaret A Savage 27 S Acc Acc d/o James R & Ann on 26 Nov 1873 at Pungo: by EM Bryan

PHILLIPS Wm L 23 S Oysterman Acc Acc s/o Saml & Mary to Mary P Justice 19 S Acc Acc d/o Saml L & Rose Ann on 25 Jan 1877 at Guilford by JB Merritt

PHIPPS Emory 22 S Surfman US Life Saving Station Wor Co MD Acc s/o Abner to Janie Russell 16 S Acc Acc d/o Charles & Elizabeth Russell now Eliz'th Jester on 8 Jan 1887(?) at Chinco: Isld by SU Grimsley Certificate returned 12 Jan 1889

PITTS Alonzo Col 19 S Wage-earner Acc Acc s/o Henry Harmon to Ellen Savage Col 21 S Acc Acc d/o Comfort on 3 Jan 1892 at Locust Mount by RH Coleman

PITTS Edward T Col 52 S Farmer Acc Acc s/o Margaret to Sarah E Pitts Col 54 S Acc Acc d/o Adah on 17 Jan 1895 at Acc by AJ Satchell

PITTS Harris (Col) 25 S Oysterman Acc Acc to Elizabeth Read 38 S Acc Acc d/o Betsy Douglas on 22 Jun 1870 near Horntown by S Marshall

PITTS Henry 24 S Laborer Acc Acc s/o Tengle & Adah Gunter to Margaret Perkins 21 S Acc Acc d/o Lewis & Mary on 11 Mar 1868 at Acc by JH Huges

PITTS John Col 23 S Sailor Acc Acc s/o Rachel Bevans to Lottie West Col 21 S Acc Acc d/o Mary A West on 27 Jan 1876 at Belle Haven by RH Govans

PITTS Levi Col 22 S Wage-earner Acc Acc s/o John & Ellen to Rosie Parramore Col 21 S Acc Acc d/o Henry & Lillie on 19 May 1889 at Onancock by JH Offer

PITTS Thomas G 26 S Farmer Acc Acc s/o Wm C & Ann M to Morion E Savage 17 S Acc Acc d/o James T & Mary on 15 Mar 1882 at Oak Grove Ch by CD Crawley

PLANTER Frederick Col 28 S Farmer Acc Acc s/o Littleton & Agnes to Lina Byrd Col 22 S Acc Acc d/o Zadock & Bridget on 30 May 1882 at Temp'ville by M Oldham

POINTER James 21 S Oysterman Acc Acc s/o James & Rebecca to Rebecca Watson 17 S Acc Acc d/o George W & Ann on 2 Nov 1894 at Chinco: Isld by RB Sanford

POINTER James B 22 S Sailor Lewis Town Chinco: Isld s/o Boyed & Catharine to Lydia Snead 23 S Chinco: Isld Chinco: Isld d/o Robt & Briget on 29 Jun 1860 at Chinco: Isld by P Bowdin Sr (John A M Whealton says both over 21)

POINTER James Jr 22 S Oysterman Acc Acc s/o James & Lydia A to Ellen Andrews 18 S Acc Acc d/o Isaac & Sarah on 22 Dec 1888 at Chinco: Isld by SU Grimsley

POLLITT James (Politte) to Anna Maria Matthews d/o George lic: 17 Nov 1856 John Allen says both over 21

POLLITT Joseph C Col 34 S Miller Som Co MD Som Co MD s/o Joseph & Charlotte to Sarah Chandler Col 24 S Acc Acc d/o Tanear on 24 May 1893 at Onancock by GHT Byrd

POLLITT Stephen L [Polliet] 24 S Oysterman MD Acc s/o Benj L & Eleanor to Clara F Taylor 17 S Acc Acc d/o Oliver L & Mary on 1 Jul 1885 near New Church by TM Poulson

POOL Otho C 25 S Mechanic MD New York City s/o Wm W & Mary E to Lena V Savage 17 S Acc Acc d/o Thos H & Maggie on 25 Dec 1892 near Temp'ville by JW Nicholson

POOLE Edward Col 27 S Farmer Acc Acc s/o Jas & Ann to Mary E Savage Col 21 S Acc Acc d/o Henry Elizth on 15 Jan 1879 at Horntown by JC Cluff

POOLMAN James Col 20 S Laborer Acc Acc s/o Henry Mason to Susan Finney Col 23 S Acc Acc d/o Mary on 12 Oct 1873 at Metompkin by A Joynes

POST Thomas 30 S Seaman Treste Austria Chinco: Isld s/o Thomas & Mary to Julia [Stubs] Stubbs 17 S Chinco: Isld Chinco: Isld d/o Andrew & Caroline on 9 Apr 1885 at Chinco: Isld by SU Grimsley

POTTS Andrew J 25 S Mariner Norfolk VA Chinco: Isld s/o George & Nancy to Sarah A Andrews 22 S Chinco: Isld Chinco: Isld d/o Joseph & Nancy on 25 Dec 1876 at Chinco: Isld by WP Thornton

POTTS Andrew J 42 W Surfman Acc Acc s/o John G L & Nancy B to Lizzie E Daisey 18 S Acc Acc d/o Arden & Nancy on 17 Jan 1895 at Chinco: Isld by SU Grimsley

POTTS Thos Jeff 32 S Sailor Acc Acc s/o Jean G & Nancy B to Martha B Mitchell 19 S DE Acc d/o James & Lizzie on 13 Dec 1893 at Wachapreague by JR Sturgis

POULSON Benjamin Col 23 S Laborer

Acc Acc s/o Martha to Melissa [Stram] Stran Col 35 S Acc Acc d/o Jno & Esther on 29 Mar 1879 at bride's home by A Handy

POULSON Edmond Col 21 S Farm Laborer Acc Acc s/o Letitia to Tilla Snead Col 20 S Acc Acc d/o Hester on 28 Dec 1884 at Acc by JWA Elliott

POULSON Edmond A [Polson] 24 S Carpenter Acc Acc s/o Jno E & Mary E to Mary A Northam 17 S Acc Acc d/o Wm E & Drucilla on 23 Jan 1884 at Acc by M Oldham

POULSON Edmund 27 S Farmer Acc Acc s/o Maria to Mary Ames 25 S Acc Acc d/o Lucy Ames on 12 Jun 1867 at Acc by WT Tull

POULSON Edmund J Col 70 S Farmer Acc Acc s/o Annie to Hettie Bundick Col 67 W Acc Acc d/o Sallie Tyler on 4 Dec 1892 near Mappsville by AJ Satchell

POULSON Erastus 22 S Farmer Acc Acc s/o Thos & Mary Ellen to Ella East 22 S Acc Acc d/o George & Sarah on 8 Jan 1879 at Heady Nk by JW Hilldrup

POULSON Erastus P 20 S Farmer Acc Acc s/o Marion J & Sarah to Nancy Chase 16 S Acc Acc d/o Wm K & Elizabeth on 25 Dec 1887 at Temp'ville by M Oldham

POULSON Henry Col 22 S Waterman Acc Acc s/o Rose Ann to Harriet D Savage Col 21 S Acc Acc d/o Sarah on 24 Dec 1876 near News Town by A Joynes

POULSON Isaac J Col 39 W Day Laborer Acc Acc s/o Charlotte Parker to Margaret A Dix Col 28 S Acc Acc d/o Betsy on 24 Jul 1881 at Drum'tn by PM Lewis

POULSON Isaiah Col 24 S Wage-earner Acc Acc s/o Tamar to Mary Susan Taylor Col 22 S Acc Acc d/o George & Sarah on 28 Jun 1891 near Parksley by LE Toulson

POULSON James 28 S Farmer Acc Acc s/o Jno & Eliza to Rachel Miller 18 S Acc Acc d/o Wm & Mary on 12 Dec 1877 at Cashville by JH Amiss

POULSON James Alma 21 S Farmer N'hamp: Acc s/o William & Mary Ann to Rebecca Catharine Harris 24 S Acc Acc d/o John & Virginia on 10 Jan 1895 at Acc by JR Sturgis

POULSON James Henry 24 S Laborer Acc Acc s/o Jacob & Mary to Mary Riley 22 S Acc Acc d/o Solomon Wise & Mary Riley on 30 Jun 1869 at Acc by WF Williams

POULSON James Hy Col 30 S Sailor Acc Acc s/o Tamar Seymour to Harriet Hopkins Col 30 S Weston VA Acc d/o Leah Lankford on 11 Mar 1876 at Onancock by JK Plato

POULSON Jno H widr to Margt Mason d/o Jacob (Decd) on 12 Jan 1854 by J Allen (Edmd Mason says she over 21)

POULSON John 24 S Plasterer Onancock Onancock s/o John & Elizabeth to Elizabeth S Williams 25 S N'hamp: Onancock d/o John & Hester on 23 Jan 1861 at Onancock by D Felton (James L Beloat says both over 21)

POULSON John Col 27 S Carpenter Acc Acc s/o Mary to Sarah Mills Col 21 S Acc Acc d/o Eliza on 27 Dec 1874 at Modest Town by A Joynes

POULSON John E to Mary E Killman d/o Erastus(?) but Samuel(?) Kilman gave consent for his duaghter Mary E lic: 31 Jan 1859 John C Wessel says he over 21

POULSON John E 23 S Laborer Acc Acc s/o Thos & Rose to Susan Ann West 25 S Acc Acc d/o Charles on 29 Mar 1866 at Acc by G Bradford

POULSON John J Col 22 S Farmer Acc Acc s/o Eleana to Leah Topping Col 19 S Acc Acc d/o Jennie on 21 Jan

1883 at Onancock by JC Ayler
POULSON John T Col 25 S Laborer Acc Acc s/o Ann to Leah J Allen Col 20 S Acc Acc d/o Easter Mears on 16 Sep 1885 at Acc by CA Horsey
POULSON Joseph Col 63 S Farmer Acc Acc s/o Rosey to Mary Phillips Col 50 S Acc Acc d/o Abbie on 23 Dec 1874 at Savageville by JK Plato
POULSON Lorenzo 24 S Farmer Acc Acc s/o Thos & Ellen to Lizzie H Smith 18 S Acc Acc d/o Thos & Sally on 24 Dec 1885 at Oak Hall by DM Wallace
POULSON Louis Col 21 S Laborer Acc Acc s/o Sarah Poulson alias West to Fanny Tankard Col 21 S Acc Acc on 9 Jan 1878 near Boston Ch by TW Nettles
POULSON Marion J 22 S Farming Acc Acc s/o Erastus & Trephany to Sarah Trader 18 S Acc Acc d/o Parker (Decd)& Nancy on 28 Sep 1861 at Acc by JC Mears (George W Bird gave above information and says he over 21)
POULSON Millard T 24 S Waterman Acc Acc s/o John E & Mary to Geneva J Russell 20 S Acc Acc d/o Robert T & Lizzie J on 5 Jul 1893 at Mappsville by JL King
POULSON Robert 22 S Farmer Acc Acc s/o Patience to Emma Wharton 17 S Acc Acc d/o Sophia on 16 May 1869 at Acc by D Titlow
POULSON Robert S 25 S Farmer Acc Acc s/o John W & Eliz'th to Rebecca J Gray 20 S Acc Acc d/o James & Betsy on 24 Dec 1890 at Onancock by GW Burke
POULSON Samuel E Col 33 S Wage-earner Acc Acc s/o Esaw & Juliet to Hester J Bayly Col 21 S Acc Acc d/o Mary on 9 Oct 1894 at Acc by PW Lee
POULSON William Col 21 S Wage-earner Acc Acc s/o Elijah & Mary to Lauretta Ann Young Col 17 S Baltimore Co MD Acc d/o James A & Mary E on 22 Aug 1895 at Onancock by SW Watkins
POULSON William F 25 S Oysterman Acc Acc s/o John H & Jane to Martha F Fisher 22 S Acc Acc d/o Thorogood & Tabitha on 27 Dec 1893 at Acc by JL King
POWELL Alfred T Col 24 S Farmer Acc Acc s/o Mary Twiford to Mary S Major Col 21 S Acc Acc d/o Lollie on 25 Dec 1892 at Savageville by JH Offer
POWELL Alva H 38 D Oysterman Wor Co MD Acc s/o Levin & Mary to Sarah J Powell 25 S Acc Acc d/o Solomon & Elizabeth on 11 May 1895 at Chinco: Isld by SU Grimsley
POWELL Edward 21 S Farmer Acc Acc s/o Nathl & Juliet to Sally Watkinson 17 S Acc Acc d/o Levin & Sally on 11 Nov 1885 at Acc C H by W Chinn
POWELL Edwin T 22 S Merchant Acc Acc s/o J T & Arinthia to Fannie W Nock 16 S Acc Acc d/o Levin W & Sarah on 4 Aug 1875 near Locust Mount by JWA Elliott
POWELL George W 25 S Farmer Acc Acc s/o Littleton & Bell to Joice Susan Fowler 24 S Acc Acc d/o John & Mary on 15 Dec 1875 at Ganetsons Chp by JE Humphreys
POWELL George W 38 W Farmer Acc Acc s/o Littleton & Bette to Catherine S Bradford 17 S Acc Acc d/o Maggie S on 5 Dec 1888 at Acc by JER Riddick
POWELL James 22 S Farmer Acc Acc s/o William & Amanda to Lilly Bunting 17 S Acc Acc d/o Geo W on 28 Dec 1892 at Temp'ville by JW Nicholson
POWELL James E 35 S Farmer Acc Acc s/o Littleton T & Eliz'th to Clara M Kellam 22 S Acc Acc d/o Thomas

A & Mary A on 18 Dec 1889 at Garrisons Ch by JM Anderson

POWELL James H 23 S Farmer Acc Acc s/o Nathaniel & Juliet to Lee Jane Watkinson 18 S Acc Acc d/o Geo & Margt A on 26 Dec 1883 at Acc by JG Anderson

POWELL John H 23 S Farmer Acc Acc s/o Littleton Thomas & Elizath Powell to Emma L Duncan 22 S Acc Acc d/o William J & Emaline on 29 Dec 1880 at Onancock by SC Boston

POWELL John T widr to Mary S Barnes lic: 21 Jul 1859 Elijah W Hickman says she over 21

POWELL Laban 23 S Carpenter Acc Acc s/o William & Amanda to Virginia S Mears 17 S Acc Acc d/o Bagwell C & Eliza A on 6 Feb 1889 at Acc by WJ Twilley

POWELL Nathaniel [Powel] (Powell) 31 W Shoemaker b: Acc s/o Jesse & Peggy to Julia A (Juliet) Mears 20 S b: Acc d/o Jas & Molly on 1 Oct 1856 at r/o W J Mears by BT Ames

POWELL Nath'l T 22 S Farmer Acc Acc s/o Nathaniel & Juliet to Bettie P Watkinson 16 S Acc Acc d/o Levin & Sally on 23 Sep 1891 at Acc by JT Moore

POWELL Samuel A 39 S Merchant s/o Wm & Narcissa to Emma A Bedell 24 S lic: 12 Oct 1864

POWELL Thomas J 30 S Merchant Acc Acc s/o George W & Margaret A to Sarah E Boggs 29 S Acc Acc d/o John W & Laura A on 28 Nov 1894 at Onancock by GE Booker

POWELL William s/o Wm to Amanda Baker d/o Shephard & ward/o Wm H Dix who gave consent lic: 18 Feb 1861 Wm H Dix says he over 21

POWELL William P 33 S Merchant Acc St Marys Co MD s/o John T & Mary S to Elizabeth Custis 32 S Acc Acc d/o Thomas E C & Bettie M on 5 Apr 1894 at Onancock by HL Derby

PRESCOTT Asa 24 S Farmer Acc Acc s/o John & Henrietta to Laodicea Taylor 18 S Acc Acc d/o Asa & Maria on 27 Nov 1867 at Acc by M Oldham

PRESCOTT Levin R 34 S Farmer Acc Acc s/o John & Hester to Mary A Taylor 24 S Acc Acc d/o Shadanck & Nancy on 20 Mar 1873 at Acc by M Oldham

PRUITT George 50 W Oysterman Acc Acc s/o Geo & Leah to Ellen Crockett 35 W Acc Acc d/o William & Rhoda on 6 Sep 1874 at Acc by RC Jones

PRUITT George Col 48 S Carpenter Acc Acc s/o Betsy to Nancy Bundick Col 34 S Acc Acc d/o Sarah on 1 Jun 1881 near Cross Rd by PM Lewis

PRUITT George 21 S Oysterman Acc Acc s/o Raymond & Margaret to Novella Crockett 19 S Acc Acc d/o John & Jane on 3 May 1893 at Tangier Isld by ZH Webster

PRUITT George B 21 S Sailor Acc Acc s/o Rebecca & Nellie to Mary [Parks] Parkes 17 S Acc Acc d/o Jno E & Eliza on 13 Aug 1882 at Tangier Isld by IG Fosnocht

PRUITT Jno H 21 S Waterman Acc Acc s/o Wm & Rachel to Chloe (Chles) Dies 18 S Acc Acc d/o Peter & Elizabeth on 18 Jan 1864 at Acc by D Titlow

PRUITT John B 32 S Minister Williamsboro NC Acc s/o Alexander & Martha W to Sabra M Pitts 21 S Acc Acc d/o Thos C & Elizabeth on 3 Mar 1892 at Onancock by AJ Fristoe

PRUITT John P 25 S Fisherman Acc Acc s/o William & Ellen to Nellie Crockett 22 S Acc Acc d/o John C & Sally on 4 Jun 1890 at Tangier Isld by J Connor

PRUITT John S 19 S Sailor Acc Acc s/o Edmond & Emily to Maggie H

Marriages   271

Landing 18 S Acc Acc d/o Arthur C & Maggie on 1 Apr 1891 at Tangier Isld by J Connor

PRUITT John S Jr 22 S Oysterman Acc Acc s/o John S & Mary A to Lilly Booth 18 S Acc Acc d/o Burton & Euphemia on 24 Jul 1890 at Chinco: Isld by GE Wood

PRUITT Joshua 26 S Oysterman Acc Acc s/o William & Ellen to Julia A Crockett 23 S Acc Acc d/o Elishia & Margaret on 21 Dec 1890 at Tangier Isld by J Connor

PRUITT Joshua T [Pruoitt] 30 W Waterman Acc Acc s/o Wm & Ellen to Amanda [Parks] Parkes 19 S Acc Acc d/o W R & Amanda on 30 Nov 1892 at Tangier by ZH Webster

PRUITT Levin Col 42 S Waterman Acc Acc s/o Abram & Bethany to Mary Bayne Col 41 W Acc Acc d/o Peter & Amy Snead on 17 Sep 1874 at Wiseville by A Joynes

PRUITT Major 30 W Steam Mill Fireman Wor Co MD Acc to Elizabeth Custis 18 S Acc Acc d/o James & Sarah on 28 Dec 1881 at Acc by TM Poulson

PRUITT Raymond T 25 S Oysterman Acc Acc s/o Raymond & Margaret to Eliza J [Parks] Parkes 18 S Acc Acc d/o Thomas & Sally on 22 Dec 1888 at Tangier Isld by GL Hardesty

PRUITT Reuben 21 S Sailor Acc Acc s/o Raymond & Margt to Arinthia Dies 17 S Acc Acc d/o Jno & Catharine on 20 May 1877 at Tangier Isld by WJ Duhadway

PRUITT Severn T 20 S Sailor Acc Acc s/o Stephen E & Emily to Emma J Wheatley 19 S Acc Acc d/o Mathew & Ann on 23 Dec 1894 at Tangier Isld by WR Gwinn

PRUITT Stephen E 22 S Sailor Acc Acc s/o Raymond & Margaret to Eva Jane Evans 17 S Acc Acc d/o George E & Ann on 12 May 1889 at Tangier Isld by J Connor

PRUITT Stephen T [Preuitt] 23 S Sailor Acc Acc s/o Wm & Ellen to Julia Williams 19 S Acc Acc d/o Seth & Sarah E on 25 Dec 1883 at Tangier Isld by CS Baker

PRUITT Thomas 21 S Sailor Acc Acc s/o Wm & Rachel to Mary Pruitt 21 S Acc Acc d/o Geo & Eliza on 7 Jun 1865 at Acc by D Titlow

PRUITT Thos H 22 S US Life Saving Service Acc Acc s/o Jno S & Mary A to Rebecca J Jester 17 S Acc Acc d/o Redeema A Carpenter on 6 Jun 1886 at Chinco: Isld by SU Grimsley

PRUITT Tubman B 24 S Waterman Acc Acc s/o William & Ellen to Sadie B Crockett 14 S Acc Acc d/o Wm H H & Arabella on 2 Dec 1891 at Tangier Isld by J Connor

PRUITT Wallace 23 S Ship Carpenter Wor Co MD Wor Co MD s/o Benj & Sinenar to Elizabeth Whealton 19 S Chinco: Isld Chinco: Isld d/o Eba & Elizth on 7 Apr 1858 at Chinco: Isld by P Bowdin (Joshna Wishart says he over 21)

PRUITT William S 22 S Sailor Acc Acc s/o Ruben & Nellie to Polly A [Parks] Parkes 20 S Acc Acc d/o Thomas & Sally on 13 May 1888 at Tangier Isld by GL Hardesty

PRUITT Wm Henry (PREWIT) 26 S Carpenter Gloucester Co Acc s/o Henry & Patsey to Henrietta Mills Feddeman 23 S Acc Acc d/o Jno Wm & Elizth D on 5 May 1858 at Temp'ville by JF Chaplain (Wm S Byrd says both over 21)

PRYOR Levin R [Prior] 19 S Farmer Acc Acc s/o Joseph C & Eliz'th H to Mary H Salisbury 17 S Acc Acc d/o Henry & Mary on 20 Dec 1893 near Onancock by PA Leatherbury

PRYOR Wm T 19 S Farmer Acc Acc s/o Colombus & Elizth to Amelia T Mister 18 S Acc Acc d/o Wm S &

Sarah C on 27 Sep 1882 at Leatherbury Chp by PA Leatherbury

PRYOR Wm T [Prior] 22 W Oysterman Acc Acc s/o Columbus & Elizabeth to Viana F Justice 18 S Acc Acc d/o Revel J & Sallie on 25 Oct 1885 at Acc by HG Cowan

PURNELL Cujar Col 31 S Acc Acc s/o George & Rose to Martha Merrill Col 30 S Acc Acc d/o Geo & Hettie on 30 Jul 1879 at New Church by JC Cluff

PURNELL Edmund Col 27 S Wor Co MD Acc s/o George & Rosey to Sarah Ann Marshall Col 25 S Acc Acc d/o James & Harriet on 26 Sep 1870 near New Church by TM Poulson

PURNELL Edward [Purniel] Col 42 W Farmer Acc Acc to Hannah Mapp Col 40 S Acc Acc d/o Rosey Purnell on 25 Dec 1879 at New Church by TM Poulson

PURNELL Jesse S [Parinell] 25 S Sailor Acc Acc s/o Wm & Annie to Janie Lewis 25 S Acc Acc d/o Reamon on 29 Nov 1882 at Acc by LB Betty

PURNELL John Col 22 S Laborer MD Acc to Rosa Garrison Col 26 S Acc Acc d/o Maria on 9 Mar 1876 at Locustville by HT Rich

QUILLEN Benton 27 S Oysterman Wor Co MD Chinco: Isld s/o John & Ann to Henrietta Whealton 18 S Chinco: Isld Chinco: Isld d/o Joshua & Nancy on 24 May 1885 at Chinco: Isld by JD Reese

QUILLEN Lombard 31 W Sailor MD Acc s/o Lombard to Ida Isabel Hickman 14 S DE Acc d/o Isaiah & Sarah E on 12 Oct 1873 at Metompkin Township by EM Bryan

QUILLEN Saml E 21 S Sailor Wor Co MD Acc s/o Hillary P & Jane E to Elizth Thornton 18 S Acc Acc d/o James W & Delilah on 24 Sep 1879 at Chinco: Isld by IT Adkins

QUINBY Thomas B 23 S Attorney-at-Law Acc Acc s/o Upshur B & Georgie E to Katie D Bagwell 21 S Acc Acc d/o Edmond C & Maggie D on 18 Jun 1890 at Onancock by J McNabb

QUINBY Upshur B 23 S Attorney Acc Acc s/o A B & Elizth U to Georgie G Richardson 19 S Wash City DC Acc d/o Thos S & Margt B on 23 Nov 1864(?) at Acc by WG Coe Certificate returned 22 Jan 1866

RAYFIELD Asa FN to Jane Scarborough FN lic: 26 Mar 1855

RAYFIELD Asa FN to Sally Broadwater FN lic: 3 Feb 1858 John W Taylor says both over 21

RAYFIELD Frisby W 23 S Shoemaker N'hamp: N'hamp: s/o Edward & Margt to Mollie W Gillespie 23 S Acc Acc d/o John L & Esther on 13 Dec 1866 at Acc by P Warren

RAYFIELD George to Mary Mears wid lic: 29 Dec 1856 Benjamin Parkes says he over 21

RAYFIELD George Col 20 S Farmer Acc Acc s/o Stephen & Leah to Nelly Burton Col 21 S Acc Acc d/o Levi & Lucy on 23 Dec 1875 at Deep Ck by A Joynes

RAYFIELD Henry T 22 S Farmer Acc Acc s/o James & Sally to Ella K Beloate 20 S Acc Acc d/o Benj T & Susan on 24 Jan 1883 at Andrew Chp by SC Boston

RAYFIELD Jas T 25 S Carpenter b: Acc s/o Levi & Ann to Sally A Killman 24 S b: Acc d/o Edwd & Jane on 27 Dec 1854 at Acc by JH Addison (John E Parker says both over 21)

RAYFIELD Jno T 22 S Oysterman b: Onancock s/o Saml & Nancy to Jane Guy 24 S (W) b: Onancock d/o Wm & Susan on 12 Jul 1854 at Onancock M E Ch by C Hill

RAYFIELD John 19 S Farmer Acc Acc

Marriages

s/o Jno T & Jane to Virginia Ward 18 S Acc Acc d/o Wm P & Margt on 30 Aug 1877 at Hacks Nk Ch by JH Amiss

RAYFIELD John L 25 S Merchant Acc Acc s/o Frisby W & Mollie W to Rose L Gillespie 23 S Acc Acc d/o George T & Lalia on 17 Jan 1894 at Acc by JL King

RAYFIELD John R 26 S Farmer Acc Acc s/o Major & Elizth to Mary E Nelson 19 S Acc Acc d/o James H & Eliath on 24 May 1882 at Mappsville Bapt Par by JW Hundley

RAYFIELD Levi 23 S Oysterman Acc Acc s/o Major & Elizabeth to Lenora A Killman 15 S Acc Acc d/o Lorenzo & Ruth P on 14 Nov 1894 at Acc by GE Booker

RAYFIELD Major 23 S Oysterman Acc Acc s/o Levi & Ann to Elizabeth Hart 20 S Acc Acc d/o John & Elici on 30 Jun 1858 at Onancock by JF Chaplain

RAYFIELD Oscar F 27 S Farmer Acc Acc s/o George & Mary to Emma R Abbott 21 S Acc Acc d/o Daniel P & Mary W on 9 Sep 1894 at Acc by JL King

RAYFIELD Sam'l J 33 S Merchant Acc Acc s/o George & Mary to Mollie W Rayfield 43 W Acc Acc d/o John L & Esther Gillespie on 18 Nov 1891 at Mappsville by JL King

RAYFIELD Solomon FN to Tamar T Chandler FN lic: 26 Dec 1855 Sabra Chandler says both over 21

RAYFIELD Thomas Col 24 S Wage-earner Acc Acc s/o Sarah to Susan Tunnell Col 23 S Acc Acc d/o Thomas & Harriet on 28 Dec 1890 at Acc by AJ Satchell

RAYFIELD William Col 24 S Farm Laborer Acc Acc s/o Leah Griffin to Sally Burton Col 22 S Acc Acc d/o Lucy on 26 Apr 1885 at Metompkin Bapt Ch by AJ Satchell

RAYFIELD William T 26 S Wheelwright Acc Acc s/o Major & Edith to Kate V Mears 20 S Acc Acc d/o George S G & Marigima on 4 Sep 1889 near Pungo: by JW Hundley

RAYFIELD Williams 19 S Farmer Acc Acc s/o Jno T & Mary jane to Williamma Fisher 20 S IL Acc d/o G S on 18 Dec 1878 at Hacks Nk by CC Wertenbaker

READ Alma J [Read] (Reed) 19 S Farmer Acc Acc s/o Richd P & Sally to Virginia W Martin 19 S Acc Acc d/o Smith K & Louisa on 25 Feb 1869 at Acc by E Hebard

READ Cyrus [Reid] 22 S Oysterman Wor Co MD Acc s/o Littleton to Nancy Benson 17 S Acc Acc d/o Wm J & Elizth on 23 Nov 1879 at Chinco: Isld by TAH O'Brien

READ Edmund [Reed] Col 42 S Laborer Acc Acc s/o Rachel to Gaddie Major Col 50 S Acc Acc on 11 Nov 1874 at Belle Haven by JE Humphreys

READ Emanuel Col 21 S Laborer Acc Acc s/o George & Martha to Peggy Savage Col 24 S Acc Acc d/o Sally on 1 Aug 1875 at Savageville by JK Plato

READ Eugene J 20 S Farmer b: Acc s/o Richd P & Mary E to Tabitha A W Smith 17 S b: Acc d/o Jas P & Margt S A on 7 Feb 1855 at Belle Haven by M Oldham

READ George [Reed] Col 20 S Laborer Acc Acc s/o John & Elizth to Maria Marshall Col 24 S Acc Acc d/o Edwd & Elizth on 3 Jun 1875 at Horntown by S Johns

READ George [Reid] 23 S Oysterman Acc Acc s/o Joshua W & Charity to Amy Jester 18 S Acc Acc d/o John & Sally on 4 Feb 1888 at Chinco: Isld by SU Grimsley

READ George D Col 21 S Wage-earner

Acc Acc s/o James & Ellen to Maggie Finney Col 17 S Acc Acc d/o Charles & Maria on 10 Mar 1890 near Savageville by JB Lewis

READ George L [Reed] Col 21 S Farmer Acc Acc s/o Any to Julia [Gaskin] Gaskins Col 21 S Acc Acc d/o Rachel on 11 Jan 1881 at Drum'tn by PM Lewis

READ Henry [Reed] Col 22 S Laborer Acc Acc s/o Emma to Margaret Floyd Col 26 S Acc Acc on 7 Mar 1881 at Pungo: by TW Nettles

READ Isaac H [Reed] 22 S Oysterman Acc Acc s/o John L & Eliz'th A to Effie H Thomas 17 S Acc Acc d/o Corbin & Sarah on 21 Oct 1895 at Sykes Isld by ML Williams

READ Jacob Col 23 S Day Laborer Acc Acc s/o Emma to Sarah Snead Col 21 S Acc Acc d/o Nancy on 12 Aug 1883 at Acc by P Sheppard

READ Jno R 24 S b: Acc s/o Richd P & Margt Matha to Mary F Henderson 22 S b: Acc d/o Wm (Decd) & Sally on 24 Jan 1855 at Acc by M Oldham (Richd J Ayres says both over 21)

READ John D [Reed] 24 S Farmer Acc Acc s/o John & Elizabeth to Amanda A Colonna 20 S Acc Acc d/o Edward & Sarah A on 5 Oct 1881 at Andreson's Chp by JC Watson

READ John E [Reid] 24 S Oysterman Acc Acc s/o Littleton & Mary to Annie [Tindal] Tindall 17 S Acc Acc d/o J H & Elmira on 7 Jan 1883 at Chinco: Isld by OS Walton

READ Joseph T [Reid] 22 S Oysterman Acc Acc s/o Joshua W & Charity to Nancy V Hall 18 S Acc Acc d/o George & Sallie on 4 Dec 1891 at Chinco: Isld by JW Turner

READ Joshua [Reid] 19 S Oysterman Acc Acc s/o Joshua W to Mary Anna [Reid] Read 15 S Acc Acc d/o Littleton on 26 Aug 1877 at Chinco: Isld by P Bowdin Sr

READ Latus Col 60 W Laborer Acc Acc s/o Rachel to Dinah Thomas Col 45 S Acc Acc d/o Gaddie Major on 2 Mar 1887 at bride's home by TW Nettles

READ Littleton D 28 S Farmer Acc Acc s/o Richd P to Henrietta S Doughty 17 S Acc Acc d/o John R & Mary R on 6 Feb 1867 at Acc by E Hebard

READ Robert Col 21 S Laborer Acc Acc s/o Frank & Emma to Margaret Coleburn Col 22 S Acc Acc d/o John & Clara on 9 Sep 1883 at Onancock by R Davis

READ Samuel Col 21 S Laborer Acc Acc s/o Emma to Fanny Sample Col 21 S Acc Acc d/o Sally on 1 Jul 1877 at Bapt Ch by TW Nettles

READ Thomas Col 31 S Wage-earner Acc Acc s/o Arthur Read & Mary Kellam to Georgianna Hack Col 30 S Acc Acc d/o Sarah on 11 Nov 1888 at bride's home by TW Nettles

READ Timothy [Reid] 22 S Oysterman Acc Acc s/o Revel & Susan to Euphemy [Mungo] (Munger) Munger 19 S Acc Acc d/o Parker & May on 4 Feb 1871 at Chinco: Isld by P Bowdin Sr

READ William 25 S Sailor Chinco: Isld Chinco: Isld s/o William & Phamie to Jane Hammons (Hudson) 30 W Chinco: Isld Chinco: Isld d/o Phillip & Mary Hudson on 5 Jul 1873 at Chinco: Isld by WP Thornton

READ William [Reed] 19 S Oysterman Acc Acc s/o Joshua W & Charity to Ibby Catharine Cherricks 17 S Acc Acc d/o Arthur & Caroline on 12 Jan 1873 at Chinco: Isld by P Bowdin Sr

READ William G [Reed] 22 S Oysterman Acc Acc s/o Timothy T & Euphemia to Sarah A Williams 16 S Acc Acc d/o William W & Henrietta on 17 Jun 1894 at Chinco: Isld by SU Grimsley

READ William J [Reed] 38 W Sailor

Acc Acc s/o Littleton & Mary A to Virginia Hickman 22 S Wor Co MD Acc on 8 Jan 1894 at Acc by GP Jones

READ William K 31 S Sailor Acc Acc s/o John R & Mary to Margie B Ames 20 S Baltimore City MD Acc d/o George T & Bettie B on 27 Jan 1890 at Acc by JM Anderson

READ William P [Reid] 43 W Dealer in Oysters Acc Acc s/o Joshua W & Charity to Eva K Moore 15 S Acc Acc d/o Wm B & Aralanta on 28 Dec 1893 at Chinco: Isld by RB Sanford

READ Wm P [Reid] 21 S Oysterman Wor Co MD Wor Co MD s/o Littleton & Mary A to Zipporah Sharpley 16 S Wor Co MD Wor Co MD d/o John A & Matildy on 1 Aug 1880 at Chinco: Isld by TAH O'Brien

RESPAES Walter B 21 S School Teaching Matthews Co Matthews Co s/o Rich'd Hy & Sarah C to Matilda Conworton 17 S Acc Acc d/o Patrick H & Matilda P on 27 Dec 1893 at Tangier by ZH Webster

REVELL Frank [Revel] Col 21 S Waterman Acc Acc s/o Lewis Revel & Millie Lidsey to Hester Kellam Col 18 S Acc Acc d/o George & Lucindar on 29 Mar 1874 at Onancock by R Davis

REVELL John W 22 S Farmer Acc Acc s/o Levin H & Medora to Middie T Fisher 18 S Acc Acc d/o John D & Delilah on 18 Dec 1895 at Red Bank by JL King

REVELL Louis [Revel] 38 W Laborer Acc Acc s/o Frank & Esther to Susan Parker 25 S Acc Acc d/o Wm & Adah on 11 Mar 1868 at Acc by JH Huges

REVELL Saml J 34 S Carpenter MD Acc s/o Leamuel H & Elizth to Cora Warner 25 S Acc Acc d/o Solomon & Arinthia on 17 Dec 1884 at Assawoman Hill by A Woodyard

REW Charles A 26 S Farmer Acc Acc s/o Richard S & Nancy to Sallie B Arlington 23 S Acc Acc d/o John & Mary on 23 Jan 1878 at Warrinton's Br by SC Boston

REW Edwd T 22 S Farmer Acc Acc s/o Henry & Hanah to Margt A Baker 21 S Acc Acc d/o Ezekiel (Asa & Tabitha) on 25 Sep 1863 at Acc by GH Ewell

REW Francis T 25 S Farmer Acc Acc s/o James A & Mary to Scynthia E Byrd 22 S Acc Acc d/o Richd P & Nancy on 16 Apr 1873 at Acc by EM Bryan

REW George H 20 S Farmer Acc Acc s/o James H & Margaret A to Marcialla A Trader 18 S Acc Acc d/o Thomas & Sarah on 10 Sep 1890 at Mappsville by WA Street

REW George R 21 S Farmer Acc Acc s/o Geo S & Margt to Maggie S Phillips 17 S Acc Acc d/o Saml & Mary on 23 Jan 1881 at Guilford Ch by LB Betty

REW Henry Col 23 S Farmer Acc Acc s/o Eliza to Sallie Savage Col 19 S Acc Acc d/o John & Jane on 4 Jan 1893 at Acc by AJ Satchell

REW Henry S 38 S Farmer Acc Acc s/o James H & Mary to Birnetta L Byrd 26 S Acc Acc d/o Richd P & Nancy on 23 Feb 1871 at r/o Richd P Byrd by DA Woodson

REW James S Col 21 S Farmer Som Co MD Acc s/o Peter Rew & Leah Taylor to Sally Jones Col 22 S Acc Acc on 11 Sep 1892 at Acc by JC Cluff

REW James T 20 S Farmer Acc Acc s/o Wm & Eva to Ella F Nock 17 S Acc Acc d/o Edwd & Mary on 19 Dec 1871 at Acc by DA Woodson

REW Jas H Jr 23 S Farmer Acc Acc s/o Saml & Henny to Margaret A Bloxom 19 S Acc Acc d/o Geo (of G)

& Narcissa on 4 Jan 1866 at Acc by JE Bundick

REW Jesse 26 S Farmer Acc Acc s/o James & Betsey to Sarah Gray 18 S Acc Acc d/o James & Elizabeth on 29 Nov 1866 at Acc by ES Grant

REW Jesse Col 22 S Wage-earner Acc Acc s/o Handy & Ellen to Mary [Wessels] Wessells Col 19 S Acc Acc d/o George & Laura on 14 Jul 1895 at Acc by AJ Satchell

REW John Col 20 S Laborer Acc Acc s/o Fanny to Hannah Lewis Col 17 S Acc Acc d/o Ann Bawen on 10 Apr 1877 at Temp'ville by M Oldham

REW John 26 S Farmer Acc Acc s/o Revel & Jane to Cordelia Williams 16 S Acc Acc d/o Thomas & Margaret on 1 Sep 1880 near Onancock by JG Anderson

REW John Jr to Tabitha Moore lic: 31 Dec 1859 Sylvester Johnson says both over 21

REW John Savage Col 23 S Farm Labor Acc Acc s/o Hesiah to Mary Corbin Col 18 S Acc Acc on 15 Jul 1883 at Oak Hall by JC Cluff

REW Peter 36 S Laborer Acc Acc s/o Bettie to Leah E Taylor 22 S Acc Acc d/o Margaret Dennis on 3 May 1868 at Acc by JO Moss

REW Thos H 22 S Carpenter Acc Acc s/o Edwd T & Margt to Priscilla E [Sommers] Summers 22 S Acc Acc d/o Saml & mary on 22 Dec 1886 at Acc by WA Street

REW Tilley 19 S Farmer Acc Acc s/o Edward T & Margaret to Effy S Young 19 S Acc Acc d/o Wm T & Mary on 4 Nov 1891 at Mappsville by JL King

REW Upshur Col 45 S Farmer Acc Acc to Marion Hickman Col 30 S Acc Acc d/o Susan on 25 Dec 1872 at Acc by A Joynes

REW William 25 S Farmer Acc Acc s/o Jas H & Mary to Mary T Wessells 18 S Acc Acc d/o Thomas & Elizth on 28 Dec 1865 at Acc by ES Grant

REW William 22 S Laborer Acc Acc s/o Maria to Martha Warner 23 S Acc Acc d/o Hannah on 1 Jun 1868 at Acc by A Joynes

REW Wm A 22 S Farmer Acc Acc s/o Geo S & Margt S to Sally T Bayly 20 S Acc Acc d/o Edwd & Lovey on 28 Feb 1877 near Onancock by RC Jones

REW Wm J 24 S Waterman Acc Acc s/o Jesse K & Sarah to Edith T Powell 16 S Acc Acc d/o James H & Emma on 13 Sep 1891 at Acc by GW Burke

REYNOLDS Isaac 21 S Oysterman Acc Chinco: Isld s/o Richd & Eliza to Sarah E Williams 15 S Acc Chinco: Isld d/o Wm & Henrietta on 17 Feb 1886 at Chinco: Isld by JD Reese

REYNOLDS Joshua 20 S Sailor Acc Acc s/o Richard P & Eliza to Mary Ann Birch 17 S Acc Acc d/o Wm F & Phoebe on 7 Mar 1889 at Chinco: Isld by SU Grimsley

REYNOLDS Richard P to Eliza Lewis wid lic: 27 Feb 1860 Wm P Thornton says he over 21

REYNOLDS Richard P [Raynolds] 22 S Shoe & Book Milton DE Chinco: Isld s/o Wm E & Louisa to Eliza Lewis 32 W Chinco: Isld Chinco: Isld d/o Joshua & Sally Whealton on 29 Feb 1860 at Chinco: Isld by P Bowdin Sr (Wm P Thornton say he over 21)

REYNOLDS William to Tabitha Sharpley d/o Henry & ward/o Wm M Feddeman who gave consent lic: 31 Jan 1860 Wm M Feddeman said he over 21

RHODES Henry M 20 S Oysterman Long Island NY Acc s/o George W & Mary E to Cora J Mears 18 S Acc Acc d/o Lorenzo T & Sally on 4 Feb 1888 at Powelton by JWA Elliott

RICH Benjamin S s/o Mulford to Rachel

S Shield d/o James dec'd lic: 20 Mar 1855 Benjamin was born 10 Sep 1828 & Wm T Ashby says she over 21

RICH Wm H 30 S Photographer Guild Hall VT Salsbury s/o Chas & Diana to Blanch E B Rich 22 S Acc Acc d/o Benj S & Rachael on 19 Aug 1886 at Acc by WC Vaden

RICHARDS Gordon C 23 S Shoemaker Wor Co MD Acc s/o John S & Mary to Jenima Taylor 18 S Acc Acc d/o Thomas & Eliza on 26 Jul 1875 at Chinco: Isld by P Bowdin Sr

RICHARDSON Bowdin (Ritcherson) 26 S Farming Acc Acc s/o Severn & Eliza to Charlotte Lewis 21 S Acc Acc d/o Edwd & Eliza on 30 Jan 1871 near Oak Grove by JWA Elliott

RICHARDSON Francis W 23 S Sailor b: Acc s/o Waltas & Sally to Marie A Hutchinson 38 W b: Acc d/o Henry & Polly Mason on 11 Apr 1855 near Pungo: by M Oldham

RICHARDSON Geo Michael Col 38 S Farming Acc Acc s/o Mary to Eleshea Ann Harmon Col 35 S Acc Acc d/o Lukey on 25 May 1873 at Burton's by N Morris

RICHARDSON George W 35 S Carpenter Acc Acc s/o James & Elizabeth to Sarah E Coleburn 28 S Acc Acc d/o Thomas & Elizth on 13 Jan 1868 at Acc by LK LeCato

RICHARDSON Isaiah 20 S Laborer Acc Acc s/o Isaiah & Mary to Harriet S (Susan) [Bonewell] Bonnewell 18 S Acc Acc d/o Chas & Cathr on 29 Jan 1863 at Acc by D Titlow

RICHARDSON John Col 20 S Laborer Acc Acc s/o Comfort Jubilee to Lottie Smith Col 21 S Acc Acc d/o Aham & Anna on 1 Oct 1876 near Belle Haven by JE Humphreys

RICHARDSON John 28 S Oysterman Acc Acc to Lee Northam 21 S Acc Acc d/o John W on 16 Mar 1890 at Sykes Isld by JS Wallace

RICHARDSON John T 23 S Mechanic Acc Acc s/o Jno & Mary to Cathr J Ward 22 S Acc Acc d/o Lewis & Mary on 22 Oct 1862 at Acc by JWA Elliott

RICHARDSON John T (J) 35 W Carpenter Acc Acc s/o Wm J & Elizabeth to Salony S Mapp 26 W Acc Acc d/o John L & Leah D Mears on 20 Dec 1871 near Locust Mount by JWA Elliott

RICHARDSON John W 24 S Life Saving Station Acc Acc s/o William H & Rachel to Alice B Jones 27 S Acc Acc d/o Geo T & Cora M on 11 Jan 1888 at Powelton by CD Crawley

RICHARDSON Joseph A 27 S Farmer Acc Acc s/o Jno T & Mary to Mary Ann Grinnalds 17 S Acc Acc d/o Jno C & Mary Ann on 23 Dec 1868 at Acc by LK LeCato

RICHARDSON Joseph A 48 W Farmer Acc Acc s/o John T & Mary to Susan Smith 45 W Acc Acc d/o Asa Taylor on 30 Oct 1895 at Acc by DGC Butts

RICHARDSON Levin H 44 S Merchant Acc Acc s/o James & Elizth to Mary Hartman 30 S Acc Acc d/o Charles & Margaret on 20 May 1885 at Acc by JWA Elliott

RICHARDSON Major R 25 S Farmer b: Acc s/o Jas & Mary to Catharine T Hall 22 S b: Acc d/o Wm & Sally on 2 Mar 1859 at Ayres Chp by ES Grant

RICHARDSON Nathan to Matilda Bratcher d/o Hambleton lic: 6 Sep 1856 J P Thomas says both over 21

RICHARDSON Saml 22 S Farmer Acc Acc s/o Margt to Maggie P Scott 22 S Acc Acc d/o James E & Elizth on 10 Jun 1877 near Onancock by PA Leatherbury

RICHARDSON Thomas S 81 W Farmer Acc Acc to Mary E Walker 53 S Acc

Acc d/o Jas on 16 May 1878 at Locust Mount by JWA Elliott

RICHARDSON William to Rachel Ward lic: 1 Aug 1860 Littleton R LeCato says both over 21

RICHARDSON Wm 23 S Farmer Acc Acc s/o Polly to Mary Lingo 23 S Acc Acc d/o Robt & Mary on 9 Feb 1854 at r/o Polly Richardson by J Burton

RIGGS John Revel 19 S Wheelwright Acc Acc s/o Joseph R & Melissa C to Lula Susan Wessells 18 S Acc Acc d/o Oliver F & Mary J on 9 Dec 1894 at Acc by DGC Butts

RIGGS Joseph R 22 S Clerking Acc Acc s/o Jos & Betsy to Malissa Parkes 18 S Acc Acc d/o Jno & Nancy on 30 Dec 1868 at Acc by JET Ewell

RIGGS Joseph R 43 W Merchant Acc Acc s/o Joseph & Elizabeth to Campsey D Russell 23 S Acc Acc d/o John E & Sally on 9 Dec 1888 at Crowsontown by HS Dulany

RILEY Edward Col 21 S Wage-earner Acc Acc s/o Eliza to Georgianna Fosque Col 16 S Acc Acc d/o Susan on 1 Aug 1889 near Acc C H by AJ Satchell

RILEY George Henry Col 23 S Farmer Acc Acc s/o Henry to Mary Ewell Col 21 S Acc Acc d/o James & Ann on 25 Jan 1893 at Acc by JW Cook

RILEY Henry Col 62 S Laborer Acc Acc s/o Solomon & Sarah Bagwell to Tabitha [Roley] Rowley Col 44 S Acc Acc d/o M on 5 Jun 1873 at Horntown by S Johns

RILEY James H Col 21 S Farm Laborer Acc Acc s/o Eliza Hickman to Grace Lee Lewis Col 21 S Acc Acc d/o Dina Coard on 18 Jul 1880 near Metompkin Ch by A Joynes

RILEY John F 26 S Farmer Acc Acc s/o Wm M & Elizth A to Frances Tignal 26 S Acc Acc d/o Saml & Eliath on 10 Oct 1867 at Acc by BT Ames

RILEY John H 27 S Merchant Acc Acc s/o Raymond R & Margsaret A to Ida G Watson 18 S Mechlenburg VA Acc d/o J Carson & Annie on 23 May 1881 at Onancock by JC Watson

RILEY Parker Col 40 S Oysterman Acc Chinco: Isld s/o Henry & Nancy to Mary E Crippen Col 20 S Acc Chinco: Isld d/o Govy Selby & Rose Crippen on 26 Sep 1880 at Chinco: Isld by R Williams

RILEY Raymond R 34 W Merchant Acc Onancock s/o Raymond & Sallie to Sarah A Mears 40 S Acc Onancock d/o Thos & Cath on 7 Feb 1861 at Onancock by JA Massey (John M Fosque Jr says she over 21)

RILEY Samuel Col 23 S Farm Laborer Acc Acc s/o Leah to Susan Custis Col 15 S Acc Acc d/o Sallie on 28 Dec 1884 near Deep Ck by CA Horsey

RILEY Sidney F 22 S Farmer Acc Acc s/o Raymond H & Eliz'th J to Mary L Hurst 24 S Acc Acc d/o John & Mary on 15 Sep 1890 at Onancock by GW Burke

RILEY William M 37 S Farmer Acc Acc s/o Wm M & Elizth to Mary A Daugherty 25 S Acc Acc d/o Jas A & Eleshea A on 20 Dec 1883 at Acc C H by JG Anderson

RILEY Wm H 23 S Oysterman Ireland Acc s/o Wm to Amanda L Thorns 23 S Acc Acc d/o Wm & Margt on 12 Apr 1882 at Guilford by MS Read

RISLEY William 59 W Farmer Atlantic Co NJ Atlantic Co NJ s/o Saml & Mary to Josephine Whealton 40 W Acc Acc d/o Thos & Mary C Birch on 26 May 1886 at Chinco: Isld by SU Grimsley

RITTERE Wm 23 S Seaman DE Acc to Juliet Ann Beasley 22 S Acc Acc d/o

Wm & Susan on 21 Sep 1884 at Acc by WC Vaden

ROACH William W 30 S Carpenter DE Acc s/o Thomas L & Angeline M to Priscilla May Milliner 18 S Acc Acc d/o James H & Elizabeth on 31 Mar 1890 at Wachapreague by JT Moore

ROBERTS Augustus 25 S Miller s/o Wm & Mary to Sarah Budd 21 S d/o Kealy & Sally lic: 31 Aug 1868 marr: 31 Aug 1868

ROBERTS Augustus F 23 S Gentleman Acc Acc s/o Lewis S & Ann to Mary S Taylor 15 S Acc Acc d/o Charles W & Melina & (ward/o Geo W Mason) on 30 Jun 1858 at Onancock by JF Chaplain (Wm J Roberts says he over 21)

ROBERTS Carlie M 22 S Farmer Acc Acc s/o Augustus & Susan to Bettie S Budd 17 S Acc Acc d/o Wm H & Susan A on 28 Mar 1883 near Locustville by JWA Elliott

ROBERTS Horace E 31 S Farmer Acc Acc s/o Edwin S & Elizabeth to Maggie A Stores 29 S Prince George Co Acc d/o Wm T & Sarah on 12 Jan 1870 near Garrisons Chp by JE Humphreys

ROBERTS Horace E 42 W Farmer Acc Acc s/o Edwin S & Elizth to Elizabeth Ashby 41 S Acc Acc d/o David & Ada on 2 Jan 1881 at Bells Nk by JE Humphreys

ROBERTS James Col 23 S Laborer Acc Acc s/o Mary to Elizabeth Taylor Col 21 S Acc Acc on 8 Nov 1882 at Horntown by JC Cluff

ROBERTS John E 23 S Farmer Acc Acc s/o Clinton & Jane to Julia M Beloate 20 S Acc Acc d/o Louis S & Mary S on 30 Jan 1889 at Oak Grove Ch by JH Riddick

ROBERTS John T 21 S Sailor N'hamp: N'hamp: s/o Authur E & Margt A to Mary Ann Doughty 19 S Acc Acc d/o James A & Margaret L on 12 Feb 1871 near Onancock by DA Woodson

ROBERTS Levin Col 24 S Wage-earner Acc Acc s/o Matilda to Bettie Parker Col 18 S Acc Acc d/o Ellen Bivens on 9 Aug 1891 at Franktown by T Peeden

ROBERTS Moses FN to Martha Kellam FN lic: 31 Dec 1860 S R Chandler says both over 21

ROBERTS Preson Col 31 S Teamster Acc Acc s/o Polly Barker to Eleanor Harmon Col 35 S Acc Acc d/o Susan on 16 Feb 1876 at St John Ch by SP Whittington

ROBERTS Preson Col 40 W Oysterman Acc Acc s/o John Roberts & Polly Barker to Comfort A Matthews Col 35 S Acc Acc d/o John & Mary on 18 Sep 1889 at Temp'ville by JC Cluff

ROBERTS Samuel 26 S Laborer s/o Rachel to Margaret Ellen Wise 23 S d/o Leah lic: 20 Apr 1868

ROBERTS William E 43 S Farmer N'hamp: Acc s/o Augustus & Eliza to Ida H Wessells 18 S Acc Acc d/o William H on 25 Apr 1892 at Modest Town by WW Wood

ROBERTSON Edgar W 24 S Physician Som Co MD Acc s/o William & Mary D to Sue H Fisher 22 S N'hamp: Acc d/o Fredine B & Rose on 19 Sep 1870 at r/o Benj T Gunters by H Petty

ROBERTSON Jno Hy Col 26 S Wage-earner Richmond Acc to Tabitha Allen Col 22 S Acc Acc d/o Mary on 6 Sep 1891 at Acc by BJ Hargarves

ROBERTSON John H 33 W Farmer b: Wor Co MD s/o John & Elizth to Sally Tull 25 W b: Acc d/o Saml & Charlott Johnson on 3 Feb 1858 at Acc by T Waters

ROBERTSON William J Col 39 S Teamster Som Co MD Acc to

Alexius Garrison Col 26 S Acc Acc d/o Reuben on 16 Nov 1892 at Locust Mount by RH Coleburn

ROBINS Kendal S 28 S Merchant Acc Acc s/o Jno S & Durcilla to Edna Terry 19 S Acc Acc d/o Jones T & Mary on 4 Jun 1879 at Pocomoke Nk by JW Hilldrup

ROBINS LaFayette 30 S Merchant Acc Norfolk s/o Arthur to Susan A Roberts 25 S Acc Acc d/o Lewis on 21 Dec 1860 at Locust Mount by JWA Elliott (J Benj(?) Floyd says both over 21)

ROBISON James 24 S Laborer Acc Acc s/o Sarah to Mary Ann Webb 21 S Acc Acc d/o Gilbert & Peggy on 8 Jul 1868 at Acc by JH Offer

ROGERS Arthur M [Rodgers] 35 S Farmer Acc Acc s/o Wm W & Rachel to Elizabeth Phillips 18 S Acc Acc d/o Levi (Levin) W & Susan on 24 Nov 1858 at Acc by P Warren (Smith K Martin says he over 21)

ROGERS Charles H 23 S Carpenter Sussex Co DE Sussex Co DE s/o Jonathan & Clarissa to Manie M Miles 18 S Acc Acc d/o Richd W & Jane on 23 Dec 1885 at Acc by DM Wallace

ROGERS Charles H 35 W Farmer Acc Acc s/o William S & Elizabeth F to Mollie E Beloate 22 S Acc Acc d/o Julius D & Edna B on 11 Jan 1888 at Savageville by RA Compton

ROGERS Charles H [Rodgers] 26 S Farmer Acc Acc s/o Wm L & Elizth to Margt H Boggs 26 S Acc Acc d/o Jno & Leah on 12 Jun 1879 at Slutkill Nk by JC Watson

ROGERS Edmond 22 S Laborer Acc Acc s/o Lucy to Leah Custis Col 20 S Acc Acc d/o Lewis & Mary on 22 Jul 1881 at Savageville by JC Ayler

ROGERS George Col 38 S Laborer Acc Acc s/o Nannie to Mary Finney Col 36 S Acc Acc d/o Ann on 19 Jun 1873 at Acc by WF Talbott

ROGERS George Col 21 S Laborer Acc Acc s/o Chas & Letty to Belle S B Hatton Col 17 S Acc Acc d/o Caroline on 14 Oct 1883 at Bells Nk by JE Humphreys

ROGERS Henry [Rodgers] Col 38 S Laborer Acc Acc to Clarissa Garrison Col 42 S Acc Acc on 16 Jun 1876 at Craddockville by WH Corbin

ROGERS Isaiah Col 24 S Wage-earner Acc Acc s/o Nathaniel & Arena to Mary Jane Wise Col 21 S Acc Acc d/o William & Sarah on 29 Dec 1889 at Savageville by JB Lewis

ROGERS John 22 S Blacksmith b: Acc s/o John to Emma S Drummond 19 S b: Acc d/o Wm & Mary (T) on 14 Nov 1855 at Acc by M Oldham

ROGERS John [Rodgers] Col 25 S Day Laborer Acc Acc s/o Phoebe to Henny Turlington Col 24 S Acc Acc d/o Malinda Shield on 1 Oct 1882 at Acc by JWA Elliott

ROGERS John H Col 22 S Farmer Acc Acc s/o Louis & Mary to Maggie E Bayly Col 18 S Acc Acc d/o Joyce Finney on 24 May 1893 at Onancock by FW Overton

ROGERS John W 21 S Sailor York Co VA Acc s/o Wm & Elizth to Sarah M Cobb 22 S Acc Acc d/o James & Leah on 29 Dec 1870 at Acc by LK LeCato

ROGERS Lewis Col 21 S Farmer Acc Acc s/o Mary to Fanny Boggs Col 22 S Acc Acc d/o Lucy on 23 Feb 1884 at Acc by P Sheppard

ROGERS Nathaniel Col 25 S Farmer Acc Acc to Margaret Ames Col 23 S Acc Acc d/o Sally on 1 Nov 1874 at Pungo: by JK Plato

ROGERS Nathaniel [Rodgers] Col 37 S Farmer Acc Acc s/o Tabitha to Susan Church Col 39 S Acc Acc d/o Bridget Bayly on 30 Jun 1887 at Acc

Marriages

by L Duncan
ROGERS Spencer F 25 S Merchant Acc Acc s/o Wm S & Elizth F to Alice T Pitts 21 S Acc Acc d/o Thos C & Elizth on 11 Jan 1882 at Onancock Bapt Ch by SC Boston
ROGERS Thomas Col 24 S Laborer Acc Acc to Malinda Ayres Col 21 S Acc Acc d/o Sarah on 31 Mar 1880 at Locust Mount by JWA Elliott
ROGERS William T [Rodgers] 29 S Captain Acc Acc s/o Wm S & Elizth F to Cordie F Mason 27 S Acc Acc d/o Zorabale C & Esther A on 25 Feb 1880 at bride's home by CC Wertenbaker
ROGERS Wm F [Rodgers] 23 S Farmer Acc Acc s/o John K & Eliza to Carrie W Chandler 20 S Acc Acc d/o Sylvester R & Mary on 11 Jan 1871 at Acc by AC Bledsoe
ROOM Henry to (-----) (-----) lic: 4 Jun 1864
ROSE Wm H 31 S Mechanic Baltimore MD Acc s/o Jno & Mary to Arinthia S J Bell 33 S Acc Acc d/o Wm & Rachel on 29 Dec 1863 at Acc by JWA Elliott
ROSELLE Joseph Col 24 S Cook N'hamp: Acc s/o James & Jane to Lottie Sample Col 21 S Acc Acc d/o Burlie Savage on 12 Oct 1884 at Acc by P Sheppard
ROSS David C 25 S Carpenter Acc Acc s/o Gilbert & Polly to Sallie A Smith 20 S Acc Acc d/o William S & Margaret on 15 Mar 1888 at Temp'ville by WF Hayes
ROSS Edward T 18 S Farmer Acc Acc s/o Levin & Nancy to Dulany A Killman 18 S Acc Acc d/o Saml & Nancy on 19 Jan 1870 at Acc by JET Ewell
ROSS Elbridge J 42 S Carpenter Acc Acc s/o Levin T & Nancy to Nellie P Fisher 37 S Acc Acc d/o Meshack & Rachel on 28 Dec 1890 at Mappsville

by WA Street
ROSS Ezekiel H 22 S Farmer Acc Acc s/o Levin J & Eliz'th to Alice N Tull 17 S Acc Acc d/o Frank G & Mary on 30 Sep 1891 at Mappsville by JL King
ROSS Gilbert P s/o Levin T to Polly C Northam d/o Gillet who gave consent lic: 10 Jan 1859
ROSS Henry 22 S Farmer Acc Acc s/o John H & Mary E to Mary E Miles 17 S Acc Acc d/o Elijah J & Sally on 15 Nov 1882 at Bethel Ch by JW Hundley
ROSS Jacob 24 S Carpenter Acc Acc s/o Levin T & Nannie to Elizabeth Tatham 18 S Acc Acc d/o Ezekiel & Cornelia on 21 Jan 1868 at Acc by M Oldham
ROSS Jacob [Rossa] (Ross) 24 W Farmer PA Acc to Elizabeth A Turner 25 S Acc Acc d/o John R & Mary on 7 Sep 1865 at Acc by D Titlow
ROSS James P 22 S Oysterman Acc Acc s/o Parker & Emily J to Clara J Warner 20 S Acc Acc d/o Solomon & Arinthia on 5 Dec 1883 at Oak Hall by RB Beadles
ROSS John to Mary West d/o Margaret who gave consent lic: 30 Apr 1856 Wm S(?) Fletcher says he over 21
ROSS Levin Col 23 S Laborer Acc Acc s/o Ezer Garrison & Esther Ross (Col to Juliet Wise Col 25 S Acc Acc d/o Simon & Edith (Col) on 30 Dec 1870 at Drum'tn by A Joynes
ROSS Levin T 22 S Railroading Acc Acc s/o Gilbert & Polly to Effie E Godwin 22 S Acc Acc d/o James & Elizabeth on 4 Apr 1888 at Downings Ch by TG Pullen
ROSS Louis J 30 S Farmer Acc Acc s/o Jacob M & Sarah A to Indiania S Watson 25 S Acc Acc d/o John R & Cath on 12 Nov 1873 at Acc by O Littleton

ROSS Martin 23 S Laborer Acc Acc to Mary Custis 19 S Acc Acc d/o Hannah on 18 Aug 1869 at Acc by TM Poulson

ROSS Parker 46 W Farming Acc Acc s/o William Ross & Sally Taylor to Emily Brittingham 20 S Acc Acc d/o Thos Brittingham & Mary Waterfield on 3 Oct 1860 at Acc by T Waters

ROSS Robert M 25 S Oyster Planter Acc Acc s/o Jno & Mary to Drucilla J Bundick 26 S Acc Acc d/o Geo T & Drucilla H on 10 Dec 1884 at Acc by A Woodyard

ROSS Samuel T 43 S Lawyer Acc Acc s/o Jacob M & Sarah A to Margaret A Melson 30 S Acc Acc d/o John D & Margaret on 27 Jan 1887 at Acc C H by W Chinn

ROSSEY Charles H 21 S Farmer Acc Acc s/o Jacob & Elizth to Ida V Abrams 19 S Acc Acc d/o John & Eliz'th on 16 Nov 1892 at Onancock by EC Atkins

ROWELL Wm Col 32 S Laborer Acc Acc to Hester Northam Col 25 S Acc Acc d/o Rosy Hope on 4 Feb 1877 near News Town by A Joynes

ROWINS William 23 S Merchant Easton MD Chinco: Isld s/o Francis H & Elizth to Eusina (Euxina) Mumford 25 W Berlin MD Chinco: Isld d/o Jno P & Martha Marsahll on 25 Mar 1873 at Chinco: Isld by P Bowdin Sr

ROWLES James E 28 S Printer Baltimore City MD Acc s/o Walter W & Helen A to Fannie J Gillespie 26 S Acc Acc d/o John W & Sallie A on 10 Aug 1887 at Mappsville by WA Street

ROWLEY Charles [Rawley] 27 S Oysterman Acc Acc s/o Chas to Susan Marshall 19 S Acc Acc d/o Stephen & Patience on 26 Dec 1875 at Bethel Ch by DA Woodson

ROWLEY Emerson 30 S Oysterman Acc Acc to Georgianna Thomas 26 S Acc Acc d/o Elizabeth on 25 Mar 1880 at Muddy Ck by JE Bundick

ROWLEY George Col 28 S Laborer MD Acc to Hester Lyon Col 31 S Acc Acc on 26 Oct 1870 at Horntown by S Marshall

ROWLEY Henry Col 27 S Laborer Acc Acc s/o Elaviora to Sarah Wharton Col 23 S Acc Acc d/o Jacob & Mary on 5 Dec 1874 at Horntown by S Johns

ROWLEY John A 67 W Farmer Acc Acc s/o Wm & Mary to Virginia A Robins 40 S Acc Acc d/o Jno S & Drucilla on 17 Dec 1879 at Cedar Ave by JW Hilldrup

ROWLEY John W 27 S Merchant Acc Acc s/o Jno W & Eliza to Cordelia M Duncan 24 S Acc Acc d/o Wm T & E W on 1 Sep 1881 at Acc by CC Wertenbaker

RUEDIGER Frederick E [Rusdiger] 26 S Clerk US Coast Survey Prussia Germany Acc s/o Ernest & Augusta to Emeline [Kelley] Kelly 26 D Acc Acc d/o Josiah & Comfort Holstin on 21 Oct 1889 at Chinco: Isld by EH Miller

RUNGE Frederick E 25 S Salesman Hamburg Germany Acc s/o Adolph & Augusta to Sophia J Spence 26 S Acc Acc d/o Lewis J & Elizabeth L on 3 Jul 1895 at Acc by HS Dulany

RUSSELL Avory (Avery) 18 S Oysterman Acc Acc s/o John & (Elizabeth) to Rebecca Jester 15 S Acc Acc d/o James & Euphemia on 13 Feb 1869 at Acc by P Bowdin Jr

RUSSELL Carol 22 S Sailor Acc Acc s/o George & Clarissa A to Virginia Nelson 21 S Acc Acc d/o William & Mary Ann on 29 Sep 1880 at Mr Wm Moore's by JC Watson

RUSSELL Charles 19 S Oysterman Acc Acc s/o Jno & Eliz to Elizabeth [Clavelle] Claville 17 S Acc Acc d/o

Jas & Mary on 20 Jun 1862 at Acc by P Bowdin

RUSSELL Charles 24 S Oysterman Wor Co MD Acc s/o Charles & Elizabeth to Florence Phipps 18 S Acc Acc d/o Abner & Emma on 3 Jan 1889 at Chinco: Isld by SU Grimsley

RUSSELL Charles Col 22 S Wage-earner Acc Acc s/o Jane to Lola Snead Col 17 S Acc Acc d/o Mary on 3 Mar 1895 at Acc by ET Outen

RUSSELL Clayton C 18 S Oysterman Acc Acc s/o John T & Mary to Jane Turlington 17 S Acc Acc d/o Charles & Margaret on 7 Feb 1889 at Chinco: Isld by SU Grimsley

RUSSELL David 22 S Oysterman Acc Acc s/o Avery & Rebecca to Ema [Jeffreys] Jeffries 17 S Acc Acc d/o Elva & Mary A on 4 Nov 1894 at Chinco: Isld by RB Sanford

RUSSELL Edward D 20 S Sailor Acc Acc s/o John E & Sallie A to Maggie E Hinman 17 S Acc Acc d/o John R & Susan J on 29 Dec 1892 at Acc by HJ Wilson

RUSSELL Edward J 22 S Sailor Acc Acc s/o Thos & Sarah to Vienna Mason 18 S Acc Acc d/o Wm & Tabitha on 7 Jun 1866 at Acc by ES Grant

RUSSELL Elijah 21 S Sailor Chinco: Isld Chinco: Isld s/o Jno & Betsey to Charlotte Sharpley 17 S Chinco: Isld Chinco: Isld d/o Teagle & Fanny on 13 Apr 1855 at r/o Minister by P Bowdin

RUSSELL Geo W 25 S Farmer Acc Acc s/o Geo Thomas & Mary to Sallie J Matthews 15 S Acc Acc d/o Z S & Sally on 15 May 1878 near Zion Ch by DA Woodson

RUSSELL James A 23 S Oysterman Acc Acc s/o Geo T & Mary to Belle Middleton 18 S Acc Acc d/o Revel P & Ellen on 6 Jan 1892 at Lee Mont by AJ Fristoe

RUSSELL James E 20 S Oysterman Acc Acc s/o Jas T & Susan J to Peggy D Custis 22 S Acc Acc d/o Jno H & Sally on 3 Jan 1867 at Acc by JE Bundick

RUSSELL Jno T 22 S Mariner b: Acc s/o Thos & Sally to Mary S (Susan) Rew 20 S b: Acc d/o Wm & Julia Rew on 22 Feb 1855 at Wm Reid's by ES Grant

RUSSELL John 19 S Oysterman Acc Acc s/o Jno & Mary to Mary Ida Watson 15 S Acc Acc d/o Lambert Quillen & Harriet Waftson on 9 Jan 1883 at Chinco: Isld by WP Thornton

RUSSELL John (W) [Russel] 23 S Sailor b: Acc s/o Seven Russell & Nancy Maonger to Hanah S (Hannah) Bull 21 S b: Acc d/o George Bull & Sarah Nottingham on 7 Jan 1857 at r/o Abbot Ashby by LK LeCato (Southey Milliner says he over 21 & Wm Lewis says she is over 21)

RUSSELL John E 24 S Mariner s/o George & Margaret to Sarah A Trehearn 21 S lic: 4 Jan 1865 marr: 5 Jan 1865 at Accomack

RUSSELL John Jr [Russel] 21 S Waterman Chinco: Isld Chinco: Isld s/o John & Elizth to Mary Hill 14 S Chinco: Isld Chinco: Isld d/o Timothy (Sen) & Rebeca on 1 Apr 1858 at Chinco: Isld by P Bowdin (John A M Whealton says he over 21)

RUSSELL John T 23 S Laborer Acc Acc s/o Geo T & Mary to Emma Simpson 22 S Acc Acc d/o Wm & Elishea on 3 Sep 1872 at r/o Mary Branch by EM Bryan

RUSSELL John T 37 W Laborer Acc Acc s/o George T & Mary to Mary C Hart 35 W Acc Acc d/o Mrs Evans on 16 Jan 1887 at Acc by CA Grice

RUSSELL John W 38 S Carpenter Acc

Acc s/o Elizabeth to Sallie Vernelson 25 S Acc Acc d/o Nannie on 29 Oct 1868 at Acc by JET Ewell

RUSSELL John W Col 25 S Wage-earner Acc Acc s/o Jane to Mary Nock Col 18 S Acc Acc d/o Levi & Sarah on 10 Jan 1888 at Acc by JA Haynes

RUSSELL Josiah T 43 W Sailor Acc Acc s/o Thomas & Eleanor to Susan Beasley 25 S Acc Acc on 13 May 1877 at Hunting Ck by FH Mullineaux

RUSSELL Robert 22 S Oysterman Acc Acc s/o James to Elizabeth Lewis 23 S Acc Acc d/o Elizabeth on 23 May 1867 at Acc by JE Bundick

RUSSELL Samuel E 22 S Carpenter Acc Acc s/o George T & Mary to Emaline S Barnes 19 S Acc Acc d/o James W & Mary J on 28 Dec 1884 at Acc by AJ Walter

RUSSELL Severn Col 22 S Laborer Acc Acc s/o Mary to Charlotte Hatton Col 23 S Acc Acc d/o Hetty on 5 Jun 1878 at Drum'tn by A Joynes

RUSSELL Sidney P 23 S Seaman Acc Acc s/o Thomas & Sarah to Elizabeth E Barnes 16 S Acc Acc d/o John & Sally on 2 Sep 1869 at Acc by JC Martin

RUSSELL Sylvanus W to Polly Hinman d/o Mary who gave consent lic: 5 Feb 1856

RUSSELL Thomas F 20 S Farmer Acc Acc s/o William (of W) & Catherine to Tabitha [Justis] Justice 17 S Acc Acc d/o Revel J & Sally on 3 Feb 1889 at bride's parents' by JW Norris

RUSSELL Thos 32 S Waterman b: Acc s/o George (Decd) & Sally to Delila Silverthorn 37 S b: Acc d/o Wm & Tabitha on 7 Jan 1858 at r/o Saml Taylor by ES Grant (David Taylor says both over 21)

RUSSELL William to Fanny Dix lic: 31 Dec 1855 Isaac Russell says both over 21

RUSSELL William 25 W Oysterman Acc Acc s/o Wm to Catharine Custis 25 S Acc Acc d/o Jno H & Sally on 3 Jan 1867 at Acc by JE Bundick

RUSSELL William [Russel] 40 W Farmer & Oysterman b: Accomac s/o Benjamin & Rachel to Nancy Bayly 23 S b: Accomac d/o Zadock on 20 Jan 1855 at Acc by GH Ewell (Robert Russell of R says both over 21)

RUSSELL William J 20 S Farmer Acc Acc s/o William & Catherine A to Laura L Wessells 18 S Acc Acc d/o Arthur & Mary on 28 Dec 1890 at Parksley by HS Dulany

RUSSELL William S 20 S Farmer Acc Acc s/o Thomas & Sally to Mary E Showard 17 S Acc Acc d/o Southy & Susan on 20 May 1869 at Acc by JET Ewell

RUSSELL Wm 25 S Farmer Acc Acc s/o Geo T & Mary to Virginia E Shrieves 21 S Acc Acc d/o Wm & Caroline on 11 Apr 1877 at Reese Chp by FH Mullineaux

RYAN William T 28 S Tonsorial Artist Kent Co DE Acc s/o Thos & Catharine to Fannie A Voyles 16 S Martinsville IN Acc d/o Rebecca on 9 May 1894 at Belle Haven by JG Lennon

SADLER George Col 30 S Farmer Acc Acc s/o Harriet Boberts to Eliza Blake Col 23 S Acc Acc d/o Sally on 9 Oct 1881 at New Church by JC Cluff

SAMPLE Asa 23 S Farmer Acc Acc s/o Littl & Margt to Laurella Case 24 S Acc Acc d/o Chas & Nancy on 26 Dec 1866 at Acc by AB Dolly

SAMPLE Asa Col 36 W Farmer Acc Acc to Tinnie E S [Rosel] Rosell Col 20 S N'hamp: Acc d/o James & Jane

Marriages

on 30 Apr 1879 at Acc by JW Diggs
SAMPLE Charles Col 25 S Farm Laborer Acc Acc s/o Alice Richardson to Mary E Tankard 22 S Acc Acc on 2 Apr 1885 at Craddockville by GHT Byrd
SAMPLE Charles Col 77 S Wage-earner Acc Acc s/o Peter Edwards & Deborah Samples to Emaline Gaskins Col 50 S Acc Acc d/o Zorobabel Matthews & Susan Gaskins on 21 Dec 1892 near Savageville by JH Offer
SAMPLE Charles L Col 22 S Merchant Acc Acc s/o Asa to Alice E Upshur Col 18 S Acc Acc d/o William & Lizzie on 18 Feb 1890 at Acc by L Duncan
SAMPLE Charlie FN single Laborer Acc Acc s/o Charles & Rachel to Elizabeth Sample FN single Acc Acc d/o Isaac & Margaret on 2 Jan 1856 at Pungo: by M Oldham (Charles Case says they over 21)
SAMPLE Elijah Col 28 S Wage-earner Acc Acc s/o William & Sally to Loretta Moore Col 22 S Acc Acc d/o Ezekiel & Ibby on 22 Apr 1891 at Hacks Nk by WB Sample
SAMPLE Ezra FN 26 S Sailor Acc Acc s/o Fanny to Agnes Revell FN 25 S Acc Acc d/o Millie on 13 May 1866 at Acc by P Warren
SAMPLE Frank R Col 21 S Farmer Acc Acc s/o Mary to Willie Doughty Col 18 S Acc Acc d/o Dorey & Nancy on 20 Apr 1892 at Acc by L Duncan
SAMPLE Geo H Col 21 S Farmer Acc Acc s/o Geo & Mary to Annie Sample Col 18 S Acc Acc d/o Stratton & Mary on 10 Dec 1890 at Acc by L Duncan
SAMPLE George Col 22 S Farmer Acc Acc s/o Jno & Mary to Elizabeth Ashby Col 26 S Acc Acc d/o Charles & Mary on 20 Feb 1881 at Drum'tn by PM Lewis
SAMPLE George of J Col 26 S Laborer Acc Acc s/o Isaac & Margaret to Mary Phillips Col 18 S Acc Acc d/o Edward & Mary on 20 Dec 1874 at Savageville by JK Plato
SAMPLE Horace Col 22 S Wage-earner Acc Acc s/o George & Eliza to Olivia Harmon Col 21 S Acc Acc d/o John & Sabra Harmon on 2 Jan 1895 at Acc by L Duncan
SAMPLE Isaac Col 25 S Farmer Acc Acc s/o John & Mary to Maggie [Hateny] Hateney 22 S Acc Acc d/o Margaret Snead on 29 Dec 1895 at Acc by JN Waters
SAMPLE James Col 43 S Laborer Acc Acc s/o Eaphernia to Louisa Ewell Col 26 S Acc Acc d/o Sarah on 5 Aug 1873 at Horntown by S Johns
SAMPLE James Henry Col 39 S Laborer Acc Acc s/o Isaac & Mary to Laura Ellen Ames Col 32 S Acc Acc d/o Laura on 6 Jan 1875 at Pungo: by JK Plato
SAMPLE James J Col 21 S Wage-earner Acc Acc s/o James & Emma to Emma Ames Col 21 S Acc Acc d/o Tarleton & Juliet on 28 Dec 1892 at Locustville by RH Coleman
SAMPLE John A Col 25 S Laborer Acc Acc to Annie [Bevans] Beavans Col 18 S Acc Acc d/o John on 15 Nov 1883 at Acc by TW Nettles
SAMPLE John E Col 23 S Farmer Acc Acc s/o Emma to Margaret S Kellam Col 17 S Acc Acc d/o Samuel & Emma on 16 Feb 1881 at Onancock by JW Diggs
SAMPLE John Henry 23 S Sailor Acc Acc s/o Comfort to Georgianna [Scarburgh] Scarborough 18 S Acc Acc d/o Sarah on 26 Dec 1866 at Acc by JH Addison
SAMPLE John Henry Col 21 S Wage-earner Acc Acc s/o John & Mary to Louisa F Stratton Col 20 S Acc Acc d/o William & Eliza on 30

Jan 1890 at Onancock by GHT Byrd

SAMPLE John T Col 21 S Laborer Acc Acc s/o Polly to Racilia Kellam Col 21 S Acc Acc d/o Mary on 21 May 1876 at Savageville by JK Plato

SAMPLE Levin Col 21 S Laborer Acc Acc s/o John & Mary to Hester Ann Chandler Col 19 S Acc Acc d/o Bowdoin & Jane on 13 Feb 1887 at Acc by JA Haynes

SAMPLE Litt FN 27 S Cook Acc Acc s/o Litt & Margt to Mary Susan Outten FN 21 S Acc Acc d/o William & Tinney on 10 Jan 1866 at Acc by JH Johnson

SAMPLE Littleton (of L) Col 28 S Wage-earner Acc Acc s/o Littleton to Anna LeCato Col 29 S N'hamp: Acc on 31 Jan 1889 at Acc by L Duncan

SAMPLE Littleton S Col 45 W Merchant Acc Acc s/o Littleton & Margaret to Mary A Becket Col 42 S Acc Acc d/o Harriet on 8 Sep 1886 at Acc by A Pinder

SAMPLE Nathaniel S 21 S Farmer Acc Acc s/o Eliza to Ann Jacobs 21 S Acc Acc d/o Ibby on 30 Dec 1868 at Acc by C Burriss

SAMPLE Obediah Col 22 S Oysterman Acc Acc s/o Littleton & Sarah to Susan Church Col 25 S Acc Acc d/o Abram & Margaret on 17 Mar 1891 near Pungo: by L Duncan

SAMPLE Simon Col 21 S Farm Laborer Acc Acc s/o Nellie Ward to Emma Kate Kellam Col 14 S Acc Acc d/o Samuel & Emma S on 8 Jan 1885 at Drum'tn by LW Lee

SAMPLE Thomas Col 51 S Farmer Acc Acc s/o Ann to Jane Bull Col 50 S Acc Acc d/o Martha on 23 Jun 1892 at Acc by L Duncan

SAMPLE William (FN) 28 S Laborer Acc Acc to Mary E Joynes (Jones) (FN) 21 S Acc Acc d/o Kessey (who gave consent) on 5 Aug 1860 at Acc by JH Addison (William Jellason says he over 21)

SAMPLE William Col 58 S Wage-earner Acc Acc s/o Margaret Nedab to Leah Kellam Col 47 S Acc Acc d/o Mary Burton on 24 Oct 1892 at Wardtown by J Savage

SAMPLE William T Col 24 S Farmer Acc Acc s/o Mary to Zipporah Parker Col 21 S Acc Acc d/o John & Mary on 7 Dec 1890 at Acc by L Duncan

SAPP Reuben (Saph) 30 S Mechanic DE DE to Mary T Byrd 23 S Acc Acc d/o Selby & Amanda on 13 Jan 1869 at Acc by JET Ewell

SARGENT Fred 21 S Merchant Drummer Manchester NH Boston MA s/o J F & Mary to Jennie E Ayres 23 W Acc Acc d/o Smith & Sarah Hyslop on 21 Jun 1886 at Pungo: by L Rosser

SATCHELL Abel E Col 19 S Farmer Acc Acc s/o Abel J & Maria to Lavirta Godfrey Col 19 S Acc Acc d/o John & Betsy on 21 Dec 1893 at Drum'tn by R Davis

SATCHELL Abraham Col 22 S Farmer Acc Acc s/o Edmond Satchell & Lizzie Custis to Laura Whealton Col 21 S Crisfield MD Acc on 12 Jan 1891 near Acc C H by AJ Satchell

SATCHELL Caleb Col 45 S Farmer Acc Acc s/o Rhoda to Mary Ewell Col 50 S Acc Acc d/o Milly on 4 Nov 1875 near Mary Branch by JW Ruff

SATCHELL Charles Col 25 S Laborer N'hamp: Acc s/o Ann to Elizabeth Beavans Col 20 S Acc Acc on 11 Oct 1871 at Acc by R Davis

SATCHELL Christopher 37 S Miller Acc Acc s/o Susan to Susan Charnock 31 S Acc Acc d/o Hessy on 11 Dec 1872 at Wiseville by JET Ewell

SATCHELL Edward Col 24 S Wage-earner Acc Acc s/o William &

Sarah to Lucy Ayres Col 23 S Acc Acc d/o Jay & Sarah on 20 Oct 1895 at Acc by JN Waters

SATCHELL George Col 25 S Laborer Acc Acc s/o Wm & betsey to Neely West Col 22 S Acc Acc d/o Bridget on 15 Mar 1883 at Drum'tn by LW Lee

SATCHELL George O 19 S Laborer Acc Acc s/o Wm Henry & Eliza to Missouri Fannie Mears 16 S Acc Acc d/o Edward S & Mary on 21 Jan 1875 at Leatherbury Chp by PA Leatherbury

SATCHELL Henry Col 25 S Laborer Acc Acc s/o Adal to Mary Colonna Col 23 S N'hamp: Acc d/o Lilia Colonna on 27 Jul 1871 at Acc by TM Cole

SATCHELL James Col 48 S Laborer Acc Acc s/o Sarah to Mary Johnson Col 38 S Acc Acc d/o Ibby Custis on 25 Dec 1877 at Modest Town by A Joynes

SATCHELL James H 26 S Farmer Acc Acc s/o Wm H & Eliza to Mary E Nock 18 S Acc Acc d/o James & Rachel on 1 Apr 1877 at Zion Bapt Ch by DA Woodson

SATCHELL James T 23 S Farmer Acc Acc s/o Geo T & Lucretia to Amanda Wessells 20 S Acc Acc d/o Ephraim & Nancy on 26 Dec 1872 at Acc by JET Ewell

SATCHELL John Col 50 S Laborer Acc Acc s/o Saml Ross & Violet Johnson to Lavinia Phillips Col 45 S Acc Acc d/o Geo Sherevis & Phoebe Joynes on 6 Nov 1870 at r/o Lavinia Philp's by C Burriss

SATCHELL John H Col 21 S Farming N'hamp: Acc s/o Agnes to Marian Byrd Col 22 S Acc Acc d/o Fanny on 29 Jan 1879 at Acc by JW Diggs

SATCHELL John T Col 26 S Farmer Acc Acc s/o Eliza Parker to Rachel Walters Col 26 S Acc Acc d/o Mary on 31 Dec 1884 at Craddockville by GHT Byrd

SATCHELL Leonard Col 26 S Laborer Acc Acc s/o Lydia to Nancy Gaskins Col 23 S Acc Acc d/o Sarah on 20 Mar 1878 near Pungo: by JE Humphreys

SATCHELL Samuel [Satchel] Col 53 S Laborer Acc Acc to Dolly [Jacob] Jacobs Col 48 S Acc Acc on 19 Jan 1873 at Acc by C Burriss

SATCHELL Southly Col 20 S Laborer Acc Acc s/o Fanny to Betsy West Col 21 S Acc Acc d/o Keziah on 13 Jan 1878 near Boston by TW Nettles

SATCHELL Thomas P 28 S Farmer Acc Acc s/o Susan to Mary E Watson 30 S Acc Acc d/o Edward R & Elizth on 21 Feb 1867 at Acc by JH Addison

SATCHELL Williams [Satchel] (FN) 43 S Laborer to Betsey (Poolman) Pontman (FN) 28 S on 24 Aug 1856 at Wachapreague by J Burton (C H Robbins says both over 21)

SAULSBURY Henry 28 S Farmer Acc Acc s/o John & Mary to Mary S Justice 29 S Acc Acc d/o Emily on 16 Dec 1875(?) at Chesconessex by JH Amiss Certificate returned 5 Apr 1877

SAUNDERS Arthur 27 S Farmer N'hamp: N'hamp: s/o James T & Helen to Elizabeth Susan Kelly 18 S Acc Acc d/o George W & Elizabeth C on 3 Oct 1894 at Onancock by HL Derby

SAUTLER George Wm 38 S Farming Germany Acc s/o Fred & Ida to Margaret Evans 33 S Acc Acc d/o Dennard & Sally on 9 Aug 1882 at Chesconessex by PA Leatherbury

SAVAGE Adam Col 27 S Wage-earner Acc Acc s/o Abram & Sallie to Melissa Ann Godwin Col 23 S Acc Acc d/o Alfred & Hester on 17 Aug 1892 at Temp'ville by JC Cluff

SAVAGE Alfred F Col 21 S Farmer Acc Acc s/o John & Annie to Maggie S Poulson Col 19 S Acc Acc d/o Isaac J & Margaret Ann on 8 Aug 1894 at Acc C H by R Davis

SAVAGE Arthur Col 30 S Laborer Acc Acc s/o Leah to Mary Hatton Col 28 S Acc Acc d/o Mary on 21 Apr 1878 at Onancock by PA Leatherbury

SAVAGE Arthur Col 32 S Laborer Acc Acc s/o Leah to Mary J Drummond Col 21 S Acc Acc d/o Caroline on 5 Jun 1881 near Onancock by RJ Waters

SAVAGE Bagwell 30 S Farmer b: Acc s/o Bagwell Savage & Margt Kelly to Margaret Floyd 33 S b: Acc d/o Thos Floyd & Sarah Ashly on 27 Dec 1858 at r/o Wm Pruitt by LK LeCato (George G Fox says both over 21)

SAVAGE Benjamin T 22 S Farmer Acc Acc s/o Wm J & Margaret A to Nona C Hope 19 S Acc Acc d/o John T F & Catherine A on 26 Feb 1890 at Acc by JA Barker

SAVAGE Caleb Col 43 S Laborer Acc Acc s/o Sarah to Frances Aydelotte Col 22 S Acc Acc d/o Eliza Holmes on 9 Jul 1873 at Horntown by S Johns

SAVAGE Calvin Col 22 S Farmer Acc Acc s/o Edmund & Mary to Clara Hope Col 21 S Acc Acc d/o Emma Northam on 17 Nov 1889 at Temp'ville by JC Cluff

SAVAGE Charles B 24 S Farmer Acc Acc s/o Edward & Elizth to Mary C Parkes 24 S Acc Acc d/o John Y & Catharine on 10 Mar 1875 at Conquest Ch by M Oldham

SAVAGE Custis Col 44 W Waterman Acc Acc s/o Candice to Rachel Fosque Col 35 W Acc Acc d/o Abe Nat Smith on 19 Dec 1894 at Acc by TW Nettles

SAVAGE Daniel Col 22 S Farmer Acc Acc s/o Wm & Rosey to Eva Davis Col 19 S Acc Acc d/o Saml & Sarah on 10 Feb 1886 at Acc by CA Horsey

SAVAGE Dennis Col 24 S Sailor Acc Acc s/o Ann to Ann Watson Col 19 S Acc Acc d/o Sina on 7 May 1876 at Modest Town by A Joynes

SAVAGE Edward Col 30 S Farm Laborer Acc Acc s/o Mary Baker to Tabitha Parramore Col 32 S Acc Acc d/o Lucy on 25 Nov 1885 at Drum'tn by LW Lee

SAVAGE Edward Thomas Col 24 S Farmer Acc Acc s/o Wm T & Rosa to Tabitha Bayly 20 S Acc Acc d/o Wm & Alice on 18 Dec 1895 at Onancock by SW Watkins

SAVAGE Edwd 23 S Laborer Acc Acc s/o Bagwell & Polly to Elizabeth East 21 S Acc Acc d/o Mahaly on 2 Jan 1859 at Acc by JWA Elliott (Wm T Turlington says both over 21)

SAVAGE Edwd J 20 S Farmer Acc Acc s/o Richd & Levinia to Tishue C Summers 19 S Acc Acc d/o Wm & Lerena on 3 Jan 1877 at Muddy Ck by DA Woodson

SAVAGE Edwd J 35 S Farmer Acc Acc s/o Edwd J & Mary E to Cordie D Beloate 22 S Acc Acc d/o Wm & Susan on 23 Nov 1884 at Acc by A Woodyard

SAVAGE Edwd M (Edward) 26 S Farmer Acc Acc s/o Major & Susan to Cath R (Catharine) Beach 23 S Acc Acc d/o George & Rosey on 26 Jan 1859 at r/o William Beach by JWA Elliott (Abel Mears of A says both over 21)

SAVAGE Elijah Col 22 S Laborer Acc Acc s/o Sally to Harriet Bayly Col 18 S Acc Acc d/o Polly Smith on 11 Oct 1874 at Belle Haven by JE Humphreys

SAVAGE Elijah Col 22 S Laborer Acc Acc s/o Comfort to Alice Fosque Col 21 S Acc Acc d/o Lucy on 26 Dec

1876 at Belle Haven by RH Govans
SAVAGE Elijah Col 35 W Wage-earner Acc Acc s/o Comfort to Caroline Hatton Col 40 W Acc Acc d/o Henry & Eliza Smith on 30 Jun 1888 at Acc by L Duncan
SAVAGE Frederick 28 W Farmer Acc Acc to Margaret Savage 22 S Acc Acc d/o Henry & Elizth on 10 Jan 1870 at Acc by S Marshall
SAVAGE Geo D Col 20 S Laborer Acc Acc s/o Ann to Susan Riley Col 20 S Acc Acc d/o Meriann on 3 Feb 1876 at News Town by A Joynes
SAVAGE George Col 28 S Dredger Acc Acc s/o Leah to Mary Ann [Justis] (Jestis) Justice Col 17 S Acc Acc d/o Bettie on 31 Dec 1873 at News Town by A Joynes
SAVAGE George Col 21 S Day Laborer Acc Acc s/o Sarah Abbott to Mary Pitts Col 24 S Acc Acc d/o Sarah Wright on 13 Oct 1881 near Modest Town by AJ Satchell
SAVAGE George B 20 S Farmer Acc Acc s/o Edward M & Kate to Indie A Mapp 23 S Acc Acc d/o G Columbus & Rose on 8 Jan 1890 at Acc by JT Moore
SAVAGE George F Col 28 S Wage-earner Acc Acc s/o Harvey & Eliz'th to Josephine Williams Col 18 S Acc Acc d/o Sally on 2 Jan 1895 at Temp'ville by GHT Byrd
SAVAGE George H Col 23 S Farmer Acc Acc s/o John & Jeannette to Mary E Joynes Col 21 S Acc Acc d/o Levin & Sarah on 4 Aug 1895 at Acc by SW Watkins
SAVAGE George S 19 S Merchant Acc Acc s/o George & Rachel to Catharine J Taylor 15 S Acc Acc d/o Joseph B & Elizabeth on 9 Nov 1859 at Acc by JH Addison (John T Rayfield wintnessed for both)
SAVAGE George William Col 29 W Wage-earner Acc Acc s/o William T & Rosa to Susan White Col 18 S Acc Acc d/o Emma on 11 Nov 1888 at Acc by JK Adams
SAVAGE Harry 21 S Laborer Acc Acc s/o Jane Roberts to Rose Bayly 21 S Acc Acc d/o Jane on 31 Aug 1881 at Locust Mount by JWA Elliott
SAVAGE Harry Col 27 W Farmer Acc Acc s/o Ricahrd Savage & Jane Roberts to Mary LeCato Col 21 S Acc Acc d/o George & Arsen on 12 Jan 1887 at bride's home by L Duncan
SAVAGE Henry 20 S Sailor Acc Acc s/o Isaac J & Patience to Mary V Tarr 16 S Acc Acc d/o James E & Mary C on 8 Mar 1892 at Chinco: Isld by JF Wooden
SAVAGE Horace Col 21 S Laborer Acc Acc s/o Comfort to Bettie Jubilee Col 21 S Acc Acc d/o Henny on 19 Dec 1877 near Hawk's Nest by JE Humphreys
SAVAGE Isaac 22 S Oysterman Wor Co MD Acc s/o Elisha & Nelly to Patience Ann Jones 17 S Acc Acc d/o Burton & Mary Jane on 1 Mar 1870 at Acc by P Bowdin
SAVAGE Isaac Col 22 S Farmer Acc Acc s/o Louis & Sarah to Clara Fosque Col 16 S Acc Acc d/o Henry & Henrietta on 1 Feb 1891 near Mappsville by AJ Satchell
SAVAGE Isaac J 47 W Dealer in Oysters Sussex Co DE Acc s/o Elisha & Ellen to Lydia A Jones 26 S Acc Acc d/o Burton & Sarah A on 17 Apr 1890 at Chinco: Isld by GE Wood
SAVAGE James black 50 S Farmer s/o Esther to Hannah Parramore black 39 S d/o Agnes lic: 24 Dec 1872 marr: at Hell Town
SAVAGE James Col 24 S Laborer Acc Acc to Lucy Ashby Col 20 S Acc Acc on 30 Dec 1875 near Locust Mount by HT Rich

SAVAGE James D 26 S Farmer Acc Acc s/o Geo S & Margaret S to Maggie E Braidwood 18 S Som Co MD Acc d/o John & Pricella on 6 Mar 1872 at Acc by JE Humphreys

SAVAGE James E 25 S Farmer Acc Acc s/o Edwd G & Elizth to Ella Budd 17 S Acc Acc d/o Wm H & Susan on 28 Jan 1880 at Mr LeCato's by LK LeCato

SAVAGE James F 21 S Farmer Acc Acc s/o Major Savage & Susan Edmond to Mary M LeCato 21 S Acc Acc d/o Nathl B Lacato & Elizth G Walls on 27 Jan 1861 at r/o Nathal Lecato by LK LeCato (John T Finney says he over 21)

SAVAGE James T 31 W Farmer Acc Acc s/o Major & Susan to Virginia C Mapp 23 S Acc Acc d/o John D & Ann T on 25 Jan 1870 at Acc by JE Humphreys

SAVAGE Jas Hy Col 30 S Farmer Acc Acc s/o Geo Wm & Rosa to Marg't A Drummond Col 22 S Acc Acc d/o Parnell & Ann on 14 Dec 1892 at Acc by JW Cook

SAVAGE Jeremiah J 23 S Farming b: Acc s/o Griffin & Mary Ann to Mary M (wid/o Solomon Decd) Wilkerson 23 W b: Wor Co MD d/o Lemaul & Margaret Dennis on 19 May 1857 at Acc by T Waters (Wm W Selby says he over 21).

SAVAGE Jno T 27 W Farmer Acc Acc s/o Richd T & Leaviner to Polly F Summers 19 S Acc Acc d/o Wm J & Arena on 19 Dec 1878 at Capt Wm Summers' by DA Woodson

SAVAGE John 28 S Sailor b: Acc s/o Bagwell & Polly to Susan Heath 21 S b: Acc d/o George & Margaret on 3 Jan 1856 at r/o Geo Heath by LK LeCato (Geo Heath says both over 21)

SAVAGE John Col 26 S Farmer Acc Acc s/o Mary Baker to Jane Hinman Col 23 S Acc Acc d/o Labra on 26 Jan 1882 at Bay Side Par by RJ Waters

SAVAGE John Col 45 S Farmer Acc Acc s/o Elizabeth to Elizabeth Poulson Col 35 S Acc Acc d/o Tamar on 6 Jan 1886 at Onancock by PA Leatherbury

SAVAGE John H 20 S Farmer Acc Acc s/o Edward of A & Eliz'th to Sallie Bundick 20 S Acc Acc d/o Elijah & Maggie on 31 Dec 1890 at Acc by JWA Elliott

SAVAGE John R 24 S Sailor Acc Acc s/o Thomas & Elizabeth to Josephine Gardner 16 S Acc Acc d/o James & Betty on 12 Jul 1893 at Acc by AJ Reamy

SAVAGE John T 24 S Farmer Acc Acc s/o Richd T & Lavinia to Manie H Hickman 22 S Acc Acc d/o Jno H & Elizth on 17 Nov 1875 at Acc by DA Woodson

SAVAGE John T Col 22 S Farmer Acc Acc s/o John Kerr & Margaret Savage to Annie Matthews Col 21 S Acc Acc d/o Geo Henry & Sarah on 9 Feb 1890 at Acc by JH Thomas

SAVAGE John T W 43 S Oysterman Acc Acc s/o James K & Ann B to Lucy B Evans 18 S Acc Acc d/o Wm S & Mary C on 10 Aug 1876 at Wise Point by PA Leatherbury

SAVAGE John W 22 S Farmer Acc Acc s/o Wm B to Sarah V Thornton 16 S Acc Acc d/o Wm & Elizth A on 18 Feb 1866 at Acc by GW Matthews

SAVAGE John W Col 21 S Laborer Acc Acc s/o Rose to Mary Jane Custis Col 21 S Acc Acc d/o Eleanor on 28 Oct 1875 at Deep Ck by HT Rich

SAVAGE John W 26 S Farmer Acc Acc s/o William J & Margaret A to Ella Gracie Drummond 18 S Acc Acc d/o Louis D on 1 Jan 1890 at Grangeville by JM Anderson

SAVAGE Littleton 60 W Farmer Acc Acc s/o Jacob & Susan to Comfort Colonna 38 S Acc Acc d/o Thomas F & Ann on 28 Dec 1873 at Acc by EM Bryan

SAVAGE Littleton Col 21 S Laborer Acc Acc to Margaret S Savage Col 18 S Acc Acc d/o Geo &Catharine on 4 Sep 1880 at Acc by TW Nettles

SAVAGE Lloyd J 26 S Merchant Acc Acc s/o Edwd & Elizabeth to Sadie D Parkes 23 S Acc Acc d/o Geo & Mary E on 30 Jun 1886 at Onancock by JW Hundley

SAVAGE Lloyd W 25 S Merchant Acc Hutchine TX s/o Jas K & Amm B to Susan A Stott 25 S Acc Acc d/o John & Sarah on 7 Oct 1875 at Onancock by FR Boston

SAVAGE Lorenzo Col 21 S Wage-earner Acc Acc s/o Sarah Duffy to Sally Mason Col 19 S Acc Acc d/o Alice on 23 Dec 1888 at Acc by AJ Satchell

SAVAGE Parker Col 30 W Farmer Acc Acc s/o Susan White to Mahala Wise Col 40 S Acc Acc d/o Esther on 30 Dec 1891 at Acc by AJ Satchell

SAVAGE Peter FN 27 W Farming Acc Acc s/o Peter & Patience to Fannie Martin FN 18 S Acc Acc d/o Jon (James)& Fanny Marting on 9 Jan 1861 at Acc by JWA Elliott

SAVAGE Richard Col 25 S Laborer Acc Acc s/o Sam Jubilee & Comfort Savage to Arinthia Jones Col 35 W Acc Acc d/o Wm & Henny Jubilee on 4 Nov 1885 at Acc by JB Lewis

SAVAGE Robert Col 22 S Sailor Acc Acc s/o Edie to Caroline West Col 21 S Acc Acc d/o James & Caroline on 10 Jan 1877 at Belle Haven by RH Govans

SAVAGE Robert T 34 S Farmer Acc Acc s/o Henry to Elizabeth R Barnes 27 S Acc Acc d/o Arthur & Annie on 25 Mar 1874 at Onancock by O Littleton

SAVAGE Samuel S 40 S Farming Acc Acc s/o John & Sally to Mary Ann Pitts 27 S Acc Acc d/o Wm & Betsy on 1 Sep 1861 at Acc by G Bradford (Samuel J Savage give information above)

SAVAGE Theordore J 23 S Farmer Acc Acc s/o J J & Mary to Dollie Coleburn 19 S Acc Acc d/o Jno W & Annie C on 16 Jun 1886 at Downings Ch by DM Wallace

SAVAGE Thomas 21 S Oysterman DE Chinco: Isld s/o Jane to Mary Hill 17 S Chinco: Isld Chinco: Isld d/o Timothy & Zipporah on 13 Jun 1883 at Chinco: Isld by EH Miller

SAVAGE Thomas Col 24 S Laborer Acc Acc s/o Mary Spires to Georgianna Walter Col 27 S Acc Acc on 1 Mar 1887 at bride's home by TW Nettles

SAVAGE Thos H B 32 S House Maker Acc Acc s/o Saml & Elizth to Kate Humphreys 22 S Acc Acc d/o Joshua & Elizth on 18 Dec 1878 near Belle Haven by E Hebard

SAVAGE Thos P Col 26 S Farm Laborer Acc Acc s/o Abel & Lizzie to Milkey Miles Col 30 W Acc Acc on 10 Jan 1885 at Lee Mont by CA Horsey

SAVAGE William Col 25 S Farmer Acc Acc s/o Leah to Clarissa Crowson Col 22 S Acc Acc d/o Fanny Parker on 20 Nov 1872 at Lilliston's Mill by A Joynes

SAVAGE William Col 21 S Laborer Acc Acc s/o Elizabeth to Susan Drummond Col 23 S Acc Acc d/o Sarah on 27 Jun 1875 at Deep Ck Mill by HT Rich

SAVAGE William Col 22 S Hostler Acc Acc s/o Wm & Rose to Laura Young Col 18 S Acc Acc d/o Tabitha on 6 Jul 1884 at Acc by GHT Byrd

SAVAGE William (J) 27 S Farmer b:

Acc s/o Bagwell Savage & Margt Kelly to Margt (I) Richardson 27 S b: Acc d/o (Mary) on 29 Dec 1858 at r/o Thos Kellam by LK LeCato (James B Groton says both over 21)

SAVAGE William B widr to Rebecca J Trader d/o Henry lic: 27 Feb 1857 John W Nock says both over 21

SAVAGE Wm T Col 49 S Farmer Acc Acc s/o Malinda Mears to Rose Ann Savage Col 40 S Acc Acc d/o Fanny on 2 Nov 1884 at Acc by CA Horsey

SAVAGE Richard K 24 S Merchant Acc Acc s/o Richard T to Charlotte J Walsh 18 S NY Acc d/o Wm & Mary on 12 Jun 1887 at Mappsville by R Walsh

SAWYER Heber Col 35 S Sailor Norfolk Acc s/o John & Mary to Rosina Beloate Col 25 S Acc Acc d/o Frank & Eliza on 15 Oct 1893 at Pungo: by JM Anderson

SCARBOROUGH Albert 24 S Farmer Acc Acc s/o Isaac & Maria to Laura Burton 21 S Acc Acc d/o Sarah on 17 Nov 1867 at Acc by WT Tull (lic: 15 Jun 1867 which states marr: 19 Jun 1867)

SCARBOROUGH Benjamin Col 23 S Wage-earner Acc Acc s/o Samuel & Elizabeth to Fannie H Savage Col 25 S Acc Acc d/o Wm T & Rosa on 10 Jul 1892 at Acc C H by BJ Hargarves

SCARBOROUGH Charles [Scarburgh] Col 52 S Farmer Acc Acc to Louisa West Col 55 S Acc Acc d/o Lottie Snead on 22 Feb 1893 at Savageville by JH Offer

SCARBOROUGH Edmond B 26 S Brick Layer Acc Acc s/o Mitchell T & Hannah M to Maggie P Mears 20 S Acc Acc d/o Arthur T & Ellen on 23 Dec 1891 at Wachapreague by JR Strugis

SCARBOROUGH Frank Col 22 S Laborer Acc Acc to Catharine Hall Col 25 S Acc Acc on 27 Oct 1880 at Acc by SMG Copeland

SCARBOROUGH Geo D 46 W Farmer Acc Acc s/o Americus & Mary to Eleanor D Keaton 42 W Acc Acc d/o Thos & Juliet Chandler on 17 Aug 1892 at Onancock by AC Berryman

SCARBOROUGH George D 26 S Farmer Acc Acc s/o Amenicus & Mary to Virginia E Watson 24 S Acc Acc d/o John & Catharine on 21 Dec 1870 at Acc by AC Bledsoe

SCARBOROUGH George T [Scarburgh] 31 S Physician Acc Nansemond Co s/o Geo P & Mary S J to Henrietta E Blackstone 25 S Acc Acc d/o John J & Margt D on 21 Mar 1867 at Acc by JD Thomas

SCARBOROUGH Henry A 22 S Farmer Acc Acc s/o Mitchell T & Hannah to Retta Stiles 18 S NJ Acc d/o Jacob & Marchie W on 20 Dec 1883 at Powelton by JW Stiff

SCARBOROUGH Peter Col 27 S Sailor Acc Acc s/o Albert & Juliet to Sally Boggs Col 15 S Acc Acc d/o Grace on 21 Feb 1872 at Acc by R David

SCARBOROUGH Samuel Col 21 S Farmer Acc Acc s/o Maria to Louisa Floyd Col 16 S Acc Acc d/o Katie on 28 Mar 1875 at Burton's by HT Rich

SCARBOROUGH Samuel Col 50 W Farmer Acc Acc to Rachel Drummond Col 50 S Acc Acc on 6 May 1880 at Deep Ck by RJ Waters

SCARBOROUGH Samuel Jr Col 20 S Farming Acc Acc s/o Samuel & Rachel to Mary Conquest Col 27 S Acc Acc d/o Ellen on 3 May 1874 at Morris Chp by PA Leatherbury

SCARBOROUGH Thomas J 20 S Farmer Acc Acc s/o Bennett W & Margt to Fannie M Humphreys 23 S Acc Acc d/o Joshua E & Elizth S on 19 Nov 1873 near Oak Grove Ch by LK LeCato

SCARBOROUGH Thomas J 23 W

Farmer Acc Acc s/o Bennitt W & Anne to Virginia F West 19 S Acc Acc d/o William & Emily on 18 Oct 1876 at Acc by RC Jones

SCORAH Frederick J 28 S Engineer Liverpool England Philadelphia PA s/o Jno Wm & Eliza C to Josephine Cropper 22 S Acc Acc d/o Wm F R & Mary E on 16 Dec 1895 at Chinco: Isld by RI Watkins

SCOTT Albert J 23 S Farmer Acc Acc s/o Thomas & Caroline to Sallie W Marshall 18 S Acc Acc d/o Salathiel & Maggie A on 5 Nov 1893 at Acc by JL King

SCOTT Alfred T 17 S Farmer Acc Acc s/o Wallas & Melinda to Mary A Taylor 16 S Acc Acc d/o Edwd & Sally S on 24 May 1866 at Acc by P Warren

SCOTT B F 42 W Oysterman N'hamp: Chinco: Isld s/o Charles & Margaret to Mary Jane [Clarke] Clark 25 S Atlantic Co NJ Chinco: Isld d/o Thomas & Elizth on 5 Jun 1880 at Chinco: Isld by WP Thornton

SCOTT David 38 W Farmer Acc Acc s/o Major & Mahala to Ida Fox 23 S Acc Acc d/o James & Nellie on 21 Jun 1882 near Onancock by PA Leatherbury

SCOTT David W 28 S Farmer Acc Acc s/o Major & Mahala to Peggy Fox 27 S Acc Acc d/o James & Nellie on 6 Sep 1871 at Reese Ch by ST Ferguson

SCOTT Francis E 22 S Farmer Acc Acc s/o Walter W & Margaret S to Malissa H Wright 27 S Acc Acc d/o Charles & Margaret on 26 Oct 1892 at Acc by SU Grimsley

SCOTT George T 21 S Farmer Acc Acc s/o James & Elizabeth to Susan Hargis 16 S Acc Acc d/o Belle S Ames on 14 Jun 1885 near Onancock by PA Leatherbury

SCOTT George T 25 S Farmer Acc Acc s/o John A & Polly E to Mamie Emily Lewis 18 S Acc Acc d/o Leonidas & Sally H on 4 Sep 1887 at bride's home by JW Norris

SCOTT Henry T 30 S Salesman Acc Chinco: Isld s/o Thos & Mary to Jane Booth 21 S Chinco: Isld Chinco: Isld d/o Wm & Elizabeth on 17 Jun 1878 at Chinco: Isld by R Williamson

SCOTT James to Elizabeth Bishop d/o Henry dec'd & ward/o Charles Mason who gave consent lic: 14 Feb 1854

SCOTT James 19 S Farmer Acc Acc s/o James E & Elizabeth to Arinthia Watkinson 17 S Acc Acc d/o Levin & Sally on 28 Nov 1880 at Acc C H by JG Anderson

SCOTT James Edward (W) 21 S House Carpenter Onancock Onancock s/o James S & Hester A to Mary Ann Poulson 24 S Onancock Onancock d/o John H & Eliza on 24 Aug 1859 near Onancock by D Titlow

SCOTT James H 30 S Sailor Acc Acc s/o James E & Mary A to Maggie A Drummond 30 S Acc Acc d/o Richard & Susan on 26 Oct 1892 at Acc by AC Berryman

SCOTT John A 23 S Mariner b: Acc s/o Jno & Tabitha to Polly Lewis 24 S b: Acc d/o Major & Elizth on 29 Jul 1858 at r/o Jno Hall by ES Grant (George L Rew says both over 21)

SCOTT John David 22 S Oysterman Acc Acc s/o Nancy to Cora E Givens 18 S Acc Acc d/o Benjamin B & Clara J on 28 Mar 1888 at Onancock by JW Easley

SCOTT John J 22 S Farmer Acc Acc s/o Geo Robert & Margt J to Lucy E Lawson 19 S Som Co MD Acc d/o John J & Hattie E on 27 Nov 1895 at Acc by HS Dulany

SCOTT John N 35 W Merchant N'hamp: N'hamp: s/o John T P & Virginia to Laura E [Killmon]

Killman 23 S Acc Acc d/o Thos & Laura on 22 Nov 1893 at Acc by JET Ewell

SCOTT John R 40 W Farmer b: Acc s/o Polly to Sally [Stephens] Stevens 40 S b: Acc d/o John & Ann on 23 Apr 1856 at Acc by JH Addison (Major Rayfield says both over 21)

SCOTT John T 26 S s/o John to Arinthia J Lankford 18 S d/o Selby & Margaret lic: 22 Mar 1865 marr: 23 Mar 1865

SCOTT John W 27 S Shoemaker Acc Acc s/o Geo & Sally to Margaret Read 17 S Acc Acc d/o Sanuel & Elizth on 5 Dec 1866 at Acc by JH Addison

SCOTT John W 18 S Farmer Acc Acc s/o Tully & Tabitha to Sarah Guy 18 S Acc Acc d/o Wm & Susan on 20 Dec 1868 at Acc by JH Addison

SCOTT John W 24 W Waterman Acc Acc s/o Tully & Tabitha to Mary C [Reed] Read 19 S Acc Acc d/o Samuel & Catharine on 29 Jan 1873 near Onancock by PA Leatherbury

SCOTT Luther D 22 S Sailor Acc Acc s/o James E & Mary A to Manie E Crockett 16 S Acc Acc d/o Thomas W & Cordelia on 8 Oct 1890 at Onancock by RA Compton

SCOTT Luther J 38 W Waterman Acc Acc s/o John H & Eliza to Kate M Beloate 36 W Acc Acc d/o Jas H & Susan Hurst on 26 Dec 1893 near Onancock by PA Leatherbury

SCOTT Major S 25 S Sailor Acc Acc s/o John H & Eliza to Ellen Johnson 16 S Acc Acc d/o Joshua & Rachel on 23 Apr 1875 at Deep Ck by PA Leatherbury

SCOTT Obed D 22 S Sailor Acc Acc s/o William D & Nervilla to Minnie C Fletcher 16 S Acc Acc d/o Eliz'th S on 29 Nov 1893 at Locust Mount by JWA Elliott

SCOTT Oswald T 26 S Farmer Acc Acc s/o Thomas & Caroline to Virginia Powell 22 S Acc Acc d/o William & Amanada on 27 May 1894 at Mappsville by JL King

SCOTT Robert 30 S Sailor Acc Acc s/o Major & Mahala to Maggie Melson 22 S Acc Acc d/o John R & Catharine on 9 Aug 1871 at Acc by J Carroll

SCOTT Shalmanezer 22 S Farmer Acc Acc s/o Walter & Melinda to Margaret Fosque 22 S Acc Acc d/o James & Emma on 24 Feb 1874 near Locustville by LK LeCato

SCOTT Thomas 45 W Farmer Acc Acc to Caroline Showard 25 S Acc Acc on 10 Jan 1866 at Acc by P Warren

SCOTT Thomas C 21 S Shoemaker Acc Acc s/o Tully & Tabitha to Henrietta Guy 19 S Acc Acc d/o Jno W & Susan on 15 Nov 1865 at Acc by D Titlow

SCOTT Thomas C 27 W Shoemaker Acc Acc s/o Tully B & Tabitha to Elizabeth P Parker 24 S Acc Acc d/o James & Susan on 19 Jun 1871 at Onancock by J Carroll

SCOTT Thomas D 30 S Mariner Acc Acc s/o Major & Mahola to Sally C Salisbury 1875 near Onancock by PA Leatherbury

SCOTT Tully J 24 S Farmer Acc Acc s/o Jno A & Polly E to Sudie A Ayres 26 S Acc Acc d/o Levin R & Susan M on 12 Nov 1884 at Acc by IG Fosnocht

SCOTT Tully P 28 S Oysterman Acc Acc s/o John H & Eliza to Hennie Elizth Johnson 21 S Smith Isld MD Acc d/o Joshua & Rachel Johnson on 14 May 1873 at Deep Ck by PA Leatherbury

SCOTT Tully W 24 S Carpenter Acc Acc s/o Tully & Tabitha to Rachel W Harrison 19 S Acc Acc d/o James & Margaret on 30 Oct 1878 at Slugtkill Nk by JH Amiss

SCOTT Walter W 25 S Shoemaker Acc Acc s/o Walter & Milinda to Margt S Walker 19 S Acc Acc d/o Levin & Eliza on 8 Mar 1868 at Acc by ES Grant

SCOTT Washington 30 S Sailor Acc Acc s/o Geo W & Eliz to Elizth Charnock 18 S Acc Acc d/o William on 15 Dec 1880 at Pungo: by CC Wertenbaker

SCOTT Wellington M 25 S Shoemaker Acc Acc s/o Geo & Betsy to Bettie S Drummond 18 S Acc Acc d/o Richd T & Susan on 4 Dec 1878 at Andrew Chp by SC Boston

SCOTT Willard F 23 S Operator Acc Acc s/o John T & Arinthia J to Annie K [Burch] Birch 22 S Acc Acc d/o James T & Sally on 15 Apr 1891 near Temp'ville by WF Hayes

SCOTT William 24 S Farmer Acc Acc s/o Jas & Hester Ann to Nervilla Smith 16 S Acc Acc d/o John & Lizzie on 22 Nov 1865 at Acc by P Warren

SCOTT William D 20 S Farmer Acc Acc s/o James E & Elizabeth to Lottie W Watkinson 18 S Acc Acc d/o Levin & Sally on 12 Jan 1890 at Drum'tn by WJ Twilley

SCOTT William H 24 S Farmer Acc Acc s/o Tully & Tabitha to Delila Crosley 23 S Acc Acc d/o Thomas & Mary on 21 Apr 1875 at Slugtkill Nk by JH Amiss

SCOTT William J 26 S Farmer Acc Acc s/o John Thos & Caroline to Martha F Young 20 S Acc Acc d/o William T & Mary W on 1 Feb 1888 at Mappsville by WA Street

SCOTT William T 26 S US Life Saving Service N'hamp: Acc s/o B F & Pauline Ann to Mrina Adams 26 S Acc Acc d/o Wm J & Lizzie on 8 Aug 1889 at r/o Major Jones' by BP Truitt

SCOTT Wm T Col 34 S Laborer Nansemond Co Acc s/o Venice to Mary Brickhouse Col 22 S Acc Acc d/o Esther on 20 Aug 1876 at Belle Haven by RH Govans

SCOTT Wm T 21 S Acc Chinco: Isld s/o Benj F & Leah to Roxilla [Burch] Birch 17 S Chinco: Isld Chinco: Isld d/o Thos L & Anna on 15 Sep 1883 at Chinco: Isld by EH Miller

SEBRA Joseph 22 S Waterman b: N'hamp: s/o William to Emiline Susan Hart 18 S b: Slutkill Nk d/o James & Mary on 20 Jun 1855 at Onancock by J Allen

SEDGEWICK Alexander F 35 W Sawyer Sussex Co DE Acc s/o Joseph & Sally to Lizzie A Wright 30 S Mecklenburg Co Acc d/o James & Amanda on 27 Dec 1894 at Pungo: by JR Griffith

SELBY Albert P 24 S Acc Acc s/o Albert P & Margt J to Mary E Payne 21 S Acc Acc d/o Edwd L & Elizth on 7 Jan 1878 at Temp'ville Par by JB Merritt

SELBY George Col 40 S Millwright Acc Acc to Eliza Blake Col 30 S Acc Acc on 26 Apr 1885 near New Church by JC Cluff

SELBY James Col 28 S Oysterman Snow Hill MD Chinco: Isld s/o Colmore Spence to Charlotte Hornenton Col 21 S Snow Hill MD Chinco: Isld d/o Leah on 4 May 1879 at Chinco: Isld by R Williamson

SELBY John H 41 S Farmer Acc Acc s/o Wm H to Virginia Mason 31 S Acc Acc d/o Stephen on 12 Dec 1886 at Acc by JR Strugis

SELBY John O 33 S Acc Acc s/o Outten to Emily F Marshall 19 S Acc Acc d/o Solomon & Elizabeth on 22 May 1871 at Solomon Marshall's by WT Wilkerson

SELBY McHenry Col 26 S Sailor Acc Acc s/o Sarah to Mary L Snead Col 24 S Acc Acc d/o Sally on 7 Oct

SERVIES Grifford 24 S Sailor NJ Acc s/o Job & Anna to Mary E Sharpley 20 S Acc Acc d/o Jno T & Susannah on 26 May 1881 at Chinco: Isld by OS Walton

SEYMOUR Ephraim Col 26 S Farmer Acc Acc s/o William & Rosa to Mary Glenn Col 25 S Acc Acc d/o Louis & Hettie on 21 Dec 1890 at Acc by N Morris

SEYMOUR George Col 22 S Wage-earner Acc Acc s/o Clarissa to Etta [Connor] Conner Col 17 S Acc Acc d/o Harriet on 1 Jan 1893 at Acc by BJ Hargarves

SEYMOUR Hugh Gordon Col 22 S Laborer Acc Acc s/o Clarissa to Annie Franklin Col 20 S NC Acc d/o Thos & Rachel Hanes on 3 May 1883 at Drum'tn by LW Lee

SEYMOUR James Col 22 S Farmer Acc Acc s/o Tabby Young to Susan White Col 22 S Acc Acc d/o Rachel on 5 Dec 1883 at Acc by AJ Satchell

SEYMOUR Thos Col 21 S Farmer Acc Acc s/o Abraham & Tabbie to Marg't Sarah Harmon Col 16 S Acc Acc d/o William & Tinney on 6 Sep 1891 at Savageville by JH Offer

SEYMOUR William A Col 23 S Farmer Acc Acc s/o Abraham & Tabitha to Elizabeth Floyd Col 22 S Acc Acc d/o John & Catherine on 26 Mar 1890 near Savageville by JB Lewis

SEYMOUR Wm Col 40 S Farmer Acc Acc s/o Molly to Rosa Warner Col 49 S Acc Acc d/o Arintha on 3 Nov 1877 at White Marsh by JK Plato

SEYMOUR Wm Henry Col 23 S Farmer Acc Acc s/o Wm & Rose to Juliet Harmon Col 17 S Acc Acc d/o Tiney on 6 Jun 1886 at Locust Mount by JWA Elliott

SHARPLEY John O 20 S Merchant Chinco: Isld Chinco: Isld s/o Parker & Mary to Matilda [Dazy] Daisey 17 S Chinco: Isld Chinco: Isld d/o James & Matilda on 8 Oct 1855 at r/o Parker Bowdin by P Bowdin

SHARPLEY Joshua T 29 S Ship Carpenter Wor Co MD Acc s/o Wm J M & Sarah E to Minnie H Gibb 23 S Acc Acc d/o Thomas B C & Henrietta on 28 Apr 1891 at Greenback by RS Williamson

SHARPLEY Luke 21 S Oysterman Acc Acc s/o Teagle & Fanny to Rebecca A Jester 19 S Acc Acc d/o Kindal & Betsy on 6 Dec 1874 at my house by P Bowdin

SHARPLEY William John 22 S Oysterman Acc Acc s/o John W & Elizabeth to Nancy Andrews 22 S Acc Acc d/o Joseph & Nancy on 5 Dec 1888 at Chinco: Isld by SU Grimsley

SHARPLEY Wm John 27 W Oysterman Chinco: Chinco: s/o John W & Eliz'th to Lydia A Thornton 18 S Chinco: Chinco: d/o Wm H & Hester M on 21 Feb 1892 at Chinco: Isld by JW Turner

SHAW George 23 S Oysterman Acc Acc s/o Wm & Tabitha to Flora E Crockett 16 S Acc Acc d/o John & Rachel A on 2 Oct 1892 at Acc by RB Scott

SHAW Wm [Shaws] 28 S Sailor Acc Acc to Tabitha Martin 18 S Acc Acc d/o Geo & Elizth on 5 Dec 1866 at Acc by JE Bundick

SHAY Custis to Emma Stant d/o John who gave consent lic: 30 Mar 1859 John J Bloxom says he over 21

SHAY George L 22 S Farmer Acc Acc s/o William & Annie to Ella Godwin 18 S Acc Acc d/o Julius A & Adaline on 21 Dec 1892 at Pocomoke M E Ch So by RB Scott

SHAY John W T 24 S Farmer Acc Acc s/o Teackle & Eliza to Oceasina [Marriner] Mariner 18 S Acc Acc d/o George & Elizth on 5 Feb 1878 near

Atlantic P O by TM Poulson
SHAY William 49 W Farmer Acc Acc s/o Elijah & Rebecca to Sallie Hancock 35 W Acc Acc d/o Shepherd Bunting on 17 May 1892 at Acc by RB Scott
SHELTON Fostner Col 24 S Laborer Patrick Co VA Acc s/o Fortner & Amanda to Tiney Parker Col 21 S Acc Acc d/o Tabitha Seymour on 2 Aug 1885 at Drum'tn by LW Lee
SHEPHERD Irving 54 W Farmer MD Acc s/o Elijah & Dollie to Sarah Marshall 40 W DE Acc d/o Jno & Elizth Davis on 17 Dec 1884 at Atlantic by A Woodyard
SHEPHERD John H 23 S Farmer New Castle on Tyne Acc s/o Benj & Annie to Susan Heath 27 S Acc Acc d/o Jno D & Peggy on 17 Mar 1886 at Acc C H by W Chinn
SHEVERS Edward H 23 S Farmer NJ Acc s/o John & M A to M L Massey 18 S Acc Acc d/o Jno & Maria Z V on 11 Dec 1878 at Horntown by M Oldham
SHIELD Augustus [Shields] Col 30 S Laborer Acc Acc s/o Levin & Jane to Annie Major Col 23 S Acc Acc d/o George Major & Charlotte Bayly on 17 Aug 1887 at Onancock by JEW Moore
SHIELD Benjamin W 34 S Merchant Acc Acc s/o Asa & Elizth to Manie Johnson 24 S Acc Acc d/o Wm J & Margaret B on 3 Jun 1885 at Acc by A Woodyard
SHIELD Dennis Col 56 W Painter Acc Acc to Amy Downing Col 41 W Acc Acc on 7 Jul 1872 near Pungo: by WA Clayton
SHIELD Edmund Col 52 S Farmer Acc Acc s/o Louisa to Sarah Burton Col 49 S Acc Acc d/o Harriet on 9 Jun 1891 at Acc by N Morris
SHIELD George Henry [Shields] Col 22 S Laborer Acc Acc s/o Isaac Shields & Arena LeCato to Juliet Edmonds Col 22 S Acc Acc d/o Perry Edmonds & Leah Turner on 2 Oct 1887 at Acc by L Duncan
SHIELD Isaac 30 S Lawyer Acc Acc s/o Patience to Mary Perkins 30 S Acc Acc d/o Lizzie on 7 Jun 1868 at Acc by JE Humphreys
SHIELD Jacob 27 S Farmer Acc Acc s/o Lousia to Georgeanna Garrison 24 S Acc Acc d/o Resiah on 3 Jul 1881 at St Luke Ch by PM Lewis
SHIELD James B [Shields] 20 S Farmer Acc Acc s/o Jesse J & Parcilia to Martha E Bunting 17 S Acc Acc d/o Jacob C & Mary on 10 Jan 1882 at Piney Forks by SC Boston
SHIELD Jerusalem [Shields] Col 25 S Farmer Acc Acc s/o Edmond & Sarah to Mary Susan Mears 25 S Acc Acc d/o Letitia on 25 Dec 1895 at Acc by JN Waters
SHIELD Jesse 24 S Carpenter Acc Acc s/o James & Elizabeth to Pamelia Badger 21 S Acc Acc d/o James Badger & Charlott James & (ward/o John Ward who gave consent) on 15 May 1860 at r/o L K LeCato by LK LeCato
SHIELD John [Shields] Col 20 S Wage-earner Acc Acc s/o Isaac & Mary to Annie [Sommers] Summers Col 22 S Acc Acc d/o Asia Ferby on 20 Sep 1889 at Belle Haven by JE Humphreys
SHIELD Littleton A [Shields] 22 S Merchant Acc Acc s/o Peter E & Virginia to Emma L Warner 23 S Acc Acc d/o Solomon & Arinthia D on 27 Dec 1891 at Messongo Bridge by JL King
SHIELD Peter (black) 31 S Laborer Acc Acc to Harriet Finney Col 35 S Acc Acc on 30 Mar 1872 near Towers's Store by N Morris
SHIELD Thomas S [Shields] Col 24 S Wage-earner Acc Acc s/o Susan to

Annie Sample Col 22 S Acc Acc d/o Nellie West on 13 Sep 1893 near Savageville by JH Offer

SHIVES Alfred A 22 S Farmer NJ Acc s/o John & Mary A to Willianna Fields 18 S Acc Acc d/o Wm B & Mary J on 2 Feb 1876 at Horntown by IT Adkins

SHORES Charles S 22 S Sailor Acc Acc s/o Gabriel & Amelia to Ida J Marshall 17 S Acc Acc d/o William & Melissa on 2 May 1892 at Tangier by ZH Webster

SHORES Petty F 18 S Sailor Acc Acc s/o Babel & Amelia to Mary Crockett 21 S Acc Acc d/o David & Jane on 26 Aug 1876 at Tangier Isld by RC Jones

SHORES Solomon S 22 S Waterman Acc Acc s/o Gabriel & Nellie to Phoebe Laird 20 S Acc Acc d/o John T & Zippora on 20 Aug 1892 at Tangier by ZH Webster

SHORES William A 18 S Oysterman Acc Acc s/o Bobet & Pamelia to Catharine Dies 17 S Acc Acc d/o John & Ann on 10 Sep 1874 at Tangier Isld by RC Jones

SHORT Alfred W 32 S Teacher Sussex Co DE Acc s/o Wm & Annie Short to Alice C Mason 19 S Acc Acc d/o Thorogood & Elizabeth on 12 Mar 1876 near Guilford by M Oldham

SHORT James R 41 W Travelling Salesman Westmoreland Co Baltimore City MD s/o Benj F & Mary J to Edith M Leatherbury 21 S Acc Acc d/o Perry A & Leah A on 16 Nov 1892 at Onancock by EC Atkins

SHOWARD Alfred W 23 S Laborer Acc Acc to Martha Lewis 22 S Acc Acc on 23 Dec 1869 at Onancock by JC Martin

SHOWARD Alfred W 27 W Farmer Acc Acc to Laura Payne 25 W Acc Acc d/o Edward Mason on 25 Dec 1878 at Horntown by JW Hundley

SHOWARD Alfred W 39 W Merchant Acc Acc s/o Wm & Sally to Martha Green 20 S Baltimore MD Acc d/o Chas A & Mary on 12 Apr 1886 at Oak Hall by DM Wallace

SHOWARD George 21 S Sailor Acc Acc to Rose Caruthers 40 W Acc Acc d/o Zadock & Betsy Lewis on 29 Mar 1866 at Acc by JH Addison

SHOWARD Joseph C 32 S Laborer Acc Acc to Rose Underhill 45 W Acc Acc d/o Elijah & Margaret Wright on 30 Nov 1882 at Acc by SC Boston

SHOWARD Levin 21 S Laborer Acc Acc to Margaret E Crowson 20 S Acc Acc d/o Levin & Maria on 14 Jan 1877 at Slutkill Nk by JH Amiss

SHOWELL John D 21 S Farmer Berlin MD Berlin MD s/o Wm & Mary to Bettie R West 22 S Acc Acc d/o Richard & Sally on 10 Jun 1885 near Guilford by JW Hundley

SHRIEVES Augustus D [Shreives] 20 S Oysterman Acc Acc s/o Wm of Wm & Caroline to Emma C Russell 25 S Acc Acc d/o Geo T & Mary on 7 Jan 1883 at Acc by WA Crouse

SHRIEVES Bowdin 22 S Farming Acc Acc s/o Wm & Jane to Mary A Hickman 22 S Acc Acc d/o Robt & Ann on 29 Dec 1870 at Acc by JET Ewell

SHRIEVES Edward C 22 S Farmer Acc Acc s/o Wm & Jane to Susan Barnes 21 S Acc Acc d/o Alfred & Mary on 21 Jun 1883 at Drum'tn by SC Boston

SHRIEVES Eldredge T 24 S Oysterman Acc Acc s/o John Thos & Marg't to Annie B Twiford 14 S Acc Acc d/o George D & Eliz'th on 28 Dec 1892 at Acc by HJ Wilson

SHRIEVES Hanson F 21 S Sailor Acc Acc s/o William & Susan to Maggie S Russell 22 S Acc Acc d/o George T & Mary on 13 Aug 1890 at

Marriages

SHRIEVES Henry [Shreaves] 21 S Farmer Acc Acc s/o Wm & Jane to Nannie W Onley 19 S Acc Acc d/o Edwd T & Sally on 25 Dec 1879 at Modest Town by JW Hundley

SHRIEVES Henry F 20 S Oysterman Acc Acc s/o John T & Margaret to Cora L Barnes 18 S Acc Acc d/o Wm J & Nettie on 6 Jan 1895 at Acc by JET Ewell

SHRIEVES James T 25 S Laborer Acc Acc s/o George & Hetty to Mary T Barnes 17 S Acc Acc d/o Samuel & Lydia on 2 Dec 1869 at Guilford by JET Ewell

SHRIEVES Jno T 23 S Waterman Acc Acc s/o Wm & Jane to Margt A Silverthorn 20 S Acc Acc d/o Sanl & Mary on 22 Oct 1863 at Acc by ES Grant

SHRIEVES John 21 S Sailor Acc Acc s/o Wm & Sarah to Virginia Justice 18 S Acc Acc d/o Wm & Sally on 31 Dec 1863 at Acc by ES Grant

SHRIEVES John 25 S Shoemaker Acc Acc s/o Abram to Fannie Savage 18 S Acc Acc d/o Littl & Cath on 20 Dec 1868 at Acc by JH Addison

SHRIEVES John E 21 S Farming Acc Acc s/o Savage to Dorothea Hope 18 S Acc Acc d/o Wm L & Jane on 10 Oct 1872 at Modest Town by JET Ewell

SHRIEVES John E [Shreives] 19 S Farmer Acc Acc s/o Jno & Elizth to Lovey T Gray 21 S Acc Acc d/o Jas & Elizth on 13 Apr 1881 at Onancock by LE Barrett

SHRIEVES Lewis [Shreaves] 23 S Sailor Acc Acc to Nancy Northam 18 S Acc Acc d/o H B on 28 Feb 1862 at Acc by JC Mears

SHRIEVES Lewis L 33 W Mariner Acc Acc s/o Wm & Polly to Euphemia C Marshall 22 S Acc Acc d/o Stephen & Patience on 24 May 1877 near Parksley by HS Dulany

Modest Town by DA Woodson

SHRIEVES Louis F 22 S Farmer Acc Acc s/o Wm & Jane to Susan Lilliston 17 S Acc Acc d/o Natalia on 5 Jan 1868 at Acc by ES Grant

SHRIEVES Michael [Shreves] Col 22 S Farmer Acc Acc s/o Southey & Sarah to Mary Laws Col 19 S Acc Acc d/o Arilla on 14 Jan 1890 near Temp'ville by JC Cluff

SHRIEVES Saml R 35 S Farmer Acc Acc s/o Abram & Lavinia to Maggie Killman 33 S Acc Acc d/o Saml & Katy on 10 Jan 1878 at Pungo Ch by CC Wertenbaker

SHRIEVES Sidney B 23 S Waterman Acc Acc s/o William & Caroline to Sallie R Lewis 19 S Acc Acc d/o James T & Mary on 9 Jun 1889 at Bloxom Sta by WF Hayes

SHRIEVES Southley [Shreaves] Col 39 S Farmer Acc Acc s/o Charlotte Wimbrough to Sarah Northam Col 38 S Acc Acc d/o Hester on 25 Dec 1879 at Modest Town by A Joynes

SHRIEVES Thaddeus W 21 S Oysterman Acc Acc s/o William & Caroline to Dany H (Damey) Trader 22 S Acc Acc d/o William & Nancy on 21 Dec 1871 at Hunting Ck by J Carroll

SHRIEVES Thomas 23 S Farmer Acc Acc s/o Wm S & Tabitha to Bettie A Mason 16 S Acc Acc d/o Zadoc & Leah on 6 Jan 1870 at Acc by JET Ewell

SHRIEVES Tully [Shrives] 22 S Waterman Acc Acc s/o Wm & Caroline to Mary E Russell 24 S Acc Acc d/o Geo T & Mary on 8 May 1878 near Woodstock by FH Mullineaux

SHRIEVES William [Shreives] 22 S Farmer Acc Acc s/o William & Jane to Polly Dix 20 S Acc Acc d/o Thomas of Geo & Margaret on 26 Dec 1869 at r/o Thomas Dix by JET

Ewell

SHRIEVES William J [Shreeves] 21 S Waterman Acc Acc s/o James H & Margaret S to Bettie S Rew 18 S Acc Acc d/o Jesse K & Sarah C on 25 Dec 1889 at Onancock by GW Burke

SHRIEVES William M [Sheaves] 20 S Oysterman Acc Acc s/o John & Elizth to Maggy Gray 18 S Acc Acc d/o James & Elizth on 9 Dec 1869 at Acc by JET Ewell

SHRIEVES William S [Sheaves] 21 S Waterman Acc Acc s/o John T & Margaret to Mary C Mason 17 S Acc Acc d/o Edward P & Susan on 29 Dec 1892 at Acc by HJ Wilson

SHRIEVES William T [Sheaves] 21 S Waterman Acc Acc s/o James H & Mary to Mary A Young 25 S Acc Acc d/o George & Susan on 13 Jan 1895 at Acc by DGC Butts

SHRIEVES Wm T [Shreves] 22 S Waterman Acc Acc s/o Wm & Caroline to Marcella Howard 18 S Acc Acc d/o Wm H & Mary E on 20 Dec 1893 at Acc by JET Ewell

SHRIEVES Zadock Otho [Shrevis] 24 S Merchant Acc Acc s/o Thos & Bettie to Louisa Baker 21 S Acc Acc d/o Sam'l & Hester on 4 Dec 1895 at Modest Town by WW Wood

SHRIVER James 25 S Book-keeper Hightstown NY Acc s/o Samuel S & Caroline to Emma Susan Hoffman 19 S Acc Acc d/o William G & Mary E on 28 May 1891 at Acc by JM Anderson

SILVERTHORN Chas H 28 S Farmer Acc Acc s/o John & Sarah to Mary A Taylor 22 W Acc Acc d/o Jesse & Elizth R Hopkins on 9 Dec 1868 at Acc by GW Matthews

SILVERTHORN Chas H 37 W Acc Acc s/o John & Sarah to Jeanie Pitchard 22 S MD Acc d/o Lamuel & Anna on 10 Oct 1877 at Atlantic P O by CC Wertenbaker

SILVERTHORN Edward T 22 S Sailor Acc Acc s/o Saml & Mary to Sallie Justice 18 S Acc Acc d/o Revel & Nancy on 23 Nov 1871 at Acc by ST Ferguson

SILVERTHORN John C 26 S Mechanic Acc Acc s/o Samuel & Mary to Emma A Barnes 18 S Acc Acc d/o John & Sally on 5 May 1870 at Guilford by JET Ewell

SILVERTHORN John D 30 S Oysterman Acc Acc s/o John W & Sarah A to Marie Ann Meelham 16 S Perth Anboy NJ Acc d/o George on 5 Feb 1873 near Horntown by WT Wilkerson

SILVERTHORN John W 22 S Oysterman Acc Acc s/o John C & Emma to Addie S Williams 18 S Acc Acc d/o Thomas H & Margaret on 10 Jan 1894 at Acc by JET Ewell

SILVERTHORN Winfield S 32 S Oysterman Acc Acc s/o Elizth to Lillie A Anderton 16 S Acc Acc d/o Edwd H & Elizth on 25 Dec 1879 at Mr Anderton's by JW Hilldrup

SIMPKINS Charles Col 21 S Day Laborer Acc Acc to Ellen Martin Col 25 S Acc Acc d/o Charlotte on 13 Jan 1886 at Acc by P Sheppard

SIMPKINS George W Col 23 S Wage-earner Acc Acc s/o Isaac & Susan to Susie Bayly Col 18 S Acc Acc d/o Mason & Mary on 27 Nov 1895 at Acc by T Turlington

SIMPKINS William Col 25 S Laborer Acc Acc s/o Lewsy to Sarah Satchell Col 21 S Acc Acc d/o Hettie Kerr on 4 Jul 1880 at Mrs H Negab's by PM Lewis

SIMPSON John A 25 S Oysterman Acc Acc s/o Richard F to Malvina Hart 25 S Acc Acc d/o Richd on 8 Jan 1863 at Acc by GH Ewell

SIMPSON Reuben 32 S Laborer Acc Acc s/o Charles & Betsy to Jane Berry 28 S Acc Acc d/o Charles &

Margaret on 23 Jun 1870 at New Town by JET Ewell

SIMPSON Revel J 23 S Oysterman Acc Acc s/o Hetty to Mary White 19 S Acc Acc d/o William on 31 Dec 1862 at Acc by GH Ewell

SIMPSON Revel J 33 D Oysterman Acc Acc s/o Hetty to Ellen Marshall 23 S Acc Acc d/o Robt & Eliza on 15 Jul 1873 near Bethel Ch by JE Bundick

SIMPSON Southey 23 S Farmer Acc Acc s/o Chas to Mary Showard 19 S Acc Acc d/o Sally on 1 Jan 1863 at Acc by GH Ewell

SIMPSON Southey 35 W Farmer Acc Acc to Margaret Mears 35 D Acc Acc d/o Arthur on 8 Sep 1870 at Acc by JET Ewell

SIMPSON Thomas 25 S Farm Labor Acc Acc s/o Elizabeth to Troy Brown Lilliston 22 S Acc Acc d/o Mahala A on 25 Dec 1880 at Acc C H by JG Anderson

SIMPSON William (Jr) 38 S Farmer Acc Acc s/o Chas & Betsy to Margt A Simpson 28 S Acc Acc d/o Wm & Elishea on 13 Oct 1865 at Acc by ES Grant

SINGLETON William J 27 W Farmer Acc Acc s/o William H & Elizabeth to Eva C Bloxom 23 S Acc Acc d/o Thomas H & Phoebe on 18 Dec 1887 at Modest Town by JW Ward

SINGLETON Wm J 25 S Farmer Acc Acc s/o William H & Elizth to Sally W Jacobs 24 S Acc Acc d/o Wm B & Sally on 22 Feb 1882 at Modest Town by MS Read

SLOCOMB Elijah Col 54 S Laborer Acc Acc s/o Agnes to Maria Logan Col 52 S Acc Acc d/o Eliza on 22 Oct 1874 near New Church by S Johns

SLOCOMB John W 29 S Merchant Acc Acc s/o William C & Susan A to Manie Beloate 18 S Acc Acc d/o James L & Mary on 11 Jul 1894 at Onancock by GE Booker

SLOCOMB Samuel B 25 S Farmer Acc Acc s/o Thos & Sallie E to Ella F Taylor 21 S Acc Acc d/o Goodwin & Sallie on 9 Jan 1883 at Oak Hall by RB Beadles

SLOCOMB Thos H 30 S Merchant Acc Acc s/o Thomas & Sallie E to Margt Blanche Johnson 27 S Acc Acc d/o Horce J (of J) & Marg't on 18 Nov 1891 at Acc by WW Wood

SMALL Arsemus 35 W Oysterman Acc Acc s/o Handy & Maria to Betsy Colonna 35 S Acc Acc d/o James on 25 Sep 1870 at r/o E T Ewell by JET Ewell (David Mason said she over 21)

SMALL James S 21 S Waterman Acc Acc s/o Marcellus & Sally to Arinthia J Marshall 21 S Acc Acc d/o Parker & Comfort on 29 Dec 1889 at Acc by JW Ward

SMALL Jno 24 S Farmer b: Acc s/o Stewart to Susan Lewis 20 S b: Acc d/o Edward & Francis on 20 Jan 1859 at Reese Chp by ES Grant (Alfred Bundick says he is over 21)

SMALL John J 31 S Farmer Acc Acc s/o Solomon & Sally to Sallie Linton 21 S Acc Acc d/o Elias & Charlotte on 11 May 1871 near New Church by TM Poulson

SMALL Orsemores (Orseymous) 23 S Waterman b: Acc s/o Handy & Maria to Amanda Hickman 25 S b: Acc d/o Richd & Polly on 25 Oct 1858 near Reese Chp by ES Grant (George S Rew says both over 21)

SMALL Sebastian 21 S Oysterman Messongo Messongo s/o Solomon to Sally Ann Chesser 21 S Messongo Messongo d/o Sallie on 4 Jan 1865 at r/o James Toppin by GH Ewell

SMALL William H 20 S Farmer Acc Acc s/o Sabastain & Sally to Ella Gladding 16 S Acc Acc d/o Oliver J & Danvers J on 9 Feb 1890 at Bethel

Ch by JE Bundick

SMITH Abraham Col 42 W Farmer Acc Acc s/o Abraham & Ann to Henrietta Jubilee Col 35 W Acc Acc d/o Thos & Peggy Hack on 20 Oct 1869 at Acc by JE Humphreys

SMITH Albert F 24 S Farmer Acc Acc s/o Ralph & Nancy to Mary Jane Lewis 21 S Acc Acc d/o Danil & Eliz on 9 Jul 1863 at Acc by ES Grant

SMITH Alexander H 22 S Waterman Acc Acc s/o James H & Sally F to Willie A Scott 21 S Acc Acc d/o Thomas & Caroline on 11 Aug 1895 at Acc by JL King

SMITH Alfred Col 22 S Wage-earner Acc Acc to Bettie LeCato Col 20 S Acc Acc d/o George & Arrina on 4 Dec 1892 at Bells Neck by M Nichols

SMITH Benjamin Col 23 S Farmer Acc Acc s/o Dina to Sarah Smith Col 21 S Acc Acc d/o Henry on 27 Dec 1874 at Belle Haven by R Davis

SMITH Charles Col 29 S Farmer Acc Acc s/o Arena to Elizabeth Channer Col 30 S Acc Acc d/o Mary on 6 Dec 1876 at Acc by JK Plato

SMITH Charles 21 S Farmer Acc Acc s/o William to Amecrica H East 16 S Acc Acc d/o Wm L & Elizth on 12 Apr 1882 at Onancock by SC Boston

SMITH Charles 22 S Sailor Acc Acc s/o Wm & Sally to Emily L Thornton 17 S Acc Acc d/o Wm Thornton of W & Emeline Ailworth on 23 Jan 1884 at Oak Hall by RB Beadles

SMITH Charles Col 22 S Wage-earner Acc Acc s/o Julius & Louisa Snead to Ethel [Hateny] Hateney Col 15 S Acc Acc d/o Thomas & Margaret on 11 Feb 1894 at Acc by ET Outen

SMITH Charles S 21 S Merchant Acc Acc s/o Custis & Rose Anna to Lillian O Moore 21 S Acc Acc d/o Laban C & Mary J on 26 Dec 1894 at Jenkins Bridge by HS Simmerman

SMITH Custis to Rose Ann Bunting d/o Shepherd who gave consent lic: 21 Jan 1856 Wm P Brittingham says he over 21

SMITH D R Col 38 S Sailor Brownsville TX Acc s/o John & Maria to Sarah Townsend Col 21 S Stockton MD Acc d/o John & Mary on 29 Aug 1892 at Chinco: Isld by HL Elderdice

SMITH Dixon 22 S Farmer Acc Acc s/o Noah & Susan to Belle Hickman 18 S DE Acc d/o Frank A & Indiana S on 4 Jul 1895 at Acc by JC Watson

SMITH Edgar J 21 S Farmer Acc Acc s/o James & Sarah to Julia A Mears 18 S Acc Acc d/o Alfred J & Leah A on 8 Dec 1875 at Ames Ridge by BW Dougherty

SMITH Edwd 28 S Farmer b: Acc s/o Thos Smith & Ally Kelly to Caty E (Moore) More 24 S b: Acc d/o Thos & Susan More Roilbarday on 18 May 1854 at New Church by T Waters (Purnell Chesser says both over 21)

SMITH Edwin Sumter 32 S Teacher Fanquier Co Bedford City VA s/o Henry & Francine E to Elizabeth Walter Quinby 23 S Acc Acc d/o Upshur B & Georgie G on 28 Jun 1893 at Onancock by AC Berryman

SMITH Erastus S (Seymour) 21 S Oysterman Acc Acc s/o Jas & Sally F to Trephenia J [Bonewell] Bonewell 20 S Acc Acc d/o Geo P & Margt Ann on 21 May 1873 near Messongo by JE Bundick

SMITH Ernest W 22 S Farmer Acc Acc s/o Noah & Susan to Martha Florence Hill 18 S Acc Acc d/o John F & Mary Jane on 25 Dec 1895 at Acc by GD Edmonston

SMITH Francis S 29 S Farmer Acc Acc s/o Hugh G & Margt E to Emma S LeCato 22 S Acc Acc d/o Littleton K & Mary on 26 Jan 1871 at Acc by JE Humphreys

SMITH Geo Col 21 S Farm Laborer Newbern NC Acc to Margaret Ames Col 18 S Acc Acc d/o Jane on 10 Aug 1884 at Acc by TW Nettles

SMITH George 24 S Oysterman Acc Acc s/o Valentine & Betsy to Jenetta Killman 21 S Acc Acc d/o James & Emeline on 30 Apr 1876 at Messongo Nk by JE Bundick

SMITH George Col 23 S Wage-earner Acc Acc s/o Moses Smith & Margaret Floyd to Jennie F Richardson Col 17 S Acc Acc d/o Lot on 23 Nov 1890 at Acc by TW Nettles

SMITH George 27 S Farmer Jersey City NJ Acc s/o Nicholas to Annie Groton 22 S Acc Acc d/o Thomas & Harriet on 6 Feb 1894 at Acc by HL Derby

SMITH George Edward 23 S Carpenter Acc Acc s/o Edmund & Catherine to Elizabeth [Andertson] Anderton 17 S Acc Acc d/o E H on 18 Jun 1890 at Sanford by WF Hayes

SMITH George O 21 S Farmer Acc Acc s/o William H & Virginia S to Annie Coxton 23 S Acc Acc d/o William H & Virginia on 26 Oct 1887 at Drum'tn by J McNabb

SMITH George W 27 S Farmer Acc Acc s/o Geo W & Elizth S to Annie F Guy 19 S Acc Acc d/o Major & Susan on 11 Dec 1879 at Hacks Nk by CC Wertenbaker

SMITH George W Col 36 S Wage-earner Acc Acc s/o Nath'l Rogers & Arena Leatherbury to Rachel Costin Col 28 S Acc Acc on 25 Sep 1889 at Onancock by JH Offer

SMITH George W 27 S Waterman Acc Acc s/o William & Ann to Mary J Watson 19 S Acc Acc d/o David F & Jennie F on 13 Apr 1892 near Belle Haven by T Burton

SMITH Harry Col 28 S Laborer Acc Acc s/o Judy Kellam to Elishea Taylor Col 21 S Acc Acc on 25 Dec 1877 at Modest Town by A Joynes

SMITH Harvey D 23 S Farmer New York City N'hamp: s/o E J & Minnie to Elizabeth Truitt 24 S Acc Acc d/o James & Ellen on 20 Sep 1894 at Eastville by PH Pernell

SMITH Henry 22 S Farmer Acc Acc s/o Lucy Turner to Eliza Smith 21 S Acc Acc d/o Elishia on 25 Dec 1867 at Acc by JH Offer

SMITH Henry Col 25 S Farmer Acc Acc to Fanny West Col 27 S Acc Acc d/o Agnes on 16 Jun 1876 near Craddockville by WH Corbin

SMITH Henry Col 60 S Farmer Acc Acc s/o Sarah to Bridget Rew Col 30 S Acc Acc on 31 Dec 1876 at Belle Haven by RH Govans

SMITH Isaac Col 50 S Farmer Acc Acc s/o Nat West to Frances West Col 48 S Acc Acc d/o James Wise on 9 Oct 1889 at Onancock by GHT Byrd

SMITH Isaac T Col 22 S Farmer Acc Acc s/o Isaac & Frances to Alice E Bayly Col 19 S Acc Acc d/o Susan on 11 Jul 1888 at Acc by JA Haynes

SMITH James 25 S Laborer Acc Acc s/o Elisha to Jane Stokely 21 S Acc Acc d/o Mary on 3 Jan 1869 at Acc by JE Humphreys

SMITH James E 22 S Farmer Acc Acc s/o Ezekiel G & Margaret to Margie S White 18 S Acc Acc d/o Louis & Mary on 29 Jan 1887 at bride's home by RA Compton

SMITH James E 30 S Farmer Acc Acc s/o James T C & Georgie to Macaria J Nottingham 20 S N'hamp: Acc d/o Severn & Lucretia on 25 May 1887 at Jos Bull's by JR Strugis

SMITH James H Col 30 S Laborer Acc Acc to Margaret Armstrong Col 40 S Acc Acc on 8 Jul 1875 at Horntown by S Johns

SMITH James H 21 S Farmer Acc Acc s/o Custis & Rose to Secilia Hall 18

S Acc Acc d/o Thos & Jane on 31 Dec 1879 at Downings Ch by JW Hilldrup

SMITH James Henry 38 S Wheelwright Kent Co DE Acc s/o Wm B & Catharine to Rebecca Bundick 22 S Acc Acc d/o Wm & Eliza on 3 Jan 1877 at Modest Town by DA Woodson

SMITH James T 23 S Seaman Acc Acc s/o James & Sally to Annie C Byrd 20 S Acc Acc d/o Obed S & Hetty C on 31 May 1882 at Conquest Ch by M Oldham

SMITH James T C 27 S Farmer b: Acc s/o John & Elizabeth to Georgianna C Boggs 24 S b: Acc d/o James & Elizabeth on 16 Jan 1856 at Acc by JH Addison (Mitchell W West says both over 21)

SMITH Jno H 33 S Waterman Acc Acc s/o Jas & Sophia to Virginia S Rayfield 18 S Acc Acc d/o Saml & Nancy on 23 Dec 1863 at Acc by D Titlow

SMITH John Col 21 S Farmer Acc Acc s/o Washington & Tersy to Letty Custis Col 19 S Acc Acc d/o Ann on 16 Jan 1873 at Onancock by R Davis

SMITH John Col 24 S Farmer Acc Acc s/o Polly to Emma Sample Col 21 S Acc Acc d/o Peggie on 12 Nov 1893 at Pungo: by JM Anderson

SMITH John Col 23 S Wage-earner Acc Acc s/o Sally Woten to Elizabeth Bayly Col 26 S Acc Acc d/o Lucy Gunter on 15 Oct 1890 at Savageville by JB Lewis

SMITH John T 20 S Farmer Acc Acc s/o William L & Catherine to Effie Julia East 19 S Acc Acc d/o James T & Julia A on 30 Dec 1891 at Acc by JB Pruitt

SMITH John W 23 S Carpenter Acc Acc s/o Geo W & Eliz'th to Bessie Sarah Parker 16 S Acc Acc d/o Thos H & Sarah on 29 Nov 1893 at Acc by EC Atkins

SMITH Joseph A 22 S Farmer Acc Acc s/o Ezekiel Y & Margaret to Alice I Poulson 21 S Acc Acc d/o John W & Elizabeth on 12 Apr 1893 at Onancock by AC Berryman

SMITH Joseph E 22 S Waterman Acc Acc s/o William T & Nicelly to Maggie Linton 20 S Acc Acc d/o John & Margaret on 16 Jul 1893 at Sykes Isld by RB Scott

SMITH Joshua Col 32 S Laborer Acc Acc s/o Hennie to Nicy Ashby Col 30 S Acc Acc d/o Adah on 9 Oct 1881 at Bells Nk by JE Humphreys

SMITH Julius Lee 29 S Farmer Acc Acc s/o Thos & Sally to Manie Drummond 17 S Acc Acc d/o Constantine on 16 Dec 1891 at Mathews Co by JW Nicholson

SMITH Lloyd M 24 S Sailor Acc Acc s/o Zekiel Y & Margaret to Mary E Fisher 20 S Acc Acc d/o G S & Tabitha on 10 Nov 1880 at Hollies Ch by SC Boston

SMITH Nathaniel 52 W Farmer Acc Acc s/o Geo & Elizabeth to Sarah (Mary) Ann Elliott 18 S Acc Acc (ward/o said Nath S Smith) on 29 Sep 1857 near Locust Mount by JW Ewell

SMITH Nathaniel L Col 25 S Wage-earner Acc Acc s/o Nathaniel & Arena to Maria Anna Wise Col 17 S Acc Acc d/o George & Betty on 19 Jun 1892 at Acc by T Turlington

SMITH Nathaniel W Col 48 S Shoemaker Acc Acc s/o Nathaniel & Nicey to Annie Wise Col 37 S Acc Acc d/o Lifco & Leah on 10 Jan 1889 at Onancock by JH Offer

SMITH Noah 25 S Farmer Acc Acc s/o Noah & (Nancy) to Susan Taylor 19 S Acc Acc d/o Asa & (Maria) on 21 Dec 1864 at r/o George H Ewell by GH Ewell

SMITH Parker Col 26 S Laborer Acc

Acc s/o Anna Rogers to Arena Nock Col 38 S Acc Acc d/o Jennie on 1 Oct 1884 at Acc by P Sheppard

SMITH Ralph F 25 S Oysterman Acc Acc s/o Albert F & Mary J to Lola F Evans 15 S Acc Acc d/o Thomas H & Mary on 11 Nov 1891 at Acc by GW Burke

SMITH Richard Col 22 S Laborer Acc Acc s/o Elisha to Rachel Smith Col 22 S Acc Acc d/o Sarah Savage on 9 Sep 1874 at Acc by JE Humphreys

SMITH Samuel 35 S Cordwainer Acc Acc s/o Edwd & Mahala to Frances Colonna 30 S Acc Acc d/o Jas & Charlotte on 20 Jun 1886 at Woodbury by JW Carroll

SMITH Thomas 50 S Laborer to Nancy (Ease) East 50 S lic: 24 Jul 1867

SMITH Thomas Col 70 S Laborer Acc Acc to Frances Martin Col 29 S Acc Acc d/o Charlotte on 9 Feb 1881 in the Public Road by PM Lewis

SMITH Thomas H 26 S Dealer in Oysters Wake Co NC Acc s/o John W & Augusta A to Levenia Andrews 21 S Acc Acc d/o John & Rachel A on 20 Dec 1893 at Temp'ville by JR Tillery

SMITH Thos 26 S Shoemaker b: Acc s/o Thos Smith & Ally Kelly to Sally [Glading] (Gladding) Gladding 22 S b: Acc d/o Geo W Glading & Holly Wheately on 24 Jun 1854 at New Church by T Waters (Michell W Gladding said both over 21)

SMITH Thos Berkeley 37 S Farmer Acc Acc s/o Thomas W & Susan C to Sally M Miles 22 S Acc Acc d/o William H & Nancy R on 17 Dec 1890 at Acc by W Chinn

SMITH Walter H 30 S Farmer Acc Acc s/o Michael & Maria C to Emaline Baker 25 S Acc Acc d/o James on 8 Mar 1876 at Modest Town by CV Waugh

SMITH William C 24 S Farmer Acc Acc s/o Wm C Sr & Rose Ann to Florence Mears 20 S Acc Acc d/o Zadock S & Julia on 27 Dec 1893 at Sanford by JR Tillery

SMITH William H 26 S Farmer Acc Acc s/o Jno W & Melinda to Virginia Moore 21 S Acc Acc d/o Geo & Ann on 18 Oct 1865 at Acc by JH Addison

SMITH William S to Margaret A White d/o William who gave consent lic: 26 Dec 1857 Henry Smith says he over 21

SMITH William S 24 S Oysterman Acc Acc s/o Wm S & Margaret to Susan A Melson 15 S Acc Acc d/o John H & Susan on 30 Dec 1885 at Onancock by CA Grice

SMITH William T 28 S Sailor s/o Thomas to Catharine Ann Archy(?) 21 S d/o Charles & Rachel lic: 11 Apr 1865 marr: 12 Apr 1865

SMITH William W 40 W Farmer Acc Acc s/o James & Sophia to Catharine A Young 23 S Acc Acc d/o Jonathan & Sophia on 2 Dec 1868 at Acc by EG Irvin

SMITH Wm W 33 S Soldier Acc Acc s/o Jas & Sophia to Mary E Savage 27 S Acc Acc d/o Jesse & Henny White on 18 Feb 1864 at Acc by D Titlow

SNEAD Andrew J Col 40 W Laborer Lancaster Co VA Acc s/o Simon & Maria to Susan Snead Col 26 S Acc Acc d/o Sally on 15 Jul 1882 at Onancock by JC Ayler

SNEAD Edmund Col 21 S Laborer Acc Acc s/o Saba Lewis to Eliza Drummond Col 17 S Acc Acc d/o Chas & Lucy on 22 Oct 1879 near Bull Run by RJ Waters

SNEAD Edward Col 25 S Farmer Acc Acc s/o Edward & Sarah to Silry Downing Col 20 S Acc Acc d/o Shepherd & Amy on 2 Feb 1887 at A J Satchell's by AJ Satchell

SNEAD Edward G Col 23 S Wage-earner Acc Acc s/o Hannah to Mary Mapp Col 22 S Acc Acc d/o Mary on 19 Dec 1888 at Locust Mount by JWA Elliott

SNEAD Edward K 45 W Lawyer Acc Acc s/o Edwd Smith & Susan Snead to Helen R Jarvis 21 S Acc Acc d/o Thos B & Mary H on 16 Dec 1872 at Onancock by J Atkinson

SNEAD Edward R s/o Edward S dec'd to Mary D Wallop d/o David dec'd lic: 22 Nov 1854

SNEAD Fred H Col 20 S Farmer Acc Acc s/o James & Jane to S Eliz'th B Hatton 19 S Acc Acc d/o James & Missouri on 23 Dec 1895 at Acc by J Duckett

SNEAD George E Col 24 S Laborer Acc Acc s/o Nancy to Rachel Holland Col 23 S Acc Acc d/o Tabby on 11 May 1872 at Oak Grove by N Morris

SNEAD George W Col 31 S Laborer Acc Acc s/o Hannah to Mary Jane Poulson Col 35 S Acc Acc d/o Neubia Mapp on 6 Sep 1880 at Locust Mount by JWA Elliott

SNEAD Horace C Col 21 S Farmer Acc Acc s/o George & Rachel to Madeline Mapp Col 17 S Acc Acc d/o James & Louisa Burton on 13 Jun 1892 at Wachapreague by RH Coleman

SNEAD James 42 W to Mary (Cherichs) Cherricks 19 d/o Daniel who gave consent lic: 31 Dec 1860

SNEAD James Col 19 S Laborer Acc Acc s/o Monia to Jane Kellam Col 17 S Acc Acc d/o Lucinda on 26 Dec 1872 at Onancock by R Davis

SNEAD James (black) 62 S Laborer Acc Acc s/o Sylvia to Fannie [Mathews] Matthews (black) 54 S Acc Acc d/o Sarah on 4 Mar 1874 at Horntown by S Johns

SNEAD James Col 24 S Farmer Acc Acc s/o Henry Smith to Charlotte Martin Col 45 S Acc Acc on 28 Dec 1880 near Onancock by JW Diggs

SNEAD James Col 30 D Laborer Acc Acc s/o Mariah to Alicia Parker Col 21 S Acc Acc d/o Patsy on 26 Oct 1884 at Acc by P Sheppard

SNEAD James 21 S Oysterman Chinco: Isld Chinco: Isld s/o Thos & Alice to Dolly Munger 18 S Chinco: Isld Chinco: Isld d/o Martha on 2 Oct 1886 at Acc by BF Jester

SNEAD James 25 W Oysterman Acc Acc s/o Thomas & Alice to Drucilla Whealton 21 S Acc Acc d/o Daniel & Mary A on 21 Nov 1890 at Chinco: Isld by JW Turner

SNEAD John 37 W Sailor Acc Acc s/o Jas & Lydia to Sarah Lewis 42 W Acc Acc d/o George & Sarah Claville on 24 Sep 1867 at Acc by WP Thornton

SNEAD John 19 S Oysterman Acc Acc s/o Thomas & Alice to Elizabeth Jester 16 S Acc Acc d/o Isaac Jester & Margaret Merritt on 4 Jun 1887 at Chinco: Isld by SU Grimsley

SNEAD John H Col 38 S Farmer Acc Acc s/o Mary to Lucy Guy Col 27 S Acc Acc d/o Sarah Poulson on 8 Jul 1885 at Acc by CA Horsey

SNEAD John J 20 S Oysterman Chinco: Isld Chinco: Isld s/o Robert & Bridget to Charlotte A Hall 17 S Chinco: Isld Chinco: Isld d/o Thomas & Mahala on 26 Nov 1871 at Chinco: Isld by P Bowdin Sr

SNEAD John J 28 S US Life Saving Station Chinco: Isld Chinco: Isld s/o Jno & Charity to Nancy Melvin 16 S Chinco: Isld Chinco: Isld d/o Thos & Lydia Ann on 2 Feb 1886 at Chinco: Isld by JD Reese

SNEAD John O Col 21 S Farmer Acc Acc s/o Maria to Tabitha Bayly Col 21 S Acc Acc d/o Danl & Mary on 10 Nov 1886 at Acc by JA Haynes

SNEAD Joseph 22 S Oysterman Acc Acc s/o John R & Charlotte to Emma Andrews 18 S Acc Acc d/o Comfort on 20 Jan 1895 at Chinco: Isld by SU Grimsley

SNEAD Julius Col 22 S Laborer Acc Acc s/o Hannah Snead to Ann Finney Col 25 S Acc Acc d/o Ann Finney on 22 Feb 1874 at Locust Mount by JWA Elliott

SNEAD Julius Col 35 S Farmer Acc Acc s/o Hannah to Margaret Hateney Col 31 S Acc Acc d/o Harriet Mears on 18 Nov 1883 at Burtons Ch by GW Young

SNEAD Levi 30 S Laborer Acc Acc s/o Asa Sturgis to Margt Manuel 30 S Acc Acc on 16 Aug 1868 at Acc by D Titlow

SNEAD Robert 30 S Laborer Acc Acc s/o Henry to Martha Wise 24 S Acc Acc d/o Mahala on 16 Jan 1867 at Acc by WT Tull

SNEAD Thomas 22 S Waterman Chinco: Isld Chinco: Isld s/o Robert & Bridget to Ruthy Russell 16 S Chinco: Isld Chinco: Isld d/o John & Elizabeth on 28 Dec 1858 at Chinco: Isld by P Bowdin (John A M Whelaton says he over 21)

SNEAD Thos 26 S Sailor Acc Acc s/o Robt & Bridget to Alice [Russel] Russell 16 S Acc Acc d/o Jno & Elizabeth on 23 May 1863 at Acc by P Bowdin Jr

SNEAD Tully S 34 W Merchant Acc Acc s/o Tully & Elizabeth to Lousia Fletcher 28 W Acc Acc (wid/o John R) & d/o David & Mary A Broadwater on 8 Dec 1859 at Conquest Ch by W Merrill

SNEAD William Col 28 S Farmer Acc Acc s/o Wm Wise & Sarah Snead to Rachel Collins Col 20 S Acc Acc d/o Jas & Rachel on 27 Mar 1879 at Savageville by JW Diggs

SNEAD Wm Col 22 S Farmer Acc Acc s/o Mariah to Ellen [Reed] Read Col 19 S Acc Acc d/o Mary Snead on 15 Feb 1882 at Onancock by JC Ayler

SNEAD Wm Col 19 S Farm Laborer Acc Acc s/o Leah to Missouri Chandler Col 21 S Acc Acc d/o Bettie on 28 Aug 1882 at Savageville by F Wood

SNEAD Wm Col 39 S Laborer Acc Acc s/o Nancy to Martha Parramore Col 45 S Acc Acc on 6 Jun 1882 at Savageville by F Wood

SNYDER Robert 25 S Farmer Germany Acc s/o Peter & Mary F to Emma Susan Cropper 25 S Acc Acc d/o John & Sarah A on 24 Dec 1873 near Locustville by LK LeCato

SPARKS Charles A Col 28 S Sailor West Indies Isld St Thomas Acc s/o Charles & Martha to Eliza E Wise Col 21 S Acc Acc d/o Samuel & Susan on 16 Jun 1895 at Acc by AJ Satchell

SPARROW Andrew W 23 S Sailor Acc Acc s/o John R & Mary to Elizabeth M Hornsby 18 S Acc Acc d/o James & Elizabeth on 23 Jan 1889 at Pungo: by JH Riddick

SPARROW Charles A 21 S Farmer Acc Acc s/o Jno R & Jane to Bettie C Guy 20 S Acc Acc d/o Wn T & Sarah on 10 Nov 1886 at Acc by L Rosser

SPARROW David widr to Molly Bundick wid lic: 2 Feb 1857

SPARROW Fred W 26 S Merchant Acc Acc s/o John R & Mary Jane to Ella K [Killmon] Killman 20 S Acc Acc d/o Lybrant J & Susan on 12 Sep 1893 at Acc by AC Berryman

SPARROW George T 18 S Farmer Acc Acc s/o Margaret S to Bettie T Scott 23 S Acc Acc d/o James E & Betsy on 14 Sep 1882 near Lee Mont by WA Crouse

SPARROW George W s/o Eliza Satchell to Margaret (Charnick) Charnock d/o

Edward who gave consent lic: 17 Nov 1854

SPARROW George W 23 S Farmer Acc Acc s/o James W & Anna to Laura F Lilliston 20 S Acc Acc d/o Henry P & Mary on 6 Arp 1870 at Metompkin by JET Ewell

SPARROW James 20 S Farmer Acc Acc s/o Wesley & Margaret to Elizabeth Lewis 23 S Acc Acc d/o Levin & Mary on 29 Aug 1880 at Reese M P Ch by FH Mullineaux

SPARROW James W 50 W Farmer Acc Acc s/o John & Hetty to Martha Berry 18 S Acc Acc d/o John & Jane on 9 Jan 1884 at Acc by JG Anderson

SPARROW Joseph J 35 W Sailor Acc Acc s/o John B & Jane to Lula B Powell 14 S Acc Acc d/o George W & Joyce S on 4 Mar 1893 at Acc by JM Anderson

SPARROW Wesley A 22 S Farmer Acc Acc s/o Wesley & Margaret to Mary E Satchell 25 W Acc Acc on 30 Sep 1885 at Temp'ville by M Oldham

SPENCE Edward 22 S Waterman Acc Acc s/o Thomas & Polly to Avery A Evans 21 S Acc Acc d/o Severn & Eliza on 19 Aug 1894 at Acc by DJ Traynham

SPENCE Elijah 25 S Waterman r: Smith Isld MD s/o Elijah & Elizabeth to Margaret Sparrow 28 W r: Smith Isld d/o Tiler & Fanny Crockett on 19 Aug 1856 at Tangier Isld by RB Hazzard (Geo W Evans says he over 21)

SPENCE Elijah 22 S Farmer Acc Acc s/o Joshua & Rachel to Carrie L Wallace 20 S Acc Acc d/o Geo B & Eliza on 8 Nov 1893 at Acc by JR Sturgis

SPENCE George H 26 S Sailor Acc Acc s/o Joshua & Rachel to Margt Emily Evans 24 S Acc Acc d/o John & Mary on 23 Aug 1882 at Chesconessex by PA Leatherbury

SPENCE John [Spense] (Spence) 73 W Farmer Som Co MD Acc s/o James & Elizth to Anne E Evans 41 W Acc Acc d/o John & Nancy on 16 Aug 1873 at Onancock by PA Leatherbury

SPENCE John C 20 S Farm Laborer Acc Acc s/o Joshua & Rachel to Elexiue Kellam 22 S Acc Acc d/o Thomas & Mary on 26 Jul 1882 at Locust Mount by JWA Elliott

SPENCE John M [Spense] 22 S Sailor Acc Acc s/o Lewes & Elizth to Martha E [Evins] Evans Col 17 S Acc Acc d/o Dennard & Sarah on 10 Jun 1885 at Onancock by CA Grice

SPENCE John T 23 S Waterman Long Ridge VA Chesconessex s/o Elijah & Elizabeth to Sena T Evans 25 S Smith Isld VA Chesconessex d/o Richard & Gracy on 28 Feb 1861 at Chesconessex by D Titlow (E L East says both over 21)

SPENCE Joshua 20 S Farmer Acc Acc s/o Joshua T & Rachel to Elenda M Williams 15 S Acc Acc d/o Benj F & Margt on 22 Sep 1878 at Joshua T Spence's by JH Amiss

SPENCE Joshua 55 W Farmer Acc Acc s/o Elijah & Betsey to Sarah Bell 40 W Acc Acc d/o Robert & Sally Bell on 20 Dec 1888 at Locust Mount by JWA Elliott

SPENCE Mitchell A 28 S Acc Acc s/o Joshua & Rachel to Isabella S Kellam 27 S Acc Acc d/o Thos A & Mary on 6 Nov 1895 at Acc by JR Sturgis

SPENCE Randford 22 S Waterman Acc Acc s/o Richard & Adaline to Dona W Raleigh 20 S Acc Acc d/o Raymond & Emily on 23 Dec 1891 at Tangier Isld by J Connor

SPENCE Richard 19 S Farmer Acc Acc s/o Lewis J & Eliz'th to Annie Williams 16 S Acc Acc d/o Robert on 26 Jan 1891 at Onancock by GW

Burke

SPENCE Thomas 21 S Sailor s/o Elijah & Betsy to Polly Marshall 22 d/o John & Sinah lic: 29 Nov 1864 marr: 29 Nov 1864 at Accomack

SPENCE William 24 S Oysterman Acc Acc s/o Richard A & Adaline to Susan Corbett 18 S Acc Acc d/o Richard & Miranda on 3 Dec 1890 at Tangier Isld by J Connor

STANT Charles D 25 S Sailor Acc Acc s/o Wm & Sarah to Harriet Smith 25 S Acc Acc d/o Valintine & Elizth on 25 Dec 1865 at Acc by M Oldham

STANT Edgar 22 S Oysterman Acc Acc s/o Robert & Mary to Matilda L Smith 17 S Acc Acc d/o Henry & Mary on 14 Jun 1882 at Pocomoke by M Oldham

STANT Gillie 77 W Farmer Acc Acc s/o Jas & Emphunia to Nancy Harris 50 W Acc Acc d/o Eli & Lemcinda Chesser on 16 Sep 1879 at Messongo by JE Bundick

STANT James A 20 S Oysterman Acc Acc s/o Robert J & Mary to Lulie Lankford 23 W Som Co MD Acc on 25 Sep 1887 at Sanford by JW Carroll

STANT Joel T 24 S Oysterman Acc Acc s/o Wm & Sarah A to Marietta Anderton 17 S Acc Acc d/o Edwd H & Betty on 12 May 1886 at Oak Hall by DM Wallace

STANT John widr to Polly Woods d/o Nancy lic: 24 Jul 1854

STANT John G 23 S Oysterman Acc Acc s/o John & Susan to Catharine Smith 18 S Acc Acc d/o Henry & Mary on 7 Dec 1880 at Pocomoke by M Oldham

STANT John T 24 S Oysterman Acc Acc s/o Samuel & Jane to Susan T Riley 21 S Acc Acc d/o George H & Catharine R on 5 Feb 1874 at Chesconessex by WF Talbott

STANT Major H 22 S Oysterman Acc Acc s/o Edwd & Milky to Cordelia Stant 18 S Acc Acc d/o Saml J & Mary on 6 Apr 1869 at Acc by M Oldham

STANT Ramond R 23 S Sailor Pigpoint Pigpoint s/o H Stant to Sarah S White 17 S Pig Point Pig Point d/o Henry who gave consent on 13 Feb 1859 at r/o Henry White by GH Ewell (Edward H Anderton says he over 21)

STANT Raymond R 32 W Merchant Acc Acc s/o Gillett & Sallie to Esther F Marshall 23 S Acc Acc d/o Thos A & Caroline on 5 Aug 1869 at Acc by GW Matthews

STANT Raymond S 22 S Merchant Acc Acc s/o Raymond R & Sallie S to Sarah B Hickman 24 S Acc Acc d/o Elijah on 8 Jun 1887 at bride's home by J McNabb

STANT Severn R 21 S Sailor Acc Acc s/o Samuel J & Jane to Lovey Bradshaw 19 S Acc Acc d/o David & Sally on 9 Jun 1875 at Chesconessex by RC Jones

STANT Wilbur Z 22 S Oysterman Acc Acc s/o Emma Stant to Amanda L Marshall 19 S Acc Acc d/o James W & Olivia on 25 May 1887 at Sanford by JW Carroll

STANT William H 21 S Oysterman Acc Acc s/o Major H & Cordelia to Rosa F Smith 21 S Som Co MD Acc d/o John H on 25 Dec 1895 at Temp'ville by EF Garner

STANT William J 21 S Sailor s/o Samuel & Jane to Rachel Marshall 16 S d/o John & Eleanor lic: 27 Jun 1868 marr: 30 Jun 1868

STATON Levi Col 45 S Laborer Acc Acc s/o Bridget to Matilda Planter Col 44 S Acc Acc d/o Leah on 28 Apr 1881 at Acc by JC Cluff

STEELMAN James D 20 S Waterman Acc Acc s/o David & Eliz'th to Emma [Tindal] Tindall 21 S Acc Acc d/o John H & Elunica on 21 Dec 1894 at Chinco: Isld by CW Matthews

STEFFENS Joseph L 51 W Chief Engineer Koblentz Germany Acc s/o Tony & Mary to Lizzie [Reed] Read 27 S Wor Co MD Acc d/o Littleton & Mary on 15 Mar 1894 at Acc by GP Jones

STEFFINS Joseph Jr 20 S Engineer Brooklyn NY Acc s/o Joseph & Marianna to Josephine Russell 17 S Acc Acc d/o Elijah & Charlotte on 20 Oct 1891 at Chinco: Isld by JF Wooden

STENGLE Adam 21 S Farmer b: Harford Co MD s/o Markus & Mary Ann to Elizabeth P Mason 17 d/o George W & Nancy lic: 3 Dec 1864 marr: 7 Dec 1864 at Accomack

STEPHENSON Robert K 26 S Clergyman Cecil Co MD Fredenca DE s/o Robert & A M to Nicholeua L Leatherbury 24 S Acc Acc d/o Perry & Zipporah on 2 Jun 1880 at Onancock by RC Jones

STERLING Angelo 21 S Farmer Acc Acc s/o James H & Nancy to Amelia J Mason 21 S Acc Acc d/o James on 7 Oct 1891 at Parksley by GF Farring

STERLING James H 35 W Farmer Acc Acc s/o Saml & Leah to Olivia Mason 23 S Acc Acc d/o James & Sarah on 7 Feb 1878 at Bloxom Store by JB Merritt

STERLING James Hy [Starlin] (Starling) 24 S Farmer & Waterman Acc A Taylor Farm s/o Saml & Leah to Nancy Ann Bull 21 S Acc A Taylor Farm d/o Wm & Sally on 13 Jan 1859 at r/o Saml Tindal by EW Stickney

STERLING Jefferson L 23 S Sailor Acc Acc s/o James H & Nancy to Maggie E [Colna] Colonna 28 S Acc Acc d/o Wm C & Mary on 11 Oct 1885 at Modest Town by A Woodyard

STERLING John J 21 S Farmer Acc Acc s/o John J & Annie J to Ida R Powell 18 S Acc Acc d/o Nathaniel & Juliet E on 12 Nov 1890 at Wachapreague by W Chinn

STERLING Joseph 22 S Farmer Acc Acc to Martha Jane Johnson 19 S Acc Acc d/o James T on 4 Jan 1872 at Oak Hall by JC Reed

STERLING William R 22 S Farmer Acc Acc s/o Joseph & Martha to Ambert Taylor 18 S Acc Acc d/o Oliver L & Mary on 17 Jul 1895 at Mappsville by JL King

STEVENS Andrew [Stephens] 23 S Farmer Acc Acc s/o James H & Larah Ann to Mollie E Mears 18 S Acc Acc d/o James E & Virginia on 8 Mar 1894 at Wachapreague by JR Sturgis

STEVENS George A 25 S Wage-earner Acc Acc s/o Nancy to Lillie May Doughty 18 S Acc Acc d/o Richard & Lizzie on 7 Jul 1889 at Acc by L Duncan

STEVENS Jas H T 22 S Sailor Acc Acc s/o Jno T & Sally to Mary C Parker 19 S Acc Acc d/o Geo T & Tabitha on 14 Jul 1886 at Acc by L Rosser

STEVENS Jno B 30 S Oysterman Acc Acc s/o Jno B & C H to Sarah Elizabeth Shelly 18 S NY Acc d/o Zachariah on 25 Jul 1869 at Acc by P Bowdin Jr

STEVENS John to Sally Ann Bennett (ward/o Lewis C H Finney who gave consent) on 10 Nov 1858 at Acc by M Oldham (Lewis C H Finney says he over 21)

STEVENS John H 30 W Carpenter Acc Acc s/o John H & Eliz'th to Mollie H Milliner 23 S Acc Acc d/o James H & Eliz'th on 28 Dec 1892 at Locust Mount by JWA Elliott

STEVENS John O 21 S Merchant Acc Acc s/o John T & Sallie A to Rosa E

Parker 18 S Acc Acc d/o George T & Tabitha on 18 Mar 1890 at Pungo: by JM Anderson

STEVENS Joseph H 22 S Farmer Acc Acc s/o John H & Eliz'th A to Mollie A Hargis 19 S Acc Acc d/o George P & Hester P on 8 Oct 1890 at Wachapreague by WJ Twilley

STEVENS Levi T 22 S Farmer N'hamp: Acc s/o John & Betty A to Olivia J Guy 18 S Acc Acc d/o John W & Margaret on 6 Jan 1895 at Acc by EC Atkins

STEVENS Lewis Col 22 S Farmer Acc N'hamp: s/o Alicia to Cora Sturgis Col 23 S Acc Acc d/o Rosa Nutts on 14 Mar 1886 at Franktown by JB Lewis

STEVENS Louis Col 25 W Laborer Acc Acc s/o Elishia to Mary Shield Col 22 S Acc Acc d/o Gilbert on 28 Feb 1887 at bride's home by TW Nettles

STEVENS Richard B Col 21 S Farmer Acc Acc s/o Rike & Margaret to Mary Jane Harmon Col 17 S Acc Acc d/o Caroline Ashby on 24 Dec 1885 at Drum'tn by LW Lee

STEVENS Rike Col (mulatto) 44 S Farmer Acc Acc s/o Tamar Young to Margaret Bayly Col 38 S Acc Acc d/o Esther Custis on 18 Jun 1871 at Acc by N Morris

STEVENS William 25 S Farmer Acc Acc s/o Jas & Rachel to Polly A Bradford 25 S Acc Acc d/o Thos & Ann on 26 Dec 1866 at Acc by AB Dolly

STEVENSON James 33 S Farmer Acc Acc s/o Levin & Sallie to Sallie E Hall 24 S Acc Acc d/o Thomas & Esther on 4 Jan 1893 at Acc by RB Scott

STEVENSON John W 40 S Farmer Acc Acc s/o John B & Euphemia to Lottie D Poole 24 S Acc Acc d/o William & Elizabeth on 29 Oct 1890 at Acc by GF Farring

STEVENSON Saml J 24 S Mechanic Acc Acc s/o Isaac & Mollie to Florence W Gibbons 18 S Acc Acc d/o Wm & Matilda A on 7 Mar 1877 at Modest Town by DA Woodson

STEVENSON William W 25 S Blacksmith Som Co MD Jenkins Bridge s/o Jas W & Elizabeth to Sarah J Hall 19 S Acc Jenkins Bridge d/o Robert L & Jane on 19 Dec 1860 at Downings Ch by W Merrill (John W Corbin says he over 21)

STEVENSON Wm B 22 S Carpenter Acc Acc s/o Isaac K & Mary A to Crissie E Kelly 21 S Acc Acc d/o Abel G & Mary on 12 Nov 1879 at Onancock by JC Watson

STEWART James 78 W Farmer Acc N'hamp: s/o Levin & Ann to Sarah Ann Lewis 39 W Acc Acc d/o John & Henrietta Hart on 30 Dec 1858 at Acc by JF Chaplain

STEWART Thomas [Steward] Col 22 S Laborer Acc Acc s/o Jane to Lucy Coleburn Col 27 S Acc Acc d/o Jane on 25 Mar 1884 at Pungo: by GHT Byrd

STEWART Vrigil J 28 S Farmer N'hamp: N'hamp: s/o Jno L & Susan J to Mary E Dennis 19 S Acc Acc d/o Emerson & Critty Sarah on 12 Nov 1873 near Franktown by CE Watts

STILES Eayre O Jr 24 S Waterman Tuckerton NJ Acc s/o Eayre O & Masia E to Elic F Bell 26 S Acc Acc d/o Walter W & Maggie A on 9 Mar 1887 at bride's father's by WJ Twilley

STILES John W 30 S Oysterman Indiana Acc s/o Eyre O to Triffie E Spence 21 S Acc Acc d/o Joshua & Rachel on 4 Oct 1885 at Point Farris by JWA Elliott

STINGLE Charles I 23 S Accountant Acc Acc s/o Adden & Eliz'th to Willie G Roberts 19 S N'hamp: Acc

d/o Thomas & Annie on 13 Apr 1892 at Acc by JB Pruitt
STOCKLEY Abram FN to Ann (Pool) Poole FN lic: 31 May 1858 John Brittingham says he over 21
STOCKLEY Francis T 24 S Merchant Acc Acc s/o Syl R & Margt to Mary A Coleburn 26 S Acc Acc d/o Saml (of Geo) & Elizth on 25 Jan 1866 at Acc by WG Coe
STOCKLEY Francis T 48 W Merchant Acc Acc s/o Sylvester & Margaret to May S [Bird] Byrd 30 W Acc Acc d/o Wesley S & Sarah Phillips on 30 Oct 1889 at Locust Mount by JWA Elliott
STOCKLEY George W 25 S Merchant Acc Acc s/o Sylvester & Peggie to Maggie J Turlington 18 S Acc Acc d/o Peter L & Peggie on 22 Dec 1870 at Acc by JWA Elliott
STOCKLEY John Col 27 S Farmer Acc Acc s/o Abel & Ann to Neely Conquest Col 23 S Acc Acc d/o Harriet on 1 Jul 1885 near Temp'ville by JC Cluff
STOKELY Frank A Col 23 S Acc Acc s/o Jane Stokely to Annie [Connor] Conner Col 20 S Acc Acc d/o George & Mary on 11 Jan 1876 near Oak Hall by SP Whittington
STOKES George S 21 S Merchant Danville VA Danville VA s/o A Y & M M to Willia A [Browne] Brown 23 S Acc Acc d/o Peter F & Sally on 6 Jun 1872 at Acc by FA Tidball
STOTZ Henry 33 S RR Track Foreman Lancaster Co PA Acc s/o John & Mary B to Ida E Bradford 23 S Acc Acc d/o Ezra & Rachel on 11 Jun 1890 at Acc by JM Anderson
STRAN George Col 30 S Laborer Acc Acc s/o Ann to Annie Mason Col 22 S Acc Acc d/o Alsie on 18 Jul 1883 at Acc by AJ Satchell
STRAN George W [Stram] Col 22 S Wage-earner Acc Acc s/o Perry & Rosey to Eliza Sample Col 17 S Acc Acc d/o Stratton & Mary on 19 Nov 1890 at Savageville by JB Lewis
STRAN Jesse Col 47 S Farmer Acc Acc to Mary Conquest Col 22 S Acc Acc d/o Lucy Gunter on 21 Apr 1878 at Acc by A Handy
STRAN John Wm [Strann] Col 35 S Laborer Acc Acc s/o Esan & Louisa to Mary [Gillet] Gillett Col 24 S Acc Acc d/o Isaac Bagwell & Avrena on 1 Jan 1871 at Modest Town by A Joynes
STRAN Oliver [Stram] Col 21 S Farmer Acc Acc s/o Emma to Elizabeth Stran Col 16 S Acc Acc d/o Stephen & Ann on 16 Feb 1879 near Woodstock by A Handy
STRAN Perry 24 S Farmer Acc Acc to Rose Horsey 23 S Acc Acc d/o George & Mary Read on 9 Jun 1867 at Acc by JH Addison
STRAN William Col 23 S Wage-earner Acc Acc s/o John Stran & Harriet Gunter to Susan Crowson Col 18 S Acc Acc d/o Maggie Drummond on 31 Oct 1888 at Acc by AJ Satchell
STRATTON Henry Col 56 S Laborer Acc Acc to Sylvia Beach Col 50 S Acc Acc on 26 Nov 1871 at Mt Oregon Farm by N Morris
STRATTON Jacob Col 50 S Laborer Acc Acc to Willie Anna Fields Col 25 S Acc Acc d/o Sarah Ward on 9 Nov 1882 near Belle Haven by J Savage
STRATTON Jacob Col 28 S Farmer Acc Acc s/o Isaac & Mary to Ella E Bayly Col 15 S Baltimore MD Acc d/o Barbara Calman on 29 Nov 1882 at Drum'tn by LW Lee
STRATTON Jacob Col 21 S Farmer Acc Acc s/o Jacob & Tabitha to Jane Bayly Col 19 S Acc Acc d/o Levin & Hester Ann on 27 Nov 1892 at Acc by PW Lee
STRATTON John H Col 23 S Laborer

Acc Acc s/o Sabra Beach to Georgianna [Allens] Allen Col 21 S Acc Acc d/o Robert & Virginia on 9 Jul 1871 at Acc by N Morris

STRATTON Thomas Col 19 S Laborer Acc Acc s/o Salby to Rosa A Coleburn Col 20 S Acc Acc d/o Louisa on 28 Dec 1876 near Locustville by LK LeCato

STRIGLE John W 18 S Merchant Acc Acc s/o James O & Sophemia A to Dollie [Dize] Dies 18 S Acc Acc d/o Nathan & Matilda on 24 Oct 1894 at Tangier by WR Gwinn

STRNIGER Benj C (Jr) 32 W Miller Acc Acc s/o Benj & Caroline to Margaret W Marston 31 W Acc Acc d/o Wm & Susan Garrison on 3 Nov 1867 at Acc by JC Martin

STRNIGER William Col 37 S Sailor Acc Acc s/o Judis Jones to Susan Wise Col 39 W Acc Acc d/o Chlone Mason on 17 Dec 1875 at Acc by HT Rich

STUBBS Andrew 25 S Seaman Caroline Co MD Chinco: Isld s/o Richson & Rodahann to Caroline [Cherix] Cherricks 28 W Chinco: Isld Chinco: Isld d/o Jno & Nancy Hall on 20 Jun 1859 at Chinco: Isld by P Bowdin (John AM Whealton says he over 21)

STURGIS Charles Col 43 S Farmer Acc Acc s/o Charles Garrison & Ellie Bell to Hester [Harman] Harmon Col 38 S Acc Acc d/o Arthur & Rosa on 1 Apr 1885 at Acc by P Sheppard

STURGIS Charles Col 22 S Wage-earner Acc Acc s/o Charles & Love W to Sallie Boggs Col 25 S Acc Acc d/o Mary on 25 Dec 1889 at Onancock by GHT Byrd

STURGIS Charles H 23 S Farmer Acc Acc s/o Charles T & Mary to Charlotte Savage 22 S Acc Acc d/o Edward G & Elizth on 15 Nov 1873 at Oak Grove Ch by LK LeCato

STURGIS Elijah 18 S Farmer Acc Acc s/o Chas & Mary to Laura Mapp 23 S Acc Acc d/o Jno G & Ann on 21 Dec 1862 at Acc by JWA Elliott

STURGIS Elijah 26 W Farmer Acc Acc s/o Charles & Mary to Mary J Bundick 23 S Acc Acc d/o John B & Margaret on 29 Nov 1871 near Locust Mount by JE Humphreys

STURGIS Elijah W 18 S Fisherman Acc Acc s/o Elijah W & Mary J to Frances E Ayres 21 S Acc Acc d/o Edward & Sally on 15 Oct 1890 at Grangeville by JR Strugis

STURGIS Franics M 24 S Sailor Acc Acc s/o Wm S & Cath K to Polly Ann Beloate 18 S Acc Acc d/o Wm H & Kesiah on 8 Jan 1862 at Acc by BT Ames

STURGIS George Col 22 S Farmer Acc Acc s/o Charles & Willie to Maggie Mears Col 18 S Acc Acc d/o Ann on 24 Jul 1889 at Onancock by JH Offer

STURGIS George Col 21 S Farmer Acc Acc s/o John Henry & Annie to Margie West Col 21 S Acc Acc d/o George & Fannie on 27 Feb 1895 at Acc by TW Nettles

STURGIS George W 25 S Farmer Acc Acc s/o Jno W & Charlotte to Margaret E Doughty 16 S Acc Acc d/o James C & Sally on 13 Dec 1882 at Acc by JE Humphreys

STURGIS James 50 S Laborer Acc Acc to Leah Wright 50 S Acc Acc on 9 Jul 1876 at Belle Haven by RH Govans

STURGIS James B 39 S Farmer N'hamp: Acc s/o Jas & Margt to Adaline Mears 28 S Acc Acc d/o Thorogood & Mahala on 4 Aug 1872 at Acc by JE Humphreys

STURGIS James S 36 S Farmer Acc Acc s/o George & Polly to Mary J Sturgis 32 W Acc Acc d/o Jno R & Margaret Bundick on 17 Oct 1880 at Locust Mount by JWA Elliott

STURGIS Jefferson D Col 26 S Farmer

Acc Acc s/o James & Leah to Ella [Bailey] Bayly Col 19 S Acc Acc d/o Thomas & Sarah on 6 Feb 1889 at Acc by L Duncan

STURGIS John 24 S Farmer b: Ames Ridge s/o Wm (S) & Catharine to Susan Bell 19 S b: Bradford Nk d/o James & Charlotte & (ward/o James R Garrison) on 8 Jan 1856 at Garrisons Chp by J Burton (Arthur Jacob says both over 21)

STURGIS John Henry Col 38 S Farmer Acc Acc s/o Sally to Ann Nock Col 40 S Acc Acc d/o John & Mahala on 19 Aug 1889 at Acc by L Duncan

STURGIS John R 28 S Merchant Acc Acc s/o Chas T & Mary to Arinthia J Mears 24 S Acc Acc d/o David B & Juiliet A on 8 Jan 1868 at Acc by JC Martin

STURGIS John W 57 W Farmer Acc Acc s/o William & Catharine to Mary Mason 50 S Acc Acc d/o William & Betsy on 18 Nov 1891 near Pungo: by JB Pruitt

STURGIS Louis Col 22 S Farmer Acc Acc s/o Chas & Hester to Mary T Kellam Col 20 S Acc Acc d/o Geo C & Lucinda on 20 Dec 1891 at Acc by JH Offer

STURGIS Moses Col 30 S Blacksmith Acc Acc s/o Jane to Ellen Matthews Col 18 S Acc Acc d/o George & Alethia on 21 Nov 1872 at Belle Haven by JE Humphreys

STURGIS Oswald W 22 S Farmer Acc Acc s/o Wm & Catharine to Virginia R Tipton 18 S Acc Acc d/o Ephraim & ann on 15 Dec 1875 near Belle Haven by JE Humphreys

STURGIS Samuel widr to Sally Charnock wid lic: 13 Jan 1857

STURGIS Thomas 30 S Seaman Acc Acc to Margaret Savage 18 S Acc Acc d/o Catharine on 3 Dec 1870 at Acc by LK LeCato

STURGIS William Col 28 S Farmer Acc Acc s/o James & Leah to Mary A Bayly Col 29 S Acc Acc d/o Felix & Augelina on 16 Jan 1895 at Acc by L Duncan

STURGIS William K 29 S Nurseryman Acc Acc s/o Elizabeth to Mamie J Wimbrough 19 S Acc Acc d/o Wm T on 27 Dec 1891 at Acc C H by VW Bargamin

SUMMERS Alfred B [Somers] 22 S Seaman Acc Acc s/o Saml & Mary to Mary L [Kelley] Kelly 19 S Acc Acc d/o Elijah B & Evaline on 26 Dec 1883 at Temp'ville by M Oldham

SUMMERS Allen 27 S Sailor Som Co MD Acc s/o Elijah & Euphernia to Eliza A Hoffman 17 S Acc Acc d/o Wm G & Mary on 26 Dec 1870 at Acc by OP Twiford

SUMMERS Edward T 21 S Sailor Acc Acc s/o Wm & Arena to Emily S Kelly 19 S Acc Acc d/o Elijah R & Evaline on 6 Mar 1878 at Muddy Ck by DA Woodson

SUMMERS Frank P 27 S Sailor Acc Acc s/o George & Evaline to Catherine J Hughes 19 S Acc Acc d/o John H & Vianna on 16 Sep 1888 at Acc by WA Street

SUMMERS George to Eveline Wessells d/o Betsy who gave consent lic: 14 Jan 1856 John W Bird says he over 21

SUMMERS George T [Sommers] 25 S Merchant Acc Acc s/o Geo & Evaline to Mary E Mears 25 S Acc Acc d/o Jno & Virginia on 16 Dec 1883 at Conquest Ch by M Oldham

SUMMERS Isaac [Sommers] 21 S Merchant Acc Acc s/o John & Veanna to Delia F Hughes 19 S Acc Acc d/o John H & Vianna on 7 Mar 1883 at Mappsville by JW Hundley

SUMMERS John O (Sommers) 22 S Sailor Acc Acc s/o John & Vinna to Emily S Lankford 19 S Acc Acc d/o Louis J & Hester A on 7 Dec 1873 at

Modest Town by JL Lodge

SUMMERS Joshua [Somers] 26 S Sailor Sussex Co DE Chinco: Isld s/o Robt & Priscilly to Lavinia Adkins 22 S Atlantic City NJ Chinco: Isld d/o Thomas H & Nancy on 17 Sep 1873 at Chinco: Isld by P Bowdin Sr

SUMMERS Reuben Col 25 S Farmer Acc Acc s/o Elizabeth to Alberta Martin Col 21 S Acc Acc d/o James & Annie on 31 Jan 1889 at Acc by AJ Satchell

SUMMERS Richd W 22 S Sailor Acc Acc s/o Jno & Vienna to Polly A Bundick 22 S Acc Acc d/o Wm J & Soymour on 3 Jan 1877 near Fox Store (Bundick) by DA Woodson

SUMMERS Samuel s/o Elizabeth who gave consent to Mary J (Justis) Justice d/o Samuel R who gave consent lic: 22 Apr 1857

SUMMERS Wm J [Somers] 22 S Sailor Acc Acc s/o Wm & Lorona to Maggie A Mears 19 S Acc Acc d/o Susan J on 1 Dec 1875 at Muddy Ck by CV Waugh

SUNKETT John 23 S Sailor Acc Acc s/o Tabitha to Margt Smith 21 S Acc Acc d/o Julia Ann on 26 Sep 1866 at Acc by D Titlow

SUNKETT John H Col 20 S Farmer Acc Acc s/o John & Maggie to Jennie Grant Col 21 S Acc Acc d/o Edward & Mary on 11 Sep 1894 at Pungo: by JH Offer

SWIFT Reuben E 55 W Mariner Falmouth MA Chinco: Isld to Ophelea F Corbin 37 S Acc Acc d/o Peter D & Charlotte on 2 Sep 1878 at Chinco: Isld by IT Adkins

SWINDELL Robert B 22 S Sailor Washington NC Washington NC s/o Mark & Ida to Ema M Davis 18 S Acc Acc d/o Samuel G & Elizabeth on 26 May 1893 at Chinco: Isld by RB Sanford

TAILOR {Taylor?} John T 24 S Farmer Acc Acc s/o Henry W & Scarborough to Caroline H White 23 W Wor Co MD Acc d/o John & Henrietta Parks on 26 Nov 1856 at r/o Wash Matthews by RB Hazzard

TANKARD Emanuel 23 S Farmer Acc Acc s/o Mary to Rachel Read 15 S Acc Acc d/o Arthur & Maria on 13 Jan 1869 at Acc by JH Offer

TANKARD George Col 23 S Oysterman N'hamp: Acc s/o Jno & Maria to Elizabeth Stringer Col 22 S Acc Acc d/o Mary Parker on 21 Apr 1887 at Onancock by GHT Byrd

TANKARD Sacker Col 30 S Laborer Acc Acc to Georgianna Watson Col 19 S Acc Acc d/o Sarah A on 25 May 1882 at Onancock by JC Ayler

TAPMAN Wm 21 S Farmer Acc Acc s/o Isaac & Rebecca to Mary Robeta Custis 21 S Acc Acc d/o Jas T & Sarah on 31 Dec 1878 near New Church by JW Hundley

TAPPEN Frank M 22 S Carpenter Wor Co MD Acc s/o Himan R & Kate D to Eliz'th A Wright 22 S Acc Acc d/o Charles & Margaret on 8 Jul 1891 at Parksley by JF Anderson

TARR Alonzo L 19 S Oysterman Acc Acc s/o James E & Mary C to Alice J Birch 15 S Acc Acc d/o Thomas J & Comfort on 22 May 1893 at Chinco: Isld by JB Lynch

TARR Charles H 45 W Acc Acc s/o Charles & Mary of Maryland to Margaret J Dunton 43 W Acc Acc d/o Preston & Mary Mason of Maryland on 1 Jan 1882 at Temp'ville by M Oldham

TARR Charles H 52 W Farmer MD Acc s/o Charles & Mary to Sallie A Gunter 55 W Acc Acc on 3 Sep 1891 at Oak Hall by JS Wallace

TARR David T 21 S Oysterman Acc Acc s/o David & Mary to Sarah E Merritt 21 S Wor Co MD Acc d/o Saml & Isabell on 11 Jun 1881 at

Chinco: Isld by WP Thornton

TARR John 48 W Mariner Chinco: Isld Chinco: Isld s/o James & Polly to Ann Thornton 37 S Chinco: Isld Chinco: Isld d/o John & Hester on 1 Jun 1859 at Chinco: Isld by WP Thornton

TARR John R 22 S Oysterman Acc Acc s/o David & Mary to Sally M Jones 15 S Acc Acc d/o Burton & Mary on 8 Jun 1871 at Chinco: Isld by P Bowdin Sr

TARR John R 27 W Oysterman Acc Acc s/o David & Mary to Elizabeth Whealton 16 S Acc Acc d/o Joshua & Nancy on 6 Jan 1877 at Chinco: Isld by P Bowdin Sr

TARR Joshua 22 S Oysterman Acc Acc s/o David & Mary to Mary A Pointer 15 S Acc Acc d/o Jas B & Lydia on 15 Feb 1880 at Chinco: Isld by WP Thornton

TATEM Benjamin 25 S Oysterman Acc Acc s/o James & Nancy to Eliza Turlington 23 S Acc Acc d/o Parker & Mary on 19 Dec 1870 at Chinco: Isld by P Bowdin Sr

TATEM John E 25 S Sailor Acc Acc s/o James & Nancy to Mary A Mears 21 S Acc Acc d/o Luther J & Mary S on 26 Feb 1882 near Locust Mount by JWA Elliott

TATEM William J [Tatum] 26 S Sailor Acc Chinco: Isld s/o James & Ann to Cordelia (J) Sharpley 15 S Chinco: Isld Chinco: Isld d/o Wm & Harriet on 9 Oct 1860 at Chinco: Isld by P Bowdin Sr (John A Whealton says he 21)

TATHAM Elijah to Sally Hickman d/o Polly who gave consent lic: 5 Mar 1860 Perry Bloxom says he over 21

TATHAM William widr to Mary Baker d/o Ezekiel dec'd lic: 6 Feb 1855

TAYLOR Agustis 19 S Oysterman Guilford Guilford s/o Charles & Peggy to Elizabeth [Hinmon] Hinman 19 S Back Ck Back Ck d/o John & Betsey on 6 Jun 1858 at Wagram Md by GH Ewell

TAYLOR Alexander 25 S Mason Acc Acc s/o Savage & Mary to Mary Wessells 27 W Acc Acc d/o Wm & Ann Bell on 25 Dec 1870 at Acc by JET Ewell

TAYLOR Alexander Col 23 S Laborer Acc Acc s/o Mary Conquest to Esther Allen Col 25 S Acc Acc d/o Robt & Jinnie on 24 Sep 1884 at Acc by LW Lee

TAYLOR Alexander 21 S Farmer Acc Acc s/o Joseph to Sadie Duncan 27 S Acc Acc d/o William & Mary on 27 Dec 1891 at Acc by JL King

TAYLOR Alfred s/o Revel to Mary Johnson d/o James T lic: 31 Jan 1854

TAYLOR Alfred s/o James B to Virginia N Boggs d/o Francis who gave consent lic: 2 Oct 1857 Wm S Smith says he over 21

TAYLOR Alfred J 28 S Merchant Acc Acc s/o Chas & Mary to Hetty C [Parks] Parkes 18 S Acc Acc d/o Robert C & Eliza on 4 Oct 1862 at Acc by GH Ewell

TAYLOR Alfred W 23 S Farmer Acc Acc s/o Alfred J & Hetty C to Bettie W Lewis 23 S Acc Acc d/o Tully M & Elizabeth on 13 Jul 1887 at Lee Mont by JW Norris

TAYLOR Ambrose S 29 S Farmer Acc Acc s/o Henry M & Nancy to Mary C Taylor 22 S Acc Acc d/o Jno G & Elizth on 26 Jun 1867 at Acc by OF Flippo

TAYLOR Amos P 26 S Oysterman Acc Acc s/o Thomas & Patsy to Elizabeth Marshall 26 S Acc Acc d/o Henry on 12 Feb 1874 at Messongo by JE Bundick

TAYLOR Andrew J 23 S Farmer Acc Acc s/o Revel J & Lonnia to Cora N Ritter 21 S Philadelphia PA Acc d/o Peter & Mary on 30 Dec 1895 at

Temp'ville by EF Garner
TAYLOR Arcellus 24 S Oysterman Acc Acc. s/o Thos & Nancy to Mary Justice 24 S Acc Acc d/o Revel & Nancy on 10 Mar 1869 at Acc by JE Bundick
TAYLOR Arthur FN to Catherine Bayly FN d/o Custis who gave consent lic: 25 Dec 1854
TAYLOR Arthur Col 50 W Farming Acc Acc s/o Millie to Frances Collins Col 33 W Acc Acc on 16 Oct 1884 at Acc by P Sheppard
TAYLOR Augustus 29 W Oysterman Acc Acc s/o David R & Catharine to Emma Darby 20 S Acc Acc d/o James & Rebecca on 3 Nov 1895 at Acc by GD Edmonston
TAYLOR Azra 22 S Farmer Acc Acc s/o John & Caroline to Parrthena Trader 21 S Acc Acc d/o Saml & Elizth on 2 Feb 1879 at Assawoman by JW Hundley
TAYLOR Caleb Col 24 S Farmer Acc Acc s/o James to Mary [Bivins] Beavans Col 21 S Acc Acc d/o Levin & Elizabeth on 7 Jan 1874 at Pungo: by R Davis
TAYLOR Caleb I Col 38 W Merchant Acc Acc s/o Caleb Topping & Leah Taylor to Ailsu J Snead Col 23 S Acc Acc d/o Littleton & Maria on 25 Jan 1888 at Acc by JA Haynes
TAYLOR Calvin 27 S Waterman Acc Acc s/o Robt & Nancy to Caroline J Wessells 19 S Acc Acc d/o Ephrain & Sally on 4 Mar 1863 at Acc by ES Grant
TAYLOR Charles 39 S Oysterman Wor Co MD Acc s/o Tully & Elizabeth to Sally Ann Jones 36 W Acc Acc d/o Thomas & Ann Sophia Melvin on 5 Oct 1870 at Chinco: Isld by P Bowdin Sr
TAYLOR Charles 53 W Oysterman Acc Acc s/o Charles & Margaret to Nancy Dix 37 W Acc Acc d/o Justice B Taylor on 9 Dec 1874 at his house by IT Adkins
TAYLOR Charles Col 22 S Day Laborer Acc Acc s/o Maria Allen to Eliza Drummond Col 21 S Acc Acc d/o Alsie on 4 Jan 1885 at St Luke Ch by LW Lee
TAYLOR Charles H 25 S Sailor ME Acc to Sallie L Davis 22 S Acc Acc d/o Wm & Sallie on 5 Apr 1878 near New Church by TM Poulson
TAYLOR Colmore S 40 W Carpenter Acc Acc s/o Southey S & Wisie to Emily F Claville 25 S Wor Co MD Acc d/o Wm B & Ann on 30 Jan 1877 at Saml Davis' by IT Adkins
TAYLOR Columbus 24 S Oysterman Acc Acc s/o Jas S & Larinia to Ida Young 27 S Acc Acc d/o Shepard & Sally on 23 Dec 1885 at Oak Hall by DM Wallace
TAYLOR Cornelius C H 24 S Oysterman Acc Acc s/o Charles & Jane to Virginia B [Justis] Justice 17 S Acc Acc d/o Saml L & Rose Ann on 27 Oct 1870 at Acc by JET Ewell
TAYLOR Cornelius T 47 W Farmer Acc Acc s/o David C to Charlotte C Poulson 34 S Acc Acc d/o Robt J & Catharine C P on 10 Jan 1883 at Cokesbury by JG Anderson
TAYLOR Cornelius V F 18 S Oysterman Acc Acc s/o Asbury C & Caroline F to Maggie Mears 21 S Acc Acc d/o Elizabeth on 28 Dec 1890 at Parksley by HS Dulany
TAYLOR Crippen of Wm 28 S Oysterman Acc Acc s/o Wm & Mary to Jane Taylor div Acc Acc d/o Susan on 4 Oct 1875 near Guilford by JE Bundick
TAYLOR Custis 28 W Farmer Acc Acc s/o Matthew H & Carsandra to Isa Taylor 22 S Acc Acc d/o Thomas & Nancy on 29 Feb 1880 near Modest Town by JE Bundick
TAYLOR David R 56 W Teamster Acc

Acc to Jane Miller 37 W Acc Acc on 16 Apr 1884 at Temp'ville by M Oldham

TAYLOR Edgar Col 21 S Wage-earner Acc Acc s/o Savage & Mary to Carrie Bowdoin Col 17 S Acc Acc d/o Robert & Candice on 28 Oct 1888 at Drum'tn by P Sheppard

TAYLOR Edward J 31 S Gentleman Acc Acc s/o Hills & M E to Lizzie J Melvin 22 S Acc Acc d/o Jno H & Mary on 19 Dec 1872 at Horntown by WT Wilkerson

TAYLOR Edwd 30 W Mariner b: Acc s/o Saml & Mary to Cath Richardson 17 S b: Acc d/o Jas & Mary on 3 Mar 1855 at Ed S Grant's by ES Grant

TAYLOR Edwd R 24 S Farmer Acc Acc s/o Wm & Ann to Mary Ann Conquest 26 S Acc Acc d/o Nathl F & Ann on 29 Feb 1873 near Assawoman by M Oldham

TAYLOR Eliha 21 S Railroading Acc Acc s/o David R & Catherine to Cordelia Nock 21 S Acc Acc d/o George & Delila on 23 Aug 1887 at Temp'ville by M Oldham

TAYLOR Erastus C 18 S Bar Room Keeper Acc Acc s/o Augustus C & Elizth M to Annie E Barnes 18 S Acc Acc d/o Jas W & Mary J on 24 Jan 1886 at Acc by HG Cowan

TAYLOR Ezekiel J 29 S House Carpenter Acc Acc s/o Thorogood N & Sally M to Emma F Rew 21 S Acc Acc d/o John on 17 Jan 1894 at Acc by HL Derby

TAYLOR F C 20 S Farmer Acc Acc s/o Wm M & S M to M L Doughty 19 S Acc Acc d/o Jno B & R on 1 Dec 1886 at Acc by WJ Twilley

TAYLOR Filmore 18 S Laborer Acc Acc s/o George & Mara to Ann Watson 23 S Acc Acc d/o Thos & Lana on 28 Dec 1893 at Chinco: Isld by RB Sanford

TAYLOR Frank Col 22 S Laborer Wor Co MD Acc s/o Caroline to Mary Abbott Col 21 S Acc Acc d/o Betsy on 10 Oct 1882 at Drum'tn by LW Lee

TAYLOR Frank Col 22 S Wage-earner Acc Acc s/o Jacob & Margaret to Josephine Handy Col 22 S Acc Acc d/o Thomas & Comfort on 16 Mar 1890 at Wattsville by N Morris

TAYLOR Frank 28 S Sailor Acc Acc s/o James S & Lavinia to Ida Taylor 24 W Acc Acc d/o Sheppead & Sallie Young on 26 Aug 1891 at Acc by JS Wallace

TAYLOR Frank Col 40 S Laborer Acc Acc s/o Sarah to Millie Marshall Col 22 S Acc Acc d/o Davy on 28 Dec 1881 at New Church by TM Poulson

TAYLOR Frederick to Sarah Bull d/o Geo dec'd lic: 19 Dec 1854 James T Johnson says both over 21

TAYLOR Frederick 50 W Farmer Acc Acc s/o Revel & Ibby to Mary J Fisher 25 W Acc Acc d/o Mary Trader on 3 Arp 1877 at Acc by M Oldham

TAYLOR Frederick D Col 22 S Farmer Acc Acc s/o Isaac & Grace to Annie L Smith Col 18 S Acc Acc d/o Henry & Fannie on 29 Jun 1890 at Acc by L Duncan

TAYLOR Geo T Col 35 S Farmer Acc Acc s/o Geo R & Emeline Harmon to Elizabeth Bundick Col 38 S Acc Acc d/o Sally on 1 Oct 1884 at Acc by JC Cluff

TAYLOR Geo Wm Col 21 S Farmer Acc Acc s/o Arthur & Catharine to Betsy Bayly Col 18 S Acc Acc d/o Annie on 8 Aug 1883 at Acc by P Sheppard

TAYLOR George FN single Laborer Acc Acc s/o Geo Nock & Adah Taylor to Sarah Ames FN single Acc Acc d/o Geo Ames & Easter Burton on 2 Jan 1856 at Pungo: by M

Oldham (James G Smith says they over 21)

TAYLOR George 23 S Farmer Acc Acc s/o Henry & Betsy to Mary A Smith 19 S Acc Acc d/o Thos & Sally on 9 Jan 1876 near New Church by TM Poulson

TAYLOR George 20 S Sailor Acc Acc s/o Joshua & Mary to Susan A Bloxom 18 S Acc Acc d/o Elijah & Airy on 27 Dec 1879 at Chinco: Isld by R Williamson

TAYLOR George 23 S Oysterman Acc Acc s/o Henry & Louisa to Julia A Marshall 20 S Acc Acc d/o Leonard & Eliath on 17 Nov 1879 at Temp'ville by JE McSparran

TAYLOR George Dennis 23 S Farmer Acc Acc s/o William & Ann to Sally Green 24 S Baltimore City MD Acc d/o Charles & Mary E on 7 Jan 1888 at Temp'ville by M Oldham

TAYLOR George T 28 S Farmer Acc Acc s/o John & Cath to Cath L Justice 19 S Acc Acc d/o John & Cath on 7 Apr 1867 at Acc by ES Grant

TAYLOR George W 26 S Farmer Acc Acc s/o John & Mileah to Jane East 21 S Acc Acc d/o Geo T & Sarah on 5 Feb 1873 at r/o Geo M T East by TM Poulson

TAYLOR George W 23 S Merchant Acc Acc s/o Wm M & Sally to Emma S Martin 19 S Acc Acc d/o Smith K & Louisa on 22 Jan 1873 at Acc by LK LeCato

TAYLOR Gillet 23 S Farmer Acc Acc s/o Rixom & Sally to Annie Miles 21 S Acc Acc d/o Richard & Jane on 8 Nov 1881 at Acc by HC Stern

TAYLOR Gillie C 20 S Oysterman Acc Acc s/o James & Melissa to Hattie D Chandler 17 S Acc Acc d/o Malinda on 3 May 1892 at Parksley by HJ Wilson

TAYLOR Handy Col 25 S Laborer Acc Acc s/o Wm & Candace to Ellen Fosque Col 22 S Acc Acc d/o Lura on 1 Nov 1879 at Acc by A Joynes

TAYLOR Henry T 44 W Waterman Acc Acc s/o Thos (of W) & Nancy to Elizabeth Mears 40 S Acc Acc d/o Rachel Marshall on 20 Dec 1891 at Lee Mont by AJ Fristoe

TAYLOR Hy Thos 19 S Sailor Acc Acc s/o Thos & Nancy to Anne Eliza Taylor 18 S Acc Acc d/o Gillet & Betsy on 1 Jan 1868 at Acc by JH Ellegood

TAYLOR Jacob Col 58 S Laborer Acc Acc to Margaret Davis Col 48 S Acc Acc on 22 Mar 1882 near Jenkins Bridge by JC Cluff

TAYLOR James Col 21 S Oysterman Acc Chinco: Isld s/o James T & Sarah to Leah Marshall Col 21 S Acc Horntown d/o George & Hester on 5 Dec 1880 at Chinco: Isld by JC Cluff

TAYLOR James Col 30 S Laborer Acc Acc s/o Mary Coard to Mary Joynes Col 22 S Acc Acc d/o Harriet Coleburn on 31 Jul 1881 at Onancock by JC Ayler

TAYLOR James Col 45 S Teamster Som Co MD Acc to Elizabeth Garrison Col 40 S Acc Acc on 22 Oct 1882 at Onancock by JC Ayler

TAYLOR James Col 23 S Farmer Acc Acc s/o Mary to Mary H Walker Col 20 S Acc Acc d/o Lydia Pitts on 30 May 1883 at Drum'tn by LW Lee

TAYLOR James Col 25 S Farmer Acc Acc s/o James A & Jennie to Mary Wise Col 22 S Acc Acc d/o John & Caroline on 18 Nov 1891 at Savageville by JH Offer

TAYLOR James A 22 S Sailor Acc Acc s/o Edwd & Sally to Mary J Williams 17 S Acc Acc d/o Thomas H & Margaret on 26 Apr 1883 at Acc by SC Boston

TAYLOR James A 25 S Waterman Acc Acc s/o Angelo & Mahala to Minnie

F [Tindal] Tindall 21 S Acc Acc d/o James H & Mary on 10 Jan 1894 at Oak Hall by DJ Traynham
TAYLOR James B 55 W Farmer Messongo Messongo s/o Tegal to Sarah Rowley 45 W Messongo Muddy Ck on 29 Jun 1858 at r/o George H Ewell by GH Ewell
TAYLOR James H 25 S Acc Acc to Delany Dalby 35 W Acc Acc on 7 Jan 1869 at Acc by JO Moss
TAYLOR James P A 21 S Oysterman Acc Acc s/o Hy B & Nancy to Melinda J Riggs 22 S Acc Acc d/o Elizabeth on 22 Mar 1866 at Acc by M Oldham
TAYLOR James S 40 W Sailor Messongo Messongo to Levinea [Staks] (Stokes) Stokes 24 W Messongo Messongo on 14 Oct 1858 at r/o Geo H Ewell by GH Ewell
TAYLOR Jeff 22 S Farmer Acc Acc s/o Elizabeth to Mary F Smith 17 S Acc Acc d/o Noah on 23 Jan 1889 at Temp'ville by WF Hayes
TAYLOR Jerimiah 24 S Oysterman Acc Acc s/o Jas B to Mary J [Brodwater] Broadwater 19 S Acc Acc d/o Walter on 13 Jan 1869 at Acc by JO Moss
TAYLOR John to Caroline White wid lic: 24 Nov 1856 Wm B Savage says he over 21
TAYLOR John 28 S Teaching b: Acc s/o William Taylor & Esther Ames to Elizabeth Hancock 23 S b: Acc d/o William Hancock & Polly Justice on 11 Apr 1857 at Acc by P Warren (Samuel Lilleston says he over 21 & James Whealton says she over 21)
TAYLOR John 23 S Oysterman Acc Acc s/o Revel & Margt to Ellen [Bonewell] Bonnewell 22 S Acc Acc d/o Geo & Ellen on 6 Feb 1867 at Acc by JO Moss
TAYLOR John 25 S Farmer Acc Acc s/o Matthew to Pamelia Hickman 25 S Acc Acc d/o Jas & Sallie on 9 Jan 1868 at Acc by M Oldham
TAYLOR John Col 20 S Laborer Acc Acc s/o Jacob & Margt to Clara Conquest Col 16 S Acc Acc d/o Sallie Wharton on 3 Aug 1885 near Temp'ville by JC Cluff
TAYLOR John E Col 22 S Farmer Acc Acc s/o Arthur & Catharine to Mary White Col 22 S Acc Acc d/o Peter & Mary on 9 Nov 1892 near Keller by RH Coleburn
TAYLOR John J (James) 21 S Oysterman b: Guilford s/o Thos (of Wm) & Nancy to Susan Taylor 21 S b: Guilford d/o Betsey Taylor on 10 Jul 1857(?) at r/o Geo H Ewell by GH Ewell (Alfred J Taylor says both over 21) Certificate returned 8 May 1860
TAYLOR John L 22 S Oysterman Acc Acc s/o George T & Louisa C to Nanie E [Justis] Justice 16 S Acc Acc d/o Revel J & Nancy M on 24 May 1893 at Lee Mont by JET Ewell
TAYLOR John S 26 S Shoemaker Acc Acc s/o Saml E & Betsy to Margaret A Lewis 18 S Acc Acc d/o Wm L & Margaret on 6 Feb 1881 at Guilford Ch by LB Betty
TAYLOR John S 20 S Waterman Acc Acc s/o Samuel C & Melinda to Sallie G Barnes 16 S Acc Acc d/o William J & Bernetta on 25 Dec 1889 at Parksley by HS Dulany
TAYLOR John T (see TAILOR)
TAYLOR John W 24 S Oysterman Acc Acc s/o Jno & Cath to Betsy Justice 22 S Acc Acc d/o Rev & Nancy on 18 Jan 1866 at Acc by ES Grant
TAYLOR Joseph 33 S Merchant Acc Acc to Sally Lang 37 S Acc Acc d/o Alexander on 10 Apr 1862 at Acc by JC Mears
TAYLOR Joseph 28 S Sailor Acc Acc s/o John & Martha to Anna Jester 17 S Acc Acc d/o Eba & Mary on 28 May 1882 at Chinco: Isld by WP

Thornton

TAYLOR Joseph B 66 W Farmer Acc Acc. s/o Jas & Hester to Mary E Gilden 43 W Acc Acc d/o Geo & Patience Beloate on 21 Nov 1877 near Onancock by SC Boston

TAYLOR Joseph H 35 W Oysterman Acc Acc s/o John Taylor & Martha Munger to Elizabeth Thornton 23 W Acc Acc d/o Robert & Henrietta Watson on 27 Dec 1890 at Chinco: Isld by GE Wood

TAYLOR Joseph H 23 S Sailor Acc Acc s/o Prudee A & Malinda J to Maggie E Ewell 21 S Acc Acc d/o Edward & Margaret on 14 Jan 1894 at Guilford by JR Tillery

TAYLOR Joseph W 26 S Farmer Acc Acc s/o Edwd W & Mary to Mollie G Corbin 22 S Acc Acc d/o Littleton D & Mary on 19 Dec 1877 at Downings Ch by JB Merritt

TAYLOR Joseph W 31 W Farmer Acc Acc s/o Edwd W & Mary to Betsy Ann Corbin 27 S Acc Acc d/o Littleton on 3 Jan 1884 at New Church by M Oldham

TAYLOR Joseph W 25 S Farmer Acc Acc s/o Samuel T & Sarah A to Sallie D Byrd 25 S Acc Acc d/o George W & Elizabeth on 29 Oct 1890 at Mappsville by WA Street

TAYLOR Lewis 23 S Farmer Acc Acc s/o Matthew H & Cassandra to Jane Taylor 17 S Acc Acc d/o Susan on 4 Sep 1873 near Guilford by JE Bundick

TAYLOR Lewis Corbin 24 S Oysterman Acc Acc s/o Saml & Lavinia to Virginia Barnes 19 S Acc Acc d/o Jno & Sally on 6 Feb 1876 at Back Ck by JET Ewell

TAYLOR Littleton Col 23 S Farmer Acc Acc s/o Jacob to Elizabeth Copes Col 13 S Acc Acc d/o Olivia on 30 Dec 1880 at Temp'ville by JC Cluff

TAYLOR Lloyd J 21 S Oysterman Acc Acc s/o Joseph & Sarah to Charlotte Knight 17 S Acc Acc d/o Henry & Arrona on 9 Jun 1886 at Acc by JW Carroll

TAYLOR Louis C 22 S Oysterman Acc Acc s/o Thomas & Elizabeth to Mary S Young 19 S Acc Acc d/o Louis J & Mary E on 12 Jun 1892 near Nelsonia by JE Bundick

TAYLOR Louis F 27 D Farmer Acc Acc s/o Matthew H & Cassandra to Mary Jane Taylor 20 S Acc Acc d/o Thomas & Nancy on 7 Feb 1876 at Guilford by JET Ewell

TAYLOR Lynn F 27 S Life Saving Service Acc Acc s/o Oliver H & Mary W to E Josie Fox 19 S Acc Acc d/o Geo G & Susan U on 22 Aug 1889 at Wachapreague by WJ Twilley

TAYLOR Major Col 20 S Sailor Acc Acc s/o Zylia Matthews to Georgianna Matthews Col 17 S Acc Acc d/o Shadrack & Harriet on 21 May 1872 near Drum'tn by A Joynes

TAYLOR Mathew L 19 S Farmer Acc Acc s/o Custis & Mary to Maggie E Russell 16 S Acc Acc d/o Thomas F & Mary on 6 Jan 1895 at Acc by JET Ewell

TAYLOR Maury 24 S Farmer Acc Acc s/o Thomas & Patsy to Alicia Bunting 19 S Acc Acc d/o Teagle & Evaline on 25 Dec 1881 at Conquest Ch by JW Hundley

TAYLOR Neal M 26 S Acc Acc to Sallie D Hall 29 S Acc Acc on 30 Dec 1885 at Oak Hall by DM Wallace

TAYLOR Oliver H to Alice Aydelotte on 14 Mar 1876 at Nashville Acc Co by JM Anderson

TAYLOR Oliver J 32 S Farmer b: Acc s/o Revel & Ibby to Mary (Starling) Sterling 23 S b: Acc d/o Kendel & Esther on 23 Dec 1858(7) near Oak

Hall by S Powers (James B Taylor says both over 21) Certificate returned 27 Jan 1858

TAYLOR Oliver J 21 S Farmer Acc Acc s/o Oliver L & Sally Ann to Elizabeth Kelly 24 W Acc Acc d/o Burwell B & Mary Gladding on 8 Jul 1886 at Acc by JW Carroll

TAYLOR Oliver L 25 S s/o Zadock & Rachel to Sally A Chesser 22 S d/o Henry & Sally lic: 10 Apr 1864 marr: 10 Apr 1864 at Accomack

TAYLOR Oliver L 39 W Farmer Acc Acc s/o Zaddock & Rachel to Mary Landing 31 W Acc Acc d/o James & Polly Ayres on 31 Dec 1872 at Temp'ville by M Oldham

TAYLOR Oswald T 25 S Sailor N'hamp: N'hamp: s/o John & Luch Taylor to Margaret S Ward 17 S Acc Acc d/o Lancelot L & Mary A on 10 Jun 1877 at Locust Mount by JWA Elliott

TAYLOR Reuben A 21 S Carpenter Acc Acc s/o Colmore & Rose to Mary F Watson 21 S Acc Acc d/o Benj & Martha on 27 Dec 1877 near Wattsville by TM Poulson

TAYLOR Revel J 21 S Farmer Acc Acc s/o Thos & Patsy to Louisa Taylor 18 S Acc Acc d/o Asa & Mary on 27 Dec 1872 at Muddy Ck by M Oldham

TAYLOR Revel J 22 S Waterman Acc Acc s/o Socertis F & Margaret to Sallie C [Justis] Justice 19 S Acc Acc d/o Isaiah W & Margaret on 5 Jun 1887 at Mappsville by JW Norris

TAYLOR Revel James 28 S Farmer Acc Acc s/o Wm & Margaret to Virginia Nock 25 S Acc Acc d/o James & Margaret on 13 Feb 1870 at Messongo by O Littleton

TAYLOR Rixsom 46 W Farmer MD Acc s/o James & Nancy to Mary E Ailworth 17 S Acc Acc d/o Lenox & Anne on 24 Aug 1870 at Acc by TM Poulson

TAYLOR Robert J to Arinthia S Wessells d/o Sally who gave consent lic: 24 Mar 1856 Alfred J Taylor says he over 21

TAYLOR Robert S 26 S Sailor Acc Acc s/o Savage & Nancy to Vernetta S Lankford 17 S Acc Acc d/o Selby & Mary on 12 Jan 1870 at Acc by JET Ewell

TAYLOR Robert S 19 S Oysterman Acc Acc s/o Henry T & Elizabeth to Laura A Taylor 17 S Acc Acc d/o Crippen D & Jane on 24 Apr 1892 at Acc by HJ Wilson

TAYLOR Robert T 21 S Oysterman Acc Acc s/o Thomas & Eliza to Anna Coard 16 S Acc Acc d/o Salathiel & Mary on 19 Sep 1874 at bride's father's by P Bowdin Sr

TAYLOR Sabastian 23 S Farmer Acc Acc s/o Thomas & Patsy to Elizabeth Knight 22 S Acc Acc d/o Henry & Serena on 25 Dec 1881 at Conquest Ch by JW Hundley

TAYLOR Saml C 24 S Farmer Acc Acc s/o John & Cath to Melinda Ewell 22 S Acc Acc d/o Gillet & Betsy on 27 Dec 1868 at Acc by JET Ewell

TAYLOR Saml T 38 W Farmer Acc Acc to Martha W Snead 25 S Acc Acc d/o John L & Tabitha on 1 Feb 1866 at Acc by JE Bundick

TAYLOR Samuel A 21 S Farmer Acc Acc s/o Samuel T & Sara A to Ella M Bloxom 18 S Acc Acc d/o Martin & Susan on 15 Jan 1888 at Acc by WA Street

TAYLOR Samuel C 30 W Farmer Acc Acc s/o John & Catherine to Arcissa [Wessels] Wessells 25 S Acc Acc d/o Samuel & Rachel on 15 Feb 1888 at Lee Mont by JS Wharton

TAYLOR Samuel C 20 S Oysterman Acc Acc s/o Samuel C & Malinda to Mary J [Justis] Justice 17 S Acc Acc d/o John & Malinda on 19 Aug 1891 at Parksley by HS Dulany

TAYLOR Samuel T 28 S Sailor Acc Acc s/o Samuel E & Eli'th to Eula L Justice 22 S Acc Acc d/o Charles & Melissa on 9 Jun 1895 at Acc by JW Charlton

TAYLOR Savage Col 30 S Laborer Acc Acc to Sarah Twiford Col 27 S Acc Acc on 6 Feb 1876 at Metompkin Bapt Ch by A Joynes

TAYLOR Sebastian 34 W Farmer Acc Acc s/o Thos & Patsey to Susan Ann Bunting 20 S Acc Acc d/o Teagle & Eveline on 29 Oct 1893 at Messongo Bridge by JW Nicholson

TAYLOR Selby s/o David who gave consent to Jane Hart d/o Richard lic: 8 Mar 1855 Samuel T Taylor says she over 21

TAYLOR Severn J 28 W Sailor MD Acc s/o Parker & Maria to Hester Jane Ward 21 S Acc Acc d/o Geo & Susan on 23 May 1867 at Acc by GW Matthews

TAYLOR Sewell A 21 S Farmer Acc Acc s/o Teagle H & Sally F to Mattie E Pruitt 19 S Acc Acc d/o Wm H & Hennie on 26 Dec 1894 at Acc by DGC Butts

TAYLOR Shaderick Col 60 S Farmer Acc Acc s/o Ada to Jane Brown Col 40 W Acc Acc d/o Leah Fisher on 7 Jan 1880 near Atlantic by JC Cluff

TAYLOR Skinner 26 S Capenter Acc Acc s/o Rixom & Sally to Mary W Matthews 16 S Acc Acc d/o Geo W & Emily on 1 Feb 1880 at Meth Par by JW Hilldrup

TAYLOR Socrates 27 S Sailor Acc Acc s/o Chas & Maggy to Margt [Wessels] Wessells 22 S Acc Acc d/o Ephrain & Sally on 2 Jul 1863 at Acc by GH Ewell

TAYLOR Socrates F 50 W Farmer Acc Acc s/o Charles & Margaret to Christanna E Hinman 35 S Acc Acc d/o William & Elizabeth on 25 May 1887 at Geo T Ewell's by JW Norris

TAYLOR Stansbury 19 S Sailor Acc Acc s/o Thos to Elizabeth Trader 19 S Acc Acc d/o Wm P & Margt on 11 Oct 1879 near Muddy Ck by JE Bundick

TAYLOR Teackle (Jr) 22 S Oysterman Guilford Guilford s/o Teackle & Rebecker to Delia (Delila) Annis 23 S Guilford Guilford d/o Levi & Tabitha on 29 Dec 1857 at r/o George H Ewell by GH Ewell (David Taylor says both over 21)

TAYLOR Thomas widr to Nancy Chandler wid lic: 15 Sep 1857

TAYLOR Thomas B 22 S Farmer Acc Acc s/o Edwd W & Sally S to Mollie E Mears 16 S Acc Acc d/o Bagwell C & Eliza on 21 Dec 1876 at Drum'tn by JH Amiss

TAYLOR Thomas R 22 S Farmer Acc Acc s/o David R & Cartharine to Caroline F Darby 16 S Acc Acc d/o Jas L & Rebecca on 28 Jan 1883 at Atlantic by MS Read

TAYLOR Thomas T 21 S Farmer Acc Acc s/o Edward W & Mary to Mary Ann Nock 23 S Acc Acc d/o Littleton & Elizabeth N on 3 Nov 1869 at Acc by JO Moss

TAYLOR Thorogood 31 W Farming Acc Acc s/o Nancy to Sally [Rolly] Rowley 35 W Acc Acc d/o George Pruitt on 7 Sep 1861 at Acc by GH Ewell

TAYLOR Thorogood 35 S Farmer Acc Acc to Elizabeth East 37 W Acc Acc on 13 Mar 1878 near Reese Chp by JH Amiss

TAYLOR Thorogood (N) 23 S Sailor Acc Acc s/o John & Milcha to Anna M Taylor 19 S Acc Acc d/o John & Harriett & ward/o Wm S Byrd who gave consent on 6 Oct 1857 at Oak Hall by S Powers (Wm S Byrd said he over 21)

TAYLOR Thorogood N 46 W Farmer

Acc Acc s/o Thos & Nancy to Nancy Berry 36 S Acc Acc d/o Charles on 30 Jun 1878 at Ann's Cove by JB Merritt

TAYLOR Thos single Shoemaker MD Chinco: Isld s/o Peter to Eliza Snead single Chinco: Isld Chinco: Isld d/o R (Robt) W & Bridget on 31 Jan 1854 at r/o Robt Snead by P Bowdin (John Thornton says both over 21)

TAYLOR Thos 49 W Oysterman Guilford Guilford s/o Tabith Taylor to Elizabeth Taylor 35 W Hunting Ck Guilford d/o Arthur & Uphamia Barnes on 15 Nov 1864 at r/o Geo H Ewell by GH Ewell

TAYLOR Thos T 46 W Farmer Acc Acc s/o Richd & Nancy to Emeline Nelson 22 W Acc Acc d/o Justice B Taylor on 11 Jun 1865 at Acc by M Oldham

TAYLOR Walter Col 35 S Farmer Acc Acc s/o George & Sally to Annie Blake Col 27 S Acc Acc d/o Hannah on 21 May 1882 near Temp'ville by JC Cluff

TAYLOR Webster F 18 S Sailor Acc Acc s/o John W & Betsey to Maggie J East 18 S Acc Acc d/o William A & Elizabeth on 1 Jan 1889 at Hunting Ck by HS Dulany

TAYLOR William 45 S Laborer Acc Acc s/o Sarah to Candice Rew 40 S Acc Acc d/o Mary on 1 Jun 1868 at Acc by A Joynes

TAYLOR William 50 W Laborer Acc Acc s/o Sarah to Emma Bayly 40 S Acc Acc on 19 May 1881 at Acc by AJ Satchell

TAYLOR WIlliam H 22 S Sailor Acc Acc s/o John W & Ellen to Genie F Knight 22 S Acc Acc d/o Henry & Arena on 11 May 1890 at Mappsville by WA Street

TAYLOR William J 28 S Oyster Dealer Acc Lancaster Co VA s/o Thos H & Sallie to Sadie M Hutchinson 22 S Acc Acc d/o Edward W on 30 Oct 1895 at Horntown by JC Watson

TAYLOR William M Jr 33 W Farmer Acc Acc s/o Wm M & Sallie A to Maggie S Bundick 18 S Acc Acc d/o Wm T & Catherine on 22 Nov 1887 at Onancock by JW Easley

TAYLOR Wm Col 23 S Barber Acc Chinco: Isld s/o James & Sally to Ellen Douglas Ewell Col 17 S Acc Horntown d/o Wm & Mary on 24 Oct 1877 near Atlantic P O by JC Cluff

TAYLOR Wm 28 S Sailor Acc Acc to Cinda E Bowen 17 S Wor Co MD Acc d/o Wm J on 2 Feb 1879 at Wm Bowen's by JW Hilldrup

TAYLOR Wm J 21 S Farmer Acc Acc s/o Asa & Maria to Virginia A Gardner 19 S Acc Acc d/o Charlotte on 4 Jul 1877 at Conquest Ch by JB Merritt

TAYLOR Wm M 24 S Farmer Acc Acc s/o Wm M & Sally A to Elizabeth C Boggs 23 S Acc Acc d/o Levi R & Hester A on 1 Aug 1878 at Leatherbury Br by JH Amiss

TAYLOR Zadoc Thos 32 S Oysterman Acc Acc s/o Thomas & Patsey to Mary Caroline Bunting 17 S Acc Acc d/o Teagle & Eveline W on 6 Mar 1887 at Temp'ville by JW Carroll

TAYLOR Samuel T Jr 21 S Oysterman Acc Acc s/o Samuel T & Critty to Sarah Ann Taylor 22 S Acc Acc d/o Zadoc & Rachel on 31 Oct 1860 at Acc by JC Mears (Julius C Mears says both over 21)

TEAGLE Abram [Teackle] Col 31 S Farmer Acc Acc s/o Leah to Emily J Watson Col 25 S Acc Acc d/o Wm & Amelia on 24 Feb 1884 at Mappsville by AJ Satchell

TEAGLE Isaac H Col 41 S Wage-earner Wor Co MD Acc s/o Jacob & Leah Merrill to Melvina Burton Col 25 S DE Acc on 3 Apr 1892 at Temp'ville

by JC Cluff
TEAGLE John Col 22 S Farmer Acc Acc s/o Abel & Leah to Margaret [Abbitt] Abbott Col 18 S Acc Acc d/o William & Sarah on 11 Nov 1888 at Sea Side by AJ Satchell
TEAGLE Joseph Col 32 S Sailor Acc Acc s/o Leah to Emily F Mapp Col 18 S Acc Acc d/o Peter & Margt on 17 Mar 1878 at Modest Town by A Joynes
TEAGUE Arthur 23 S Laborer Acc Acc s/o Rosa Snead to Rachel Webb 21 S Acc Acc d/o Margaret on 13 Jan 1867 at Acc by JWA Elliott
TEAGUE George T Col 24 S Farmer Acc Acc s/o Arthur & Rachel to Maggie Davis Col 19 S Acc Acc d/o Richard & Juliet on 18 Apr 1891 at Acc by JWA Elliott
TEAGUE William [Tigue] Col 29 S Laborer Acc Acc s/o George & Leah to Lizzie Bell Col 21 S Acc Acc d/o Mary on 9 Nov 1881 near Locustville by LK LeCato
TENNANT John C to Sallie T Potter on 11 Jun 1858 at St James Ch Drum'tn by C Colton (George D Wise says both over 21)
TERRY Jones F 25 S Oysterman b: Warick to Mary J W Mears 17 S b: Acc d/o Robert Mears on 6 Mar 1856 at r/o John Stants by GH Ewell (Raymond R Stant says he over 21)
THOMAS Aaron S 24 S Oysterman Acc Acc s/o Julia A to Priscilla Thomas 19 S Acc Acc d/o Jno P & Caroline on 22 Sep 1878 at Tangier Isld by WJ Duhadway
THOMAS Aaron S 27 W Waterman Acc Acc s/o Joshua & Julia to Sarah Corbett 18 S Acc Acc d/o Richd & Mary M on 21 Sep 1884 at Acc by CS Baker
THOMAS Corbin 22 S Oysterman Acc Acc s/o Jno & Eliza to Sarah W Marshall 18 S Acc Acc d/o Dennard & Eliz on 28 Jun 1865 at Acc by GH Ewell
THOMAS Edward 21 S Oysterman Acc Acc s/o Corbin & Sarah to Sallie Miles 21 S Acc Acc d/o Severn P & Hester Ann on 9 Apr 1893 at Sykes Isld by RB Scott
THOMAS George W 25 S Farmer b: Kent Co MD s/o John & Mary to Caroline Mason 22 S d/o Bagwell & Margaret lic: 16 May 1865 marr: 17 May 1865
THOMAS Henry A 21 S Sailor Acc Acc s/o Jno P & Caroline to Mary A Spence 19 S Acc Acc d/o Elijah & Margt on 20 May 1877 at Tangier Isld by WJ Duhadway
THOMAS Isaiah 20 S Sailor Acc Acc s/o Lybranet H & Polly to Nellie Laird 18 S Acc Acc d/o Jno T & Melinda on 20 May 1883 at Tangier Isld by CS Baker
THOMAS James 23 S Sailor Acc Acc s/o Elizabeth to Margaret Parkes 17 S Acc Acc d/o Jno E & Eliza on 14 Feb 1886 at Tangier Isld by CS Baker
THOMAS John H Col 24 S Farmer Kinston NC Acc s/o Ailsie Jones to Georgianna Hutchinson Col 22 S Acc Acc d/o Geo & Leah on 20 Nov 1889 at Onancock by GHT Byrd
THOMAS John Parker 25 S Merchant b: Tangier Isld s/o John & Ann to Caroline Crockett 15 S b: Tangier Isld d/o Severn & Ellender on 28 Feb 1856 at Acc by JH Addison (L H Thomas says he over 21)
THOMAS John R 20 S Sailor Acc Acc s/o Edward R & Mary W to Anna S Gaskins 17 S Acc Acc d/o John S & Letitia on 28 Jan 1875 at Acc by WJ Twilley
THOMAS John W 23 S Sailor Acc Acc s/o John P & Caroline to Emma N Crockett 19 S Acc Acc d/o John M & Emma R on 1 Apr 1891 at Tangier

Isld by J Connor

THOMAS Joseph Col 25 S Laborer Anne Arundel Co MD Acc to Mary Knocke Col 35 S Acc Acc d/o Jenney on 27 Nov 1884 at Acc by P Sheppard

THOMAS Joshua 26 S Sailor Smith Isld MD Acc s/o Wm S & Mary A to Emma Susan James 20 S Acc Acc d/o Levin T & Elizth C on 22 May 1872 at Acc by PA Leatherbury

THOMAS Leband H (Lyband) 21 S Merchant Tangier Isld Tangier Isld s/o John & Ann to Polly Crockett 20 S Tangier Isld Tangier Isld d/o John & Sarah on 1 Oct 1856 at Acc by JH Addison

THOMAS Lewis 31 S Sailor Acc Acc s/o Jno & Eliza to Amanda Lewis 17 S Acc Acc d/o Revell & Polly on 20 Nov 1865 at Acc by JH Ellegood

THOMAS Lloyd F 21 S Farmer Acc Acc s/o Jas P to Mary Lee Gladding 19 S Acc Acc d/o Jas H & Mary J on 22 Jan 1880 at New Church by CS Arnett

THOMAS Lloyd F 30 S Farmer Acc Acc s/o James B & Pamelia A to Henrietta Brimer 25 S Acc Acc d/o Samuel & Jane on 29 Jun 1887 at Temp'ville by JW Carroll

THOMAS Sheppard Col 29 S Laborer Acc Acc s/o Wm to Missouri Gunter Col 23 S Acc Acc d/o Lucy on 4 Jan 1888 at Acc by JA Haynes

THOMAS Washington P 21 S Farmer Acc Acc s/o Jas B & Amelia to Ann C Whealton 21 S Acc Acc d/o Erastus & Mary on 5 Dec 1877 near Oak Hall by M Oldham

THOMAS William S 19 S Merchant Acc Acc s/o Josha & Julia to Julie Crockett 18 S Acc Acc d/o Peter & Mary on 19 Aug 1867 at Acc by WT Tull

THOMAS Wm H Col 22 S Teacher Hollidaysburg PA Baltimore MD s/o Benjamin & Serena to Margt Ann Stevens Col 17 S Acc Acc d/o Rica & Margaret on 7 Sep 1876 near Drum'tn by A Joynes

THORNS Columbus C 25 S Oysterman Acc Acc s/o Wm & Margt to Malissa Thorns 20 S Acc Acc d/o Polly on 11 Jan 1885 at Guilford by JW Carroll

THORNS Dennis 26 S Oysterman b: Acc s/o Polly Thomas to Eveline Taylor 25 S b: Acc d/o Teagle & Rebecha on 5 Nov 1854 at Geo H Ewell's by GH Ewell (Geo H Ewell says both over 21)

THORNS Henry 23 S Farmer Acc Acc s/o Gilley & Comfort to Elizth Custis 35 S Acc Acc d/o John H & Sally on 3 Jan 1877 at Guilford by JB Merritt

THORNS Jas 25 S Sailor Acc Acc s/o Zipporah Colona to Catharine Taylor 29 W MD Acc d/o Jno & Emma Zelder on 29 Mar 1863 at Acc by ES Grant

THORNS John C 23 S Acc Acc s/o Wm & Margt to Lavinia Taylor 15 S Acc Acc d/o Gilley & Elizabeth on 9 Feb 1876 at Guilford by JET Ewell

THORNS John D [Thorms] 28 S Oysterman Acc Acc s/o Dennis & Eveline to Arinthia C Ewell 24 S Acc Acc d/o James & Julia Ann on 22 Feb 1888 at Guilford by JS Wharton

THORNS Robert C 20 S Sailor & Laborer Acc Acc s/o Elizabeth to Rebecca E [Tiler] Tyler 21 S Acc Acc d/o Selby & Jane on 30 Apr 1882 at Acc by LB Betty

THORNS William R 25 S Waterman Acc Acc s/o Dennis & Margaret to Maggie May Annis 18 S Acc Acc d/o Wm F & Mary on 27 Feb 1895 at Acc by J Connor

THORNTON Alfred T 24 S Oysterman Acc Acc s/o James & Jane to Alice D ·Ewell 19 S Acc Acc d/o Jno & Sarah Ann on 26 Dec 1877 near Masonville by FH Mullineaux

THORNTON Alfred T 22 S Oysterman Chinco: Isld Chinco: Isld s/o Parker & Eliza to Ida E Daisey 16 S Chinco: Isld Chinco: Isld d/o Wm H & Mary A on 9 May 1886 at Chinco: Isld by SU Grimsley

THORNTON Benjamin 22 S Acc Acc s/o Parkes & Eliza to Arena Thornton 22 S Acc Acc d/o Wiles B & Ebby on 7 Dec 1882 at Chinco: Isld by WP Thornton

THORNTON Calhoun J 21 S Farmer Acc Acc s/o James & Mary to Willie F Bundick 15 S Acc Acc d/o Thomas & Mary on 30 Dec 1888 at Crowsontown by HS Dulany

THORNTON Charles 22 S Carpenter Acc Chinco: Isld s/o Wm & Abagil to Sarahann (Sally A) Jester 26 W Chinco: Isld Chinco: Isld d/o George & Hetty Burch on 16 Feb 1857 at r/o Parker Bowdin by P Bowdin (John Thornton says he over 21)

THORNTON Edwd 45 S Acc Acc to Mary E Matthews 28 S Acc Acc d/o Jacob & Seymour on 22 Mar 1877 at Mrs Matthews' by DA Woodson

THORNTON James 21 S Waterman Chinco: Isld Chinco: Isld s/o John (D) & Betsey to Delilah [Wimber] (Winbro) Wimbrough 16 S Chinco: Isld Chinco: Isld d/o Griffin & Betsy on 5 Oct 1857 at my house by P Bowdin (John A M Whealton says he over 21)

THORNTON James L 19 S Farmer Acc Acc s/o James & Mary to Sarah C Jenkins 17 S Acc Acc d/o Wm J & Susan on 27 Dec 1893 at Lee Mont by JET Ewell

THORNTON James T 22 S Oysterman Acc Greenbackville s/o Robt & Margt to Ella Taylor 23 S Wor Co MD Greenbackville d/o Jno & Mahala on 2 Mar 1881 at Greenbackville by WL Holmes

THORNTON James T 23 W Oysterman Acc Greenbackville s/o Robt & Margaret to Mary Elizth Ward 32 W Wor Co MD Greenbackville d/o Jas & Amanda Tull on 15 Aug 1883 at New Church by TM Poulson

THORNTON James W Jr 22 S Oysterman Acc Acc s/o Jas W Sr & Delilah to Julia Russell 15 S Acc Acc d/o Elijah & Charlotte on 22 Nov 1892 at Chinco: Isld by JF Wooden

THORNTON Jas H 24 S Oysterman Acc Acc s/o Jas & Jane to Elisha Simpson 19 S Acc Acc d/o Wm & Margt on 13 Jun 1886 at Lee Mont by WA Street

THORNTON John 20 S Sailor Chinco: Isld Chinco: Isld s/o Kendal & Sarah to Trany M Melvin 16 S Chinco: Isld Chinco: Isld d/o Saml & Elizth on 28 Jan 1877 at Chinco: Isld by R Williamson

THORNTON John 24 S Oysterman Acc Acc s/o James to Elizabeth A Kelly 21 S Acc Acc d/o Edmund & Sarah on 14 Oct 1880 at Acc by JW Hundley

THORNTON John 19 S Oysterman Acc Acc s/o John C & Mary A to Patience Thornton 16 S Acc Acc d/o Miles B & Ebba on 22 Sep 1888 at Acc by JE Bundick

THORNTON John H 20 S Laborer Acc Acc s/o Wm T & Sally to S Ellen Taylor 21 S Acc Acc d/o Nancy on 26 Dec 1882 at Conquest Ch by M Oldham

THORNTON John T 22 S Sailor Chinco: Isld Chinco: Isld s/o Ann to Sarah J Jones 16 S Chinco: Isld Chinco: Isld d/o Danl & Mary on 22 Jan 1877 at Chinco: Isld by WP Thornton

THORNTON John T 27 W Oysterman Acc Acc s/o Ann to Comfort Andrews 23 S Acc Acc d/o William & Mary on 23 Aug 1880 at Chinco: Isld by WP Thornton

THORNTON John T 26 S Oysterman Acc Acc s/o John H & Margaret to Margaret S Chesser 24 S Acc Acc d/o Smith & Margaret on 8 Feb 1882 at Mappsville by JW Hundley

THORNTON Lemuel Y 21 S Farmer Acc Acc s/o Thos & Maria to Harriet F [Tyndall] Tindall 21 S Acc Acc d/o Sepland & Ann Mary on 8 Jan 1879 at Modest Town by JW Hundley

THORNTON Lewis J 27 S Farmer Acc Acc s/o John H & Margaret to Fannie Taylor 21 S Acc Acc d/o Ambrose S & Catharine on 30 Dec 1890 at Acc by RS Williamson

THORNTON Miles 20 S Fisherman Chinco: Isld Chinco: Isld s/o Wm P & Nancy to Ebba Hall 23 S Chinco: Isld Chinco: Isld d/o John (Decd) & Mary on 22 Nov 1857 at Chinco: Isld by P Bowdin (John A M Whealton says she 21)

THORNTON Miles B 39 W Oysterman Acc Acc s/o Wm P & Nancy to Maggie E Bennett 22 S Sussex Co DE Acc d/o Wn & Sally on 13 Mar 1880 at Chinco: Isld by WP Thornton

THORNTON Robert to Margaret Taylor d/o John lic: 27 Aug 1856 Wm W Selby says both over 21

THORNTON Robt J 26 W Oysterman Acc Acc s/o Jas & Sallie to Syrena J Brimer 25 W Acc Acc d/o (-----) Taylor on 15 Jun 1862 at Acc by JE Maloy

THORNTON Silas B 23 S Oysterman Acc Acc s/o Miles & Ebba to Eliza Ann Daisey 19 S Acc Acc d/o John & Nancy M on 9 Jun 1891 at Chinco: Isld by JW Turner

THORNTON Sylvester L 22 S Farmer Acc Acc s/o John Henry & Peggy to Florence E Chesser 21 S Acc Acc d/o Erastus P & Harriet on 3 Jul 1887 at Acc by JW Ward

THORNTON Thomas to Maria Johnson lic: 2 Jun 1856 Wm B Savage says both over 21

THORNTON William Jr 20 S Mariner Chinco: Isld Chinco: Isld s/o Revel & Henrietta to Sarah Lewis 21 S Chinco: Isld Piney Isld d/o William E & Leah on 16 Mar 1857 at Chinco: Isld by P Bowdin (John Thornton says he over 21)

THORNTON William T 28 S Farmer Acc Acc s/o William T & Elizabeth to Sarah Ross 17 S Acc Acc d/o Levin J & Elizabeth on 24 Apr 1889 at Temp'ville by WF Hayes

THORNTON Wm 24 W Waterman Chinco: Isld Acc s/o Revel & Henny to Elizabeth [Russel] Russell 18 W Acc Acc d/o Jno & Elizabeth on 19 Apr 1863 at Acc by P Bowdin Jr

THORNTON Wm 20 S Waterman Acc Acc s/o Miles & Ebba to Mary Melvin 16 S Acc Acc d/o Thomas & Lydia on 24 Nov 1881 at Chinco: Isld by WP Thornton

THRONTON John to Elizabeth Watson wid lic: 30 Oct 1860 John A M Whealton says he over 21

TIDBALL Thomas A 25 S Minister Winchester Co VA Portsmouth VA s/o Scott & Cath to Mary J [Browne] Brown 25 S Acc Acc d/o Peter F & Sally on 17 Oct 1872 at St James Ch by AL Berkeley

TIFFANY Louis McLaw 34 W Physician Baltimore MD Baltimore MD s/o Henry Tiffancy & Sally J McLaw to Evelyn May Bayly 29 S Acc Acc d/o Thomas H & Eveline M on 8 Jan 1879 at Petersburg Va by CR Hains

TIGNAL George S 23 S Farmer Acc Acc s/o Samuel & Mary A to Mary N Bundick 21 S Acc Acc d/o Wm T & Katie on 16 Nov 1892 at Onancock by EC Atkins

TIGNAL Samuel 45 W Farmer Acc Acc s/o John & Mary to Mary Johnson 28 W Acc Acc (wid/o Alfred F) & d/o

(Samuel K & Sallie Thomas Lewis) on 4 Feb 1869 at Acc by ES Grant

TILGHMAN Peter M 34 D Photographer Salisbury MD Acc s/o Peter & Harriet to Annie J Lewis 17 S Som Co MD Acc d/o Asa & Susan on 11 May 1880 at Onancock by JC Watson

TILGHMAN Sylvester C 25 S Blacksmith Acc Newbery Charles Co MD s/o Alfred L & Hattie J to Mamie T Rayfield 26 S Acc Acc d/o John T & Susan on 10 Aug 1893 at Acc by AC Berryman

TILGHMAN Wm B H 21 S Green Grocer Wor Co MD Acc s/o Peter & Margt to Vectoria F [Robbins] Robins 18 S Acc Acc d/o G G on 25 Apr 1877 at Chinco: Isld by R Williamson

TIMMONS Albert 32 W Laborer Acc Acc s/o Wm & Mary to Margaret A [Colona] Colonna 28 S Acc Acc d/o John R & Eliza on 9 Jul 1882 at Nashville Acc Co by RB Beadles

TIMMONS Henry 29 S U S Lifesaving Service Wor Co MD Acc to Annie Thornton 18 S Acc Acc d/o James W & Delilah on 28 May 1882 at Chinco: Isld by WP Thornton

TINDALL Custis C [Tyndall] 22 S Merchant Acc Acc s/o John H & Eliz'th J to Nonie C Massey 21 S Acc Acc d/o James D & Ella on 9 Jan 1895 at New Church by GJ Hill

TINDALL Edward [Tindal] 21 S Oysterman Acc Acc s/o George T & Catharine to Mary E Lewis 16 S Acc Acc d/o Daniel W & Drucilla on 5 Mar 1895 at Chinco: Isld by CW Matthews

TINDALL George 21 S Shoemaker Acc Acc s/o Jno H & Nancy to Nancy Mallett 22 S Acc Acc d/o Desius & Nancy on 10 Jul 1870 at Acc by WP Thornton

TINDALL James Henry 24 S Teamster Acc Acc s/o James & Sarah Ann to Mary E Davis 23 S Acc Acc d/o George & Margaret on 29 Jun 1870 at Acc by O Littleton

TINDALL James W [Tindal] 25 S Oysterman Acc Acc s/o John W to Amy L [Burch] Birch 18 S Acc Acc d/o Thomas L & Annie on 14 Jun 1873 at Chinco: Isld by WP Thornton

TINDALL James W [Tyndall] 21 S Farmer Acc Acc s/o Sheppard D & Arinthia T to Maggie E Dennis 21 S Acc Acc d/o William H & Mary E on 3 Apr 1889 at Acc by JS Wallace

TINDALL Jno H [Tindle] 20 S Soldier Wor Co MD Acc s/o Jno W & Emily to Elmener Lewis (23) S Acc Acc d/o Isaac & Vesta on 18 Mar 1864 at Acc by JE Bundick

TINDALL John H 23 S Farmer Acc Acc s/o George & Hetty to Elizabeth J Whealton 23 S Acc Acc d/o Esastus & Mary on 12 Sep 1870 at Acc by O Littleton

TINDALL John U [Tindle] 32 W Oysterman Chinco: Isld Chinco: Isld s/o John W to Mary E Williams 22 S Chinco: Isld Chinco: Isld d/o Selby & Susan on 29 Apr 1878 at Chinco: Isld by IT Adkins

TINDALL John W [Tindal] 40 W Shoemaker MD Chinco: Isld s/o Thos & Leah to Nancy C Cluff 40 W Chinco: Isld Chinco: Isld d/o Wm & Nancy Sharpley on 11 Aug 1858 at Chinco: Isld by P Bowdin

TINDALL John W [Tindal] 20 S Oysterman Acc Acc s/o John H & Elmira to Sarah A Daisey 16 S Acc Acc d/o James H & Catharine on 27 Dec 1890 at Chinco: Isld by GE Wood

TINDALL Joseph J 35 S Farmer Acc Acc s/o Samuel J to Tabitha A Lang 35 S Acc Acc d/o Henry & Catharine on 29 Dec 1895 at Parksley by MF Sanford

TINDALL Salathiel S [Tindal] 25 S Farmer Acc Acc s/o Geo R & Hester A to Tabitha S Warren 23 S Acc Acc d/o Jno T & Tabitha on 5 Feb 1879 at Hollies Ch by SC Boston

TINDALL Saml J [Tindal] 40 W Shoemaker Wor Co MD Acc s/o Thomas & Leah to Cordelia Ann Taylor 16 S Wor Co MD Acc d/o Jas H & Louisa on 26 Dec 1875 at Wattsville by IT Adkins

TINDALL Samuel 21 S Sailor Acc Acc s/o John W & Emily to Euphamia Russell 18 S Acc Acc d/o Elijah & Charlotte on 1 Aug 1874 at Chinco: Isld by P Bowdin Sr

TINDALL Samuel J [Tindal] 24 S Farmer b: Acc s/o George & Hester A to Margaret (L S) Corbin 18 S b: Acc d/o William (H) & Ann on 6 Jan 1858 at New Church by T Waters (Edward Smith says he over 21)

TINDALL Shephard to Ann Maria McCready d/o Stephen dec'd lic: 9 Apr 1856 Samuel S Hinman says both over 21

TINDALL Shepherd D 40 W Farmer Acc Acc to Arinthia Chesser 31 S Acc Acc d/o Robert & Betsy on 23 Jan 1866 at Acc by GW Matthews

TINDALL Wm E 25 S Capenter Acc Acc s/o Sheppard & Maria to Emma L Ling 23 S Acc Acc d/o Edward & Esther on 22 Dec 1886 at Acc by BF Jester

TINGLE Samuel 21 S Oysterman DE Chinco: Isld s/o Anais & Mary to Vesta E Bloxom 17 S Chinco: Isld Chinco: Isld d/o Elijah & Ana on 30 Nov 1876 at Chinco: Isld by P Bowdin Sr

TIPTON John T 20 S Farmer Acc Acc s/o Ephrain & Ann P to Rachel C [Stephens1
1872 at Acc by JE Humphreys

TITLOW Daniel 30 S Minister b: Philadelphia s/o Jacob & Cath to Elizth S Revell 21 S b: Acc d/o Jno B & Anna W & (ward/o Robert J Poulson who gave consent) on 5 Apr 1854 at Acc by J Allen

TOPPING Caleb Col 66 S Farmer Acc Acc s/o Sarah & Riley to Lydia Poulson Col 31 S Acc Acc d/o Jno & Mary on 29 Jul 1885 near Lee Mont by CA Horsey

TOPPING Charles Col 24 S Wage-earner Acc Acc s/o Lucy to Laura Susan Bayly Col 21 S Acc Acc d/o Jane Chandler on 28 May 1890 at Acc by JB Lewis

TOPPING David to Mary T White d/o Thomas lic: 2 May 1855 Henry C White says both over 21

TOPPING Floyd H 23 S Farmer Acc Acc s/o James T & Alfred to Nettie S Byrd 15 S Acc Acc d/o Teackle L & Mary E on 12 Nov 1890 at Acc by HS Dulany

TOPPING Henry Col 22 S Farmer Acc Acc s/o Caleb &Mary to Mary H Chandler Col 21 S Acc Acc d/o Wm Drummond & Jane Chandler on 7 Jun 1891 at Acc by LE Toulson

TOPPING Levi 32 S Farmer Acc Acc s/o Edward Turnell & Sarah Topping to Mary Jane Boggs 22 S Acc Acc d/o Thomas Boggs & Rhoda Bayly on 26 May 1871 at Savageville by WF Williams

TOPPING Wash 22 S Farmer Acc Acc s/o Annie Finney to Arinthia [Bevans] Beavans 23 S Acc Acc d/o Severn & Lizzie on 23 Jan 1867 at Acc by WT Tull

TOWNSEND Alfred J 42 W Farmer Wor Co MD Wor Co MD s/o Peter & Mary to Rebecca S Tyler 23 S Acc Acc d/o John D & Mary R on 12 Jan 1871 at Acc by GT Tyler

TOWNSEND Charles W 22 S Waterman Pocomoke City MD Acc s/o Jas to Alise E Moore 19 S Pocomoke City MD Acc d/o John H

& Sarah on 24 Dec 1895 at Tangier by CP Swain

TOWNSEND John Col 34 S Oysterman Acc Acc s/o Elijah & Tabitha to Martha Fields Col 30 S Acc Acc d/o Gerturde on 4 Mar 1874 at Horntown by S Johns

TOWNSEND Joseph W Col 23 S Tonsorial Artist Som Co MD Som Co MD to Lizzie B Smith Col 20 S Acc Acc d/o Isaac & Amanda on 4 Apr 1888 at Onancock by JC Cluff

TOWNSEND Lemuel J 20 S Oysterman Acc Acc s/o Samuel J & Emaline to O Maud Corbin 18 S Acc Acc d/o George W & Missouri on 18 Dec 1895 at Greenbackville by HS Bean

TOWNSEND Levin 33 W Sailor Chinco: Isld Chinco: Isld s/o Gorah & Mary to Mary Carpenter 23 S Chinco: Isld Chinco: Isld d/o Revil & Elizabeth on 12 Apr 1860 at Chinco: Isld by P Bowdin Sr (lic: 31 Jan 1860 Wm M Feddeman said both over 21)

TOWNSEND Levin T 27 S Laborer Som Co MD Acc to Hulda Mason 24 S Acc Acc d/o Preson & Polly on 24 Dec 1861 at Acc by T Waters

TOWNSEND Littleton 56 W Farmer Acc Acc s/o Sothey & Leah to Emaline Churn 39 W Acc Acc d/o Henry & Nancy Boggs on 10 Jan 1876 near Modest Town by JE Bundick

TOWNSEND Madison D 66 W Mechanic Wor Co MD Acc s/o Charles & Edith to Drucilla Peppet 28 S Wor Co MD Acc d/o Saml & Dolly on 24 Jul 1878 near Bethel Ch by JE Bundick

TOWNSEND Oliver F 35 W Oysterman Acc Acc s/o Sam'l J & Eveline to Jennie Mariner 22 S Acc Acc d/o George & Elizabeth on 10 Oct 1893 at New Church by TM Poulson

TOWNSEND Southey 30 S Sailor Acc Acc s/o Littl & Tabitha to Sarah J Mears 23 S Acc Acc d/o Meshach & Elizth on 4 Feb 1869 at Acc by JE Bundick

TOWNSEND Stephen Col 25 S Teamster Sussex Co DE Sussex Co DE s/o Perry & Jane to Amelia White Col 25 S Acc Acc d/o Henry & Susan on 27 Feb 1895 at Drum'tn by R Davis

TOWNSEND William 35 W Mariner Acc Chinco: Isld s/o Gorale & Mary to Maria C Sharpley 18 S Chinco: Isld Chinco: Isld d/o William & Elizabeth on 4 Apr 1857 at Chinco: Isld by P Bowdin

TOWNSEND Wm 34 S Sailor MD Chinco: Isld s/o Gorah & Nancy to Nancy Sharpley 17 S Chinco: Isld Chinco: Isld d/o Wm & Elizth on 30 Aug 1854 at r/o Elizth Sharpley by P Bowdin

TRADER Dawson J 22 S Farmer Acc Acc s/o William T & Margaret A to Laura E Taylor 18 S Acc Acc d/o Wm of T H & Mary T on 17 May 1891 at Mappsville by JL King

TRADER Floyd 23 S Sailor Acc Acc s/o Thomas & Sarah A to Narcissa L Rew 20 S Acc Acc d/o James H & Margaret A on 19 Aug 1888 at Temp'ville by TM Poulson

TRADER Francis 23 S Oysterman Acc Acc s/o John T & Elizth to Olevia F Drummond 22 S Acc Acc d/o John T & Evaline on 26 Dec 1883 at Oak Hall by RB Beadles

TRADER George 26 S Farmer Acc Acc s/o James G & Elizth to Maggie F Taylor 18 S Acc Acc on 23 Jan 1878 near Atlantic P O by M Oldham

TRADER George Col 22 S Laborer Acc Acc s/o Sarah to Tabitha Davis Col 19 S Acc Acc d/o Sarah on 2 Jan 1878 at News Town by A Joynes

TRADER George Col 21 S Laborer Acc Acc s/o George & Jane to Ida Justice Col 21 S Acc Acc d/o Moses &

Mary on 26 Mar 1882 near Modest Town by AJ Satchell

TRADER Hy (Henry) 57 W Farmer b: Acc to Comfort Hudson 56 W b: Acc on 28 Dec 1854 at Comfort Hudson's by GH Ewell

TRADER James T 24 S Carpenter Acc Acc s/o John T & Elizabeth to Lida D Drummond 21 S Acc Acc d/o John T & Evelyn on 23 Jan 1889 at Acc by JS Wallace

TRADER John to Elizabeth Harris lic: 2 Dec 1859 James W Martin says both over 21

TRADER Joseph 26 S Farmer Acc Acc s/o Henry & Elizabeth to Esther Bennett 30 W Acc Acc d/o William Parker on 8 Apr 1891 at Hacks Nk by JM Anderson

TRADER Julius C 27 S Sailor Acc Acc s/o Wm & Nancy to Margaret A West 27 S Acc Acc d/o Solomon & Margt on 30 Oct 1861 at Acc by ES Grant

TRADER Parker 20 S Oysterman Acc Acc s/o Comfort to Sarah W Stokes 16 S Acc Acc d/o Wm Stokes & Lavinia Taylor on 15 Feb 1866 at Acc by GW Matthews

TRADER Ramond (Raymond) 22 S Farmer b: Acc s/o Parke (Parker) & Elizabeth to Elizabeth Chase 20 S b: Acc d/o Robert on 27 Dec 1855 at r/o Robt Chase by GH Ewell

TRADER Raymond J 35 W Oysterman Acc Acc s/o Raymond & Betsey to Martha A Smith 28 S Acc Acc d/o James & Sally on 19 Apr 1894 at Mappsville by JL King

TRADER Samuel 30 W Farmer Acc Acc to Henrietta Trader 24 S Acc Acc d/o Hy & Critty on 25 Feb 1869 at Acc by M Oldham

TRADER Samuel A 22 S Farmer Acc Acc s/o Saml & Eliz to Critty Ann Kelly 22 S Acc Acc d/o Geo W & Eliz on 3 Jul 1881 at Messongo

Bridge by JW Hundley

TRADER Sewell Col 20 S Farmer Acc Acc s/o Sally to Clarissa Byrd Col 17 S Acc Acc d/o Jane on 31 Jan 1895 at Acc by JC Cluff

TRADER Sidney 30 W Farmer Acc Acc s/o Henry & Lizzie to Polly J Evans 27 S Smith Isld MD Acc d/o Francis & Julia A on 8 Jun 1886 at Acc by L Rosser

TRADER Teackle 24 S Sailor Acc Acc s/o Raymond & Elizth to Laura Christopher 18 S Acc Acc d/o Levin & Nancy on 22 Aug 1880 at Messongo by DA Woodson

TRADER Thomas F 23 S Oystering Acc Acc s/o Wm P & Margt to Demeriah C Byrd 20 S Acc Acc d/o Geo P & Mary E on 7 Dec 1875 at Modest Town by DA Woodson

TRADER Thos 25 S Oysterman Acc Acc s/o Parker & (Nancy) to Sarah J Marshall 19 S Acc Acc d/o (Ann Marshall) on 6 Jan 1863 at Acc by GH Ewell

TRADER Washington L 20 S Waterman Acc Acc s/o Thomas & Sarah to Mary B Hurley 16 S Acc Acc d/o Robert & Ann on 8 Oct 1884 at Acc by WA Street

TRADER Whittington W 22 S Farmer Acc Acc s/o Wittington W & Rachel to Elizabeth A Justice 22 S Acc Acc d/o Teackle & Tabitha on 16 Dec 1869 at Acc by M Oldham

TRADER William S 22 S Farmer Acc Acc s/o Wn & Sarah A to Alice C Dunton 15 S Acc Acc d/o Jno T & Margt J on 7 Jan 1883 at Oak Hall by RB Beadles

TRADER William T 19 S Oysterman Acc Acc s/o Wm P & Margt to Cordelia Chesser 18 S Acc Acc d/o John & Matilda on 1 Jun 1884 at Mappsville by WA Street

TRADER Wm H 25 S Oysterman Acc Acc s/o Edwd & Rose to Virginia

Marshall 21 S Acc Acc d/o Henrietta on 14 Mar 1878 at Messongo by JE Bundick

TREHEARN Geo Franklin [Trehurn] Col 30 S Farmer Acc Acc s/o Edward & Luray to Docia Bagwell Col 35 W Acc Acc d/o Harriet Petit on 23 Jul 1893 at Acc by AJ Satchell

TREICH John B 42 W Tailor b: Pegrchoarde France s/o John B & Gennatte to Mary P Bloxom 33 W b: Acc d/o Saml Justice & Elizth Powell on 31 Mar 1858 at Onancock by P Warren

TROWER George Col 24 S Laborer Acc Acc s/o Mary to Jane Perkins Col 25 S Acc Acc d/o Lizzie on 7 Apr 1882 at Pungo: by TW Nettles

TROWER George N 26 S Farmer Acc Acc s/o Thomas L & Annie W to Maggie Elva Tunnell 19 S Acc Acc d/o William D & Elizabeth B on 17 Jan 1889 at Locustville by RA Compton

TROWER Jesse Col 48 S Farmer N'hamp: Acc s/o Jane to Jane Trower Col 38 S Acc Acc on 9 Feb 1882 at Locust Mount by JWA Elliott

TROWER John [Trowers] Col 21 S Wage-earner Philadelphia PA Acc to Carlene Johnson Col 24 S Acc Acc d/o James on 29 Oct 1890 at Savageville by JB Lewis

TROWER Thos L 28 W Farmer b: N'hamp: s/o John & Delitha to Ann W Nock 16 S b: Locustville d/o Levin W & Polly W & (ward/o Levin W Nock who gave consent) on 15 Nov 1855 at Nocks Br by A Wallace

TRUITT Benjamin J 28 S Minister Quantico MD Acc s/o Benjamin W & Martha W to Belle R Lewis 19 S Acc Acc d/o William T & Rebecca on 10 Jul 1890 at Chinco: Isld by AD Melvin

TRUITT James H 29 S Seaman DE Acc s/o Barton & Elizth to Georgie D Sterling 19 S Acc Acc d/o John & Annie S on 4 Sep 1884 at Acc by JW Hundley

TRUITT Thomas M 32 S Farmer Wor Co MD Acc s/o Isaac J & Jane B to Eliza Ellen Kollock 18 S Acc Acc d/o Wm J & Sarah A on 31 Aug 1892 at Chinco: Isld by HL Elderdice

TRUITT William 36 W Farmer b: Acc s/o Jester & Polly to Caroline Marshall 36 W b: Wor Co MD d/o John & Sallie Gillett on 21 Dec 1856 at bride's home by JM Dennis

TRUITT William 50 W Farmer Acc Acc to Sarah Davis 25 S Acc Acc on 22 Jul 1868 at Acc by JO Moss

TULL Charles U 25 S Farmer Acc Acc s/o Fredrick A & Isabella to Virginia Covington 23 S Wic Co MD Acc d/o Royston & Mary on 19 Jan 1882 at New Church by HC Stern

TULL Edward H Col single Acc Acc to Elizabeth [Jornes] Jones Col single Acc Acc on 25 Nov 1877 at Wagrases Acc Co by JB Butler

TULL Edward T Col 21 S Laborer Acc Acc s/o Wm & Anna to Emma King Col 22 S Acc Acc d/o Fitchett & Mary on 13 Jan 1895 at Temp'ville by GHT Byrd

TULL Eliha Y 25 S Merchant Acc Acc s/o William T & Catherine to Nannie B Topping 21 S Acc Acc d/o David T & Mary T on 7 Mar 1888 at Sign Post by BF Jester

TULL Harrison Col 33 S Farmer Acc Acc s/o Jesse & Gatta to Drucilla Downing Col 25 S Acc Acc d/o Stewart & Hannah on 28 Jun 1874 by S Johns

TULL Harrison Col 32 S Laborer Acc Acc s/o Galty to Sally Roberts Col 24 S Acc Acc d/o Polly on 20 Jul 1882 at Acc by JE Bundick

TULL John S s/o Geo W who gave consent to Eliz Dix d/o Wm H who gave consent lic: 25 Dec 1854

TULL John S 33 W Acc Acc s/o George to Virginia Dix 23 S Acc Acc d/o William H & Susan on 17 Jul 1870 at Conquest Ch by M Oldham

TULL Lynor 20 S Farmer Acc Acc s/o Hanison & Mary to Martha Selby 22 S Acc Acc d/o Major & Jane on 20 Feb 1881 at New Church by TM Poulson

TULL William Col 48 S Farm Laborer Wor Co MD Acc s/o Mary Merrill to Ann M Slocomb Col 26 S Acc Acc d/o Mary on 8 Oct 1880 near Oak Hall by JC Cluff

TULL William Col 62 W Wage-earner Acc Acc s/o Levy & Mary Bain to Annie Conner Col 32 W Acc Acc d/o George & Mary on 5 Nov 1890 at Wattsville by AS Amos

TUNNELL Douglas Col 20 S Wage-earner Acc Acc s/o John & Susan to Hannah F [Baily] Bayly Col 19 S Acc Acc d/o Henry & Mary on 11 Jan 1891 at Wattsville by AS Amos

TUNNELL Edmund FN to Mary Outten FN lic: 13 Jan 1858 S W Powell says both over 21

TUNNELL Edwin J 21 S Farmer Acc Acc s/o William D & Eliz'th to Eva C Bull 19 S Acc Acc d/o Eli W & Susan on 27 Dec 1893 at Onley by EF Garner

TUNNELL George W Col 26 S Farmer Acc Acc s/o Jno & Sarah to Birdie L Slocomb Col 17 S PA Acc d/o Ella M on 5 Jan 1890 at Wattsville by N Morris

TUNNELL Levin T Col 40 S Farmer Acc Acc to Elizabeth Jenkins Col 35 S Acc Acc on 22 May 1873 at Wattsville by S Johns

TUNNELL William D 23 S Merchant Acc Acc s/o Jackson & Margt to Georgie S James 19 S Acc Acc d/o Thos H & Tabitha A on 28 Nov 1865 at Acc by P Warren

TURLINGTON Charles 45 W Oysterman Acc Acc s/o Parker & Mary to Susan Powell 45 W Acc Acc d/o George & Eliza A Birch on 29 Mar 1892 at Chinco: Isld by JW Turner

TURLINGTON Field 21 S Oysterman Acc Acc s/o Arthur & Charlotte E to Rebecca [Jeffreys] Jeffries 18 S Acc Acc d/o Alva A & Mary on 22 Mar 1893 at Chinco: Isld by RB Sanford

TURLINGTON George W to Martha A Killman d/o William who gave consent lic: 5 Jun 1854

TURLINGTON George W 20 S Farmer Acc Acc s/o Wm Thomas & Sarah to Leah Susan East 17 S Acc Acc d/o James T & Julia A on 1 Feb 1888 at Acc by JWA Elliott

TURLINGTON Isaac Col 34 W Farmer Acc Acc s/o Levi & Rachel to Agnes Moore Col 35 S Acc Acc d/o Thomas & Ellen Truitt on 19 Sep 1894 at Acc by T Turlington

TURLINGTON Isaac J Col 32 S Farmer Acc Acc s/o Levi Turlington & Rachel Mears to Eliza Drummond Col 28 W Acc Acc d/o Charles & Lucy on 29 Oct 1890 at Savageville by JB Lewis

TURLINGTON Israel 25 S Oysterman Acc Acc to Mary Horsey 27 S Acc Acc on 19 May 1867 at Acc by JO Moss

TURLINGTON John Wm 22 S Farmer Acc Acc s/o John W & Amanda to Ella D Coard 22 S Acc Acc d/o John W & Nancy on 28 Oct 1885 at Woodbury by JW Carroll

TURLINGTON Louis 23 S Mechanic Acc Acc s/o John & Rachel to Susan E Bradford 23 S Acc Acc d/o Benjamin & Catharine on 6 Dec 1876 at Oak Grove Ch by JW Ewell

TURLINGTON Saml Z 20 S Farmer Acc Acc s/o Saml M & Elizth R to Sarah A F Ames 18 S Acc Acc d/o

Jos F & Nancy B on 20 Nov 1866 at Acc by LK LeCato

TURLINGTON Saml Z 22 W Farmer Acc Acc s/o Saml & Betsy to Emma Catharine Ames 16 S Acc Acc d/o Richard W & Susan on 19 May 1870 at Acc by JC Martin

TURLINGTON Samuel C 28 S Merchant Acc Acc s/o James N & Lauretta to Mary E Ames 28 S Acc Acc d/o John E & Margaret on 26 Jan 1887 at bride's home by RA Compton

TURLINGTON Thomas Col 24 S Laborer Acc Acc s/o Malinda Shield to Sylvia Ashby Col 26 S Acc Acc d/o Charles & Mary on 30 Jan 1879 at Burtons Chp by A Handy

TURLINGTON Thomas Col 37 W Minister Acc Acc s/o George T & Malinda to Mary E Lewis Col 19 S Acc Acc d/o Hiram & Emma J on 15 May 1895 at Acc by AJ Satchell

TURLINGTON Thomas W 22 S Farmer Acc Acc s/o Thomas & Sarah to Fanny D Johnson 18 S Acc Acc d/o James E & Margaret on 14 Dec 1881 at Locust Mount by JWA Elliott

TURLINGTON William M 28 S Merchant Acc Acc s/o James N & Lauretta to Annie W Mapp 20 S Acc Acc d/o William E & Catherine on 10 May 1888 at Locustville by RA Compton

TURNER Charles A Col 25 S Sailor Acc Acc s/o John & Leah to Cordelia Hutchinson Col 25 S Acc Acc d/o George & Leah on 30 Apr 1893 at Acc by T Turlington

TURNER Charles F 30 S Waterman Acc Acc s/o James & Margaret to Maggie S Smith 24 S Acc Acc d/o George & Elizabeth on 18 Mar 1891 at Acc by JM Anderson

TURNER George (A) 23 S Sailor b: Acc s/o Richard & Polly to Rosey Ann (Rosa) Chandler 21 S b: Acc d/o Edward & Mary on 9 Jul 1856 at Locust Mount by JWA Elliott (James E Turner says both over 21)

TURNER George K 42 S Farmer b: Bradford Nk s/o John & Molly to Elizth Susan Hyslop 38 S b: near Last Shift d/o James & Mary on 26 Mar 1856 at Wachapreague by J Burton (Joshua Turner says both over 21)

TURNER George K 62 W Farmer Acc Acc s/o John & Mary to Juliet S Garrison 38 W Acc Acc d/o Edwin L & Elizth Roberts on 25 Aug 1874 at Acc by JE Humphreys

TURNER George S 22 S Oysterman Acc Acc s/o Sally to Mary J Taylor 18 S Acc Acc d/o Jmaes H & Nancy on 26 Jul 1882 at Acc by JE Bundick

TURNER George T 25 S Sailor Acc Acc s/o Jas S & Margt A to Kate S Chandler 17 S Acc Acc d/o Thos R & Emily S on 23 May 1883 at Acc by WC Vaden

TURNER George T 25 S Farmer Acc Acc s/o John T & Virginia to Alice P Drummond 19 S Acc Acc d/o Joseph P & Rose A on 23 May 1895 at Acc by JR Sturgis

TURNER George W 22 S Farmer Acc Acc s/o James E & Catharine to Arinthia J Kellam 19 S Acc Acc d/o George A & Ann A on 9 May 1875 near Middlesex Acc Co by JE Humphreys

TURNER Henry Col 52 S Farmer N'hamp: Acc s/o Harriet Geddings to Jane Mapp Col 37 S Acc Acc d/o Mahala on 7 Jul 1885 at Acc by CA Horsey

TURNER James S to Margaret Parker d/o Thomas & ward/o John W Chandler who gave consent lic: 27 Nov 1854

TURNER James S 19 S Farmer Acc Acc s/o James E & Catharine to Catharine Lawrence single Acc Acc d/o John & Margaret on 20 Jan 1876 at Oak Grove Ch by LK LeCato

TURNER Jas Scarburgh 34 S Sailor b: Acc s/o Geo K & Easter to Margaret Parker 20 S b: Acc d/o Thos & Mary on 30 Nov 1854 at Acc by JH Addison

TURNER John widr Farmer Acc Acc to Sallie Wyatt 27 S Acc Acc d/o Isma on 20 Apr 1867 at Acc by BT Ames

TURNER John Col 35 S Farmer Acc Acc to Louisa Sample Col 40 S Acc Acc on 25 Sep 1891 at Acc by L Duncan

TURNER John E 23 S Sailor Acc Acc s/o James E & Margaret S to Dora C Stevens 18 S N'hamp: Acc d/o John H & Bettie A on 13 Mar 1889 at Pungo Bapt Ch by JW Hundley

TURNER John Hy Col 21 S Farm Laborer Acc Acc s/o Mary to Bettie Bibbins Col 23 S Acc Acc on 5 Aug 1885 at Acc by CA Horsey

TURNER John R 45 S Gentleman Acc Acc s/o Rosie to Susan E Mason 38 S Acc Acc on 29 Sep 1869 at Acc by D Titlow

TURNER John T 21 S Farming b: Acc s/o Samuel & Sally to Isabella Kellam 23 S b: Acc d/o Thos T & Margt on 13 Jan 1856 at Pungo: by M Oldham (Edward T Bool says both over 21)

TURNER John T 23 W Farmer Acc Acc s/o Saml & Sally to Virginia Ann LeCato 22 S Acc N'hamp: d/o Jno (Decd) & Sarah on 24 Feb 1858 at Pungo: by M Oldham (Edward T Bool says he over 21)

TURNER Joshua H 21 S Merchant Acc Acc s/o Jas S & Catharine to Emma K Taylor 18 S Acc Acc d/o Wm M & Sally on 27 Jan 1886 at Acc by L Rosser

TURNER Litey Col 20 S Farmer Acc Acc s/o John & Leah Upshur to Lucy Bayly Col 19 S Acc Acc d/o Daniel & Mary on 13 Jan 1892 at Acc by T Turlington

TURNER Richard 25 W Sailor Acc Acc s/o Richd & Polly to Mary West 21 S Acc Acc d/o Isaac & Patty on 6 Jan 1858 at Pungo: by M Oldham (John J Chandler says she over 21)

TURNER Samuel J 18 S Farmer Acc Acc s/o John T & Virginia to Marggie A [Beloat] Beloate 16 S Acc Acc d/o Edward A & Annie on 4 Dec 1895 at Acc by EE Harrell

TURNER William Col 23 S Wage-earner Acc Acc s/o John & Leah to Ann Eliza Fosque Col 21 S Acc Acc d/o Henry & Margaret on 17 Feb 1892 at Acc by T Turlington

TURNER Wm 21 S Laborer Acc Acc s/o James & Tinny Ann to Mary S Kellam 22 S Acc Acc d/o Sarah J on 1 Dec 1875 near Hank's Nest by JWA Elliott

TWIFORD Custis [Twyford] Col 22 S Laborer Acc Acc s/o Lencinda Major to Fannie Smith Col 21 S Acc Acc d/o Nancy & Esther on 10 Dec 1879 at Belle Haven by TW Nettles

TWIFORD Edgar V 32 S Sailor Acc Acc s/o Wm B & Elizabeth to Lillian M Lewis 19 S Acc Acc d/o Isaac J & Sallie M on 15 Sep 1889 at Chinco: Isld by BP Truitt

TWIFORD Geo R [Twyford] 22 S Oysterman Acc Acc s/o Julius & Annie to Maggie C Rew 17 S Acc Acc d/o Frances S on 25 Oct 1886 at Acc by AD Davis

TWIFORD George D 25 S Oysterman Acc Acc s/o George W & Margaret to Elizabeth Lewis 17 S Acc Acc d/o John & Peggy on 27 Dec 1860 at r/o Julius Twiford by ES Grant (Thomas S Lewis says he over 21)

TWIFORD Jas H 27 S Sailor Acc Acc s/o Jas & Laviana to Margaret L C Lofland 18 S Acc Acc d/o Alfred & Carry on 14 May 1862 at Acc by JH Addison

TWIFORD John W [Twyford] 24 S Waterman Acc Acc s/o Julius C & Ann to Carrie L Silverthorn 17 S Acc Acc d/o Edw'd T & Sally C on 27 Dec 1891 at Guilford Ch by JW Nicholson

TWIFORD Luther E 22 S Oysterman Acc Acc s/o Geo D & Eliz'th to Manie E Matthews 17 S Acc Acc d/o Levin F & Virginia T on 27 Dec 1893 at Lee Mont by JET Ewell

TWIFORD Philander R [Tryford] 32 S Farmer Acc Acc s/o Revel & Anna to Margaret H Parker 29 S Acc Acc d/o Jno M & Ellen on 26 Dec 1883 at Onancock Par by WC Vaden

TWIFORD Purnell O 29 S Farmer Acc Acc s/o Revel & Ann to Missouri K Hickman 22 S Acc Acc d/o Jno H & Elizth on 1 Feb 1872 at Metompkin by DA Woodson

TWIFORD Revel T 30 S Farmer Acc Acc s/o Revil & Annie to Elizabeth Budd 26 S Acc Acc d/o Wm & Sally on 6 Nov 1870 at Acc by E Hebard

TWIFORD William 24 S Farmer Acc Acc s/o Revel & Ann to Jane E Bundick 17 S Acc Acc d/o Anna on 18 Dec 1870 near Drum'tn by JB Converse

TWIFORD William J Col 35 S Sailor Acc Acc s/o Rosie Gray to Sallie Wise Col 20 S Acc Acc d/o Lizzie on 23 Oct 1890 at Onancock by GHT Byrd

TWILLEY Wm J 29 S Minister Wic Co MD Acc s/o Cabab D & Hester A to Mary A Schellinger 24 W Cape May NJ Acc d/o Jacob & Marchie Stiles on 22 Sep 1881 at Powelton by GH Ray

TYLER James H 21 S Oysterman Acc Acc s/o David & Margaret to Nancy T Hart 26 S Acc Acc d/o Richard & Annie on 5 Jan 1873 near Messongo by JE Bundick

TYLER John 21 S Oysterman b: Sexes Isld to Mary Hall 20 S b: Pig Point d/o Robt on 1 Jun 1855 at r/o Geo H Ewell by GH Ewell (Samuel T Taylor says both over 21)

TYLER John S [Tyler] (Taylor) 27 S Merchant Acc Acc s/o John D & Mary R to Rose B Walston 22 S Acc Acc d/o Wm & Ann on 7 May 1868 at Acc by HA Wise Jr

TYLER Selby [Tiler] 21 S Oysterman b: Cattail s/o David to Jane Hart 20 S b: Messongo d/o Richard on 16 Mar 1855 at r/o Geo H Ewell by GH Ewell

TYLER William 24 S Oysterman Acc Acc s/o John & Mary to Ida White 17 S Acc Acc d/o Elizabeth on 8 Jun 1882 at Cattail Nk by M Oldham

UNDERHILL James D 48 S Carpenter Acc Acc s/o Thomas & Nancy to Rose A Wright 38 S Acc Acc d/o Elijah & Margt on 31 Mar 1875 near Pungo: by FR Boston

UNDERHILL Joshua M 25 S Farmer N'hamp: N'hamp: s/o Michael & Fluvanna to Daisey C Killman 21 S Acc Acc d/o Patrick W & Lavenia on 26 Jun 1895 at Acc by JM Dunaway

UNDERHILL Thomas C 25 S Farmer Norfolk City Acc s/o Francis S & Corenia to Eugenia Harmon [Edmond] Edmonds 25 S Acc Acc d/o James W & Mollie A B on 24 Dec 1895 at Acc by EE Harrell

UPSHUR Alfred Col 29 S Laborer Acc Acc s/o Abram & Mollie to Hester Bibbins Col 22 S Acc Acc d/o Robert & Mary on 5 Apr 1876 at Belle Haven by JE Humphreys

UPSHUR Arthur D 37 S Dealer in Wood b: N'hamp: s/o Wm & Elizth to Lucretia Major 25 S b: Acc d/o Wm L & Elizth on 22 Dec 1854 at Pungo: by M Oldham

UPSHUR Henry Col 24 S Farmer Acc Acc s/o Wm & Ellen to Arinthia Savage Col 23 S N'hamp: Acc d/o

Julius on 14 Jul 1880 at Belle Haven by SMG Copeland

UPSHUR Wm FN 28 S Sailor N'hamp: Acc to Elizabeth Anthony 24 S Acc Acc on 3 Sep 1863 at Acc by JWA Elliott

VANAMAN James 26 S Coal Burner Cunberland Co NJ Acc s/o Wesley & Ann to Sarah Tatham 23 S Acc Acc d/o Ezekiel & Comelia on 30 Dec 1858 at Acc by JF Chaplain (James M(?) and Pancost(?) says both over 21)

VEASEY William H widr to Margaret A E Parker d/o George W lic: 16 Jan 1856 J H Snead says both over 21

WADDY Edward D 19 S Farmer N'hamp: Acc s/o Frederick & Maggie H to Roberta K Wilkins 17 S Acc Acc d/o William B & Manie E on 12 Nov 1890 at Acc C H by W Chinn

WALKER Asher 21 S Waterman Wor Co MD Chinco: Isld s/o Purnell & Mary to Meany Elizth Jester 21 S Chinco: Isld Chinco: Isld d/o James & Enpheney on 19 Oct 1882 at Chinco: Isld by WP Thornton

WALKER Charles T 36 W Carpenter Washington DC Acc to Emma Kate Bennett 19 S Acc Acc d/o George W & Laura on 27 Jun 1894 at Pungo: by JR Griffith

WALKER Edmond Col 25 W Farmer Acc Acc s/o Zadock & Charlotte to Rosa [Shields] Shield Col 21 S Acc Acc d/o Wm & Mary Snead on 29 Dec 1882 at Savageville by F Wood

WALKER Emanuel Col 22 S Wage-earner Acc Acc s/o George & Winnie to Sarah West Col 24 W Acc Acc d/o James & Eliza Collins on 10 Aug 1888 at Acc by L Duncan

WALKER George C 22 S Blacksmith Acc Acc s/o Wm B & Mary A to Madgie A Ward 19 S Acc Acc d/o Alex J on 24 Nov 1880 at Belle Haven by RD Stimson

WALKER Howard Col 21 S Laborer Acc Acc s/o Jennie to Arinthia Ann Lofland Col 19 S Acc Acc d/o Bernice & Jennie on 24 Jan 1888 at Acc by JA Haynes

WALKER Hy C (John) 23 S Trimmer Acc Acc s/o Hy S & Sophia Kellam to Margt E Doughty 17 S Acc Acc d/o John R & Mary Colonna on 30 May 1855 at Acc by M Oldham

WALKER Isaac 21 S Sailor Acc Acc s/o Virginia to Louisa Pitts 16 S Acc Acc d/o Sarah Kellam on 16 Jan 1867 at Acc by WT Tull

WALKER J Harry 26 S Salesman Acc Acc s/o Henry C & Margaret E to M Beach Martin 22 S Acc Acc d/o Smith K & Rose W on 24 Dec 1889 at Mrs Rose Martin's by JW Hundley

WALKER James K 48 W Acc Acc s/o Harry & sophia to Mary A Mears 32 S Acc Acc d/o Jno W A & Hetty on 23 Apr 1872 at Belle Haven by JE Humphreys

WALKER John S widr to Lydia S Hyslop d/o Smith Hyslop lic: 19 Oct 1857 C C Satchell says both over 21

WALKER Richard Col 21 S Farmer Acc Acc s/o Wm & Mary to Martha LeCato Col 21 S Acc Acc d/o George & Rena on 18 Nov 1894 at Acc by ET Outen

WALKER Robert 40 W Farmer Acc Acc s/o Teackle to Emma Sterling 22 S Acc Acc d/o Jas H & Annie on 4 Jul 1886 at Acc by JW Carroll

WALKER Robt W 24 S Farmer Acc Acc s/o Teackle & Margt to Mary T Littleton 19 S Acc Acc d/o Thos & Sarah on 7 Oct 1868 at Acc by G Bradford

WALKER Setphen Col 21 S Farmer Acc Acc s/o Purnell & Tabby to Sarah Lee Topping Col 21 S Acc Acc d/o Caleb Topping & Mary Poulson on 22 Nov 1893 at Onancock by FW

Overton

WALKER Shadrack Col 41 S Farmer Acc Acc s/o Lara to Elizth Ewell Col 32 S Acc Acc d/o Caroline on 18 May 1879 at Chinco: Isld by JC Cluff

WALKER William to Nancy Trehearn lic: 5 Apr 1858 James H Coleburn says both over 21

WALKER William Col 27 S Farmer Acc Acc to Kitty Sample Col 18 S Acc Acc d/o Isaac on 29 Aug 1878 at Savageville by JW Diggs

WALKER William Col 21 S Wage-earner Acc Acc s/o Mary to Annie Finney Col 18 S Acc Acc d/o Jennie on 5 Jul 1893 at Acc by T Turlington

WALKER William T 23 S Farmer Acc Acc s/o Teagle & Elizabeth to Mary Catharine Copes 17 S Acc Acc d/o John & Cary on 25 Dec 1873 at Acc by JE Bundick

WALKER Wm H 26 S Carriage Maker Acc Acc s/o Wm B & Mary A to Willie C Ayres 19 S Acc Acc d/o Richard L & Betsy Ann on 10 May 1882 at Acc by FM Birch

WALKLEY James T 25 S Sheet Iron Worker Birmingham England Acc s/o Thos & Mary to Keturah S J Boone 22 S Acc Acc d/o Jacob & Margt on 18 Apr 1877 at Belle Haven by HM Anderson

WALLACE Abel Washington 26 S Farmer Acc Acc s/o Daniel & Elizabeth to Emma J Guy 19 S Acc Acc d/o Robert P & Tabitha on 30 Mar 1870 at Acc by E Hebard

WALLACE Daniel 56 W Mechanic Acc Acc s/o Daniel & Tabitha to Margt Mears 37 W N'hamp: Acc d/o Wm & Elizabeth Booth on 29 Oct 1862 at Acc by JWA Elliott

WALLACE Frederick 21 S Farmer Acc Acc s/o John & Susan to Arinthia J Mears 20 S Acc Acc d/o George T & Marg't on 16 Jan 1889 at bride's home by JWA Elliott

WALLACE Jno C 23 S Sailor Acc Acc s/o Danl & Betsy to Susan A Mason 22 S Acc Acc d/o Bagwel & Molly on 9 Sep 1863 at Acc by JWA Elliott

WALLACE Jno E 21 S Sailor Gloucester Co VA Acc s/o Wm & Elizth to Lenah Thomas 20 S Acc Acc d/o Lybrand J & Polly on 19 Aug 1877 at Tangier Isld by WJ Duhadway

WALLACE John Daniel 25 S Farmer Acc Acc s/o John C & Susan J to Georgie M Mears 18 S Acc Acc d/o George T & Margaret J on 6 Mar 1895 at Locust Mount by JWA Elliott

WALLACE John E 25 S Farmer Norfolk VA N'hamp: s/o Thos D & Elizth S to Ellen M Nock 22 S Acc Acc d/o Louis & Susan on 10 Dec 1873 near Locustville by LK LeCato

WALLACE John O 19 S Farmer Acc Acc s/o Abel W & Emory to Kate Bell 26 S Acc Acc d/o John & Hester on 18 Nov 1891 at Acc by JWA Elliott

WALLACE Robt C 22 S Oysterman Acc Acc s/o Daniel & Margaret to Cora J Mears 17 S Acc Acc d/o George W & Sarah on 4 Jan 1891 at Acc by JWA Elliott

WALLACE William 21 S Farmer Acc Acc s/o Benj & Elizth to Arinthia S Mears 21 S Acc Acc d/o Abel & Elizth on 26 Mar 1879 at Pungo: by CC Wertenbaker

WALLOP Edw'd H Col 36 S Oysterman Acc Acc s/o Wm S & Lucinda to Idia J Roe Col 33 S Acc Acc d/o Henry & Lizzie on 31 Jan 1892 at Horntown by AS Amos

WALLOP Henry Col 35 S Oysterman Acc Acc s/o Lefcoe & Charlotte to Mary A Hickman Col 25 S Acc Acc d/o Spencer & Easter on 3 Oct 1872 at Acc by M Oldham

WALLOP Isaac Col 22 S Oysterman Acc Acc s/o Laura Evans to Jennie Fletcher Col 21 S Acc Acc d/o Mary Browne on 5 Dec 1879 at Horntown by PJ Adams

WALLOP John Col 49 S Farmer Acc Acc s/o Lottie to Ann Townsend Col 31 S Acc Acc d/o Elijah & Tabitha on 4 Mar 1874 at Horntown by S Johns

WALLOP John D Col 21 S Oysterman Acc Acc s/o John & Ann to Lizzie Armstrong Col 20 S Acc Acc d/o Thomas & Ellen on 8 Jan 1890 at Wattsville by N Morris

WALLOP William J H 41 S Physician Acc Acc s/o John D to Sarah R Byrd 20 S Baltimore City Acc d/o Colmore E & Mary on 7 Nov 1861 at Acc by T Waters

WALSTON Saml J 24 S Merchant Acc Acc s/o Wm & Anna G to Elizabeth T Young 21 S Acc Acc d/o Edward J & Sarah on 19 Sep 1867 at Acc by JD Thomas

WALTER Andrew J 37 S Minister Baltimore MD Acc s/o Andrew S & Lafenia to Isabella S Lewis 21 S Acc Acc d/o Alfred J & Maria on 24 Jul 1884 at Acc by SA Hobitzell

WALTER George Smith 30 S Blacksmith Acc Acc s/o John S & Lydia to Lena M Bell 18 S Acc Acc d/o Robert J & Susan on 30 Apr 1889 at Onancock by JW Hundley

WALTER James T 23 S Wheelwright Acc Acc s/o Richard & Juliet to Anna Floyd 17 S Acc Acc d/o John R & Lousia on 9 Dec 1874 at Acc by JE Humphreys

WALTER John R 27 S Merchant Acc Acc s/o John S to Rose T Holt 21 S r: Acc d/o Edwd & Margt on 11 Nov 1868 at Acc by JE Humphreys

WALTER John S 44 W Farmer Acc Acc s/o Richd & Mary to Lydia S Hyslop 23 S Acc Acc d/o Smith & Sarah on 21 Oct 1857 at Acc by M Oldham

WALTER Nathaniel F 25 S Farmer Acc Acc s/o John S & Annie to Mary E Beloate 25 S Acc Acc d/o James H & Eliza on 26 Jan 1887 at bride's father's by RA Compton

WAPLES Charles S 25 S Merchant Acc Baltimore City MD s/o Edward B & Sarah to Margaret H Finney 24 S Acc Acc d/o William (of Wm) & Margaret on 27 Oct 1890 at Acc by JB Pruitt

WAPLES Edward B Sr 65 W Milling Acc Acc s/o Samuel T & Sabra P to Elizabeth A West 46 S Acc Acc d/o Revel & Elizabeth on 17 Apr 1889 at Onancock by JW Hundley

WAPLES Edwd B Jr [Wapler] 23 S Farmer Acc Acc s/o Edwd B Sr & Sarah to Mary E Chandler 19 S Acc Acc d/o Sylvester R & Mary A on 12 Sep 1877 near Onancock by JH Amiss

WAPLES John Col 22 S Laborer Philadelphia PA Acc s/o Jas Fosque & Jane Long to Letitea Savage Col 18 S Acc Acc d/o Edwd & Mary on 22 Jul 1883 at Temp'ville by M Oldham

WAPLES O Jennings 24 S Mechanic Acc Acc s/o Edwd B & Sarah to Emma S Finney 19 S Acc Acc d/o Wm & Margt S on 15 Dec 1886 at Acc by JW Hundley

WAPLES Saml T 30 S Farmer Acc Acc s/o Edwd B & Sarah A to Elishea Anna Drummond 27 S Acc Acc d/o Jno R & Elishea on 16 Jan 1884 at Drum'tn by JW Hundley

WAPLES Thomas FN 36 S Farmer Acc Acc s/o Daniel & Comfort to Betsy Ailworth FN 31 S Acc Acc d/o Annie Ailworth on 10 Dec 1865 at Acc by TL Tomkinson

WAPLES William Col 26 S Teamster Acc Acc s/o Lydia to Willianna

Kellam Col 21 S Acc Acc d/o Mary on 16 Sep 1895 at Drum'tn by JR West

WARD Alfred C 22 S Grocer Norfolk Co VA Norfolk Co VA s/o Littleton & Elizth to Emma S Savage 21 S Acc Acc d/o Wm & Margt on 1 Dec 1886 at Acc by W Chinn

WARD David T 20 S Brick Layer Acc Acc s/o Wm & Margt to Bettie [Stakes] Stokes 22 S Acc Acc d/o Wm on 3 Jan 1878 at Oak Grove Ch by JWA Elliott

WARD George Col 31 S Steward N'hamp: Acc s/o Anatha to Mary Addison Col 21 S Acc Acc d/o Edward & Laura on 11 May 1893 at Acc by TW Nettles

WARD George G 49 S Farmer N'hamp: N'hamp: s/o James & Susan to Susan M Ward 36 W N'hamp: Acc d/o Mitchell & Betsy Matthews on 22 Jan 1891 at Belle Haven by WJ Twilley

WARD Harry J 27 S RR Employee Salisbury MD Acc s/o Cyrus & Caroline to Susan R Mears 25 S Acc Acc d/o Gilbert J & Elizabeth on 31 Dec 1885 at Acc by JW Carroll

WARD Isaac 53 W Farmer b: Som Co MD s/o Joseph & Milly to Peggy Read 50 S b: Dorchester Co d/o Major on 15 Jan 1858 at New Town/Sandy Hill by JM Dennis (John E Wise says she over 21)

WARD James Col 22 S Wage-earner Acc Acc s/o Juliet Bayly to Minnie G [Shields] Shield Col 18 S Acc Acc d/o Edmund & Sarah on 25 Feb 1892 at Locust Mount by RH Coleman

WARD James N 49 W Farmer Acc Acc s/o Wm & Margaret to Sally A Groton 29 W Acc Acc d/o Samuel & Sally Bundick on 8 Dec 1874 near Locustville by LK LeCato

WARD James W 22 S Farmer Acc Acc s/o James & Mary to Martha A East 18 S Acc Acc d/o James T & Juliet on 26 Dec 1878 near Locustville by LK LeCato

WARD Jas N 29 S Farmer b: Acc s/o Wm Ward & Margt Lewis to Mary E Shield 21 S b: Acc d/o Jas (Decd) & Elizth on 20 Dec 1854 at Burton Chp by LK LeCato (Wm R Bunting says both over 21)

WARD John 32 W Carpenter Acc Acc s/o Lancelot & Mary to Susan Bundick 39 S Acc Acc d/o John S & Jinney on 4 Apr 1858 near Garrisons Chp by JW Ewell (James G Smith says she over 21)

WARD John A Col 23 S Farmer Acc Acc s/o Ellen to Arinthia Sunket Col 22 S Acc Acc d/o Mark & Sarah on 26 Dec 1894 at Acc by J Duckett

WARD John H Col 24 S Laborer Wor Co MD Acc s/o Sarah to Ellen Wise Col 25 W Acc Acc d/o Richard & Annie Bayly on 18 Nov 1869 at Acc by A Joynes

WARD John L 50 W Farmer & Mechanic Acc Acc s/o Lamcelot & Mary to Ann Roberts 30 W Acc Acc d/o Margaret Doughty on 27 Jul 1881 at Onancock by SC Boston

WARD John T Col 21 S Farmer Acc Acc s/o John H & Nellie to Sarah Drummond Col 22 S Acc Acc d/o Abel & Leah on 4 Jan 1893 at Lee Mont by JW Cook

WARD Julius W 20 S Merchant Acc Acc s/o Alexander J & Peggy E to Margaret S Walker 19 S Acc Acc d/o Henry C & Margaret B on 12 Aug 1880 at Belle Haven by RD Stimson

WARD Levin Col 21 S Farm Labor Acc Acc s/o Ellen to Anna Ward Col 21 S Acc Acc d/o Eliza on 14 Mar 1883 at Locustville by LW Lee

WARD Lewis T 27 S Farmer Acc Acc s/o Golden & Marg A to Alice A Bell 17 S Acc Acc d/o Jno E & Esther on 31 Aug 1881 at Locust Mount by JWA Elliott

WARD Nathl J 37 S Farmer N'hamp: Acc s/o Jas & Margt to Margaret A Ward 37 W N'hamp: Acc d/o Jno & Sarah Ross on 25 May 1872 at Acc by JWA Elliott

WARD Noah T 24 S Waterman Som Co MD Som Co MD s/o Noah a & Polly A to Nancy A Hoffman 28 S Som Co MD Acc d/o Jas K & Sarah on 2 Aug 1865 at Acc by D Titlow

WARD Samuel D to Margaret Turner lic: 24 May 1858 John E Ward says both over 21

WARD Sargarent Pentice 30 S Merchant Acc Acc s/o Alexander J & Peggie E to Virginia Trechart Potter 22 S Acc Acc d/o Edmund H & Lelia T on 16 Jan 1895 at Belle Haven by REC Lawson

WARD Seymour B 27 S Dentist Acc Acc s/o Alaxander J & Lizzie to Eva R LeCato 21 S Baltimore City MD Acc d/o Littleton T & Corelis S on 24 Apr 1895 at Acc by JT Bosman

WARD Thomas D 29 S Farmer N'hamp: Acc s/o Wm S & Tabitha to Mary C Kellam 24 S Acc Acc d/o Benj J & Catharine A on 15 Dec 1886 at Locust Mount by JWA Elliott

WARD William to Sarah A Mason d/o Bagwell C lic: 26 Apr 1858 Bagwell C Mason says both over 21

WARD William P 25 S Farmer b: Acc s/o Wm & Margaret to Margaret N Phillips 22 S b: Acc d/o David & Martha on 20 Dec 1857 near Onancock by JF Chaplain (James M Watson says both over 21)

WARD Wm Douglas 18 S Farmer Acc Acc s/o L L & Margt A to Virginia H Taylor 18 S Acc Acc d/o Jno H & Lucy E on 31 Jan 1876 near Little Rest by LK LeCato

WARFIELD Milton W 28 S Physician Howard Co MD Howard Co MD s/o Philomen D & Lucutis to Mary Elizth Dawley 24 S Rochester NY Acc d/o John & Adeline on 29 Jul 1861 at Acc by J Atkinson (George T Scarburgh says both over 21)

WARNER Edmond Col 23 S Oysterman Acc Acc s/o Hannah Taylor to Jane Gibbons Col 22 S Acc Acc d/o Mary on 21 Sep 1876 near News Town by A Joynes

WARNER Edward C 23 S Clerk Acc Acc s/o Solomon & Arinthia to Maude Fisher 18 S Acc Acc d/o Jno D & Delilah on 20 May 1885 near Assawoman by A Woodyard

WARNER George Col 23 S Laborer Acc Acc s/o James & Mary to Fanny Taylor Col 22 S Acc Acc d/o Henry & Eliza on 29 Oct 1885 at Acc by AJ Satchell

WARNER John J 22 S Carpenter Acc Acc s/o Solomon & Arinthia D to E Wharton Taylor 22 S Acc Acc d/o Thomas T & Mary Ann on 20 Sep 1894 at Temp'ville by JR Tillery

WARNER Robert J 26 S Seaman Acc Acc s/o Isaac & Elizabeth to Sarah E Bloxom 31 W Acc Acc d/o James & Nancy Andrews on 16 May 1871 near Mappsville by O Littleton

WARNER Wharton Col 23 S Farmer Acc Acc s/o Mary to Annie Bloxom Col 23 S Acc Acc d/o Sabra on 3 Apr 1889 at Acc by AJ Satchell

WARREN Calvin L 34 W Teacher N'hamp: Acc s/o Patrich & Elizth to Fannie S Hopkins 20 S Acc Acc d/o Ellison A & Jane on 11 Dec 1861 at Acc by P Warren

WARREN Cyrus F 23 S Laborer Acc Wor Co MD s/o Albert H & Mary to Maggie L [Willet] Willett 19 S Acc Acc d/o John W & Polly on 30 Mar 1885 at Onancock by PA Leatherbury

WARREN Hebard L 23 S Farmer Acc Acc s/o Jno & Tabitha to Minnie D Read 18 S Acc Acc d/o Litt D & Henrietta on 13 Jan 1886 at Acc by L

Rosser
WARREN John Col 22 S Wage-earner Acc. Acc s/o Hilly & Finney to Hester [Bivens] Beavans Col 21 S Acc Acc d/o Moses & Ibby on 3 Sep 1890 at Drum'tn by BJ Hargarves
WARREN John L 28 S Farmer Acc Acc s/o Jno & Tabitha to Sarah T Smith 17 S Acc Acc d/o Walliam P & Susan on 24 Nov 1880 at Pungo: by SC Boston
WARREN John W 32 S Merchant Wor Co MD Acc s/o John S & Adaline to Ida V Whealton 28 S Acc Acc d/o John B & Mary A on 28 Dec 1892 at Chinco: Isld by GE Wood
WARREN Willard 22 S Laborer Steam Mill Sussex Co DE Acc s/o Rupes M & Mary to Mary A Hornsby 22 S Acc Acc d/o James H & Elizabeth on 8 Nov 1881 at Bells Nk by JE Humphreys
WARRINGTON Charles Col 30 S Farmer Acc Acc s/o James & Susan to Frances Roberts Col 24 S Acc Acc d/o James & Mary on 27 Jun 1874 near Onancock by S Johns
WARRINGTON Henry Col 21 S Laborer Acc Acc s/o Eliza to Emma Northam Col 20 S Acc Acc d/o Acria on 23 Jan 1876 at Modest Town by A Joynes
WARRINGTON James Col 50 S Farmer Acc Acc to Lousia Fletcher Col 50 S Acc Acc on 14 Dec 1872 at Wagram by TM Poulson
WARRINGTON James H Col 21 S Waterman Acc Acc s/o Edward & Harriet to Mary A Crippen Col 21 S Acc Acc d/o Henry & Clarissa on 14 Mar 1894 at Acc by JC Cluff
WARRINGTON Riley J Col 23 S Farmer Acc Acc s/o Charles & Frances to Julie A [Homes] Holmes Col 20 S Acc Acc d/o Lewis & Ann on 23 May 1894 at New Church by TM Poulson

WARRINGTON William 21 S Mechanic s/o John & Peggie to Virginia S Robins 21 S d/o Abraham lic: 28 Dec 1868 marr: 16 Jan 1869
WARRINGTON William [Warrenton] 22 S Carriage Mkr Acc Acc s/o John C & Margt to Nettie Mears 27 W Acc Acc d/o William & Fanny on 25 May 1871 at Acc by JE Humphreys
WASHINGTON Charles Col 22 S Sailor N'hamp: Acc to Jane Young Col 19 S Acc Acc d/o Sarah on 26 Sep 1878 near Poor House by A Joynes
WASHINGTON George Col 40 S Fireman GA Acc s/o Abram & Mary to Virginia Topping Col 35 S Acc Acc d/o Virginia on 3 Apr 1888 at Onancock by GHT Byrd
WATERFIELD James 21 S Farmer Acc Acc s/o James W & Susan to Mary Poulson 20 S Acc Acc d/o John J & E liz'th on 27 Dec 1893 at Onancock by GE Booker
WATERFIELD James W 20 S Farmer Acc Acc s/o Wm & Margaret to Lavina Susan Gray 17 S Acc Acc d/o James & Elizabeth on 18 Jan 1871 at Deep Ck by JET Ewell
WATERFIELD William 63 W Farmer Acc Acc to Rosetta Haley 60 W Acc Acc on 10 Nov 1886 at Acc by L Rosser
WATERHOUSE Frank L 22 S Sailor Acc Acc s/o Amelia to Rebecca Susan Bull 21 S Acc Acc d/o George W & Elizabeth on 27 Oct 1889 at bride's father's by JS Wharton
WATERS Edwin T 26 S Sailor Acc Acc s/o Wm C & Margt to Catharine R Finney 22 S Acc Acc d/o Wm B & Margt on 29 May 1872 at St James Ch by O Littleton
WATERS Gerge E 24 S Seaman Acc Acc s/o George & Malinda to Emma Joynes 23 S Acc Acc d/o Eliar & Sally on 2 Mar 1871 at Andrew Chp

by AC Bledsoe

WATERS Julius W Col 22 S Farmer Wor Co MD Acc s/o Thomas & Rosanna to Mary P Broughton Col 21 S Acc Acc d/o Isaac & Elizabeth on 30 Jan 1894 at Acc by JC Cluff

WATERS William F 27 S Merchant Acc Acc s/o Wm C & Margaret to Annie C Jacobs 22 S Acc Acc d/o Wm E & Charlotte on 28 Apr 1880 at Craddockville by CC Wertenbaker

WATKINSON Cornelius 22 S Farmer Acc Acc s/o Geo & Margt to Juliana Mears 21 S Acc Acc d/o Gilbert & Elizth on 14 Nov 1877 near Onancock by WJ Duhadway

WATKINSON David W 23 S Farmer Acc Acc s/o Evans & Alicia to Margaret E Beasley 25 S Acc Acc d/o Susan on 28 Dec 1881 at Acc by SC Boston

WATKINSON Evins 35 S Carpenter b: Acc s/o Cornelius & Rosey to Elizth Ann Bloxom 18 S b: Acc d/o Wm & Eliza on 15 Nov 1854 at r/o Minister by LK LeCato

WATKINSON George H 34 S Farmer Acc Acc s/o Geo & Margt to Willianna Northam 18 S Acc Acc d/o Jas M & Sarah on 28 Jan 1880 at Zion Bapt Ch by DA Woodson

WATKINSON James W 42 S Farmer Acc Acc s/o George & Sarah to Catharine J Mears 34 W Acc Acc d/o James & Molly on 3 Feb 1875 near Locustville by JH Amiss

WATKINSON John T 30 S Farmer Acc Acc s/o Geo & Sally to Eliza Ann Melson 25 S Acc Acc d/o Jas H & Elizabeth on 11 Oct 1865 at Acc by ES Grant

WATKINSON Levin 23 S Farmer Acc Acc s/o George & Sally to Sally Hargis 21 S Acc Acc d/o George & Ann (who gave consent) on 2 Jan 1861 at r/o Littlt Lacato by LK LeCato (James Wadkinson says he over 21)

WATKINSON William 28 S Farmer Acc Acc s/o William & Mary to Sarah E Johnson 21 S Acc Acc d/o Isaiah on 23 Dec 1874 at Acc by DA Woodson

WATSON Alfred 21 S Oysterman Acc Acc s/o Robert & Henrietta to Salona Cherricks 17 S Acc Acc d/o Joshua & Elizabeth on 23 Oct 1889 at Chinco: Isld by SU Grimsley

WATSON Benjamin F Col 22 S Wage-earner Acc Acc s/o Sally to Sadie E Joynes Col 17 S Acc Acc d/o Wilson & Arena on 23 Aug 1892 at Onancock by JW Cook

WATSON Charles Col 22 S Laborer Acc Acc s/o Eliza to Martha White Col 25 S Acc Acc d/o Harriet Koolman on 17 Aug 1884 at Acc by LW Lee

WATSON Charles F 24 S Farmer Acc Acc s/o Thos P & Annie B to Mollie R Mason 22 S Acc Acc d/o George W & Nancy B on 22 Nov 1882 at Savageville by IG Fosnocht

WATSON David Col 22 S Farmer Acc Acc s/o Jacob & Hetty to Mary A Planter Col 19 S Acc Acc d/o Fred & Linie on 25 Nov 1894 at Temp'ville by GHT Byrd

WATSON David T 25 S Farmer Acc Acc s/o Jno E & Elizth S to Mary F Rew 21 S Acc Acc d/o Revel & Jane on 26 Dec 1883 near Acc C H by JG Anderson

WATSON Edgar 25 S Farmer Acc Acc to Cornelia S Fisher 25 S Acc Acc d/o Abeduego T & Critty on 17 Jan 1895 at Hallwood by JL King

WATSON Edmond Col 23 S Sailor Acc Acc s/o Eliza to Mary E White Col 18 S Acc Acc d/o Harriet on 5 Jun 1881 near Onancock by JC Ayler

WATSON Ellison 25 S Farmer Acc Acc s/o Wm & Fannie to Cassie [Crocket] Crockett 22 S Acc Acc d/o Southey

& Margt on 3 Feb 1870 at Acc by JE Humphreys

WATSON George C 21 S Farmer Acc Acc s/o John R & Cath C to Susane A Chandler 20 S Acc Acc d/o Thos B & Sarah on 6 Jan 1869 at Acc by ES Grant

WATSON George D 24 S Clergyman Acc New Town MD s/o Jas H & Eveline to Evelyn M Watson 22 S Acc Acc d/o Edwd R & Elizabeth on 7 Oct 1869 at Acc by EG Irvin

WATSON George D 20 S Oysterman Acc Acc s/o David R & Annie to Lizzie Claville 17 S Acc Acc d/o James & Elizabeth on 22 May 1895 at Chinco: Isld by SU Grimsley

WATSON Golden F 36 S Sailor Acc Acc s/o John E & Elizabeth to Maggie B Mears 28 S Acc Acc d/o James & Mary on 15 Jan 1890 at Acc by W Chinn

WATSON Henry Col 35 S Acc Acc s/o Sinah to Arinthia Seymour Col 25 S Acc Acc d/o Dinah on 15 Dec 1879 at Modest Town by JE Bundick

WATSON Henry Col 46 W Farmer Acc Acc s/o John Harmon & Sinah Watson to Nicse Selby Col 33 S Acc Acc d/o Robert & Leah on 7 Jan 1888 at Mappsville by WA Street

WATSON Henry O 24 S Farmer Acc Acc s/o David & Mary to Leah Ann Riley 19 S Acc Acc d/o Geo T & Catharine W on 4 Mar 1874 near Onancock by O Littleton

WATSON Jacob Col 32 S Farmer Acc Acc s/o Ann to Hetty Conquest Col 35 S Acc Acc d/o Euphemia on 25 Dec 1879 at Modest Town by A Joynes

WATSON Jacob Col 22 S Farmer Acc Acc s/o Jacob & Nelly to Maggie Wharton Col 22 S Acc Acc d/o Mary on 22 Jul 1891 at Nelsonia by JE Bundick

WATSON Jacob Col 48 S Wage-earner Acc Acc to Elishea A Williams Col 33 S Acc Acc d/o Rachel on 26 Sep 1894 at Acc by AJ Satchell

WATSON James 38 W Farmer b: Acc s/o John & Betsy to Virginia Phillips 23 S b: Acc d/o David & Patsy on 22 Aug 1855 at Burton Ch by JWA Elliott (John W Sturgis says she over 21)

WATSON James 22 S Oysterman Acc Acc s/o Peter & Susan to Mahala Archey 22 S Acc Acc d/o Charles & Rachael on 29 Jun 1870 at Locust Mount by JWA Elliott

WATSON James R 27 S Louis(?) Farmer Acc Acc s/o Thos P & Annie B to Annie B Mason 29 S Acc Acc d/o Geo W & Nancy on 26 Jan 1881 near Savageville by LE Barrett

WATSON Jessie R 22 S Sailor Chinco: Isld Chinco: Isld s/o William T & Elizth to Catharine Andrews 16 S Chinco: Isld Chinco: Isld d/o William & Mary on 3 Jan 1875 at Acc by P Bowdin Sr

WATSON John 42 W Shoemaker Chinco: Isld Chinco: Isld s/o Robt & Sarah to Mary Taylor 22 S Chinco: Isld Chinco: Isld d/o Jacob & Sarah on 17 Jun 1860 at Chinco: Isld by P Bowdin Sr (W M Feddiman said she over 21)

WATSON John 24 S Farmer Acc Acc s/o John & Elizabeth to Elizabeth Harrison 21 S Acc Acc d/o Wm & Rachel on 27 Oct 1874 at Acc by LK LeCato

WATSON John C 44 Waterman N'hamp: Acc s/o Benjamin & Susan to Tabitha S Coleburn 28 Acc Acc d/o Jno A & Elizth on 3 Dec 1857 near Pungo: by M Oldham (Jonathan Smith says both over 21)

WATSON John H Col 26 S Wage-earner Acc Acc s/o Henry & Arinthia to Arena Nock Col 21 S Acc Acc d/o Parker & Annie on 12 Dec

1889 at Acc by JE Bundick

WATSON John N 25 S Carpenter Acc Acc s/o Elizabeth to Harriet D Byrd 23 S Acc Acc d/o Selby on 17 Oct 1866 at Acc by M Oldham

WATSON John P 21 S Oysterman Acc Acc s/o John W & Mary to Elizabeth Hancock 22 S Acc Acc d/o John & Sally on 6 Feb 1873 at Chinco: Isld by P Bowdin Sr

WATSON John T 23 S Carriage Mkr Acc Acc s/o Thos to Bettie A Evans 17 S Acc Acc d/o Thos & Esther A on 4 Apr 1867 at Acc by JO Moss

WATSON John W 55 W Oysterman Acc Acc to Martha Bowden 24 S Acc Acc d/o William & Ann N on 12 Nov 1873 at Chinco: Isld by WP Thornton

WATSON Joseph FN to Martha Tunnell FN lic: 28 Feb 1859

WATSON Joseph C 28 S Farmer Acc Acc s/o Thos P & Ann B to Maggie R Bundick 31 S Acc Acc d/o John B & Margaret E on 7 May 1891 at Acc by JR Strugis

WATSON Levin T Col 23 S Sailor Acc Acc s/o Thomas & Susan to Clyda G Davis Col 22 S Acc Acc on 3 Mar 1890 at Onancock by JH Offer

WATSON Lewis Oswald 20 S Farmer Acc Acc s/o Joseph & Elizabeth to Mary E Parker 18 S Acc Acc d/o William L & Margaret on 15 Dec 1869 near Locustville by LK LeCato

WATSON Littleton 32 W Oysterman Chinco: Isld Chinco: Isld s/o Jno W & Mary to Susan [Chericks] Cherricks 44 W Chinco: Isld Chinco: Isld d/o James & Mary Furguson on 13 Mar 1883 at Chinco: Isld by WP Thornton

WATSON Littleton W 23 S Oysterman Chinco: Isld Chinco: Isld s/o John & Mary to Ann Eliza Tatham 28 W Chinco: Isld Chinco: Isld d/o Parker & Mary Turlington on 6 Jan 1873 at Chinco: Isld by WP Thornton

WATSON Mitchell W 52 W Farmer Wor Co MD Onancock s/o John & Ann to Mary R Townsend 50 S Onancock Onancock d/o Littleton & Nancy on 15 Dec 1860 at Drum'tn by D Felton (Edward K Snead says she over 21)

WATSON Moses B 26 S Trading b: Prussia s/o M A to Leah Solms 19 S b: Prussia d/o B & Emily on 23 May 1863 at Acc by D Titlow

WATSON Robert 44 W Oysterman Acc Acc s/o Robert & Polly to Harriet Hancock 24 S Wor Co MD Acc d/o Major & Tabitha on 3 May 1874 at Chinco: Isld by P Bowdin Sr

WATSON Samuel Col 28 S Farmer Acc Acc s/o Annie to Elizabeth Dennis Col 23 S Acc Acc d/o Annie on 24 Sep 1885 near Temp'ville by JC Cluff

WATSON Smith Col 22 S Laborer Acc Acc s/o Patience to Czanna (Czarina) Planter Col 21 S Acc Acc d/o Agnes on 3 Aug 1871 at Acc by M Oldham

WATSON Thomas 23 S Oysterman Acc Acc s/o Purnell & Mary to Laney Lone 21 S Acc Acc d/o James & Elizth on 19 Jun 1867 at Acc by P Bowdin Sr

WATSON Thomas N 21 S Farmer Acc Acc s/o John N & Harriet to Ida E Grinnalds 23 S Acc Acc d/o James H & Tabitha J on 27 Mar 1889 at Temp'ville by WF Hayes

WATSON Thoro Col 29 S Wage-earner Acc Acc s/o Mary to Mary Jane Beloate Col 35 S Acc Acc d/o Mary Jane on 8 Oct 1893 at Locust Mount by JWA Elliott

WATSON William Col 32 S Laborer Acc Acc s/o Sinah to Cecillia Sample Col 24 S Acc Acc d/o Littleton & Sarah on 10 Apr 1881 at Pungo: by TW Nettles

WATSON William T 25 S Farmer Acc Acc s/o Thomas P & Ann L to Mary

Budd 21 S Acc Acc d/o William & Sarah on 16 Dec 1874 at Acc by RC Jones

WATSON Wm F 25 S Farmer Acc Acc s/o Jno E & Elizth to Harriet S Budd 26 S Acc Acc d/o Wm & Sally on 21 Oct 1886 at Onancock by JW Hundley

WATSON Wm L 30 D Oysterman Chinco: Isld Chinco: Isld s/o Robert & Henrietta to Esther Carpenter 18 S Chinco: Isld Chinco: Isld d/o Richard & Mary J on 7 Feb 1883 at Chinco: Isld by WP Thornton

WATSON Wm T 30 W Merchant b: Chinco: Isld s/o Zadoc & Frances to Elizabeth T Williams 18 S b: Chinco: Isld d/o Littl & Elizth on 12 Dec 1855 at Chinco: Isld by WP Thornton

WATTS John D 36 S Merchant Acc Acc s/o John S & Adaline to Mary E Bundick 20 S Acc Acc d/o Thos of W & Mary on 12 Feb 1890 at Zion Bapt Ch by AJ Fristoe

WATTS John Edward Col 20 S Wage-earner Acc Acc s/o Abbott & Hannah to Mary Dinah Dickerson Col 17 S Acc Acc d/o David & Amy on 8 May 1889 at Acc by AJ Satchell

WATTS Levi 22 S Wage-earner Acc Acc s/o Abbott & Hannah to Missouri Ewell 17 S Acc Acc d/o James & Ann on 4 Jun 1890 at Acc by AJ Satchell

WATTS William Abbott Col 21 S Wage-earner Acc Acc s/o Abbott & Hannah to Susan [Justis] Justice Col 17 S Acc Acc d/o Esther on 23 Mar 1893 at Acc by AJ Satchell

WEAVER George N 35 S Teacher Acc Acc s/o James C & Sally P to Kate L Lewis 24 S Acc Acc d/o John T on 11 Apr 1894 at Sykes Isld by DJ Traynham

WEAVER James T 31 S Waterman Acc Acc s/o James C & Sally P to Manie E Miles 16 S Acc Acc d/o Severn & Amanda on 8 Jan 1893 at Acc by RB Scott

WEBB Arthur (FN) 24 S Farmer Acc Acc s/o Jno & Harriet to Margt Morris (FN) 23 S Acc Acc d/o Solomon (Lavin) & Tabby Mears on 26 Mar 1864 at Acc by JWA Elliott

WEBB George (Col) 22 S Laborer Acc Acc s/o John & Harriet to Mary Bagwell (Col) 21 S N'hamp: Acc d/o George & Mary on 30 Dec 1869 near Belle Haven by JE Humphreys

WEBB George Col 36 W Farmer Acc Acc s/o Jno & Harriet to Margaret Ames Col 24 S Acc Acc d/o Mary on 29 Dec 1880 near Belle Haven by SMG Copeland

WEBB Gilbert FN 24 S Sawyer Acc Acc s/o Jno & Harriet to Ailsy Morris FN 28 S Acc Acc d/o Levin & Tabitha on 9 May 1866 at Acc by JWA Elliott

WEBB John Col 50 S Farmer Acc Acc to Lucy Foskey Col 40 S Acc Acc on 14 Dec 1871 at Belle Haven by TM Cole

WEBB John FN to Harriet Harmon FN lic: 27 Feb 1854 John E Smith says both over 21

WEBB Southey 22 S Sailor N'hamp: Acc s/o Southey & Hester to Mary C Justice 19 S Acc Acc d/o John & Melinda on 6 Dec 1874 near Foxville by JE Bundick

WEBB Southey 28 W Farmer N'hamp: Acc s/o Southey to Mary A Wright 27 S Acc Acc d/o John & Louisa on 7 Jun 1882 at Lee Mont by WA Crouse

WEBB Southey R 36 W Surfman N'hamp: Acc s/o Southy to Catharine E Adams 19 S Acc Acc d/o John E & Nancy E on 13 Aug 1890 at Acc by HS Dulany

WEBB Wm Henry FN 43 S Sawyer b: Acc s/o Molly to Milly Taylor FN 41 S b: Acc d/o Lucy Lefco on 4 May

1854 at r/o Jno W Elliotts by JWA Elliott (John E Smith said both over 21)

WELBOURN George Col 45 S (Laborer) Acc Acc s/o Betsy (Beky) to Leah Walters Col 40 S Acc Acc d/o Agnes on 2 Jun 1873 at Horntown by S Johns

WESCOTT Benj F [Wescoat] 23 S Teacher b: Frank Town s/o Hezekiah P & Susan to Hester A Savage 22 S b: Ward Town d/o Michl & Finatta on 23 Aug 1854 at Garrisons Chp by A Wallace

WESCOTT Gustave T 20 S Merchant N'hamp: Acc s/o Edward D & Virginia S to Julia A Wise 19 S Acc Acc d/o Edward S & Sarah on 27 Sep 1892 at Craddockville by JM Anderson

WESCOTT Hesckiah P (Hezekiah) [Wescot] 26 S Farmer Acc N'hamp: s/o Hesckiah (Hezehiah) & Susan to Mary S (Susan) Savage 22 S Acc Acc d/o Major & Susan on 26 Jan 1857 at r/o Abel Mears by JWA Elliott (Joseph S Wescoat says both over 21)

WESCOTT John Col 30 S Laborer N'hamp: Acc s/o Vianna to Margaret Rogers Col 25 S Acc Acc d/o Charles & Lettia on 3 Apr 1887 at Hawk's Nest by L Duncan

WESCOTT John E 23 S Merchant Acc Acc s/o Jos J & Elizth B to Maggie C Mapp 18 S Acc Acc d/o Wm C & Cath A on 27 Jan 1879 at Hawk's Nest by CC Wertenbaker

WESCOTT Joseph C 29 W Merchant Acc Acc s/o Joshus & Margt S to Sally P Weaver 30 S Acc Acc d/o James C & Sally P on 2 Sep 1885 at Acc by JW Hundley

WESCOTT Joseph J Jr 25 S Farmer Acc Acc s/o Joseph J & Betsy B to Annie M Copes 18 S Acc Acc d/o Wm T & Susan Copes on 24 Nov 1887 near Locustville by JWA Elliott

WESCOTT William W [Wescoat] 25 S Farmer N'hamp: N'hamp: s/o Jno L & Sarah to Esther Joynes 23 S Acc Acc d/o Edwd & Ann on 31 Dec 1879 at Garrisons Chp by JE Humphreys

WESSELLS Alfred 21 S Farmer b: Acc s/o Danl & Elizth to Kessey Phillips 22 S b: Acc d/o Levin & Charlotte on 8 Feb 1855 at New Church by T Waters

WESSELLS Andrew J 22 S Farmer Acc Acc s/o Ephraim W & Mary to Eva B Barnes 16 S Acc Acc d/o Alfred J & Mary on 27 Oct 1889 at bride's father's by JS Wharton

WESSELLS Arthur 27 S Mechanic Acc Acc s/o John & Susan to Mary A Wessells 15 S Acc Acc d/o Ephrain & Mary on 8 Jan 1868 at Acc by ES Grant

WESSELLS Augusta F 23 S Farmer Acc Acc s/o Arthur T & Ann to Elizabeth S Hope 20 S Acc Acc d/o Wm S & Jane on 13 Dec 1863 at Acc by ES Grant

WESSELLS Augustus F 35 W Farmer Acc Acc s/o Arthur to Elishea A Hope 19 S Acc Acc d/o Wm S on 22 Oct 1874 at Metompkin by EM Bryan

WESSELLS Charles F 22 S Farmer Acc Acc s/o Wm W & Caroline to Cora A Bloxom 21 S Acc Acc d/o Major & Clarissa on 1 Mar 1882 at Mr Martin Bloxom's by JW Hundley

WESSELLS Emory J [Wessels] 22 S Oysterman Acc Acc s/o Henry & Virnetta to Alice L Small 20 S Acc Acc d/o John J & Sarah on 4 Dec 1892 at Mappsville by JL King

WESSELLS Ephraim J 22 S Farmer Acc Acc s/o Ephraim & Mary to Mary E Parkes 20 S Acc Acc d/o Edwd J & Nancy on 28 Dec 1884 at Acc by WA Street

WESSELLS Ephraim of D 30 S Milling

Acc Acc s/o David B & Nancy to Nancy R Taylor 21 S Acc Acc d/o Calvin & Adaline on 23 Dec 1888 at Lee Mont by JW Norris

WESSELLS Ephrain 21 S Farmer Acc Guilford s/o Richard & Polly to Mary A Bell 19 S Acc Guiford d/o William (Decd)& Ann on 10 Jan 1861 at Ann Bell's by GH Ewell (Major Mason says be over 21)

WESSELLS George Col 25 S Laborer Acc Acc s/o Violet to Laura Waters Col 18 S Acc Acc d/o Major & Agnes on 10 Jan 1877 near News Town by A Joynes

WESSELLS George Col 23 S Laborer Acc Acc s/o Jno & Anne to Arinthia Downing Col 25 S Acc Acc d/o Mary Downing on 20 Apr 1882 near News Town by AJ Satchell

WESSELLS George Col 36 W Farmer Acc Acc s/o Ann to Ama Lee Patterson Col 16 S Acc Acc d/o Leah Ann on 27 Dec 1891 at Acc by LE Toulson

WESSELLS Henry C 36 S Farmer Acc Acc s/o Thos & Elizabeth to Arinthia Hickman 17 S Acc Acc d/o John E & Matilda on 30 Aug 1885 at Acc by WA Street

WESSELLS Isaac 35 S Farming Acc Acc s/o Richard & Mary to Margaret A Thomas 23 S Acc Acc d/o Gillet & Comfort on 1 Jan 1871 at Guilford by JET Ewell

WESSELLS J W 45 S Oysterman Acc Acc s/o Walter & Polly to Elizabeth Smith 27 S Acc Acc d/o Valentine & Elizth on 11 Jan 1881 at Pocomoke by M Oldham

WESSELLS Jacob [Vessels] Col 65 S Wage-earner Acc Acc to Elizabeth Nedab Col 60 S Acc Acc on 3 Feb 1893 at Acc by L Duncan

WESSELLS James Col 20 S Wage-earner Acc Acc s/o Ann to Mary Young Col 19 S Acc Acc d/o Sallie on 19 Jul 1893 at Acc by AJ Satchell

WESSELLS James T 24 S Farmer Acc Acc s/o Thos (of J) & Carlo. to Caroline Susan Parkes 16 S Acc Acc d/o Chas & Margt on 7 Jan 1866 at Acc by ES Grant

WESSELLS Jefferson D 21 S Farmer Acc Acc s/o David B & Nancy to Emily L Bundick 19 S Acc Acc d/o Wm J & Seymour on 29 Nov 1882 at Acc by JW Hundley

WESSELLS Jno C 27 S Carpenter Baltimore MD Acc s/o Jno to Laurah J Fanton 17 S r: Acc d/o Jane on 10 Apr 1862 at Acc by GH Ewell

WESSELLS John 40 S Farmer Acc Acc s/o John & Susan to Mary Taylor 30 S Acc Acc d/o Wm & Ann on 17 Apr 1873 at Guilford by JE Bundick

WESSELLS John O 41 S Farmer Acc Acc s/o Saml & Rachel to Ellen Stant 39 S Acc Acc d/o Saml & Ellen on 11 Nov 1886 at Guilford by JW Norris

WESSELLS John W 26 S Farmer Acc Acc s/o Thomas H & Elizabeth to Ocenia B Wessells 16 S Acc Acc d/o Samuel & Rachel on 15 Dec 1881 at Acc by JW Hundley

WESSELLS Judson F [Wessels] 25 S Carpenter Acc Acc s/o Augustus F & Elizabeth W to Ella J Taylor 23 S Acc Acc d/o Alfred Jackson & Hetty S on 12 Dec 1888 at Zion Ch by JS Wharton

WESSELLS Littleton E 22 S Farmer Acc Acc s/o Alfred J & Georgianna to Sarah T [Bonewell] Bonnewell 17 S Acc Acc d/o John W & Emaline E on 10 Jan 1894 at Acc C H by JM Dunaway

WESSELLS Luther J 26 S Farmer Acc Acc s/o Samuel & Virginia to Mary A Young 26 S Acc Acc d/o John S & Susan on 27 Dec 1891 near Guilford Ck by JW Nicholson

WESSELLS Luther J 27 S Oysterman Acc Acc s/o Richard & Virginia to Sallie L Mason 23 S Acc Acc d/o James & Sarah on 7 Jan 1894 at Parksley by JET Ewell

WESSELLS Oliver F 20 S Farmer Acc Acc s/o Thomas & Catharine to Mary J C Young 20 S Acc Acc d/o Samuel & Sally on 8 Jan 1873 near Guilford by JET Ewell

WESSELLS Oliver J 21 S Sailor Acc Acc s/o Ephrain & Mary to Missouri G Mears 22 S Acc Acc d/o Meshack & Betsy on 19 May 1886 at Mappsville by WA Street

WESSELLS Otho L 23 S Waterman Acc Acc s/o Betsy Young to Annie B Shrieves 18 S Acc Acc d/o Thadius W & Dannah on 25 Dec 1895 at Acc by JR Sturgis

WESSELLS Richard 29 S Farmer Acc Acc s/o Jno H & Susan to Virginia Wessells 20 S Acc Acc d/o Ephraim W & Elizth on 4 Jan 1866 at Acc by ES Grant

WESSELLS Samuel 22 S Farmer Acc Acc s/o Jno & Susan to Georgiana Young 19 S Acc Acc d/o Margt Young (Thorns) on 4 May 1865 at Reese Chp by ES Grant

WESSELLS Samuel H 21 S Sailor Acc Acc s/o Henry W & Bernitte to Cora A Gladding 18 S Acc Acc d/o Burwell B & Mary on 4 Jan 1889 at Acc by WA Street

WESSELLS Samuel T 19 S Farmer Acc Acc s/o Samuel & Georgianna to Sarah E Young 27 S Acc Acc d/o John S & Susan on 2 Jan 1889 at Woodbury Ch by WF Hayes

WESSELLS Southey Col 25 S Laborer Acc Acc s/o Violet to Hester Justice Col 40 S Acc Acc d/o Peggy on 18 Jan 1882 near News Town by AJ Satchell

WESSELLS William B [Wessels] 18 S Farmer Acc Acc s/o L Bates & Mary E to Etta L Hurst 18 S Acc Acc d/o J Wesley & Annie on 6 Nov 1895 at Acc by MF Sanford

WESSELLS William H 21 S Farmer Acc Acc s/o Oliver F & Mary J to Lillian Lee Riggs 15 S Acc Acc d/o Joseph H & Melissa on 3 Mar 1895 at Acc by DGC Butts

WESSELLS William J [Wessels] 29 W Farmer Acc Acc s/o Ephraim W & Mary to Elizabeth W Hinman 29 W Acc Acc d/o Littleton Nock on 8 Aug 1888 at Parksley by JS Wharton

WESSELLS William W s/o Walter to Catherine Justice d/o Samuel who gave consent lic: 25 Dec 1854

WESSELLS Wm J 23 S Sailor Acc Acc s/o Wm W & Caroline to Sarah E Trader 17 S Acc Acc d/o Raymond & Betsy on 30 Apr 1882 at Shiloh Ch by JW Hundley

WESSELLS Wm J 24 S Farmer Acc Acc s/o Epharim & Mary to Mary G Matthews 23 S Acc Acc d/o Samuel H & Margt on 27 Dec 1882 at Acc by JW Hundley

WEST Appie Col 60 W Farmer Acc Acc to Lizzie Conner Col 40 W Acc Acc on 17 Aug 1890 at Belle Haven by JE Humphreys

WEST Augustus S Col 22 S School Teacher Acc Acc s/o Jane to Mary S Martin Col 18 S Acc Acc d/o Sheppard & Sarah on 21 Jan 1885 near Pungo: by GHT Byrd

WEST Costella Col 22 S Laborer Acc Acc s/o Margaret Sample to Elizabeth Major Col 23 S Acc Acc d/o Gladdie on 1 Apr 1874 at Belle Haven by JE Humphreys

WEST Daniel Col 33 S Laborer Acc Acc s/o Nicy to Ida Finney Col 21 W Acc Acc d/o Mary Rodgers on 11 Dec 1879 at Onancock by JW Diggs

WEST Daniel Col 22 S Sailor Acc Acc s/o Appy & Sally to Florence Brickhouse Col 21 S N'hamp: Acc d/o Horace & Sally on 5 Jun 1890 at Shiloh Ch by TW Nettles

WEST, Edmund Col 26 S Wage-earner Acc Acc s/o Isaac to Catharine Upshur Col 29 S Acc Acc d/o Frank on 5 Jan 1892 at N'hamp: by J Savage

WEST Edward Col 21 S Sailor Acc Acc s/o Chlom to Emma Simpkins Col 17 S Acc Acc d/o Ezekiel & Louisa Rino on 16 Jul 1874 at Onancock by PA Leatherbury

WEST Edwin N 26 S Mechanic Acc Acc s/o Richard N & Sally P to Ida A Mason 20 S Acc Acc d/o William on 9 Nov 1887 at Acc by WA Street

WEST Frank A 24 S Tinner Acc Acc s/o John & Jane to Nannie Lambden 22 S Wor Co MD Acc d/o Saml & Mary on 20 Feb 1878 at Onancock by SC Boston

WEST Geo E Col 22 S Wage-earner Acc Acc s/o Nellie to Bertie Finney Col 21 S Acc Acc d/o Emma on 6 Jul 1892 at Savageville by JH Offer

WEST George Col 24 S Laborer Acc Acc s/o Louisa to Lydda Bull Col 20 S Acc Acc d/o Peggy on 28 Mar 1875 at Onancock by JK Plato

WEST George Col 26 W Sailor Acc Acc s/o Louisa to Leah Finney Col 21 S Acc Acc d/o Rachel on 8 Oct 1882 at Savageville by F Corrd

WEST George A Col 37 S Sailor Acc Acc to Elizabeth Sample Col 27 S Acc Acc on 3 Jan 1872 at Belle Haven by JE Humphreys

WEST George G 21 S Farmer Acc Acc s/o George & Susan to Eleanor E Ames 15 S Acc Acc d/o Levin & Lottie E on 15 Nov 1876 at Craddockville by JWA Elliott

WEST George T Col 33 S Farmer Acc Acc s/o Levin & Leah to Sarah Conquest Col 21 S Acc Acc d/o Missouri on 3 Jan 1895 at Acc by PW Lee

WEST George W 26 S Farmer Acc Acc s/o Edward J & Margt to Sarah E Mears 23 S Acc Acc d/o Julius C & Susan J on 8 Nov 1882 at Acc by SC Boston

WEST Isaac Col 33 S Laborer Acc Acc s/o Sarah to Nancy [Gaskin] Gaskins Col 26 S Matthews Co VA Acc on 14 Dec 1881 at Acc by TW Nettles

WEST James 22 S Laborer Acc Acc s/o Caroline to Sarah Rogers 31 S Acc Acc d/o Nariscie on 17 Aug 1870 at Acc by JE Humphreys

WEST John Col 30 S Farmer Acc Acc s/o George & Chloe to Elisie Byrd Col 22 S Acc Acc on 4 May 1871 near Reese Chp by N Morris

WEST John H 21 S Farmer Acc Acc s/o Jesse & Susan to Emma S Elliott 17 S Acc Acc d/o Geo & Ann on 6 Sep 1865 at Acc by D Titlow

WEST John W 20 S Sailor Acc Acc s/o Francis & Elizth to Sadie V Bundick 21 S Acc Acc d/o Geo T & Drucilla on 20 Jun 1877 at Modest Town by DA Woodson

WEST Julius Col 31 S Laborer Acc Acc s/o Mary to Hannah Parkes Col 40 S Acc Acc d/o Henny Lewis on 22 May 1873 at Deep Ck by N Morris

WEST Julius Col 32 W Laborer Acc Acc s/o Mary to Tamar Chandler Col 30 W Acc Acc d/o Labra on 13 Jun 1875 at Bay Side Ch by HT Rich

WEST Levin 27 S Laborer Acc Acc s/o Mary to Tamar Grant 26 S Acc Acc d/o Ann Snead on 13 Feb 1867 at Acc by JH Ellegood

WEST Lewis Col 35 S Farmer Acc Acc s/o Clara Mason to Tamar White Col 41 S Acc Acc d/o Ada on 6 Jul 1885 near Hunting Ck by CA Horsey

WEST Lorenzo 24 S Life Saving Station Acc Acc s/o George R & Jane to Vienna S Barnes 23 S Acc Acc d/o Wm G & Mary J on 5 Nov 1884 at Acc by JW Carroll

WEST Major Col 22 S Farmer Acc Acc s/o Sally to Mary Jane Harrison Col 22 S Acc Acc d/o Caroline on 21 Dec 1877 at Pungo: by TW Nettles

WEST Major Col 24 S Laborer Acc Acc to Edie Sample Col 23 S Acc Acc on 13 Oct 1878 near Pungo: by JW Diggs

WEST Orris Col 22 S Laborer Acc Acc s/o Leah to Alice Phillips Col 21 S Acc Acc d/o Malinda Walston on 2 Jan 1879 at Drum'tn by RH Govans

WEST Peter FN 33 S Laborer Acc Acc s/o Lewis Justis & Comfort West to Rachel Dix FN 21 S Acc Acc d/o Lewis & Mary on 10 Oct 1860 at Drum'tn by G Cummins (T J Rayfield says he over 21)

WEST Revil 50 W Farmer Guilford Acc s/o Revil & Susannah to Margt C Riley 33 S Pongot Acc d/o Raymond & Sally on 15 Feb 1854 at r/o Ray Riley Jr by C Hill

WEST Richard 23 S Waterman b: Acc s/o Revil & Elizth to Sarah Phillips 23 S b: Acc d/o Wm & Hester on 16 Nov 1858 at Reese Chp by ES Grant (H D Carmine says both over 21)

WEST Samuel Col 21 S Laborer Acc Acc to Priscilla Custis Col 18 S Acc Acc d/o James & Maria on 20 Feb 1879 at Parsonage by A Handy

WEST Samuel Col 40 S Wage-earner Acc Acc s/o Peter to Esther [Parks] Parkes Col 27 W Acc Acc d/o Mary Wessells on 17 Apr 1890 at Acc by AJ Satchell

WEST Samuel W Col 26 S Farmer Acc Acc s/o Albert & Kesiah to Leah J Bunting Col 28 S Acc Acc d/o Millie on 21 Feb 1894 at Savageville by JH Offer

WEST Thos C 38 W Carpenter Acc Acc s/o Paul to Rebecca S Nelson 22 S Acc Acc d/o James & Nancy on 19 Sep 1866 at Acc by P Warren

WEST William 22 S Farmer Acc Acc s/o William & Emily to Indianna F Richardson 18 S Acc Acc d/o William & Rose on 5 Dec 1871 near Onancock by LK LeCato

WEST William Col 22 S Laborer Acc Acc s/o Peter & Rachel to Nelly Moore Col 21 S Acc Acc d/o Sarah on 31 Oct 1882 near Poor House by AJ Satchell

WEST William Col 22 S Sailor Acc Acc s/o William & Maria to Annie H Sample Col 21 S Acc Acc d/o Margaret on 27 Apr 1892 at Acc by L Duncan

WEST William R Col 21 S Sailor Acc Acc s/o Nathl & Bridget to Martha M Watson Col 21 S Acc Acc d/o Thos & Susan on 9 May 1872 at Onancock by R Davis

WEST Wm C 22 S Merchant Acc Acc s/o Revel & Margt C to Annie M Parker 21 S Acc Acc d/o John E & Mary E on 4 Jan 1882 at Onancock Bapt Par by SC Boston

WHARTON Frazier Col 25 S Farmer Acc Acc s/o Tabitha to Bettie Wise Col 18 S Acc Acc d/o Agnes George on 12 Oct 1884 at Acc by R Davis

WHARTON Gabriel 26 S Oysterman Acc Acc s/o Ibby to Larna Taylor 22 S Acc Acc d/o Leah on 9 Jan 1868 at Acc by S Marshall

WHARTON George Col 31 S Sailor Acc Acc s/o Eleshea Douglass to Caroline Marshall Col 18 S Acc Acc d/o Edmund & Elizabeth on 3 Jun 1875 at Horntown by S Johns

WHARTON George Col 21 S Laborer Acc Acc s/o Mary to Jane Parker Col 18 S Acc Acc d/o Emma Conquest on 26 Dec 1877 at Horntown by JC Cluff

WHARTON George Col 34 W Oysterman Acc Acc s/o Jacob & Mary to Mary Ann Tull Col 19 S Acc Acc d/o William & Ann on 28 Aug 1890 at Horntown by JC Cluff

Marriages

WHARTON Henry Col 24 S Laborer Acc Acc s/o Sally to Scarburgh Conquest Col 21 S Acc Acc d/o Sally on 13 Aug 1871 at Acc by A Joynes

WHARTON Jacob FN to Leah Holden FN lic: 29 Dec 1856 J S D Hollands says both over 21

WHARTON James Col 24 S Wage-earner Acc Acc s/o Sally to Ida Drummond Col 19 S Acc Acc d/o Jesse & Hester on 29 Jan 1890 at Acc by N Morris

WHARTON John W Col 20 S Farmer Acc Acc s/o Martha to Margaret Rew Col 18 S Acc Acc d/o Upshur on 4 Dec 1881 at News Town by AJ Satchell

WHARTON Littleton D Col 36 W Farmer Acc Acc s/o James Henry & Rachel to Missouri Ellen Roberts Col 25 S Acc Acc d/o Moses & Martha on 2 Jan 1889 at Onancock by JH Offer

WHARTON William J Col 22 S Laborer Acc Acc to Amanda M Dickerson Col 15 S Acc Acc d/o John F & Sally F on 25 Dec 1893 at Greenbackville by AS Zeaue

WHARTON Williams Col 24 S Laborer Acc Acc s/o Mary to Maggie West Col 20 S Acc Acc d/o Bredget on 14 Sep 1880 at Acc by PM Lewis

WHEALTON Daniel 19 S Mariner Chinco: Isld Chinco: Isld s/o Eba & Elizabeth to Mary Ann [Daysey] Daisey 17 S Chinco: Isld Chinco: Isld d/o Parker J & Elizabeth on 28 Mar 1857 at Chinco: Isld by WP Thornton

WHEALTON Daniel T 27 W Sailor Chinco: Isld Chinco: Isld s/o J D & Jane to Bettie E Jones 21 S Assateague Chinco: Isld d/o John A & Airy on 14 Apr 1886 at Chinco: Isld by SU Grimsley

WHEALTON E William 24 S Farmer Acc Acc s/o Erastus & Mary to Bettie Tindall 20 S Acc Acc d/o George W & Charlotte A on 28 Sep 1887 at Oak Hall by BF Jester

WHEALTON Eba single Laborer Chinco: Isld Chinco: Isld s/o Eba & Betsey to Elizth Sharpley single Chinco: Isld Chinco: Isld d/o Teagle & Fanney on 22 Sep 1853 at r/o Teagle Sharpley by P Bowdin

WHEALTON Eba B 21 S Oysterman Acc Acc s/o Eba & Z B to Annie R B Ward 18 S Acc Acc d/o James N & Annie on 19 Nov 1882 at Acc by SC Boston

WHEALTON George 24 S Sailor Acc Acc s/o John D & Jane to Molly [Reed] Read 22 S Acc Acc d/o Littleton & Mary A on 29 May 1895 at Chinco: Isld by CW Matthews

WHEALTON James Col 24 S Oysterman Chinco: Isld Chinco: Isld s/o Samuel Aydelotte & Amelia Whealton to Maria Brinney Col 28 S Chinco: Isld Chinco: Isld d/o Ocker & Peggy on 7 May 1872 at Chinco: Isld by P Bowdin Sr

WHEALTON James E 23 S Farmer Acc Acc s/o Erustus & Mary to Margaret Smith 17 S Acc Acc d/o William & Sarah & (Sarah E Broadwater gave consent for daughter) on 8 Jan 1874 at Temp'ville by M Oldham

WHEALTON Jno B 21 S Sailor Acc Acc s/o Elias & Elizabeth to Mary A Claville 22 S Wor Co MD Acc d/o Jas & Hester on 5 Sep 1863 at Acc by P Bowdin

WHEALTON John (Jr) 22 W Sailor Chinco: Isld Chinco: Isld s/o Daniel & Elizth to Jane Hill 18 S Chinco: Isld Chinco: Isld d/o Tlmothy & Rebecka on 29 Apr 1858 at Chinco: Isld by P Bowdin

WHEALTON John B 25 W Sailor Acc Acc s/o Eba & Elizabeth to Mary H Williams 21 S DE Acc d/o Ely F & Sophy M on 27 Sep 1871 at Chinco:

Isld by P Bowdin Sr

WHEALTON John B Jr 26 S Sea Captian Acc Acc s/o John D & Jane to Manie M Birch 26 S Acc Acc d/o George C & Trany on 25 Dec 1888 at Chinco: Isld by BF Jester

WHEALTON John Jr ward/o Geo Claville who gave consent to Mary Ann Russell d/o John who gave consent lic: 11 Apr 1855

WHEALTON Joshua single Laborer Chinco: Isld Chinco: Isld s/o Eba & Betsey to Nancy [Forguson] Ferguson single Chinco: Isld Chinco: Isld d/o Jas & Patience on 1 Aug 1853 at his father's by P Bowdin

WHEALTON Levin Thos 26 S Farmer MD Acc s/o Oliver & Maria to Maggie Tarr 16 S MD Acc d/o Charles H & Mary on 6 Jan 1888 at Oak Hall by TG Pullen

WHEALTON Samuel Col 22 S Oysterman Acc Acc s/o Lemuel Aydelotte to Leah Crippen Col 18 S Acc Horntown d/o Henry on 23 Apr 1876 at Chinco: Isld by SP Whittington

WHEALTON Thomas K 35 S MD MD to Missouri C Carmine 19 S Acc Acc d/o Thomas J on 19 Nov 1875 at Onancock by FR Boston

WHEALTON Wallace L 21 S Oysterman Acc Acc s/o Daniel & Mary A to Annie Jester 18 S Acc Acc d/o Isaac & Margaret on 18 Apr 1891 at Chinco: Isld by JW Turner

WHEALTON Wm 27 S Merchant Chinco: Isld Chinco: Isld s/o Wm & Tabitha to Josephine Birch 24 S Chinco: Isld Chinco: Isld d/o Thos & Mary C on 15 Dec 1869 at Chinco: Isld by P Bowdin Jr

WHEALTON Wm 19 S Oysterman Acc Acc s/o Joshua & Nancy to Mary A Powell 22 S Wor Co MD Acc d/o Levin on 13 Nov 1882 at Chinco: Isld by WP Thornton

WHEALTON John Jr 19 S Sailor Chinco: Isld Chinco: Isld s/o Daniel & Betsey to Mary Ann [Russel] Russell 17 S Chinco: Isld Chinco: Isld d/o Jno & Betsey on 13 Apr 1855 at r/o Minister by P Bowdin

WHEATLY John 20 S Waterman Acc Acc s/o Ignadius & Ann to Jane Crockett 17 S Acc Acc d/o John C & Sallie on 14 Dec 1892 at Tangier by ZH Webster

WHITE Alfred P 29 S Merchant s/o Henry B to Susan A L Mason 18 S d/o Samuel & Adaline W lic: 14 Sep 1864

WHITE Andrew J 19 S Farmer Acc Acc s/o Elijah A J & Susan to Tabitha J Harrison 25 S Acc Acc d/o James E & Margaret A on 22 Jan 1890 near Onancock by RA Compton

WHITE Asbury Col 35 S Farmer Acc Acc s/o Sinah to Jane Bundick Col 35 S Acc Acc d/o Wm & Leah on 31 Dec 1882 at Mappsville by AJ Satchell

WHITE David F 23 S Merchant Acc Acc s/o David C & Hetty C to Medora S Melson 18 S Acc Acc d/o Henry & Emma on 27 Nov 1873 at Acc by IT Adkins

WHITE Edward Col 28 S Sailor Acc Acc s/o Sarah to Mary E Clayton Col 21 S Acc Acc d/o Harriet on 21 Sep 1882 near Lee Mont by AJ Satchell

WHITE Edward J 25 S Farmer Acc Acc s/o Jas H & Nancy to Annie A Gladding 20 S Acc Acc d/o Geo W & Sally on 14 Apr 1881 at Oak Hall by RB Beadles

WHITE Elijah J 20 S Laborer b: Acc s/o Levin White & Chassy Beloat & (ward/o Wm H Beloate) to Susan Gardner 20 S b: Acc d/o Wm Gardner & Sally Edward on 8 Feb 1856 at Acc by P Warren

WHITE George Col 25 S Laborer Acc Acc s/o Harriet to Mary Warrington

Smith Col 18 S Acc Acc d/o Leah on 31 Aug 1877 at Bowdin Chandle's by JK Plato

WHITE George Col 19 S Laborer Acc Acc s/o Mary to Annie Poulson Col 16 S Acc Acc d/o Ann on 6 Jan 1879 at Aaron Handy's by A Handy

WHITE George Col 23 S Farmer Acc Acc s/o Peter & Ellen to Catherine Taylor Col 23 S Acc Acc d/o Arthur & Catherine on 26 Dec 1888 at Acc by JA Haynes

WHITE George E Col 21 S Farm Laborer Acc Acc s/o Sina to Rosa West Col 23 S Acc Acc d/o Ellen on 19 Jun 1887 at Acc by JK Adams

WHITE George T to Fanny Ann Hope d/o Wm T or S who gave consent lic: 28 Feb 1859

WHITE George W 40 S Farmer Acc Acc s/o Geo W & Henrietta to Mary E Bradford 20 S Acc Acc d/o Ezia & Rachel J on 30 Mar 1881 near News Town by JC Watson

WHITE Harry T 32 S Merchant Acc Acc s/o Edwd T & Henrietta to Annie Matthews 17 S Acc Acc d/o Washington & Caroline F on 27 Jul 1882 at Acc by LB Betty

WHITE Harry T 39 W Merchant Acc Acc s/o Edward T & Henrietta to Kate D Hall 35 S Acc Acc d/o Henry & Amoret on 7 Jan 1890 at Norfolk VA by RN Sledd

WHITE Henry Col 21 S Waterman Acc Acc s/o Henry Moore & Martha White to Julia [Rodgers] Rogers Col 24 S Acc Acc d/o George & Tabby on 4 Jun 1871 at Sluglkill Nk by JH Addison

WHITE Henry black 23 S Laborer s/o Easter to Susan Pitts black 33 S d/o Margaret lic: 26 Aug 1874 marr: 27 Aug 1874 near Locustville

WHITE Henry Col 25 S Laborer Acc Acc s/o Fanny to Adah Hope Col 20 S Acc Acc d/o Rose on 8 Feb 1877 near News Town by A Joynes

WHITE Henry Col 19 S Laborer Acc Acc s/o Sinah to Nancy Clayton Col 17 S Acc Acc d/o Harriet on 13 Mar 1879 at Parsonage by A Handy

WHITE Henry Col 34 S Sailor Acc Acc s/o Ada to Lucy Gunter Col 24 S Acc Acc d/o Hennie on 4 Jul 1885 near Lee Mont by CA Horsey

WHITE Henry C 27 S Clerk Acc Drum'tn s/o Lovey to Elizabeth Shaffer 28 S PA Drum'tn d/o Jacob & Rebecca on 6 Sep 1859 at Onancock by AM Wiggins (W J Ayres says both over 21)

WHITE Henry T to Elizabeth B Palmer wid lic: 26 Feb 1855 John J R Blackstone says he over 21

WHITE Hugh G 21 S Laborer Acc Acc s/o Catharine Phillips to Margaret L Mears Col 25 S Acc Acc d/o Luther & Susan on 11 Jul 1881 at Locust Mount by JWA Elliott

WHITE Isaac Col 30 S Laborer Acc Acc s/o Leah to Sinah Crippen Col 27 S Acc Acc d/o Maria on 15 Oct 1873 at News Town by A Joynes

WHITE Isaac Col 25 S Laborer Acc Acc s/o Harriet to Elizabeth Allen Col 26 S Acc Acc d/o Jennie on 22 Sep 1884 at Acc by LW Lee

WHITE James 28 S Farmer Acc Acc s/o Wm A to Otellia Fox 22 S Acc Acc d/o James & Nellie on 17 Aug 1871 at Acc by PA Leatherbury

WHITE James Col 25 S Sailor Acc Acc s/o Rosey to Maggie Parkes Col 21 S Acc Acc d/o Susan on 3 Aug 1876 near News Town by A Joynes

WHITE James Col 21 S Sailor Acc Acc s/o Martha to Mary Stringer Col 21 S Acc Acc d/o Ellen on 17 Jun 1883 at Onancock by R Davis

WHITE James H 22 S Farmer Acc Acc s/o Louis H & Mary E to Emma S Cobb 21 S Acc Acc d/o William T & Virginia on 24 Dec 1893 at Acc by

AJ Reamy

WHITE James Myers 33 S Waterman Acc Acc s/o Henry C & Elizabeth to Cordie Elizabeth Shea 29 S Acc Acc d/o Custis & Emma on 13 Mar 1894 at Acc C H by JM Dunaway

WHITE John 26 S Laborer Acc Acc s/o Esther to Adaline Conquest 30 S Acc Acc d/o Mary on 12 Aug 1869 at Acc by A Joynes

WHITE John D 62 S Farmer Acc Acc s/o John & Tabitha to Elizabeth Northam 63 S Acc Acc d/o James & Millie Justice on 15 Nov 1875 near Messongo by TM Poulson

WHITE John E 27 S Farmer Acc Acc s/o Jno & Ann to Sallie G Smith 21 S Acc Acc d/o Jas G & Elizth on 7 Dec 1865 at Acc by LK LeCato

WHITE John E Col 32 S Sawyer Acc Acc s/o Hester Laws to Rebecca Fosque Col 28 W Acc Acc d/o Adam & Martha Matthews on 3 Jan 1895 at Acc by JC Young

WHITE John W 27 S Acc Acc s/o Thomas & Hester to Mary Jane Ward 17 S Acc Acc d/o Jno L & Susan on 28 Nov 1877 at Drum'tn by FH Mullineaux

WHITE Joshua Thos Col 22 S Wage-earner Acc Acc s/o Levin & Adeline to Sabra Riley Col 21 S Acc Acc d/o Margaret on 13 Apr 1892 at Acc by AJ Satchell

WHITE Julius C s/o Henry B to Margaret C Lewis d/o William dec'd lic: 4 Apr 1855

WHITE Levi Col 23 S Wage-earner Acc Acc s/o Sinah to Winnie Drummond Col 24 S Acc Acc d/o Mary on 3 Jul 1895 at Acc by W Hopkins

WHITE Levin Col 22 S Day Laborer Acc Acc s/o Martha to Susan Nock Col 21 S Acc Acc d/o Fanny on 29 Dec 1886 at Onancock by JC Williams

WHITE Levin C 37 S Blacksmith Wor Co MD Acc s/o Geo & Sarah to Caroline H Porter 20 S Wor Co MD Acc d/o Jno & Henrietta on 1 Feb 1854 near Sol Copes, T'ville by C Hill

WHITE Levin T 21 S Oysterman Acc Acc s/o James & Mary to Elizabeth Holly 19 S Acc Acc d/o Benjamin T & Charlotte on 16 Dec 1885 at Temp'ville by M Oldham

WHITE Lewis 28 W Waterman Acc Acc s/o George & Charlotte to Indianna A Mister 30 S Acc Acc d/o John & Susan on 30 Dec 1874 at Onancock by JH Amiss

WHITE Lewis Col 19 S Laborer Acc Acc s/o Fanny to Sarah Justice Col 22 S Acc Acc d/o Airy on 1 Oct 1882 near News Town by AJ Satchell

WHITE Louis H 21 S Sailor Acc Acc s/o Geo & Charlott to Mary Drummond 21 S Acc Acc d/o Jsa & Hanah on 15 Mar 1866 at Acc by JH Addison

WHITE Major Col 27 S Wage-earner Acc Acc s/o Jesse & Harriet to Mary E J Gray Col 17 S Acc Acc d/o George & Annie on 19 Mar 1893 at Acc by BJ Hargarves

WHITE Millard F 21 S Oysterman Acc Acc s/o Levin & Sophia to Elizabeth Taylor 18 S Acc Acc d/o Susan on 26 Nov 1870 at Acc by TM Poulson

WHITE Musco G 28 S Farmer Acc Acc to Nancy C Barnes 24 S Acc Acc on 4 Feb 1886 at Acc by JW Carroll

WHITE Oswald F 35 S Farmer Acc Acc s/o Napolean to Tabitha A Wilson 30 W Acc Acc d/o Wesley & Sally Archie on 15 Nov 1893 at Acc by JR Sturgis

WHITE Otho J 19 S Farmer Acc Acc s/o Elijah A J & Susan to Anna S Scott 17 S Acc Acc d/o Thomas C & Heinretta on 29 Nov 1885 at Onancock Bapt Par by JW Hundley

WHITE Peter Col 39 S Farmer Acc Acc

s/o Easter to Ellen Parkes Col 35 S Acc Acc d/o Violet on 23 Feb 1880 at Acc by RH Govans

WHITE Peter 25 W Sailor Sussex Co DE Acc s/o Robert & Lydia to Elizabeth Merritt 18 S Acc Acc d/o James & Ann on 11 Feb 1880 at the Parsonage by IT Adkins

WHITE Peter Col 24 S Farmer Acc Acc s/o William to Sarah Wise Col 23 S Acc Acc d/o Adam & Lizzie on 31 Mar 1886 at Drum'tn by CA Horsey

WHITE Peyton Col 23 S Laborer Acc Acc s/o Rasbarey & Jane to Mary Nock Col 20 S Acc Acc d/o Emma on 6 May 1883 at Modest Town by AJ Satchell

WHITE Rasberry Col 50 W Farmer Acc Acc to Hannah Savage Col 51 W Acc Acc on 21 Sep 1890 at Temp'ville by JC Cluff

WHITE Richard to Frances Baylis d/o K B who gave consent lic: 31 Aug 1857 John W Taylor says he over 21

WHITE Robert R 30 S Carpenter b: Acc s/o Jas & Matilda J to Sarah E Carmine 20 S b: Onancock d/o Jas & Elizth on 19 Mar 1856 at Onancock by J Allen

WHITE Samuel B 26 S Merchant Acc Acc s/o Samuel J & Lovey D to Nannie L Higgins 25 S Acc Acc d/o Michael H & Marianna on 1 Sep 1887 at Drum'tn by W Chinn

WHITE William to Eveline Powell d/o William lic: 23 Apr 1855 Z Chandler says both over 21

WHITE William 30 S Laborer Acc Acc s/o Amelia to Sally Chandler 28 S Acc Acc d/o Leah on 25 Nov 1869 at Acc by A Joynes

WHITE William 31 S Carpenter Acc Acc s/o Napoleon O & Eliza to Nellie Major 25 S Acc Acc d/o Wm L & Elizabeth on 23 Dec 1872 near Pungo: by O Littleton

WHITE William F 26 S Farmer Acc Acc s/o Henry T to Nettie Hiden Mears 21 S Acc Acc d/o William & Susan on 25 Dec 1888 at Onancock by JW Hundley

WHITE William J 30 S Farmer Acc Acc s/o William C & Hennie to Margaret J Coxton 26 S Acc Acc on 25 Apr 1872 at Acc by DA Woodson

WHITE William T 22 S Farmer Acc Acc s/o George T & Fanny A to Mary Della Johnson 18 S Acc Acc d/o John T & Rachel H on 19 Dec 1888 at Wachapreague by W Chinn

WHITE William T Col 34 S Wage-earner Acc Acc s/o Harriet to Susan Floyd Col 27 S Acc Acc d/o Mary on 14 Jun 1894 at Acc by PW Lee

WHITE Wm 25 S Oysterman Acc Chinco: Isld s/o Richd White & Franas Rollock to Almira Hudson 16 S Sussex Co DE Assateague Isd d/o Robert on 1 Mar 1886 at Assateague by JD Reese

WHITEHURST C W 24 S Barber Princess Ann Co VA Acc s/o Odder & jane to Laura V Cole 23 W Howard Co MD Acc d/o Peny G & Mary E on 8 Apr 1886 at Acc C H by W Chinn

WHITTINGTON Jno W Col 26 S Farmer Som Co MD Acc s/o Canvas to Harriet A Fletcher Col 27 S Acc Acc d/o Annie Rew on 6 May 1879 at Oak Hall by JW Hilldrup

WHITTINGTON John W Col 33 W Laborer Som Co MD Acc s/o Jno & Mary to Harriet F Selby Col 28 S Acc Acc d/o Wesley & Elizth on 4 Aug 1883 at Oak Hall by RB Beadles

WIDGEN James W Col 53 S Wage-earner Acc Acc s/o Drucilla to Hannah Drummond Col 39 S Acc Acc d/o Louisa on 14 Mar 1895 at Acc by AJ Satchell

WIGGINS Asa 32 S Waterman SC Acc to Vernittie Thomas 20 S Acc Acc d/o W S & Julia Ann on 14 Dec 1892 at Tangier by ZH Webster

WIGTON William 48 W Farmer Tompkins Co NY Acc s/o Wn & Elizth to Mary A Walker 28 W Acc Acc d/o Wm S Shrieves on 22 Aug 1866 at Acc by JE Bundick

WILCOX Ronland H 25 S Fisherman Stonington CT Stonington CT s/o Elias & Hannah L to Clara E Matthews 20 S Acc Chinco: Isld d/o Jas E & Martha S on 14 Mar 1883 at Chinco: Isld by OS Walton

WILKERSON Andrew 23 S Oysterman Acc Acc s/o Sewell & Sallie J to Evelyn Prescott 21 S Acc Acc d/o Asa & Thedosia on 4 Mar 1891 at Acc by WF Hayes

WILKERSON Henry F 44 S Acc Acc s/o Solomon & Menah(?) to Mary T Colony 24 S Acc Acc d/o John & Mary on 18 Feb 1885 at Acc by TM Poulson

WILKERSON John 22 S Oysterman Acc Acc s/o Sewell & Sally Jane to Emma Parkes 30 S Acc Acc d/o Mark & Elizabeth on 18 May 1886 at Temp'ville by M Oldham

WILKERSON John (Jehu) 23 S Oysterman Acc Acc s/o Shadrack & Margaret to Martha Marshall 19 S Acc Acc d/o Hetty on 20 Dec 1871 at Pocomoke by M Oldham

WILKERSON Samuel [Wilkinson] (Wilkerson) 25 S Oysterman Acc Acc s/o Shadrack & Margaret to Harriet Linton 23 S Acc Acc d/o Charlotte on 21 Dec 1871 at Messongo by M Oldham

WILKINS Southey Col 26 S Wage-earner N'hamp: Acc s/o Squire & Mary to Susan Rogers Col 24 S Acc Acc d/o Charles & Lettie on 12 Sep 1895 at Acc by J Savage

WILKINS William B 32 S Merchant Acc Acc s/o Geo W & Elizth to Mary E Powell 21 S Acc Acc d/o Jno F & Arinthia on 25 Jul 1872 at Pesbytn Chh by O Littleton

WILLET George S 25 S Farmer Acc Acc s/o Annie to Polly F Small 16 S Acc Acc d/o Jno S & Susan A on 26 Jan 1876 at Onancock by RC Jones

WILLET Jno W 20 S Farmer b: Acc s/o Wm & Polly & (ward/o Geo P Ewell) to Polly Hickman 17 S b: Acc d/o Nancy Hickman on 16 Nov 1854 at r/o E S Grant by ES Grant

WILLET Jno W 26 S Clerk Acc Acc s/o Jno & Willet to Maggie E Mister 22 S Acc Acc d/o Wm S & Sally on 20 Mar 1884 at Acc C H by JG Anderson

WILLET Onie F 30 W Laborer Acc Acc s/o Annie to Maggie Simpson 17 S Acc Acc d/o Southey on 30 Sep 1885 at Modest Town by A Woodyard

WILLET Thos R 25 S Farmer b: Acc s/o William & Polly to Eleshea A Bell 17 S b: Acc d/o Thorogood (who gave consent) & Catharine on 5 Jan 1859 at r/o Thorogood Bell by ES Grant

WILLET Tully E 24 S Sailor Acc Acc s/o Polly to Harriet J Bayly 19 S Acc Acc d/o Francis A on 20 Aug 1882 at Onancock by PA Leatherbury

WILLET William J 20 S Waterman Acc Acc s/o Thomas R & Etitia to Libby B Marvel 37 S Acc Acc d/o Nathaniel & Caroline on 13 Mar 1895 at Acc by JET Ewell

WILLETT Charles E 28 S Liquor Dealer Acc Acc s/o Thos R & Alcia to Susan R Lewis 25 S Acc Acc d/o Jas of Wm & Mary on 22 Jan 1886 at Acc by HG Cowan

WILLETT John T 24 S Sailor Acc Acc s/o Thomas R & Eletia to Mary E Lloyd 33 W Acc Acc d/o Julius & Ann Twyford on 1 Aug 1894 at Acc by JET Ewell

WILLETT Thomas 23 S Farm Laborer Acc Acc s/o Esther to Susan

Watkinson 25 S Acc Acc d/o Geo & Susan on 30 Dec 1885 at Acc by HG Cowan

WILLETT Wm M 48 S Carpenter Acc Acc s/o Polly to Annie Gladding 24 S Acc Acc d/o Polly on 23 Nov 1884 at Acc by AJ Walter

WILLIAMS Benjamin F 21 S Sailor Acc Acc s/o Jas & Elizth to Cora M Bennett 19 S Acc Acc d/o Jas H & Elizth on 16 Jan 1879 at Pungo Meth Ch by CC Wertenbaker

WILLIAMS Charles H 20 S Sailor Acc Acc s/o Seth & Emma to Lizzie Chambers 19 S Acc Acc d/o John A & Leah on 26 Dec 1894 at Tangier Isld by WR Gwinn

WILLIAMS Douglas Col 22 S Laborer Acc Acc s/o George & Drucilla to Sarah Nock Col 18 S Acc Acc d/o Margaret Nock on 2 Nov 1892 at Wattsville by ML McKenry

WILLIAMS Edward W 21 S Sailor Acc Acc s/o George W & Cordelia A to Maggie L Pruitt 21 S Acc Acc d/o Thomas & Mary on 20 Sep 1893 at Tangier Isld by ZH Webster

WILLIAMS Frank Col 22 S Sailor Acc Acc s/o Issac & Mary to Nancy Griffin Col 18 S Acc Acc d/o Mary Griffin on 21 May 1882 near Temp'ville by JC Cluff

WILLIAMS Geo H Col 25 S Oysterman Acc Acc s/o Rosy to Harriet Justice Col 23 S Acc Acc d/o Moses & Mary on 11 Nov 1877 at Modest Town by A Joynes

WILLIAMS George W 31 S Mariner Acc Acc s/o Seth & Rosey to Cordelia Evans 21 S Acc Acc d/o George & Nelly on 31 Aug 1870 at Acc by D Titlow

WILLIAMS James FN 25 Acc Acc s/o Ann Bayly to Harriet Cropper FN 15 Acc Acc d/o Mary Handy lic: 9 Oct 1862

WILLIAMS James Col 27 S Laborer Acc Acc s/o Rachel to Mary Jane Marshall Col 21 S Acc Acc d/o Milly on 22 May 1873 near Horntown by S Johns

WILLIAMS Jefferson D 23 S Oysterman Acc Acc s/o Henry & Rosa to Susan S Stant 18 S Acc Acc d/o Jno H & Susan on 29 Apr 1885 at Oak Hall by DM Wallace

WILLIAMS John Col 18 S Wage-earner Covington WV Acc s/o Geo & Susan to Ann E Finney 21 S Acc Acc d/o Judy on 29 Dec 1895 at Acc by J Duckett

WILLIAMS John Henry 22 S Sailor Acc Acc s/o Robert & Eliza to Mary Evans 17 S Acc Acc d/o John & Triffie C on 23 Dec 1888 at Tangier Isld by GL Hardesty

WILLIAMS Joseph Col 60 S Laborer Wor Co MD Acc to Mary Slocomb Col 60 S Acc Acc d/o Charity on 26 Dec 1874 at Acc by TM Poulson

WILLIAMS Joshua N 27 S Oysterman Chinco: Isld Chinco: Isld s/o Littleton & Elizabeth to Drucilla J Sharpley 21 S Chinco: Isld Chinco: Isld d/o John W & Elizabeth on 9 Nov 1873 at Chinco: Isld by WP Thornton

WILLIAMS Joshua N Jr 18 S Oysterman Acc Acc s/o Selby & Susan to Lizzie Thornton 16 S Acc Acc d/o Jno & Elizabeth on 27 Dec 1882 at Chinco: Isld by WP Thornton

WILLIAMS Littleton 22 S Oysterman Chinco: Isld Chinco: Isld s/o Selby & Susan to Vesta Carpenter 21 S Chinco: Isld Chinco: Isld d/o Richard & Mary on 6 Jun 1880 at Chinco: Isld by WP Thornton

WILLIAMS Lloyd O Col 21 S Wage-earner Acc Acc s/o Harriet Ann to Mary M Holden Col 16 S Acc Acc d/o Vienna on 6 Oct 1895 at Acc by AJ Walter

WILLIAMS Robert 20 S Sailor Acc Acc

s/o Robert & Eliza to Virginia [Streggle] Strigle 16 S Acc Acc d/o James O & Flora on 30 Sep 1888 at Tangier by GL Hardesty

WILLIAMS Robert F 25 S Merchant Richmond VA Richmond VA s/o John & Mary Ann to Isabella Wilkins 19 S Acc Acc d/o Geo W & Elizth on 6 Nov 1856 at Acc C H by WF Williams (John J Wise says he over 21)

WILLIAMS Samuel Col 25 S Laborer Acc Acc s/o Saml & Rachel to Grace [Only] Onley Col 23 S Acc Acc d/o Elizth on 2 Dec 1877 at News Town by A Joynes

WILLIAMS Samuel B 22 S Oysterman Acc Acc s/o Robert & Eliza to Lucy V Evans 18 S Acc Acc d/o John T & Maria on 25 Aug 1890 at Tangier Isld by J Connor

WILLIAMS Selby 27 S Oysterman Chinco: Isld Chinco: Isld s/o Littl & Mahala to Susan Jones 28 W Chinco: Isld Chinco: Isld d/o Jno & Peggy Lunn on 13 Nov 1854 by P Bowdin (Littleton T Williams says he over 21)

WILLIAMS Stephen E Col 31 S Laborer Acc Acc s/o George & Drucilla to Martha J [Connor] Conner Col 22 S Acc Acc d/o George & Mary on 21 Dec 1892 at Wattsville by ML McKenry

WILLIAMS Thomas 19 S Farmer Acc Acc s/o Selby & Rosey & (ward/o Arthur Mears who gave consent) to Margaret Mears 22 S Acc Acc d/o James & Molly on 7 Feb 1861 at Reese Chp by ES Grant (Arthur Mears says she over 21)

WILLIAMS Thomas 22 W Oysterman Acc Acc s/o Joshua & Virginia to Mary Sparrow 21 S MD Acc d/o Margaret on 15 Aug 1870 at Acc by J Carroll

WILLIAMS William H 22 S Shoemaker Pigpoint Pigpoint to Rosey A Stant 21 S Pig Point Pig Point d/o (Edmond) Stant on 17 Dec 1860 at Asa Hall's by GH Ewell (James W Hall says he over 21)

WILLIS Carlton V 31 S Life Saving Service N'hamp: Acc s/o John H & Margaret E to Sarah A Elliott 21 S Acc Acc d/o Thomas G & Margaret S A on 30 Jan 1889 at John E Nock's by JWA Elliott

WILLIS Edgar M 21 S Farmer Acc Acc s/o Custis & Sally to Sadie Smith Ward 19 S Acc Acc d/o Alexander J & Margaret on 26 Oct 1870 at Belle Haven by H Petty

WILLIS Henry Col 17 S Laborer Acc Acc s/o Hennie Harmon to Cordelia Burton Col 18 S Acc Acc d/o Tinney Harmon on 6 Mar 1887 at Acc by L Duncan

WILLIS Jacob Col 23 S Laborer Acc Acc s/o Mary to Fannie Brickhouse Col 18 S Acc Acc d/o Ester on 23 Jul 1871 at Acc by JE Humphreys

WILLIS John H 23 S Merchant Acc Acc s/o Lon & Ann to Margaret E Mears 17 S Acc Acc d/o Able (of Able) & Margaret on 17 May 1855 at r/o Abel Mears by JWA Elliott

WILLIS Robert 24 S Farmer Acc Acc s/o John & Margt to Amanda A Bundick 21 S Acc Acc d/o John B & Margareft E on 7 Dec 1882 at Acc by JW Stiff

WILLIS Zorobabel 27 S Merchant Acc N'hamp: s/o Edward L & Joice to Rose W Hopkins 23 S Norfolk City Acc d/o John W H & Laura H on 3 Nov 1880 at Belle Haven by RD Stimson

WILLS Parker 32 S Merchant Nansemond Co VA Norfolk City s/o N P & Ann E to Jane D Hopkins 22 S Norfolk Co VA Acc d/o Jno W M & Laura H on 17 Jan 1882 at Dr J W M Hopkins' by GW Easter

WILSON Benjamin Col 29 S Laborer Hanover Co VA Acc s/o Claussa to Eliza Bundick Col 25 S Acc Acc d/o Esther on 20 Apr 1882 near News Town by AJ Satchell

WILSON Frank Col 23 S Laborer MD Acc to Mary A Davis Col 18 S Acc Acc d/o Wm on 26 Oct 1873 at Metompkin by JE Bundick

WILSON John 32 W Painter Fayette Co OH Acc s/o James & Nancy to Tabitha Archer 20 S Acc Acc d/o Charles W & Sally on 4 Mar 1884 near Locust Mount by JWA Elliott

WILSON Lloyd F 23 S Teacher N'hamp: Acc s/o John S & Keturah G to Amanda J Robins 23 S Acc Acc d/o Arthur & Juliet on 12 Feb 1857 at Belle Haven by M Oldham (Smith K Martin says both over 21)

WILSON William J 21 S Carpenter N'hamp: Acc s/o Jas & Elizth to Florence E Churn 17 S N'hamp: Acc d/o John & Eliza on 18 Nov 1868 at N'hamp: by H Petty

WIMBROUGH Ezekiel 45 S Farmer Acc Acc s/o John to Mary Jones 35 W Acc Acc d/o Calbe & Elizth Duncan on 14 May 1868 at Acc by GW Matthews

WIMBROUGH Goldberry 21 S Farmer Wor Co MD Acc s/o Wm T & Gertrude to Indiana Bayly 17 S Acc Acc d/o Edward & Lovey on 29 Mar 1885 at Acc by WC Vaden

WIMBROUGH Jno D Col 41 W Merchant Som Co MD Acc s/o Jno & Mahala to Elizabeth Bundick Col 25 S Acc Acc d/o Wm & Eliza on 19 Mar 1876 at Wm Jas Broughton's by CV Waugh

WIMBROUGH John 35 W Sailor Acc Acc s/o Griffin & Elizth to Susanna Harrison 18 S N'hamp: Acc d/o Wm & Fanny on 28 Jan 1882 at Chinco: Isld by OS Walton

WIMBROUGH John D to Mary Ann Hope ward/o Benj T Gunter who gave consent lic: 5 Jan 1858 L G Northam says he over 21

WIMBROUGH John T 24 S Oysterman Acc Acc s/o Griffin & Betsy to Roesy [Dunston] Dunton 22 S Acc Acc d/o John & Kessay on 30 Jan 1875 at Chinco: Isld by P Bowdin Sr

WIMBROUGH Levi [Wimbro] 23 S U S Service PA Acc to Ambert Ayres 16 S Acc Acc d/o Jas & Polly on 8 Jun 1862 at Acc by TL Poulson

WIMBROUGH Oliver L 24 S Oysterman Chinco: Isld Chinco: Isld s/o Griffin & Elizabeth to Rebecca Booth 17 S Chinco: Isld Chinco: Isld d/o Jno & Adaline on 23 Jan 1886 at Chinco: Isld by SU Grimsley

WIMBROUGH Washington Col 26 W Sailor Acc Acc s/o Charlotte to Charlotte Watson Col 27 S Acc Acc d/o Ann on 16 Jun 1878 at Abel Joynes by A Joynes

WIMBROUGH William T 54 W Teamster MD Acc s/o John & Sally to Rose Lee Martin 23 S Acc Acc d/o Smith W on 30 Jan 1890 at Acc by JWA Elliott

WIMBROUGH Wm T 43 W Teamster Wor Co MD Acc s/o Jno & Sally to Ann M Parker 22 S Acc Acc d/o Geo W & Margt on 21 Jan 1879 at Onancock by SC Boston

WINDER Edwd J 25 S Farmer Acc Acc s/o John E T & Frances to Martha A Leatherbury 22 S Acc Acc d/o Perry A & Zipporah on 19 Mar 1884 at Onancock by IG Fosnocht

WINDER George Col 21 S Farming N'hamp: Acc s/o Eliza Nelson to Maggie Moore Col 21 S Acc Acc d/o Emaline on 25 Jun 1882 at Acc by F Wood

WINDER George E 23 S Carriage Mkr Acc Acc s/o Jno W & Mary to Annie R Ayres 17 S Acc Acc d/o Richd L & Elizth on 23 Dec 1874 at

Onancock by FR Boston

WINDER George W 20 S Farmer Acc Acc s/o John D & Hester to Mary E Taylor 20 S Acc Acc d/o Joseph B & Elizth on 18 Jan 1860 at Acc by JH Addison

WINDER Jno E T [Window] 24 S Farmer b: Acc s/o Jno D & Hester Ann to Frances Ann Watson 20 S b: Acc d/o Edwd R & Elizth W on 7 Mar 1855 at r/o Ed R Watson by C Hill

WINDER John Col 25 S Sailor Acc Acc s/o Wm & Elizth to Mary Fisher Col 17 S Acc Acc d/o Charles Silverthorn & Nannie Fisher on 18 May 1885 at Chinco: Isld by JD Reese

WINDER John A [Window] 42 W Farmer Acc Acc s/o George & Anna to Elizabeth Chesser 25 S Acc Acc d/o Robert & Betsy on 20 Jan 1874 at Acc by TM Poulson

WINDER John David 18 S Farmer Acc Acc s/o Jas A & Mary to Alice E Elliott 17 S Acc Acc d/o Thos G & Angelia on 10 Nov 1881 at Oak Grove Ch by JWA Elliott

WINDER John E (Window) s/o Levin to Sarah A (Window) Winder d/o John D lic: 26 Mar 1855 Henry D Carmine says both over 21

WINDER Robert H 26 S Farmer Acc Acc s/o James A & Mary to Nola S Mapp 18 S Acc Acc d/o George C & Rose on 13 Nov 1892 at Locust Mount by JWA Elliott

WINDER Thaddeus [Window] 28 S Farmer Acc Acc s/o Gillet & Ann to Julia A Mears 29 S Acc Acc d/o Thorogood & Mahala on 14 Jan 1869 at Acc by E Hebard

WINDER William S s/o (Levin) to Ellen D Joynes d/o (Edward D) on 19 Sep 1860 at Acc by M Oldham (Obed H Hanby says he over 21)

WINDFIELD John Col 34 S Wage-earner r: Acc to Mary Williams Col 22 S Acc Acc d/o Henry & Margaret on 25 Mar 1894 at Bloxom Sta by AJ Satchell

WISE Abel H Col 34 S Farmer Acc Acc s/o Rebecca Beckett to Caroline Poulson Col 34 S Acc Acc d/o Eliana Poulson on 21 Sep 1884 at Acc by PA Leatherbury

WISE Adam 26 S Farmer Acc Acc s/o Sarah to Lizzie Custis 23 S Acc Acc d/o Sarah Jane on 18 Mar 1868 at Acc by JH Huges

WISE Alfred Col 23 S Wage-earner Acc Acc s/o William W & Rachel to Catharine Jones Col 24 S MD Acc d/o Richard & Mary on 14 Oct 1893 at Acc by T Turlington

WISE Daniel Col 30 S Wage-earner Acc Acc s/o Leah Bayly to Lena Downing Col 23 D Acc Acc d/o Edmund & Sarah Snead on 22 Apr 1891 at Acc by AJ Satchell

WISE Edmond Col 24 D Farmer Acc Acc s/o Edmond Wise & Peggy Justice to Sabra J Hinman Col 18 S Acc Acc d/o Clarey on 21 Dec 1890 at Mappsville by AJ Satchell

WISE Edward Col 20 S Sailor Acc Acc s/o Edward Wise & Peggy Justice to Lucy A Byrd Col 17 S Acc Acc d/o Sarah on 23 Dec 1882 near News Town by AJ Satchell

WISE Edward Col 41 S Wage-earner Acc Acc s/o Wm W & Rachel to Candasi Moore Col 26 S Acc Acc d/o Emeline on 1 Oct 1893 at Acc by T Turlington

WISE Edward S 21 S Farmer Acc Acc s/o Edwd F & Mary to Elizabeth S [Jacob] Jacobs 18 S Acc Acc d/o Wm E & Charlotte on 1 Dec 1869 at Acc by E Hebard

WISE Ellison Col 24 S Sailor Acc Acc to Lucy Watson Col 21 S Acc Acc d/o Mary on 9 Apr 1882 at Onancock by JC Ayler

WISE Ellison Col 27 W Farmer Acc Acc s/o Harriet to Annie Bayly Col 21 S Acc Acc d/o Mark & Virginia on 20 Jul 1890 at Onancock by GHT Byrd

WISE Fillmore Col 24 S Farmer Acc Acc s/o William & Virginia to Manie Chandler Col 17 S Acc Acc d/o Alfred & Precilla on 11 May 1893 at Onancock by FW Overton

WISE George 22 S Laborer Acc Acc s/o Leah to Martha Wise 25 S Acc Acc d/o Mary on 14 Jul 1867 at Acc by WT Tull

WISE George Col 21 S Farmer Acc Acc s/o Ann Snead to Belle Susan Coleburn Col 21 S Acc Acc d/o Sinah on 12 Sep 1875 at Acc by A Joynes

WISE George D 21 S Farmer Acc Acc s/o Jno E & Elizth S to Bettie C Core 20 S Acc Acc d/o Wm T & Mary on 18 Jan 1871 at Acc by DA Woodson

WISE George D 28 W Farmer Acc Acc s/o Jno E & Elizth to Arinthia Adams 21 S Acc Acc d/o Jas C & Mary on 2 Jan 1879 at Mr Jas Adam's by JG Anderson

WISE George T Col 22 S Farmer Acc Acc s/o Jane to Etta E Johnson Col 21 S Acc Acc d/o Moses & Peggie on 13 May 1894 at Onancock by A Harris

WISE Henry Col 25 S Sailor Acc Acc s/o Edith to Lizzie Fosque Col 22 S Acc Acc d/o Lonny on 1 Jan 1882 near Modest Town by AJ Satchell

WISE Henry Col 20 S Farmer Acc Acc s/o Roda to Annie Floyd Col 17 S Acc Acc d/o Peter & Lizzie on 7 Jun 1894 at Acc by L Duncan

WISE Hezekiah Col 21 S Wage-earner Acc Acc s/o Sabra to Anna Hinman Col 22 S Acc Acc d/o Airy on 18 Dec 1889 at Acc by AJ Satchell

WISE Hillory Col 23 S Laborer Acc Acc s/o Annice to Mary Savage Col 18 S Acc Acc d/o Leah Beach on 28 Dec 1881 at Locust Mount by JWA Elliott

WISE Hy A Col 23 S Farmer Acc Acc s/o Leah to Elizth T Conner Col single Acc Acc d/o Jessy on 23 Aug 1877 at Morris Chp by A Handy

WISE Illinoise Col 19 S Sailor Acc Acc s/o John W & Eliza to Annie Chandler Col 21 S Acc Acc d/o Isaac & Grace on 15 Mar 1874 at Savageville by R Davis

WISE James E Col 23 S Wage-earner Acc Acc s/o John & Eliza to Amanda Kellam Col 17 S Acc Acc d/o Harriet Bailey on 10 Aug 1890 at Acc by J Duckett

WISE James H Col 24 S Laborer Stockton MD Acc s/o Charles Steveson & Mary Wise to Sarah Custis Col 22 S Acc Acc d/o Harvey & Hannah on 1 Jan 1888 at New Church by TM Poulson

WISE Jesse Col 28 S Wage-earner Acc Acc s/o Jahe to Ida Giddings Col 26 S Acc Acc d/o Matthew & Letty on 9 Jul 1893 at Wardtown by J Savage

WISE John FN to Ellen Bayly FN d/o Ann who gave consent lic: 11 Aug 1859 Henry C Ayres says he over 21

WISE John A Col 22 S Laborer Acc Acc s/o Ann to Ida [Beckett] Becket Col 17 S Acc Acc d/o Mary on 13 Jun 1880 at Locust Mount by JWA Elliott

WISE John H 24 S Merchant Acc Acc s/o John E & Elizth S to Bettie G Warner 23 S Acc Acc d/o Geo J & Emily J on 1 Nov 1866 at Acc by ES Grant

WISE John Henry Col 30 S Farmer Acc Acc s/o Matilda Ann Finney to Sarah Poulson Col 25 S N'hamp: Acc d/o Leah on 27 May 1894 at Acc by TW Nettles

WISE John S 22 S Farmer Acc Acc s/o Moses & Catharine to Mary A

Bunting 17 S Acc Acc d/o Jacob & Mary on 22 Dec 1875(?) near Locustville by JH Amiss Certificate returned 5 Apr 1877

WISE John William 26 S Laborer Acc Acc s/o Henry Topping & Mahala Wise to Susan Watson 27 W Acc Acc d/o Geo West & Chloe Mason on 9 Sep 1869 at Acc by WF Williams

WISE Joshua FN to Maria Wise FN lic: 26 May 1854 John E Wise says both over 21

WISE Joshua Col 24 S Wage-earner Acc Acc s/o Mary to Sarah Byrd Col 17 S Acc Acc d/o Edmund & Ann on 12 Jan 1888 at Acc by JK Adams

WISE Lee Col 24 S Wage-earner Acc Acc to Mary E Sample Col 19 S Acc Acc d/o Louisa on 25 Sep 1891 at Acc by L Duncan

WISE Levin Col 43 S Farmer Acc Acc s/o Rose Bagwell to Kesiah Bell Col 40 S Acc Acc d/o Esther Allen on 21 Dec 1881 at Drum'tn by PM Lewis

WISE Major T 22 S Mechanic Acc Acc s/o Edward T & Mary P to Bettie C Colonna 20 S Acc Acc d/o Benjamin S & Mollie on 24 Dec 1873 at Acc by O Littleton

WISE Noah Purnell Col 23 S Wage-earner Acc Acc s/o Purnell & Cynthia to Maria Eliz'th Kerr Col 24 S Acc Acc d/o Betsey Drummond on 14 Oct 1888 at Acc by JK Adams

WISE Oka Col 30 S Wage-earner MD MD s/o George & Hester to Grace Johnson Col 21 S Acc Acc d/o George & Elizabeth on 11 Nov 1888 at Horntown by N Morris

WISE Parker Col 20 S Laborer Acc Acc s/o Wm & Charlotte to Sally A Perkins Col 20 S Acc Acc d/o Charlotte on 3 Apr 1883 at Acc by GW Young

WISE Parker Col 24 W Wage-earner Acc Acc s/o Charlotte Kellam to Jane Lofland Col 19 S Acc Acc d/o Bernice on 1 Jul 1891 at Savageville by JH Offer

WISE Peter Col 24 S Wage-earner Acc Acc s/o Jane to Mary Ann Custis Col 21 S Acc Acc on 20 Jun 1895 at Onancock by SW Watkins

WISE Purnell Col 29 S Waterman Acc Acc s/o Leah to Margaret Drummond Col 30 S Acc Acc d/o Abram & Leah on 24 Jun 1895 at Acc by JR West

WISE Samuel FN to Emeline Scarborough FN d/o Albert who gave consent lic: 4 Apr 1856 Albert Scarborough says Samuel over 21

WISE Samuel Col 65 W Farmer Acc Acc to Amy Downing Col 45 S Acc Acc on 14 Aug 1887 at Horntown by N Morris

WISE Samuel H Col 31 S Laborer Wor Co MD Acc s/o Lamuel & Annie to Maggie Brinney Col 17 S Acc Acc d/o William & Jane on 30 Mar 1893 at Chinco: Isld by RB Sanford

WISE Sandy Col 21 S Laborer Acc Acc s/o Lydia to Otelia Burton Col 18 S Acc Acc d/o Ann Bunting on 19 Jan 1879 at Belle Haven by JE Humphreys

WISE Sidney Col 25 S Wage-earner Acc Acc s/o Caroline to Gabriella Parker Col 19 S Acc Acc d/o Geo W & Eliz'th on 27 Mar 1892 at Acc C H by BJ Hargarves

WISE Solomon 21 S Laborer Acc Acc s/o Fanny to Milly Rew 21 S Acc Acc on 26 Dec 1867 at Acc by ES Grant

WISE Stephen Col 24 S Farm Laborer Acc Acc to Margaret A Custis Col 18 S Acc Acc d/o Eliza Sahby on 24 Jun 1885 at Acc by AJ Satchell

WISE Theodore Col 35 S Teamster Acc Acc to Laura Kellam Col 25 S Acc Acc d/o Jane on 18 Oct 1888 at Acc by P Sheppard

WISE William FN to Mary Ann

Scarborough FN lic: 28 Dec 1857 Albert Scarborough says both over 21

WISE William Col 27 S Sailor Acc Acc s/o Leah to Virginia Bayly Col 22 S Acc Acc d/o Mary on 16 Mar 1873 at Onancock by JH Offer

WISE William Col 21 S Sailor Acc Acc s/o John & Eliza to Sarah Finney Col 18 S Acc Acc d/o George & Julia on 12 Nov 1888 at Onancock by JH Offer

WISE William M Col 21 S Wage-earner Acc Acc s/o George D & Leah to Scarborough A Wise Col 20 S Acc Acc d/o Arthur & Charlotte on 21 Apr 1889 at Acc by JH Offer

WISE Wm T 25 S Druggist Acc Acc s/o Jno E & Elizth S to Sarah P Bagwell 21 S N'hamp: Acc d/o Heley P & Sarah A on 28 Nov 1878 at Onancock by JH Amiss

WISE Edward T 65 W Farmer Acc Acc s/o Solomon & Nancy to Lucretia N Nottingham 53 W N'hamp: Acc d/o Obed Goffigon on 1 Jun 1887 at J Bull's by JR Strugis

WOODS James A (Albert) 24 S Sailor Messongo Messongo to Mary Taylor 15 S Messongo Messongo d/o James S Taylor on 27 Feb 1861 at Pigpoint Acc Co by GH Ewell (Wm S Smith says he over 21)

WOODS John 23 S Waterman Messongo Messongo to Susan Stant 22 S Messongo Messongo d/o William on 21 Oct 1858 at Tunn Isld Messongo by GH Ewell (Raymond R Stant says he over 21)

WOODWARD Wm Wallace 32 S Lawyer Middlesex Co VA Middlesex Co VA s/o Filmore F & Mary E to Kate R Drummond 27 S Acc Acc d/o John R & Eleshea on 17 Apr 1884 at Onancock Bapt Ch by JW Hundley

WOOTERS William E 24 S Painter DE Acc s/o Daniel & Martha to Allie Smith 23 S Acc Acc d/o Thomas & Sallie on 11 Dec 1888 at Pittsville by TM Poulson

WRIGHT Alfred J 28 S Farmer Acc Acc s/o Charles & Margt to Malinda C Mason 24 S Acc Acc d/o David & Cath on 26 Jul 1877 near Woodstock by FH Mullineaux

WRIGHT Custis Col 32 S Farmer Acc Acc s/o Tammy to Inez Sample Col 22 S Acc Acc on 11 Jan 1877 at Acc by RH Govans

WRIGHT David 34 S Blacksmith Acc Acc s/o Walter & Hennie to Nancy Mears 34 W Acc Acc d/o Zorobabel & Polly on 30 Dec 1874 at Woodstock by IT Adkins

WRIGHT Douglas 25 S Farmer Acc Acc s/o James B & Margaret A to Libbie L Barnes 19 S Acc Acc d/o William T & Julia on 28 Dec 1887 at Mappsville by WA Street

WRIGHT Edward 24 S Carpenter Acc Acc s/o John & Louisa to Gennet Mears 15 S Acc Acc d/o Edwd & Nancy on 16 Dec 1875 at Acc by CV Waugh

WRIGHT Edward 24 S Farmer Acc Acc s/o James B & Margaret to Vianna [Somers] Summers 22 S Acc Acc d/o John & Vianna on 22 Sep 1895 at Mappsville by JL King

WRIGHT Frederick 31 S Laborer Acc Acc to Martha Turner 21 S Acc Acc d/o Sally on 9 Sep 1881 at Hadlock VA by J Savage

WRIGHT George 30 S Farmer Acc Acc s/o John & Louisa to Melinda Justice 43 W Acc Acc d/o Henry & Catharine Wright on 17 Jun 1883 near Foxville by JE Bundick

WRIGHT George H 30 S Sailor Acc Acc s/o Jas B & Margaret to Hester Thornton 16 S Acc Acc d/o Wm & Emeline on 18 Dec 1878 at Conquest Ch by JW Hundley

WRIGHT George T Col 27 S

Wage-earner Acc Acc s/o Ann to Mary Clayton 25 S Acc Acc d/o Harry & Jane on 15 Dec 1895 at Acc by W Hopkins

WRIGHT Isaac 53 W Farmer b: Acc s/o Parker & Nancy to Rachel Garrison 41 S b: Acc d/o Abel Garrison & Margt Kellam on 20 Dec 1854 at Locustville by LK LeCato (Thomas P Copes says she over 21)

WRIGHT Isaac T 35 S Farmer Acc Acc s/o Elijah & Margaret to Virginia Lee Poulson 19 S Acc Acc d/o John W & Elizabeth on 2 May 1883 at Acc by WC Vaden

WRIGHT John B 24 S Sailor Acc Acc s/o James B & Margaret A to Catharine [Sommers] Summers 22 S Acc Acc d/o Samuel & Mary on 17 May 1891 at Mappsville by JL King

WRIGHT Samuel 21 S Farmer Acc Acc s/o Henry to Eleshea Chandler 20 S Acc Acc d/o Jno B & Sally on 24 Jan 1872 at Acc by M Oldham

WRIGHT Southey Col 26 S Laborer Acc Acc s/o Leah to Elizabeth Jacobs Col 22 S Acc Acc d/o Elizabeth on 13 Mar 1881 at Acc by TW Nettles

WRIGHT William T 33 S Farmer Acc Acc s/o Thos (S) & Rebecca to Mary S Carey 24 S Acc Acc d/o Sam] S & Mary on 18 Nov 1857 at Drum'tn Meth Ch by JF Chaplain (John J Blackstone says both over 21)

WYANT Claudius N 32 S Teacher Rockingham Co Acc s/o Augustine & Amanda F to Blanche A Northam 29 S Acc Acc d/o Thos A & Virnetta on 19 Jul 1892 at Onancock by HL Derby

WYATT Edward Col 27 S Farmer Acc Acc to Sarah Savage Col 21 S Acc Acc on 5 Sep 1895 at Bacon Hill by W Dixon

WYATT Frazier Col 22 S Sailor King William Co VA Acc s/o Silas & Sally to Henrietta Wise Col 18 S Acc Acc d/o Jno A & Eliza on 5 Apr 1877 near Onancock by PA Leatherbury

WYATT George W 22 S Carpenter Acc Acc s/o Wm & Elizth to Susan A Watson 19 S Acc Acc d/o Edwd & Elizth on 8 Oct 1861 at Acc by ES Grant

WYATT John L 22 S Carpenter Acc Acc s/o Joshua B & Tabitha to Indiana Roberts 20 S N'hamp: Acc d/o Nathaniel & Ann Turner & (ward/o A J Ward who gave consent) on 23 Feb 1857 at Pungo: by M Oldham

WYATT William F 20 S Farmer N'hamp: Acc s/o William J & Amelia C to Kate E Ames 24 S Acc Acc d/o James S on 30 Dec 1891 near Belle Haven by T Burton

YOUNG Alfred 24 S Farmer Acc Acc s/o Shepperd & Sallie to Janie Young 21 S Acc Acc d/o Benjamin & Betsey on 28 Dec 1887 at Mappsville by WA Street

YOUNG Alfred D 26 S Sailor Acc Acc s/o David & Margt to Susan Jane Bloxom 23 S Acc Acc d/o John J & Mary A on 29 Nov 1874 at Temp'ville by M Oldham

YOUNG Andrew 23 S Laborer Acc Acc s/o Jno & Mary to Elizabeth S White 18 S Acc Acc d/o Elijah A J & Susan on 23 Apr 1879 at Onancock by SC Boston

YOUNG Benjamin 21 S Sailor b: Guilford s/o David & Margaret to Elizabeth Northam 20 S b: Acc d/o Eljah on 29 Mar 1885 at r/o Elijah Northam by GH Ewell

YOUNG Benjamin Col 30 S Laborer Acc Acc s/o Harriet to Margaret Downing Col 22 S Acc Acc d/o Mary on 19 Apr 1880 at Parsonage by RJ Waters

YOUNG Dennis Col 24 S Laborer Acc Acc s/o Wm Abbott & Leah Young to Demariah White Col 22 S Acc Acc d/o Isaac & Sarah on 3 Oct 1885 at Acc by AJ Satchell

YOUNG Edward Col 35 S Wage-earner Acc Acc to Virginia Finney Col 28 W Acc Acc on 18 Sep 1889 at Onancock by JH Offer

YOUNG Edward J widr Doctor to Sally T Ailworth wid lic: 28 Sep 1859

YOUNG Edw'd D 24 S Telegraphy N'hamp: Acc s/o John T & Bettie L to Bessie B Walter 20 S Acc Acc d/o John R & Rosa F on 11 Nov 1891 at Keller by JR Strugis

YOUNG Eli Col 26 S Wage-earner Acc Acc s/o Eli Sr & Eliz'th to Sally Wise 18 S Acc Acc d/o Patience on 29 Dec 1895 at Acc by AJ Satchell

YOUNG Ezekiel Col 45 S Farmer Acc Acc s/o Violet to Susan Mears Col 52 S Acc Acc d/o Martha on 7 Oct 1880 at Drum'tn by PM Lewis

YOUNG Ezekiel Col 60 W Farmer Acc Acc to Rosena Bloxom Col 39 S Acc Acc d/o Hetty on 1 Dec 1886 at Acc by P Sheppard

YOUNG Francis Col 21 S Laborer Acc Acc s/o Sarah to Letty Savage Col 22 S Acc Acc on 9 Oct 1884 at Acc by CA Horsey

YOUNG George Col 48 S Farmer Acc Acc s/o Nisy to Ann Walker Col 52 S Acc Acc d/o Katy on 15 Nov 1873 near Modest Town by A Joynes

YOUNG George H 27 S Sailor Guilford Guilford s/o Richd & Polly to Susan Young 23 S Guilford Guilford d/o Robt & Arella (Belle) on 1 Jun 1865 at r/o Samuel Taylors by GH Ewell

YOUNG George T 22 S Sailor Acc Chinco: Isld s/o Henry & Ann to Comfort Whealton 20 S Chinco: Isld Chinco: Isld d/o Eba & Elizth on 31 May 1855 at r/o Parker Bowdin by P Bowdin (John J Bloxom says both over 21)

YOUNG George T 42 W Sailor Acc Acc s/o Henry & Anna to Mary Jane [Law] Laws 30 W Acc Acc d/o Eba & Elizabeth Whealton on 22 Mar 1874 at Chinco: Isld by P Bowdin Sr

YOUNG George T 22 S Farmer Acc Acc s/o Isaac & Sallie to McCartie Lee Gray 18 S Acc Acc d/o Dennis W & Amanda on 8 Jan 1890 at Parksley by HS Dulany

YOUNG Gillie 25 S Farmer Acc Acc s/o Samuel & Rachel to Annie Hickman 17 S Acc Acc d/o Robert W & Elizabeth on 26 Jan 1892 at Acc by AJ Fristoe

YOUNG Isaac Wesley 22 S Sailor Acc Acc s/o Samuel & Sally to Louisa J Linton 18 S Acc Acc d/o John & Margaret Jane on 18 Oct 1874 at Pocomoke by M Oldham

YOUNG Jas R 19 S Farmer Acc Acc s/o Jno & Laura to Maggie S Matthews 18 S Acc Acc d/o Zorobabel S & Sally on 27 Feb 1878 near Guilford by FH Mullineaux

YOUNG Jesse D 22 S Farmer Acc Acc s/o George to Julia B Young 17 S Acc Acc d/o Francis S on 25 Dec 1895 at Acc by JR Sturgis

YOUNG John 26 S Farmer b: Acc s/o Jonathan & Lavinia to Mary Rayfield 19 S b: Acc d/o Levi & Ann & (ward/o John Arlington who gave consent) on 3 Jan 1855 at Acc by JH Addison

YOUNG John s/o Richard to Susan Clayton d/o Thomas R who gave consent lic: 12 Mar 1855 Richard Young says he over 21

YOUNG John Col 23 S Laborer Acc Acc s/o Sarah to Lydia Drummond Col 22 S Acc Acc d/o Leah Young on 1 Aug 1872 near Acc C H by A Joynes

YOUNG John 64 W Farmer Acc Acc s/o Jonathan & Catharine to Susan A Harrison 53 W Acc Acc d/o Levin & Elizth Moore on 13 Oct 1886 at Sluytkill Nk by JW Hundley

YOUNG John 72 W Farmer Acc Acc s/o Jonathan & Catharine to Mary Morehead 62 W Acc Acc d/o Leah East on 14 Dec 1892 at Acc by AC Berryman

YOUNG John E 22 S Farmer Acc Acc s/o William & Susan to Mary E Watson 18 S Acc Acc d/o John E & Elizabeth on 31 Dec 1873 at Acc by LK LeCato

YOUNG John H 28 S Oyster Planter Acc Acc s/o John H & Maria to Emma E Tull 15 S Acc Acc d/o Wm H & Eliz'th C on 5 Mar 1890 at Greenbackville by BF Jester

YOUNG John Shephard s/o Samuel who gave consent to Susan Riggs ward/o Thomas Wessels (of Jas) who gave consent lic: 12 Jan 1859

YOUNG John T 23 S Farmer N'hamp: N'hamp: s/o Thos & Margt to Elizth L Ashby 19 S Acc Acc d/o Albert G & Bettie on 31 Oct 1866 at Acc by P Warren

YOUNG Littleton D 20 S Sailor Acc Acc s/o Samuel & Sally to Susan F Middleton 18 S Acc Acc d/o Jno & Julia on 27 Jan 1870 at Acc by JET Ewell

YOUNG Lorenzo Col 22 S Wage-earner Acc Acc s/o Lura to Charlotte Boggs Col 18 S Acc Acc d/o Otho & Harriet on 5 Oct 1890 at Acc C H by BJ Hargarves

YOUNG Milton 26 S Oyster Dealer Long Isld NY Acc s/o Ezra K & Hannah A to Flora A Risley 20 S NJ Acc d/o Daniel B & Annie E on 27 Jan 1886 at Acc by WH Stone

YOUNG Richard to Susan East d/o William who gave consent lic: 29 Aug 1860 James T Nock says he over 21

YOUNG Richard 21 S Waterman Acc Acc s/o George H & Susan A to Eliza Ellen Justice 16 S Acc Acc d/o James T & Marg't J on 20 Dec 1891 near Lee Mont by GF Farring

YOUNG Robert Col 26 S Railroad Laborer N'hamp: Acc s/o Margt Addison to Millie Kellam Col 26 S Acc Acc d/o Candace on 19 Oct 1884 at Acc by GHT Byrd

YOUNG Robert J 23 S Farmer Acc Acc s/o John S & Susan to Martha J Barnes 19 S Acc Acc d/o Thomas H & Nancy on 4 Jan 1888 at Guilford by WF Hayes

YOUNG Robert W 27 S Oysterman Acc Acc s/o Samuel & Sally to Elizabeth S Wessells 21 S Acc Acc d/o Thos & Cath on 26 Sep 1875 at Guilford by M Oldham

YOUNG Rudolph W H 22 S Oyster Planting Acc Acc s/o John H & Maria to Mary E Taylor 24 S MD Acc d/o Skinner & Mahala on 8 Feb 1888 at Franklin City by CH Williams

YOUNG Saml 20 S Farmer Acc Acc s/o Wm & Susan to Manie Satchell single Acc Acc d/o Geo & Luky on 19 Dec 1883 at Acc by JG Anderson

YOUNG Saml J 21 S Laborer Acc Acc s/o Saml & Rachel to Mary A Ewell 25 S Acc Acc d/o Geo T & Elizth on 25 Dec 1879 at Geo T Ewell's by FH Mullineaux

YOUNG Samuel s/o Gillet to Rachel Mason d/o Zorobabel lic: 17 Dec 1855 David Mason said both over 21

YOUNG Samuel widr to Mary Bloxom lic: 26 Dec 1855 Matthew Taylor says she over 21

YOUNG Samuel T 20 S Farmer Metompkin Guilford s/o Southey (Samuel who gave consent) to Margaret Mason 26 S Guilford Guilford d/o Major & Nancy on 2 Feb 1859 at r/o Southey Grinals by GH Ewell (Throgood Mason says she over 21)

YOUNG Sheppard s/o Elizabeth Northam who gave consent to Sally

(Shreaves) Shrieves d/o John T who gave consent lic: 17 Dec 1855

YOUNG Theodore 20 S Sailor Chester Co NJ Chinco: Isld s/o Benj & Cath to Mary Watson 20 S Chinco: Isld Chinco: Isld d/o Jno Watson & Sarah Thornton on 19 Jan 1858 at Chinco: Isld by P Bowdin (Joshna Wishart says he over 21)

YOUNG Theodore Col 35 S Farmer Acc Acc s/o Harriet to Edie White Col 22 S Acc Acc d/o Sina on 14 Oct 1886 at Acc by AJ Satchell

YOUNG William 23 S Farmer Acc Acc s/o William & Susan to Julia West 29 S Acc Acc d/o Edward & Virginia on 25 Nov 1876 at Drum'tn by DA Woodson

YOUNG William Col 18 S Wage-earner Acc Acc s/o John & Harriet to Nicey Hatton Col 15 S Acc Acc d/o James T on 29 May 1895 at Acc by AJ Satchell

YOUNG William D Col 19 S Laborer Acc Acc s/o Sarah Taylor to Ellen Poulson Col 22 S Acc Acc on 12 Feb 1880 at the Parsonage by RJ Waters

YOUNG William T 24 S Sailor s/o David & Margaret to Mary W Byrd 20 S d/o John W Byrd & Nancy Bloxom lic: 14 Feb 1865 marr: 16 Feb 1865

YOUNG Wm R 20 S Laborer Acc Acc s/o Richard W & Susan to Neely Gardner 17 S Acc Acc d/o Benjamin Gardner & Elizth Gladden on 25 Dec 1881 at Acc by SC Boston

YOUNG Wm S 22 S Farmer Acc Acc s/o Severn J & Mary L to Margaret E Doughty 22 S Acc Acc d/o Major & Catharine on 30 Nov 1881 at Pungo: by CC Wertenbaker

ZELL George B 26 S Dentist Delaware Co PA Delaware Co PA s/o George B & Debie J to Blanche Hall 16 S Acc Acc d/o Anthony L & Eliz'th on 4 May 1892 at Acc by RB Scott

ZEMBER John 21 S Farmer Australia Acc s/o Louis to Margaret Taylor 13 S Acc Acc d/o Joseph & Elizabeth S on 11 Jan 1891 at Acc by JWA Elliott

Bride Index

(-----)
(-----) 157, 281
  Easter (FN) 90
Abbott
  Elizabeth S 58
  Emma R 273
  Jane (Col) 257
  Margaret (Col) ... 325
  Mary (Col) 318
  Mollie A 133
  Sarah A (Col) 202
Abdell
  Bettie H 175
Abrams
  Ida V 282
Ackley
  Amanda P 214
  Willianna 49
Adams
  Alice P 182
  Arinthia 363
  Catharine E 347
  Eleanor L 199
  Emma L 63
  Lizzie S 238
  Maria A 205
  Mary A 245
  Mary S 38
  Mrina 295
  Nancy 196
Addison
  Mary (Col) 341
Adkins
  Lavinia 315
  Mary A 263
Ailworth
  Amanda 218
  Betsy (FN) 340
  Charlotte 218
  Charlotte A 145
  Laura 230
  Mary E 322
  Sally T 367
  Sarah (Col) 186

  Sarah Ann 254
Allen
  Amanda M 258
  Anna (Col) 42
  Bettie (Col) 165
  Daisey (Col) 29
  Elizabeth (Col) ... 355
  Ella (Col) 28
  Esther (Col) . 266, 316
  Georgianna (Col) .. 313
  Leah J (Col) 269
  Maggie (Col) 117
  Mary (Col) 145
  Mary A (Col) 148
  Patience L (Col) .. 233
  Rachel (Col) 29
  Rebecca 253
  Rose L 98
  Sally (Col) 45
  Susan (Col) 160
  Tabitha (Col) . 89, 279
Ames
  Ann (Col) 35
  Annie T 91
  Bettie B 191
  Bettie E L 224
  Cath S 72
  Charlotte (Col) ... 48
  Charlotte E C 264
  Eleanor E 351
  Elizabeth 36
  Ella C (Col) 89
  Emma (Col) 285
  Emma Catharine .. 335
  Hester (Col) 59
  Isabella Sarah 30
  Julia A 194
  Kate E 366
  Laura (Col) 120
  Laura A 177
  Laura Ellen (Col) .. 285
  Leah (Col) 74
  Lottie 91
  Lottie E 50

  Louisa F 69
  Maggie E 112
  Margaret (Col)
   ... 105, 280, 303, 347
  Margaret C 223
  Margaret Jane 196
  Margaret S 82
  Margaret Susan ... 136
  Margaret T 185
  Margie B 275
  Maria (Col) 247
  Mary (Col) 136
  Mary 118, 268
  Mary E 123, 335
  Minnie G 193
  Nervilla E 34, 89
  Rachel (Col) 107
  Rebecca A 118
  Rose A 125
  Sarah 216
  Sarah (FN) 318
  Sarah A F 334
  Sarah E (Col) 64
  Susan M 193
  Tabitha 265
  Tillie (Col) 107
  Virginia S 235
Anderson
  Mary Lizzie (Col) . 169
Anderton
  Elizabeth 303
  Lillie A 300
  Marietta 309
Andrews
  Annie 91
  Arinthia 49
  Catharine 345
  Charlotte A 225
  Comfort 327
  Eliza 216
  Elizabeth A 200
  Ellen 267
  Emma 307
  Levenia 305

Lizzie 41, 108
Mary 95, 108
Matilda 55
Nancy 296
Rebecca J 60
Sarah 61
Sarah A 155, 267
Sarah E 342
Annis
  Betty (Col) 166
  Catharine E 214
  Cornelia Ann (Col) 231
  Delia 323
  Lena T 190
  Maggie May 326
  Mary A 208
  Sarah Jane 87
  Susan 55
Anthony
  Eliza Jane (Col) ... 255
  Elizabeth 338
Applegate
  Mary 79
Archer
  Tabitha 361
Archey
  Mahala 345
Archie
  Tabitha A 356
Archy
  Catharine Ann 305
Ardis
  Emma F 254
  Sarah F 98
Arlington
  Sallie B 275
Armstrong
  Adeline 215
  Ann (FN) 119
  Lizzie (Col) 340
  Margaret (Col) ... 303
  Margaret (FN) ... 135
Ashby
  Amanda (Col) 247
  Bridget (Col) 74
  Caroline (Col) 50
  Clara (Col) 143
  Colline (Col) 73
  Eliza (Col) 46
  Elizabeth 279
  Elizabeth (Col) ... 285
  Elizabeth L 368
  Esther (Col) 94

Fannie (Col) 94
Juliet Ann 42
Louisa 43
Louisa (Col) 250
Lucy (Col) 289
Maggie (Col) 111, 192
Margaret (FN) ... 164
Mary E 193
Mary Susan (Col) . 75
Mary T 30
Nicy (Col) 304
Rose (Col) 35
Sarah J (Col) 47
Sylvia (Col) 335
Aydelotte
  Alice 321
  Frances (Col) 288
  Harriet 129
  Mary 166
Ayres
  Ambert 361
  Ambret 38
  Annie R 361
  Bettie P 100
  Elizabeth L 71
  Elizabeth S 243
  Frances (Col) 141
  Frances E 313
  Ida M 133
  Jennie E 286
  Licia A 38
  Louisa 68
  Lucretia 82
  Lucy (Col) 287
  Malinda (Col) 281
  Margaret S 89
  Martha S (Col) ... 124
  Mary 322
  Mary Jane 201
  Olive E 253
  Rose (Col) 34
  Sally A 206
  Sally Virginia 173
  Sudie A 294
  Susan E 266
  Theodosia 85
  Willie C 339
Babbitt
  Mary F 75
  Mary Montgomery . 228
Badger
  Annie 235
  Easter (Col) 48

Julia Ann (Col) ... 250
Lavenia 204
Mary A 264
Pamelia 297
Bagwell
  Annie D 158
  Bettie M 203
  Catharine (Col) ... 125
  Docia (Col) 333
  Irene 255
  Kate (Col) 93
  Katie D 272
  Lillian W 79
  Margaret R 203
  Mary (Col) 94, 262, 347
  Narcissa M 205
  Rosa (Col) 137
  Sally W 186
  Sarah P 365
  Susan (Col) 123
Baker
  Amanda 270
  Annie L 166
  Catharine 70
  Ella 202
  Emaline 305
  Emma 38, 255
  Hester 106
  Ida M (Col) 138
  Louisa 300
  Margaret A 275
  Mary 255, 316
  Mary A 27
  Olive P 40
  Olivia A 178
  Sophia S 207
Ballard
  Annie (Col) 248
Banks
  Mary (Col) 136
Barger
  Melissa 163
Barnes
  Annie E 318
  Annie M 167
  Arinthia C 172
  Arinthia C L 134
  Arinthia F 199
  Arinthia J 211
  Cora L 299
  Elizabeth 324
  Elizabeth E 284
  Elizabeth R 291

Bride Index

Elizabeth S 190
Elizabeth Susan . . . 225
Ella Cora 154
Emaline S 284
Emma A 300
Eva B 348
Eva L 238
Fanny 163
Julianna A 116
Juliet A 199
Kate E 183
Libbie L 365
Margaret Jane 198
Martha J 368
Mary 209, 251
Mary F 202
Mary R 259
Mary S 270
Mary T 299
Melissa 187
Missouri 259
Nancy C 356
Pamelia Mary 226
Ruth T 56
Sallie E 40
Sallie G 320
Sally 208
Sarah A 260
Susan 298
Susan A 40
Vienna S 351
Virginia . . . 210, 321
Barrett
  Lizzie A 61
Bateman
  Seneth 167
Battaile
  Ann Hay 159
Battails
  Ellen Z 167
Baum
  Kate E 212
Baylis
  Frances 357
Bayly
  Adah (Col) 90
  Alice E (Col) 303
  Annie (Col)
  . . . . . . 122, 177, 363
  Annie J 122
  Bernetta (Col) . . . 206
  Betsy 161
  Betsy (Col) 318

Caroline (Col) 94
Carrie F 175
Catharine 257
Catherine (FN) . . . 317
Cordelia (Col) 194
Cornelia (Col) 193
Drucilla 253
Drucilla (Col) 93
Elizabeth 181
Elizabeth (Col) . . . 304
Ella (Col) 314
Ella E (Col) 312
Ellen (Col) 341
Ellen (FN) 363
Emeline 38
Emeline (FN) 98
Emma 324
Emma (Col) 123
Evelyn May 328
Fanney (Col) 129
Gracie (Col) 58
Hannah F (Col) . . . 334
Harriet 246, 251
Harriet (Col) . 187, 288
Harriet J 358
Hester J (Col) 269
Hetty 148, 220
Ida (Col) 178
Indiana 361
Jane (Col) 312
Laura Susan (Col) . 330
Louisa Ann (Col) . . 75
Lucinda (Col) 191
Lucy (Col) 336
Lydia (Col) 216
Maggie E (Col) . . . 280
Margaret (Col)
  . . . . 28, 48, 155, 311
Margaret Ann 250
Margaret H 58
Maria (Col) 122
Mary (Col) . . 120, 139
Mary A 149
Mary A (Col) . 75, 314
Mary Ann (Col) . . 47
Mary E 165
Mary S (Col) 92
Missouri 85
Nancy 284
Peggy (FN) 231
Polly (Col) 80
Rebecca (Col) 258
Rose 289

Rosetta (Col) 194
Sally F (Col) 175
Sally T 276
Sarah (Col) 216
Sarah Alice (Col) . . 37
Seml Ann 197
Susan (Col) . . . 85, 99
Susan E 119
Susie (Col) 300
Tabitha (Col) 288, 306
Virginia (Col) 365
Virginia S 240
Bayne
  Annie V (Col) 125
  Charlotte A 116
  Mary (Col) 271
Beach
  Adah (Col) 254
  Catharine R 288
  Ella F 111
  Henny (Col) 112
  Margaret R 159
  Sarah (black) 234
  Susan 30
  Sylvia (Col) 312
Beasley
  Corinthia 198
  Juliet Ann 278
  Margaret E 344
  Susan 284
  Willianna 128
Beavans
  Amy (Col) 249
  Annie (Col) 285
  Arinthia 330
  Elizabeth (Col) 126, 286
  Ella (Col) 49
  Emma (Col) . . 78, 137
  Hester (Col) 343
  Larretta (Col) 217
  Maggie S (Col) . . . 146
  Margaret 44
  Margaret (Col) . . . 64
  Margaret Ellen (Col) 139
  Mary (Col) 317
  Mary S (Col) 177
  Nelly (FN) 247
  Peggy (Col) 250
  Sarah 265
  Tinny (Col) 266
Becket
  Ann (Col) 263
  Caroline (Col) 34

Eliza (Col) 159
Ida (Col) 363
Lizzie (Col) 248
Lucy Jane (Col) . . . 197
Lukie (Col) 181
Luky 46
Maggie (Col) 257
Maggie S (Col) . . . 45
Martha (Col) 46
Mary (Col) . . 164, 233
Mary A (Col) 286
Polly (Col) 177
Polly (FN) 49
Recie (Col) 89
Sallie (Col) 36
Sarah Ann 59
Bedell
  Emma A 270
Beeby
  Comfort A 54
  Ellen 57
Bell
  Alice A 341
  Ann 232
  Arinthia S J 281
  Cordelia A 193
  Dinah (Col) 165
  Dorothy A 243
  Drucilla 176
  Eleshea A 358
  Elic F 311
  Elizabeth 117
  Elizabeth B 69
  Elizabeth H 226
  Ella (Col) 142
  Emaline (Col) 165
  Emma (Col) 145
  Emma C 234
  Georgeana 118
  Juliet 265
  Kate 339
  Kesiah (Col) 364
  Lena M 340
  Lena S 184
  Lizzie (Col) 325
  Lizzie E 215
  Mamie 161
  Margaret S 129
  Maria 181
  Mariah 63
  Mariah Jane 120
  Mary 316
  Mary A 124, 349

Mary E 73
Mary Elizabeth . . . 265
Mary T 219
Missouri E 222
Rockzanah T 150
Sallie 222
Sarah 119, 308
Sarah E 49
Susan 219, 314
Beloate
  Alice L 52
  Bertha L 35
  Clara M 163
  Clarissa (FN) 145
  Cora L 199
  Cordelia J 165
  Cordie D 288
  Ella K 272
  Gabillia E 234
  Julia M 279
  Kate M 294
  Lola M 70
  Manie 301
  Margaret D 233
  Margaret Sarah . . . 235
  Marggie A 336
  Mary A 194, 235
  Mary E 321, 340
  Mary Eliza 147
  Mary Jane (Col) . . 346
  Mary V 41
  Mollie E 280
  Patience 233
  Polly Ann 313
  Rosina (Col) 292
  Sarah 237
  Sarah E 34, 168
  Susan 52
  Virginia E 31
  Virginia S 238
  Virginia Susan . . . 225
Bennett
  Annie D 197
  Cora M 359
  Emma Kate 338
  Esther 332
  Indiannia D 197
  Lillie C 52
  Maggie E 328
  Margaret A 42
  Minnie C 105
  Sally Ann 310
Benson

Mary E 61
Nancy 273
Berry
  Jane 300
  Maggie R 206
  Martha 308
  Mary 92
  Matilda 116
  Nancy 324
  Permelia 209
  Sarah A 27
Bibbins
  Bettie (Col) 336
  Hester (Col) 337
  Sarah Ann (FN) . . 75
Birch
  Alice J 315
  Amy L 329
  Annie K 295
  Annie M 175
  Airylanta 246
  Elizabeth 180
  Elizabeth E 184
  Hettie F 185
  Jane 172
  Josephine . . . 278, 354
  Lillie A 91
  Lizzie J 86
  Maggie Virginia . . 140
  Malinda 184
  Manie M 354
  Mariah C 62
  Martha 103
  Mary 108
  Mary A 64
  Mary Ann 276
  Mary C 240
  Mary E 104
  Mary G 111
  Matilda 149
  Nancy M 200
  Patsy 62, 245
  Rebecca 61, 184
  Roxilla 295
  Sadia 83
  Sarahann 327
  Susan 180, 334
Bishop
  Elizabeth 293
  Esther (Col) 120
  Hetty J 81
  Maggie E 88
  Mary 208

Bride Index

Mary L 175
Sudie W 152
Blackstone
  Elizabeth W 96
  Henrietta E 292
  Kitty C 246
  Margaret D 51
  Margaret Susan . . . 96
  Rachel W 92
Blackwell
  Anna M 212
Blades
  Mary 168
Blake
  Annie (Col) 324
  Eliza (Col) . . 284, 295
  Jane (Col) 37
  Lena 146
  Martha (Col) 134
  Missouri (Col) . . . 170
Blossomgale
  Mary 115
Bloxom
  Alice W 70
  Annie (Col) 342
  Arinthia E 77
  Bettie B 210
  Caroline E 176
  Caroline W 181
  Carrie O 260
  Clara T 214
  Comfort 62
  Cora A 348
  Cordie E 262
  Elizabeth 86
  Elizabeth Ann 344
  Elizabeth S 194
  Ella M 322
  Eva C 301
  Gertrude A 144
  Hetty 138
  Jannie E 53
  Julia Ann 120
  Lizzie E 140
  Manie 61
  Margaret A 275
  Mary 168, 368
  Mary (Col) 117
  Mary A T 234
  Mary D 240
  Mary E 55
  Mary G 111
  Mary P 333

Mary T 228
Ora V 248
Patience 92
Peggy (Col) 77
Rosena (Col) 367
Rosy (Col) 113
Sallie S 38
Sarah E 342
Susan A 319
Susan Jane 366
Vesta E 330
Virginia W 116
Boggs
  Agnes M 83
  Annie (Col) 105
  Betsy (Col) 107
  Caroline A 249
  Charlotte (Col) . . . 368
  Cordie (Col) 36
  Edith G 122
  Elizabeth C 324
  Elizabeth M 45
  Ella (Col) 105
  Emaline 331
  Emma S 136
  Emma T 59
  Eveline J 86
  Fanny (Col) 280
  Georgianna C 304
  Judah (FN) 136
  Leah S 255
  Lillian L 204
  Margaret H 280
  Martha (Col) 178
  Mary (Col) 48
  Mary E 249
  Mary E (Col) 28
  Mary Jane 330
  Pearl Elizabeth . . . 137
  Sallie (Col) 313
  Sally (Col) 292
  Sarah E 270
  Susan (Col) 110
  Susan Ann 124
  Virginia (Col) 137
  Virginia N 316
Bohn
  Josephine 125
Bonnewell
  Bettie Eva 196
  Elizabeth 68
  Ellen 320
  Harriet Susan 277

Rachel Ann 32
Sarah T 349
Trephenia J 302
Booker
  Bridget J (Col) . . . 206
  Emma J (Col) 134
Boone
  Keturah S J 339
  Margaret 237
Booth
  Elizabeth . . . 109, 144
  Jane 293
  Janie 200
  Lilly 271
  Margaret 339
  Maria 265
  Mary 61, 84
  Rebecca 361
Bowden
  Annie 114
  Comfort J 62
  Della 85
  Elizabeth 53, 61
  Elizabeth J 171
  Grace W 27
  Hester Ann 240
  Jane 60
  Malissa (Col) 61
  Martha 346
  Martha E 84
  Mary 61, 209
  Mary Ann 49
  Mary Nancy 215
  Rebecca 216
  Sarah J 240
Bowdoin
  Carrie (Col) 318
  Maria (Col) 44
  Martha (Col) 45
  Virginia B 181
Bowen
  Ailsey (FN) 39
  Cinda E 324
Bowers
  Jennie E 236
Bowles
  Mary Jane (Col) . . 158
Bradford
  Catherine S 269
  Elizabeth S 75
  Hetty L 118
  Ida E 312
  Maggie L 265

Margaret 88
Margaret S 207
Mary Ann 128
Mary E 355
Mary S 93
Mary V 158, 212
Peggy 181
Polly A 311
Rachel H 182
Sarah (Col) 35
Sudie A 141
Susan E 334
Bradshaw
   Lovey 309
   Maggie L 247
Braidwood
   Maggie E 290
Brasure
   Lucinda 55
   Maria 91
Bratcher
   Matilda 277
Brickhouse
   Emeline (Col) 258
   Esther (Col) 43
   Fannie (Col) 360
   Florence (Col) . . . 350
   Mary (Col) 295
Brimer
   Henrietta 326
   Laceretta 121
   Mary 97, 261
   Mary Ann 150
   Mary E 233
   Syrena J 328
Brinney
   Charlotte 103
   Juliet 243
   Maggie (Col) 364
   Maria (Col) 353
Briscoe
   Mary Ellen 102
Brittingham
   Anna E 110
   Ellen James 250
   Emily 282
   Emily J 73
   Emily Jane 92
   Girtie 152
   Mary (Col) 170
   Mary (FN) 103
Broadwater
   Comfort E 123

Elizabeth (Col) . . . 181
Jane 222
Julia D 139
Letita R B 146
Louisa 307
Margaret 67
Mary C 156
Mary E 138
Mary Inez 248
Mary J 320
Mary L 157
Sally (FN) 272
Broughton
   Alice (Col) 63
   Hester (Col) 97
   Josephine (Col) . . . 77
   Mary Jane 79
   Mary P (Col) 344
   Sarah H 114
Brown
   Alice 199
   Betsy (Col) 231
   Georgianna (Col) . . 210
   Ida F 198
   Jane (Col) 323
   Josephine (Col) . . . 89
   Louisa 138
   Mary F (Col) 229
   Mary J 328
   Mary R 101
   Rachel 87
   Rose (Col) 115
   Sarah (Col) 164
   Vernulia (Col) 117
   Virginia Ann 224
   Willia A 312
Broxton
   Annie M 128
Budd
   Arinthia A 173
   Bettie S 279
   Catharine 34
   Elizabeth 337
   Ella 290
   Ellen T 236
   Emma 59
   Ethel V 209
   Harriett S 347
   Kessy 131
   Mary 347
   Mary E 97
   Sally 209
   Sarah 279

Sarah E 171
Bull
   Alice M 105
   Ann 257
   Ann (Col) 218
   Bettie S 173
   Birdie Amanda . . . 243
   Charlott E 31
   Drucilla C 96
   Edna 208
   Elethea 167
   Elizabeth 127
   Elizabeth L 143
   Ellen (Col) 53
   Esther 59
   Eva C 334
   Hannah 283
   Harriet 212
   Hester 66
   Hester B 212
   Jane (Col) . . 144, 286
   Jennie 163
   Jennie C 91
   Josephine 172
   Lydda (Col) 351
   Manie A 35
   Manie E 191
   Margaret (Col) . . . 210
   Mart V 30
   Mary B 198
   Mary F 185
   Nancy Ann 310
   Phebe Elizabeth . . . 57
   Polly G 74
   Rebecca Susan . . . 343
   Rebecca T 144
   Ruth 85
   Sally 244
   Sarah 318
   Sarah C 29
   Susan 128
Bullman
   Leonora G 56
Bundick
   Adaline 173
   Alice L 188
   Amanda A . . 69, 360
   Betsey (Col) 72
   Betsy 58
   Betsy (Col) 107
   Caroline 187
   Drucilla J 282
   Eliza (Col) 361

Bride Index

Elizabeth 128
Elizabeth (Col) 318, 361
Elizabeth F W 262
Ella F 203
Emily L 349
Eudie S 166
Fluvanna J 150
Hettie (Col) 268
Jane (Col) 354
Jane E 337
Kelsy 76
Lacy M 242
Lancy M 188
Leah (Col) 71
Leah (FN) 264
Louisa 261
Lucretia 50
Lucy (Col) 72
Maggie E 117
Maggie R 346
Maggie S 324
Margaret 40
Margaret E S 76
Mary 91, 141
Mary A 259
Mary E . 163, 231, 347
Mary J 195, 313
Mary N 328
Matilda S 194
Molly 307
Nancy (Col) 270
Nannie A 70
Oceana 243
Ocianna 56
Polly A . 72, 232, 315
Rebecca 304
Rosa (Col) 114
Sadie V 351
Sallie 290
Sally (Col) 111
Sarah (Col) 68
Sarah A 152
Sarah Ann .. 153, 189
Susan 341
Susan (Col) 63
Susan A 129
Susan B 171
Tabitha (Col) 136, 147
Willie F 327
Bunting
  Alicia 321
  Ann 139
  Ann (Col) 41

Annie 166
Caroline 249
Ella F 157
Emma E 168
Hennie E 79
Julia F 41
Laura F 64
Leah J (Col) 352
Lilly 269
Lydia (Col) 149
Mamie M 96
Martha E 297
Mary 51
Mary (FN) 74
Mary A 364
Mary Caroline ... 324
Mary E 246
Mary E (Col) 75
Mary F 261
Mary V 227
Nancy (Col) 119
Rose Ann 302
Sallie 297
Susan 239
Susan Ann 323
Susan Jane 73
Virginia 249
Virginia M 136
Burr
  Ida C 241
Burroughs
  Emma J 97
  Mary P 200
Burrse
  Elizabeth 102
Burton
  Ada (Col) 165
  Ann 210
  Anna M 127
  Cordelia (Col) 360
  Elizabeth A 240
  Fannie E 182
  Laura 292
  Louisa A 54
  Maggie 184
  Maggie S (Col) ... 191
  Marianna 220
  Mary A (Col) 149
  Mary Jane (Col) .. 42
  Mary M K 245
  Melvina (Col) 324
  Missouri (Col) ... 29
  Nelly (Col) 272

Otelia (Col) 364
Rowena F 112
Sally (Col) 273
Sarah (Col) 297
Sarah E 54
Selby (Col) 45
Susan C (Col) 216
Willie (Col) 218
Busby
  Mary O 55
Byrd
  Annie C 304
  Annie Suan 196
  Bettie 241
  Bettie D 152
  Bettie S 83
  Birnetta L 275
  Caroline (Col) 204
  Clarissa 57
  Clarissa (Col) 332
  Demeriah C 332
  Elisie (Col) 351
  Eliza (Col) 114
  Elizabeth C 252
  Elizabeth M 77
  Elizabeth P 256
  Ellen 232
  Emma (Col) 215
  Eveline 195
  Floney 115
  Florence N 148
  Harriet D 346
  Henrietta 47
  Ida (Col) 112
  Ida Grace 225
  Indianna F 199
  Lina (Col) 267
  Lucy A (Col) 362
  Lulie 84
  Malinda A 199
  Margaret 49
  Margaret J 79
  Maria (Col) 33
  Marian (Col) 287
  Martha F 249
  Mary (Col) 29
  Mary A 131
  Mary E 139, 221
  Mary Ella (Col) ... 135
  Mary Frances 85
  Mary S 312
  Mary T 286
  Mary W 369

Minnie L 219
Nettie S 330
Rachel (Col) 34
Rachel Ann (Col) . . 188
Rosana (Col) 99
Sadie E 49
Sallie 78
Sallie D 321
Sallie E 155
Sarah 202
Sarah (Col)
. . . . 120, 125, 364
Sarah R 340
Scynthia E 275
Susanna 114
Tabitha S 157
Thealey Ann 126
Callahan
  Mary 141
Campbell
  Lela M 77
Carey
  Mary S 366
Carmine
  Annie C 201
  Annie L 237
  Elizabeth R 66
  Elnora R 99
  Maggie A 160
  Mary 67
  Mary C 132
  Missouri C 354
  Sarah E 357
  Tabitha S 104
Carpenter
  Annie 180
  Elizabeth 185
  Estella 137
  Esther 347
  Mahala 157, 240
  Mary 331
  Nancy 182
  Sarah E 87
  Vesta 359
Carter
  Betsy (FN) 203
  Mamie M 86
  Susan (Col) 126
Caruthers
  Frances S 86
  Rose 298
Case
  Ann 42

Bethany (Col) 68
Betsey (FN) 145
Laurella 284
Sarah (FN) 119
Caulk
  Bertie 243
  Halcyone 98
Cave
  Lydia J 116
Chambers
  Lizzie 359
  Racelia S 175
Chance
  Elizabeth S 165
  Emma 103
Chandler
  Ada (Col) 94
  Ann F 123
  Anngeler 58
  Annie (Col) 363
  Annie B 218
  Annie J 175
  Berlie T 106
  Betsy 150
  Bettie U 35
  Carrie W 281
  Cecilia M 193
  Eleanor D 292
  Eleshea 366
  Elizabeth F 33
  Hattie D 319
  Hester Ann (Col) . . 286
  Ida (Col) 174
  Kate S 335
  Kesiah S 151
  Keturah James 59
  Lena T 165
  Maggie 176
  Maggie S 119
  Manie (Col) 363
  Margaret A 162
  Martha (Col) 153
  Mary (Col) 215
  Mary A (Col) 106
  Mary C 61
  Mary E 340
  Mary Elizabeth . . . 43
  Mary H (Col) 330
  Missouri (Col) . . . 307
  Mollie L 238
  Nancy 323
  Rose B 132
  Rosey Ann 335

Sally 357
Sarah (Col) 267
Susan (Col) 185
Susan E 92, 199
Susane A 345
Tamar (Col) 351
Tamar T (FN) 273
Channer
  Elizabeth (Col) . . . 302
Charnock
  Betsy Davis 52
  Eliza A 83
  Elizabeth 295
  Hettie 247
  Julia E 242
  Maggie L 248
  Malinda 165
  Margaret 36, 116, 307
  Polly 187
  Sally 314
  Sarah Ann 52
  Susan 286
Chase
  Anna 77
  Anna E 202
  Clarinda S 149
  Comfort J 221
  Elizabeth 332
  Lucy 29
  Nancy 268
  Sallie A 229
  Sarah 110
Cherricks
  Anna 184
  Caroline 313
  Charlotte A 86
  Cornelia 179
  Elizabeth 80, 183, 206
  Ibby Catharine . . . 274
  Margaret 240
  Martha E 57
  Mary 245, 306
  Mary E 206
  Nancy R 32
  Salona 344
  Susan 346
Chesser
  Arinthia 330
  Cecelia 221
  Cordelia 332
  Elizabeth 85, 362
  Ellen 73
  Florence E 328

Bride Index

Julia Ann 238
Margaret S 328
Martha J 39
Matilda 232
Nancy 161, 309
Ocia 196
Rachael 138
Sally A 322
Sally Ann 301
Susan 122
Susan A 247
Virginia 131
Christian
  Florence F 176
Christopher
  Emeline 79
  Emily 28
  Laura 332
  Mary (Col) 39
  Sally A 223
Church
  Emma (Col) 146
  Georgie (Col) 134
  Sally A (Col) 215
  Susan (Col) . 280, 286
Churn
  Clara T 87
  Emaline 331
  Florence E 361
  Margaret E 177
  Melinda 195
  Sarah A 207
  Sarah E 211
Clark
  Harriet 53
  Mary Jane 293
Claville
  Annie 202
  Elizabeth
    . . . 162, 168, 180, 282
  Emily F 207, 317
  Jane 81
  Lizzie 345
  Lydia A 205
  Mary A 353
  Matilda 27
  Nancy 140
  Rebecca 54
  Sarah 180, 306
Clayton
  Caroline K 224
  Catharine E 214
  Elizabeth C 227

Hetty T 226
Laura S 56
Mary 366
Mary (Col) 136
Mary E (Col) 354
Nancy (Col) 355
Sallie (Col) 178
Sally (Col) 114
Sally J 54
Sally M 56
Sarah E 211
Susan 367
Cluff
  Adah 132
  Josephine 168
  Nancy C 329
Coard
  Alice Lee 51
  Anna 322
  Annie E 59
  Dina (Col) 96
  Elizabeth C 38
  Ella D 334
  Ida V 239
  Jane S 29
  Laura 162
  Maria (Col) 29
  Mary (Col) 219
  Mary J 262
  Maud S 40
  Susan E 150
Cobb
  Elizabeth 255
  Emma S 355
  Leah 194
  Sarah M 280
  Virginia G 145
Cole
  Laura V 357
Coleburn
  Annie W 35
  Arinthia (Col) 165
  Belle Susan (Col) . . 363
  Bettie 98
  Bettie (Col) 261
  Catharine Ann 176
  Dollie 291
  Emily E 116
  Georgianna (Col) . . 144
  Harriet (Col) 107
  Leah (Col) 116
  Lelia G 90
  Louisa A 226

Lucy (Col) 311
Lula O 113
Margaret (Col) . . . 274
Margie (Col) 29
Mary A 312
Rachel C 63
Rosa A (Col) 313
Sarah E 277
Sinah (Col) 262
Susan (Col) 81
Susan B 176
Tabitha S 345
Collins
  Cornelia 90
  Delilah (Col) 192
  Elizabeth 230
  Emma 241
  Frances (Col) 317
  Hester 174
  Hester (Col) 96
  Ida 32
  Lillie C 115
  Maggie (Col) 146
  Margaret Sarah (Col)178
  Martha 57
  Mary E 75, 183
  Mary Indianna . . . 209
  Mary Jane 141
  Matilda E 247
  Melissa 163
  Rachel (Col) 307
  Sarah 32
  Sarah (Col) 39, 246, 338
  Sarah I 205
Colonna
  Amanda A 274
  Anna 260
  Betsy 301
  Bettie C 364
  Catherine 32, 70
  Comfort 291
  Elizabeth C 210
  Elizabeth E 184
  Emily J 73
  Emma F 126
  Frances 305
  Henriette (Col) . . . 116
  Jennie 131
  Lillian M 145
  Maggie E 310
  Margaret (Col) . . . 48
  Margaret A 329
  Mary (Col) 287

Medora 257
Roberta H 129
Rose (Col) 224
Sadie G 172
Sally A 226
Susan B 251
Susan R 161
Virginia 85
Colony
   Mary T 358
Connaway
   Louisa 113
Conner
   Angeline M 55
   Annie (Col) . 312, 334
   Elizabeth J 109
   Elizabeth T (Col) . . 363
   Etta (Col) 296
   Frances (Col) 220
   Harriet (Col) 229
   Jennie 101
   Leah J (Col) 137
   Lizzie (Col) 350
   Martha J (Col) . . . 360
   Mary 262
   Sarah Ann (Col) . . 89
Conquest
   Adaline 356
   Alice J 63
   Catharine (Col) . . . 95
   Clara (Col) 320
   Clarissa (Col) 135
   Cordelia (Col) 257
   Electra (Col) 139
   Ella (Col) 214
   Ella J 65
   Ellen (Col) 76
   Emma (Col) 120
   Emma Q 230
   Eveline J 66
   Harriet (Col) 215
   Hetty 169
   Hetty (Col) 345
   Ibby (Col) 105
   Louisa (Col) 158
   Lovie A (Col) 219
   Mary (Col)226, 292, 312
   Mary Ann 318
   Mary E 195
   Mary P 151
   Neely (Col) 312
   Sarah (Col) 351
   Scarburgh (Col) . . . 353

Conworton
   Marthella 38
   Matilda 275
Cook
   Mary Jane 264
Copes
   Annie M 348
   Arena 204
   Elizabeth (Col) . . . 321
   Ida 244
   Laura V 120
   Louisa 181
   Lovey C 156
   Margaret Arinthia . 45
   Margaret D 230
   Martha J (Col) . . . 140
   Mary Catharine 243, 339
   Nannie 183
   Olivia (Col) 256
   Sarah (Col) 249
Corbett
   Eliza 161
   Sarah 325
   Susan 309
Corbin
   Annie R 227
   Betsy Ann 321
   Bettie A 148
   Elizabeth 131
   Ellen L 216
   Grace (Col) 56
   Harriett 69
   Ida V 60
   Margaret L S 330
   Mary (Col) 276
   Mary (FN) 103
   Mary C 59
   Mary E 210
   Mollie (Col) 241
   Mollie G 321
   Nora 183
   O Maud 331
   Ophelea F 315
   Sally 65
   Sally Ann (Col) . . . 113
   Susan Ann 187
Core
   Alice 262
   Alice L 244
   Bettie C 363
   Comfort (Col) 262
   Elizabeth 139
   Ella J 256

Loretta Lee 176
Lula Lee 154
Mary W 181
Sallie A 239
Coryell
   Laura J 74
Costin
   Rachel (Col) 303
Covington
   Virginia 333
Coxton
   Annie 303
   Elizabeth 167
   Lelia L 162
   Margaret J 357
   Margaret S 100
   Tabitha 38
   Virginia 243
Creak
   Elizabeth (Col) . . . 238
Crippen
   Betsy (Col) 188
   Darkey (Col) 170
   Elizabeth (Col) . . . 55
   Esther (Col) 149
   Harriet (Col) 159
   Leah (Col) 354
   Mary A (Col) 215, 343
   Mary E (Col) 278
   Sally Ann (Col) . . . 98
   Sarah (Col) 97
   Sarah D (Col) 232
   Sinah (Col) 355
   Surena (Col) 57
   Tittie (Col) 217
Crockett
   Amanda Jane 130
   Ann 101
   Annie 182
   Annie F 109
   Bettie 64
   Caroline 325
   Cassie 344
   Catharine 261
   Clara E 261
   Cordie L 132
   Dona 259
   Educy 133
   Eliza 261
   Eliza E 131
   Elizabeth A 197
   Ellen 100, 260, 262, 270
   Emeline 132

Bride Index

Emily 103
Emma N 325
Fanton J 200
Flora E 296
Hettie J 83
Jane 354
Julia 115
Julia A 271
Julie 326
Laura 259
Leanah 132
Lucy 101
Maggie H 162
Maggie L 127
Malissa F 144
Manie E 294
Marcha 64
Margaret
.... 99, 101, 246, 308
Margaret A 129
Margaret E 258
Maria 102
Mary 100, 154, 197, 298
Mary C 99
Mary E 210
Mary Jane 219
Melissa D 95
Nellie 185, 270
Nellie W 218
Nelly 103
Novella 270
Olivia 101
Polly 326
Polly J 262
Rachel 101, 221
Rebecca (Col) 102
Sadie B 271
Sallie 232
Sallie J 115
Sally 36
Sarah .. 99, 100, 102
Sippora 215
Susan E 261
Susan S 245
Theressa 96
Zipporah 199
Zipporah A 223
Cropper
Alice B 171
Annie T 152
Atta Ann 51
Aynes 93
Emma Susan 307

Harriet (FN) 359
Josephine 293
Margaret S 194
Mary (Col) 105
Melissa 47
Melissa D 161
Crosley
Delila 295
Fanney H 178
Mary E 235
Minerva 172
Rose Ella M 256
Croswell
Ann (Col) 208
Elizabeth (Col) ... 67
Crowns
Elizabeth (Col) ... 258
Crowson
Anna S 160
Clarissa (Col) ... 291
Emma J 81
Maggie (Col) ... 125
Margaret E 298
Mary 29
Mary E 37
Susan (Col) 312
Cullen
Amanda F 127
Blanche L 226
Peggy M 200
Custis
Annie (Col) .. 28, 151
Annie M 51
Bettie (Col) 110
Caroline (Col) 33
Catharine 284
Comfort E (Col) .. 142
Elizabeth 270, 271, 326
Elizabeth (Col)
.... 44, 158, 231
Elizabeth T 130
Ellen (Col) 82
Emma (Col) 263
Emma C (Col) ... 112
Emma J (Col) ... 141
Esther (Col) 145
Florence M 153
Henrietta M 188
Jennie M 236
Julia Ann (Col) ... 58
Leah (Col) 280
Letty (Col) 304
Lillian M 131

Lizzie 362
Louisa 159
Lucy 223
Maggie D 58
Maggie V 105
Margaret . 59, 80, 260
Margaret (Col) ... 153
Margaret A (Col) .. 364
Margaret S 123
Martha J (Col) ... 37
Mary 73, 282
Mary (Col) ... 30, 247
Mary Ann (Col) .. 364
Mary Jane (Col) .. 290
Mary Roberta 315
Nancy (Col) 117
Peggy D 283
Priscilla (Col) ... 352
Rachel Ann (Col).. 136
Rachel E (Col) ... 93
Sadie (Col) 77
Sarah 250
Sarah (Col)
.... 182, 204, 363
Susan (Col) 278
Cutler
Ann (Col) 35
Ella M 150
Lizzie Catherine .. 109
Rosa A 123
Daisey
Adelaide 185
Eliza Ann 328
Elizabeth
..... 49, 87, 108, 206
Elizabeth A 32
Ellen 84
Ida 240
Ida E 327
Jane 108
Lizzie 179
Lizzie E 267
Lydia A 108, 173
Maria 54, 180
Mary A 167, 227
Mary Ann 353
Mary J 174
Matilda 296
Nancy 61
Sarah 32
Sarah A 329
Dalby
Delany 320

Elenor 83
Damlin
  Margaret E 162
  Rachel A 109
  Susan 162
Darby
  Caroline F 323
  Emma 317
  Sarah Jane 213
Daugherty
  Alicia R 69
  Mary A 278
  Sallie A 143
Davis
  Agnes (Col) 206
  Alexine M 128
  Ann (Col) 139
  Clyda G (Col) 346
  Critty 150
  Damariah 150
  Elisha (Col) 133
  Elizabeth Ann 211
  Ellen (Col) 77
  Ema M 315
  Emily Catharine (Col) 57
  Emory E 49
  Eva (Col) 288
  Ida J 50
  Jane (Col) 28, 112, 230
  Jennie W 176
  Lillie J 105
  Lucy (Col) 176
  Maggie (Col) 325
  Margaret (Col) 234, 319
  Margaret A (Col) .. 111
  Margaret E (Col) .. 138
  Mary 79, 168
  Mary (Col) .. 234, 237
  Mary A 236
  Mary A (Col) 361
  Mary E 329
  Middie (Col) 203
  Mileah Ann 229
  Millie (Col) 266
  Nancy (Col) 114
  Phoebe (Col) 76
  Rachel 172
  Rose (Col) 150
  Rosie (Col) 75
  Sadie E 131
  Sallie L 317
  Sarah 83, 215, 297, 333
  Sarah A (Col) 157
  Sarah Ann (Col) .. 201
  Sarah M 222
  Tabitha (Col) 331
  Vernetta E 39
  Virginia F 100
  Virginia S 243
Dawley
  Mary Elizabeth ... 342
Dawson
  Ida 117
Dean
  Virginia M 31
Dennis
  Annie L 28
  Arinthia J (Col) ... 29
  Elizabeth (Col) ... 346
  Emily 222
  Emma B (Col) 178
  Hester (Col) 168
  Jane (Col) 90
  Leah A (Col) 149
  Lydia (Col) 72
  Maggie E 329
  Martha E 57
  Mary (Col) 172
  Mary E 311
  Mary Elizabeth (Col)164
  Mary Jane (black) . 158
  Mary M 290
  Matilda J 129
  Minnie 185
  Peggie S (Col) ... 178
  Rosey M 264
Derby
  Mary C 35
Dickerson
  Amanda M (Col) .. 353
  Ellen (Col) 189
  Esther (Col) 136
  Harriet (Col) 138
  Leah (Col) 137
  Louisa (Col) 242
  M Ida (Col) 93
  Martha (Col) 111
  Mary (Col) 136
  Mary Dinah (Col) . 347
  Mary M S (Col) .. 150
  Mary O 123
  Sallie 164
  Sarah (Col) 97
  Virginia (Col) 119
Dies
  Annie 182
  Arinthia 271
  Catharine 298
  Charlet 100
  Chloe 270
  Dollie 313
  Ellen 100
  Jane 101, 130
  Julia ....·..... 83
  Maggie W 27
  Mary J 83
  Mary L 260
  Mary V 118
  Melitha Ann 133
  Nellie 261
  Sarah F 100
  Scany 259
  Sevenia 102
Dix
  Ann (Col) 142
  Anna 57
  Arinthia T 116
  Bettie (Col) 97
  Catherine A 147
  Elizabeth 333
  Ella (Col) 122
  Emma (Col) 245
  Esther (Col) 260
  Fanny 284
  Fanny (Col) 104
  Hester (Col) 45
  Jeanette M 259
  Leah Susan (Col) .. 152
  Margaret 187
  Margaret (Col) ... 89
  Margaret A (Col) .. 268
  Mary 65, 71, 91
  Mary (Col) 44
  Mary Frances 195
  Mary L 175
  Matilda 85
  Mattie S 67
  Nancy 317
  Pollie 253
  Polly 299
  Rachel (Col) 105
  Rachel (FN) 352
  Sally 190
  Sarah 49
  Virginia 334
Dixon
  Catharine 155
Dorne
  Sarah (Col) 156

Bride Index

Doughty
  Alaha Omega 70
  Alice (Col) 159
  Ann 341
  Bettie B 30, 191
  Catharine S 251
  Elizabeth (Col) ... 111
  Ella (Col) 176
  Emma (Col) 31
  Henrietta S 274
  Josephine 154
  Julia 158
  Lillian S 31
  Lillie May 310
  M L 318
  Margaret A 209
  Marg't E 313, 338, 369
  Margaret V 82
  Mary 79
  Mary Ann 279
  Mary F 78
  Mary J 187
  Mary S 74
  Rose S 50
  Sally A 224
  Sarah F (Col) 247
  Susan W 31
  Virginia (Col) 119
  Willie (Col) 285
Douglass
  Atty (Col) 151
  Clara (Col) 119
  Emma (Col) 48
  Esther 123
  Georgianna (Col) . . 119
  Hannah (Col) 33
  Harriet Ann (Col) . 88
  Jane (Col) 257
  Margaret C (FN) . . 125
  Mary J (Col) 94
Downes
  Joanna 258
Downing
  Alice (Col) . . 147, 169
  Amy (Col) . . 297, 364
  Ann 245
  Ann (Col) .. 171, 183
  Arinthia (Col) 349
  Charloltte M 30
  Cordelia (Col) 265
  Drucilla (Col) 333
  Elizabeth (Col) 76, 161
  Hannah (Col) 78

  Harriet (Col) . . 87, 251
  Jannie F 234
  Juliet 89
  Leah 119
  Leah (Col) ... 95, 169
  Lena (Col) 362
  Lesh (FN) 48
  Lizzie 258
  Margaret (Col) 126, 366
  Martha (Col) 53
  Mary (Col) 87
  Mary (FN) 44
  Mary E (Col) 233
  Nancy (Col) 44
  Silry (Col) 305
  Susan (Col) 192
Drewer
  Rebecca 102
Druer
  Rebecca (Col) 102
Drummond
  Alice (Col) 45
  Alice L 142
  Alice P 335
  Annie (Col) 106
  Araminta (Col) ... 94
  Augusta 205
  Betsey (Col) 242
  Bettie S 295
  Caroline 154
  Carrie L 232
  Charlotte 119
  Cordelia B 60
  Elishea Anna 340
  Eliza 174
  Eliza (Col)
  ... 170, 305, 317, 334
  Eliza Ann (Col) ... 249
  Elizabeth C 105
  Elizabeth S 255
  Ella Gracie 290
  Ellen (Col) ... 30, 263
  Emma S 280
  Euginia 239
  Hannah (Col) 357
  Harriet (Col) 113
  Harriet A 186
  Ida (Col) 353
  Kate R 365
  Lavania C 148
  Leah (Col) 185
  Lida D 332
  Louisa (Col) 135

  Lydia (Col) 367
  Maggie A 293
  Maggie S 264
  Malinda 123
  Manie 304
  Margaret (Col) ... 364
  Margaret A (Col) . . 290
  Martha (Col) 258
  Mary 356
  Mary (Col) 82, 151, 186
  Mary A (Col) 140
  Mary C 51
  Mary E (Col) ... 223
  Mary Jane 168
  Mary Y (Col) ... 288
  Mollie 59
  Olevia F 331
  Polly (Col) 227
  Rachel (Col) 292
  Roseann T 152
  Sarah 123
  Sarah (Col) . . 160, 341
  Sarah A 107
  Sarah A (Col) 195
  Serena 187
  Susan (Col) 291
  Tamar (Col) 156
  Virginia (Col) 161
  Winnie (Col) 356
Dryden
  Mary E 64
Duer
  Matt L M 195
Duffy
  Agnes (Col) 226
  Mary 137
  Sally (FN) 96
  Sarah (Col) ... 37, 103
Duncan
  Ann (Col) 97
  Bertie Ann 170
  Cordelia M 282
  Elizabeth (Col) ... 191
  Emma L 270
  Jane 157
  Julila F 249
  Mary 361
  Mary S (Col) 92
  Rebecca A 76
  Sadie 316
Dunton
  Alice C 332
  Margaret J 315

Margaret T 185
Mary F 238
Mollie B 59
Rosey 361
Sallie 90
Sarah (Col) 33
East
  Alsie 88
  Amecrica H 302
  Annie 135
  Caroline 252
  Effie Julia 304
  Elizabeth 144, 288, 323
  Elizabeth L 173
  Ella 268
  Hetty (Col) 117
  Jane 319
  Julia Ann 127
  Leah Susan 334
  Lydia S 41
  Maggie J 324
  Maggie S 56
  Manie A 40
  Martha A 341
  Mary 368
  Mary J 263
  Melissa E 218
  Nancy 305
  Sarah 241
  Sarah F 258
  Susan 165, 368
  Susan J 148
  Tabitha A 47
Edmonds
  Eugenia 337
  Juliet (Col) 297
Edwards
  Cora (Col) 172
  Lena E 219
  Maggie T 228
  Mary (Col) 33
  Nellie (Col) 124
  Rosa (Col) 122
  Susan E 195
Eichelberger
  Elizabeth S 204
  Nannie (Col) 216
Ellett
  Fanny J 207
Elliott
  Alice E 362
  Emma S 351
  Harriet 249

Henrietta (Col) . . . 236
Leah (FN) 187
Louisa 56
Maggie A 62
Margaret Jane 196
Margaret S 27
Mary 304
Sarah A 250, 360
Sarah Ann 304
Ellis
  Sarah E 157
  Virginia 142
Estridge
  Helen 262
Evans
  Adaline 261
  Alexine 132
  Amanda L 107
  Anne E 308
  Annie H 135
  Avery A 308
  Bettie 260
  Bettie A 346
  Carolin A 104
  Cordelia 359
  Delia 53
  Effie L 28
  Eliza 79
  Elizabeth D 127
  Emma C 179
  Esther (FN) 130
  Ettie J 211
  Eva Jane 271
  Gertrude 65
  Kate M 250
  Lena 100
  Lola F 305
  Lucy A 50
  Lucy B 290
  Lucy H 76
  Lucy V 360
  Maggie H 198
  Maggie L 244
  Malinda 255
  Manie 34
  Margaret
   . . . 35, 175, 246, 287
  Margaret Emily . . 308
  Martha E (Col) . . . 308
  Mary 115, 359
  Mary Ann 245
  Mary C 283
  Mary Rebecca 151

Mary S 130
Mary Washington . 115
Melissa A 176
Minnie J 115
Mollie H 251
Nellie T 42
Polly J 332
Rhoda L 101
Sally 101
Sarah 100
Sarah C 198
Sena T 308
Sophia M 190
Susan 131
Susan (FN) 48
Triffie 99
Triphemia A 35
Virginia 259
Zipporah 85
Ewell
  Alice D 326
  Arinthia C 326
  Cordelia F (Col) . . 123
  Elizabeth 71
  Elizabeth (Col) . . . 339
  Elizabeth Y 27
  Ellen D (Col) 91
  Ellen Douglas (Col) 324
  Emily L 205
  Emma (Col) 186
  Emma S (Col) 94
  Evaline T 231
  Ida C 74, 241
  Jannetta (Col) 125
  Leah (Col) 56
  Lizzie (Col) 142
  Louisa (Col) . 178, 285
  Maggie E 321
  Marceline E 197
  Margaret 40
  Margaret A 253
  Martha A 225
  Mary 34
  Mary (Col) 64, 278, 286
  Mary A 368
  Mary Ann . . 213, 245
  Mary Ann (Col) . . 103
  Mary F 204
  Mary L (Col) 212
  Matilda 166
  Melinda 322
  Missouri 347
  Sadie 57

Bride Index

Sally E 227
Sarah (Col) 153
Susie V 70
Fanton
   Laurah J 349
Farrow
   Elizabeth 238
Feddeman
   Annie C 203
   Elizabeth 264
   Henrietta Mills . . . 271
   Louisa (Col) 103
   Maggie (Col) 95
   Martha S 229
   Mary 103
   Mary E 173
Fedford
   Rosina M 110
Fenrrick
   Johanna 60
Ferguson
   Mary 183
   Nancy 354
   Susan 84, 346
Fields
   Eleshea (Col) 140
   Emma (Col) 162
   Hester (Col) 123
   Lizzie (Col) 66
   Martha (Col) 331
   Sarah (Col) 229
   Willianna 298
   Willie Anna (Col) . 312
Finney
   Ann (Col) 116, 142, 307
   Ann E (Col) 359
   Annie (Col) . . 58, 339
   Bertie (Col) 351
   Catharine M (Col) . 142
   Catharine R . 214, 343
   Elishia (Col) 116
   Eliza (Col) 81
   Emma (Col) 136
   Emma S 340
   Euphemia 52
   Eva (Col) 200
   Harriet (Col) 297
   Henrietta (Col) 31, 106
   Ida 98
   Ida (Col) 350
   Leah 37
   Leah (Col) 351
   Louisa (Col) 29
   Maggie (Col) 182, 274
   Maggie S 177
   Margaret E 105
   Margaret H 340
   Martha (Col) 238
   Mary 57
   Mary (Col)
   . . . . 73, 125, 248, 280
   Matilda (Col) 44
   Matilda A 181
   Nellie (Col) 124
   Rose Ann 217
   Sallie W 201
   Sally (Col) 106
   Sally V S (Col) . . . 260
   Sarah (Col) 365
   Susan (Col) 267
   Susan C 173
   Tabbie (Col) 106
   Virginia (Col) 367
   Willianna (Col) . . . 164
Fisher
   Agnes (Col) 77
   Amanda M (Col) . . 127
   Cornelia S 344
   Easter (Col) 65
   Elizabeth 148
   Henrietta 264
   Ida V F 57
   Jane (Col) 323
   Laura C 213
   Malinda C 253
   Margaret 32
   Martha F 98, 269
   Mary 78
   Mary (Col) 362
   Mary (FN) 93
   Mary E 78, 304
   Mary J 318
   Maude 342
   Middie T 275
   Nellie P 281
   Sarah Ann 264
   Sue H 279
   Susan E 118
   Susan J 152
   Willianna 273
Fitchett
   Junie W 211
   Lula W 69
   Maggie S (Col) . . . 146
   Manie S 148
   Marie 237
Martha L 126
Mary (Col) 203
Rachel T 130
Sally A 219
Sudie L 110
Susan (Col) 191
Fitzgerald
   Elizabeth M 202
   Margaret J 181
   Martha 82
   Ruth 158
   Willianna 95
Flawbush
   Ellen 101
Fleming
   Laura A 180
Fletcher
   Anna D 67
   Betsy (Col) 205
   Elizabeth S 141
   Ella A 149
   Harriet A (Col) . . . 357
   Henrietta (Col) 96, 159
   Jennie (Col) 340
   Louisa 307
   Lousia (Col) 343
   Margaret (Col) . . . 241
   Mary (Col) . . . 36, 141
   Mary A (Col) 170
   Mary E 190
   Minnie C 294
   Rose Ann (Col) . . . 160
   Sarah (Col) 182
   Sarah Jane (Col) . . 96
Flick
   Burniette 97
   Ella T 200
Floyd
   Anna 340
   Annie (Col) . . 42, 363
   Bettie (Col) 235
   Elizabeth (Col) . . . 296
   Emma Susan (Col) . 75
   Indie 111
   Laura E 213
   Louisa (Col) 292
   Maggie (Col) 147
   Margaret 288
   Margaret (Col) . . . 274
   Mary 99
   Mary (Col) . . . 34, 230
   Mary (FN) 33
   Sarah Elizabeth . . . 119

Susan (Col) 357
Foreman
  Georgianna (Col) .. 156
  Mary (Col) ... 97, 160
Foskey
  Lucy (Col) 347
  Margaret 142
Fosque
  A E 58
  Alice (Col) 288
  Ann 240
  Ann Eliza (Col) ... 336
  Catherine S 243
  Ceorgianna (Col) .. 278
  Clara (Col) 289
  Ellen (Col) 319
  Laura A 59
  Lizzie (Col) 363
  Loretta (Col) 182
  Louisa (Col) .. 82, 142
  Louisa E (Col) ... 250
  Margaret 294
  Margaret (Col) 36, 261
  Mary H (Col) 124
  Rachel (Col) 288
  Rebecca (Col) 356
  Sarah V (Col) 43
Fowler
  Bettie F 175
  Joice Susan 269
Fox
  Annie E 261
  Bettie S 211
  E Josie 321
  Elizabeth 173
  Harriet (Col) .. 99, 159
  Ida 293
  Jennie 203
  Keziah 173
  Mary 74, 178
  Olivia 201
  Otellia 355
  Peggy 293
  Susan S 68
Francis
  Eliza 144
Franklin
  Annie (Col) 296
  Mittie C 50
Furniss
  Ellen Maud 107
Gainer
  Rachel (Col) 156

Galloway
  Lottie E 32
Gardner
  Armenia 249
  Elizabeth 40, 148
  Florence A 263
  Josephine 290
  Julia A 154
  Maggie S 190
  Mame 198
  Mary 50
  Mollie 159
  Neely 369
  Sadie E 227
  Sudie 162
  Sudie V 162
  Susan 354
  Virginia A 324
Garrison
  Alexius (Col) 280
  Arinthia J 154
  Bettie (Col) 249
  Clarissa (Col) 280
  Elizabeth (Col) ... 319
  Emma Laura 197
  Garrison (Col) 237
  Georgeanna 297
  Georgie E 192
  Juliet S 335
  Lottie 42
  Lucy (Col) 121
  Margaret (Col) ... 262
  Margaret W . 222, 313
  Mary (Col) 44
  Mary S (Col) 123
  Matilda 152
  Rachel 366
  Rosa (Col) 272
Gaskill
  Maggie F 56
Gaskins
  Anna S 325
  Eliza Ellen 241
  Emaline (Col) 285
  Julia (Col) 274
  Mary (Col) 203
  Nancy (Col) . 287, 351
  Rachel (Col) 73
  Rachel A (Col) ... 263
  Susan 48
George
  Elizabeth (Col)
  .... 64, 66, 105

Gibb
  Minnie H 296
  Susan J 254
Gibbons
  Annie (Col) 114
  Ayrie (Col) 37
  Caroline (Col) 178
  Elizabeth A 143
  Evaline 100
  Fannie 107
  Florence W 311
  Georgianna 115
  Jane (Col) 342
  Mary A 249
  Mary E 163
  Nancy 60
  Sally W 40
Giddings
  Ida (Col) 363
  Mary A (Col) 31
Gilden
  Mary E 321
Gillespie
  Fannie J 282
  Mary E (Col) 111
  Mollie W ... 272, 273
  Rose L 273
  Susan J 172
Gillett
  Annie S 256
  Caroline 333
  Elizabeth D 55
  Esther (Col) 128
  Mary (Col) 312
Givens
  Cora E 293
Gladding
  Adeline J 253
  Amanda A 173
  Annie 359
  Annie A 354
  Cora A 350
  Elizabeth ... 155, 322
  Elizabeth J 110
  Elizabeth P 256
  Ella 301
  George Anna ... 198
  Harriet (Col) 181
  Levinia C 227
  Maggie J 76
  Malvina 78
  Margaret (Col) ... 250
  Marseally 84

Bride Index

Mary E 196	Maggy 300	Rose Ann (Col) . . . 39
Mary Lee 326	Mary 41, 51	Gunter
Nellie E 73	Mary E J (Col) . . . 356	Carrie S 88
Polly 67	McCartie Lee 367	Clarissa (Col) 29
Rebecca E 155	Nancy 36	Lucy (Col) 355
Sally 305	Nancy S 162	Lydia (Col) 43
Susan 78	Rebecca J 269	Margaret (Col) . . . 118
Glenn	Rose A 207	Mary 71
Alice C (Col) 247	Sallie L 224	May 128
Ann (black) 247	Sally L 92	Missouri (Col) 136, 326
Betsey (Col) 149	Sarah 276	Roas (Col) 260
Maggie (Col) 82	Virginia T 51	Sallie A 315
Mary (Col) 296	Green	Sarah (Col) 183
Godfrey	Ella F 162	Sarah A 220
Ella (Col) 159	Martah 298	Susan (Col) 250
Lavirta (Col) 286	Mary L 134	Susan A (Col) 145
Marian (FN) 121	Sally 319	Susan M 35
Miriam (FN) 124	Griffin	Willianna (Col) . . . 114
Godwin	Ann (Col) 124	Guy
Amy (Col) 155	Betsy (Col) 215	Annie F 303
Annie U 146	Elizabeth (Col) . . . 106	Bettie C 307
Arra (Col) 95	Emma (Col) 264	Daisy D 128
Bertha L 263	Esther (Col) 114	Emma J 339
Effie E 281	Hester A (Col) . . . 110	Henrietta 294
Elizabeth (Col) . . . 96	Kate E 121	Jane 272
Ella 296	Maggie (Col) 187	Kate C G 60
Eugenia C 252	Martha (Col) 114	Lillie L 106
Martha F 75	Mary (Col) 225	Lucy (Col) 306
Melissa Ann (Col) . 287	Metosa Augusta (Col) 71	Manie A 52
Millie 41	Nancy (Col) 359	Margaret B 47
Sallie A 259	Sabra 53	Margaret S . . 101, 202
Goffigon	Sarah (Col) 182	Mary E 115
Ella F 34	Sarah Elizabeth (Col)225	Nancy 242
Lucretia N 365	Grinnalds	Nancy C 236
Martha (Col) 203	Adah 106	Olivia J 311
Olivia S 266	Elizabeth 153	Rebecca L 127
Grant	Elizabeth P 260	Sarah 294
Annie A 88	Eveline T 133	Sarah F 118
Jennie (Col) 315	Henrietta 69	Violet (FN) 37
Sarah E (Col) 192	Ida E 346	Hack
Tamar 351	Jane C S 68	Ann (Col) 159
Gray	Leigh V 239	Betsy Ann 36
Annie (Col) 151	Mary A 180	Georgianna (Col) . . 274
Bettie (Col) 94	Mary Ann 277	Henrietta (Col) . . . 302
Bettie J 229	Virginia Lee 121	Mary 31
Elizabeth 127	Groton	Nellie 245
Ella D 211	Annie 303	Rachel (Col) 76
Hennie (Col) 142	Georgianna 214	Sabra C 177
Ida A 240	Maranda W 117	Sally Upshur 35
Lavina Susan 343	Margaret J 266	Haley
Lovey T 299	Mary A 40	Emeline (Col) 160
Lucretia 82	Sally A 341	Emma L 81
Maggie A 243	Gumby	Emma S 51

Helen G (Col) 160
Mary Ann 81
Onie (Col) 257
Polly G 74
Rosetta 343
Sarah A 163
Hall
  Ann E 220
  Annie 252
  Annie Lee 96
  Arra (Col) 95
  Bernetta Susan ... 149
  Blanche 369
  Caroline 313
  Catharine (Col) ... 292
  Catharine T 277
  Celicia F 65
  Charlotte A 306
  Clara V 171
  Cornelia 111
  Demeria 144
  Ebba 328
  Elishea 162
  Elizabeth ... 188, 200
  Emma Jane 104
  Hortense 97
  Julia Ann 175
  Kate D 355
  Mahala 240
  Malinda 265
  Mary 89, 337
  Mary (Col) 142
  Mary A 108
  Mary E 58
  Mary S 104
  Matilda L 59
  Melissa 75
  Milcah A 156
  Nancy V 274
  Rebecca J 76
  Reina 262
  Riley 131
  Sallie D 321
  Sallie E 311
  Sally C 200
  Sarah (Col) 241
  Sarah J 311
  Secilia 303
  Violet (Col) 241
Hammonds
  Margaret 80
Hammons
  Jane 274

Hamons
  Mary J 175
Hancock
  Elizabeth ... 320, 346
  Harriet 346
  Mary 98
  Mary E 134
  Sallie 297
  Sally A 252
  Tabitha 69
Handy
  Emaline (Col) 103
  Josephine (Col) ... 318
  Sallie (Col) 202
Hardis
  Rosa 248
Hargis
  Annie (Col) 121
  Annie E 254
  Carrie L 154
  Harriet 129
  Margaret 46, 210
  Mary H (Col) 90
  Milly (Col) 88
  Mollie A 311
  Polly 263
  Roxanna 212
  Sally 344
  Susan 293
  Susan (Col) 218
Harmanson
  Kate A 233
  Rose (Col) 246
Harmon
  Alsie (Col) 42
  Anne (Col) 192
  Annie (Col) 66
  Catharine (Col) ... 141
  Deliah Ann (Col) .. 67
  Eleanor (Col) 279
  Eleshea Ann (Col) . 277
  Elizabeth 119
  Elizabeth (Col) 47, 256
  Elzey (Col) 241
  Emma Susan (Col) . 146
  Harriet (FN) 347
  Hester (Col) 313
  Ida A 135
  Ida N 243
  Juliet (Col) 296
  Laura (Col) 46
  Margaret A 49
  Margaret Sarah (Col)296

Mary 246
Mary (Col) .. 188, 217
Mary Jane(Col) 155, 311
Nancy (black) 225
Olivia (Col) 285
Sarah (Col) 30
Sarah Elizabeth(Col) 110
Susan 224
Susan (Col) 56
Harris
  Ann B 51
  Atta Ann 51
  Catharine 268
  Elizabeth 332
  Fannie L 43
  Melissa 47
  Nancy 309
  Susan 52
  Susan S 52
Harrison
  Annie E 254
  Caroline W 246
  Elizabeth ... 150, 345
  Eller 60
  Laura S 105
  Lou Emma 104
  Mary Jane (Col) .. 352
  Rachel W 294
  Susan 86
  Susan A 367
  Susanna 361
  Tabitha J 354
  Willianna 107
Hart
  Arminda 47
  Eleshea Ann 92
  Elisha E 176
  Elizabeth ... 183, 273
  Emiline Susan 295
  Jane 323, 337
  Lillie E 196
  Malvina 300
  Mary Ann 224
  Mary C 283
  Mary Jane 264
  Melvina 80
  Missouri 99
  Nancy Emily 104
  Nancy T 337
  Nellie S 68
  Nelvira 206
  Sarah A 195
  Sarah Ann 311

Bride Index

Seney A 246
Hartman
   Mary 277
Hateney
   Ethel (Col) 302
   Harriet (Col) 44
   Maggie 285
   Margaret (Col) . . . 307
   Martha (Col) 29
   Mary (Col) 126
   Sarah A (Col) 46
Hatton
   Ann 204
   Belle S B (Col) . . . 280
   Caroline (Col) 289
   Charlotte (Col) 216, 284
   Elizabeth B 306
   Lottie (Col) 37
   Mary (Col) . . 233, 288
   Nicey (Col) 369
   Rachel (Col) 193
   Rose 80
   Sarah Frances 217
Hayle
   Otelia J 128
Hayman
   Annie O 184
Hayward
   Lucinda (Col) 76
Heath
   Georganna 241
   Georgianna (Col) . . 164
   Missouri (Col) . . . 227
   Olivia 201
   Rose (Col) 165
   Susan 290, 297
Henderson
   Esther 219
   Mary 98
   Mary Ann 218
   Mary F 274
   Patsy C (Col) . . . 246
   Sallie 91
   Sally L 217
   Sarah A (Col) 59
   Susan L 147
Henson
   Phoebe E 79
Hickman
   Alice A 82
   Amanda 301
   Ann E 98
   Anne 248

Annie 209, 367
Annie L 199
Annie W 71
Arinthia 349
Belle 302
Burnetta J 28
Carrie J 166
Elizabeth 53
Emma Susan 197
Ida Isabel 272
Lida (Col) 249
Lovey 71
Manie E 91
Manie H 290
Manie J 198
Margaret (Col) . . . 141
Margaret A 35
Marion (Col) . . . 276
Mary 148
Mary (Col) 137
Mary A 298
Mary A (Col) 339
Missouri E 190
Missouri K 337
Pamelia 320
Polly 358
Polly D 156
Rosa Ann (Col) . . . 99
Rosey A 39
Ruth 199
Sadie U 131
Sallie A 201
Sally 244, 316
Sarah B 309
Susan (Col) 251
Tiffany 254
Virginia 275
Virginia (Col) 242
Virginia A 238
Higgins
   Nannie L 357
   Sudie L 194
Hill
   Amy 228
   Ary L 212
   Demariah 109
   Jane 353
   Lydia A 205
   Manie F 180
   Martha Florence . . 302
   Mary 283, 291
   Mary A 167
   Mary J 80

Molly 169
Rebecca . 41, 180, 211
Sarah 108
Hinman
   Anna (Col) 363
   Arinthia G 56
   Arinthia S 262
   Bettie C 51
   Christanna E 323
   Eliabeth W 350
   Elizabeth . . . 229, 316
   Jane (Col) 290
   Laura 233
   Leah (Col) 95
   Maggie 138
   Maggie E 283
   Margaret A 220
   Martha (Col) 114
   Mary 106
   Mary A (Col) 39
   Mary E 107
   Nancy J 210
   Nancy L 106
   Polly 284
   Rachel (Col) 228
   Sabra J (Col) 362
Hoffman
   Eliza A 314
   Emma Susan 300
   Nancy A 342
Holden
   Arinthia (Col) 55
   Emma (Col) 112
   Henrietta (Col) . . . 184
   Isabella (Col) 225
   Leah (FN) 353
   Lydia (Col) 96
   Mary (Col) 169
   Mary M (Col) 359
   Sally Jane (Col) . . . 153
   Susan (Col) 133
   Susan June (Col) . . 161
Holland
   Alice L 93
   Clara E W 31
   Henrietta (Col) . . . 222
   Laura 258
   Rachel (Col) 306
   Sarah (Col) 141
   Sarah E 111, 166
   Susan A 67
Holloway
   Jane 90

Marriage Records of Accomack County, VA, 1854-1895

Holly
  Eliza 213
  Elizabeth 356
  Ella D 32
Holmes
  Emma (Col) 212
  Julie A (Col) 343
Holstin
  Emeline 282
Holt
  Elizabeth E 184
  Fanny 161
  Mary H 128
  Rose T 340
Hope
  Adah (Col) 355
  Ary (Col) 143
  Clara (Col) 288
  Dorothea 299
  Elishea A 348
  Elizabeth S 348
  Emma (Col) 252
  Esther (Col) . 114, 136
  Fanny Ann 355
  Hester A (Col) ... 70
  Lucy 142
  Margaret 131
  Margaret J 117
  Marie J 152
  Martha (Col) 254
  Mary Ann 361
  Mary E 226
  Minnie F 171
  Nona C 288
  Ocia (Col) 161
  Sadie Annie 217
  Sarah (Col) 32
Hopkins
  Addie E 243
  Alice 46
  Bernetta 154
  Effie M 95
  Emma A 163
  Esther A 223
  Fannie S 342
  Georgianna 81
  Harriet (Col) 268
  Jane D 360
  Julia A 242
  Leah Gennie 186
  Lena E 210
  Mary 28, 54
  Mary A 300

  Mary F 54
  Missouri I V 67
  Mollie 152
  Polly 108
  Rose W 360
  Susan 229
  Susan C 178
Hornenton
  Charlotte (Col) ... 295
Hornsby
  Alexius 263
  Elizabeth M 307
  Gertrude 218
  Mary A 343
Horsey
  Eliza Susan 107
  Hester (Col) 168
  Mary 334
  Rose 312
Houston
  Emaline 195
Houten
  Sarah (Col) 112
Howard
  Marcella 300
Hudson
  Almira 357
  Bertie 228
  Comfort 332
  Jane 274
  Mary 54, 108
  Mary Hester 38
  Mary M (Col) 64
  Sadie W 228
  Susna J 164
Hughes
  Catharine J 314
  Delia F 314
Humphreys
  Fannie M 292
  Kate 291
Hundley
  Cordelia H 107
  Elizabeth 166
  Sarah 162
Hurat
  Anna M 254
Hurley
  Beatie 155
  Hetty 148
  Indiana 220
  Mary B 332
Hurst

  Arinthia A 239
  Catharine 51
  Emma C 238
  Etta L 350
  Kae C 37
  Kate M 294
  Mary L 278
  Sally 206
  Sarah Jane 51
  Susan 176
Hutchinson
  Cordelia (Col) 335
  Elizabeth J 236
  Georgianna (Col) .. 325
  Hester A 121
  Lizzie (Col) 31
  Marie A 277
  Mary R 47
  Sadie M 324
Hyslop
  Elizabeth Susan ... 335
  Jane 63
  Jane (Col) 53
  Jennie E 286
  Lydia S 338, 340
  Mary (Col) 69
  Rosa Ann 191
Insley
  Willie 151
Jackson
  Matilda E 247
Jacobs
  Ann 286
  Annie C 344
  Arinthia (Col) 64
  Dolly (Col) 287
  Elizabeth (Col) ... 366
  Elizabeth S 362
  Ida C (Col) 144
  Laura A (Col) 37
  Maggie (Col) 35
  Margaret (Col) ... 126
  Sally W 301
James
  Eliza B 191
  Elizabeth B 143
  Emma S 193
  Emma Susan 326
  Georgia T 56
  Georgie S 334
  Jannie M 75
  Julia A 69
  Maggie 160

Bride Index

Manie E 237
Margaret E 129
Mary 32
Mary Frances (Col) 145
Mary Jr (Col) 231
Mary Susan 243
Sarah A 160
Victoria (Col) 110

Jarman
  Mollie A 252

Jarvis
  Helen R 306
  Jennie (Col) 119

Jeffries
  Ema 283
  Rebecca 334

Jenkins
  Elizabeth (Col) . . . 334
  Sarah C 327

Jester
  Amy 273
  Anna 320
  Annie 205, 354
  Drucilla . . . 127, 216
  Elizabeth
    . . . . . 53, 84, 183, 306
  Ellie 38
  Emma E 149
  Margaret 216
  Mary A 169
  Mary J 171
  Meany Elizabeth . . 338
  Nancy 214
  Patsy 62, 245
  Rachel 63
  Rebecca 201, 282
  Rebecca A 296
  Rebecca J 271
  Redemia A 80
  Sarah 155
  Sarah Ann 214
  Sarah E 90
  Sarahann 327

Johnson
  Abbie R 164
  Arinthia 104
  Carlene (Col) 333
  Charlotte H 161
  Clara V 196
  Cynthia Anna 176
  Easter (Col) 192
  Elizabeth (Col) . . . 95
  Elizabeth A 108

Ella P 262
Ellen 175, 294
Emma P 232
Etta E 263
Etta E (Col) 363
Eva 144
Fanny D 335
Florence M 65
Grace (Col) 364
Harriet (Col) 33
Hennie Elizabeth . . 294
Henrietta 36
Hester 189
Hester (Col) . . 45, 165
Ida Lee 265
Jennie A 79
Jimma (Col) 47
Laura T 195
Libbie D 208
Louisa (Col) 207
Maggie (Col) 104
Manie 297
Manie (Col) 58
Margaret (Col) . . . 153
Margaret Blanche . 301
Margaret C 224
Margaret H 223
Maria 328
Mariah 63
Martha Jane 310
Mary 39, 176, 316, 328
Mary (Col) . . . 48, 287
Mary A 261
Mary Della 357
Mary E 135, 173
Sallie T 224
Sally 44, 279
Sally A 162
Sarah A (Col) 122
Sarah E 344
Susan 132
Susan V 135
Virginia C 153

Jones
  Alice B 277
  Annie 183
  Arinthia (Col) 291
  Bettie E 353
  Catharine 56
  Catharine (Col) . . . 362
  Charlotte (Col) . . . 141
  Cornelia 111
  Drucilla 175

Elizabeth 57, 180
Elizabeth (Col) . . . 333
Elizabeth J 38
Hennie (Col) 194
Henny (Col) 153
Ida V 89
Lavinia E 60
Lydia A 289
Margaret C 170
Martha A M 54
Mary 212, 361
Mary A 73
Mary E . . . 61, 62, 84
Mary J 193
Patience Ann 289
Rachel 221
Rebecca 61
Sally (Col) 275
Sally Ann 317
Sally M 316
Sarah 108, 205
Sarah J 327
Silvy Ann (Col) . . . 113
Sophia 129
Susan 54, 360

Joynes
  Adeline (Col) 146
  Arinthia S 184
  Ellen D 362
  Emma 124, 343
  Emma (FN) 186
  Esther 348
  Florence (Col) . . . 252
  Hester (Col) 97
  Maggie (Col) 151
  Margaret (Col) . . . 251
  Mary (Col) . . . 33, 319
  Mary E (Col) 289
  Mary E (FN) 286
  Pamilia 105
  Sadie E (Col) 344
  Sarah (Col) 30
  Sarah A 122
  Tabbie M S 202
  Tillie J (Col) 66
  Vinetta 146
  Vinettae 160
  Virginia S 27, 30

Jubilee
  Arinthia (Col) 291
  Arinthia J (Col) . . . 184
  Bettie (Col) 289
  Henrietta (Col) . . . 302

Hester (FN) 120	McCreany J 106	Isabella S 308
Margaret H (Col) . . 185	Melinda 365	Jane (Col) . . . 63, 306
Mary (Col) 30	Nanie E 320	Josephine 81
Mary E (Col) 192	Pamelia A C 41	Katie Susan (Col) . . 78
Vandalia A (Col) . . 43	Rose Ann 86	Laura (Col) 364
Justice	Sallie 72, 300	Leah (Col) 286
Arinthia L 261	Sallie C 322	Lelia M (Col) 88
Arinthia V 213	Sarah (Col) 356	Lena Y 252
Bernetta 227, 260	Susan (Col) . . 90, 347	Maggie S 79
Betsy 320	Susan Ann 139	Mamie J 170
Brunetta 41	Tabitha 284	Manie 72
Caroline T 212	Tamar (Col) 114	Margaret 161
Carrie S 188	Viana F 272	Margaret S 71, 89
Catharine L 319	Virginia . . . 259, 299	Margaret S (Col) . . 285
Catherine 350	Virginia B 317	Martha (FN) 279
Clarissa (Col) 172	Zilla (Col) 202	Mary 256
Eliza 196	Kearney	Mary (Col) 43
Eliza Ellen 368	Lillie B 104	Mary A 69, 83
Elizabeth 67, 169	Keaton	Mary C 342
Elizabeth A . . 65, 332	Eleanor D 292	Mary G 122, 126
Elizabeth P 232	Kellam	Mary J 127
Elizabeth S 260	Adah 122	Mary S 336
Ella 206	Addie J 85	Mary S (Col) 137
Emaline 40	Alice V 107	Mary T (Col) 314
Emma (Col) 169	Amanda (Col) 363	Millie (Col) 368
Emma L 207	Ann R 53	Missouria A 193
Eula L 323	Annie (Col) . 250, 256	Oceanna (Col) 87
Harriet (Col) 359	Arinthia J 335	Phoebe A (Col) . . . 128
Hester (Col) 350	Arinthia S 75	Racilia (Col) 286
Hetty Catharine . . . 246	Bettie S 129	Roberta 233
Ida (Col) 331	Bettie W 193	Romenia O 145
Ida S 151	Charlotte (Col) . . . 126	Sally A 63
Julia C 133	Clara M 269	Sally Ann 81
Lacy M 242	Cordelia C 233	Sarah (Col) . . 177, 193
Laura (Col) 171	Cordelia S 178	Sarah A 55
Laura E 167	Elexiue 308	Sarah C 125
Laura F (Col) 130	Eliza (Col) 143	Sarah E 92
Lea 167	Elizabeth 126	Sarah G (Col) 133
Liney A 229	Elizabeth S . . 118, 183	Susan A K (Col) . . 186
Manie J 39	Ella B (Col) 94	Virginia (Col) 223
Margaret S 197	Ella E 31	Virginia F 235
Mary 317	Ellen T 106	Willianna (Col) 202, 341
Mary (Col) 66	Emma 205	Willianna M 225
Mary A 144, 212	Emma Kate (Col) . . 286	Yula B 118
Mary Ann (Col) . . 289	Esther F 45	Kelly
Mary C 347	Georgie A 60	Ann Elizabeth J . . . 233
Mary E 155, 172	Hadda 74	Annie W 78
Mary Ellen 133	Harriet 74	Catharine 208
Mary H (Col) 43	Henrietta W 201	Crissie E 311
Mary Ida 251	Herriet T 144	Critty Ann 332
Mary J . . . 315, 322	Hester (Col) . . 94, 275	Elizabeth 80, 231, 322
Mary P 266, 333	Indiana S 129	Elizabeth A 327
Mary S 287	Isabella 336	Elizabeth Susan . . . 287

Bride Index

Emeline 282
Emily S 314
Juliea 187
Kezíah A 233
Manie 234
Martha (Col) 114
Mary C 180
Mary E 250
Mary Jane 39
Mary L 314
Matilda F 132
Rebecca C 113
Sarah P 39
Sudie S 259
Susan 127
Susan C 188
Tabitha 139
Kelso
  Margaret Ann 132
Kerr
  Maggie (Col) 49
  Maria Elizabeth (Col)364
  Rachel (Col) 124
  Sally (Col) 106
Kerry
  Harriet J 146
Kidd
  Sally A 223
Killman
  Ann E 41
  Anne J 167
  Arinthia 111
  Bettie 52
  Betty 226
  Comfort 190
  Daisey C 337
  Dulany A 281
  Elizabeth A 198
  Ella K 307
  Emeline 263
  Emma 134
  Eveline 162
  Indiana Susan 128
  Isabella 40
  Jane 124
  Jenetta 303
  Kate L 103
  Laura E 294
  Lelia E 187
  Lenora A 273
  Lew E 189
  Maggie 170, 299
  Martha A 334

  Mary 52
  Mary E 226, 268
  Mary W 104
  Melissa 32
  Miranda T 57
  Sally A 272
  Susan . . 57, 163, 225
  Tabitha 255
  Tabitha S 236
Kimmerle
  Eva 161
  Margie 233
King
  Emma (Col) 333
  Flora A 192
Knight
  Charlotte 321
  Elizabeth 322
  Genie F 324
  Mary E 196
  Mary J 149
Knock
  Susan 194
Knocke
  Mary (Col) 326
Kollock
  Ellen 333
Laird
  Nellie 325
  Phoebe 298
Lambden
  Atty (Col) 151
  Nannie 351
Landing
  Adaline 152
  Elishea Ann 220
  Elizabeth 252
  Elsie 182
  Maggie H 271
  Mary 322
  Sallie 65
  Sarah A 252
Lane
  Virga A 178
Lang
  Critty 195
  Fanny P 217
  Grace (Col) 170
  Laura 243
  Mollie S 136
  Olevis (Col) 111
  Sally 320
  Tabitha A 329

Langedale
  Indianna (Col) 159
Lankford
  Alice M 181
  Annie E 84
  Arinthia J 27, 294
  Emily S 314
  Laura E 230
  Lulie 309
  Manie K 84
  Vernetta S 322
Lawrence
  Annie L 198
  Catharine 335
  Catharine S 68
  Hennie A 167
  Margaret F 199
Laws
  Amanda (Col) 248
  Annie F J A (Col) . 47
  Eliza (Col) 249
  Elizabeth (FN) . . . 149
  Ella (Col) 114
  Hester (Col) 78
  Martha (Col) 42
  Mary (Col)218, 237, 299
  Mary Elizabeth . . . 185
  Mary Jane 367
  Racilia (Col) 153
  Sally (Col) 114
  Sarah (Col) . . 112, 156
  Virginia (Col) 244
Lawson
  Lucy E 293
  Rebecca E 95
Leary
  Lizzie (Col) 146
Leatherburry
  Amie C 45
Leatherbury
  Edith M 298
  Martha A 361
  Mary (Col) 150
  Nicholeua L 310
  Virginia A (Col) . . 137
LeCato
  Anna (Col) 286
  Bettie (Col) 302
  Emma S 302
  Esther 50
  Eva R 342
  Ida 135
  Jemina (Col) 204

394 Marriage Records of Accomack County, VA, 1854-1895

Martha (Col) 338
Mary (Col) 289
Mary F 126
Mary M 290
Nannie (Col) 105
Patience P 213
Sadie A 68
Sarah (Col) 33
Virginia Ann 336
Lewis
   Alberta 148
   Alexine D 261
   Amanda 221, 326
   Amanda W 155
   Amelia A 242
   Amy 228
   Ann (Col) 63
   Anna 72, 265
   Anna A 86
   Annie J 329
   Annie W 139
   Ara 184
   Arinthia A 158
   Arinthia J 156
   Arinthia S 181
   Arrena J 266
   Belle R 333
   Bettie S 127
   Bettie W 316
   Caroline 37
   Caroline M 236
   Carrie L 70
   Catharine 172
   Caty F 201
   Celia Ann (Col) . . . 169
   Charlotte 277
   Charlotte A 206
   Cora E 205
   Cordie A 90
   Cornelia D 139
   Cynthia A 82
   Eliza . . . 108, 213, 276
   Eliza Ellen 60
   Elizabeth
   . 98, 235, 284, 308, 336
   Elizabeth A 222
   Ella Lee 234
   Ella M 208
   Ella N 174
   Ellen H 222
   Elmener 329
   Emily 195
   Emma 265
   Emma C 205
   Eveline 168
   Georgianna 41
   Georgianna (Col) . . 214
   Grace Lee (Col) . . 278
   Hannah (Col) 276
   Harriet (Col) 136
   Henrietta 223
   Hester 208
   Hester Jane 213
   Indianna 207
   Isabella S 340
   Jane 189
   Janie 272
   Jennie 257
   Julia A 172
   Kate L 347
   Laura V 179
   Lelia L 98, 162
   Lillian M 336
   Lydia A 62
   Maggie A 66
   Mamie Emily . . . 293
   Marcella A 189
   Margaret . . . 129, 252
   Margaret A 320
   Margaret C 356
   Margaret Cath . . . 151
   Margaret R 205
   Mariah R 248
   Martha 298
   Martha J 182
   Mary 207, 328
   Mary (Col) 93
   Mary A 67, 72, 180, 210
   Mary E 329
   Mary E (Col) 335
   Mary Emily 209
   Mary Hester 38
   Mary J O 86
   Mary Jane . . . 40, 302
   Mary O 114, 123
   Mary S 197, 239
   Mary W 156, 234
   Melissa W 80
   Melvina 80
   Pamelia Mary . . . 226
   Polly 293
   Rebecca A 208
   Rose 298
   Sadie D 40
   Sallie P 134
   Sallie R 299
Sally 104, 148
Sarah . . 208, 306, 328
Sarah A 90, 134
Sarah Ann 311
Sarah E 241
Sarah J 40
Sudie M 97
Susan 212, 301
Susan R 358
Tabitha 263
Trany M 54
Ursula T 173
Virginia 213, 219
Lilliston
   Anna M 254
   Catharine T 86
   Catharine W 56
   Charlotte 83
   Ellen T 43
   Emma L 141
   Jane 244
   Juliett 145
   Laura 126
   Laura F 308
   M Virginia 167
   Margaret A 46
   Mary 98
   Mary (Col) 106
   Mary L 263
   Olivia W 124
   Sadie 132
   Susan 299
   Susan A 139
   Theresa C 153
   Troy Brown 301
Ling
   Elizabeth 182
   Emma L 330
   Sallie A 235
   Virga 98
Lingo
   Catharine 226
   Margaret 208
   Margaret E 256
   Mary 278
Linton
   Arrella 132
   Brunitta 223
   Harriet 358
   Isabella 144
   Jane 221
   Louisa J 367
   Maggie 304

Bride Index

Mary A 242
Mary Ann 245
Mary C 102
Mary E 191
Rachel 211
Rachel Ann 101
Sallie 301
Sarah 242
Triphemia A 144
Littleton
  Lisman 237
  Marcelleus 173
  Margaret A 133
  Mary T 338
  Vernetta S 266
Lloyd
  Mary E 358
Loan
  Caroline C 54
Lofland
  Amelia 59
  Arinthia Ann (Col) . 338
  Jane (Col) 364
  Margaret L C 336
  Mary E 80
Logan
  Charlotte (Col) . . . 220
  Elizabeth (Col) . . . 98
  Jane (Col) 99
  Maria (Col) 301
  Mary (Col) 99
  Mary Ann (Col)103, 134
  Sarah 227
  Susan L 147
Lone
  Laney 346
Long
  Alicia C 203
  Henrietta (Col) . . . 65
  Mary Grace 253
Lord
  Elizabeth 130
Louden
  Elizabeth 151
Loun
  Elizabeth C 86
Lucas
  Cath 31
  Clara 78
  Clara W 230
  Sally A 248
  Virginia A 203
Lungren

Sarah J 142
Lunn
  Susan 360
Lurton
  Ann 130
  Ann (Col) 138
  Annie (FN) 121
  Elizabeth 130
Lyon
  Hester (Col) 282
Maddox
  Lavinia Frances . . . 110
Major
  Ann (FN) 223
  Annie (Col) 297
  Arinthia (Col) 167
  Betsy Ann (Col) . . 53
  Camilla 121
  Charlotte (Col) . . . 229
  Elizabeth (Col) 216, 350
  Gaddie (Col) 273
  Lottie (Col) 37
  Lucretia 337
  Margaret (FN) . . . 256
  Mary (Col) 177
  Mary S (Col) 269
  Mary Susan (Col) . 161
  Nellie 357
  Rosena (Col) 130
Mallett
  Mary 185
  Nancy 329
Manuel
  Margaret 307
  Rose (Col) 150
Mapp
  Annie L 178
  Annie W 335
  Belle S 233
  Bettie L 235
  Bettie V 118
  Caddie S 253
  Emily F (Col) 325
  Emma S 234
  Fannie (Col) 202
  Florence (Col) . . . 265
  Hannah (Col) 272
  Hester A 59
  Indie A 289
  Jane (Col) 335
  Kate (Col) 235
  Kate R 69
  Laura 313

Leah Ann 233
Louisa (Col) 74
Madeline (Col) . . . 306
Maggie A 172
Maggie C 348
Manie C 118
Marietta M 68
Mary (Col) 33, 238, 306
Mary S 218
Melissa (Col) 187
Nola S 362
Rachel (Col) 182
Sadie A 265
Salony S 277
Sarah (Col) 27
Sudie (Col) 177
Susan 30
Virginia C 290
Mariner
  Esther 240
  Jennie 331
  Oceasina 296
Marsh
  Dora C 128
  Harriet E 176
  Triphema A 35
  Triphenia A 131
Marshall
  Alice 28
  Amanda 208
  Amanda L 309
  Amy (Col) 220
  Ann 221
  Arcnea 200
  Arinthia 175
  Arinthia J 301
  Caroline 333
  Caroline (Col) 352
  Cora T 78
  Danverse Jane 148
  Elizabeth 29, 220, 316
  Ellen 213, 301
  Emily F 295
  Esther (Col) 55
  Esther F 309
  Euphemia C 299
  Eusina 282
  Florence 206
  Georgie A 170
  Harriet (Col) 103
  Harriet E 119
  Hattie M 143
  Ida J 298

Jane (Col) 99
Jennie Ellen 209
Josephine 232
Julia A 319
Leah (Col) 319
Lizzie B (Col) 252
Mahala Jane 213
Margaret E 129
Margaret S (Col) .. 135
Maria (Col) 273
Martha 358
Mary 251
Mary A 68
Mary E 211
Mary Jane (Col) .. 359
Matilda J 219
Melissa D 95
Millie (Col) 318
Missouri D 223
Narcissa 222
Nellie 33
Oliva E 113
Polly 309
Rachel 309
Rachel Ann 209
Sallie W 293
Sarah 297
Sarah (Col) 243
Sarah A 221
Sarah Ann (Col) .. 272
Sarah J 332
Sarah W 325
Susan 157, 282
Susan A 183
Virginia 333
Zenie C 61
Marston
  Margaret W 313
Martin
  Alberta (Col) 315
  Alice L 266
  Amanda S 206
  Annie 135
  Charlotte (Col) ... 306
  Drusilla 244
  Edna B 52
  Elizabeth 221
  Ellen (Col) 300
  Emma S 319
  Emma T 143
  Euphemia 164
  Fannie (FN) 291
  Florence 149

Frances (Col) 305
Henrietta 127
Jinnie (Col) 160
Juliet (FN) 266
Laura 219
Lelia A 213
M Beach 338
Maggie A 265
Mary A 77
Mary E 193
Mary S 52
Mary S (Col) 350
Mary Susan (FN) .. 48
Olivia A 149
Phoebe (FN) 216
Rose Lee 361
Sarah 100
Susan (Col) 193
Tabitha 296
Virginia W 273
Marvel
  Libby B 358
Mason
  Adaline 60
  Alice C 298
  Amanda Louise ... 82
  Amelia J 310
  Ann Eliza 50
  Anna (Col) 226
  Annie (Col) 312
  Annie B 345
  Arinthia 88
  Bernetta 260
  Bettie A 299
  Bettie M 79
  Caroline 95, 325
  Catharine 109
  Charlotte A 34
  Cordie F 281
  Elizabeth
  ... 210, 213, 234, 251
  Elizabeth (Col) ... 112
  Elizabeth H 181
  Elizabeth P 310
  Ella (Col) 116
  Emily Susan 179
  Eveline T 133
  Florence E (Col) .. 225
  Hulda 331
  Ida A 351
  Jane (Col) 125
  Julia 237
  Kitty (Col) 187

Laura 298
Lelia L 78
Lena J 260
Lizzie (Col) 116
Lizzie E 240
Maggie N 77
Malinda C 365
Margaret 230, 268, 368
Margaret Ann 172
Margaret J 315
Marharet J 126
Marie A 277
Mary 41, 314
Mary (Col) 76
Mary Ann .. 109, 115
Mary C 300
Mary E 174
Mary J 41
Mollie R 344
Nancy 234
Olivia 310
Polly 152
Rachel 368
Sabra (Col) 56
Sadie M 177
Sallie L 350
Sally 151, 190
Sally (Col) 291
Sally L 92
Sarah (Col) 125
Sarah A 342
Sarah C 205
Susan 364
Susan (Col) 313
Susan A 339
Susan A L 354
Susan E 336
Susan J 196
Susan M 110
Tabitha S 123
Vienna 150, 283
Virginia 295
Virginia L 87
Virginia T 230
Massey
  Carrie C 97
  M L 297
  Mary Elizabeth ... 135
  Nonie C 329
  Sarah Emma 258
Matthews
  Adah (Col) 77
  Anna Maria 267

Bride Index

Annie 355	McCready	Hester (Col) 137
Annie (Col) 290	Elizabeth 124	Hester A 158
Betsy 139	Maria 330	Hetty 38
Blanche 251	Oshia A 242	Ida L 53
Caroline 212	Vianna 165	Indiana 67
Caroline (Col) 32	McGee	Indie 237
Caroline W 94	Rachel E 215	Joice M 52
Charlotte Emory . . 75	McLane	Julia 30
Clara A 263	Mary S 118	Julia A 76, 270, 302, 362
Clara E 358	McMath	Juliana 344
Comfort A (Col) . . 279	Amelia Emma 91	Kate V 273
Dora (Col) 218	Rebecca L 66	Laura 46
Elizabeth A 120	Willie A 91	Laura T 208
Ellen (Col) 314	Mears	Leah A (Col) 146
Emma W 215	Adaline 313	Louisa 239
Euphemia Ann . . . 124	Adaline F 149	Lula A 262
Fannie (black) 306	Adeline (Col) 191	Maggie 317
Georgianna (Col) . . 321	Alberta (Col) 229	Maggie (Col) 313
Harriet (Col) 174	Angeline (FN) 44	Maggie A 315
Henrietta (Col) . . . 65	Ann 238	Maggie B 345
Ida 184	Anna 214	Maggie E 50
Ida J 125	Annie L 68	Maggie P 292
Isorah 41	Annie L (Col) 160	Maggie S . . . 113, 198
Jane 41	Arinthia 264	Manie E 71
Janie T 42	Arinthia J . . . 314, 339	Margaret
Maggie E 39	Arinthia S 339	. . . . 50, 301, 339, 360
Maggie S 367	Arinthia T 219	Margaret Ann 206
Manie E 337	Belle Sarah (Col) . . 36	Margaret E 360
Margaret 266	Bettie B 219	Margaret L (Col) . . 355
Margaret S 239	Bettie S 143	Margaret T 154
Martha 109	Catharine 70	Maria (FN) 202
Martha W 89	Catharine A 81	Mary 272
Mary 108	Catharine J 344	Mary (Col) 218
Mary (Col) 51	Catherine E 50	Mary A
Mary A (Col) 202	Caty 38	. . . 231, 256, 316, 338
Mary E 171, 327	Charlotte . . . 158, 171	Mary B 177
Mary E (Col) . 94, 240	Cora J 276, 339	Mary C 182
Mary G 350	Courithea S 118	Mary E 221, 314
Mary J 180	Drucilla 50, 176	Mary Ellen 159
Mary W 323	Drusilla 69	Mary J W 325
Missouri E 70	Eliza S 77	Mary S 118, 232
Ocia (Col) 161	Elizabeth 197, 213, 319	Mary Susan 297
Othelia (Col) 169	Elizabeth Sarah . . . 235	Mattie 160
Rebecca (Col) 356	Ella 194	Mildred Lee 143
Rebecca F (Col) . . 142	Emma 229, 237	Missouri 158
Sallie J 283	Emma Cora 75	Missouri Fannie . . 287
Sally 241	Emma Laura . 145, 197	Missouri G 350
Sally A 149	Fannie A 191	Mollie 41
Sarah 95, 113	Florence 305	Mollie E . . . 310, 323
Sarah (Col) 169	Geneva F 254	Nancy 365
Sarah A 112	Gennet 365	Nettie 343
Susan (Col) 240	Georgie M 339	Nettie Hiden 357
Susan M 341	Harriet 181	Phillis (Col) 234

Rathalia A 140
Sally 165
Salony S 277
Sarah A 31, 278
Sarah E 351
Sarah J 227, 331
Sarah Jane 87
Sophronia 217
Susan 63
Susan (Col) . 204, 367
Susan F 234
Susan R 341
Tabitha A 265
Vandalia E 29
Vernetta 233
Virginia S 270
Virginia Susan ... 225
Willie A 221
Meelham
  Marie Ann 300
  Mary A 148
Melson
  Catharine 239
  Comfort 206
  Eliza Ann 344
  Ellen F 211
  Hester Ann 242
  Jeralean F 210
  Julia J 208
  Maggie 294
  Margaret A 282
  Mary H 80
  Mary Susan 197
  Medora S 354
  Nancy 36
  Sallie E 204
  Sarah 104
  Scarborough 53
  Sudie E 211
  Susan A 305
Melvin
  Ann S 180
  Elizabeth 108
  Georgianna (Col) .. 121
  Josephine 212
  Lizzie A 171
  Lizzie J 318
  Mary 109, 328
  Nancy 306
  Sally Ann 317
  Sarah E 93
  Trany M 327
  Venice 139

Merrill
  Annie Elizabeth ... 220
  Hetty (Col) 117
  Martha (Col) 272
  Olivia Jane 92
Merritt
  Elizabeth 357
  Jennie E 61
  Maggie E 185
  Sarah Bell 62
  Sarah E 315
Metcalf
  Anna 154
Middleton
  Belle 283
  Bettie J 253
  Elizabeth C 188
  Maria 260
  Martha 169
  Nancy R 190
  Susan F 368
  Virginia J 190
Milbourn
  Adaline (Col) 241
  Annie (Col) 256
  Delilah (Col) 159
  Harriet (Col) 215
Miles
  Annie 319
  Dolly 209
  Drucilla H 71
  Georgianna 224
  Georgianna (Col) .. 74
  Jane 83
  Lizzie G 70
  Manie E 347
  Manie M 280
  Mary 189
  Mary (Col) 223
  Mary A 189
  Mary E 281
  Milca (Col) 153
  Milkey (Col) 291
  Missouri 97
  Olivia 73
  Pamalia 220
  Rennie 211
  Sallie 325
  Sally M 305
  Sarah A 132
  Susan 220
  Virginia 209
Miller

Jane 318
Louisa (Col) 214
Mary (Col) 214
Nannie G 154
Rachel 268
Rachel A 63
Sarah 177
Milliner
  Annie M 63
  Arivenia E 69
  Emeline Edna ... 60
  Evelina S 172
  Henriette P 139
  Mollie H 310
  Nannie 225
  Nannie J 201
  Priscilla May 279
  Sarah 27
  Sarah A 97
  Susan 266
  Tabitha 182
  Virginia D 157
Mills
  Eliza (Col) 66
  Harriet (Col) 158
  Sarah (Col) 268
  Sarah W 264
Mister
  Amelia T 271
  Elizabeth 35
  Emily J 194
  Indianna A 356
  Jane 131
  Judia A 147
  Lizzie 35
  Maggie E ... 248, 358
  Malissa 218
Mitchell
  Clara S 33
  Martha B 267
Moore
  Agnes (Col) 334
  Alabama 179
  Alise E 330
  Candasi (Col) ... 362
  Cath Jane 253
  Catharine 83
  Caty E 302
  Elizabeth 197
  Elizabeth S 123
  Eva K 275
  Hester (Col) 49
  Lillian O 302

Bride Index

Loretta (Col) 285
Lucy (Col) 99
Maggie (Col) . . . 361
Martha 259
Nelly (Col) 352
Rachel A 102
Sadie E 219
Sallie 239
Sarah T 186
Susan 162
Susan A 367
Tabitha 276
Virginia 305

Morehead
  Mary 368

Morgan
  Annie F B P 232

Morris
  Ailsy (FN) 347
  Harriet 251
  Margaret (FN) . . . 347

Mumford
  Eusina 282
  Hattie 74
  Mary E 54

Munger
  Dolly 306
  Euphemy 274
  Mary Ann 54
  Rosetta 138

Murphy
  Eliza 130

Myers
  Agnes 102

Nedab
  Elizabeth 117
  Elizabeth (Col) . . . 349
  Hester C (Col) . . . 155
  Susan Ann (FN) . . 47
  Venice (Col) 258

Neely
  Leah (Col) 263

Nelson
  Augusta 205
  Bettie A 151
  Clara L 162
  Edith M 209
  Emeline 324
  Emma C 166
  Harriet 265
  Kate 221
  Leah Ann 203
  Margaret 69

Mary 167
Mary E 273
Rebecca S 352
Salley 227
Virginia 282

Nettles
  Frances (Col) 33

Nicholson
  Henrietta S 207

Nock
  Adah (FN) 130
  Alice 116
  Ann (Col) 314
  Ann W 333
  Annie W 246
  Arena (Col) . 305, 345
  Arinthia 153
  Arinthia (Col) 65
  Bertie B 130
  Bettie F 85
  Charlotte 152
  Cordelia 318
  Eliza (Col) 174
  Elizabeth W . 169, 350
  Ella F 275
  Ellen (Col) . . . 33, 170
  Ellen M 339
  Ellen T 105
  Emma (Col) 159
  Fannie W 269
  Ibby (Col) 53
  Ida 228
  Julia E 236
  Lizzie (Col) 248
  Lizzie W 46
  Maggie S 110
  Margaret C 139
  Margaret L 198
  Maria (Col) 43
  Maria L 96
  Mary (Col) 48, 284, 357
  Mary Ann 323
  Mary E . 85, 107, 287
  Mary F 170
  Mary R 189
  Mary T 108
  Polly (Col) 77
  Rachel (Col) 193
  Rachel Ann (Col) . . 136
  Rose (Col) 165
  Sallie A 57
  Sally C 196
  Sarah 211

Sarah (Col)
  . . . 188, 225, 262, 359
Susan (Col) 356
Virginia 322
Virginia (Col) 120, 188
Virginia M 108
Wessie E 127

Northam
  Airy (Col) 66
  Anna (Col) 252
  Arinthia 156
  Arinthia J 207
  Blanche A 366
  Clara F 45
  Elizabeth
  . . . . 28, 251, 356, 366
  Emma 188
  Emma (Col) 343
  Emma J 147
  Henrietta 254
  Hester (Col) . . 43, 282
  Jane 107
  Leah (Col) 111
  Lee 277
  Lena J 128
  Maggie S 218
  Maggie V (Col) . . . 99
  Margaret A 78
  Mary (Col) . . 136, 203
  Mary A 152, 268
  Mary E 157
  Mary E (Col) 112
  Nancy 299
  Polly 38, 248
  Polly C 281
  Rhoda (Col) 250
  Sally A 152, 183
  Sally C 163
  Sarah (Col) 299
  Sarah W 186
  Susan 85, 166
  Willianna 344

Nottingham
  Harriet Susan 27
  Lucretia N 365
  Macaria J 303
  Margaret F 217
  Mary M 191
  Willie E 68

Ocher
  Leah (FN) 65

Oldham
  Mary E 66

Olive
  Lucretia 166
Oliver
  Virginia Elizabeth . 143
Onions
  Virginia S 156
Onley
  Dame A 72
  Elizabeth (Col) . . . 156
  Grace (Col) 360
  Jane (Col) 230
  Lidai H 74
  Lovey 112
  Mary J 242
  Nannie W 299
  Sinah 116
Otwell
  Annie F 132
Outten
  Jane (Col) 90
  Margaret (Col) . . . 245
  Mary (FN) 334
  Mary Susan (FN) . . 286
  Sophia (Col) 92
Owens
  Gretrude 46
Palmer
  Elizabeth B 355
Parker
  Alicia (Col) 306
  Ann M 361
  Annie M 352
  Annie Wharton . . . 98
  Bessie Sarah 304
  Bettie (Col) 279
  Bettie J 68
  Candice (Col) 28
  Caroline 129
  Caroline S (Col) . . 173
  Charity (Col) 190
  Cora (Col) 264
  Cornelia (Col) 113
  Cornelia Page 253
  Cynthiana 39
  Effie 264
  Elizabeth 237
  Elizabeth (Col) . . . 230
  Elizabeth P 294
  Ella (Col) 186
  Ellen P 186
  Emma (Col) 191
  Esther 332
  Frances 97

Gabriella (Col) . . . 364
Harriet A 76
Hester 52
Ida 127
Jane 166
Jane (Col) 352
Katie N 200
Lenn (Col) 155
Lula F 198
Margaret
  . . . 142, 155, 335, 336
Margaret A E 338
Margaret H 337
Margaret Va (Col) . 34
Martha (Col) 36
Mary 243
Mary Alice 201
Mary Ann 94
Mary C 310
Mary E 346
Mary H 258
Mary J (Col) 42
Mary S (Col) 244
Mary Susan (Col) . 153
Mollie (Col) 171
Nancy 211
Neville (Col) 45
Patience (Col) . 45, 145
Patience Elenora (Col)82
Peggie E 97
Rosa E 311
Ruth 258
Sabra Jane (Col) . . 87
Sarah (Col) 43
Sarah A 225
Sarah Ann 88
Sarah S 107
Sudes C 140
Susan 128, 275
Susan Ann (Col) . . 113
Susan P 257
Susan W 105
Tiney (Col) 297
Victoria (Col) 224
Viola S 178
Zipporah (Col) . . . 286
Parkes
  Alitia 47
  Amanda 271
  Amy (Col) 200
  Arinthia J 39
  Betsy Ann 83
  Bettie 115, 259

Burnetta J 199
Caroline H 315
Clara F 204
Cora D 73
Cynthia 188
Danice R 57
Edna 194
Elenor 134
Eliza J 271
Elizabeth 57, 106, 260
Elizabeth S 189
Ellen (Col) 357
Emma 200, 358
Emma M 224
Esther 201
Esther (Col) 352
Esther A 165
Eulalia S 227
Florence (Col) . . . 186
Gertrude F 228
Hannah (Col) 351
Hetty C 316
Ibby Jane (Col) . . . 73
Ida Susan 226
Indiana R 133
Josephine 230
Laura 199
Lizzie E 77, 140
Lula K 207
Maggie (Col) 355
Maggie B 83
Maggie S 130
Malissa 278
Marceline C 238
Margaret 325
Margaret S 81
Martha 188
Mary 97, 115, 200, 270
Mary (Col) 120
Mary A 226
Mary C 288
Mary E 97, 348
Mary S (Col) 49
Mary T 254
Mary Virginia 92
Nancy 38
Olivia 101
Olivia S 40
Polly A 271
Rosey (Col) 156
Rosy (Col) 190
Sadie D 291
Sallie J 115

Bride Index 401

Sally J 214
Sarah 102
Sarah Jane 239
Susan 208, 349
Tabitha J 151
Virginia S 201
Zipporah 259
Parramore
   Clara (Col) 36
   Cordie (Col) 218
   Ella (Col) 232
   Hannah (black) . . . 289
   Lucy (Col) 96
   Margaret (Col) . . . 34
   Martha (Col) 307
   Mary (Col) 187
   Rosie (Col) 267
   Sallie Seymour . . . 141
   Sally (Col) 42
   Sophia 129
   Tabitha (Col) 288
Pate
   Susan S 133
Patterson
   Ama Lee (Col) . . . 349
Paul
   Ann 112
   Cordelia 102
Payne
   Anna 168
   Laura 298
   Lillie R 165
   Mary E 295
   Nellie 156
   Nina M 156
   Susan 102
   Virginia 244
Pecos
   Mary A 44
Pennewell
   Bertie 193
Pepper
   Mary (Col) . . 106, 212
Peppet
   Drucilla 331
Perdie
   Mattie 117
Perkins
   Jane (Col) 333
   Margaret 267
   Martha 246
   Mary 297
   Sally A (Col) 364
Pettitt
   Esther (Col) 151
   Mary 53
   Mary J 231
Peyton
   Leah L 91
Phillips
   Alice (Col) 352
   Alsey 265
   Ann S 68
   Annie (Col) 256
   Catharine L (Col) . 77
   Charlotte 206
   Eley 265
   Elizabeth 280
   Elizabeth Amanda . 224
   Elizabeth H 203
   Ella (Col) 108
   Emma (Col) 99
   Emma S 255
   Florence (Col) . . . 191
   Josephine F (Col) . 146
   Kessey 348
   Laura (Col) 223
   Lavinia (Col) 287
   Llewellyn 178
   Maggie S . . . 233, 275
   Margaret E 143
   Margaret N 342
   Mary 237, 264
   Mary(Col) 140, 269, 285
   Mary E 213, 255
   Mary J (Col) 94
   Mary S 77, 312
   Mary S (Col) 47
   Pheby (FN) 224
   Phoebe 216
   Sarah 255, 352
   Susan 194
   Susan A 137
   Virginia 345
   Williana (Col) 136
   Willianna (Col) . . . 164
Phipps
   Florence 283
Piper
   Jane (FN) 220
Pitchard
   Jeanie 300
Pitts
   Alice T 281
   Annie (Col) 83
   Indiana W (Col) . . 104
Louisa 338
Mary (Col) 289
Mary Ann 291
Rosa 37
Sabra M 270
Sarah E (Col) 266
Sudie (Col) 111
Susan (black) 355
Susan (Col) 250
Susan A 236
Susan E 241
Planter
   Annie 112
   Comfort (FN) 65
   Czanna (Col) 346
   Mary A (Col) 344
   Matilda (Col) 309
Pointer
   Mary A 316
Pontman
   Betsey (FN) 287
Poole
   Ann (FN) 312
   Christie 177
   Harriet (Col) 181
   Lottie D 311
Poolman
   Betsey (FN) 287
Porter
   Airy 86
   Caroline H 356
Potter
   Sallie T 325
   Virginia Trechart . . 342
Potts
   Nannette 74
Poulson
   Alice I 304
   Amelia F 84
   Ann (Col) 161
   Annie 215
   Annie (Col) 355
   Caroline (Col) 362
   Catharine 140
   Charlotte (Col) . . . 192
   Charlotte C 317
   Clarissa (Col) 204
   Elizabeth (Col) 244, 290
   Ellen (Col) 369
   Gertie F 111
   Harriet E 197
   Indie A 166
   Julia Ann 257

Lydia (Col) 330
Maggie S (Col) ... 288
Martha W 128
Mary 343
Mary (Col) ... 93, 136
Mary Ann 293
Mary E 226
Mary Jane (Col) .. 306
Peggy 161
Permelia S 175
Rachel A 63
Rose (Col) 48
Rose Ella (Col) ... 71
Sadie (Col) 43
Sarah (Col) 363
Susan J 150
Vernulia (Col) 117
Violet (Col) 199
Virginia Lee 366
Powell
  Alicia A 150
  Anna W 254
  Cath C 45
  Edith T 276
  Eliza C 236
  Emma 169
  Evelin J 36
  Eveline 357
  Georgie E 173
  Hellen M 67
  Hester Ann 244
  Ida R 310
  Linnie S 263
  Lola 110
  Lula B 308
  Maggie L 127
  Mary A 354
  Mary E 358
  Mary S 154
  Minnie C 125
  Nancy M 175
  Sarah J 269
  Susan 334
  Triphenia 159
  Virginia 294
Prescott
  Evelyn 358
  Hester 252
  Pamelia 196
Pruitt
  Annie 131, 185
  Catharine 100
  Cora A 38

Delilah 83
Eliza J 103
Helen 262
Jane 259
Lelia 113
Lura Emma (Col) . 113
Maggie L 359
Maria 131
Martha 184
Mary 271
Mary E 102
Matilda A 95
Mattie E 323
Polly J 260
Sally 323
Winnoa 92
Purnell
  Laura M C 241
  Lovey 159
  Minie 174
Pusey
  Laura E 91
Quinby
  Elizabeth Walter .. 302
  Margaret H ... 144
Raleigh
  Dona W 308
Rally
  Emily 103
Rayfield
  Annie (Col) ... 110
  Elishua 194
  Elizabeth 246
  Elizabeth A ... 233
  Ella T 200
  Henrietta (Col) .. 56
  Kate A 58
  M Birditta 170
  Mamie T 329
  Manie V 247
  Maria 246
  Mary 367
  Mary Ann 154
  Mary E 40
  Mollie W 273
  Nancy 117
  Nannie A 253
  Sallie J 247
  Sally 77
  Sarah 112
  Sarah (Col) ... 260
  Sarah L 56
  Susan 162

Virginia S 304
Read
  Arinthia (black) ... 217
  Arinthia (Col) 217
  Catharine A 135
  Drucilla J 240
  Elizabeth 266
  Elizabeth S 144
  Ella Susan 176
  Ellen (Col) 307
  Emma (Col) 105
  Fannie 224
  Frances 155
  Jane 154
  Julia C 259
  Lizzie 310
  Lottie (Col) 46
  Lucy (Col) 247
  Lucy L 61
  Margaret 294
  Margaret (Col) .. 119
  Martha (Col) 171
  Mary 191
  Mary (Col) 214
  Mary Ann 214
  Mary Anna 274
  Mary C 294
  Minnie D 342
  Molly 353
  Nancy 185
  Peggy 341
  Rachel 315
  Rosa 131
  Sallie A 118
  Sarah (Col) 72
  Susan A 147
  Virginia (Col) ... 46
Reeder
  Minnie S 33
Revell
  Agnes (FN) 285
  Elizabeth S 330
  Ellen (Col) 216
  Mary (Col) 255
Rew
  Annie J 222
  Bettie 134
  Bettie S 300
  Bridget (Col) ... 303
  Candice 324
  Emma F 318
  Jane T 212
  Leah (Col) 203

Bride Index

Maggie A 239
Maggie C . . . 179, 336
Margaret (Col) . . . 353
Martha A 163
Mary A (Col) 37
Mary F 344
Mary H (Col) 34
Mary S 283
Milly 364
Nancy 88
Narcissa L 331
Rachel 207
Rebecca D 145
Sallie D 104
Sally M 56
Sophia (Col) 50
Susan 168, 244

Rhodes
  Hattie 235
  Mary E 86

Rhuark
  Amanda R 248

Rich
  Blanch E B 277
  Maude M 158

Richardson
  Bettie A 66
  Catharine . . . 196, 318
  Elizabeth 246
  Elizabeth Susan . . . 80
  Essie Thomas 158
  Georgie G 272
  Harriet 67
  Inda A 138
  Indianna F 352
  Jennie F (Col) 303
  Louilla (Col) 236
  Margaret I 292
  Mary A B 30
  Mary C 218

Riggs
  Lillian Lee 350
  Melinda J 320
  Susan 368

Riley
  Ada (Col) 231
  Amy (Col) 226
  Frances Ann 238
  Grace (Col) 56
  Leah Ann 345
  Margaret C 352
  Mary 268
  Mary (Col) 250

Mary E 132
Purcilla (Col) 64
Sabra (Col) 356
Sarah 81
Susan (Col) 289
Susan T 309

Risley
  Flora A 368

Ritter
  Cora N 316

Roane
  Harriet (FN) 49

Roberts
  Ann 341
  Catharine S 217
  Effie 217
  Frances (Col) . . . 343
  Indiana 366
  Isabella (Col) 187
  Juliet S . . . 145, 335
  Lanetta 218
  Leah (Col) 215
  Maggie E 244
  Margaret C 244
  Marianna 235
  Mary (Col) 222
  Mary (FN) 103
  Mary Susan 179
  Missouri Ellen (Col) 353
  Sally 209
  Sally (Col) 333
  Sarah A (Col) 134
  Sue F 143
  Susan A 280
  Victoria C 217
  Virga E 46
  Willie G 311

Robins
  Amanda J 361
  Maggie O 31
  Susan 171
  Vectoria F 329
  Virginia A 282
  Virginia S 343

Roe
  Idia J (Col) 339

Rogers
  Addie M 42
  Fannie (Col) 139
  Fannie L 69
  Ida (Col) 350
  Josephine (Col) . . . 177
  Julia (Col) 355

Margaret (Col) . . . 348
Margaret S 236
Mary E (Col) 250
Missouri (Col) . . . 164
Sarah 351
Sarah W 192
Susan (Col) 358

Rosell
  Cordie (Col) 216
  Tinnie E S (Col) . . 284

Ross
  C Annie 37
  Emily Jane 92
  Leah (Col) 129
  Maggie 72
  Malvina 78
  Margaret A 342
  Sarah 328
  Sarah A 89
  Susan 196

Rossey
  Mary C 46

Rowins
  Zenie C 61

Rowley
  Sally 323
  Sarah 320
  Tabitha (Col) 278
  Virginia A 229

Russell
  Alice 84, 307
  Annie E 135
  Arinthia S 134
  Campsey D 278
  Clara 231
  Elenor D 114
  Elizabeth 88, 180, 328
  Elizabeth C 38
  Emma C 298
  Ester 239
  Euphamia 330
  Geneva J 269
  Harriet A 175
  Ida M 147
  Janie 266
  Josephine 310
  Julia 327
  Leah Ann 174
  Lillie 168
  Maggie E 321
  Maggie S 298
  Margaret 260
  Mary A 179

Mary Ann 354
Mary E* 299
Olivia 251
Rebecca 180
Ruthy 307
Sarah A 166
Susan 131
Willie 164
Salisbury
  Mary H 271
  Sally C 294
Sample
  Ann (Col) 121
  Anna L (Col) 214
  Annie (Col) . 285, 298
  Annie H (Col) 352
  Cecillia (Col) 346
  Comeliac (Col) ... 42
  Cornelia (Col) 193
  Edie (Col) 352
  Eliza (Col) .. 165, 312
  Elizabeth (Col)
  .... 43, 94, 351
  Elizabeth (FN) ... 285
  Emma (Col) 304
  Fanny (Col) 274
  Hester (Col) 202
  Inez (Col) 365
  Jane (Col) 48
  Josephine (Col) ... 92
  Kessie (Col) 48
  Kitty (Col) 339
  Liney (FN) 177
  Lottie (Col) 281
  Louisa (Col) 336
  Maggie (Col) 130, 183
  Margaret (Col) ... 122
  Mary (Col) .. 118, 216
  Mary (FN) 90
  Mary E (Col) ... 364
  Rachel 69
  Rachel (FN) 251
  Rosy (Col) 143
  Sarah (Col) 216
  Sarah (FN) 129
  Susan (Col) .. 33, 257
Satchell
  Betty 189
  Eve (Col) 192
  Lucretia 50
  Maggie 71
  Manie 368
  Margaret 239

Margaret E (Col) .. 104
Mary E 308
Nancy (Col) 47
Sarah (Col) 300
Saunders
  Maria 232
Savage
  Addie (Col) 43
  Alice 137
  Annie (Col) . 222, 250
  Arinthia (Col) . 46, 337
  Bettie (Col) 119
  Bettie U 191
  Burley (Col) 142
  Catherine 30
  Charlotte 313
  Cordie (Col) 126
  Elexine (Col) 256
  Eliza (Col) 122
  Elizabeth 100
  Elizabeth (Col) ... 194
  Elizabeth A 120
  Ellen (Col) 266
  Emma (Col) 91
  Emma J 196
  Emma S 341
  Fannie 299
  Fannie H (Col) ... 292
  Florence (Col) ... 114
  Hannah (Col) 357
  Harriet D (Col) ... 268
  Hester A 348
  Ida (Col) 95
  Jane 54
  Jannie 106
  Julia 85
  Laura 64
  Lena V 267
  Letitea (Col) 340
  Letty (Col) 367
  Levania F 178
  Lizzie (Col) 117
  Louisa 103
  Lucy (Col) 245
  Lucy A 50
  Maggie C 52
  Maggie L 95
  Maggie T 144
  Manie W 70
  Margaret 95, 289, 314
  Margaret A 266
  Margaret S ... 50, 237
  Margaret S (Col) .. 291

Margaret Susan ... 198
Margie (Col) 37
Martha (Col) 76
Mary 179
Mary (Col) 47, 129, 363
Mary A 163
Mary A (Col) 106
Mary E 27, 305
Mary E (Col) 267
Mary J 161
Mary M 248
Mary S 88
Mary Susan 348
Morion E 267
Nannie (Col) 139
Otelia E 81
Peggy (Col) 273
Rose Ann (Col) ... 292
Sabra 155
Sallie (Col) 275
Sally (Col) 155
Sarah (Col) .. 188, 366
Willianna A 81
Scarborough
  Ella (Col) 187
  Emeline (FN) ... 364
  Georgianna 285
  Jane (Col) 81
  Jane (FN) 272
  Kate M 182
  Laura E (Col) 216
  Maggie (Col) 146
  Manie (Col) 73
  Margaret (Col) ... 91
  Mary A 186
  Mary Ann (FN) ... 365
  Sarah 178
  Susan 28
Schellinger
  Mary A 337
Schley
  Martha J 57
Scott
  Anna 171
  Anna S 356
  Arinthia J 27
  Azie S 254
  Bettie T 307
  Demeriah 150
  Eliza (Col) 146
  Eliza F C 145
  Elizabeth 28, 115
  Elizabeth H 181

Elizabeth M 260
Ella N 63, 201
Ellen 175
Emma S 231
Harriet E 83
Henrietta 36
Henrietta E 227
Laura 201
Lavinia 199
Lillie C 197
Maggie P 277
Malinda 249
Marion J 113
Mary 30, 49
Mary Anna 154
Miranda W 91
Olivia B 197
Polly B 251
Rebecca E 212
Sallie L 144
Sally 65
Sarah W 98
Tabitha S 199
Willie A 302
Selby
　Annie E 112
　Caroline (Col) 95
　Gertrude (Col) ... 120
　Harriet A (Col) ... 357
　Hester (Col) 185
　Margaret (Col) ... 228
　Martha 334
　Mary A P 230
　Mary C (Col) 217
　Nicse (Col) 345
Seymour
　Amanda (Col) 186
　Arinthia (Col) 345
　Eliza (Col) 225
　Ida (Col) 186
　Margaret (Col) ... 124
　Mary 134
　Mary (Col) 104
　Sarah Elizabeth ... 119
　Sarah Frances (Col) 191
Shaffer
　Elizabeth 355
Sharpley
　Charlotte 283
　Cordelia J 316
　Drucilla J ... 205, 359
　Elizabeth 353
　Euphamia 60

Jane Caroline 109
Maggie A 66
Maria C 240, 331
Mary 168
Mary A ... 54, 80, 84
Mary Ann .. 109, 214
Mary E 296
Nancy 60, 331
Nancy C 329
Phebe 184
Tabitha 245, 276
Zipporah 275
Shaw
　Mary (Col) 147
Shay
　Nancy 221
Shea
　Cordie Elizabeth .. 356
Shears
　Elizabeth A 100
Shelly
　Nancy Amelia 180
　Sarah Elizabeth ... 310
Shepherd
　Elizabeth (FN) ... 159
　Lee 231
　Mary (Col) 249
　Sallie 91
Sherwood
　Eve (Col) 87
Shield
　Bertha M 72
　Cardilia E (Col) ... 121
　Elizabeth 198
　Emma L 196
　Henny (Col) 249
　Josephine H 94
　Maggie A 158
　Mary (Col) 311
　Mary E . 34, 173, 341
　Minnie G (Col) ... 341
　Rachel S 277
　Rosa (Col) 338
　Silvary (Col) 160
　Virginia 148
Shores
　Amelia J 201
　Jennie 220
Short
　Mary E (Col) 30
Showard
　Caroline 294
　Catharine 82

Georgie A 234
Hester 65
Lizzie Ann 36
Margaret 240
Mary 301
Mary A 250
Mary E 284
Shrieves
　Adaline 225
　Ann Eliza 53
　Annie 163
　Annie B 350
　Annie N 215
　Bernettie S 208
　Cassandra 206
　Clara 231
　Cornelia 173
　Cynthiana 188
　Elizabeth A 207
　Ellen E 227
　Emma 71
　Eva A 208
　Eva S 189
　Jennie 127
　Julia A 219
　Laura H 52
　Lovey H 248
　Maggie 58
　Maggie C 189
　Margaret 248
　Mary 52, 72, 171
　Mary A 259, 358
　Mary F 35
　Mary J W 248
　Mary T 72
　Otelia S 95
　Rachel S 52
　Sallie M 239
　Sallie S 230
　Sally 225, 369
　Sarah Ann 199
　Sarah B 117
　Soulie E 260
　Sudie E 211
　Susan 208
　Susan L 92
　Virginia E 284
Sicker
　Emma 236
Silverthorn
　Carrie L 337
　Delila 284
　Margaret A 299

Mary A 148
Susan J 134
Synthia J 134
Vienna 190
Simpkins
  Emma (Col) 351
  Mary A (Col) 155
  Patsy (Col) 28
Simpson
  Alvertia 162
  Annie 71
  Catharine 205
  Elisha 327
  Emma 283
  Jane 60
  Maggie 358
  Margaret 98
  Margaret A 301
  Melvina C 69
  Sallie V 190
  Vianna S 163
Singleton
  Emma S 213
Slocomb
  Ann M (Col) 334
  Birdie L (Col) ... 334
  Lavania C 148
  Leah (Col) 125
  Levinia C 227
  Mary (Col) 359
  Mary E 133
  Susan B 118
  Zenette 184
Small
  Alice L 348
  Eliz 189
  Elizabeth 59, 189
  Elizabeth P 232
  Elizabeth S 70
  Emeline 74
  Matilda 116, 232
  Polly F 358
  Sally R 117
  Sarah 244
  Sarah J 235
  Susan E 262
Smart
  Mary E 221
Smith
  Alice E 120
  Alice L 220
  Allie 365
  Ann (Col) .. 161, 229

Anna 126
Annie 183
Annie (Col) 254
Annie L (Col) 318
Annie R 257
Ayrie (Col) 119
Betsy 206
Bunetta 239
Caroline (Col) 289
Catharine 309
Cordie E 204
Eliza 303
Elizabeth 349
Elizabeth (Col)
  ...... 103, 118, 253
Ellen 50
Emma (Col) 58
Emma E 141
Emma F 124
Fannie (Col) 336
Florence V 240
Hannah R 84
Harriet 309
Harriet (FN) 258
Harriet A 55
Hennie (Col) 35
Jane S 64
Josephine M 128
Leticha 44
Lizzie B (Col) 331
Lizzie H 269
Lottie (Col) 277
Louisa J 168
Maggie S 335
Mamie E 156
Manie 58
Margaret 194, 315, 353
Margaret (Col) ... 120
Martha 99
Martha A 332
Mary (Col) 67, 74
Mary A . 186, 222, 319
Mary Ellen (Col) .. 129
Mary F 320
Mary J (Col) 48
Mary Nancy 108
Mary R 218
Mary Sue 140
Mary Warrington (Col)
  355
Matilda L 309
Missouri 178
Mollie M 200

Nervilla 295
Nice (Col) 192
Rachel (Col) . 142, 305
Rosa F 309
Sallie A 281
Sallie G 29, 356
Sally 65
Sarah (Col) .. 137, 302
Sarah J 69
Sarah L 146
Sarah T 343
Sophia (Col) 204
Sue M 79
Susan 277
Susan A 97, 187
Susan J 245
Susan M 143
Tabitha A W 273
Snead
  Ailsu J (Col) 317
  Amy (Col) 257
  Annie (Col) 257
  Burlena (Col) ... 121
  Cordelia (Col) 42
  Easter (Col) 28
  Eliza 86, 324
  Eliza (Col) 157
  Ellen 87
  Georgianna 192
  Henrietta (Col) ... 85
  Leah 82
  Lena (Col) 362
  Lola (Col) 283
  Lydia 267
  Martha W 322
  Mary 61, 271
  Mary (Col) 35, 74, 256
  Mary Ann 179
  Mary Ann (Col) .. 257
  Mary E (Col) 192
  Mary L (Col) 295
  Nellie (Col) 146
  Polly 187
  Rachel (Col) 247
  Sarah (Col) .. 250, 274
  Sarah A (Col) 45
  Susan (Col) 305
  Tabitha 159
  Tilla (Col) 268
Solms
  Leah 346
Sparrow
  Caroline 228

Bride Index

Laura 126
Margaret ... 116, 308
Mary 360
Mary E 72
Mary S 93
Sally 234
Sarah C 147
Spence
  Betsy 195
  Bettie F 115
  Kissey 252
  Margaret Ann 163
  Maria 221
  Mary 102, 252
  Mary A 325
  Matilda J 102
  Miranda J 242
  Missouri 241
  Sophia J 282
  Susan 132
  Susan J 183
  Triffie E 311
Stant
  Catharine 45
  Cordelia 309
  Dolly P 71
  Elizabeth J ... 31, 242
  Ellen 349
  Emma 296
  Ida 205
  Julia A 169
  Lula C 244
  Margaret J 102
  Marina F 66
  Nancy 200
  Rosey A 360
  Susan 365
  Susan S 359
  Willieanna 91
Staton
  Matilda (Col) 190
  Sarah A (Col) 39
Steelman
  Annie 62
  Mary A 109
  Sarah E 180
Sterling
  Daisy B 32
  Emma 338
  Georgie D 333
  Jane 147
  Margaret 182
  Mary 168, 321

Ocia 181
Rachel J 50
Stevens
  Ann 166
  Annie 153
  Bettie (Col) 151
  Dora C 79, 336
  Eveline C 237
  Margaret Ann (Col) 326
  Margaret Susan ... 237
  Mary E (Col) 255
  Mattie R 163
  Rachel 128
  Sally 294
  Sarah Ann (Col) .. 89
  Sarah Ann (FN) .. 93
  Sarah E 154
Stevenson
  Elizabeth J 133
  Mary E (Col) 67
  Sarah Elizabeth ... 58
Stewart
  Georgianna (Col) .. 43
  Mary G 122
  Tinny A (Col) 167
Stiles
  Carrie F 76
  Mary A 337
  Retta 292
  Sally M 157
Stockley
  Alice Lee 69
  Mary B 177, 235
  Rebecca (Col) 181
Stokely
  Jane 303
  Rachel (FN) 122
Stokes
  Bettie 341
  Levinea 320
  Sarah W 332
Stores
  Maggie A 279
Stott
  Susan A 291
Stran
  Elizabeth (Col) 312
  Emma Kate (Col) .. 245
  Esther 225
  Fannie (Col) 47
  Laura (Col) 105
  Mary (Col) 44, 48
  Melissa (Col) 268

Sarah (Col) 247
Stratton
  Louisa F (Col) ... 285
  Rose Ann (Col) ... 244
Strigle
  Eliza J 255
  Virginia 360
Stringer
  Elizabeth (Col) ... 315
  Mary (Col) 355
  Mary M 193
Stuart
  Rhoda (Col) 141
Stubbs
  Julia 267
  Mary J 113
Sturgis
  Annie L 67
  Cora (Col) 311
  Elizabeth 96
  Elizabeth J 177
  Elizabeth M 141
  Ella N 173
  Lottie C 226
  Maggie A 193
  Margaret 95
  Margaret S 121
  Mary J 313
  Susan (Col) 45
  Virginia C 192
Summers
  Annie (Col) 297
  Annie E 259
  Bettie A 77
  Catharine 366
  Malissa S 228
  Mary E 201
  Mollie 167
  Oshie E (Col) ... 179
  Polly F 290
  Priscilla E 276
  Tishue C 288
  Vianna 365
Sunket
  Arinthia (Col) 341
  Margaret (Col) ... 78
Swanger
  Mary 141
  Sadie P 75
  Theresa 70
Tankard
  Annie Elizabeth(Col) 165
  Clara (Col) 107

Fanny (Col) 269	Dora 253	Louisa (Col) . 133, 230
Hester (Col) 63	E Wharton 342	Maggie 49
Mary E 285	Easter (FN) 56	Maggie F 331
Tarr	Edna E 228	Mahala Jane 237
Maggie 354	Elishea (Col) 303	Margaret
Margaret Jane 93	Eliza 86	. 40, 65, 210, 328, 369
Martha Ann 64	Eliza (Col) . . 133, 160	Margaret J 33
Mary E 183	Elizabeth	Margaret S . . 126, 188
Mary V 289	164, 212, 246, 324, 356	Maria 88
Nancy M 62	Elizabeth (Col) . . . 279	Mary
Roxanna A 62	Elizabeth (FN) . . . 36	. 65, 117, 345, 349, 365
Sarah 90	Elizabeth A 107	Mary A . . 87, 222, 258
Tatham	Elizabeth D 212	. . . . . . 270, 293, 300
Ann Eliza 346	Ella 327	Mary Ann (Col) . . 191
Critty 138	Ella F 301	Mary C 316
Elizabeth 281	Ella J 349	Mary Cath 85
Jane 213	Ella L 209	Mary E 362, 368
Mary Ann 182	Ellen 327	Mary J 241, 335
Nancy 38	Elzey (Col) 150	Mary J (Col) 221
Rebecca 109	Emeline 324	Mary Jane 321
Sallie A 201	Emily F 207	Mary R 220
Sarah 338	Emma 85, 195, 230, 248	Mary S 112, 279
Susan 80	Emma J 157	Mary Susan 179
Tatman	Emma K 336	Mehaleh (Col) 170
Ella L 157	Eveline 326	Melissa 32
Taws	Eveline R 174	Milly (FN) 347
Neely 115	Fannie 328	Nancy . . 117, 242, 317
Taylor	Fanny (Col) 342	Nancy R 349
Amanda 150, 255	Gertrude 85, 228	Narcissa 222
Amanda Jane 32	Henny 202	Nettie J 117
Ambert 310	Henrietta 48	Nora (Col) 136
Anna M 323	Hester 65	Rebecca 253
Anne Eliza 319	Ida 173, 229, 318	Roney J 163
Annie E 242	Ida F 146	Sallie A 33
Annie E W 58	Ida L 95	Sally 71, 248
Annie L 32	Isa 317	Sarah (Col) 125
Annie Lee 38	Isabella (Col) 67	Sarah (FN) 214
Arinthia P 34	Jane 108, 168, 317, 321	Sarah A 89
Arinthia S 190	Jane (Col) 54, 90, 254	Sarah Ann 324
Arminida 82	Jeanette F 259	Sarah Ann (Col) . . 29
Carvilla T 241	Jenima 277	Sarah E 133
Catharine 326	Julia 251	Susan111, 277, 304, 320
Catharine J 289	Julia P 233	Susan (Col) . 142, 268
Catherine (Col) . . . 355	Juliet (Col) 89	Susan E 123, 142
Caty (FN) 164	Laodicea 270	Syrena J 328
Cecilia 124	Larna 352	Trifany A S 238
Charlotte (Col) . . . 64	Laura A 322	Virginia H 342
Charlotte A 240	Laura E 331	Virginia L 134
Clara F 267	Lauretta 46	Virginia W 93
Comfort Ann (Col) 264	Lavinia 326	Zipporah 85
Coraline F 238	Leah E 276	Teaser
Cordelia Ann 330	Litia A (Col) 145	Annie 95
Delia 146	Louisa 322	Terry

Bride Index

Edna 280
Manie P 71
Thomas
  Amanda D 103
  Anna 209
  Bettie L 100
  Dinah (Col) 274
  Effie H 274
  Eliza 108
  Ethel 197
  Eveline 101
  Frances P 101
  Georgianna 282
  Julia 261
  Julia F 100
  Lena 339
  Margaret A 349
  Margaret J 200
  Mary (Col) 48
  Mary A 135
  Mary J 115
  Mary Jane 246
  Melissa 213
  Nellie A 99
  Olevia 220
  Priscilla 325
  Susan 133
  Vernittie 357
Thompson
  Eliza Ann 42
  Elizabeth A 204
  Hannah (Col) 224
  Louisa (FN) 216
  Mary (FN) 113
Thorns
  Amanda L 278
  Cora Belle 82
  Cornelia J 32
  Malissa 326
  Nancy J 163
Thornton
  Alice B 204
  Ann 108, 316
  Annie 147, 329
  Arena 327
  Caroline 72
  Carrie J 169
  Delilah 93
  Demeriah D 62
  Eliza 84
  Elizabeth
    . . . . 88, 183, 272, 321
  Ellen 86, 135

Emeline 79
Emily 28
Emily L 302
Gozelle 84
Henrietta 55
Hester 365
Hester A 79
Lizzie 359
Louesianna 108
Lydia A 296
Maggie E 246
Manie S 58
Margaret 80, 221
Maria 109
Mary J 80
Mary Jane 168
Mary W 73
Matilda Ann 109
Olivia Jane . . . 92, 240
Patience 327
Phoba 55
Sarah 202
Sarah E 245
Sarah V 290
Susanna 74
Tignal
  Frances 278
  Margaret 58
  Willie 151
Timmons
  Mary E 54
Tindall
  Airy E 110
  Airylanta 246
  Annie 274
  Annie May 182
  Bettie 353
  Emma 42, 309
  Harriet A 176
  Harriet F 328
  Julia E 36
  Mary 184
  Minnie F 320
  Susan 85
Tipton
  Carissa Ann 154
  Emma Jane 153
  Lottie L 153
  Mary F 92
  Virginia R 314
Topping
  Hetty 148
  Leah (Col) 268

Mary 258
Nannie B 333
Sarah 89
Sarah Lee (Col) . . . 338
Virginia (Col) 343
Townsend
  Ann (Col) . . 190, 340
  Gallie (Col) 90
  Leah 238
  Maria 241
  Maria C 240
  Mary E 139
  Mary R 346
  Sarah (Col) 302
  Sarah J 227
  Victoria (Col) 220
Trader
  Adeline 252
  Bettie 34
  Burnetta 148
  Dany H 299
  Dosia (Col) 229
  Drucilla 44, 107
  Elizabeth 323
  Elizabeth A . . 76, 251
  Elizabeth L 226
  Emeline 198, 263
  Euphernia 227
  Eva 195
  Henrietta 332
  Jane 76
  Lavinia S 254
  Lizzie J 195
  Marcialla A 275
  Mary 138
  Mary (Col) 94
  Mary J 318
  Mollie J 132
  Nancy 247
  Parrthena 317
  Polly 67, 148
  Rebecca J 292
  Sallie 76
  Sarah 269
  Sarah E 350
  Willianna 202
Trehearn
  Maggie (Col) 202
  Melissa (Col) 125
  Nancy 339
  Sarah A 283
Trower
  Annie D 217

Jane (Col) ... 30, 333
Jennie (Col) 74
Lena E 29
Polly W 120
Truitt
　Elizabeth ... 264, 303
　Sallie C 73
　Sarah M 222
Tull
　Alice N 281
　Elizabeth 327
　Emma E 368
　Maria L V 228
　Mary Ann (Col) .. 352
　Missouri E 157
　Mollie W 152
　Sally 279
　Sarah E 111
Tunnell
　Adah (Col) 231
　Arinthia (Col) ... 158
　Elizabeth (Col) ... 219
　Henrietta J 222
　Maggie Elva 333
　Martha (FN) 346
　Mary Lynn 69
　Ritie (Col) 140
　Susan (Col) 273
Turlington
　Ann (Col) 260
　Ann Eliza 346
　Bettie R 68
　Eliza 316
　Elizabeth S 235
　Florence Susan (Col) 223
　Henny (Col) 280
　Jane 283
　Jennie (Col) 193
　Joyce 64
　Leah J 96
　Lizzie S 223
　Louisa (Col) 204
　Maggie J 312
　Mary 49
　Mary (Col) 223
　Missouri 51
　Sarah (Col) 238
　Susan (Col) 160
Turner
　Adalaide 46
　Bettie 78
　Catharine S 68
　Dora C 79

Elizabeth 192
Elizabeth A 281
Levinia S 64
Lizzie Jane 81
Maggie S 177
Margaret 342
Martha 365
Mary (Col) .. 117, 143
Mary E 68
Mary J 31
Mary Susan 204
Matilda Ann 183
Missouri (Col) ... 147
Olivia E 218
Priscilla 81
Rosa 46
Sallie F 253
Sarah Ann 63
Susan 239
Tabitha Rachel (Col) 151
Twiford
　Ann 67
　Anna 120
　Anna E 119
　Annie B 298
　Annie C 89
　Clara D 40
　Edith L 130
　Elizabeth (Col) ... 187
　Elizabeth B 232
　Lizzie S 40
　Maggie A 210
　Maggie C 179
　Margaret 32
　Martha A 214
　Mary E 214, 358
　Minnie G 89
　Roberta S 151
　Rose D 37
　Sally A E 231
　Sarah (Col) .. 125, 323
Tyler
　Agnes (Col) 77
　Bettie S 93
　Hettie (Col) 268
　Martha 111
　Priscilla 221
　Rebecca E 326
　Rebecca S 330
　Sallie 101
Underhill
　Rose 298
Upshur

Alice E (Col) 285
Catharine (Col) ... 351
Maria (FN) 30
Martha A (Col) ... 44
Mary Ann 43
Vernelson
　Sallie 284
Voyles
　Fannie A 284
Walden
　Mary B 157
Walker
　Alice M 211
　Ann (Col) .. 191, 367
　Anna 242
　Annie (Col) 192
　Charlotte A J 129
　Docia (Col) 36
　Maggie S 37
　Margaret S .. 295, 341
　Mary A 358
　Mary Catharine ... 243
　Mary E 277
　Mary H (Col) 319
　Mary Ida 127
　Rose E 140
　Sarah S 217
　Sarah Walker 55
Wallace
　Carrie L 308
　Clara 174
　Elizabeth (Col) .. 245
　Elizabeth A 256
　Fannie E 227
　Leah V 264
　Mary A 257
　Mary Jane 265
　Nettie F 256
　Sarah J 92
Wallop
　Harriet A 131
　Leah (FN) 70
　Mary D 306
　Mary M (Col) ... 172
Walsh
　Charlotte J 292
Walston
　Rose B 337
　Sarah P 55
Walter
　Bessie B 367
　Emma 257
　Frances (Col) ... 255

Bride Index 411

Georgianna (Col) . . 291
Louisa 115
Mary E 232, 249
Sarah (Col) 146
Walters
  Emily E 116
  Harriet (FN) 170
  Leah (Col) 348
  Rachel (Col) 287
Waples
  Lydia (Col) 185
Ward
  Amanda E 210
  Amanda F 233
  Anna (Col) 341
  Anna J 244
  Annie R B 353
  Belle (Col) 71
  Caroline (Col) 159
  Catharine 196
  Catharine J 277
  Elizabeth C 195
  Henny 230
  Hester Jane 323
  Jane (FN) 65
  Louisa (Col) 167
  Madgie A 338
  Maggie (Col) 194
  Margaret A 342
  Margaret S . . 234, 322
  Margaret Susan . . . 103
  Martha Ann 64
  Mary 185
  Mary A 60
  Mary E 154
  Mary Elizabeth . . . 327
  Mary Jane 356
  Nannie L 164
  Phebe (Col) 129
  Rachel 278
  Sadie Smith 360
  Sarah F 217
  Susan 51
  Susan M 341
  Tabitha A 236
  Theodecea 50
  Virginia 273
Warner
  Annie L 188
  Arinthia D 96
  Bettie G 363
  Clara J 281
  Cora 275

Elizabeth 247
Emma L . . . 196, 297
Ida D 201
Lucy (Col) 137
Martha 276
Mary 27
Rosa (Col) 296
Sally 147
Warren
  Elizabeth A 50
  Ella (Col) 228
  Ella J E 36
  Tabitha S 330
  Virginia 66
Warrington
  Emily 51
  Georgianna (Col) . . 156
  Margaret C 223
Washington
  Lillie (Col) 39
Waterfield
  Elizabeth J 47
  Maggie 79
  Mareitta 261
Waterhouse
  Permelia 209
Waters
  Agnes (Col) 116
  Annie (FN) 121
  Catharine R 214
  Emma 124
  Laura (Col) 349
  Mary Ann 245
Watkinson
  Alice 207
  Arinthia 293
  Bettie P 270
  Lee Jane 270
  Lottie W 295
  Margaret 243
  Mary 89, 159
  Mary E 79
  Rebecca S 209
  Sally 269
  Sarah Ann 63
  Susan 158, 359
  Susan Ann 235
Watson
  Adeline 174
  Ann 318
  Ann (Col) 288
  Belle (Col) 33
  Catharine 239

Catherine (Col) . . . 65
Charlotte (Col) . . . 361
Clarissa (Col) 138
Elizabeth
  . . . . 47, 112, 321, 328
Elizabeth (Col) . . . 252
Ella Lee 109
Ellen (Col) 216
Emily J (Col) 324
Emma (Col) 135
Emory J (Col) 170
Evelyn M 345
Fannie E 53
Florence 174
Frances (Col) 254
Frances Ann 362
Georgianna (Col) . . 315
Harriet (Col) 59
Hattie (Col) 66
Henrietta 54
Hester Ann (Col) . . 66
Ida G 278
Ida V 184
Indiania S 281
Jane (Col) 257
Laura F 235
Leah (Col) 255
Louisa (Col) 98
Lucy (Col) . . 203, 362
Lula M 175
Martha 61
Martha M (Col) . . . 352
Mary . . . 169, 209, 369
Mary A 254
Mary E
  . . . . 84, 171, 287, 368
Mary F 322
Mary Ida 283
Mary J 303
Mary Jane (Col) . . 192
Mary M 152
Mary R 196
Nancy 60
Rebecca 267
Rebecca A 79
Rhoda 166
Rowena (Col) 132
Sadie E 160
Sally (Col) 160
Susan 127, 364
Susan A . . . 196, 366
Virginia (Col) 251
Virginia E 292

Watts
  Annie (Col) 137
  Ellen S 259
  Estelle J 72
  Maggie (Col) 114
  Mary M 172
Weaver
  Sally P 348
  V Lee 232
Webb
  Arinthia (Col) 224
  Elizabeth (Col) . . . 216
  Emma 121
  Emma Jane (Col) . . 206
  Lucy Jane (Col) . . . 208
  Margaret (Col) . . . 62
  Margaret S (FN) . . 121
  Mary Ann 280
  Nancy A (Col) . . . 149
  Rachel 325
Webster
  Alice D 34
Weeks
  Frances (Col) 45
Wescott
  Elizabeth S 150
  Maggie C 59
  Mamie E 119
  Nannie 125
  Rosa Ann 157
Wessells
  Adaline W 189
  Amanda 262, 287
  Arcissa 322
  Arinthia J 234
  Arinthia S 322
  Caroline J 317
  Charlotte 205
  Eliza (Col) 121
  Elizabeth 211, 368
  Elizabeth J 156
  Ella J 177
  Ellen 31
  Esther (Col) 352
  Evelin T 167
  Eveline 243, 314
  Eveline C 195
  Evelyn E 245
  Genettie G 116
  Henrietta 228
  Ida H 279
  Jane (Col) 187
  Jenetta S 143

  Laura C 138, 213
  Laura L 284
  Margaret 189, 213, 323
  Margaret A 78
  Margaret Ann 261
  Mary . 57, 72, 138, 316
  Mary (Col) . . 133, 276
  Mary A 219, 348
  Mary J 166
  Mary S 87
  Mary T 276
  Nancy 41
  Ocenia B 349
  Sarah E 201
  Sarah K 88
  Susan 242, 278
  Viola J 166
  Virginia 350
  Virginia S 258
West
  Alice Lee 82
  Alicia Anna (Col) . 186
  Ann (Col) 73
  Betsy (Col) 287
  Betsy A 237
  Bettie R 298
  Caroline (Col) 291
  Cordelia (Col) 45
  Eleshea A C 173
  Elizabeth (Col) . . . 204
  Elizabeth A 340
  Elizabeth Sarah (Col) 53
  Ella 167
  Emma (Col) 122
  Emma L 209
  Fanny (Col) 303
  Frances (Col) 303
  Henrietta V 223
  Joanna T 203
  Julia 369
  Kitty 257
  Kitty (Col) 90
  Laura E (Col) 118
  Lottie 91
  Lottie (Col) 267
  Louisa (Col) 292
  Maggie (Col) 257, 353
  Maggie E (Col) . . . 78
  Margaret A 332
  Margaret Ann (Col) 136
  Margaret R 110
  Margaret Rachel . . 45
  Margie (Col) 313

  Mary . . . 71, 281, 336
  Mary (Col) 43, 123, 126
  Mary Ann 73
  Mary F (Col) 123
  Mary Jane (Col) . . 155
  Mary Jane (FN) . . . 256
  Mary S (Col) 121
  Nancy 196
  Nancy (FN) 48
  Nancy E 27
  Nannie C 215
  Nannie S 137
  Neely (Col) 287
  Nellie (Col) 203
  Pearl Lena (Col) . . 236
  Rachel (Col) 105
  Roberta 135
  Rosa (Col) 355
  Sally A (Col) 202
  Sally R 255
  Sarah (Col) 338
  Sopha (FN) 254
  Sophia (Col) 92
  Sudie E 222
  Susan 364
  Susan Ann 268
  Virga 98
  Virginia 244
  Virginia F 293
Wharton
  Adaline F (Col) . . . 140
  Elizabeth 256
  Elizabeth (FN) . . . 179
  Emma 269
  Frany 54
  Harriet (Col) 111
  Harriet (FN) 170
  Henrietta (Col) . . . 142
  Ibby (Col) 247
  Lulie (Col) 158
  Maggie (Col) 345
  Mary A 89
  Mary A (Col) 224
  Nancy E 87
  Sarah (Col) 282
  Tamer Eliz (Col) . . 226
Whealton
  Ann C 326
  Anna 148
  Anna M 86
  Comfort 367
  Drucilla 306
  Eliza 276

Bride Index 413

Elizabeth . . 57, 144, 207
. . . . . . 231, 271, 316
Elizabeth J 329
Erista E B R 87
Gertrude 183
Henrietta 272
Hester A 264
Ida V 343
Josephine 278
Julia 179
Laura (Col) 286
Margaret E 55
Mary 86
Mary A 174, 227
Mary A (Col) 174
Mary E 179
Mary Jane 367
Sarah 205, 208
Sarah Ann 168
Tabitha 68, 263
Wheatley
  Emma J 271
Wheeler
  Mary 54
  Mary Ann 174
White
  Alice (Col) 134
  Amelia (Col) 331
  Anna (Col) 110
  Annie (Col) . 138, 153
  Arrena (Col) 261
  Belinda 221
  Caroline 320
  Caroline H 315
  Charlotte (Col) . . . 249
  Demariah (Col) . . . 366
  Edie (Col) . . . 51, 369
  Elitia A 109
  Eliza Ann (Col) . . . 114
  Elizabeth 264
  Elizabeth E 62
  Elizabeth S 366
  Emma (Col) . 153, 227
  Esther E 215
  Evelin J 36
  Frances A 200
  Georgianna (Col) . . 230
  Harriet (Col) . 107, 174
  Harriet A (Col) . . . 149
  Harriet Ann (Col) . 44
  Ida 337
  Jane E 226
  Kate A 130

Kitty (Col) 87
Leah S (Col) 263
Lizzie A 179
Lucretia A 183
Lucy A (Col) 172
Maggie (Col) 108
Maggie E (Col) . . . 29
Mania D J (Col) . . 55
Margaret A . . 34, 305
Margaret Cath 151
Margaret T 152
Margie S 303
Martah (Col) 122
Martha (Col) 344
Mary 68, 301
Mary (Col) 320
Mary A 190
Mary C (Col) . . . 103
Mary E (Col) 344
Mary E S (Col) . . . 156
Mary S 194
Mary T 330
Matilda A 147
Mattie A 207
Rebecca A 82
Sabra (FN) 37
Sallie F (Col) 142
Sally 170
Sally (Col) 87
Sally A 147
Sarah A 161
Sarah A (Col) 39
Sarah S 309
Susan (Col) . 289, 296
Tabitha 215
Tamar (Col) 351
Virginia C 103
Whittington
  Margaret A (Col) . . 140
  Mary Elizabeth (Col) 140
  Mary V 88
  Tamen Ann (Col) . 140
Wigton
  Mary 72
Wilgus
  Nancy 62
Wilkerson
  Alice A 68
  Clarinda 221
  Emma (Col) 231
  Florence 210
  Mary C 189
  Mary M 290

Roxanna 223
Wilkins
  Isabella 360
  Roberta K 338
Willett
  Betsy 264
  Georgianna 81
  Maggie L 342
  Sarah Jane 88
Williams
  Addie S 300
  Annie 308
  Belle B 252
  Charity 181
  Cordellia 276
  Elenda M 308
  Elishea A (Col) . . . 345
  Eliza J 211
  Elizabeth 222
  Elizabeth (Col) . . . 93
  Elizabeth S 268
  Elizabeth T 347
  Henrietta 49
  Hester 174
  Hester A 128
  Josephine (Col) . . . 289
  Julia 271
  Leonra S 210
  Lucinda 75
  Margaret Ann (Col) 94
  Mary 168
  Mary (Col) . . 103, 362
  Mary E 329
  Mary H 353
  Mary J 319
  Mary T 51
  Mila (Col) 113
  Minor 53
  Nancy 80
  Rose (Col) 82
  Sallie (Col) 48
  Sally 104
  Sarah 253
  Sarah A 61, 274
  Sarah E . 101, 197, 276
  Tabitha T 132
  Vianna (Col) 138
Willis
  Amanda A 69
  Elizabeth C 126
  Maggie I 27
  Margaret R 159
Wilson

Rosina 224
Sarah A 163
Tabitha A 356
Wimbrough
   Ambert 38
   Delilah 327
   Elizabeth 67
   Henrietta 179
   Mamie J 314
   Susan 86
Winder
   Betsy (Col) 122
   Clara 85
   Elizabeth ... 182, 212
   Ella B 164
   Julia 30
   Mary (Col) 71
   Sarah A 362
Windsor
   Sarah M 131
Winger
   Laura 150
Winslow
   Atty (Col) 151
Wise
   Agnes (Col) 146
   Anna (Col) 231
   Annie (Col) . 122, 304
   Bertie (Col) 39
   Bettie (Col) 352
   Betty (Col) 48
   Cath C 45
   Catharine 239
   Catharine (Col) . 74
   Cordelia (Col) .. 110
   Eliza E (Col) ... 307
   Ella B 28
   Ellen (Col) . 110, 341
   Emma S (Col) 158
   Fannie (Col) 137
   Fannie E (Col) .. 229
   Harriet (Col)
       ...... 43, 167, 192
   Henrietta (Col) . 366
   Julia (Col) 256
   Julia A 348
   Juliet (Col) 281
   Leah (Col) 138
   Leah J (Col) 92
   Lucy (Col) 256
   Maggie L (Col) .. 231
   Maggie V 154
   Mahala (Col) 291

Margaret (Col) ... 58
Margaret Ellen ... 279
Maria (FN) 364
Maria Anna (Col) . 304
Martah 307
Martha 363
Martha (Col) 42
Mary (Col) 44, 169, 319
Mary Jane (Col) .. 280
Mary S 130
Rose 235
Sallie (Col) 337
Sally 367
Sally (Col) 161
Sarah (Col) .. 227, 357
Sarah (FN) 44
Scarborough A (Col) 365
Susan (Col) 313
Tillie (Col) 114
Viola (Col) 255
Witham
   Nellie F 174
Woods
   Luzetts 236
   Oceanna 155
   Polly 309
Wright
   Belle S (Col) ... 141
   Bertha L 70
   Elizabeth 147
   Elizabeth A 315
   Hester 38
   Hester (Col) 116
   Leah 313
   Lizzie A 295
   Maggie A 197
   Maggie S 116
   Malinda 189, 365
   Malissa H 293
   Mary A 347
   Mary E 236
   Mary F 28
   Rose 298
   Rose A 337
   Sallie D 72
   Susan S 147
   Willie D 71
Wyatt
   Georgie C 266
   Sadie M 164
   Sallie 336
   Susan A 196

Young
   Annie 63
   Annie (Col) 125
   Catharine ... 183, 191
   Catharine A 305
   Clara C 76
   Cornelia 88
   Darkey (Col) 170
   Effy S 276
   Elizabeth ... 228, 253
   Elizabeth P 229
   Elizabeth T 340
   Emily C 112
   Emma S 73
   Ethel 207
   Georgiana 350
   Hannah 171
   Ida 317
   Ida S 78
   Jane (Col) 343
   Janie 366
   Julia B 367
   Laura 198
   Laura (Col) 291
   Lauretta Ann (Col) . 269
   Maggie L 180
   Margaret 80, 145
   Margaret (Col) .. 189
   Martha F 295
   Mary (Col) 349
   Mary A . 97, 300, 349
   Mary C 56
   Mary G 232
   Mary J (Col) 186
   Mary J C 350
   Mary S 321
   Mollie B 151
   Phoebe E 195
   Polly Susan 39
   Rose Emma 237
   Sallie A 70
   Sally D 134
   Sarah (Col) 124
   Sarah E 350
   Sarah M 254
   Sophia 138
   Sophy Anna 62
   Susan 367
   Susan W 229
   Williana 88
Zelder
   Catharine 326

Other books by the authors:

Abstracts of the Wills and Administrations of Accomack County, Virginia, 1800-1860
Barry W. Miles and Moody K. Miles, III

Cemeteries of the City of Hampton, Virginia, Formerly Elizabeth City County
Barry W. Miles

Cemeteries of the City of Newport News, Formerly Warwick County, Virginia
Barry W. Miles and Gertrude Stead

Colonial Families of the Eastern Shore of Virginia, Volume 1
Mary Frances Carey, Barry W. Miles and Moody K. Miles, III

Colonial Families of the Eastern Shore of Virginia, Volume 2
Mary Frances Carey, Barry W. Miles and Moody K. Miles, III

Tombstone Inscriptions of Upper Accomack County, Virginia
Mary Frances Carey with Moody K. Miles, III and Barry W. Miles